The Concept of Honor in the Language of Early Arabic Poetry

ŁÓDŹ STUDIES IN LANGUAGE

Edited by Barbara Lewandowska-Tomaszczyk and Łukasz Bogucki

VOLUME 72

PETER LANG

Bartosz Pietrzak

The Concept of Honor in the Language of Early Arabic Poetry

A Cultural Linguistic Study

PETER LANG

Bibliographic Information published by the Deutsche Nationalbibliothek
The Deutsche Nationalbibliothek lists this publication in the Deutsche Nationalbibliografie; detailed bibliographic data is available online at http://dnb.d-nb.de.

Library of Congress Cataloging-in-Publication Data
A CIP catalog record for this book has been applied for at the Library of Congress.

This publication was financially supported by the Faculty of Philology of the Jagiellonian University in Kraków.

Cover illustration: Courtesy of Benjamin Ben Chaim.

This book is based on a PhD thesis which has been reviewed by: Janusz Danecki (University of Warsaw) and Marek Dziekan (University of Łódź).

ISSN 1437-5281
ISBN 978-3-631-88290-0 (Print)
E-ISBN 978-3-631-89223-7 (E-PDF)
E-ISBN 978-3-631-89267-1 (EPUB)
DOI 10.3726/b20341

Peter Lang – Berlin · Bruxelles · Lausanne · New York · Oxford

This publication has been peer reviewed.

www.peterlang.com

to my life companion, MJK
and to my parents, Renata & Andrzej

Contents

Acknowledgements

If I have seen further it is by standing on the shoulders of Giants.

Isaac Newton

This book would not have been written without the guidance of the "Giants" of Polish Arabic studies. It is a record of my Ph.D. thesis I wrote under the supervision of prof. Elżbieta Górska, to whom I would like to express my deepest thanks. It could not have been accomplished without her constant support as my mentor, scientific advisor, and a source of inspiration. Also, I would like to extend my gratitude to the reviewers of the thesis, prof. Janusz Danecki and prof. Marek M. Dziekan. Their invaluable critique helped me shape and refine the ideas I present in this book.

A big thank to those who contributed unknowingly: family and friends.

Technical notes

In the body of the text in this book, I will differentiate between English lexemes and names of the concepts/schemata these lexemes refer to in English. The former will be rendered always in italics, whereas the latter in small caps. In the case of Arabic, since small caps do not always work with the special characters used in the transcription, I decided not to make any graphical difference between names of the concepts/schemata and the lexemes that refer to them. Thus, by HONOR, I will mean the entire notion of this phenomenon, whereas *honor* is my way of mentioning English lexeme used in reference to it. In Arabic, however, by *ʕirḍ* I will mean either a transcription of Arabic عِرْض or the concept/ schema this Arabic lexeme refers to. In my work, I understand the *lexeme* in the traditional way as a lexical (or dictionary) item that stands for a cluster of textual forms, i.e., different nominal/adjectival (e.g., plural) and verbal (aspectual, modal, etc.) forms.

Sometimes in the text, I use so-called curly brackets, i.e., {}, to depict a propositional conceptualization, i.e., a statement of knowledge. Thus, {*karīm* is the best of his people} is an encoded chunk of culturally shared knowledge, which served as a basis for different kinds of inferences.

When it comes to the transcription of the text in Arabic, I decided to limit it only to particular lexemes. The supporting examples quoted in Arabic are not transcribed, since in my opinion, in a semantic study, in which none syntactic or morphological dependencies are of great importance, the transcription seems to be unnecessary.

The supporting examples are fully translated and commented on in the main body of text. The translation – if not indicated otherwise – is mine. I aimed to render the intended meaning of Arabic sentences in the manner as faithful as it was possible. This, however, could be achieved in most of the cases only on the expense of the artistic value of the translation. Thus, instead of providing more or less coherent interpretation of Arabic verses, I choose to render as rigid literary, verbatim reading of the text as it was possible. Consequently, I often resort to use of square brackets [], in which I provide – sometimes cumbersome – complements needed for the faithful rendition of Arabic sentences, especially in the frequent cases, in which appellatives are omitted by poets for sake of the poetic license (cf. Kowalski 1997: 55).

While transcribing Arabic lexemes and the concepts they refer to, I use italics. In my transcription, I followed ISO-233 (1984 version) and Górska (2015: 13–4) with minor exceptions. I transcribe *ʔalif maqṣūra* (ى) as *à*. *Tāʔ marbūṭa* (ة) in the absolute state is rendered as *ẗ* only if it follows a long vowel *ā* (e.g., حَيَاة = *ḥayāẗ*).

Otherwise, it is not transcribed (e.g., كَرَامَة = *karāma*). In the construct state, it is always rendered as *t*. The short-vowel inflectional endings are rendered only if the context requires it. In the case of the *hamza*, I consequently render any instance of *hamzat al-qaṭʕ* – even when it occurred at the beginning of a word (e.g., أَعْرَاب = *ʔaʕrāb*) – except for Arabic proper names, in which I omit any initial *hamza*, including *hamzat al-qaṭʕ* (e.g., الأعرابي = al-Aʕrābī). The Arabic proper names are not italicized.

The table below presents the general rules I applied in my transcription.

Transcription of Arabic text

ء	*ʔ*	ط	*ṭ*
ا	*ā*	ظ	*ẓ*
ب	*b*	ع	*ʕ*
ت	*t*	غ	*ġ*
ث	*ṯ*	ف	*f*
ج	*ǧ*	ق	*q*
ح	*ḥ*	ك	*k*
خ	*ḫ*	ل	*l*
د	*d*	م	*m*
ذ	*ḏ*	ن	*n*
ر	*r*	ه	*h*
ز	*z*	و	*w* *ū*
ش	*š*	ي	*y* *ī*
س	*s*	ى	*à*
ص	*ṣ*	ة	-/*ṫ*[1] (status absolutus)
ض	*ḍ*		*t* (status constructus)

1 Only in the ـاة ending.

1. Introduction: the case study

This book is about meaning of certain words and expressions used in the language of Early Arabic Poetry in reference to honor. It means that it is about something that for many might be controversial in a lot of different ways and for a lot of different reasons.

First of all, the method of studying the meaning I will present in this book is at the center of a heated debate that has been running since at least 19th c. This is because in this book I argue that meaning is not universal, what is a troubling statement making many linguists uneasy to the point some of them choose to withdraw from studying meaning whatsoever (Wierzbicka 1996: 3–8). But can we really imagine the study of language without studying meaning? Because what is language, if not – as Anna Wierzbicka (1992: 3; 1996: 3) put it – a "tool", an "instrument for conveying meaning"? Isn't it that the sole purpose of our language is to express "our thought, our feelings, our perceptions (Wierzbicka 1992: 3)" to share them with others, be them those with whom we are here and now, or those distant in time and space? In language, while speaking, expressing utterances, first and foremost, we *mean*. So, can one "professionally" study language without any reference to meaning? Wouldn't such a study be "like studying road signs from the point of view of their physical properties, (…) or like studying the structure of the eye without any reference to seeing (Wierzbicka 1996: 3)"?

Thus, in this book, the meaning is at the center of the linguistic inquire. Moreover, this meaning is claimed to affect the shape of the language system as a whole; and it is strongly held to be culture-specific. The latter claim was at the core of a long-lasting debate between universalist and relativist linguists, which became so well embedded in academic discourse (and its social perception) that it has even traveled into the realm of internet meme strings. Thus, in my opinion, the best epitome of universalist approach to meaning is the following meme by an anonymous Tumblr user:

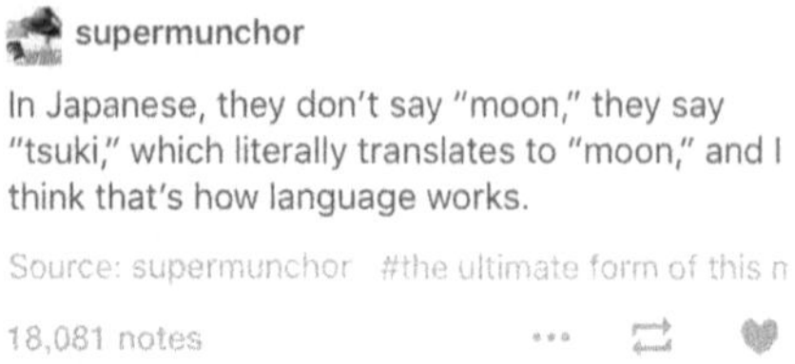

source: Tumblr[1]

This meme clearly tells us that the way languages work does not have too much to do with meaning in general. Meaning seems here a matter of quite redundant labels attached to words and expressions of different linguistic shape that are implicitly presented here to be of much more importance for professionals who intent to study "how language works". One can read the message implied in the meme as a statement: there nothing about meaning worth a serious linguistic inquiry.

I claim contrary to that. Language is a phenomenon much more complex than a mere record of grammatical and syntactical functions – and meaning is what makes a particular language itself. It is true that English *moon* and Japanese 月-*tsuki* are – dictionary-wise – replaceable. Still, does English *moon* evoke the same whole universe of associations as Japanese 月-*tsuki* does? Can we replace them easily by Arabic *qamar*, which refer to the same celestial body? If so, then why is it that in Arabic, the phrase "oh my moon (*ya qamarī*)" would be a way of referring to one's lover rather than praying to the satellite of our Planet? Thus, do *moon* and *qamar* still have *the same* meaning?

---

1 It seems the post was first posed by *supermunchor*, who later deleted it (cf. https://supermunchor.tumblr.com/post/129429267709 [20-07-2022]). Its earliest (since April 2015) and still existing occurrence can be traced to https://otakuanilog.tumblr.com/post/126523203792/10-attack-on-titan-facts [20-07-2022]. It follows a template of a meme first occurring in 2013 (cf. https://knowyourmeme.com/memes/in-france-they-dont-say-i-love-you [20-07-2022]). With time, memes using this template started commenting on some supposed culture-specific pragmatic meaning conveyed in different languages. A good example of the use of this template in this way is the Polish meme saying: "In Poland we don't say "*Here's your change*", we say "*Grosik będę winna*" [lit., "I'll owe you one Polish grosz," (1/100 of 1 Polish zloty) – it's what one can frequently hear from a cashier at the checkout, since it's easier for them to make the change round] and I think it's beautiful."

My answer to this question is negative, and in this book, I will try to prove that any other answer is simply not possible. That is because the meaning I discuss in the following chapters is a much more complicated thing than most of us are used to imagine. It cannot be described by a definition or an explication. In fact, what I propose in the following chapters might resemble more an encyclopedia entry or an ethnographic report rather than a dictionary. This is because my goal was not to suggest how one could render some Arabic words in their native language, but to understand a complex way, in which Arabic language encoded the knowledge about some elements of the social life of people who used it.

The meaning, which I intend to describe is thus encyclopedic in nature. We should read it that while *meaning*, we always *mean* what we *know* about the world. This was noticed already centuries ago by Islamic scholar, ar- Rāzī († 1210), who said:

> للألفاظ دلالات على ما في الأذهان لا على ما في الأعيان ولهذا السبب يقال: الألفاظ تدل على المعاني، لأن المعاني هي التي عناها العاني، وهي أمور ذهنية
>
> [People's] utterances refer to what is in [their] minds and not to what [appears] in [their] eyes, and for that reason we say: the utterances point towards the meanings (*maʕānī*), since the meanings are what is meant by the one who means (*ʕanā-hā al-ʕānī*) – and [thus] they are mental phenomena (ar-Rāzī 1981: 31).

In other words, ar- Rāzī insisted that while talking, one never *means* things, which are "out there" – which they see with their eyes – but they can talk only about the way they *perceive* those things. We do not talk about the "objective" world, but – to use Ray Jackendoff's term – about our "conceptualized world" (Jackendoff 2002: 304), *das Ding an mich* of Immanuel Kant. And this conceptualized reality is not our own – we share it with others, participating in a complicated, constantly evolving system we call *culture* (cf. Kövecses 2017: 308).

Thus, this book is about such a meaning – a complex structure, which emerges as a part of the shared knowledge of people, and by that – to a certain extent – it is relative to their culture. Such a meaning is a powerful factor in shaping our linguistic behaviors, since it contains not only the more dictionary- like information, but also the encodement of the place of a given concept within a thick network of the *conceptualized world*. Therefore, I will not present just definitions of the analyzed vocabulary, but – perhaps more importantly – I shall reconstruct all the connections between domains of knowledge that account for everything (or at least most) the people who used some words *meant*. What I want to show is the native perspective of these people – the way they *perceived* the world – which was encoded in their language and linguistic practices they performed. Hence, my study is an example of Cultural Linguistics, being a culture-focused branch of cognitive linguistics. Its major focus is then on the conceptual system – the culture – which shapes a particular language in a unique way.

***

Of course, this book is not about such a meaning in general. As I mentioned, it presents a case study that examines the way, in which pre-Islamic Arabs used to talk about honor – or more precisely – what they *meant* while using different linguistic tools to express their thoughts about this social phenomenon. Hence, my study is an example of the application of Cultural Linguistics in Arabic philology, which follows the long tradition of oriental studies, the methodology of which "is primarily a translation of one culture to another" (Dziekan 2008: 20). Being the analysis of a past stage of Arabic language, my research is certainly a historical study, yet in the most part it is not diachronic. This is because I am interested mostly in the synchronic features of the conceptual system persisting in a specific moment in time, rather than in how this system evolved or came to be. Nevertheless, sometimes, I could not hold myself from positing etymological hypotheses, especially where they seemed helping in the overall argumentation.

I focus on language and culture of Arabs of the so-called al-Ǧāhiliyya period, which extended up to a century and half back before the rise of Islam (Dziekan 2008: 32). I decided to so, because of the importance of this period for the development of the whole Arabic and Arabo-Muslim civilization. Even though it was named by Muslim scholars *al-ǧāhiliyya*, i.e., [the time of] ignorance or barbarism, by no means was it ever intended to be forgotten (Dziekan 1998: 88–9). In fact, the opposite is true – the whole Arabic culture after the emergence of Islam would always refer to it as an undisputed reference point (Dziekan 2008: 82). Therefore, in studying it I was motivated by the belief expressed by Marek M. Dziekan (2008: 81) that "more comprehensive knowledge of al-Ǧāhiliyya can afford better understanding of some phenomena, which are usually considered Islamic, however, they bear in their nature an early Arabic pagan imprint". Such a phenomenon explored in this work is honor.

As I have mentioned, I employed in my case study the methods and theoretical frame of Cultural Linguistics. It means that although my focus was always on the language and its use, in fact, my analyses could be seen aiming twofold. On the one hand, I intended to describe the repertoire of lexical tools available to pre-Islamic Arabs in their discourse on honor. On the other one, however, I was interested in the way they used to perceive this social phenomenon. This second goal might be considered a more ethnographic in nature, and it correlates with goals of numerous anthropological studies, in which the descriptive approach was adopted (cf. Stewart 1994: 5). Nevertheless, this ethnographic interest was rooted in the linguistic one since the description of the native perception of honor served characterizing encyclopedic meanings of analyzed lexical items.

Following Cultural Linguistics, and more precisely, one of its major theoretics, Farzad Sharifian, I prose to describe these meanings in terms of *cultural conceptualizations*. i.e., (cultural) schemata, categories, metaphors, and metonymies. They might be understood in the simplest way as conceptual devices encoding certain pieces of knowledge of people. In other words, my case study – like any cultural linguistic examination – aimed to define the way, in which a particular piece of the cultural knowledge was encoded, and how this encoded knowledge affected the language – most importantly its lexicon – by being in fact the whole meaning meant by speakers of this language. Consequently, in whole, I depicted so-called semantic frames, i.e., encodement of this piece of knowledge, as well as linguistic items associated with it.

Therefore, in short, one can see my methods as describing the way some people – i.e., pre-Islamic Arabs – used to think and talk about a certain social phenomenon – i.e., honor. Perhaps even better, one can say that I intended to characterize – semantically and ethnographically – all linguistic choices that Arabs of al-Ǧāhiliyya were provided with to convey their thinking about honor. For the examination in my study, I selected five most obvious of such choices, i.e., lexemes *karam*, *karāma*, *ḥasab*, *šaraf*, and *ˁirḍ*, which by Edward Lane, were rendered as somehow the closest correlates of English lexeme *honor/honour*. My selection was further refined in a pre-study on Classical Arabic dictionaries explications. Consequently, I included in my analysis also the concept of *mağd* "fame, glory", closely related to pre-Islamic Arabic conception of honor. Moreover, in order to complete – or at least to attempt to complete – this conception, I also decided to represent the conclusions of my preliminary study on the most important profiles of pre-Islamic Arabic SHAME-DISHONOR, i.e. the concepts of *ˁayb*, *ˁār*, and *ḥayāʔ* (cf. Pietrzak 2022).

All in all, my sole goal was to contribute to the understanding of pre-Islamic Arabic honor – linguistically and anthropologically – by applying relatively novel methods, which have not been used yet in studying Arabic language functioning before Islam. Consequently, by this case study, I intend to submit the cultural linguistic approach for discussion as a methodological frame for future studies in Arabic and other oriental languages of the past and present.

Naturally, one can ask a question why I decided to make HONOR the theme of my study. I must admit my choice was dictated by a more or less common belief that honor, dignity, sense of pride – all of these phenomena – are at the core of the interests of people, whose way of life might be subsumed under the umbrella term of Arabic culture (although, I am aware how much oversimplifying this term is).

Sometimes, this culture is even termed as *honor culture* (cf. Osh et al. 2013: 334), that is, a culture, in which "[i]nsults to honor should be retaliated against quickly and with force (Osh et al. 2013: 334)." Because of that I found it very interesting to take a closer look at the origin of this Arabic sentiment of honor, which must naturally trace back *at fontes* of Arabic culture, i.e., to al-Ǧāhiliyya.

The impression that honor, dignity, sense of pride plays such a special role for Arabic and Muslim people definitely can be ascribed to the honor killing[2] practice, which – especially in Europe – from time to time, makes headlines. The ubiquity of honor killing as a theme in media could be supported by the data from corpus analysis. The lexeme *killing* is the second most frequent nominal modifier of the American English *honor*, and British English *honour*.[3] It is also a theme of many, sometimes unreliable, reportages or novels, which contributed to the spread of a certain stigma of honor killing, attached to Arabic and Muslim culture.

Consequently, I wanted to examine a possible contrast between the Arabic and European understanding of honor. I intended then to see how much the historical and modern forms of this concept resemble the pre-Islamic understanding. I must admit I expected to find profound (or at least significant) differences, which could explain the historical and (presumed) modern Arabic respect towards this notion. What is yet interesting is the fact that the conclusions I arrived at – which I will present in the following chapters– might turn to be quite surprising for many.

1.1. Pre-Islamic Arabs, their poetry and their (?) language

In short, my case study concerns the native understanding of honor among pre-Islamic Arabs and the way, in which this understanding shaped the language – or more precisely, the means of linguistic expression – of those people. A topic defined in such a way, however, involves several questions, which – although many has attempted to answer them – are still a source of so many uncomfortable

---

2 An insightful account of honor killing and the governing role of shame in this practice in modern Pakistani culture is presented in Wilson & Lewandowska-Tomaszczyk (2021).

3 Based on the corpus *English Web 2015* (available on *SketchEngine*, https://www.sketchengine.eu [08-07-2021]). Interestingly, in Polish corpus *zabójstwo honorowe* "honor killing" is not that frequent, and according to frequency, the lexeme *zabójstwo* "killing" places 47th on the list of collocates of *honorowy* "honor" (cf. the corpus *Polish Web 2015* available on *SketchEngine*, https://www.sketchengine.eu [08-07-2021]).

doubts. The most important of them are the identification of *pre-Islamic Arabs* and the authenticity of existing records of their poetry.

Although it might sound surprising, we still do not precisely know how it came to be that Arabs started referring to themselves as *ʕarab* (cf. Hoyland 2017). In general, it is commonly accepted that the Semitic root √ʕRB did link to the notion of desert and its dwellers. Thus, in Biblical Hebrew, one can find such lexemes as *ʕărābā*, being the desert in the territory of modern Jordan (Danecki 2001: 19), or *ʕărābī* – someone, who obviously led a life of a nomad (cf. Is13:20). Similarly, *aribi* indicated a desert-dweller in Assyrian texts (Hoyland 2001: 8).[4] Consequently, at the beginning of the common era, the term *Arab* became strongly attached to the former lands of Nabatean kingdom, which after the Roman conquest were turned into the province of *Arabia*. Thus, with time, the people, who lived in its towns and cities, began to be referred to as *Arabs* (Hoyland 2017: 127–8). Nevertheless, it is worth noting that many times in the ancient texts, variations of the name Arab can have diverse signification, sometimes difficult to explain, such as the instance of its application in the reference to a religious cult (cf. Retsö 2013: 363, 2010: 285–6).

The aforementioned remarks can explain only why others used to refer to Arabs in the way we still do. In fact, some scholars, such as Webb, proposed that the use of the Arabic lexeme *ʕarab* as an endonym, i.e., in reference to Arab people by Arabs themselves, is a rather later development, which took place after the Islamic conquest (al-Jallad 2020a: 423). However, it might well be the case that only the chronology of this development is wrong. Already in the famous Old Arabic inscription of an-Namāra, one can see the use of *ʕrb* – *ʕarab* – as an ethnicon rather than a toponym (al-Jallad 2020a: 423). Moreover, as reported recently by al-Jallad (2020a), there is a Safaitic inscription, in which similar reading is suggester for the term *ʔʕrb* – *ʔaʕrāb*.

These two terms – *ʕarab* and *ʔaʕrāb* – frequently assigned to sedentary *ʕarab* and Bedouin *ʔaʕrāb* respectively (Danecki 2001: 20), might be found in the Holy Qurʔān, which was written *bi-lisānin ʕarabiyyin mubīn* "in an eloquent Arabic tongue (Q26: 195)." As noticed by Retsö (2013: 362) as well as Zwettler (1978: 163), the adjective *ʕarabī* "Arabic", derived from *ʕarab*, that occurs in this verse, stands obviously in opposition to *ʔaʕǧamī*, which although usually is

4 What is quite important, these designations were primarily used exclusively in reference to the inhabitants of the Syrian desert (Hoyland 2001: 5), and only with time more and more area of what we call nowadays the Arabian Peninsula became referred to as Arabia, and the people who inhabited it as Arabs.

translated as "a foreigner (Greek or Persian)", used to referred to someone "who cannot speak clearly[5]". Thus, *ʕarabī* meant simply the one who could properly speak the Arabic language (Sālim 1988: 60), i.e., the one who was able to speak in a *faṣīḥ* "pure" way.[6] Consequently, we could infer that the Qurʔānic Revelation produced "in an eloquent Arabic tongue" occurred as something for certain people in their own idiom, "in sharp contrast to previous non-Arabic scriptural revelations (Zwettler 1978: 163)." It means then that for those people Arabic language was an index for self-identification.

In other words, even though the term *ʕarabī* was likely an exonym, with time it was adopted as the endonym by people who shared common identity founded on the use of a common language – Arabic language – *ʕarabiyya*. Nevertheless, one fact complicates this assertion: no inhabitant of the 6th and 7th century Arabian Peninsula is believed to have been the native speaker of this particular idiom (cf. Zwettler 1978: 101).

Perhaps better then, one could say that it was the ability of comprehending and – to a lesser extend – using *ʕarabiyya* that served as an important index for self-identification of pre-Islamic inhabitants of Arabian Peninsula in terms of more or less consciously existing *Kulturnation* (Zwettler 1978: 164). It was the case due to fact that *ʕarabiyya* – though being a mother tongue of no one – was the language variety used in the composition of the oral poetry, which undeniably played a key role in bringing those people together as one culture community of "Arabs". Consequently, we can perceive this poetry as the identifier that made a mass of people, who led a similar lifestyle and occupied a similar time and space, one people of a more or less unitary culture. It was then an "invisible bond between diverse clans" of Arabian people (al-Azzam & al-Kharabsheh 2013: 288). In other words, the easiest way to answer the question of who *pre-Islamic Arabs* were, is to say that they were the recipients of that oral poetry – often referred to as Early Arabic Poetry – that was composed and transmitted in the language known as *ʕarabiyya*.

1.1.1. Early Arabic Poetry (EAP) – the *register* of Arabs

Naturally then, the corpus of this poetry must be the best source for studying the culture of pre-Islamic Arabs (Mahrān 1980: 46). It is known for later generations

5 According to Retsö (2013: 362), this claim could be also supported by a similar use of the lexeme *ʕagūm*, a Hebrew Midrash cognate of Arabic *ʔaʕǧamī*.

6 Such a meaning of *ʕarabī* might be also deduced based on the contexts of use of the lexeme *faṣīḥ* "pure, eloquent" in Early Arabic Poetry (cf. t23A:70; t36A:204; t28A:125).

as *dīwān al-ʕarab* "the register of Arabs", meaning that it is the only existing first-hand record of the culture of these people (Mahrān 1980: 48). In fact, most of what we know about them comes from this *dīwān* (Dziekan 2008: 84). It tells us about their life, religion, customs, traits of character, and even about their ways of thinking (Sālim 1988: 40; Mahrān 1980: 47).

Usually, the term Early Arabic Poetry (EAP) is applied to the oral poetry composed by the first *ṭabaqa* "layer" of Arabic poets, who according to medieval Arabic writer al-Ǧāḥiẓ, lived during 150 years before Islam, in 6th and 7th century (Dziekan 2008: 81). Nevertheless, as a whole, it is deeply rooted in the past of pre-Islamic Arabs (Knauf 2010: 242). The development of EAP was certainly related to court centers of such royalties as Laḫmids, ruling in al-Ḥīra (Danecki 1998: 21), Ġassānids from Levant (Kowalski 1997: 40), or even the kings of the tribal congregation of Kinda, existing in Naǧd in 5th/6th c. CE (al-Sharkawi 2017: 54–5). Thus, from among its major themes one can find eulogy, yet the thematic scope of EAP was by far more diverse and covered satire, as well as so-called *ḥamāsa*, i.e., encouragement to fight, addressed to the poet's tribesmen (ʕAlī 1993c: 341).

The oral poetry played a crucial role in the society of pre-Islamic Arabs. One can say that it was one of the major *foci* of their culture, which was as an essential part of its definition as ancestor cult, combat, honor, natural environment, or constant migration (Dziekan 2012: 18). In fact, poets served a key function within a tribe. They were the spokespersons of the entire group – sometimes its *pars-pro-toto* (cf. Danecki 2001: 58–9), and, frequently, they played a role of modern publicists or commentators (Bielawski 1968: 28), or even journalists (Hitti 1970: 25). For that, poets were venerated by their tribesmen – up to the point of fear. Moreover, it could be perhaps quite justified to say that EAP actually functioned in a simile to modern social media. The poems, passed from mouth to mouth were means, by which pre-Islamic Arabs shared information (quite frequently in the form of "fake news"), promoted their self-image, and – of course – insulted each other.

Having been an oral phenomenon, EAP has not been recorded until so-called *tadwīn* period, between 8th and 10th c. (Dziekan 2012: 11). Before that, it was being preserved and transmitted – still orally – by professional reciters known as *ruwāẗ* (sg. *rāwī*), who did "memorize, authenticate, verify and narrate the poetry of a particular poet or several poets" (al-Sharkawi 2017: 28). The *tadwīn* period was deeply linked to the growing interest in EAP among medieval Arabic scholars, who believed it was composed in a language variety akin to that one of the Qurʔān (al-Sharkawi 2017: 28). Thus, it was crucial for their work aiming to assure the proper understanding of the Holy Text.

Nonetheless, the long oral transmission – lasting at least 150–200 years –must have risen doubts as for the authenticity or originality of the text recorded during the *tadwīn* period. Already in the Middle Ages, scholars such as al-Ǧumaḥī († 845) suggested that poems constituting the corpus of EAP were misattributed by its early compilers, i.e., Ḥammād ar-Rāwiya († 771/2 c.) and Ḫalaf al-Aḥmar († 796/7), or even that they were fabricated altogether (Mahrān 1980: 51).

In modern times, the doubts raised around the Early Arabic Poetry have been of much gravity, reaching the point of the dismissal of the existence of such a phenomenon at all. Scholars such as Ṭaha Ḥusayn or D. S. Margoliouth considered the corpus of the poetry of al-Ǧāhiliyya as a later, Islamic creation, which only with time was romanticized as the original literary composition of Arabs from before the Revelation (Monroe 1972: 1–4). In fact, as noted by Rabin (1955: 21), we cannot deny that there are signs of some editing in the corpus of EAP, which can be inferred from the discrepancies between the corpus we have and some of the quotations scattered in works of medieval Arabic scholars. This is probably why so many modern philologists of Arabic language and Qurʔān researchers tend to ignore the texts of EAP (Bauer 2010: 700). This distrust persists even today (cf., e.g., Owens 2006: 8), even though scholars seem to have come to consensus in dismissing the doubts about the originality of the Early Arabic Poetry (Bauer 2010: 700).[7] Indeed, they were not taken too seriously by medieval Arabic philologists, who resorted to numerous quotations of the al-Ǧāhiliyya poems, e.g., in their dictionaries and lexicons (Dziekan 2008: 83).

1.1.2. Authenticity of EAP and its oral-formulaic nature

In general, I strongly believe that in the case of EAP, we should concur with Marek Dziekan (2012: 17) who maintains that "one can compose a number of poems in a specific manner or style, yet it is impossible to invent the whole civilization". But how can we know for a fact that what has reached us thanks to the *tadwīn* efforts of medieval Arabic philologists is an authentic pre-Islamic creation? The answer, I believe, should be sought in the characteristics of EAP as an oral poetic tradition. And that's the answer first given by James T. Monroe (1972) and later by Michael Zwettler (1978) in their analyses of formulaicity of EAP and its language.

They both decided to adopt a theory of oral-formulaic composition proposed by two scholars, Milman Parry and Albert Lord, who studied Homeric and

7 For details of debunking the claims by Ṭaha Ḥusayn and D. S. Margoliouth cf. Monroe (1972: 4–5).

Yugoslavian epics. With time, their theory found its application to a variety of oral traditions, such as Greek poetry (Hesiod, Delphic oracular utterances), Old and Middle English poetry, medieval French and German epics, Old Testament verse, Babylonian, and Hittie epic (Zwettler 1978: 5). What connects all those creations is their seemingly longevity across (sometimes countless) generations that commonly is ascribed to the "fantastic memories" of illiterate people who were their creators and later transmitters (Zwettler 1978: 4). What Parry and Lord proposed is a different explanation for their astonishing preservation that instead of being seen as a product of "fantastic memories" of illiterate people should be seen as a result of the "modes of *composition* that are distinctly oral, rather than literary" (Zwettler 1978: 4).

Those modes relied heavily on existence of a set of so-called formulas that up to date have been characterized in several ways. Parry defined a formula as "a group of words which is regularly employed under the same metrical conditions to express a given essential idea (in Zwettler 1978: 6).[8]" In other words, a formula might be seen as a "mental template underlying the production of [orally composed verses] (Nagler in Zwettler 1978: 7)", thereby prescribing certain "verbal configurations of sounds, rhythm, syntax, diction, meaning, and (…) context", and persisting by that as a "recurrent verbal phenomen[on]" (Zwettler 1978: 9). In more modern version, however, the formula is being defined as "a sequence, continuous or discontinuous, of words or other meaning elements, which is, or appears to be, prefabricated: that is, stored and retrieved whole from memory at the time of use, rather than being subject to generation or analysis by the language grammar (Wray & Perkins in Lancioni 2009: 222)."

Perhaps, the best way to understand the formulas is to see them as "rhythmic aids", what was proposed by Monroe (1972: 11). The "oral-formulaic technique of verse composition" was based on the use of such aids, the pre-existing formulas. In the oral verse creation, a poet used those formulas-aid, knowing that each of them is a formula of a certain type. A poem produced in such a way was "not composed *for* but *in* performance (Lord in Zwettler 1978: 8)" that was spontaneous from start to finish (Monroe 1972: 11). These formulas-rhythmic aids were part of an ongoing oral tradition – and thus a poet was both a creator and a transmitter of poetry, who underwent a training that meant mainly the "unconscious absorption of hundreds of lines containing units – verbal, metrical, and syntactic – that are not necessarily identical, but that exhibit strong 'family' resemblance (Nagler in Zwettler 1978: 8)."

---

8 For more definitions of *formula* cf. Lancioni (2009: 222–5).

Parry and Lord's theory must naturally pertain to the question of the authenticity of the studied texts, which for long had been orally transmitted until the time of their final recording in a form of a written text. In fact, they proposed to see this written final text not as a preserved, faithful image of the "original" creation, but rather as the reflection of "a single moment in the tradition (Lord in Zwettler 1978: 5)", which resulted in emergence of a fixed text. Before that, however, the text must have existed in a plethora of variants, being again and again (re-)created during performances of poets-singers. Still, every of such "variant" of a text – an online variation composed in a performance in a specific place and time, for a specific audience – was nevertheless always recognized as a performance of the same poem or song (Zwettler 1978: 10). Moreover, it is safe to say that a given performance was not a "variant" of a particular poem – since there was seemingly no "original version" of this poem at the first place. The oral tradition was fluid: poems-songs were composed orally (a poet – an illiterate person – did not write them down at any time), so from the very beginning they have existed in a variety of forms, more or less alike in their underlining patterns design – the formulaic composition. Thus, as claimed by Lord, the conception of originality cannot be logically consistent with the oral tradition (Zwettler 1978: 10). Consequently, the question whether the written record of a poem preserved its "original" form is meaningless. Such a record is nothing more than a record of a single performance of a poem (Zwettler 1978: 10). Still, beyond any doubts, it was by any means the performance of this exact poem: its substance was transmitted intact, and the only alterations, which occurred from times to times in different performances of the poem "involved addition, omission, and transposal of lines or material as a result of variations in style, training, or background from one poet to another or from one period in a poet's career to another (Lord in Zwettler 1978: 10)." Nevertheless, the poem was still *the same poem*, assured to be that by the performer, who "would empathetically claim that his presentation (…) is a verbatim "recitation" of it as he heard or performed it before (Zwettler 1978: 25)." Having said that, we must bear in mind that although a given performance was claimed to be a recitation of a particular poem-song, the oral transmission was not entirely based on memorization (Zwettler 1978: 18). The poem was re-created as a formulaic composition: a more or less fixed collection of formulas. It was the same text performed anew, in which the recitation of the memorized texts was performed in an improvised style.

Such a phenomenon – the orally composed poetry, transmitted through generations of poet-singers known by different names – psalmists, rhapsodes, *ruwāẗ* (sg. *rāwī*), jongleurs, guslars, skalds (Zwettler 1978: 18) – could be definitely seen as folk poetry (Zwettler 1978: 32). Such folk poetry is what EAP could be called as well. This was already proposed by such Arabic philologists as Karl Petráček or Alfred Bloch (Zwettler 1978: 33). Zwettler agrees with them, adding his assertion that not only was EAP folk poetry, but also the oral-formulaic tradition. He goes on presenting his case study on the *muʕallaqa* by Imruʔ al-Qays. He demonstrates how EAP passes the test for oral-formulaic composition (Zwettler 1978: 41): its verses are characterized by the rare enjambement, the presence of formulaic techniques and "well-established themes for rapid composition (Lord in Zwettler 1978: 41)." Together they were factors "of great value both to the oral-formulaic poet and to the mnemonically oriented transmitter or reciter (Zwettler 1978: 31)." The limited study by Zwettler was later recreated on the larger body of texts by Paoli (2001), who confirmed that EAP poems were orally composed and transmitted "with the aim of rendering a previously heard poem as excellently and as accurately as possible (Zwettler 1978: 32)."

Everywhere in EAP, one can notice the presence of the formulaic techniques: "[i]dentical or similar word- groups, corresponsional phonetic or syntactic phrases, appearance of like syntactical or grammatical units in the same metrical position (Zwettler 1978: 41)." Yet, the thematic formulaicity can be also observed in this poetic tradition. Most of its poems follows a fixed thematic model of *nasīb-waṣf-qaṣd*: the beginning with a nostalgic opening, often a description of a deserted campsite, followed by the description of a camel/horse/wine/hunting etc., and the end with a "purpose" verses, i.e., eulogy (*madḥ*) or satire (*hiǧāʔ*) (Kowalski 1997: 49, 61–9). Moreover, all these conventionalized units also kept occurring in a close set of recurrent "motifs, images, and stylistic figures or speech [that] disclose the common tradition (Zwettler 1978: 79)."

All in all, EAP poems seem to have been a good example of oral-formulaic folk composition, despite that they certainly differ in size from Homeric or Slavic epics analyzed by Parry and Lord. This difference could only mean that the verbatim memorization played more significant role in their transmission (Monroe 1972: 40), "greatly reduc[ing] the urgency of the poet's need for a rigidly economical system of formulas (Zwettler 1978: 55)." Thus, all the members of a pre-Islamic Arabic tribe or clan could play to a certain degree a role in transmitting the poems composed by their poets (Zwettler 1978: 30).

Therefore, EAP might and should be considered an authentic pre-Islamic phenomenon – despite all the doubts casted over centuries on the uncertain attribution of al-Ǧāhiliyya poems. In fact, this uncertainty of the attribution seems to be the only issue that has troubled some Arabic and Western philologists (Zwettler 1978: 196) to the point that while falsifying it, some of them went a step further, denying the existence or authenticity of the whole corpus of EAP (Monroe 1972: 6). Yet, the uncertainty of poetry attribution is an inevitable part of the oral-formulaic tradition (sic!). The attribution issue is always linked to the pursuit after the original version of a poem. However, as I mentioned, originality is logically inconsistent with the oral composition that is characterized by built-in fluidity, existence in variations – from the very moment, in which a poem was conceived. Though, its creator – an illiterate poet – did not write down its "original version" and from the beginning, his or her performance must have differed from one instance to another (cf. Monroe 1972: 14).

This variation must have continued later within the oral transmission by *ruwāt* that were not only mere transmitters, but also poets themselves (Zwettler 1978: 83), who as pointed out by Goldziher, "contributed to the perfection (Zwettler 1978: 86)" of transmitted compositions. In fact, as noticed by Bräunlich, the relationship between a *šāʕir*-poet and a *rāwī*-transmitter should be rather considered in terms of the relationship between a master and a student. Such a relationship inevitably resulted in emergence of poetical "schools" of poets bound by a long chain of *šāʕirs* and *rāwīs* (Zwettler 1978: 86). The poems passed down such a string of illiterate creators must have existed in variants – thus the variation, as noted by Blachère, was inescapably inherent to EAP.

The fact that this poetry was created within strings of poets-transmitters perfectly justifies considering it a "collective" or "folk" tradition (Zwettler 1978: 81). It also explains so-called *intiḥāl*, i.e., using verses attested in poems by other author/s. It was not then any verse "theft" – *sariqa* – but rather the evidence for the existence of a common poetical heritage, from which oral poets drew (cf. Zwettler 1978: 83). They shared yet the same stock of formulas they employed in their compositions, and "these formulaic elements may be the surest proof that we are dealing, by and large, with an *authentic and conscientiously recorded* body of poems composed and rendered within an oral tradition as it has come to be understood (Zwettler 1978: 198).[9]"

1.1.3. Language of Early Arabic Poetry (LEAP)

Yet, what does such an authenticity of EAP tell us about the language of its composition? Can we consider it also *authentic* pre-Islamic variety of language used by pre-Islamic Arabs?

---

9 Let us note, in passing, that the formulaicity of EAP is sometimes used as an argument against its authenticity. For instance, Owens (2006: 8) dismisses EAP as a valid source of data for the historical studies on Arabic, supporting his view with the conclusions presented in Zwettler (1978), which – as evidently shown in here – rather argues straightforwardly in favor of the authenticity of EAP.

Technically speaking, this variety – as I mentioned, known as *ʕarabiyya* – is usually covered by the umbrella term of Classical Arabic (CA) that might be define as the language of Arabic texts produced between 6th and the end of 8th c. (Danecki 1998: 7). These texts include not only EAP, but also the Holy Qurʔān, as well as the poetry composed during the Umayyad era. Sometimes however, the language of EAP is singled out within this complex, even though from the perspective of morphology and syntax,[10] there is no plausible argument to do so.

Due to the character of my study – focus of which is placed on the semantic culture-bound content conveyed in language – I also follow this distinction in my research, referring to the variety of CA employed in EAP simply as Language of Early Arabic Poetry (LEAP). I decided to use this straightforward term, even though this variety has gone by different names, such as "pre-Islamic Arabic poetic *koiné*" (Danecki 1998: 22) or "pre-Classical Arabic" (al-Sharkawi 2017: 49–50). This is because they both are rather imperfect. "Pre-Classical Arabic" connects too easily with the "classicism" of CA, i.e., "an ideological construct like each and every other linguistic environment polluted by the concept of something "classical" (i.e., diachronically normative) (Knauf 2010: 248)." The adjective "classical" should be seen rather as a sociolinguistic label (Larcher 2010: 269) that tells us something only about the value attached to this language variety by the much later scholars. "Pre-Islamic Arabic poetic *koiné*", however, is quite unfortunate due to the nature of the LEAP. The term *koiné* suggests some relatedness to Greek *koiné*. The problem is that in contrast to that language, LEAP was not a spoken variety (Rabin 1951: 17). It was rather a sociolect of pre-Islamic poets "made for the poets and comprehended by themselves above all (Brockelmann in Zwettler 1978: 101)."

In other words, LEAP was the *Kunstsprache* and *Hochsprache* of pre-Islamic Arabic society, mastered by "word- smiths" of al-Ǧāhiliyya: poets, orators, soothsayers, and prophets (Zwettler 1978: 135). Thus, it was by far affected by the oral- formulaic specificity of the texts those "word- smiths" produced. Consequently, one can explain some of its peculiarities – and further, some of the peculiarities of CA – only as a result of conventionalizing certain formulaic way of the expression of particular meaning (cf. Lancioni 2009: 220).

As the *Kunstsprache* and *Hochsprache*, LEAP was also the mean of trans- or intertribal communication (Zwettler 1978: 111), playing by that the role of the nexus binding speakers of different Arabic dialects into a single cultural

10 Although, Bloch held that one should differentiate between CA and the language employed in EAP based on syntactical discrepancies observed in between (Zwettler 1978: 103).

group – becoming, as I mentioned, an index for their self-identification. Consequently, it can actually resemble Homeric Greek – the *Kunstsprache* of ancient Greeks – sharing with it two important traits (Zwettler 1978: 97). Both are closely related to the process of formulas conventionalization. They might seem contradictory: on the one hand, LEAP and Homeric Greek preserved many of the archaic features that ceased to function in spoken varieties; on the other hand, however, they have also incorporated throughout time many dialectal elements from different spoken vernaculars (Zwettler 1978: 102). Both preservation and incorporation have been resulting from the process of conventionalizing linguistic units within the stock of poetical oral formulas. In other words, some archaisms and dialectal features stuck in LEAP and Homeric Greek because "they adequately and quite satisfactory functioned in specific prosodic contexts (Zwettler 1978: 112)."

In LEAP, the incorporated dialectal features are usually some variants of morphological units, such as demonstratives, patterns for broken plural or verbal nouns (Zwettler 1978: 111). Additionally, in this variety, as dialectal elements one can perceive the stock of synonyms and near-synonyms. In both cases, the individual tribal linguistic items were "absorbed into the common poetic vocabulary of Arabic-speaking poets (Zwettler 1978: 111)." The conventionalization of these dialectal elements was responsible for the emergence of a wide spectrum of replaceable items, which can be employed in specific rhythmic and metrical environments without the alteration of conveyed meaning (Zwettler 1978: 103).

On the other hand, the preservation of archaic features was dictated by the sheer fact of their usefulness for certain prosodic contexts. From among such features, in LEAP, the most important one is so-called *ʔiʕrāb*, i.e., the system of word-final short vowels used for marking grammatical case in nominal and verbal (modal) inflection. As argued by al-Jallad and van Puten (2017), this system is a feature that can be traced back to Proto-Semitic language. This could mean that its preservation in LEAP is quite remarkable. Nevertheless, it would be not preserved – as it was the case of the spoken vernaculars of Arabic – if it was not "a functional and vital element of skilled poetic rendition (Zwettler 1978: 145)." Thus, *ʔiʕrāb* was preserved only because it was an irremovable element of oral formulas of EAP (loc. cit.).

The preservation of archaic features and the absorption of dialectal elements makes it clear that LEAP cannot be simply considered as a stage of the development of Arabic language (Zwettler 1978: 148). Nevertheless, it was – together with the language of Qurʔān – the base for later deduction and codification of CA by the philologists and grammarians of 8th and consecutive centuries

(Zwettler 1978: 148). Therefore, as noted by Lancioni (2009: 220, 223), the oral-formulaic nature of EAP can contribute to our understanding of specifics not only of this pre-Islamic mean of a special communication, but also of CA and further of Modern Standard Arabic (MSA). LEAP was deeply affected by this mode of poetic composition. In fact, it became with time specifically convenient for such creation due to its schematic – "patterned" – morphology that "allows for a high degree of interchangeability of lexical parts (Zwettler 1978: 55)", playing by that an important role in respect of both the formulaic composition and its later transmission (Zwettler 1978: 32). This, however, means that not only LEAP preserved some archaic features and absorbed others from dialects, but also that it bears many other – sometimes odd – linguistic traits[11] that have arisen from the oral-formulaic nature of its use (cf. Lancioni 2009: 223).

Consequently, my answer to the question of the authenticity of LEAP is positive: this variety of Arabic language was in fact a pre-Islamic variety – preserved within the stock of formulas of EAP in composition and re-composition of folk poetry of al-Ǧāhiliyya. Still, its history is vague and full of uncertainty. It must obviously predate the poets from 6th c., whose names were passed down by the tradition. At this point, however, the obviousness ends – anything else one could tell about this language is unfortunately a matter of many hypotheses.

1.1.4. The history of LEAP: a hypothesis

In my opinion, the most interesting of those hypotheses was presented by Knauf (2010) and Durie (2019), who attempted to recreate a link between ancient spoken Arabic vernacular of Nabatean Kingdom and *ʕarabiyya*.

Knauf believed that both LEAP, as well as the variety of Arabic, in which the Qurʔān was composed, were distant descendants of the ancient dialect of Nabateans – people, who created a strong kingdom and a trading empire that existed in between 3rd c. BCE and 2nd c. CE. It is rather certain that they were Arabs – at least for Greeks and Romans (Durie 2018: 4–5). Consequently, they rather spoke some variety of Arabic, which seems to have been characterized by the use of *(ʔ)l-* definite article (al-Jallad 2018: 325). Although their statehood ceased to exist in 108 CE, their presence is still attested in Roman writings from

11 Some of the examples of such traits, such as dual agreement marking in verbs and adjectives, or singular form of 3rd person verb with plural nominal subject, were discussed in Lancioni (2009: 225–36).

4th c., such as by Epiphanius, who noted that Nabateans were singing hymns in Arabic to their virgin goddess known as "Kaabou[12]" (Hoyland 2007: 53–4).

This spoken vernacular of Nabateans – Nabatean Old Arabic – became with time a certain variety of prestige, which was used alongside other Arabic vernaculars known as Ancient North Arabian dialects (Knauf 2010: 228). In other words, the diglossia – as understood by Ferguson (Mejdell 2018: 333) – was the major feature of the linguistic situation as much of the society of ancient Arabs as of those living today (Knauf 2010: 229). Nabatean Old Arabic was elevated as the dialect of prestige due to the sociopolitical influence of the trading empire of Nabateans, whose commercial network covered the whole Arabian Peninsula. Primarily, as a *koiné* dialect, it was, however, only a spoken variety, perhaps limited to the use by traders and shippers (Knauf 2010: 229). From this trading variety, Early Standard Arabic emerged – a later *koiné* dialect used in intertribal commercial communication by the dwellers of the Arabian Peninsula (Knauf 2010: 231).

Nevertheless, there is evidence that Nabataean Old Arabic was not limited only to the trading activities. It seems that it – or its variation – was also utilized in religious cult. It definitely can be observed in the famous text of En Avdat inscription from 1st/2nd c. CE. It is a Nabatean text written in Aramaic, in which a "three stichoi of early Arabic poetry" in the meter *ṭawīl* were inserted (Knauf 2010: 233). These Arabic verses – although their proper deciphering is still debated – seems to be linked to a cultic context. It could correspond with what aforementioned Epiphanius of Salamis said about post-Nabateans – namely that they sang hymns in Arabic to their deities. Similar observations were also made by St. Jerome. Thus, we can hypothesize that up to 4th/5th c. CE, people living in the former realm of Nabatean kingdom used Arabic in their religious practices (Knauf 2010: 235).

Perhaps, then, as proposed by Retsö (2010: 290), primarily, *ʕarabiyya* was a variety of language reserved for cultic purposes. Therefore, in al-Ǧāhiliyya, this dialect was reserved for *kāhin*s, i.e., pagan diviners or soothsayers, who used it in uttering their prophecies. With time however, as noted by Goldziher, from this cultic institution a secular one emerged – it was the institution of a *šāʕir*-poet

12 According to Joan (2018) *Kaabou* was an Arabic goddess styled as a black stone. The evidence for her existence were found in one of the tombs at Petra in 1989. It was seemingly a virgin goddess (cf. Arabic *ǧarya kāʕib* "the girl whose breasts are beginning to swell (Lane 1968g: 2616)"), possibly cognate of Venus/Ishtar. Joan upholds that there is a straightforward link between black-stone goddess *Kaabou* of Nabateans and the Meccan sanctuary of Kaʕba and its Black Stone.

(Kowalski 1997: 46). Al-Ǧāhiliyya poets kept using *ʕarabiyya* in their poetic creation, which evolved from religious to fully secular poetry, such as it was persisting in 6th c. and onward (Kowalski 1997: 46–9). The suggestion that in the past the functions of *kāhin*-diviner and *šāʕir*-poet could have persisted united is embedded in the very term *šāʕir* "poet" (Dziekan 2012: 18) that meant literarily "feeling (more)" or perhaps "oversensitive" or even "inspired" (Knauf 2010: 247). Nevertheless, even after the "secularization" of poetry, a poet still enjoyed a semi-religious status, for instance, they were believed to possess his or her own jinni (Dziekan 2012: 18).

This "secularization" might have been related to the de-Hellenization of the Middle East, which began in 4th c. CE. As noted by Knauf (2010: 239), this social development also involved the change in the mode of addressing the public. Previously employed stone inscriptions started disappearing, and as a consequence, a new "public forum" of poetry emerged. This poetry became a "pan-Arabic means of expression and communication" and it developed from the earlier Nabatean cultic poetry (Knauf 2010: 239).

Thus, in fact, in al-Ǧāhiliyya, according to Knauf, at least two pan-Arabic varieties were in use that can be, I think, covered by the umbrella term of *ʕarabiyya*. Among those varieties, there was aforementioned Early Standard Arabic, i.e., a *koiné* of city-based traders, and the poetic and religious language, which appears to have been an "intertribal language of prestige of the Bedouin society" (Knauf 2010: 241, 246–7). The latter underwent solidification at the royal courts of Kinda (Rabin 1951: 3), Laḫmids (Danecki 1998: 21), and Ġassānids (Kowalski 1997: 40), and eventually turned into what I call LEAP. Alongside these two varieties, Arabs spoke their everyday dialects (Retsö 2010: 282), which could have descended from other variants of Arabic spoken at the beginning of the common era, including so-called Ancient North Arabian dialects. What is quite interesting, both Knauf (2010) and Durie (2019), suggest that it was Early Standard Arabic – not LEAP – that was employed by Muḥammad in reviling His Message.[13] Later on, after the rise of Islam, LEAP became the language of prestige

13 Knauf (2010:247) seems to suggest that Qurʔān was actually composed in a variety of Early Standard Arabic strongly influenced by LEAP. He says: "The orthography of the Qur'an firmly places its language in the context of [Early Standard Arabic] which, however, was not yet an all-Arabian standard [since it was restricted to trading activities]. The Prophet wanted to create an Arabic holy scripture, so he had to take recourse to the only written form of Arabic that existed in his time. At the same time, he produced a religious text, so it was necessary to recite the written in a manner as close to Poetic Old Arabic [i.e., LEAP] as possible, necessitating occasional claims that the Prophet

for tribal aristocracy and feudal lords, and Early Standard Arabic laid the foundation for Standard Arabic, the language of commerce and administration (Knauf 2010: 248) that later was merged with LEAP into the construct of CA.

Perhaps, a distant echo of the fact that LEAP was derived from Nabatean variety of Arabic can be the meaning of the adjective *nabaṭī* "Nabatean", which in modern Bedouin communities also serves to denote oral poetic composition and performance. Perhaps, as hypothesized by Durie (2019: 9–10), this name is a remnant of an ancient metonymy, in which the whole poetic composition was referred to by the term used to define the language used by a poet. It is worth noting that this modern Bedouin oral poetry is also composed in a special poetic variety of Arabic, removed from spoken vernaculars. In fact, this special dialect resembles somehow LEAP, possibly being its descendant that underwent around 1500 years long development (cf. Monroe 1972: 13).

Consequently, I believe, it is fair to say that the oral-formulaic nature of LEAP might be traced back to its cultic ancestor employed in (pan-)Arabic pagan cult at least in the remnants of the Nabatean Kingdom. In fact, other oral-formulaic traditions – such as Delphic oracular utterances or Old Testament verse (Zwettler 1978: 5) – were also related to cultic forms. The formulas of EAP were then first developed within the religious context that perhaps was also an important factor in the preservation of archaic linguistic features. It is possible then that although with time the stock of formulas must have undergone thematic evolution, some old patters – morphological, syntactical, but also lexical and conceptual – could have got preserved and thus, via LEAP, perpetuated in CA and later in its descendant, MSA.

1.2. Studying LEAP and the culture of pre-Islamic Arabs

All in all, *ʕarabiyya* as LEAP began to serve as the index of the self-identification for certain people living in particular time and space. These people were Arabs of al-Ǧāhiliyya, the recipients of EAP. Therefore, this book – to put in another way – is about the language that brough together those people into one culture "nation". Studying a fragment of it – its semantic frames for discourse about

---

was nevertheless no poet (*shāʿir*), i.e., inspired pagan". Durie (2019), in turn, states that definitely Qurʔānic language was the *koiné* of merchants and traders. He also presents an extensive argument, supporting this thesis, mostly based on the observation on so-called Qurʔānic Consonantal Texts (QCT) and the rhyme rules, which points towards the inconsistency of the later punctation. At the same time, he demonstrates the compatibility of QCT and Nabatean or post-Nabatean variety.

honor – give us the opportunity to see some pieces of the perspective pre-Islamic Arabs had while perceiving the reality. But is such a study justified enough?

Even if EAP is not "original" in the sense of being 1:1 reflection of poems created and first performed in 6th and 7th c., its language – LEAP – might be consider actually "original", or as close as it gets to "original". This is because EAP was an oral-formulaic folk tradition – composed and later transmitted by means of fixed formulas. Therefore, following Monroe (1972: 17), I would risk a hypothesis that LEAP as recorded in those formulas was a preserved semi-closed linguistic system, which retained certain archaic linguistic features as well as was constantly absorbing new material along the way of the history of its use as a poetic prestige variety. In other words, although the corpus of EAP might not be entirely frozen in time, the language used in its composition could be perceived so.

My study pertains to meaning encoded in this language. Naturally, I deduce it partially based on the corpus of "fluid" EAP. To a certain extent, poems traditionally ascribed to pre-Islamic or early Islamic poets, were altered with time in respect to verse order, verse addition/omission, or lexical substitution – all of which must have comply with the rhythmic and metrical intent of "original" author. Nevertheless, such alteration generally did not disturb the meaning intended by this author (Zwettler 1978: 190). Naturally, although quite rarely, one can find in EAP some later addition of Islamic provenance – especially in the discourse on religious life of Arabs. Thus, in some al-Ǧāhiliyya poems, we encounter "elimination of pagan theophoric names or substitution of the name *Allāh*, allusions to Qurʔānic passages or Islamic concepts or rituals (Zwettler 1978: 221)." These intrusions were a result of adjusting the poetical creation and transmission to the new sensibility of poets-transmitters' audiences, who were now Muslim (Zwettler 1978: 221). Nonetheless, to quote Zwettler,

> (…) these reflections of a post-*jāhilī* outlook are relatively rare and are really quite accidental, in general, to the spirit and substance of the poems in which they occur. The faithfulness of the seventh- to tenth-century Bedouin *rāwī*-poets to the tradition of their pre-Islamic forebears remained for the most part unquestioned. In all essential features – form, themes, imagery, style, language, and point of view – the recorded renditions that we call pre-Islamic poetry were, and still can be, accepted and recognized as equivalent to what those earlier poets had first uttered. Among the unlettered Bedouins, despite their formal adherence to Islam, the art and technique of oral verse composition and rendition persisted alive and intact. The continuity and integrity of the tradition of the poetry was assured because its traditional oral-formulaic mode of existence continued unchanged (Zwettler 1978: 222).

Thus, the subject of my study – the meaning, or intent (ar. *maʕnà*) – was rather undisturbed within the texts of EAP. The language that conveyed it, however, could undergo a limited "standardization" procedure, by later Arabic philologists – especially those affiliated with the Baṣran school, such as al-Aṣmaʕī. This procedure would entail "occasional grammatical normalizations (Zwettler 1978: 208)" of linguistic features found in the corpus of EAP that did not fully conform to the system discernible as dominant within the whole corpus of CA. Nevertheless, these "normalizations" were not invented by those philologists, nor were they introduced based on their whim. In my understanding, they were instances of "correcting" linguistic anomalies, i.e., features preserved within the transmission of some poems, yet not conventionalized (or simply widespread enough) as fully-accepted elements of some pan-Arabic poetic formulas. As a consequence, I imagine, some of these anomalies were "adjusted" to the more prevalent conventionalized forms – as long as such adjustments did not interfere with the rhythmic and metrical constitution of a given text. Therefore, I believe, even after the standardization procedure performed by medieval Arabic philologists, LEAP was still the authentic language of pre-Islamic Arabic oral poetic composition.

Moreover, since my study is semantic or conceptual in nature, it is worth mentioning that at these two levels, LEAP is a well-preserved pre-Islamic variety. This is because as noticed by Zwettler, the oral-formulaic formulas encoded also "significant number of recurrent motifs, images, situations, episodes, relationships, and contexts – all of which can certainly be considered "formulaic" on the conceptual, if not verbal, level (Zwettler: 1978: 77, cf. also 53)."

Therefore, I believe, it is safe to say that formulas actually encoded certain conceptualizations: cognitive schemata and categories, or conceptual metaphors and metonymies. These are usually encoded on the "verbal level" in form of a set of linguistic choices, associated with certain cognitive schemata (Fillmore 1975: 124). Consequently, I would risk saying that EAP oral formulas must have functioned in the simile to constructions evoking semantic frames available for certain concepts in the memory of the speaker (cf. Fillmore 1976: 25; Petruck 2013: 1) – here a poet (cf. Monroe 1972: 17). In other words, studying the stock of oral formulas of EAP might be considered as research aiming to describe semantic frames available to the users of LEAP. Furthermore, I propose to see such an enterprise as another application of Oral Tradition theory in linguistics. As noted by Lancioni (2009: 220), this approach is not employed too often in linguistic scholarship, yet it can afford so much better explanation for many peculiarities of languages known to have been used in oral-formulaic composition. In the case of my study, such an explanation is proposed to be presented as for the specifics of some of the semantic frames in LEAP, i.e., of the semantics of this variety of Arabic language.

Nevertheless, one should approach LEAP with caution, since as proved by Zwettler (1978: 209), there are instances, in which the standardization imposed by medieval philologists onto the text affects also the imagery intended in it. Similarly, one should be cautious with respect to synonyms or near-synonyms. It is certain that the popular perception of Arabic as the language most abundant in detailed vocabulary should be rather considered a folk theory. Most of the synonyms are absorptions from spoken vernaculars, which got conventionalized as parts of certain formulas due to their prosodic properties (Zwettler 1978: 55). Because of that, meanings of a given set of synonyms was rather generalized, and thus they cannot be seen as highly specialized vocabulary (Zwettler 1978: 113). Nonetheless, I believe that even so, the study on those (near) synonyms might be very beneficial for our understanding of pre-Islamic Arabic culture since the synonymous lexical items – even bearing the same conceptual content – reflect in fact different facets of experience of people of al-Ǧāhiliyya. In other words, the same concept could be referred to in different spoken vernaculars by different lexemes or expressions that – altogether – manifest different ways of experiencing a given phenomenon – all of which were yet pre-Islamic in nature.

At last, one could rise some objection as for the validity of my study due to its interest in a language variety that by no means was a native language or even a spoken vernacular of any inhabitant of pre-Islamic Arabian Peninsula in 6th and 7th c. Consequently, can I claim that my study examines the relationship between a certain language and the culture of those people? I believe, the answer is positive, because LEAP was not a secret language of pre-Islamic Arabic poets – it was a register of Arabic employed in a special means of communication between people. Despite the fact that, as I have already observed, it was functionally restricted – and its intelligibility must have differed from one person to another – it is still the most authentic record of linguistic behavior of Arabs living in al-Ǧāhiliyya. This is because EAP was the social media of those people – the poets always intended to address public, even though in doing so, they used a different – perhaps weird, archaic – language. EAP was not composed for an elite circle of poets only! And what they were creating was immersed in the conceptual system those poets shared with their audiences. This conceptual system might be called pre-Islamic Arabic culture.

And even if what I did was studying a sociolect, which could not faithfully reflect the whole spectrum of cognitive phenomena persisting in the society of pre-Islamic Arabs, I still strongly believe that we do not possess any other source of data I could've examined to enhance our understanding of the native perception – cultural cognition – shared by Arab people living in the times of al-Ǧāhiliyya. Thus, even though the texts constituting the corpus of EAP – *dīwān al-ʕarab* – probably underwent a process of morphosyntactic adjustments, I still uphold that they provide the most authentic picture of the conceptual world of those people.

Consequently, I believe that LEAP – the formulaic sociolect of al-Ǧāhiliyya poets – is the most suitable material for cultural linguistic study, since it could be seen as a vehicle that caried the authentic pre-Islamic cultural conceptualizations through generations, up until today. Those conceptualizations – schemata, categories, metaphors, and metonymies – were encrypted by the formulas that came to be the common heritage of Arabic poets, from which they drew in their creation and constant re-creation of oral folk poetry of al-Ǧāhiliyya.

Therefore, following Bauer (2010: 703), I believe that study of Early Arabic Poetry should not be yet abandoned, since there is still so much to be studied – in the field of historical anthropology, ethnology, and history of mentalities – in the only native – authentic – voice left after pre-Islamic Arabs.

1.3. Cultural Linguistic case study on HONOR in LEAP

To sum it up, in this book, I will present a case study, in which I applied the Cultural Linguistic methodology into the examination of HONOR in LEAP. My goal is to represent the encodement of cultural conceptualizations of HONOR in this variety of Arabic language. These conceptualizations can be understood as chunks of knowledge about HONOR shared by Arabs living in al-Ǧāhiliyya. In other words, my study aims to scrutinize the linguistic reality of those people from the point of view of their culture, which shaped this reality.

Being a case study, first and foremost, the aim of this presentation is to discuss the applicability of the Culture Linguistic model in research on historical stages of Arabic language. Moreover, I believe the conclusions I arrived at might serve as a starting point for many studies in synchronic and diachronic schema, both comparative – on related and unrelated languages – and descriptive – on Arabic varieties. Somehow, on the margin of my intentions, there was also a wish to prove that the studies on EAP, which in recent decades, gained some notoriety in the field of Arabic studies (especially, Arabic linguistics), are still a fruitful area of research, in which one can yet produce valuable conclusions. In a way then, I was inspired by Bauer's defense of this compartment of Arabic philology (Bauer 2010: 703). Following him, I fully agree that it can still bring in some important data on pre-Islamic Arabic life, deriving from such methodological schema as historical anthropology, ethnology, or history of mentalities.

For the case study, I selected the phenomenon of honor, yet I decided to focus on the most essential elements of this concepts that I could place within a coherent cultural model of honor as it functioned in the society of pre-Islamic

Arabs. Thus, I focused on the semantic frames organized around the following Arabic concepts: *karam*, *karāma*, *ḥasab*, *šaraf*, *ʕirḍ*, *mağd*, *ʕayb*, *ʕār*, and *ḥayāʔ*. One can noticed that I did not include among them any conception of PRIDE, which naturally can be perceived as relating to HONOR. This is because in this particular study I decided to focus only on the description of the conceptualizations of some social phenomena, without providing detailed insight into feelings or emotions triggered by them. Thus, insofar as I use the definition of these emotions in the models I present in my study, I did not intend to focus in it on the cultural specifics of these emotions, nor on their linguistic expression. Naturally, I am aware that research aiming specifically to define the emotional elements of the conceptualizations of HONOR could be of much benefit. Nevertheless, I decided to leave this area of LEAP conceptualizations for further studies.

As far as the state-of-the-art presentation is concerned, I decided to divide it in two sections, which will be included in the next two chapters. The first of them – **2. Theories and Methods** – is meant to bring closer the main ideas of Cultural Linguistics and its focus of the relationship between culture and language. In this chapter, I present the state of the cultural linguistic studies on Arabic language (cf. section 2.1.3.), as well as I describe the analyzed materials and the research procedure. The following chapter – **3. Honor** – presents the anthropological conclusions on the major theme of this book, i.e., honor. It presents the state of our understanding of honor, mostly based on the data from European cultures. In it, I also included the summary of research done on honor in the context of Arabic culture, as well as on the conceptualizations of HONOR encoded in language.

The remaining chapters will present my study on LEAP HONOR, which consisted in the most part of lexical analysis on lexemes and idiomatic expressions. As I mentioned, for the examination, I chose five HONOR-related lexemes – *karam*, *karāma*, *ḥasab*, *šaraf*, and *ʕirḍ* – as well as *mağd*, and SHAME-related *ʕayb*, *ʕār*, and *ḥayāʔ*. All in all, I aimed to describe their semantic content in terms of cultural conceptualizations, so as to represent a coherent cultural model of the system of honor as it persisted in the culture and language of pre-Islamic Arabs.

First of all, in Chapter 4. ***Karam* – *Karīm* – *Karāma*,** I discuss the most important element of this model, that is, the HONORABLE/NOBLE BEHAVIOR, which seems to be metonymically structured by the cultural script of GENEROSITY-HOSPITALITY. The chapter also includes the description of the equally essential concept of HONOR/RESPECT-PAID. Following that, being a logical extension of the former, Chapter 5. ***Ḥasab* – *Ḥasīb*** discusses the notion of HONOR-VALUE of someone derived from HONORABILITY. Both chapters 4. and 5. serve preparing the ground for the discussion of the most significant profiles of HONOR, being

PRECEDENCE and RIGHT TO RESPECT. The former is discussed in Chapter **6. *Šaraf* – *Šarīf***, and the latter in **7. *ʕIrḍ***. Chapter 6 also presents some conclusions on the conceptualizations of *mağd*, which were related to the schema of *šaraf*. At last, in Chapter **8. Shame & Dishonor**, I present my preliminary results from the analyses on LEAP schema SHAME, which include description of three concepts: *ʕayb*, *ʕār*, and *ḥayāʔ*.

In the summary of this book, in Chapter **9. Conclusions: HONOR and SHAME in LEAP**, I sum up my findings in the form of the essential structure of the cultural model of HONOR as it was functioning in LEAP (and al-Ğāhiliyya culture). Moreover, by adding in the preliminary data on pre-Islamic Arabic model of SHAME-DISHONOR, I will suggest existence of a subsuming model/script a of SOCIAL EVALUATION of WORTHINESS.

Eventually, the model I rendered is juxtaposed with the data on the European conception of HONOR, which by most part will be discussed in Chapter 3. This, however, will allow me to present some hypotheses on the possible consequences of such a juxtaposition for our more general understanding of HONOR and some social phenomena, which nowadays might not be seen as related to it at all. In such a way, I believe, my study can contribute not only to the enhancement of our knowledge of Arabic al-Ğāhiliyya, but also of our own social life.

2. Theories and methods

> *To study language is to hear clamor of culture grappling with raw experience.*
>
> G. Palmer, *Toward Theory of Cultural Linguistics, 1996, p. 6.*

Before I dive into the description of how the culture of pre-Islamic Arabs shaped their linguistic expression of HONOR, I would like to present an introduction to the major theoretical and methodological assumptions of my study. These were entirely based on the theory of so-called *Cultural Linguistics* (CL), which is a growing subfield of cognitive linguistics research. It is focused on the description of cultural grounding of language, i.e., the way, in which language is affected by culture. As one can see, the most important assumption of such theorem must be that of the existence of a firm relationship between language and culture.

In this chapter, I will present some theoretical conclusions CL researchers proposed in defining this particular relationship, pointing towards the mutual relevance culture and language bear to each other. After that, I would like to present some major premises of CL as a subfield of *Cognitive Linguistics* (CogL), as well as the brief history of its development. Later, I will define in detail analytical tools employed by CL and derived from CogL theory of language and human cognition. At last, I will present how CL predefines objectives of my research, and how I have met those through my research design.

2.1. Culture, cultural cognition, and language

First however, I feel obligated to elaborate on the aforementioned assertion that there is a relationship existing between language and culture. In order to do so, let me start form shedding some light on what in this statement is meant by *culture*.

The concept of culture is one of those vague terms everyone uses freely both in everyday and in scientific discourse. Perhaps, this is the reason why the major theorist of CL, Farzad Sharifian, avoided it, promoting the use of the term *cultural cognition* instead. In fact, what is really interesting for CL is human cognition that is shaped to a great extent by culture (Athanasiadou 2017: 112), which itself seems to be a broader phenomenon. Perhaps, then, one can define *culture* in two senses – in a narrow one as the cultural cognition, i.e., as a set of patterns of knowledge shared by some people, which "provide the ground for linguistic and nonlinguistic behavior (Athanasiadou 2017: 112)", and in the broader one, as a collection of all artifacts – narratives, ideologies, worldviews, art, etc. – in which this knowledge is encoded (Wilson & Lewandowska-Tomaszczyk 2017: 247–8).

Culture in the narrow sense, as the cultural cognition, is a kind of conceptual system (Kövecses 2017: 309) shared by people, who constitute a cultural group. The cognition itself – the conceptual system – "is both a process and a product (Kövecses 2017: 308)." As a process it can be understood as a set of cognitive operations of *making sense* of experience that lead to emergence of knowledge about the world, governing individual's apprehension and their behavior. This knowledge might be equated with the cognition being a product, and it is to a great extent shared by members of the same community – it is "a set of shared understandings (Kövecses 2005: 1)" of the reality.

The aforementioned cognitive operations are sometimes termed as *conceptualization*, which is described as a mental activity, which in a way, turns the *objective* world into *our* conceptualized world (cf. Jackendoff 2002: 294–332), being the (culturally) constructed knowledge of this world. In other words, (cultural) cognition is what accounts for the fact – acknowledged since at least Emmanuel Kant – that the only world we know is the one seen with our eyes. The *objective* world – *das Ding in sich* – is forever unavailable to our understanding.

Elements of this conceptualized world – or perhaps better, patterns of the knowledge originating from *making sense* of experience – are what we usually termed as *concepts*. However, CL prefers to name them *conceptualizations*, to accentuate their dynamic nature. Naturally, CL acknowledges the fact that these conceptualizations residue primarily in an individual (Sharifian 2008: 111). However, it emphasizes that they are largely influenced by culture. This influence comes from within the culture group, to which a given individual belongs, since their conceptualizations (concepts) are a subject of constant negotiations with the members of this group. To put it in other words, their "conceptualized world" is constantly *tuned* to the conceptions prevailing in this group (cf. Jackendoff 2002: 330). In this manner, members of a cultural group exchange their concepts about their experience of the reality, arriving eventually at a sort of consensus concerning the knowledge of the world. As a result, the members of that group share a conceptual system, which consists of conceptualizations making them "think, so to say, in one mind (Sharifian 2003: 187)".

Sharifian cultural cognition more precisely as a cognitive network of representations distributed heterogeneously across minds of the members of a culture group (Sharifian 2003: 190). It is what constitutes "the cultural knowledge that emerges from the interaction between [those] members (...) across time and space (Sharifian 2015: 476)". It is then and emergent and dynamic system, since it emerges from these interactions, in which the members of the cultural group negotiate and renegotiate constantly its content (Sharifian 2015: 476). In turn, human conceptualizations, being dynamic patterns of understanding of experience, which are mediated by the members of the cultural group, are mostly – however not entirely – cultural, and those *cultural conceptualizations* are at the heart of CL studies on language.

However, being units of organization of shared cultural knowledge (Sharifian 2008: 116), cultural conceptualizations are not distributed evenly across the cultural group. They are dispersed heterogeneously (Sharifian 2003: 192) and therefore, not all its members possess exactly the same understanding of the reality (Sharifian 2008: 112). This means that a cultural group is not determined in size – it might range from a size of a family or a tribe to the extent of a nation or nations (Sharifian 2003: 191). The fuzzy borders of culture groups are a result of the fact that some people share more or less of conceptualizations constituting bigger or smaller cultural entities such as civilizations, national cultures, local cultures, subcultures, etc.

All in all, culture defined in a narrow sense as a conceptual system or a shared cognition allows people belonging to the same culture group "[to make] sense of (…) experiences in a more or less unified manner (Kövecses 2017: 309)". In other words, what makes a culture is the similar understanding of the reality drew from common experience of those people and encoded in heterogeneously distributed conceptualizations. It is then the knowledge, according to which people behave, as well as, which they apply in their apprehension of the behavior of others (Sharifian 2008: 114); it is what makes people of a certain group think and even feel (Wilson & Lewandowska-Tomaszczyk 2017: 247) in a comparable way – or simply stated, experience the world in a similar manner.

As I mentioned, the culture in a broader sense might be seen as not only encompassing cultural cognition and cultural conceptualizations shared by a group of people, but also the means, in which those conceptualizations are expressed, such as literature, painting, and other arts. Among these means, however, language has a prominent position.

The major assumption of CL is that "language is a central aspect of cultural cognition (Sharifian 2015: 476)", since it largely embodies conceptualizations of its speakers (Sharifian 2008: 116), being by that "the tool by which cultural cognition is stored and communicated (Wilson & Lewandowska-Tomaszczyk 2017: 248)". In other words, cultural cognition is "instantiated in the content and the use of language (Sharifian 2008: 122)", and one can see language as serving as a "collective memory bank" of a cultural group, which keeps *in it* its conceptualization through time and space (Sharifian 2015: 476). Some of those conceptualizations stored in language are fossilized aspects of shared cognition of distant generations of the past (Sharifian 2015: 476), which in a way, still constitute actual shared cognition of a given cultural group.

Cultural conceptualizations are then encoded in language (Sharifian 2008: 123), and this encodement exists at all the levels of linguistic system. The most obvious instance of it takes place in the lexicon of a language, since in their encyclopedic meaning, words evoke evidently different conceptualizations (Sharifian 2008: 123; Kövecses 2017: 309). Thus, one can say that in fact the meaning in language comes down to the conceptualizations (Athanasiadou 2017: 112), from among which most are cultural in nature. Similarly, the use of these words in form of metaphors or metonymies is also largely – yet not entirely – motivated by cultural cognition (Sharifian 2008: 124–5). In some languages, the encodement happens also at the morpho-syntactic level and take form of cultural formation of grammatical categories or other grammatical features evoking different cultural models for experience.

Cultural conceptualizations encoded in broadly understood semantic components of linguistic structure account for the native categories and schemata. Language as embodying cultural conceptualizations might then be seen as something, which *speaks* its native speakers' minds – something articulating their imageries, which could be expressed by any means of human expression (Palmer 1996: 115). It is a mean of communicating the way they see certain phenomena – elements of the landscape, natural and social events, social roles, etc. – and sense them in form of feelings, tastes, and impressions (Palmer 1994: 1). Language then tells us about the way its native speakers experience the world – it manifests their folk knowledge about this world. In other words, it speaks out their culture – the conceptual system made up out of their shared experience. Therefore, language never really refers to things, which *objectively* are *out-there*, but rather to our conceptions about them (Jackendoff 2002: 303–10) – our conceptualizations of them, or our imageries – ways of imagining them (cf. Maalej 2008: 412). A similar conception could be also found in the medieval Arabic scholarship, such as in ar-Rāzī's *Mafātiḥ al-Ġayb*, quoted in the previous chapter. In fact, one can see language as a mirror of the culture of its native speakers (cf. Deutscher 2011).

Equally evident, the encodement of cultural conceptualizations occur at the pragmatic level – the level of language use (Sharifian 2008: 125). Culture seems to stipulate the pragmatic devices available for users of a given language. It governs the discourse mostly by means of discourse scenarios and other event schemata, which stipulate the way interlocutors use language while engaging in a communication. The context of a particular language use[1] is always presumed

1 Quite an extensive description of the role of culture as the context of a language use is provided in Kövecses (2017).

by culture, since "culturally constructed, conventional (…) imagery of world-view (…) provides the stable point of reference for the interpretations of discourse (Palmer 1996: 6)". In other words, any discourse in any language is structured by the cultural knowledge of particular interlocutors participating in it. Misunderstandings happen when discourse participants refer to different cultural models of experience, consequently interpreting partner's utterances in accordance with different set of culturally defined expectations (cf. Sharifian 2008: 121–2). Therefore, to understand a given texts, not only do we need to know the language, in which it was produced, but also the imageries, which stipulated its production – its form and content (Palmer 1996: 115).

The language plays yet one important role in its relationship with culture. As we know, cultural conceptualizations "arise from the interaction between the members of a cultural group (Sharifian 2003: 190)". What is quite important is the fact that this interaction is largely linguistic in nature. As I mentioned earlier, people constantly negotiate and renegotiate their understanding of the reality within their cultural group (Sharifian 2008: 118). This negotiation on its turn happen mostly by means of the elaboration of shared conceptualizations in discourse. In other words, it is mostly in language use in communication with others how we *tune* our "conceptualized worlds", so as to make them match the "worlds" of the members of our cultural group (Jackendoff 2002: 330). Thus, "linguistic interactions are crucial to the development of cultural conceptualizations", because they enable people to "construct and co-construct meanings of their experiences" (Sharifian 2017: 5).

2.1.1. Cultural Linguistics (CL) in a nutshell

As we could see, culture defined as a conceptual system or cultural cognition is in a mutual relationship with language – language is the major mean of storing, transmitting and negotiate cultural conceptualization, whereas culture as a system of such conceptualizations is what makes up language content and governs its use (cf. Palmer 2007: 1047) – or alternatively, what motivates its structures (Sharifian 2011: 47). I believe the statement that culture is what actually makes a given language itself is not farfetched. In other words, cultural cognition shapes the linguistic system and makes it used in a way it is actually used.

What is CL then? I think the easiest way to define it is to say that it is a linguistic inquiry that lays its major interest onto cultural conceptualizations (cf. Kövecses 2017: 307) as formative and governing elements of linguistic system. In other words, it investigates the relationship between the cultural conceptualizations and language (Sharifian 2017: 2), studying by that socio-cultural grounding of language (Sharifian 2017: 47) – its grounding in cultural cognition (de Silva, Cuenca, & Romano 2017: 348). As a result, CL aims to understand specificity of a given language and its use. It does so through the description of cultural conceptualizations that structure the means of expression available to speakers of this language.

Its major part consists then of a kind of ethnographic enterprise (cf. Sharifian 2017: 41), which aims to describe the encyclopedic meaning of linguistic structures (cf. Palmer 2007: 1047; Palmer 1996: 290). Therefore, first and foremost, it maps cross-linguistic differences "in construal of categorization of common experience (Palmer 2007: 1047)", which are perceived as largely cultural in nature. In other words, CL is interested in "how people frame experiences and abstract meanings from them (Palmer 1996: 36)". Thus, from among methods of CL, ethnographic tools are equally important as linguistic ones (Palmer 1996: 36). Moreover, CL acknowledges the role of culture as grounding pragmatic variations existing between languages as well as languages varieties. It recognizes the fact that the discourse and our linguistic behavior is to a large degree dependent on the culture of interlocutors, which in form of mostly scenarios or event schemata, governs the language use in a particular situation (Sharifian 2008: 125–6).

As I mentioned, the core of the interest of CL is the notion of cultural conceptualizations – a subclass of conceptualizations being aspects of human cognition. Such conceptualizations are understood as cognitive operations, from which CL is interested mostly in schematization, categorization, metaphorization and metonymization, and conceptual blending (Sharifian 2003: 188). The most important from among these processes are schematization and categorization. The schematization is "a process that involves the systematic selection of certain aspects of a referent to present the whole, disregarding the remaining aspects (Talmy, in Sharifian 2003: 188)". Its results are conceptualizations termed as schemata, which might be seen as structures constituting one's knowledge (understanding, expectations, etc.) of certain phenomena (such as events, social roles, etc.). On its turn, the categorization entails treatment of different individual referents as somehow equal (Sharifian 2003: 188), resulting in creation of categories of elements of the reality (both natural and social), in which an individual perceived the world. Those schemata and categories are the conceptualizations, which are usually evoked by words in their meanings. Of course, CL does not study any kind of schemata or categories. It is interested only with those, which might be rendered *cultural*, i.e., which are co-constructed by negotiations and re-negotiations taking place within a cultural group, or alternatively, that has cultural basis (De Silva, Ceuanca, & Romano 2017: 350). Other cultural conceptualizations studied by CL are cultural (conceptual) metaphors and metonymies, as well as culturally specific blends (Sharifian 2003: 188). Further in this chapter, I will elaborate the characteristic of cultural schemata, cultural categories, and cultural metaphors and metonymies.

The notions of schemata, categories, metaphors, and metonymies might bring to our attention the fact that CL should be rather perceived as an ethnographically oriented subfield of CogL. In fact, scholars of CogL were always somehow culture-oriented. Langacker, for instance, stated that "language is an essential instrument and component of culture, whose reflection in linguistic structure is pervasive and quite significant (in Palmer 2007: 1045)". Since CogL is a theory of grammar, in which a central role is ascribed to the meaning, one can assume that this reflection of culture should be sought in the semantic characteristics of language. According to CogL, meaning originates not only from different biological cognitive processes, including the process of embodiment, but also from cultural traditions (Palmer 2007: 1045). In other words, CogL acknowledges the fact that some conceptualizations of human experience are embodied in language (Sharifian 2008: 116). Moreover, it admits that as long as the characteristics of the operations or the processes of conceptualization are universal, they ultimately emerge at large in a form of culturally negotiated conceptualizations (Sharifian 2008: 117-8; Palmer 1996: 116). This means that, in fact, CogL accepts possibility that some of the semantic components of grammar are shaped by culture of language users (Palmer 2007: 1046).

Sharifian (2008: 473) himself defined CL as an attempt to integrate CogL with ethnography-oriented research. Consequently, he postulated employment of analytical tools developed within the theory of CogL – i.e., schemata, categories, metonymies, and metaphors – in ethnolinguistics (Sharifian 2015: 475, 477). Nevertheless, one could imagine a more complementary relationship persisting between CL and CogL. For intendance, Zoltàn Kövecses (2017: 308), considered them both as linguistic inquiries concerned with the specifics of human linguistic practice, yet the latter focuses on more universal, cognitive aspects of this practice, whereas the former analyzes its cultural aspects.

2.1.2. History of Cultural Linguistics

Both major theorists of CL, Gary Palmer (1996: 4–5; 10) and Farzad Sharifian (Sharifian 2015: 474) considered it as directly growing out of and integrating three 20th century ethnographic approaches in linguistics and anthropology. They were Boasian linguistics or linguistic relativity, ethnosemantics or ethnoscience, and ethnography of speaking. What hold these three diverse research approaches together was their common conviction about cultural relativity as well as empiricism of their methodologies. Nevertheless, the interest in the relationship between language and culture might be traced back at least to 16th c. (Sharifian 2017: 111), and it was always – at least in the West – treated with a sort of reservation, or even with animosity, due to its anti-universalistic scent (Sharifian 2015: 20).

From among the aforementioned approaches in linguistics, the most controversial one used to be – and perhaps still is – the linguistic relativity theory that stemmed from the linguistic school of Franz Boas and was represented at its best by two American researchers, Edward Sapir and Benjamin Lee Whorf. One should search for roots of Boasian linguistics long before Franz Boas though in a philosophical stream within German romanticism in form of Herder's notion of *Volksgeist* (Sharifian 2015: 22). This conception was an ethnocentric belief that nations are governed by "nation souls" or "spirits", which were embodied in languages these nations speak. This vague philosophical idea was later adopted and promoted by Wilhelm Humboldt, who also saw in language "the outer appearance" of a nation spirit (Sharifian 2015: 22), which articulates this spirit and gives shape to thoughts of people belonging to that nation (Dirven, Wolf, & Polzenhagen 2007: 1203).

The ideas of Humboldt influenced German linguist Franz Boas, who brought them to the United States, where he found an opportunity to test them empirically. This opportunity was presented to him in the languages of Native Americans. Their uniqueness made him and his followers convinced that culture and language are inseparable, and that specificity of one always implies the distinctiveness of the other. Boas' theory was later developed by other students of these languages, from among whom the most recognizable were Sapir and Whorf. Sapir added to the discipline the notion of the negotiation of shared imageries resulting in the fact that linguistic classification was socially constructed (Palmer 1996: 11–12). This notion, as we know, became in time one of the core conceptions of CL. He was also strongly convinced of relativity – not only of linguistic forms, but also of conceptual ones. Therefore, he believed that "[t]he worlds in which different societies are distinct worlds, nor merely the same world with different labels attached (Sapir, in Wierzbicka 1992: 4)".

Both students of Boas are perhaps best recognized as authors of a theory christened by Harry Hoijer "Sapir-Whorf hypothesis" (Blount 2009: 32). It is considered the cornerstone of the linguistic relativity theory, which might be summarized as a conviction that one's mother tongue restricts somehow thinking process of this someone – in other words, our language makes us unable to think of certain things. In such a way, Sapir and Whorf supposedly formulated the claim that a language restricts its native speaker's ability of thinking.

Such an accusation seems to be an overinterpretation of statements produced by Sapir and Whorf, by mixing them with German neo-Humboldtian explicit linguistic solipsism (Leavitt 2015b: 26). It seems that neither of scholars associated with the American school of anthropological linguistics – neither Boas, nor Sapir, nor Whorf – claimed that language put any restrictions on what one can conceptualize. Sapir, for instance, openly claimed that all thoughts – even such complex as Kant's theory – might be formulated in all languages, even those considered the most "primitive" (judging them by early 20th c. standards) (Sapir 2003: 78). Thus, if all might be formulated in every language, the statement that a language can restrict some thoughts seems simply contrary. In all fairness, Whorf might be seen close to such a conception in his theory of habitual thoughts – the "lazy" thoughts, which are more readily available to us, and which are categorized by categories already available in our language and culture (Leavitt 2015b: 25). But Whorf has never dismissed the fact that beside such habitual thoughts, human thinking process entails "potentialities of thoughts", which are unlimited (Leavitt 2015b: 25). In other words, Whorf noticed what is quite sensible and perhaps is even a truism: it is easier to think of and imagine scenarios involving objects to which we can refer in words (and concepts) already available in our dictionary. It is enough to consider, for instance, specialized languages, which are perfect tools of describing phenomena of which it would be hard to think in terms of everyday language (cf. Jackendoff 2002: 292). As noticed by Blount (2009: 32), Whorf did not mean anything truly controversial, what can be seen in "a very clear exposition of Whorf 's claims" by John Lucy, whose idea Blount summarized as follows:

> Whorf argued that the ontological categories upon which important language distinctions are based, such as tenses and classifiers, are habitually used by speakers and that the habitual use itself predisposes them to see their physical and cultural world through the categories. For example, an individual who conceptualizes linear distance in terms of miles will tend to 'think' in terms of those units, whereas someone whose experience is with kilometers will 'think' in terms of that category (Blount 2009: 32).

The overinterpretation of Sapir's and Whorf's theory led to confusing linguistic relativism with linguistic solipsism, which was a part of neo-Humboldtian approach to language. It is worth noting moreover that neo-Humboldtian linguists gained deserved notoriety by being involved in Nazi propaganda (Leavitt 2015b: 26). The linguistic relativism shared this notoriety, what deeply affected its development in the second half of 20th c.

However, relativism of Boas, Sapir, and Whorf did not mean they believed that a language defines boundaries of thinking of its native speaker or their fate, abilities, or character traits. The real meaning of it was stressing the fact that a language must be analyzed in its own terms, without imposing external (to that language) perspective of the researcher, who studies it (Leavitt 2015b: 18). In fact, linguistic relativity should be seen as a metaphor deriving from Einstein's theory of relativity (Leavitt 2015b: 18) that at its center states simply that time and space are "relative" to the observer. In the same manner, language is "relative": a researcher- observer's language (cf. time and space) is by no means universal (cf. the same for all observers), but specific. Thus, while studying a different language, the researcher-observer should not apply their own linguistic categories but try to describe the language in the categories of native speakers of this language.

Boas, Sapir, and Whorf died before the end of the first half of 20th c. After their death, in 50', universalistic psycholinguists coined the notorious "Sapir-Whorf" hypothesis, triggering by this the demise of the ethnographically oriented approach in linguistics. Both Chomsky's Generative Grammar and early CogL rejected the hypothesis and the whole theory of linguistic relativity as wrong (Leavitt 2015a: 26) and obviously contradicting facts. As Leavitt (2015a: 27) says, in 70', the linguistic relativity – and the whole school of anthropological linguistics – was seen only as a "sad ghost of the past".

Despite such unfavorable atmosphere however, some research in the relationship between culture and language was still conducted. For instance, in 60' and 70' ethnosemantics/ ethnoscience and ethnography of speaking were somehow thriving. The former was "the study of the ways in which different cultures organize and categorize domains of knowledge, such as those of plants, animals, and kin (Palmer 1996: 19)", whereas the latter focused on the cultural grounding of language use, i.e., pragmatics. Moreover, in 70' and 80', the interest in relative, culturally specific organization of knowledge encoded in language was yet again revived – this time by the efforts of Anna Wierzbicka and her Natural Semantic Metalanguage (NSM) methodology (Leavitt 2015a: 62). She herself (Wierzbicka 1992: 22) stated that the best description of her study was encapsulated in the title of one of her books: *Universal human concepts in culture- specific configurations*, which obviously refers to the Boasian interest in the culture- specific organization of meaning. NSM, being a metalanguage consisting of hypothetically yet empirically tested universal "semantic prime" – i.e., words- meanings (Goddard & Wierzbicka 2014: 12), might be defined as a culture-independent tool of semantic analysis, which allows to "pin down subtle meaning difference" (Goddard & Wierzbicka 2008: 205–6). Due to its culture-transparency, it serves as a *tertis comparationis* for semantic analysis of culture-specific meanings (Goddard & Wierzbicka 2008: 206) embodied in lexical and grammatical structures, as well as in behavioral scripts or scenarios. Thus, using NSM, a researcher can conduct "a systematic investigation into language-specific patterns of lexicalization (Goddard & Wierzbicka 2008: 217)".

In fact, Wierzbicka might be considered one of the first linguists who readopted the all-shamed theory of Boas, Sapir, and Whorf. In 90', one could also observe the beginning of attempting to analyze so called "Whorf effects", i.e., the effects of one's mother tongue on their thinking processes (Leavitt 2015b: 27). In about the same time, first Gary Palmer (cf. 1996), and later Farzad Sharifian (cf. e.g., 2017), proposed a coherent theory of CL as we know it today.

In this place, I would like to mention yet another area of linguistic research influenced by Boasian (and Humboldtian) theory of language and culture, which is normally omitted in general elaboration of CL's background. This area is Polish methodology known as Linguistic Image of the World (in Polish, *Językowy Obraz Świata*, JOŚ) or Linguistic Worldview (cf. Danaher, Głaz & Łozowski 2013). In most basic words, JOŚ is a research field aiming to analyze the aforementioned Linguistic Image of the World, which might be defined as "a set of regularities contained in combination of grammatical categories (…) as well as in the semantic structures of the lexis (Tokarski 1995: 7)". JOŚ studies then a kind of "interpretation of the reality", which is "encapsulated in language" (Bartmiński 2006: 12). It employs mostly different kind of ethnographic and semantic methods (cf. Bartmiński 2006: 13) to postulate "cognitive definition" of meaning of a word or grammatical structure (cf. Bartmiński 2009: 47), which will reflect folk interpretation of a given fragment of the reality, conceptualized in that meaning (Bartmiński 2006: 14). As one can see, this research enterprise seems quite akin to what we call nowadays CL. However, in the department of theory, JOŚ lacks the clearness of CL. The vagueness of the notion of the subject of this field – the Linguistic Image of the World – led to criticism (cf. Bobrowski 1995 & 2010), some of which seems justified. For instance, what I find to be the most troubling problem of JOŚ is that in fact, it postulates existence of a somehow redundant structure that is supposed to be present in language. Its redundancy comes down to its relationship with culture. In fact, the Linguistic Image of the World seems to be simply the culture itself, defined as a conceptual system. Therefore, there is no need to term it "linguistic" (cf. Bobrowski 1995).

Another example of such a frequently neglected ethnographically oriented linguistic research is so-called axiolinguistics, which was promoted as a part of the JOŚ project by Jadwiga Puzynina (1992). The interest of this subfield of JOŚ is particularly relevant to my current study since its major focus was placed on the lexicalization of certain values in language. Currently, as the major researcher of this field one can name Beata Raszewska-Żurek (2010, 2012, 2016, 2019).

2.1.3. Current development of Cultural Linguistics. State of CL research in Arabic language

The current stage of CL research development was summarized in Sharifian (2017). Besides some theoretical synopsis and considerations, it contains examples of application of diverse linguistic methods into studies on cultural grounding of particular languages, such as English, Chinese, Greek, Bulgarian, Hungarian, Polish, Portuguese, Spanish and others. The methods used in these studies were e.g., different kinds of discourse analyses, corpus analysis (corpus linguistics), ethnographic methods, contrastive analysis, conceptual analysis, and narrative analysis (Sharifian 2017: 9–7).

CL studies focus on the description of cultural conceptualizations – schemata, categories, metaphors, metonymies, and blends – and their linguistic instantiations. Most of them concentrate on the cross- linguistic variations, studying a particular language discourse separately or comparatively. Some of the researchers also study variations within a language, foregrounding the impact of a given culture on the emergence of a particular variant. An example of such research are studies on World Englishes (cf. Sharifian 2011: 60–77).

The application of CL theoretical and methodological framework to Arabic language and culture is still very limited. The most noteworthy example of studies in this field is the work of Zouhair Maalej (e.g., 2007; 2009; 2008; 2011), who investigates the cultural grounding of embodied cognition based on analysis of conceptual metaphors in Tunisian Arabic and MSA. In general, the notion of cultural conceptualizations is not yet broadly applied within Arabic studies. Therefore, my research might still be considered as one of the first examples of employment of the CL assumptions to Arabic, and as the first attempt of CL analysis on LEAP and the culture of pre-Islamic Arabs. All in all, my analyses are an exploratory attempt at application of CL methodological frame to historical stages of the development of Arabic language and culture. Similarly, my study might be also considered the first application of JOŚ and axiolinguistics premises into examination of the value of HONOR and its lexicalization in LEAP.

2.2. Tools of Cognitive Linguistics for studying cultural grounding of language

As defined earlier, CL might be seen as a subfield of CogL, due to adopted theoretical assumptions and applied methods. In this section, I would like to elaborate on those, by presenting my understanding of the notions of schemata, categories, metaphors, and metonymies.

2.2.1. Cultural Models and Cultural Schemata

The notion of cultural schemata is the most crucial one for the entire theoretical framework of CL. In all fairness, it might seem to be a quite messy part of its theory, especially taking into consideration terminology used by theoretics – mostly those of CogL. Still, the notion of a "schema" (plural: schemata) seems sometimes to be used interchangeably with the notion of a "model", depending on the researcher's choice. Following Sharifian – or at least his statement expressed in Sharifian (2008: 251) – I consider a "model" being a broader phenomenon, which "characterize[s] higher nodes of our conceptual knowledge and that encompass[es] a network of schemas, categories and metaphors". In my study, I represent a skeletal form of such a model, by which one can depict the pull of LEAP conceptualizations of HONOR. Nevertheless, in fact, as noticed by Palmer (1996: 62) the notion of "schemata" and "models" are to a great extent relative, since both "may be more or less complex and more or less abstract, so that the distinction between them tend to blur (Palmer 1996: 62)". In other words, one can say that a model is simply a more complex schema (Wilson & Lewandowska-Tomaszczyk 2017: 248).

2.2.1.1. Cognitive schemata

As I mentioned, the most important notion of CL is that of a "schema". The notion seems to refer to a conceptual phenomenon known in many cognitive theories under plethora of different names, such as script, scenario, frame, Idealized Cognitive Model, scene, semantic field of potential mental space (Tuggy 2007: 104), or simply (conceptual) domain (Cienki 2007: 170) – all of which are meant to signify the encodement of encyclopedic knowledge or "a simplified stories (Sweetser 1987: 44)" about something.

Cognitive schemata are results of the process of conceptualization of experience (Sharifian 2008: 117), and might be understood as "fixed template[s] for ordering specific information (Oakley 2007: 216)", or in other words, as "building blocks of cognition that help organize, interpret, and communicate information (Sharifian 2017: 11)". They are hierarchical abstraction, i.e., they can provide more or less information, yet never more than that contained in a given real-world experience (Palmer 1996: 29). Therefore, one can define them as "mental representations of some regularities in our experience (Palmer 1996: 68)", which serve us in interpretation of novel real-world experiences and in appropriation of our behavior while facing them. Schemata might be linked to one another, constituting in such a way more complex knowledge encoding structures, which might be called models (Palmer 1996: 68).

The most informative elaboration of the theory of schema was presented in Casson (1983), therefore in this section, I follow his understanding of this notion. To enhance the apprehension of this theory, I use the example quoted also in Casson (1983), that is, the schema COMMERCIAL EVENT.

Casson (1983: 430) considers schemata as "conceptual abstractions", being very general or even fundamental conceptual phenomena "that mediate between stimuli received by the sense organ and behavioral responses", serving as "the basis for all human information processing", such as perception, comprehension, categorization, recognition, problem-solving, and decision making. Using our example, the schema COMMERCIAL EVENT is what governs our behavior in a situation, which is an instance of what we call a commercial event (e.g., buying bread in a bakery). It mediates between our perception (i.e., observation of a given real-world situation, which takes place in a bakery, after we entered it to buy a loaf of bread) and our understanding of how we should act in a given real-world context (e.g., how we should act while buying bread). The schema is then a kind of a representation of stereotypical situation, object, sequence of events, etc., which structures our knowledge of the instances of these situation, object, or sequence of events (Casson 1983: 431). Of course, the schema COMMERCIAL EVENT is abstract, and it accounts for all possible commercial events, which we might encounter. Those events will obviously differ in detail, but they will contain some common elements, such as BUYER, SELLER, EXCHANGE, GOODS, PAYMENT, etc. These common elements are what is abstracted from particular real-world experiences in the process, which constituted the schema COMMERCIAL EVENT as a part of our knowledge of the world. As one can see, such a schema is very abstract – it might be applied to both buying a loaf of bread in a bakery or buying an apartment or a share in a company. Each of these events is structured in a bit different fashion and as such constitutes itself a cognitive schema (SHOPPING IN BAKERY, PURCHASING APARTMENT, and PURCHASING COMPANY SHARE ON MARKET). These schemata might be then considered as subschemata of the more general, more abstract schema COMMERCIAL EVENT. Thus, schemata constitute hierarchies of higher- and lower-level elements – "[t]he higher level of schemata are fixed and represent invariant aspects of concepts (Casson 1983: 431)", knowledge of which they encode. In other words, elements of the abstract schema COMMERCIAL EVENT are unchangeable – if we are to consider a particular situation as a commercial event, it must possess some elements, which all commercial event possess. Whereas, the lower-level schemata, i.e., subschemata, characterize in having "terminals" or "slots", which "must be filled by specific instances of data (Casson 1983: 431)". In other words, "they have variables that are associated with, or "bound by" elements in the environment in particular instantiation of the schema (Casson 1983: 431)". Thus, the subschema SHOPPING IN BAKERY is one of those "down-to-earth" elements of the schematized knowledge of the world. It inherits the fixed elements of the COMMERCIAL EVENT, but it is also what is directly applied to a real-world experience – a situation, in which we found ourselves. It contains the variables – "slots" – for particular real-world elements, which derive from the fixed elements of the schema COMMERCIAL EVENT. Thus, SHOPPING IN BAKERY contains such slots as CUSTOMER (=BUYER), BAKER (=SELLER), EXCHANGE, BAKED GOODS (=GOODS), MONEY (= PAYMENT). In a particular real-world situation, all those slots must be filled by real-world element so that we could recognize the situation as an instantiation of the schema SHOPPING IN BAKERY, being a subschema of COMMERCIAL EVENT. The instantiation is then this matching between the slots and the real-world objects and events, or "binding particular elements to particular variables on particular occasions (Casson 1983: 432)". The variables in the schema – in our example: CUSTOMER, BAKER, EXCHANGE, BAKED GOODS, MONEY – contain some conditions of which real-world elements can be bound (i.e., matched) with them. Therefore, one knows that CUSTOMER and BAKER can be filled only with human beings, MONEY with cash or card payment, and BAKED GOODS with things like bread, rolls, cookies, but not chairs, hammers, books, etc. Moreover, they encode knowledge of the relationship between the variables (Casson 1983: 432) (e.g., one knows that CUSTOMER EXCHANGES MONEY with BAKER for BAKED GOODS). They also contain certain prototypical values (i.e., stereotypical objects, events, etc.), which are instantly used while one deals with incomplete data (Casson 1983: 432) (i.e., if one entered a place called "Bakery", they assume that they can buy bread there, even if they do not actually see it displayed in the shopwindow). Such prototypical values are weakly bound to a variable, and as soon as matching data is provided, they are replaced by them (Casson 1983: 432).

Schemata are then complex hierarchical structures consisting of more or less concrete subschemata (Casson 1983: 436). In our example, the most abstract schema is that of COMMERCIAL EVENT, whose subschema SHOPPING IN BAKERY is more concrete. It is not, however, atomic – it consists of the elements (CUSTOMER, BAKER, EXCHANGE, BAKED GOODS, MONEY), which – although termed variable above – themselves might be seen as subschemata. For instance, BAKER organizes our knowledge of who might be a baker (i.e., what are the conditions, which stipulates our possible reference to someone as *baker*), and EXCHANGE is itself a structured scenario in which there are at least two actors, which act in a certain way, etc. In my understanding, these lowest-level subschemata should not be equated immediately with the variables or the slots to fill with the data from the real-world experience. They should, however, be seen as the structures, which as their parts contain those slots. In other words, e.g., BAKER is a schema of our knowledge of what makes someone a baker, but it also possesses a slot we fill with a real-world person, who matches that knowledge – i.e., who meets our expectations of who a baker is.

The hierarchical organization of schemata might be of different kind (cf. Casson 1983: 437). The most obvious one is the taxonomical relationship between schemata, such as that between COMMERCIAL EVENT (superordinate element) and SHOPPING IN BAKERY (subordinate element). Other hierarchical grouping might entail part-whole relationship (e.g., SHOPPING IN BAKERY and BAKER) or sequential organization (e.g., COMMERCIAL EVENT is preceded by two event schemata BUYER HAS MONEY and SELLER HAS GOODS, and might be followed by other scenarios, such as RETURNING HOME).

What is quite important, "schemata are not only data structures, [but] they are also data processor (Casson 1983: 438)". In other words, a schema is "a pattern *of* an action" and "a pattern *for* an action" (Casson 1983: 438). This means that schemata might be processed in both ways, bottom-up and top-bottom, and both processes are normally run simultaneously. What it means is that processing of schemata, which are our patterns of understanding of the real-world experiences, is initiated with the outside (usually sensory) input. In such a way, the schemata are processed bottom-up, i.e., from raw data, which triggers a particular lowest-level schema up to the more and more abstract schemas subsuming the lower ones. Once the processing reached the higher level of abstraction, it starts run top-bottom, i.e., it initiates our understanding and behavior based on the schema and its subschemata down to the variables and the elements of the real world, which are being bound to them in the process (cf. Casson 1983: 438–9).

In our example, supposedly, we have just realized we run out of bread at home. This is a sensory input – raw data[2] – which triggers our bottom-up processing of the schema BREAD, which is a subschema of BAKING GOODS (taxonomical relationship). In such a way, we arrive at the element of the more abstract schema – BAKERY (part-whole relationship), from which we climb up to even more abstract schema SHOPPING IN BAKERY. Now, the processing is run top-bottom, from SHOPPING IN BAKERY to all those different schemata, which makes

---

2 In fact, such data is quite complex. It consists of all sensory and conceptual inputs, which make us realize we run out of bread (such as the observation of an empty bread box, the knowledge of the bread box and the fact that it is a usual storage place for bread in our home). I'm fully aware of the complexity of such sensory input data, and in my example, it is used only as more or less *pars-pro-toto*.

us think and act appropriately to the situation, in which we run out of bread, and we want to get it. In other words, we decode from our schemata that BREAD is a kind of BAKING GOOD, and BAKING GOODS can be acquired in a BAKERY, which is a place, in which we perform SHOPPING IN BAKERY that is a kind of COMMERCIAL EVENT. In such a way, we can infer that, in order to get BREAD, we have to BUY it. This inference, our deduction, was yet another instance of the top-bottom processing (from COMMERCIAL EVENT to the BREAD we lack). Another example of the top-bottom processing will be our action governed by other schemata sequentially related to SHOPPING IN BAKERY, such as LEAVING HOME or DRIVING A CAR. At last, our schema SHOPPING IN BAKERY is what will govern our behavior during actual shopping for bread. Our schematized knowledge processing runs then all the time up and down from raw data or more concrete schemata to more abstract ones. In such a way, we constantly deal with the real-world experiences – we make assumptions on them and act in accordance with those or we react based on our expectations concerning what we are dealing with.

To sum it up, one can say that schemata are abstract systems of information abstracted from repetitive experience of an individual (Oakley 2007: 216). They emerge as top-down-and-bottom-up "frames for constituting different facets of experiences (Oakley 2007: 216)" or "frames [which] impose particular ways of seeing the world (Kövecses 2017: 317)". As such, they establish "an organized framework of objects and relations which have yet to be filled with concrete detail (D'Andrade 1996: 122)". In other words, schemata are cognitive wholes, which encode knowledge about the world, and by that, they "capture believes, norms, rules, and expectations of behavior as well as values relating to various aspects and components of experience (Sharifian 2017: 7)", governing our understanding and reactions.

2.2.1.2. **Cultural schemata**

All in all, cognitive schemata are universal phenomena pertaining to the universal machinery of human cognition. How can we then understand the notion of "cultural schema"?

The simplest definition could be the statement that cultural schemata are schemata that are culturally specific (cf. Palmer 2007: 1046) or constituting "culturally constructed subclass of schemas (Sharifian 2015: 478)". Of course, immediately, one would ask a question what it means to be "culturally specific". The answer to this could be that it means a cultural schema is "a cognitive schema that is intersubjectively shared by a social group (D'Andrade 1987: 112)". This brings us back to Sharifian's understanding of cultural cognition as a subject of constant negotiations and re- negotiations taking place in a cultural group. Cultural schemata are simply those schemata, which encode something one can call common knowledge shared by people within his cultural group or knowledge obvious for members of this group (D'Andrade 1987: 113). Thus, cultural schemata, being "abstracted from collective cognitions associated with a cultural group (Sharifian 2015: 478)", might be seen as containing folk theories of the world (Dirvern, Wolf, & Polzenhagen 2007: 1204), and as structures, in which "culture's collective wisdom and experience is laid down (Dirvern, Wolf, & Polzenhagen 2007: 1204)". Of course, still the locus of such schemata is in an individual and they are still established based on the individual experience (Sharifian 2015: 478). However, their nature is far from being idiosyncratic, since they are subject of constant negotiations within a group. In other words, after having emerged in an individual mind based on their individual experience, a schema becomes shared with this individual's cultural group members. These members contrast this schema with their own schemata (abstracted from their own experiences), co-creating in such a way common understanding (and handling) of the experience. Thus, an idiosyncratic schema becomes communal after having been adjusted by social interactions, such as e.g., communicative discourse, which "tunes" individual cognitions into a heterogeneously shared, more or less identical, cultural cognition of the world.

2.2.1.3. Cultural schemata and language: encyclopedic meaning and semantic frames

The connection between schemata and human cognition brings into our focus the relation between the cognitive/cultural schemata defined above and linguistic structure. One can see the importance of schemata for language in two interrelated cognitive linguistic phenomena: encyclopedic meaning and framing.

Simply stated, since cultural schemata are structures of encodement of cultural knowledge, they must be what accounts for meaning understood as encyclopedic in nature. One of the major assumptions of CogL is that there is not such a thing as linguistic meaning as opposed to more complex meaning constituting our understanding of a given phenomenon (cf. Jackendoff 2002: 285–7; 2007: 658). Meaning in language overlaps with our knowledge to the extent that postulating existence of purely linguistic meaning is redundant. What we mean in our linguistic utterances about something is by all means what we think about it, i.e., a kind of conceptual product of the inferences deriving from our overall knowledge. Meaning is then obviously a part of our conceptual system (Jackendoff 2002: 271–5).

If so, schemata must play crucial role in structuring the meaning in language. A cultural schema, understood as "[t]he pool of knowledge that forms a web of concepts (Sharifian 2015: 480)" of a given phenomenon, might be seen as what "capture[s] encyclopedic meaning that is culturally constructed for many lexical items of human languages (Sharifian 2015: 480)". Schemata – and in a broader sense, cognitive models – serve then definition of elements of our lexicon (Palmer 1996: 122) – lexemes, expressions, and other meaningful structures. In other words, meaning is relative to cognitive models constituted in part by schemata (Palmer 1996: 290), since cognitive schemata represents our concepts of the world, which are what we refer to as meanings in our linguistic utterances (cf. Kövecses 2017: 313).

Therefore, the meaning of the English lexemes *baker* and *cash* is encoded in schemata BAKER and CASH, which are subschemata of a broader scenarios such as SHOPPING IN BAKERY, or COMMERCIAL EVENT. What it means is that, in order to decode the meaning of these words, we must refer to the whole schema that encompasses them. Thus, *baker* and *cash* might be defined only in relation to the schema SHOPPING IN BAKERY, which defines as its elaborations the subschemata BAKER and CASH. The meaning of *baker* contains then all the information we have about someone, who might be referred to as *baker*. In other words, seeing a schema as "a coherent set of interrelated concepts", we can say that decoding the meaning happens, as one "singles out" some entities within this schema "or in relations to" it for profiling (Tuggy 2007: 104) – the schema constitutes a base for profiling the meaning of its components (cf. Langacker 2006: 31, 34). In such a way, meaning of the lexemes *baker* or *cash* will be what we know about these entities in respect to the schema subsuming them (i.e., for example, SHOPPING IN BAKERY). It means that "in a particular instance of usage each word corresponds to a part of some schema or a perspective on a schema (Palmer 1996: 66)". Words connect to schemata in their meanings, which compromise bigger or smaller parts of them.

In other words, following Charles J. Fillmore, one can say the word meaning can be characterize only "in terms of experience-based schematizations of the speaker's world (Petruck 2013: 1)." What it entails is that our words always evoke particular schemata (Sweetser 1987: 44) and can be decoded only relative to them (Fillmore 1976: 27). This corresponds with the aforementioned characteristics of schemata processing as simultaneously bottom-up-and-top-bottom: a given word evokes a particular schema (bottom-up processing), and the schema defines meaning to this word (top-bottom processing). This bottom-up-and-top-bottom process is at the core of the notion of *semantic frame* as it is defined in Frame Semantics (Petruck 2013: 1).

In his article form 1975, Ch. J. Fillmore proposed existence of *frames* within his *scene-and-frame paradigm* for the theory of semantics (Fillmore 1975). The frame in that paradigm was defined as a "system of linguistic choices – the easiest cases being collections of words, but also including choices of grammatical rules or linguistic categories – that can get associated with prototypical instances of scenes (Fillmore 1975: 124)." The notion of *scene*, however, was understood by Fillmore as "not only visual scenes but also familiar kinds of interpersonal transactions, standard scenarios defined by the culture, institutional structures, enactive experiences, body image, and, in general, any kind of coherent segment of human beliefs, actions, experiences or imaginings (Fillmore 1975: 124)." The scene in this paradigm can be then perceived as in fact synonymous to what I described as schema. Fillmore postulates that such scenes-schemata always are associated in the minds of language users with the aforementioned linguistic frames, i.e., sets of certain linguistic elements. This association enables the users to decode the meaning conveyed in utterances by placing the linguistic items – words and phrases – within a frame that is mapped onto elements of the associated scene-schema. These elements provide then the meaning for the employed linguistic items. At the same time, however, these uttered linguistic items – by means of the same associative relationship – call up the associated scene-schema shaping the ongoing discourse in a specific way. The associations between linguistic choices and different schemata provide the interlocutors with tools to navigate through the conversation both thematic-wise and by supplying relevant linguistic means of expression (Fillmore 1975: 125–6). To put it bluntly, words and phrases call up specific parts of our knowledge so as we could talk appropriately to the discourse, in which we participate. By calling the schema, they not only make us understand them – decode their meanings – but also link to the associated frames that provide us with related pieces of knowledge and other words and phrases mapped onto them. Such understanding neatly matches the aforementioned bottom-up-and-top-bottom processing of schemata. It extends it however, by accentuating the relationship of our schemata with linguistic system in forms of scene-frames associations.

Nowadays, in Frame Semantics, the discipline of linguistics founded by Fillmore, the term *frame* or *semantic frame* functions more or less in the sense of a (cognitive) schema (cf. Fillmore 1976: 25; Petruck 2013: 1). Nevertheless, it seems to stress the aforementioned fact that the elements of a particular schema "have linguistic reflexes (Fillmore 1976: 29)", or in other words, "are indexed by words that evoke the frame [i.e., the schema] (Petruck 2013: 1)." It means that Frame Semantics puts more accent onto the aforementioned bottom-up-and-top-bottom processing of a given cognitive schema-frame that serves "for both encoding and decoding purposes (Petruck 2013: 1)." In my understanding, one can interpret the *semantic frame* as a notion covering both a cognitive schema and a set of "linguistic choices" associated with it. This set – at least at the origin of Frame Semantics – could be termed a *linguistic frame* (cf. Fillmore 1975: 124, 125–6), being "the specific lexico-grammatical provisions in a given language for naming and describing the categories and relations found in schemata" (Palmer 1996: 61).

As I have said, our choice of words directs attention of our interlocutors towards specific parts of our knowledge. Moreover, it highlights certain areas within a particular culled-up schema, while leaving behind its other elements (Casson 1983: 433). Such focusing of direction within a discourse was defined by Fillmore as *framing* (cf. Fillmore 1976: 27), and it accounts for the fact that sometimes words "evoke the same general scene [i.e., schema] in different way (Cienki 2007: 172)". Taking our schema of SHOPPING IN BAKERY as an example, let as consider the use of two lexemes which evoke its subschema MONEY: *cash* and *card*. Both, CASH and CARD conceptualize the method of payment and as such, both stands for the elaboration of the schema MONEY. Both words, *cash* and *card* might be used by someone while describing their visit in a bakery. Still, the choice of a particular word – say, *cash* – will activate totally different parts of the schema SHOPPING IN BAKERY (a subschema of COMMERCIAL EVENT). If the lexeme *cash* is used, a different set of expectations are being activated in the minds of the interlocutors of the speaker. Thus, the interlocutors retrieve their knowledge of all schemata associated to CASH, expecting the speaker to talk about such concepts as CHANGE, BILLS, COINS, CASH REGISTER, etc. None of those concepts, would appear in their minds, if the speaker used the word *card*. This lexeme, on its turn, would evoke different schemata – those related to CARD – such as TERMINAL, PIN CODE, CREDIT CARD, DEBIT CARD, etc. Moreover, the speaker could leave all those schemata inactive, if they chose not to mention any of the elaboration of the subschema MONEY. In such a case, the interlocutors would simply assume the stereotypical value of the variable contain by this subschema, without further specification.

In other words, a particular use of words or other linguistic structures in an utterance always "selects particular aspects of the schema for highlighting or foregrounding, while leaving others in the background unexpressed (Casson 1983: 433)".

2.2.1.4. Major types of Cultural Schemata

Casson (1983: 441–9) listed only three types of cognitive schemata: object schemata, orientation schemata, and event schemata. In fact, one can present more detailed classification. In this subsection, I will briefly describe the major types of cultural schemata as used in CL. My description includes also so-called image-schemata, which tend to be defined as a separate phenomenon, not related to the notion of schema. I decided to include it in this section, due to its importance for structuring of certain conceptualizations (Sharifian 2003: 195), in which image-schemata cooperate with cognitive schemata. Despite the image-schemata, my description will include event schemata (scenarios or scripts), object schemata, role schemata, and proposition schemata.

2.2.1.4.1. Event schemata

Event schemata, rendered sometimes as scenarios or scripts, are complex schemata consisting of subschemata sequentially linked with each other (Casson 1983: 438). They cover a variety of actions, situations, events, etc., which might be more or less complex (Casson 1983: 446) and they are abstracted from our experience of certain events (Sharifian 2003: 194). In general, they encode the knowledge of what can and will happen in a given situation, defining our expectations of proceeding in it (Palmer 1996: 68) Cultural event schemata are then "culturally defined sequence[s] of action (Palmer 1996: 75)", which govern our understanding of encountered situations and our behavior in it. The aforementioned schema SHOPPING IN BAKERY and its superordinate schema COMMERCIAL EVENT are both examples of event schemata. As I mentioned, such schemata usually contain subschemata of different kind, some of which are also event schemata.

2.2.1.4.2. Object schemata

Although Sharifian did not mention object schemata in his papers on CL, I think they one can include them in a list of cultural schemata. In my understanding, such schemata encode our knowledge of wide range of objects – animated and unanimated ones – together with our understanding of relationships between them. These relationships are all the classification systems, such as taxonomy, partonomy (part- whole relationship), functional classification, etc. (Casson 1983: 441–3). In other words, such schemata encode our knowledge about categories of what there is in the world. The schemata MONEY, GOODS, and BAKERY might be seen as examples of object schemata.

2.2.1.4.3. **Role schemata**

Role schemata encode our knowledge of types of people. In other words, they define our expectations regarding "specific role positions in a cultural group" (Sharifian 2003: 194). Nishida defines it moreover as a "set of behaviours that are expected of people in particular social positions" (Sharifian 2003: 195). From among the schemata, I mentioned earlier, BAKER, BUYER, and SELLER are all examples of role schemata.

2.2.1.4.4. **Proposition schemata**

Proposition schemata are less intuitive to the previous types. Sharifian (2003: 196) defines them as "abstractions which act as models of thought and behaviour", which "might provide a basis for different patterns of reasoning across cultural group". Quinn saw them as "template[s] from which any number of propositions can be constructed" (Palmer 1996: 105). In other words, proposition schemata are the knowledge structures, from which and based on which we derive our inferences about the world. Perhaps, we could term them as our assumptions about the world, which are a basis for our reasoning. The simplest structure of a propositional schema takes form of an argument and a predicate, which might be further augmented with some logical operations, such as quantification, conjunction, negation, etc. (Cienki 2007: 178). As examples of propositional schemata, Sharifian (2003: 196) provides FAMILIES SHARE FOOD WITHOUT EXPECTATIONS, WORDS ARE POWERFUL, and ANCESTOR SPIRITS MADE THE LAW FOR US AND TOLD US HOW TO LIVE. As we can see, such schemata seem to be regular statements. Nevertheless, one should not consider them so – the form WORDS ARE POWERFUL is not a statement but only a linguistic approximation of some people's belief (Sharifian 2003: 196). The limited extent of verbalization is a characteristic trait of propositional schemata (Palmer 1996: 105) – they are not statements, but the templates, from which we generate inferences, which we express as linguistically uttered statements (i.e., propositions). Propositional schemata seem to be substantial element of other schemata, such as events, objects, and roles, since they "allow the conceptualization of (…) [certain phenomena] in terms of models of thoughts and human behaviour, living entities, natural and supranatural forces and physical or immaterial objects (De Silva, Cuenca, & Romano 2017: 351)".

2.2.1.4.5. **Image-schemata**

As I mentioned, image-schemata are regularly treated separately as a phenomenon somehow different from cognitive schemata. Nevertheless, following

Sharifian (2003), I decided to include the description of them as a type of schemata, since image-schema are also structures, which in a way organize our knowledge. It happens primarily because image-schemata "provide structures for certain conceptualizations (Sharifian 2003: 195)", from among which the most obvious are metaphors. For instance, Qurʔānic Arabic conceptualization of heart (*qalb*) includes the metaphor HEART IS CONTAINER, which is structured by image-schema CONTAINER (Maalej 2008: 400). Similarly, conceptualization of Persian *del* 'heart' also includes the image-schema CONTAINER together with its more culture specific elaboration in form of SIX-SIDED CONTAINER (Sharifian 2017: 27). As one can see, image-schemata connect to images, but they are nor rich images – merely abstract ones, which cannot be imagined "concretely" (Palmer 1996: 65). They do not specify "actual magnitude, shape, or material (Oakley 2007: 217)" of the "imagined" objects. Mark Johnson, who introduced the notion of an image-schema to cognitive science, defined one as "a recurring, dynamic pattern of our perceptual interactions and motor programs that gives coherence and structure to our experience" (Cienki 2007: 178). In other words, image-schemata are recurring visual templates, which are constitutive parts of some of our conceptualizations. One can consider them as "distillers" of our special and temporal experience (Oakley 2007: 215). Oakley (2007: 217) lists the following major image-schemata: CONTAINER, BALANCE, COMPULSION, BLOCKAGE, COUNTERFORCE, RESTRAINT, REMOVAL, ENABLEMENT, ATTRACTION, MASS-COUNT, PATH, LINK, CENTER-PERIPHERY, CYCLE, NEAR-FAR, SCALE, PART-WHOLE, MERGING, SPLITTING, FULL-EMPTY, MATCHING, SUPERIMPOSITION, INTERACTION, CONTACT, PROCESS, SURFACE, OBJECT, and COLLECTION. Each of those image-schemata might be defined. For example, Szwedek (2018: 63) defines the image-schema OBJECT as "bounded matter whose density is primarily *expressed* by touch". Additionally, he represented it as a circle or circumference, which symbolizes boundedness of the matter. Moreover, as the aforementioned example of *del* shows, image-schemata can be more or less specific. They ubiquitously underlie linguistic forms, e.g., they govern our use of preposition. As noticed by Wierzbicka (1992: 56), the English preposition *on* is linked to the image-schema SURFACE, whereas *in* is linked to that of CONTAINER. The use of particular preposition is bound to the conceptualization of category one refers to. Thus, observing a class of categories – e.g., Arabic lexemes used to refer to time, such as *fatra* 'a period (of time)', *sāʕa* 'an hour', *yawm* 'a day', *sana* 'a year' – one can hypothesize about their conceptualization structured by image-schemata. Since, in Arabic all or most of such time-related categories are usually preceded by the proposition *fī* 'in', one can infer that TIME is conceptualized in Arabic as CONTAINER.[3]

2.2.1.5. **Cultural Models vs. *Idealized Cognitive Models* (ICMs)**

Although sometimes the notions of "schemata" and "models" seem to be used interchangeably by linguists, I assume them not to be the same phenomenon. My understanding of a "cultural schema" was presented in the former subsections. Whereas following Sharifian (2008: 251), quoted earlier, as a "cultural model", I will understand a structure "that encompass[es] a network of schemas, categories and metaphors". In other words, a cultural model "reflects (…) [the] cultural conceptualizations exploiting image-schema, metaphor, and metonymy (Maalej 2008: 423)". Such a model comes close to what in CogL is known as Idealized Cognitive Model (ICM). ICM might be also described "schematically, metaphorically, or metonymically (Maalej 2008: 402)", what as a result, connects it somehow with the aforementioned notion of cultural model, or at least indicates that a cultural model might be considered being an ICM (Maalej 2008: 423).

The notion of ICM was introduced by Georege Lakoff (1987) as "a complex structured whole", which organize our knowledge (Lakoff 1987: 68). He hypothesized that it "uses four structuring principles": propositional structure (corresponding to Fillmore's notion of *frame*), image-schematic structure, metaphoric mappings, and metonymic mappings (Lakoff 1987: 68). In fact, although at the beginning ICM was exclusively used by Lakoff to refer to such an understood "complex structured whole", with time he started using the notion an ICM or a model in reference to the "structuring principles" structures as well (Palmer 1996: 61). In such a way, one can frequently find such terms as *metaphoric models* or *metonymic models* used frequently in the CogL literature (cf. Maalej 2008: 411).

The similarities between Sharifian's understanding of a model and Lakoff's ICM are quite obvious. Lakoff himself (1987: 69) admitted the possibility of matching propositional ICMs (i.e., propositional structures) with the notion of schemata. Moreover, according to Lakoff (1987: 68), concepts might be defined only relative to an ICM, i.e., they can be explicated only in respect to such an entity, which again call up an important characteristic of cognitive schemata.

Ergo, how shall I understand the notion of cultural model in my study? For me, a model consists of schemata of different types (including image-schemata)

---

3 Based on the corpus ArabicWeb2012, available at SketchEngine (https://sketchengine.eu/, [24-08-2021]).

linked with each other by means of metaphorical and metonymic mappings (or models). In other words, I will postulate the model as being more or less analytical (not real) construct, which encapsulates the description of schemata as being interrelated – in form of either metaphors (relations between conceptually distant schemata) or metonymies (relations between subschemata subsumed by a coherent schema).

The notion of metaphors brings into our attention an important element of the discussion on the cultural models, i.e., that on the role of conceptual metaphors within models. Primarily, as suggested by Quinn (cf. Palmer 1996: 105), metaphors were postulated to be only derivations of more basic propositional content which, in fact, constitutes a model. In such understanding, conceptual metaphors merely reflect the model content (Kövecses 2005: 205) or are derived from our knowledge about something (Dirven, Wolf, & Polzenhagen 2007: 1205–6). The opposite stand was adopted by Lakoff and Kövecses (Dirven, Wolf, & Polzenhagen 2007: 1206) who postulated that "conceptual metaphors hold the constitutive role" in a model (Dirven, Wolf, & Polzenhagen 2007: 1206). Zoltàn Kövecses (1995) in his study on the American model of FRIENDSHIP, notices that "the concept [of friendship] lies at the intersection of several systems of metaphor, the relevant part of which make up the abstract domain that is called friendship (Kövecses 1995: 319)". In a similar fashion, he postulates the English model of ANGER, in which different metaphorical mappings constitute the structure of schemata defining properties of this feeling (Kövecses 2005: 197). In other words, he theorizes that metaphors "lend" or provide "skeletal structure" for the model of concepts (Kövecses 2005: 198–9), mostly for those abstract in nature (Kövecses 2005: 203).

In my study, I will follow the assumptions of Lakoff and Kövecses, which means I will use the metaphorical mappings as "skeletal" structures, which organize the knowledge of a particular phenomenon.

All in all, cultural models might be perceived as analytical construals, which subsume different kinds of cultural conceptualizations. It means then that such models represent the properties of conceptual system encompassing a particular culture (Kövecses 2017: 309).

2.2.2. Cultural categories

As I mentioned earlier, categorization is one of the two most important operations of human cognition, second being the process of schematization elaborated above. One can see it as an association procedure, in which an object (in a broad sense) is perceived as a kind of another object (Sharifian 2008: 117).

The categorization results in emergence of categories, which together with schemata are the major tools of organizing our knowledge of the world (Sharifian 2008: 117). Categories might then be seen as "mental referential points", i.e., they serve us as a basis for comparison, while encountering new experience (Lewandowska-Tomaszczyk 2007: 149). We categorize all kinds of objects, not only things, but also "events, settings, mental objects, properties relations and other components of experience" (Sharifian 2017: 15), or more precisely "colours, emotions, attributes, food, stuffs, kinship terms (…) etc. (Sharifian 2017: 7)".

In fact, there are two types of categorization (cf. Palmer 1996: 291; Lewandowska-Tomaszczyk 2007: 156–7). The first one might be perceived as similar to schematization, since it entails elaboration. It is then the categorization procedure, by which one tries to list the examples (i.e., elaborations) of a particular category. This type is known in linguistics under the name of taxonomy. In other words, we do categorize by elaboration, when for instance, we list the instances of the category BAKING GOODS as BREAD, ROLLS, BREAD CRUMBS, CAKE, etc. The second type of the categorization is somehow different. It entails extension of the category in question, i.e., evaluation of how well the experienced object fit the category. We categorize by extension, when we refer to different phenomena as being somehow identical – for instance, when use the lexeme *school* to refer to such meanings as "a building, in which children are thought", "a teaching institution", "a trend in science or art (e.g., Boasian school of linguistics)" etc., all of which might be seen as falling under the category SCHOOL (i.e., they are all a *type* of school). As one can see, the categorization by extension is the basis of a word's polysemy, i.e., it accounts for the fact that some words have more than one meaning.

Although these two types of categorization look different, the mechanism driving them both is the same: the experiencer perceives some objects as somehow identical or equal. Both are also organized around a prototypical instance of a category. Prototype is a notion introduced to cognitive science by Eleonor Rosch, who noticed that human categorization process entails judgement "of goodness of membership" in a particular category (Palmer 1996: 78). One can understand a prototype as "a stereotypic, or generic, representation of a concept that serves as a standard for evaluating the goodness-of-fit" of objects perceived as falling under the category in question (Casson 1983: 434).

CogL rejects the classical theory of classification in terms of sufficient and necessary features, which account for evaluating an object as falling under a category. It accepts the fact that the categorization is prototypical in nature, i.e., it entails evaluation or judgement of how similar a thing is to the best example of a category (Lewandowska-Tomaszczyk 2007: 145). It means then that membership in a category is gradable – there are better and worse examples of it, and that categories are blurred at the edges, i.e., sometimes it is difficult to delimit two categories, when their least fitting instances seem to fall under them both (Lewandowska-Tomaszczyk 2007: 145). In the category BAKING GOODS, there are better and worse examples of fitness. For example, BREAD seems more fitting to it than CAKE, which, on its turn, falls at the edge of the category, and might be actually categorized as an instance of either BAKING GOODS or SWEETS. In such a theory of categorization, we cannot establish a fixed set of features, possession of which can guarantee fitness to a particular category. What makes instances of the category fall under it, is family resemblance, or overlapping sets of features, from among which some are more silent than the other (Lewandowska-Tomaszczyk 2007: 146). The theory entails then a kind of metonymy, in which one of the members of the category (i.e., its prototype) stands for all its elements (Lakoff 1987: 78).

As I have mentioned, the categorization by extension gives rise to polysemy, which might be in fact perceived as "as an instance of categorization (…), [in which] category-members form (…) chains of related senses (Lewandowska-Tomaszczyk 2007: 158)". A category structured by such a process forms a radial network of interrelated meanings of a given word (e.g., *school*) (Lewandowska-Tomaszczyk 2007: 147). In such a network, a central place is occupied by the most prototypical instance of the category, i.e., the meaning of the word, which is the most salient (Lewandowska-Tomaszczyk 2007: 147). In our example, this central meaning is "a teaching institution". Remaining meanings – "a building, in which children are thought" and "a trend in science or art" – fall around the central member, which "motivates noncentral senses" (Lewandowska-Tomaszczyk 2007: 148), "in the sense that they bear family resemblance to it (Lakoff, in Lewandowska-Tomaszczyk 2007: 148)". To "to account for the types of links between the central and noncentral category members", we ought to employ all kinds of cognitive models (in the sense of Lakoff's ICMs) – propositional, metaphorical, metonymic, and image-schematic (Lewandowska-Tomaszczyk 2007: 148). In other words, "a building, in which children are thought" might be categorized as a type of SCHOOL, based on a metonymic model, in which name of the "teaching institution" stands for the name of its own seat. In such a theory of polysemy, some extensions of the central category of a sense are considered predictable – like e.g., in the case of *mother* used in reference to "biological mother", "stepmother", or "adoptive mother" (Lewandowska-Tomaszczyk 2007: 148). Remaining senses – e.g., *mother* as "a title of a nun" – are not predictable and are conditioned by the culture (Lewandowska-Tomaszczyk 2007: 148). In other words, we can say that the prototype of such a radial category is the meaning, which covers all (or most of) models in the sense of ICMs, which encodes the knowledge of a given category (Lakoff 1987: 83). Such coverage entails being at the intersection of most of the schemata, in relation to which this category is defined.

In fact, one can perceive a category – of any type – as a node within cognitive schemata (cf. Lakoff 1987: 69). It means that categories are in fact subschemata of more or less abstract schemata, which are interconnected or interwoven with one another by means of metaphor, metonymy, or conceptual integration.[4] "The properties of the category would depend on many factors: the role of that node [i.e., this category] in a given schema, its relationship to other nodes in the schema, the relationship of that schema to other schemas, and the overall interaction of that schema with other aspects of the conceptual system (Lakoff 1987: 69–70)". Some of the categories are lexicalized (Sharifian 2017: 7), i.e., we possess lexical means of their expression in form of, e.g., words. Therefore, in order to define a word – its meaning, i.e., the (conceptual) category, to which it refers – we have to provide all the schemata, in which this category appears as a subschema (a node), determining the relationships between this category and other elements its subsuming schemata, as well as the relationships between those schemata themselves.

Such an understood category might be perceived as the elaboration system – the second type of the categorization procedure. In fact, it comes down to what we know as taxonomy, i.e., the operation of organizing items as *kinds* of something (Palmer 1996: 88). Thus, we do categorize things in hierarchies of a superordinate and its subordinates, which corresponds in linguistics to a hypernym and its hyponyms. As I said, we can also see such categories as schemata – more precisely, object schemata (cf. Casson 1983: 441). In fact, being a schema, a category underlies a classification system, which can take form of aforementioned taxonomy, or other types of hierarchical organization such as partonomy (part-whole relationship) or functional classification ("X is used for Y" classification) (Casson 1983: 441–3). As I mentioned, such understood category might subsume not only things but also other types of real-word items, such as events. Thus, event schemata (scenarios) might also form categories (Casson 1983: 449).

In other words, a notion of category is somehow related to that of schema, since "[a]ll humans schematize their experience and organize their schemas into complex categories, chains, and hierarchies (Palmer 1996: 293)".

4 For more about conceptual integration or blend theory, cf. Turner (2007).

What is quite important, both categorization processes – extension and elaboration – are usually at play in the case of a particular category. Such double procedure results in emergence of a schematic model of a category, in which it is organized by both the extension and elaboration (Lewandowska-Tomaszczyk 2007: 157). Thus, the category of SCHOOL might subsume the meanings of "a building, in which children are thought" and "a teaching institution", as well as its instances being ELEMENTARY SCHOOL, HIGH SCHOOL, and UNIVERSITY. In both categorization procedure prototypical effects are at play.

The notion of taxonomy based on the categorization by elaboration, brings us closer to the concept of cultural category. It will be truism to say that categories differ immensely across cultures and languages. We find it obvious mostly in the phenomenon of unmatching meanings what accounts for the fact that words in different languages are so often barely translatable (Wierzbicka 1992: 20). In other words, we can detect different categorization – cutting the real-world into coherent conceptual pieces – by looking into lexicons of languages. It is possible because categories are usually lexicalized (cf. Sharifian 2017: 7), i.e., they are "labeled" by lexical items (Sharifian 2015: 480).

A cultural category is then a type of cultural conceptualization – a result of negotiation within a culture group over the division of the world into classes of objects. In other words, cultural categories are what indicates culturally constructed division of the reality (Sharifian 2015: 480). It is the most obvious in the case of taxonomies (categorization by elaboration), which reflect "folk ontologies that define the essential nature of things for each culture (Palmer 1996: 8)". But also, in the case of polysemy (categorization by extension), the impact of culture on language is noticeable. The motivation of the extension from a central sense (meaning) is not natural, but cultural (cf. Lewandowska-Tomaszczyk 2007: 148), being affected by constant negotiations within a cultural group.

2.2.3. Cultural metaphors

As we learned in the previous sections, schematization and categorization are two major cognitive procedures consisting human cognition of the world. Their results – schemata and categories – are the basics of our conceptualization of experience. Nevertheless, human cognition is much richer in operations it performs. Thus, sometimes, it sets up connections between existing schemata and/or categories, which results in emergence of new conceptualizations (Sharifian 2008: 117). From among such connections, conceptual metaphor is the most obvious phenomena, which has been studied in the framework of CogL since 80' of the last century, when George Lakoff and Mark Johnson published their famous *Metaphors We Live By* (Lakoff & Johnson 2013), and recently elaborated and extended by such scholars as Zoltán Kövecses (2021).

They defined the essential understanding of their theory of metaphor, by stating that "metaphor is understanding and experiencing one kind of thing in terms of another" (Lakoff & Johnson 2013: 5). Basically speaking, it means that (conceptual) metaphors are strategies or devices, by which we conceptualize non-physical reality – phenomena of social, political, psychological, or emotional nature (De Silva, Cuenca, & Romano 2017: 350). In general, by metaphor, one understands a systematic correspondence between two theoretically non-related domains of experience (Grady 2007: 189). One of those domains – a source (domain) – serves as a "source" of conceptualization of another domain – a target (domain). In other words, elements of the source are mapped (or are projected, or map) onto the elements of the target, providing by that "language and imagery which are used to refer to (...) [this target domain] which is actually at use in the discourse" (Grady 2007: 189). Such a correspondence – a mapping – is unidirectional (Grady 2007: 191) and motivated by our experience of some sort of similarity between the physical source and (more) abstract target (Kövecses 2005: 5). This connecting sense of experience was termed in the theory *experiential basis* of the mapping (Kövecses 2005: 5–6), and is what tells us about how the target is somehow experienced by people, even though it is not something one can easily experience per se.

Although for ages, metaphors have been considered a linguistic phenomenon, they are in fact something much more than simply that. Perhaps, the most important discovery of Lakoff & Johnson (2013: 3–4) is that metaphors are primarily conceptual in nature and language is only the department, in which they manifest (possibly in the easiest way). Metaphors are functions of thinking, not speaking. Nevertheless, linguistic studies on metaphors are essential (Kövecses 2005: 32) since the existence of conceptual metaphors is usually postulated on the basis of analyzed linguistic expression (Kövecses 2005: 8). Of course, such postulations should be treated as mere hypotheses, since in fact each metaphor is not only linguistic phenomenon, but also conceptual, socio-cultural, bodily, and neural one (Kövecses 2005: 8).

Conceptual metaphors are bodily, because they primarily rely on our human experience of our own body (Kövecses 2005: 18). Such bodily experience might seem primary one, and thus metaphors, which emerged motivated by it, are frequently referred to as *primary metaphors* (Kövecses 2005: 3). They are seen as "building blocks of mental experience" being patterns, "which map fundamental perceptual concepts into equally fundamental, but not directly perceptual ones"

(Grady 2007: 192). One of the many examples of such primary metaphors is a very well-known ANGER IS A PRESSURIZED FLUID IN A CONTAINER, which might be deduced from such English expressions of ANGER as *he is boiling*, *he hit the roof*, etc. It is based on our basic experience of our body, in which while experiencing anger, we feel rising temperature and blood pressure. Such metaphors seem to be to a certain degree universal, since our human body is by all means of universal design (Grady 2007: 194).

Primary metaphors are the foundation of the hierarchical system of metaphors, which constitutes a great deal of our conceptual system. The hierarchies of metaphors are organized by the extent of their position on the abstraction-specificity spectrum, which also pertain to the context of the use of a given metaphor (Kövecses 2021: 135). Consequently, a metaphor might be highly schematic, abstract – it is then a primary metaphor, based on an image-schematic model – or "detailed, rich, and specific", bound to a given context and functioning at the level of a particular mental space[5] (Kövecses 2021: 135). In between, the metaphors are more or less specific, nevertheless the lower-level ones always inherit the general properties of the more abstract mappings (Grady 2007: 191).

As I mentioned, metaphors are also neural phenomena, i.e., it has been proven that there are some neural correlates, which correspond to conceptual metaphors (Kövecses 2005: 23). In other words, our brain considers the source domain and target domain to be actually connected, or as if they were the same type of phenomena. This means that conceptual metaphor is a mental operation, which has its basis in human brain, and as such it must be accounted for by evolutionist.[6]

Since conceptual metaphor are primarily functions of thinking, they must be strictly related to our cognitive schemata and categories. In fact, one can understand a metaphor also as a systematic correspondence between schemata and/or categories. In other words, in a metaphor, the source domain schema specifies

5 For more about conceptual integration or blend theory, cf. Fauconnier (2007).

6 In fact, Steven Mithen suggested that primarily human brain was domain-specific, i.e., humans were not able to think metaphorically about the world and themselves. However, in the Upper Paleolithic (100 000 – 30 000 years ago), they ability of establishing long-lasting links between unrelated concepts in form of metaphor must have developed. As the argument for that, Mithen provides the emergence of anthropomorphism and totemism attested in the art works of humans, which naturally rely on metaphorical thinking – anthropomorphism on the metaphor ANIMALS AND PLANTS ARE PEOPLE and totemism on PEOPLE ARE ANIMALS (Kövecses 2005: 24–5).

some elements (subschemata) of the target domain schema, which – being "derived systematically from" the source – mimic its elements (subschemata) (Casson 1983: 450). Such systematic correspondence – mapping – might be seen as the "skeletal structure" of a cognitive model, in which concepts from two schemata are linked with each other by a set of metaphoric correlations (Kövecses 2005: 199). It means, that a certain schema "lends" its structure to another schema, organizing by this our knowledge about more abstract phenomena (Kövecses 2005: 198). Thus, linguistic metaphor can be also defined as a linguistic expression that evokes not one but two schemata simultaneously (Palmer 1996: 66). In such a way, the knowledge about a particular, more physical object is mapped onto the knowledge of more abstract one (Palmer 1996: 223). Researchers postulated that in fact, models of all abstract phenomena must use metaphors in organizing their knowledge. In such models, metaphors play crucial role defining different elements of the conceptualization, constituting ontological, casual, epistemic, expressive, and other parts of the model (Kövecses 2005: 197).

Most frequently, the schema, which lend the structure to another schema, is an image-schema. Thus, *qalb* "heart" in Qurʔānic Arabic is conceptualized by the metaphor *qalb*-HEART IS CONTAINER, which links the imagery of the *qalb*-HEART with the image-schema of CONTAINER (Maalej 2008: 400). Such linkage is of a great deal of importance since it governs linguistic expression of the category *qalb*-HEART. It is also a basis for further inferences on a given concept, which together constitute a complex model of it in form of schemata linked with each other by metaphors, which derive from the central metaphor of *qalb*-HEART IS CONTAINER. Thus, one can see *qalb* as a CONTAINER, into which God can POUR many things, such as FAITH, HYPOCRISY, IGNORANCE, SICKNESS, etc. (Maalej 2008: 400), understanding it as the residuum of human mental and emotional capacities, which might be affect by God.

What is quite interesting, metaphors observed across languages many times seem strikingly similar to each other. For instance, the way we conceptualize ANGER AS BOILING of a certain fluid is far too common to be a mere coincident. Thus, in English we say *he was boiling with anger*, in Polish *gotował się ze złości*, and in Arabic *ġalà min al-ġaḍab* (Dziekan 2003: 141) – and all these expressions, formulated in rather distant languages, mean in fact the same. This makes us ask the question about whether conceptual metaphors are universal or not.

Universality of metaphors might be assumed first and foremost because the most primary experiential foundation of our metaphorical thought is our body. Human body is universal in its design and thus, metaphors motivated by our universal bodily perception must be universal too (Kövecses 2005: 17–18; 34).

In other words, the universality of conceptual metaphors was perceived as motivated by their embodiment.

Thus, it seems embodiment motivates the most abstract of our metaphors – those rendered as primary, which as a result might be seen as fairly universal (Kövecses 2005: 4). Nevertheless, their universality is by all means a debatable matter. In fact, many scholars noticed that even the primary metaphors can be affected by culture. Bodily experience seems to be used selectively in conceptualization of abstract phenomena. This selectiveness is by far a result of culture and its ideologies, which can "override" embodiment (Kövecses 2005: 4), which itself might be to a certain degree shaped by a given culture (Maalej 2007: 90–2). Therefore, perhaps more accurately, one should perceive embodiment more as a phenomenon situated in a given socio-cultural context (cf. Dirven, Wolf, & Polzenhagen 2007: 1210) instead of a purely universal one.

So, if even the primary metaphors are to a certain degree affected by culture and its ideologies, one can expect that more specific, more concrete metaphors must be also shaped by a particular culture (Kövecses 2005: 65). In fact, the metaphors above the generic-level seem to more or less culture-specific. The reason of their variation across languages comes down in the most part to the differences in shared experience of a phenomena within a given cultural group (Kövecses 2005: 231). These differences entail differentiation of the context (environmental, social, etc.), as well as of the historical experiences the group (Kövecses 2005: 232–6, 241). The culture specificity of metaphors involves different types of variation, which were painstakingly described in detail by Kövecses (2005). In general, one can categorize these types as either cross-cultural or cross-linguistic. Cross-cultural variation (cf. Kövecses 2005: 67–87) entails emergence of different metaphors, which might (but do not have to) be derived from more generic and thus universal ones. In turn, cross-linguistic variation (Kövecses 2005: 151–162) is the situation, when in two languages, one and the same conceptual metaphor occurs, yet it seems to be treated differently.

What is important for us at this point is that all conceptual metaphors, which can differ between one language and another or can be treated differently in those languages, might be termed *cultural metaphor* (cf. Sharifian 2015: 481). In other words, conceptual metaphors are cultural conceptualizations, which capture some culturally defined knowledge of the speakers of a particular language. They govern to a significant extent the use of this language, and they also allow as to understand how native speakers of this language see some schemata as linked with each other by the means of a kind of similarity.

This linkage between schemata should be, however, postulated with a great caution, since what might seem a metaphor for an outsider, may be not seen like that by the natives (Sharifian 2017: 21, 34). In my opinion, in order to properly assess existence of a metaphoric linkage between two schemata, we have to examine the content (mostly propositional one) of the target schema. For instance, Aboriginal expression *ancestors are crying*, which is used in reference to RAIN, should not be a reason for postulating the metaphor RAIN IS TEARS OF ANCESTORS, since the schema RAIN already encompass as one of its subschemata the propositional schema in form of RAIN IS TEARS OF ANCESTORS (Sharifian 2017: 34). Therefore, RAIN IS TEARS OF ANCESTORS is not a metaphor but a part of Aboriginal knowledge of the world encoded in the schema RAIN.

Besides the cross- cultural and cross- language variation, metaphors might also differ within one culture and one language due to within- culture- group differences in age, gender, education, etc. (cf. Kövecses 2005: 88–104). One can also think of highly contextualized metaphors, functioning at the metal space level, which derive, yet bear a local, context- bound characteristics (Kövecses 2021: 136–7). In fact, such contextualized, novel metaphors are coined by us constantly – not only in form of structures characterizing *licentia poetica*. Creative metaphors are nonetheless deeply rooted in the conceptual system shared by the cultural group (cf. Kövecses 2005: 260– 2), since as more specific, they nevertheless draw from the more abstract, supraindividual or subindividual (image-schematic) metaphors (Kövecses 2021: 134– 5, 137). Naturally, although being a product of one's creativity, they were created in order to communicate. Even poetry is a mean of communication between someone – a poet – and someone else – a reader or a hearer. Thus, even while analyzing a poetic text, one can postulate some cultural metaphors based on the metaphoric expressions used by a poet. All in all, the novel – local – linkage laid between concepts by a poet are preestablished by the existing schemata and categories constituting this poet's conceptual system, which by far is shared by members of their cultural group (cf. Berrada & M'sk 2007: 35).

2.2.4. Cultural metonymies

Apart from the linkages between two knowledge schemata, our cognition can also create links between conceptual structures within one schema. Such operation is known in CogL as metonymy. Traditionally, metonymy was seen as "a semantic link between two senses of a lexical item that is based on a relationship of contiguity between the referents of the expression in each of those senses" (Panther & Thornburg 2007: 237). In other words, two senses of the word *crown*, "an ornament worn by a monarch" and "a power of a monarch", are linked by the proximity in the real world between what a monarch wears while exercising their sovereignty, which is symbolized by this something. In such a model of metonymy, it is a referential tool operating by a "stands-for" relationship between objects, which involves simple substitutions of referents (Panther & Thornburg 2007: 237).

In CogL, however, the operation of metonymy is considered as something more than a mere tool of substitution (Panther & Thornburg 2007: 238). Conceptual metonymy is a cognitive process, which operates in a given context, in which there is a target concept (e.g., "a power of a monarch") subsumed by a conceptual structure (i.e., a schema) containing another concept (e.g., CROWN "an ornament worn by a monarch"), known as source, vehicle, or reference point. More precisely, one can define it as a "process [, which] consists in mental accessing one conceptual entity via another entity (Radden & Kövecses 1999: 19)", or after Langacker, as a process, "in which one conceptual entity, the reference point, affords mental access to another conceptual entity, the desired target (Langacker, in Radden & Kövecses 1999: 19)".

The metonymic mapping – in contrast to the metaphoric one – is by principle bidirectional (Radden & Kövecses 1999: 22). It means that a vehicle can usually be equally accessed by the associated target. However, this rule is not universal, and some metonymies cannot be easily reversed. In general, the interpretation of the proper reading of a concept – target vs. vehicle – is achieved only based on evaluation of a particular context (Radden & Kövecses 1999: 22).

Nevertheless, similarly to conceptual metaphor, conceptual metonymy is by no means a merely linguistic phenomenon and its linguistic expression is only the manifestation of a cognitive process. From a semiotic point of view, metonymy is an indexical operation, which establishes a link between an index (e.g., a red face) and its referent (e.g., being angry) (Panther & Thornburg 2007: 242). As such it can function outside of the realm of language, accounting for any "stands-for" association in the real world based on our experience (cf. Sharifian 2017: 31).

Thus, to sum up, metonymy is an operation linking two concepts based on our knowledge of a relation holding between them (cf. Palmer 1996: 232). In other words, metonymy links two elements of a cognitive schema encoding some knowledge, which subsume these concepts and their relationship (cf. Palmer 1996: 232). In metonymy, one uses one of those elements – a source or a vehicle – in order to evoke another or even the whole schema (cf. Lakoff 1987: 78; Panther & Thornburg 2007: 238). For instance, if asked by George *How did you come here?*, Mark responds: *I borrowed a car from my brother*, without causing any confusion, George would understand that Mark arrived by a car. This is because, Mark's answer is an instance of metonymy, in which the subschema HAVING A

CAR is employed to evoke the whole schema DRIVING A CAR (one has to HAVE A CAR in order to be able to DRIVE it) (Lakoff 1987: 79).

Therefore, the most important principle of conceptual metonymy is contiguity, by which one should understand a contiguity within an ICM (Radden & Kövecses 1999: 19) or simply, a cognitive schema. Of course, not every single concept within one schema can be metonymically accessed via any other concept subsumed by this schema. Even though NOSE and MOUTH are a part of a schema FACE, one cannot use the former in other to evoke the latter (Radden & Kövecses 1999: 29–30). It seems then that "metonymy may only arise when the intended target is uniquely accessible (Radden & Kövecses 1999: 30)". Moreover, the more contrast between two concepts within a schema there is, the more readily available they are for a metonymic mapping of one another. Therefore, the most frequently occurring metonymy is that following the part-for-whole and whole-for-part models (Radden & Kövecses 1999: 30). In other words, quite often, in a metonymy, the whole schema stands for its particular part or a part of a schema stands for the whole schema. Thus, despite being traditionally differentiated from metonymy, synecdoche (*pars-pro-toto* relationship), is considered in CogL as a type of conceptual metonymy (Panther & Thornburg 2007: 238). Nevertheless, alongside part-for-whole/whole-for-part model, there is also a number of metonymies, in which the vehicle and the target are parts of the same schema (Radden & Kövecses 1999: 30), and do not contain each other.

As I said metonymy is not only a referential tool of substitution. We can perceive it as a phenomenon, in which conceptual elements of a schema interact with each other, giving rise by that to a complex meaning. Therefore, some scholars – such as Radden & Kövecses (1999: 19) – suggest that instead of considering metonymy in terms of substitution, we should consider it as a conceptually additive process. This would mean that the use of *crown* in reference to "a power of a monarch" implies not only this particular signification, but also manifests our conceptualization of "a power of a monarch" as being exercised by someone, who – while doing so – wears a strictly and culturally defined ornament. Similarly, by saying *She is just a pretty face*, we do not merely mean that a woman is beautiful, but we also hint at the fact that in the most stereotypical scenario, we evaluate someone's beauty primary by looking at their face (cf. Radden & Kövecses 1999: 19). Therefore, in the metonymy, "both the vehicle and the target are conceptually present", yet one of them – the vehicle – seems to be more salient than another (Radden & Kövecses 1999: 19).

The aforementioned additive property of metonymy accounts for tangible pragmatic advantages over the literal reference (Panther & Thornburg 2007: 250), which can explain the ubiquity of the use of this linguistic tool.

Because it is not a mere substitution, metonymy could be preferred because it might be "more immediately useful for the given purpose in the given context (Lakoff 1987: 84)", by providing us with some gains in form of contextual effects (Panther & Thornburg 2007: 250). For instance, this is the case of the metonymy, which operates based on the online attribution taking place in a discourse. Thus, while talking with Mark, George can refer to their friend Ronald as *curmudgeon* (e.g., George: *Mary told me she hasn't see the curmudgeon for ages.*), if in the course of the conversation, Mark had already attributed Ronald using this adjective (e.g., Mark: *Ronald is such a curmudgeon!*). In such a way, not only did George referred to Ronald, but also maintained important information about him without additional effort. Similar effect could be observed also in the aforementioned metonymic answer *I borrowed a car from my brother*. This expression provides much more information ("I arrived here by car, which I had borrower from my brother") than non-metonymic, literal one ("I arrived here by a car"), by virtually the same processing effort.

Moreover, metonymy might be preferred in a particular utterance, because of the decreased processing effort of its production. Such situation takes place whenever the source concept, the vehicle, is "easier to understand, easier to remember, easier to recognize" than the target (Lakoff 1987: 84). It is especially useful when the available information about the source is limited and we have to find the way to decrease the processing effort of referring to it – like in a situation, when waiters name customers by the numbers of their tables (e.g., in the expression *The number five ordered a steak*). The smallest effort would be exercised if the waiters knew names of the customers. In the situation, in which this information is not available, the easiest way to refer to the customers is the metonymy NUMBER OF THE TABLE FOR THE CUSTOMER/S SITTING AT THE TABLE (Panther & Thornburg 2007: 250).

In other words, metonymy either facilitates the reference, when the information about the referent is limited, or provides more information about the referent with the smallest possible processing effort. In both cases, the metonymy foregrounds or highlights the conceptual content of the target – which appears more salient – and backgrounds the conceptual content of the source (Panther & Thornburg 2007: 242). Therefore, when the waiters call someone *the number five*, they do not actually think of any number – the semantic content of the concept NUMBER FIVE is shadowed. Still, due to the additive nature of conceptual metonymy, it is by no means absent from the reference. The waiters might think of a particular customer, yet this customer is still sited at the table *number five*. Both information are then conveyed with the minimal processing effort.

In my study, I was particularly interested in the cultural aspects of the motivation of metonymic mappings I analyzed. In other words, I postulated existence of some cultural metonymies, which encode important information (i.e., chunk of knowledge) shared by pre-Islamic Arabs. This encodement results from the culture-related "principles governing the selection of preferred vehicle" (Radden & Kövecses 1999: 44, 48–50). Usually, these principles – cultural preferences of a vehicle – come down to a choice of a particular part of a schema to represent the whole (PART FOR WHOLE metonymies). Such a choice often reveals some culture-based inclination for distinguishing one member of a category in order to perceive it as its prototype. This distinguishing, however, implies always either certain stereotypical knowledge shared within a given group, or the evaluation of category members in terms of ideal, typical, and other – culture-bond – dimensions.

From among these dimensions, the stereotype is the most significant one (cf. Haiman 1993: 300). A social stereotype might be seen as a metonymy, which conditions the category extension, in which "a subcategory has a socially recognized status as standing for the category as a whole, usually for the purpose of making quick judgement about people (Lakoff 1987: 79)". This subcategory might be seen as a culturally recognized prototype of a whole category or schema (Radden & Kövecses 1999: 18). The culture-specific metonymic extension might be observed, for instance, in popular tautologies, such as *boys will be boys* (Panther & Thornburg 2007: 255), which evoke some stereotypical value of the category (here, NAUGHTY, MISBEHAVING BOYS). In other words, the stereotype might be seen as a value ascribed to a category by default based on expectations formulated for its members by a cultural group (Lakoff 1987: 81). The easiest way in detecting it is so-called BUT-test. For instance, Lakoff (1987: 79–81) postulated that a stereotypical value of the category MOTHER in English is HOUSEWIFE. The observation was based on a test consisting of two sentences (1) and (2):

(1) *Mary is a mother,* BUT *she isn't a housewife.*
(2) *Mary is a mother,* BUT *she is a housewife.*

From among these sentences, (1) sounds (or perhaps used to sound) more natural for a speaker of English, whereas (2) sounds somehow weird. It is because BUT is a copula introducing a statement, which contradicts a preceding clause. The preceding clause predicates that Mary falls into the category of MOTHER. Therefore, only in (1), BUT seems to be used properly, since it introduces a statement contradicting the predication of the first clause, i.e., it states that Mary is not a HOUSEWIFE. Thus, HOUSEWIFE seems to be a default value implied by the category MOTHER. In other words, one can say that by predicating *Mary is mother*, one actually asserts that Mary is mother and housewife, because stereotypically every MOTHER is considered to be a HOUSEWIFE. Ergo, the use of BUT in (2) is simply redundant and thus pragmatically incorrect, since it violates 2nd Gricean maxim – "no more information than what is necessary" (cf. Panther & Thornburg 2007: 248).

Metonymy is especially important in my study, since EAP is abundant in it, most often due to the use of substantivized adjectives (Zwetler 1978: 80; e.g., *ṣārim* "sharp, piercing" for "a sword") in place of appellatives (cf. Kowalski 1997: 55). In fact, the modern conception of metonymy as encoding certain stereotypical – thus cultural – knowledge has been already proposed ages ago in 11th c. by medieval Arabic scholar al-Ǧurǧānī in his definition of a tool of indirect expression known in Arabic as *kināya* (al-Ǧurǧānī 1984: 66). He understood this tool as a mean of reference, in which a meaning (concept) was indicated not by its conventional designation, but by a lexical item, which refers to another concept/ meaning that "follows" or "neighbors" the intended one (*huwa tālī-hi wa-ridfu-hu*) in "the existing reality (*fī al-wuǧūd*)". In other words, for al-Ǧurǧānī *kināya* was also something that operates on what we would call nowadays cognitive schemata, subsuming our knowledge of some parts of the reality. Such an understanding neatly matches the modern theory I summarized earlier.

Moreover, al-Ǧurǧānī seems to have recognized that *kināya*-metonymy is an operation, in which a certain prominent imagery or conceptualization serves as a vehicle of access to the whole concept/schema. For instance, he explains the use of the expression *naʔūm aḍ-ḍuḥà* "[she] who is well asleep at the forenoon" in the meaning of "a rich woman", by pointing towards a certain stereotypical property of the scene SLEEPING IN LATE for the whole role schema of a RICH WOMAN – someone, who does not have to manage errands in the morning, because she possesses servants doing it for her. Thus, similarly to the conception of conceptual metonymy, al-Ǧurǧānī's theory of *kināya* acknowledged that the metonymic mapping can only exist based on some shared understanding of the reality and of the relationships existing in it. Most importantly, al-Ǧurǧānī (1984: 72) insist that the salience of a vehicle imagery (e.g., SLEEPING IN LATE) within the whole knowledge schema (e.g., RICH WOMAN) must be a well-known and evident matter (*al-ʔamr ẓāhir maʕrūf*). This salience should be understood in terms of stereotypicality of a certain element within a particular cognitive schema.

2.2.5. Metaphors and metonymies – summary

In general, both metaphors and metonymies can be characterized as cognitive operation, in which some cognitive structures are being linked. Such a linkage accounts for emergence of cognitive models. Both types of models – metaphoric and metonymic – are responsible for extension of a category, which results in development of polysemy (cf. Lewandowska- Tomaszczyk 2007: 148). They might be then seen as "one of the *cognitive construals* mechanism" of meaning construction (Wilson & Lewandowska-Tomaszczyk 2017: 262).

The only difference between metaphor and metonymy lays in the elements they link together. Metaphor links two separate schemata, which, in most of the instances, are conceptually distant from each other, whereas metonymy operates within one schema only (Panther & Thornburg 2007: 238). Some scholars argue that the difference between these two cognitive phenomena is blurred (Panther & Thornburg 2007: 239; Maalej 2008: 421), which might be seen reasonable due to the difficult to define notion of conceptual distance. In fact, many times, while studying conceptual metaphors and metonymies, one can encounter such linkages between schemata, which are not easy to classify. It is so, because schemata might be subsumed by a more generic schema, turning by this into subschemata. In such a case, what previously seemed to be a metaphor between two schemata might be a metonymy linking elements of one more general schema. One deals definitely with such a situation, while examining the primary metaphors (cf. Panther & Thornburg 2007: 244–5). The metaphor AFFECTION IS WARMTH might be easily seen as a non-linguistic indexical metonymy WARMTH FOR AFFECTION, since in fact the motivation of the metaphor is the bodily experience of warmth accompanied strong feelings.

Nevertheless, metaphors and metonymies interact with each other in many ways establishing very complex linkages between schemata and their subschemata. Such a complex linking phenomenon was termed by Louis Goossens (2003) as *metaphtonymy*. For instance, sometimes, in case of *metonymy within metaphor* (Goossens 2003: 363– 4), source and/ or target concepts of metaphoric mappings might be elaborated by means of metonymy. Panther & Thornburg (2007: 243) provide as an example of such a case the expression *Don't bite the hand that feeds you*, in which BITE and FEED are both metaphors, whereas HAND stands obviously for a PERSON. Similarly, Tunisian *qalbū žiʕān* meaning "he is greedy" (lit. "his heart is hungry") is constructed as an interplay of the metonymy *qalb*-HEART FOR PERSON and the metaphor HUNGER IS GREED (Maalej 2008: 241). Alternatively, one can also observe such a phenomenon as *demetonymisation inside a metaphor* (Goossens 2003: 365–6) or rather rare *metaphor within metonymy* (Goossens 2003: 366– 7). Another type of an interaction between metaphors and metonymies are so-called post-metonymies and post-metaphors postulated by Nick Riemer (2003). They are such instances of metaphors or – less often – metonymies, which originally used to function as metonymies or metaphors respectively. For instance, the modern English metaphor *beat one's breast* meaning "make a noisy open show of sorrow" is not a real conceptual metaphor structuring a certain social behavior with an imagery, but it is rather a post-metonymy, i.e., an old, "dead" metonymy that ceased to be recognized as a metonymy due to the historical change of social practices (Riemer 2003: 389). The original – nowadays "dead" – metonymy encoded a certain stereotypical scene/imagery of public expression of sorrow – BEATING ONE'S BREAST – that is no longer recognized as so. Thus, the category BEATING ONE'S BREAST is no longer a part of the schema EXPRESSION OF SORROW, and by that the expression founded on a link between them might be interpreted only as metaphor (cross-domain mapping), and not as metonymy (intra-domain mapping).

2.3. Applied methods

In the previous sections, I defined the major concepts of the methodology I decided to apply in my study. Now, I would like to present in detail objectives of my research, as well as the actual methodological design of my analysis and the analytical procedures I conducted in it.

2.3.1. Objectives

In short, in my study, I aimed to portray cultural conceptualizations of HONOR in LEAP. Therefore, I tried to describe in detail cultural models subsuming the knowledge of HONOR shared by the speakers of LEAP. The notion of HONOR used in here (and in the title of my study) should be seen by all means as an approximation only, since in LEAP one cannot find sufficient equivalent of this European concept. Thus, in fact, in my study, I will render the cultural model of different yet closely related phenomena, which in European languages were more or less conceptualized as HONOR. Moreover, as I mentioned in the previous chapter, LEAP being a poetic and perhaps religious variety of Arabic was not a language used in everyday communication. Therefore, the notion of its speakers should not be understood literarily. Nevertheless, LEAP is by all means the most suitable subject of such an analysis, since it solely served transmission of cultural knowledge among pre-Islamic Arabs in form of poetic discourse of EAP (cf. Sharifian 2003: 190).

In the study, I intended to reconstruct cultural schemata, which encapsulate schematized pre-Islamic knowledge of HONOR together with any conceptual linkages, in which they persisted, encoded by metaphoric and metonymic models. My goal is then to represent the whole encyclopedic meaning of HONOR shared by Arabs in al-Ǧāhiliyya, which affected the LEAP lexicon by giving rise to category extension (i.e., polysemy), and which shaped the semantic frames: the analyzed schemata and sets of linguistic choices associated with them. My examination of the latter – the effect on semantic frames – will be limited to the effects of metaphoric and metonymic mappings only. This is because the most obvious of manifestations of the semantic framing – the collocation – due to some technical obstacles I will discuss further in this chapter, was not possible to be rigidly analyzed.

In other words, I wanted to present two interrelated phenomena: the cultural or folk assumptions on HONOR, which circulated in the Arabic society during the time of the second al-Ǧāhiliyya, and the way, in which these assumptions shaped the language use in the discourse about HONOR in form of some prescribed linguistic choices, one had to made in order to say something about it in LEAP. Of course, the medium of transmission and negotiation of these schemata and associated frames was the EAP.

Thus, the first objective of my research was to reconstruct all cultural schemata encoding pre- Islamic Arabic knowledge of HONOR. I started my study from selecting several LEAP lexical categories, which seem to be in proximity to European conceptualizations of HONOR. These categories are lexicalized in LEAP in form of the following nouns: *ʕirḍ*, *šaraf*, *ḥasab*, *karam*, and *karāma*. Starting from these categories (i.e., nodes withing some schemata), I reconstructed around them the whole schemata in a linguistic study encompassing dictionaries and corpus analyses on the aforementioned four lexemes. In order to accurately render the encyclopedic meaning of the selected lexical items, in my description, I included metaphors, which played structuring role in some of the analyzed schemata, as well as metonymies, which encode the culture-specific knowledge in form of stereotypes, and perception of idealness or typicality. My linguistic conclusions were supplemented with ethnographic data from existing historical literature. Moreover, to enrich the quality of my findings, I decided to juxtapose such reconstructed schemata with some schemata encoding the knowledge of SHAME, the opposite of HONOR. Such schemata were reconstructed around few other categories I choose to represent the concept of SHAME.

These cultural schemata rendered around selected categories are what encapsulate the encyclopedic meaning of all the lexical items used in reference to different HONOR- and SHAME-related phenomena. In other words, this part of my study might be seen as aiming to provide definition of HONOR-related lexis.

In my description of the semantic frames that used to govern the language use in the discourse about HONOR (and SHAME) in EAP, I focused on two different elements. First of all, I signalize which categories (i.e., nodes) encompassed by the schemata were actually lexicalized in LEAP. In other words, in my description of the cultural schemata, I point towards the words strictly related to primarily selected categories lexicalized as *ʕirḍ*, *šaraf*, *ḥasab*, *karam*, and *karamā*. For instance, defining the cultural schema of *karam*, I showed the lexical choices a LEAP speaker had, while talking about *karam*, in the form of such lexemes as *karīm*, *makruma*, *laʔīm*, etc. Such lexicalized categories might be termed "cultural categories" since they reflect culture-specific classification of some (social) phenomena.

Moreover, in my study, I link the characteristics of the reconstructed cultural schemata with the description of meaning extension of the cultural categories. This was achieved in the analysis of conceptual metaphors and metonymies. On the one hand, such a description provides an insight into the relation between the analyzed cultural schemata and the other parts of the conceptual system. It defines then how metaphors – certain encodement of cross-schematic linkages – shape the semantic frame, by implying some readily available associations evoked by the categories of HONOR. Furthermore, by studying the metonymies, it also describes the entrenched relations between elements of those schemata, mostly by identifying stereotypical and other salience-based linkages between a category and a schema subsuming it.

On the other hand, however, my study helps specifying the linguistic choices of a figurative nature prescribed by the analyzed schemata. In other words, it explains the motivation behind the use of figurative language in form of metaphorical expressions and metonymies. In the case of conceptual metaphors, my description demonstrates how metaphorical models – i.e., metaphorical mappings – prescribe grammatical and lexical choices of LEAP user. For example, conceptualization of *šaraf* in form of the metaphor *šaraf* IS ELEVATED PLACE, precisely defines the lexical options one had, while talking about becoming a man of *šaraf*, in form of such verbs as *samā*, *ṣaʕida*, *tasallaqa*, or *tasannama*, all of which refer to the concept of ASCENDING or CLIMBING. Similarly, analyses of metonymical models also pointed towards possible linguistic choices defined by the encoded knowledge of contiguity between conceptual entities. Thus, while referring to *karam*, one could also use the lexeme *ḥasab*, because of the existence of a metonymy *ḥasab* FOR *karam*. This metonymy derives from a CONTAINER-CONTENT relationship encoded by the schema *ḥasab*, which encloses the knowledge that *ḥasab* is a VALUE based on the COUNT of one's DEEDS of *karam*. In other words, using *ḥasab* to refer to *karam*, one could mention their commitment to the code of *karam*, pointing towards their VALUE, being established by it.

In such a way, I believe, I succeeded in representing the pre-Islamic Arabic knowledge of HONOR-related phenomena, together with the way, in which this knowledge underlies the use of LEAP in a discourse about them. In other words, I described cultural semantic frames for pre-Islamic Arabic HONOR, providing not only the answer to the semantic question about meaning of particular words and expressions, but also pointing towards the predefined choices, LEAP user had, while talking about HONOR. All in all, the research aiming to achieve such objectives clearly follows the methodological outline of CL.

2.3.2. Methodology of the study on cultural conceptualizations of HONOR in LEAP

At last, I will describe in detail the research procedures, which resulted in drawing the conclusion presented in the further chapters.

As I mentioned earlier, the starting point of my research was a linguistic study on four Arabic lexemes – *ʕirḍ*, *šaraf*, *ḥasab*, *karam*, and *karāma* – which might be interpreted as referents of phenomena subsumed by European notion of HONOR. It consisted of three separated stages: dictionaries analysis, corpus-based analysis, and integration of acquired data.

2.3.2.1. Dictionaries analysis

In my study on meaning of the selected lexemes, I employed three types of dictionaries. Primarily, I used a representative choice of lexicons composed by medieval Arabic philologists. First of these lexicons is the famous *Kitāb al-ʕAyn* (KtA) by al-Ḫalīl Ibn Aḥamd al-Farāhīdī († 786) considered the first Arabic dictionary (KtA1: 3) and perhaps one of the first dictionaries– in the world in general (Haywood 1960: 39–40). The version of KtA I used in my study is a four volumes edition oversaw and "re-ordered in alphabetic order" by ʕAbdalḥamīd Hindāwī and published in Beirut by Dār al-Kutub al-ʕIlmiyya. As noticed by Hindāwī in the preface to this edition (KtA1: 5), many meanings and words recorded by later lexicographers are missing from KtA, which might be interpreted as the indication of their later development. Thus, KtA was in my study always a starting point of discussion since it could be seen as the closest to the state of the Arabic lexicon persisted in al-Ǧāhiliyya.

Remaining lexicons I used were *Kitāb Ǧamharat al-Luġa* (AlG) by Ibn Durayd († 933) and *Aṣ-Ṣiḥāḥ* (*Tāǧ al-Luġa wa-Ṣiḥāḥ al-ʕArabiyya*; AsS) by al–Ǧawharī († 1003). I choose these two dictionaries, because they might be perceived as subsequent development stages of Arabic lexicography. Thus, KtA represents more or less the state of lexicographic knowledge of 9th c., AlG of 10th, and AsS of 11th.

In my study, I resorted also to *Lisān al-ʕArab* (LsA) by Ibn Manẓūr († 1311), which although deriving to a certain extent from AsS by al-Ǧawharī, presents material from other sources absent from the aforementioned dictionaries (EAL&L: 33). I used it generally in a complementary way.

The second type of dictionaries I employed were onomasiological dictionaries – so-called topic-based lexicon (*maʕāǧim mawḍūʕiyya*) or books of utterances (*kutub al-ʔalfāẓ*). In my study, I employed three of such lexicons: *Kitāb al-Alfāẓ* (iSk) by Ibn as-Sikkīt († 858), *Kitāb al-Alfāẓ al-Kitābiyya* (aHm) by al-Hamaḏānī († 938/9), and *Al-Muḫaṣṣaṣ* (mHs) by Ibn Sīdah († 1066). As one can guess, these lexicons enlist lexical items – both lexemes and expressions – ordered in accordance with the semantic domains they refer to. In other words, they depict Arabic semantic frames (or at least some parts of them) for discourses around several different concepts/topics, representing linguistic choices available to a speaker of Arabic language.

As one can see, both types of dictionaries are rather later creations. Thus, it might seem controversial to use them as a source of conclusions for LEAP. Nevertheless, I decided to do so, because of the fact of the amazing and painstaking work the compilers of these lexicons performed in order to reach "the purest" of Arabic "languages" used – in their belief – in the composition of Qurʔān. As we know, in this work, they used EAP as a "golden standard" for this language (Durie 2018: p.7), and thus, they tried to keep their conclusions as close as it was possible to the variety used in this poetic composition of al-Ǧāhiliyya. Moreover, as noticed by Bauer (2010: 715), they work seems to have been aiming more than just explaining the peculiarities of some Qurʔānic verses – most of the words, they provided in their dictionaries, do not show up in Qurʔān after all. In fact, they rather aimed "to preserve the most distinguish part of their heritage, their literature (Bauer 2010: 715)". Thus, in a way, their lexicons could be seen as a proper philological source of arguments in the discussion over LEAP. Nonetheless, despite this, I decided to treat their conclusions more as hypotheses, especially in the situation, when I could not find a textual argument for their soundness in the corpus of EAP.

Moreover, one could question my choice as for the particular set of employed dictionaries and lexicons. Perhaps most importantly, one could notice the lack of such works as *Fiqh al-luġa* by aṯ-Ṯaʕālibī († 1035), or *Maqāyis al-Luġa* by Ibn Fāris († 1004). I must admit that in my selection I aimed to provide only a representation from within the rich lexicographical tradition of Arabic philology, following to a certain extent the choice made by Haywood (1960) in his elaboration of this tradition. I recognize especially the value of *Maqāyis al-Luġa*, which is a dictionary aiming to define the common properties of derivatives of a given Arabic root. Nevertheless, in my study, I decided not to resort to it, since I tried to focus on synchronic characteristics of Arabic lexis, downplaying – to a certain degree – the conceptualizations encoded in LEAP through the derivational motivations.

At last, in my study, I also used a choice of bilingual CA dictionaries. I selected two of them: the dictionaries by Edward Lane (1968a-h) and by Hans Wehr (edited by J. Milton Cowan)[7] (Wehr & Cowan 1976). The bilingual dictionaries served only a limited, complementary role in my analyses. Therefore, I used only two examples of such lexicons – those, which based on my personal experience, I judge as the most convenient ones. Consequently, I did not resort to such great Arabic bilingual dictionaries as the lexicons by Ullmann (1983) or Baranov (1984).

In the text of this book, I refer to CA dictionaries, using the abbreviation CAD, whereas topic-based dictionaries are referred to by TBD.

The procedure of the dictionaries analysis was quite simple. Based on CAD, I listed all meanings of a given analyzed lexical item, noting all possible meaning extension (i.e., polysemy) that could signalize existence of metaphoric or metonymic models. Consequently, I proposed a working hypothesis as for the existence of a certain radial network of the particular category, proposing the possible vectors of its semantic development. Following that, I used TBD to recreate a repertoire of linguistic elements of a semantic frame associated with this category. TBD conclusions were always incorporated into the main body of my particular argumentation, whereas CAD data on radial networks was presented in separate sections.

The table below (Tab. 1.) presents the list of the employed dictionaries together with their authors and the abbreviations used in the text in reference to them.

7 The choice of English translation of the original German dictionary by Wehr was dictated by the fact that I intended to write this book in English. I decided to resort to Cowan's intuition as for the translation of entries provided by Wehr in German due to my intention of avoiding additional possible conceptual inferences that could occur in the translation rendered by me, a non-native speaker of English.

Tab. 1. Dictionaries used in the analysis of meaning and meaning extension

	Title	Author	Abbreviation in the text (numerals indicate volumes)
Classical Arabic Dictionaries (CAD)	*Kitāb al-ʕAyn*	al-Ḫalīl Ibn Aḥamd al-Farāhīdī († 786)	KtA; KtA1-4
	Kitāb Ǧamharat al-Luġa	Abū Bakr Muḥammad Ibn al-Ḥasan Ibn Durayd († 933)	AlG
	Aṣ-Ṣiḥāḥ (Tāǧ al-Luġa wa-Ṣiḥāḥ al-ʕArabiyya)	Abū Naṣr Ismāʕīl Ibn Ḥammād al-Ǧawharī († 1003)	AsS
	Lisān al-ʕArab	Muḥammad Ibn Mukarram Ibn ʕAlī Ibn Manẓūr († 1311)	LsA; LsA1-15
Topic-based Dictionaries (TBD)	*Kitāb al-Alfāẓ*	Yaʕqūb Ibn Isḥāq Ibn as-Sikkīt († 858)	iSk
	Kitāb al-Alfāẓ al-Kitābiyya	ʕAbd ar-Raḥmān Ibn ʕIsà Ibn Ḥammād al-Hamaḏānī († 938/9)	aHm
	Al-Muḫaṣṣaṣ	Ibn Sīdah (Abū al-Ḥasan ʕAlī Ibn Ismāʕīl) († 1066)	mHs; mHs1-17

2.3.2.2. Corpus-based study

In my study, I employed a textual corpus consisting of texts of so-called *dīwāns*, i.e., poetry compilations, of poets, who lived and created during the time of al-Ǧāhiliyya and the early Islamic era. Following Zwettler, I treat these texts as the final record of the long tradition of EAP, oral-formulaic poetry of pre-Islamic Arabs. Although Zwettler rather opted for greater or lesser extent of anonymity persisting within this tradition (cf. Zwettler 1978: 200, 202–4), I follow the intuition of Monroe (1972: 42) as for possibility of detecting at least some traces of the existence of different schools of poets, if not individual traits of particular poets. Therefore, in my work I decided to follow the finding of medieval Arabic philologists regarding the attribution of the EAP poems. I decided to do so, since I found it rather unlikely that following these findings could possibly affect my conclusions. This is because, for the most part in my analysis, I focus almost entirely on so-called discourse context (i.e., the co-text), as well as the conceptual cognitive contexts (i.e., the culture), and the social situational context (cf. Kövecses 2021: 139–40) that can be interpreted as the context of EAP as a certain social institution. Consequently, I do not take into consideration the authorship-related context of a particular use of the analyzed lexis. I do that only rarely, in case of such authors as ˁAntara Ibn Šaddād, whose Black identity was important for interpretation of some of the lines attributed to him. Thus, while presenting textual samples in the body of the text, I sometimes omit the traditional attribution whatsoever.

Following the application of Oral Theory to EAP, I decided to include in my corpus texts recorded by medieval Arabic philologists and attributed to authors traditionally places within the time frame of 6th and 7th c., up to the initial phase of the Umayyad Caliphate. The demarcation line I arbitrarily drew between the texts of EAP was based on the presumed date of birth of the alleged poets, and it was the year of Prophet Muḥammad's hijra, i.e., 622. This means that in my corpus the latest timewise texts were those attributed to two Islamic caliphs, ˁAlī († 661, born in 599) and Muˁāwiya Ibn Abī Sufyān († 680, born in 608). I am fully aware how controversial such a choice is, since the poems attributed to both caliphs are more than likely to be composed by later poets. I decided to include them, however, based on my conviction as for the formulaicity of EAP as a whole. Moreover, as I said, in the analyses of the contexts of the use of analyzed lexis, I did not intend to take into consideration the identity of alleged authors of the texts. Therefore, the fact that poems of these two caliphs were not composed by them did not affect in any way the conclusions I drew. Furthermore, from among all the analyzed contexts of the use of the HONOR-related vocabulary in EAP only ca. 4 %[8] of them happened to occur in the poems controversially attributed to these two Islamic caliphs. This indicates that is rather unlikely that the conclusions derived based on these contexts could eventually affect the overall results of my study.

In the following chapters, I will refer to this corpus of pre-Islamic and early Islamic poetical texts as Corpus of Early Arabic Poetry (CEAP). It was compiled personally by me based on two corpora – *King Saud University Classical Arabic Corpus (KSUCAC)* created by the team led by Maha S. Alrabiah (2014), and a corpus prepared by Abeer Alsheddi (2016) as a part of his M.A. thesis.[9]

8 I analyzed 27 contexts from the poems attributed to caliph ˁAlī, and 5 from those attributed to caliph Muˁāwiya.

9 In fact, one could argue that instead of CEAP, I should have employed other databases for LEAP research. The most important of those is Analytical Database of Arabic Poetry (ADAP) presented by Kirill Dmitriev in 2020 as a conclusion of his research project "Language–Philology–Culture. Arab Cultural Semantics in Transition" (https://arts.st-andrews.ac.uk/arsem [25-08-2022]). Nevertheless, up until November 2021, when I finally concluded my analyses, ADAP did not seem fully functional. Moreover, after achieving full functionality, ADAP proved not to be of a great help for my conclusions. It seems to provide much less data on the lexis I analyzed than CEAP. For instance,

It consists of 50 text files encompassing poems attributed to 40 poets, most of which – 40 files – were derived from Alsheddi (2016). From KSUCAC, I copied only texts of so-called *muʕallaqāt*, since they were the only texts in this corpus matching the time frame, I was interested in. All in all, CEAP size is 282,650 words. It is then a rather small corpus, and therefore, whenever I provide a normalized word count (NWC), I use the 10,000 as a reference point.[10]

The reason I employed the files derived from the aforementioned corpora is their availability. I am fully aware that there is possibly better material for analyses I performed, yet such works as the amazing *Al-Muʕǧam al-Mufaṣṣal fī Šawāhid al-Luġa al-ʕArabiyya* by Imīl Badīʕ Yaʕqūb (1996) is not available in the formats that allow corpus linguistic analysis. Nevertheless, I sincerely hope that this incredible poetry compilation will one day be available for such research, providing a great source of data on LEAP and conceptualizations encoded in it.[11]

The table below (Tab. 2.) presents the list of all poets included in my CEAP together with the information on the quotation style I used the following chapters. Most of the quotations from the texts of CEAP are accompanied by the reference to a *dīwān*, i.e., a collection of poems attributed to a particular author, usually supplemented with a philological commentary (*šarḥ*). This commentary served as an important reference point for my translations and consequently, my understanding of the given textual context. Therefore, each instance of the quotation of a passage within a corpus contains always the information about its author (i.e., the poet), and the corresponding *dīwān*. For instance, "t22A:25" is the reference to the passage on the page 25 in the *dīwān A* (i.e., t22A) for the text by Zuhayr Ibn Abī Sulmà, indexed in CEAP as t22. In the situation, when I could not localize a given passage in such a *dīwān*, the reference to a particular text contains the letter χ (cf. t22χ). The corpus in form of TXT files is fully available online on the platform *SourceForge*.[12]

ADAP provides only 9 occurrences of the lexeme *ʕirḍ*, whereas CEAP 76 (https://www.arabicpoetry.ac.uk/poem.php#senses=2c97a669a533042b8ca69f06d8f0f8f2%205725b00f9f8e0d5fee27674e16304bb7%209ce2b21eb0376004aa1db45157e8c497&search=1 [25-08-2022]). Nevertheless, I definitely find ADAP to be a tool that can greatly enhance and facilitate the study on EAP, as well as on Arabic poetry in general.

10 Such a NWC calculation is recommended for relatively small corpora (cf. *The Grammar Lab*, http://www.thegrammarlab.com/?p=160 [05-05-2021]). 10,000 English words is roughly 20 pages A4 of a single-spaced text (cf. *WordCounter*, https://wordcounter.io/faq/ [08-07-2021]).

11 I would like to thank prof. Janusz Danecki, the reviewer of my Ph.D. thesis, for pointing towards the great value of the dictionary by Yaʕqūb (1996) for studies on LEAP.

12 The corpus files are available at https://sourceforge.net/projects/ceap-bp/files/ [25-08-2022].

Tab. 2. Corpus of Early Arabic Poetry (CEAP) used in the study and the reference to the corresponding dawāwīn with commentaries

Poet	Text file name	Corresponding *dīwān* – reference
Uḥayḥa	t01	t01A
aš-Šanfara	t02	t02A
Taʔabbaṭa Šarran (Ṯābit Ibn Ǧābir)	t03	t03A
al-Muhalhil	t04	t04A
as-Samawʔal	t05	t05A
Imruʔ al-Qays	t06, t06x	t06A
Ṭarafa Ibn al-ʕAbd	t07, t07x	t07A
Hudba Ibn al-Ḫašram	t08	t08A
al-Ḫirniq Bint Badr	t09	t09A
al-Mutalammis	t10	t10A
al-Ḥāriṯ Ibn Ḥilizza	t11, t11x	t11A
ʕAmr Ibn Kulṯūm	t12, t12x	t12A
ʕAdī Ibn Zayd	t13	t13A
Bišr Ibn Abī Ḫāzim al-Asadī	t14	t14A
ʕAbīd Ibn al-Abraṣ	t15, t15x	t15A
al-Aswad an-Nahšalī	t16	t16A
an-Nābiġa aḏ-Ḏubyānī	t17, t17x	t17A
as-Sulayk	t18	-
Ḥātim aṭ-Ṭāʔī	t19	t19A
		t19B
		t19C
ʕUrwa Ibn al-Ward	t20	t20A
		t20B
ʕAntara Ibn Šaddād	t21, t21x	t21A
		t21B
Zuhayr Ibn Abī Sulmà	t22, t22x	t22A
		t22B
Ṭufayl	t23	t23A
Abū Ṭālib	t24	t24A

(*Continued*)

Tab. 2. Continued

Poet	Text file name	Corresponding *dīwān* – reference
Qays Ibn al-Ḫaṭīm	t25	t25A
		t25B
		t25C
Aws Ibn Ḥağar	t26	t26A
al-Ḥādira	t27	t27A
al-Aʕšà	t28, t28x	t28A
ʕĀmir Ibn aṭ-Ṭufayl	t29	t29A
Labīd Ibn Rabīʕa	t30, t30x	t30A
		t30B
ʕAmr Ibn Maʕd Yakrib	t31	t31A
aš-Šammāḫ Ibn Ḍirār	t32	t32A
al-Ḫansāʔ	t33	t33A
Kaʕb Ibn Zuhayr	t34	t34A
		t34B
ʕUrwa Ibn Ḥizām	t35	t35A
Ibn Muqbil	t36	t36A
Caliph Ali	t37	t37A
Ḥassān Ibn Ṯābit	t38	t38A
		t38B
al-Ḥuṭayʔa	t39	t39A
Caliph Muʕāwiya Ibn Abī Sufyān	t40	t40A

Besides the *dīwāns*, in the understanding of some textual contexts, in the case of *muʕallaqāt*, I also used translations by either Polish (Witkowska & Danecki 1981) or English (Arberry 2017) authors.

In my work on CEAP, I employed two corpus analysis tools – the software *AntConc* and the online tool *SketchEngine*.[13] Although Alfaifi & Atwell (2016) claimed that the latter is the best available tool for Arabic corpora processing, personally, I did not find any of existing corpus-processing applications – even those strictly designed for Arabic, like *Ghawwas* – compatible with CEAP. That

13 https://www.sketchengine.eu/ [05-05-2021].

is, I believe, because of the format of the encoded texts, which uses *scriptio plena* (i.e., vocalization of the consonantal text). What is worth stressing, the vocalization in CEAP is by no means consistent, i.e., the same word could be vocalized randomly rather than consistently (e.g., *ʕirḍ* could be spelled as عِرْض, عِرض, or even عرْض) or it can be left in *scriptio defectiva*. Unfortunately, none of the existing tools was able to process properly texts encrypted in such a way. Therefore, I conducted my corpus-based study in two steps. First, I used *AntConc*, which works with *scriptio plena*, in order to allocate occurrences of a given lexeme (e.g., *ʕirḍ*), by searching for items represented in all possible spelling variants (i.e., عِرْض, عِرض, عرْض, and عرض). Afterwards, I evaluated the acquired data using *SketchEngine*, which operates on *scriptio defectiva*. In such a way, I was able to avoid situation, in which a given word being misspelled in the corpus was omitted in the occurrences analysis.

Due to such technical problems, I must have resigned from the quantitative analysis, i.e., that on the collocation. Unfortunately, the manual calculation of collocates turned out to be too risky to be undertaken as a sound scientific procedure.

Moreover, I also used *SketchEngine* provide some reference points, derived from English, Polish, and MSA corpora.

The corpus study based on CEAP came down to the analysis of contexts of all occurrences of the selected lexemes – *ʕirḍ*, *šaraf*, *ḥasab*, *karam*, and *karāma*. Each analyzed context consisted of at least one *bayt* (i.e., a verse of a poem), however, in most of the cases, I included a broader co-text of an analyzed item. In total, I analyzed 827 of such contexts.

2.3.2.3. Data integration

Using CAD, TBD, and CEAP, I was able to describe the semantic frames for the pre-Islamic Arabic discourse about honor. All in all, in the data integration procedure, I was following so-called *Grounded Theory*, a methodological framework used in qualitative studies, which prescribes analytical procedure of abstraction of more coherent conceptions from raw data (in my case, CAD definitions, TBD observations, and CEAP contexts) (cf. Charmaz 2006).

I first used all the data acquired from dictionaries analyses. Based on CAD, I proposed a skeletal structure of a particular schema in form of more or less precise definition of the meaning of a given lexical items. CAD allowed me also to postulate existence of some metaphorical and metonymic models (i.e., category extensions). This postulation was further elaborated in some cases in a study on TBD. In such a way, based purely on different dictionaries, I was able to posit a hypothetical shape of a cultural schema together with metaphorical mappings structuring it and metonymies functioning within it.

Such a hypothetical schema was the subject of my consecutive study on CEAP. My observations on the contexts, in which a given word occurs, allowed me to acquire all sorts of data about the cultural conceptualizations associated with the schema it evokes. First of all, the analysis allowed me to observe the contextual meaning of this lexeme, supplying data on schematic knowledge encoded in this associated schema. Moreover, from those contexts, I was able to derive information about the image-schematic conceptualization of the particular category, as well as the metaphorical and metonymic models linking it to other schemata and categories.

In such a way, the hypothetical cultural schema was elaborated and afterwards juxtaposed with the ethnographic data I derived from existing historical literature. For the most part, I referred to *The Encyclopedia of History of Arabs before Islam* by Ǧawād ʕAlī (1993a-c),[14] although in particular cases, I also employed works by different authors, both modern such as Dziekan (2008), Danecki (2001), Retsö (2003), Hoyland (2001), and classical ones, such as Jacob (1897) and Wellhausen (1987). Sometimes, I also resorted to *Encyclopedia of Islam* (EoI).

After having postulated a particular cultural schema, I tried to integrate it into more complex system of different subschemata and subsuming schemata. Some of them are the schemata evoked by other analyzed lexemes. Others, however, are mostly subsuming schemata, which I hypothesized partially based on the ethnographic data and partially based on the internal logic of the schemata I postulated. In this fashion, I hope, I manages to represent a cohesive system of conceptualization of HONOR persisting in the pre-Islamic Arabic society.

Presentation of particular cultural schemata contains already description of elements of an associated linguistic frame. It includes enumeration of all the conceptual categories (i.e., nodes within the schemata), which were lexicalized in LEAP lexicon, and as such were the primary lexical options in the language use in the discourse on honor. Moreover, it also points towards the linguistic choices prescribed by the metaphorical and metonymic mappings, presenting associated lexemes, as well as the way the analyzed vocabulary could be actually used.

14 I decided to use the Encyclopedia by ʕAlī due to its exhaustiveness, although often it only repeats the conclusions presented earlier by Muḥammad Šukrī Al-Alūsī (2009).

3. Honor

My study is the first attempt to apply the methods of CL in studying the relationship between pre-Islamic Arabic culture and LEAP. Therefore, as I said, perhaps, its subject could not be different than honor. Pre-Islamic Arabic society always seemed to its students to be circulating around this very notion (cf. Dziekan 2008: 84–94). In fact, some of the scholars ascribe Arabs of al-Ǧāhiliyya with such a veneration of honor that it resembled in their eyes a religious cult (cf. Farès 1938: 96). Even nowadays Arabic society is also almost by default associated with honor – and rarely is this association positive. Such a linkage between honor and Arabic society seems so strong perhaps because of the honor-killing crimes, which frequently make headlines in the Western media. This phenomenon definitely might be traced back to the times of al-Ǧāhiliyya (cf. Górecka 2009: 82–3). It was not, however, the case of Arabic society only and honor, in fact, as an unstoppable power was responsible for far more atrocity and violence than the sole Arabic honor-killings.

It may occur to someone that *honor* is an abstract term and not a forceful factor stirring the life of people. It might be so, since in the West, honor as a value is on its way to decline. For instance, in German, the word *Ehre* "honor" is used rarely, mostly in literature and for many, seems to refer to an archaic concept without any link to nowadays life (Sotirov 2017: 19). In fact, what we can observe in European cultures is the final stage of a shift from the understanding of HONOR as a marker of one's standing to seeing it as a collective of some moral qualities (Stewart 1994: 48), and thus reducible to such concepts as INTEGRITY or MORAL COMPASS (Stewart 1994: 51). This shift is, however, a relatively late phenomenon (Stewart 1994: 45–6), being a result of a development from local to global scale culture and it might be link to the process of individualization of the modern society.

This development is clearly responsible for the variation in the extent of significance attached to honor in modern communities. For instance, it has been noted that more individualistic cultures (e.g., Dutch) differ from the more collective ones (e.g., Spanish) in the expression and sharing of honor-related emotions, such as shame, pride, and anger (Mosquera, Manstead & Fischer 2016). It has already been noticed by Peristiany (1965:10), who claimed that some communities refer to HONOR more frequently than other, implying that the honor is more present in their everyday life. Those communities are usually "small scale, exclusive" and they tend to be characterized by "face to face personal, as opposed to anonymous, relations", in which "the social personality of the actor is as significant as his office" (Peristiany 1965: 11). In such communities, solidarity between members of a group – be it a village, a pueblo, a tribe, a clan – has a great importance. And thus, in such a group strictly depending on actions and reactions of others, a code of behavior is well-defined – what makes its evaluation straightforward. In such communities, honor of others is at constant scrutiny. Consequently, one can consider these communities as epitomizing what can be termed as *honor culture* (cf. Mosquera, Manstead & Fischer 2016: 834).

In more and more modern societies, however, an individual is free (or at least freer) from such a constant examination. It is because we do not have one way of life or one model for an ideal behavior. Thus, it is impossible to judge others by standards limited only to us (cf. Peristiany 1965: 10). It was not naturally the case for the most of the communities of the past. Such a freedom of a social scrutiny is a quite recent phenomenon. Before the mid of 20th c., most people used to live in groups of much smaller scale, in which evaluation of one's behavior was by all means a case. In such groups, HONOR played still a substantial role and it was far from the decline one can observe nowadays in the West. It was valued extensively to the point its veneration could seem religious in nature (Peristiany 1965: 34–5). And this special veneration is what we can observe in the society of Arabs of al-Ǧāhiliyya. Pre-Islamic society was a collection of such small communities – tribes, clans, families – and thus naturally, HONOR must have been an important factor in the life of pre-Islamic Arabs.

However, before examining this importance of HONOR for Arabs of al-Ǧāhiliyya, I think it is crucial to understand what kind of a social phenomenon HONOR is in general. What is quite interesting, despite the diversity of cultures, in which one can find some traces of it, HONOR seemed strikingly similar for a pre-Islamic Arab, a Medieval Islandic warrior, or a mid-20th century Spaniard. Nowadays, this similarity might perhaps be clouded by the ambiguity of HONOR-related lexis of European languages, or perhaps more precisely, by the ambiguity of this notion itself. Thus, in this chapter, I would like to examine further the general concept of HONOR, and how it might seem to us obscure or ambiguous, so that I could accurately juxtapose pre-Islamic Arabic conception of it with its European counterparts.

3.1. The essence of HONOR

HONOR as a social construct has been a subject of numerous studies, mostly anthropological, such as Peristiany et al. (1965), Stewart (1994), or Nisbett (1996), but also philosophical, such as the work by Kwame A. Appiah (2010).

The simplest definition of HONOR one can propose, based on these studies, is that it is the RIGHT TO RESPECT (Stewart 1994: 54), which one can lose (cf. Stewart 1994: 54) or one can be deprived from (Baroja 1965: 85). Although such definition of HONOR in terms of RIGHT might at the first glance seem surprising, it was certainly more intuitive for the language users of the past. This can be deduced, for instance, from the synonymy existing in Medieval German, where the term *rechtloss* "[people] without rights" sometimes was being swapped with the adjective *ehreloss* "[people] without honor" (Stewart 1994: 38–9). Thus, following such understanding, my HONOR is upon what I can demand respect. At whom though, should I seek this respect? The easiest answer is that HONOR is the RIGHT TO RESPECT by equals, that is, my peers. This is quite essential for understanding this notion, so much that Stewart (1994: 54) categorized such a basic type of HONOR as HORIZONTAL HONOR – the RIGHT which is possessed and executed only among equals. Therefore, HONOR was so substantial for many generations of people, since it was what granted them appreciation of those, with whom they used to live. It was so important, since HONOR was not RIGHT to any kind of RESPECT (Stewart 1994: 23) – it was what might be seen as "the right to be treated as a full or equal member (Stewart 1994: 54)" of a group. Denying someone HONOR – the RIGHT TO RESPECT – was to disdain them, show them that they do not deserve to be part of the community (cf. Bourdieu 1965: 197–8). Thus, as a result, HONOR was establishing a collective of people, who were equal in HONOR – that is, they all had the same RIGHT to be respected. Stewart (1994: 54) named such a collective *the honor group*. But the sole belonging to this group did not bestow one with HONOR – communities allocated this RIGHT always according to some rules (Stewart 1994: 23). These rules – or better, standards – were what is generally known as a code of honor or a code of honorable conduct. It means that an honor group consisted in fact of people who followed the same code of behavior and for that they acquire HONOR – the RIGHT TO RESPECT by other followers of this code (Stewart 1994: 54).

But who was there to judge those people whether they deserved HONOR or not? The answer is simple: those people themselves. As Pitt-Rivers (1965: 27) stated: "public opinion forms (…) a tribunal before which the claims to honour are brought". He termed this tribunal as "the court of reputation". An individual was then constantly "on show", being evaluated by their equals (Peristiany 1965: 11), who compared the behavior of this individual to a certain conduct perceived as ideal in their joint community (Peristiany 1965: 10). Thus, the HONOR was ascribed to the individual based on a certain WORTH OR VALUE resulted from this evaluation (Pitt-Rivers 1965: 21; Stewart 1994: 21). This WORTH guaranteed being considered a full member of the group. In other words, HONOR depended always on others' acknowledgement of one's claim to be RESPECTED (Pitt-Rivers 1965: 21), which was achieved by recognizing this someone as meeting the standards of the community.

Although sounding quite high-pitched, the code of honor was in fact a collection of such standards – i.e., bare minimum of decent behavior – not of idealized, heroic norms (cf. Stewart 1994: 54). Thus, breaking these rules, not following these standards, must have resulted in ostracizing the wrongdoer by their community (Stewart 1994: 111), since not only did they act dishonorably, but also – and perhaps primarily – they broke commonly accepted rules. The standards, however, were applied only to the members of the same honor group (cf. Pitt-Rivers 1965: 51). They were certain ideals, in which members of that group wanted to see themselves, and with which they wanted to be associated. Therefore – although being the bare minimum of a decent conduct – they were still ideal in the sense of a certain aspiration to be seen as better – more ideal – than others. This, however, was because the whole group had its own HONOR. This group HONOR was in a bidirectional relationship with each member of the community. On the one hand, an individual derived much of their HONOR from the HONOR of their group. On the other, however, the HONOR of the group was based on its members' conduct (Pitt-Rivers 1965: 35). Thus, the standards consisting of codes of honor might have seemed idealistic – simply stated, any community wanted to be perceived as ideal or heroic.

The size of such a HONOR-related group was not precisely defined and an individual belonged simultaneously to several of them – the most nuclear being family, and the most general, a nation or a state. Family HONOR was a most basic GROUP HONOR, from which an individual could derive their claim to the RIGHT TO RESPECT. Therefore, by their behavior, members of a family protected each other's HONOR (Pitt-Rivers 1965: 28) and were responsible – in front of each other – to maintain the GOOD NAME of the family – its WORTH OR VALUE. HONOR was then a "hereditary quality" (Pitt-Rivers 1965: 55). Thus, protecting family HONOR was in many cultures among the first commandment of the code of honorable behavior (Bourdeiu 1965: 201).

To sum it up, one's HONOR was their RIGHT TO RESPECT in their community, which recognized this someone as its full member based on their WORTH or VALUE. This VALUE was assigned to this individual in the process of the EVALUATION performed by other members of the community, who scrutinized this someone's behavior by comparing it to the certain standards of conduct the community followed. The standards were considered a bare minimum of a decent behavior and they were some ideals, in terms of which the community tended to define itself. They were also what the community prided itself with, or in other words, what the community members wanted to think their actions are. Therefore, the community based its HONOR on realization of those standards by its members, who themselves derived their HONOR-RIGHT TO RESPECT from the HONOR of their community. To put it in other words, HONOR was a positive pole of an evaluation system (Peristiany 1965: 9), whose sole purpose was to maintain the GOOD NAME of a group in eyes of other groups based on EVALUATION of its members' actions in terms of a certain standards of behavior.

3.2. The ambiguity of European notion of HONOR

At the very first glance, one can notice that the definition of HONOR presented in the previous section does not fully exhaust our (European) understanding of HONOR, to which we refer with such lexemes as English *honor*, Polish *honor*, German *Ehre*, etc.

First and foremost, one can point towards the etymological evidences that *honor* had little to do with opinion of someone's peers. In fact, historically speaking, HONOR was primarily a RIGHT TO RESPECT bestowed by some authority – normally a ruler or a state in general (Pitt-Rivers 1965: 23). It was still RIGHT TO RESPECT, but it was not by any means granted by one's equals. Such HONOR was referred to e.g., by Greek *timē*, which meant the RIGHT TO RESPECT one acquired due to the fact that they proved being superior – better – than others (Stewart 1994: 60). Similarly, the very Latin lexeme *honor* could also have the meaning of "the right to special respect that arises from superior rank (Stewart 1994: 60)". Such HONOR might be termed HONOR-PRECEDENCE, since it is a kind of claim to excellence, in which one demands precedence over others based on their real (or just presupposed) excellent qualities (Pitt-Rivers 1965: 23–24). Stewart (1994: 59) named it, however, "vertical honor" or "rank honor", since it implied existence of a hierarchy of honor based on ranks, functions, wealth, or anything else, which divided people into better and worse. The Medieval European hierarchy of such a kind granted the most HONOR to God, then to the monarch, and at last, to people in accordance with their social standings (Pitt-Rivers 1965: 23–4). In fact, it was normally bestowed by the superior – typically the king – in a ritual, which resembled a rite of passage from one level of HONOR-PRECEDENCE to another. Such a ritual usually involved touching the honored one – by sword or – like in Oxford University – even by a book (Pitt-Rivers 1965: 24).

HONOR-PRECEDENCE was then at the core of the social system of feudal Europe. Therefore, it was usually attached by birth to nobility – as it was the case of ancient Greek *timē* itself (Korus 2017: 33), and the later concepts, such as Polish *honor* (Grzeszczak 2017: 118). It was what made noblemen stick to their own code of honor, neglecting those codes, which their inferiors followed (cf. Pitt-Rivers 195: 62). Thus, superior saw it belittling to accept a challenge issued by their subject (Pitt-Rivers 1965: 57). Accepting such a challenge was beneath them, since they derived their RIGHT TO RESPECT based on something, the inferior could not challenge.

Nevertheless, HONOR-PRECEDENCE persisted in a strong relationship with the HORIZONTAL HONOR, since it was in a way protected by it (Stewart 1994: 61). In other words, people, who derived their RIGHT TO RESPECT based on PRECEDENCE, still were scrutinized by their peers – equally bestowed with the same HONOR. Thus, one's VERTICAL HONOR was somehow dependent on their horizontal one. This points yet towards something very essential – HONOR-PRECEDENCE could be increased or decreased, i.e., one could constantly increase their RIGHT TO RESPECT, by showing more and more excellency surpassing the standing of their peers, and thus, making one of more and more of such RIGHT (Stewart 1994: 62). This characteristic is a consequence of the hierarchical nature of HONOR-PRECEDENCE. HORIZONTAL HONOR – RIGHT TO RESPECT of peers – could not be increased (Stewart 1994: 59). It was binary – either one had it, or one was deprived of it.

Another facet of the European notion of HONOR is that it implies a certain REPUTATION. It was the case of HONOR-PRECEDENCE – like ancient Greek *timē* – to which an esteem of excellence was attached (Stewart 1994: 60). Similarly, Latin *honor* referred generally to prestige and esteem, which was usually derived first and foremost from public dignities and offices (Baroja 1965: 82). However, more interesting for us is Greek *timē* – HONOR and a kind of fame, in name of which heroes of ancient Greece used to fight and sacrifice their life (Korus 2017: 31). It was derived from the verb *tamáo* "to perceive something as a certain value" (Korus 2017: 36), and thus, might be simply understand as a VALUE – of a person or – as it was also a case – of stolen goods (Korus 2017: 36). Therefore, one can see HONOR as a VALUE of a person, which is ascribed to them by their peers (Pitt- Rivers 1965: 21). Such a conceptualization, perhaps, might also be seen in two Spanish HONOR-related term *valer más* "greater worth" and *valer menos* "lesser worth" (Baroja 1965: 88). One's HONOR was then this someone's WORTH in eyes of their equals, who – as I said in the previous subsection – constantly evaluated each other's behavior, by comparing it to the code of ideal(ized) conduct. Sometimes, such HONOR was referred to in the anthropological literature as "outer honor" (cf. Stewart 1994: 123), which comprises the public opinion on someone, their behavior, way of life, etc. (Stewart 1994: 14) or simply, their reputation (Stewart 1994: 18) or fame (Baroja 1965: 85). One can see it as a certain public image of an individual (cf. Bordieu 1965: 208), which might have been the reason why in many languages – such as in Polish – *honor* could metonymically be employed to refer to female sexual purity (cf. Grzeszczak 2017: 118). Such a metonymy seems to be motivated by the fact that female sexual chastity seems to be ubiquitous element of HONOR codes in many cultures (cf. Pitt-Rivers 1965: 45–6).

HONOR was also perceived as an inner quality, which one can see as the value of an individual it their own eyes (Pitt-Rivers 1965: 21). Such HONOR was referred to in anthropological studies as "inner" or "subjectified honor" (Stewart 1994: 15, 18), and might be in fact seen as a type of feeling, which in European languages, is frequently referred to as "a sense of honor" (Stewart 1994: 17). This sense – or a feeling – was based on one's self-evaluation, which resulted in a belief in one's VALUE. Such VALUE could be attached to different facets of the social self of an individual: their family, masculinity/femineity, or social independence (Osh et al. 2013: 335). As such, the sense of honor dictated one to protect this VALUE in all those aspects, primarily through the attachment to the code of honorable behavior (Stewart 1994: 146). In Greek, such a concern for one's honor is referred to as *egoismos* and it might be understood as "the inner necessity and obligation to achieve identity with the image of the ideal self (Cambell 1965: 149)". The ideal self – in all its facets: family, masculinity/femineity, and social independence – was what one perceived as their *timē* – their HONOR and VALUE, upon which the HONOR was founded, and it was based on one's beliefs as for the HONORABILITY of their conduct. The own perception of one's WORTH resulted in strong attachment to it and, as a consequence, in the devotion in protecting it by all costs. Therefore, HONOR, being RIGHT TO RESPECT, was reflexive, i.e., demanded a reaction – usually violent – whenever it was attacked or challenged (Stewart 1994: 64; Pitt-Rivers 1965: 26).

Such sense of HONOR – sense of one's VALUE derived from one's evaluation of their own conduct – was then a certain moral sense. It dictated one to stick to the honorable behavior, avoiding a devaluation in one's and their peers' eyes. Sometimes, in many European languages, such sense or feeling that one has to protect their HONOR by sticking to the honorable conduct was conceptualized by a metonymy as SHAME. This is the case of Spanish, in which *vergüenza* means both, shame – i.e., "shyness, blushing" – and something "what makes a person sensitive to the pressure exerted by public opinion" (Pitt-Rivers 1965: 42) – or in other words, a sense of honor. Thus, people deprived of HONOR – the RIGHT TO RESPECT – frequently, were referred to as shameless – in Spanish, *los sin vergüenza* (Pitt-Rivers 1965: 40–1, 50). This metonymy foregrounds the fact – derived from reflexiveness of HONOR – that lack of one's concern for their reputation is shameful, i.e., dishonoring (cf. Pitt-Rivers 1965: 43). In other words, people who do not have SHAME, are not people free from it, but those, who cannot be SHAMED, since they are not concerned with their reputation, and thus, they fall beyond the scope of SOCIAL EVALUATION (Pitt-Rivers 1965: 50). This also means that an attack on one's HONOR launched by a shameless one should not be avenged, since it would imply that the offended party recognizes HONOR – and a certain WORTH – in HONOR- and WORTH-less offender. This, however, was an indication that the offended individual sees themselves at the same level as the shameless one – and since HONOR was an element of dialectics among equals, by this, they dishonored themselves (Bourdieu 1965: 200).

The sense of honor is then the feeling about one's self. It tells this someone that they have a certain WORTH, which is based on their honorable behavior. Therefore, it dictates this someone to keep sticking to this behavior, being socially approved conduct. No wonder then that HONOR might be perceived as simply INTEGRITY of an individual (cf. Campbell 1965: 141; Stewart 1994: 51) – it can be seen as a VALUE of a person, who sticks to the code of the proper action.

Such a person might be described by the expression *a man of honor*, which points towards yet another understanding of HONOR, which is widespread in Europe. It suggests that HONOR is actually a certain VIRTUE. In fact, sometimes it is difficult to distinguish HONOR from the VIRTUOUS CONDUCT it is based upon (Pitt-Rivers 1965: 36). HONOR was founded on one's proper – i.e., VIRTUOUS – behavior and, based on the aforementioned sentiment of honor – concern for repute – having HONOR obligated its bearer to stick to that very VIRTUOUS behavior. Even HONOR-PRECEDENCE, HONOR bestowed by the authority, was perceived as obligating one to honorable conduct (Pitt-Rivers 1965: 23). Someone of HONOR-PRECEDENCE could not simply show they are not virtuous, because it would have been a prove that they do not deserve the RIGHT TO RESPECT (Pitt-Rivers 1965: 37). Thus, between HONOR and VIRTUE, there was a quite unclear relationship, which contributed with time to blurring the understating of the notion of HONOR. The blurring occurred due to a certain shift in allocating HONOR by the society. Previously, it was bestowed primarily based on some external qualities, such as one's rank, position, office. With time, it was more and more related to one's behavior so that it ended up being almost entirely associated with it (Stewart 1994: 34). This transition from external to internal qualities is the reason of what Stewart (1994: 51) termed as "collapse" of HONOR in the West. In other words, with time, HONOR was less and less seen as a RIGHT TO RESPECT, and more as a certain VIRTUE, perhaps INTEGRITY or HONORABLENESS – sticking to certain rules of appropriate behavior (Stewart 1994: 51–3). The expression like *man of honor* and *sense of honor* definitely suggests so (Stewart 1994: 46). Especially, *sense of honor* seems to indicate that, since one cannot *sense* a RIGHT, but they can sense an inner feeling of obligation to certain standards. It should not be then surprising that responders of the survey conducted in recent years in Central and Eastern Europe associated HONOR not with a certain RIGHT, but with "a collection of moral traits", such as dignity, sincerity, reliability, justice, responsibility, loyalty, solidarity, tolerance, etc. (cf. Sotirov 2017: 19).

HONOR has yet another meaning, which is nowadays mostly visible in derivatives from its major designation, namely, it can be seen as HONOR-PAID by the society (cf. Pitt-Rivers 1965: 38). Such HONOR is what someone, who acquired HONOR-RIGHT TO RESPECT of their peers, received from them. It is a certain treatment – the very RESPECT – a HONORABLE one attains in return for their HONORABILITY (Pitt-Rivers 1965: 38). In every society, there are some rules, in accordance with which people of HONOR should be treated (Stewart 1994: 24). Those rules specify the way of HONORING someone – i.e., expressing the RESPECT an HONORABLE person deserves. The existence of these rules accounts for the strong sentiment – anger, wrath – felt by a dishonored person, who does not feel it because someone offended them, but rather because that someone failed "in the duty of respect" (Stewart 1994: 28) they deserved for being HONORABLE. Again, the duality of HONOR is here at play – being dishonored and the anger about it can be traced back to the sense of honor, which is based on the individual's private perception of their own HONORABILITY. This facet of HONOR – HONOR-PAID – is the social, external validation of that perception, and as such, it is the validation of one's status as a person of HONOR, i.e., a person deserving to be RESPECTED (cf. Pitt-Rivers 1965: 43, 72). Therefore, in accordance with the logic of HONOR, words uttered by people are of such importance that they become insults or affronts – simply stated, they are the most obvious "expressions of attitude which claim, accord or deny honour (Pitt-Rivers 1965: 27)". In European languages, the scenario of HONOR-PAID evokes a number of lexical items, such as English expressions *to honor someone*, *to pay honor to someone* or *to be honored*.

One could say that HONOR-PAID is to what HONOR- RIGHT TO RESPECT entitles someone, whose behavior was evaluated by their peers as HONORABLE, i.e., suitable for someone, who has HONOR-VIRTUE-INTEGRITY or who acquired the RIGHT TO RESPECT due to their HONOR-PRECEDENCE. This sentence quite neatly depicts the ambiguity of the European notions of HONOR referred to by multiply lexemes and expressions, which seem to fall – semantically speaking – in a proximity to each other. HONOR is first and foremost a RIGHT TO RESPECT, which is allocated to someone based on external or internal factors, which both indicate a certain WORTH or VALUE of a person deserving this RIGHT. In the context of European conceptualizations, the external factors were primary and comprised status symbols such as wealth, rank, or excellency of an individual, who surpassed others. The internal factors were the inner qualities of someone, which were materialized in their behavior being in line with a given community (normally idealized) standards of behavior. One can call the HONOR bestowed based on the external factors HONOR-PRECEDENCE or VERTICAL HONOR. The one based on the internal factors was personal HONOR and it was a special instance of HORIZONTAL HONOR. The uniqueness of the personal HONOR lays in the fact that it was not RIGHT to any type of RESPECT, but TO RESPECT of one's equals. In other words, it was the official open recognition of someone in terms of the full membership in their community. This recognition implied actually recognizing this someone as VALUABLE or of WORTH, which constituted this someone's REPUTATION, esteem or prestige. It was also a WORTH or VALUE this someone saw in themselves, feeling a sentiment – the sense of honor – which, on the one hand, assured them of being WORTH the RESPECT of others, and on the other hand, obligated them to stick to the code of HONOR. This sentiment – perhaps something as INTEGRITY – was the reason people of honor behaved in a certain way, which for the most part in the European history might have been considered a VIRTUOUS behavior. All in all, people who behaved in this way received HONOR-PAID, i.e., the RESPECT and acknowledgement of their HONOR-RIGHT by the members of their community. This payment was due to the realization of the community standards of behavior, which was supposed to be how this community wanted to be seen outside. Thus, HONOR of an individual naturally extended into the HONOR of their community – be it their family, clan, tribe, or nation.

3.3. Studies on HONOR in Arabic context

As I mentioned, one of the motivations to carry on a CL study on HONOR-related LEAP lexis was in fact the general assumption of the great importance of HONOR for pre-Islamic Arabs. This assumption is not, however, just a common belief, which – as it is frequently the case of such beliefs – is not entirely true. In fact, pre-Islamic Arabic veneration has been studied by many scholars – philologists, anthropologists, and historians.

Perhaps, in the context of my particular project, the most important from among those studies was the research by a sociologist and orientalist Bichr Farès (1932), summarized also in his entry on *ʕirḍ* "honor" in the Encyclopedia of Islam (Farès 1938). Farès – similarly to my study – focused on the pre-Islamic poetry to analyze philologically the notion of *ʕirḍ* as it was presented in the poems of al-Ǧāhiliyya. His study focused primarily on the lexeme *ʕirḍ* and the concept it referred to, what found some critiques among orientalists contemporary to

Farès (cf. Guillaume 1934). Although, it seems the critique was mostly directed towards Farès's belief in originality of EAP, which – as we learned – was contested for a while. In general, the most important conclusion presented in his work was that of the semi-religious character of pre-Islamic HONOR veneration, which was supposed to be the case due to weak religious sentiment among Arabs (Farès 1938: 96). He described it in the following way:

> ʕ*irḍ* took the place of religion at the gathering held for contests of honor called *mufāḫarāt* and *munāfarāt*, to keep alive among Arabs that state of intense social life in which their feelings underwent a transfiguration (Farès 1938: 96).

What is noticeable is Farès's narrowed interest in the phenomenon of pre-Islamic HONOR, which focused virtually only on the analysis on the concept of ʕ*irḍ*. My study, although still being more lexical than conceptual (cf. Stewart 1994: 5), focuses on more HONOR-related concepts, and its major interest in not these phenomena *per se*, but the way they were encoded in LEAP.

Beside Farès (1932 & 1938), pre-Islamic HONOR has not been thoroughly studied. The information about it – in form of scattered entries – one can find also in more general historical literature on al-Ǧāhiliyya, such as ʕAlī (1993b: 407–8, 572–585) or Jacob (1897: 220). On the contrary, HONOR seems to much better analyzed as a phenomenon persisting in the modern Arabic communities.

From among the most important studies on modern Arabic HONOR, we should mention the book by Abu-Lughod (1986), in which the author depicted the life circulating around HONOR in a Bedouin community from Western Egypt. Her conclusions, in fact, were very helpful in providing proper description of the HONOR-related phenomena analyzed in this book. Especially, in the case of such concepts as *karam* and *šaraf*, they allowed me to hypothesize about a certain continuity across history between pre-Islamic and modern Bedouin conceptualizations.

Moreover, HONOR in modern Arabic contexts was analyzed in several papers such as by Dodd (1973), in which the author, in fact, summarized the state of knowledge about ʕ*irḍ* as for the early 70' of the last century. In his article, he tried to capture the effect of modernization of Arabic societies on the notion of HONOR. HONOR was also a subject of the anthropological studies by Abou-Zeid (1965), who– almost two decades earlier than Abu-Lughod – studied a similar Bedouin community in the Egyptian West, and by Stewart (1994), who conducted field research among Bedouins of Sinai. We can add to this group of works the paper by Wikan (1984), in which she claimed the priority of SHAME over HONOR in modern communities of Cairo and Oman, as well as a book by Górecka (2009), portraying the understanding of female HONOR in the society of nowadays Jordan. A short yet very insightful description of the phenomenon of HONOR in Yemeni society was also provided by Sławek (2011).

In contrast to all the aforementioned research, my study is linguistic in nature. What it means is that the ethnographic description is a merely starting point of the analysis, aiming to depict the encodement of conceptualizations of knowledge in language. In my study, I rendered encyclopedic definition of pre-Islamic Arabic HONOR-related phenomena in order to specify the effect their cultural conceptualizations had on LEAP – in form of lexical field division (cultural categories), polysemy (metaphors and metonymies), and limitation on linguistic choices (linguistic framing). Of course, such characteristics is due to its CL design. In other words, the anthropological description – although still at the core of my thesis – plays only a role of interlude to the actual conclusions on the subject. The aim of my project is to depict the language as bound to the cultural conceptualizations – those "ethnographic" qualities – by analyzing its lexicon and the way it was structured by pre-Islamic Arabic understanding of HONOR. Naturally, this understanding must come first – nevertheless, in my analysis, it is not its end. Therefore, in this paper, the most important conclusions are those regularly omitted in anthropological studies, i.e., the statements of metonymies and metaphors, which help us understand not only the content of analyzed schemata, but also provide in a way an insight into first-person experience of them. Thus, I am generally interested in facts like that *ʕirḍ* is conceptualized as a POSSESSED OBJECT or a SIDE (OF A BODY), or that *karam* "generosity-hospitality" was so important for pre-Islamic Arabs that it was used also to call up the whole schema of HONORABLENESS-NOBILITY, and not only that one of actual GENEROSITY-HOSPITALITY. Nevertheless, as we will see in the following chapter, I decided not to divide these two elements – ethnographic encyclopedic description and linguistic conclusions – since they the point of CL is to show how deeply they are interwoven. Therefore, my ethnographic conclusions will blend with linguistic ones to show that it is very difficult to say where language ends and culture starts. The boundary between these two is not only fuzzy, but almost not existing. This is because it is hard to be definite about placing the meaning – the main theme of this book –on either of two sides – language or culture.

Moreover, as for the very ethnographic part of my study, I decided to extent the scope of interest presented by earlier research to include some of the concepts, which rarely are taking into consideration while talking about HONOR. Namely, besides such obvious choices as *ʕirḍ* and *šaraf*, I decided to analyze also schemata referred to by *ḥasab*, *karam*, *karāma*, and *murūʔa* as well as – in a limited fashion – by *mağd*. The reason of such extension stems from the understanding of HONOR hold by the speakers of European languages. In Europe, HONOR – as we learned – was an ambiguous phenomenon, which is why, in order to properly juxtapose it with its Arabic counterpart, one should address all of its facets in form of HONOR-PRECEDENCE, HONOR-VIRTUE, HONOR-REPUTE, or HONOR-PAID.

3.4. Linguistic studies in conceptualization of HONOR

As I mentioned in the previous chapter, my study was the first attempt to apply the methods of CL to LEAP. It is not, however, the first study on the conceptualization of HONOR and its lexicalization in language.

Probably, the most comprehensive linguistic analysis of this subject was conducted as a part of the scientific project titled EUROJOS, led by Jerzy Bartmiński (2015–2017). Its results were published in a form of a volume of *Axiological Lexicon of Slavs and their Neighbors* (*Leksykon aksjologiczny Słowian i ich sąsiadów*) edited by Sotirov and Ajdačić (2017). It contained data gathered from extensive research on conceptualizations of HONOR, which was based on the JOŚ methodology mentioned in the previous chapter. As one can expect, the studies presented in the volume were conducted mostly on Slavic languages – Polish, Croatian, Russian, etc. – but it also included papers on HONOR in ancient Greek, German, and Lithuanian. The conclusions presented in this work suggest a general unity of the notion of HONOR in the cultures of the Central and Eastern Europe, pointing towards its dual nature (inner vs. outer honor), as well as the fact that its presence in the value systems is fading.

Another example of a linguistic study on HONOR, which might be seen as related to CL in a way, was the analysis and explication of the meaning of Polish lexeme *honor* proposed by Anna Wierzbicka (1992: 2018–21). It is an example of the presentation of the prospects of Wierzbicka's NSM methodology in the realm of the definition of axiological and emotional vocabulary. As such, her analysis consisted of author's native speaker insight into the meaning as well as complementary excerpts from the literature. Using her semantic primes, Wierzbicka explicated Polish *honor* in the following way:

> honor
> it is like a part of a person
> if something bad happens to a person
>   nothing bad can happen to this thing
> if one doesn't do something that one should do
>   something bad can happen to this thing
> if something bad happened to this part
>   one cannot think good things about oneself anymore
>   and one cannot want people to think good things about one anymore
> it is better if bad things happen to a person
>   than if something bad happens to this thing (Wierzbicka 1992: 220–1).

Although the NSM methodology seems very promising, I decided not to follow it due to some problems I encountered, while attempting to apply it in my study. Mainly, I had difficulties in providing explications, which will be both intelligible and yet limited only to Wierzbicka's semantic primes. Nevertheless, I think a translation of my conclusions into NSM explication could actually be a very interesting scientific exercise.

All in all, although HONOR seems to be so well studied in both contexts – the historical and anthropological Arabic, as well as the linguistic one – I believe the conclusions I present in this book might still be very valuable. Not only my examination followed a quite recently developed methods of CL and CogL, but it also broadens the scope of the analysis of HONOR in Arabic context, by focusing on concepts rarely studied as up to date. Therefore, I hope that it will prove that, even though it appears to be singing the same old song, the study on LEAP and Early Arabic Poetry can still yield worthwhile and useful results for our understanding of Arabic past and present.

4. Karam – Karīm – Karāma

While attempting to translate the English word *honor* into Arabic, we would not consider the lexeme *karam* as our first choice. Nowadays, *karam* is mostly seen as a more or less accurate translation of the concept of GENEROSITY. Nevertheless, a brief look at its derivatives – *karīm* and *karāma* – might bring into our attention its more HONOR-related nature. The lexeme *karīm* sometimes is being translated as "noble", which in his study on the Arabic vocabulary on generosity, Stephan Guth (2015: 191) interpret as "nobility" of character. Referring to either generosity, or to nobility, *karam* was certainly one of the key concepts of the pre-Islamic Arabic culture (Guth 2015: 179), and its importance was transitioned into Islam. Thus, both – the God and the Holy Qurʔān – were ascribed with *karam*, being attributed by the lexeme *karīm*.

If considered as "noble" or "of noble character", *karīm* seems to refer to a person of special virtues, from among which generosity occupies a prominent place. Such understood nobility – the nobility based on virtues – has more than few common points with the concept of HONOR, whose understanding by the Western anthropologists I presented in the previous chapter. As we learned, European HONOR is a bit confusing concept, encapsulating several profiles, from among which HONORABLENESS – HONOR-VIRTUE or HONOR-VIRTUOUS CONDUCT – occupies a an important place. In this chapter I will attempt to demonstrate how by means of a certain cultural metonymy, the concept of *karam* might be precisely seen as corresponding to this fundamental notion, upon which one's RIGHT TO RESPECT was founded. In other words, *karīm* may be understand as being *noble* in the sense of being *a man of honor* or simply *honorable*. Consequently, one should understand *karam* as more or less referring to the pre-Islamic Arabic cultural script of NOBLE – i.e., HONORABLE – BEHAVIOR. I think it is safe to say that such a script might be perceived as a "code of honor".

As I mentioned, besides *karīm*, *karam* is somehow more visibly related to HONOR by the concept of *karāma*. This notion, however, does not seem to refer to the concept of HONORABLENESS or VIRTUOUS CONDUCT, and connects in fact to yet another profile of European HONOR – that of HONOR-PAID. As we saw in the previous chapter, HONOR was primarily understood as RIGHT TO RESPECT by one's peers, and this very RESPECT was referred to by *honor*-related lexis. In LEAP, the situation seems similar, although RESPECT OF PEERS, i.e., "honoring someone", derives its lexical expression from the idea of HONORABLENESS. Perhaps, the fact of such derivation results from the stress which is to be found within notion of HONOR in many cultures – namely, that EQUALITY is an essential element of the CODE OF HONOR: showing no RESPECT to one's EQUALS was being non-HONORABLE at all (cf. e.g., Bordieu 1965: 198). Thus, to put in in LEAP terms: showing no *karāma* was by all means not being *karīm*. As we will see, in general, the cultural script of *karāma* involved for the most part reciprocity of the script of *karam*.

As I said, in this chapter, I will discuss first and foremost a certain cultural metonymy, which I believe is grounded in the social reality of pre- Islamic Arabs. The metonymy depicts *pars-pro-toto* relationship between the cultural script (event schema) of *karam*-GENEROSITY-HOSPITALITY and encapsulating it script of *karam*-NOBILITY-HONORABLENESS (HONOR-VIRTUOUS CONDUCT-based NOBILITY). Moreover, I will try to explain further semantic extension of the category of *karīm* by means of other conceptual metonymies, which foreground different conceptualizations constituting the schema *karīm*-HONORABLE. In fact, metonymy is the most frequently occurring conceptual device in the context of the *karam*-related lexis, what can reflex the fact that in general EAP employs as a major tool of expression "a specific form of metonymy (Bauer 2010: 705)". Additionally, I will present conceptualizations of *karam* and *karīm* in form of image-schematic and metaphoric models, which complimentarily, account for the specificity of linguistic frames associated with these schemata. Last but not least, I will represent the cultural conceptualizations of LEAP *karāma*.

4.1. The concepts of *karam*, *karīm*, and *karāma* in CAD

As pointed by Guth (2015: 174), the root √KRM is polysemous, and it encompasses two rather distinguishable etymons – √KRM$_1$ and √KRM$_2$. The most notable derivation of √KRM$_1$ is *karm*, roughly speaking, "vine(yard)" or "grapes", whereas √KRM$_2$, which is in our main interest, might be subsumed as a derivation basis for all the meaning somehow related to *karam*, i.e., to "nobility of one's action" and "generosity". Etymologically speaking, the relation between √KRM$_1$ and √KRM$_2$ is rather unlikely. Nevertheless, perception of affinity of *karm* and *karam* seems to be quite widespread in the times of the Prophet Muḥammad – at least according to what reports Ibn Manẓūr in his lexicon:

فَخَفَّفَت العَرَبُ الكَرْمَ وهُم يُرِيدُونَ كَرَمَ شَجَرَةِ العِنَب لِما ذُلِّلَ مِن قُطُوفِه عِندَ اليَنْع وكثرة من خَيْرِه في كُلّ حال وأنّه لا شَوْك فِيه يُؤْذِي فنهى النبي (...)عَن تَسْمِيَتِه بِهَذا لِأنه يعتَصِر منه المُسْكِر المُنَهى عن شُرْبِه (...) قال أبو بكر:يُسَمَّى الكَرْم كَرْمًا لِأنَّ الخَمْر المُتَّخِذَة منه تَحُثُّ على السَخاء والكَرَم وتَأْمُرُ بمَكارِم الأخْلاق فَاشْتَقّوا له اسمًا من الكَرَم لِلكَرَم الذي يتولّد منه (...)

Arabs simplified [the word] *karm* ["grape-vine"], having in mind *karam* [i.e., goodness] of the grape bush – and that's because of the fact that [its branches] hang down while

> being harvested after having ripen [and they are easy to be plucked], and because of the many good things [derived] from it in any case, as well as because of the fact it doesn't have any thorns, which might harm the harvester. The Prophet [Muḥammad] (…) banned calling it by this name because of the fact that the forbidden intoxicator is pressed out of it (…). Abū Bakr once said: grape-vine is called *karm*, because wine, which is acquired from it, encourages [one] to generosity and noble behavior (*karam*), and it dictates [one to follow his] good dispositions. Thus, [Arabs] derived for [grape-vine] a name from *karam* because of all the goodness (*karam*), which is brought in from it (LsA12: 606).

Such etymological claims should be treated rather as folk etymology. The evidence from the comparative studies on other Semitic languages suggests keeping those two etymons apart (Guth 2015: 175). The etymology of √KRM$_2$ is unfortunately impossible to reconstruct. It might be true that originally it signified COPIOUSNESS of rain as in Ethiosemitic derivates meaning "a rain season" (Ge'ez *kərämt*, Tigre *krämti*, and Amharic *kərämt*) (Guth 2015: 179), or CA *karuma* as in *karuma as-siḥāb ʔiḏā ǧāʔa bi-l-ġayṯ* "the cloud brought abundance of rain" (AsS: 996). Thus, its primary meaning would be more of physical nature and only afterwards, it has developed metaphorically into GENEROSITY (Guth 2015: 179). Eventually, by generalization of meaning, it began to signify NOBILITY OF CONDUCT. Of course, such deliberations are highly hypothetical, since there is no data disqualifying the claim that the etymological development might have occurred in a reverse course – from GENEROSITY to COPIOUSNESS (Guth 2015: 179).

In the dictionary by Wehr & Cowan (1976: 821), *karam* is defined as "noble nature; high- mindedness, noble- mindedness, noble- heartedness, generosity, magnanimity, kindness, friendliness, amicability, liberality, munificence", which in fact is a quite accurate definition considering the cultural schemata I will render below. AlG (798) and AsS (996) define it rather vaguely as the opposite of *luʔm*, which in AsS (1021) is defined as "anything, in which one is meager [or scanty], because of its goodness – it might be house belongings etc." Thus, they seem to equalize *karam* and GENEROSITY. In KtA4 (24), *karam* is defined as "a fertile stoneless land" and "*šaraf* [high social status] of a man" that brings us closer to the concept of *karam* as linked to the HONOR of someone. The first meaning seems to relate somehow to GOODNESS. LsA provides three meaning of this lexeme. Quoting Ibn Sīdah (LsA12: 602), it repeats that *karam* is the opposite of *luʔm* and states that "it is in the man himself, even if he does not have [noble] ancestors". However, the concept of *luʔm* is defined in LsA12 (627) as the opposite of *karam* and *ʕitq*. This does not really help us understanding what *karam* is, since LsA12 (602) says that it is also "used in reference to horses, camels, trees and other valuable things, when ʕitq is meant – the origin [of such a derivation is the *karam*] in men". I believe that the lexeme of ʕ*itq* in this place refer to roughly speaking the concept of EXCELLENCE. The third signification provided in LsA12 (606) is the definition of a fertile, stoneless land provided in KtA4 (24). At this point, one can notice that *karam* is described as related to two separate (yet I believe interrelated) concepts: GENEROSITY and GOODNESS-EXCELLENCE. Ibn Manẓūr (LsA12: 602) – after Ibn Sīdah – also mentions the fact that *karam* might be possessed by a man who does not have noble ancestry, i.e., who is not noble or of noble origin.

In all CAD, *karam* is also defined as a verbal noun of the verb *karuma* "being *karīm*" (KtA4: 24; AlG: 798; AsS: 996; LsA12: 602). The lexeme *karīm* is explicated by Lane (1968h: 2999) as "generous; liberal; honorable, noble; high-born (both in the opposition to *laʔīm*)", "a noble, a high-bred, a well-born, or an excellent, horse, etc.; a horse of generous, high, or good, breed or quality", "a thing highly esteemed or prized or valued; excellent, precious, valuable, or rare", "productive (said about land)", and "in high estimation at his owner (said about a camel)". These meanings are also cognates of the concepts of GENEROSITY and GOODNESS- EXCELLENCE. KtA4 (24) derives meaning of *karīm* from *karam*, which might be interpreted as *karīm* being the man of *karam*. Similarly, both AlG (798) and AsS (996) derive the meaning of *karīm* from *karam* (a *karīm* person is a person of *karam*). Still, AsS (996) adds that *karīm* equals *ṣafūḥ*, which Lane (1968d: 1696) translates as "one who has the quality of turning away from the crimes, sins, faults or offences". This would link *karīm* via the concept of GOODNESS-EXCELLENCE to the concept of HONOR acquired by following a certain code of VIRTUOUS conduct. In LsA, Ibn Manẓūr begins from defining *karīm* as an epitaph of God. He states (LsA12: 602) that God's being *karīm* means that He is "of much goodness (*ḫayr*), generosity, [He is] the giver whose giving will never run out". In other words, he says that "[God] is the absolute *karīm*". It much brings the concept of *karīm* back to the notion of GENEROSITY. Other significations he mentions are more related to the concept of HONORABLENESS. Thus, the lexeme of *karīm* might also mean "the one who kept (*karrama*) himself from being spoiled [i.e., dishonored] by something like disobedience of his Lord (LsA12: 606)" (which seems to relate to the meaning of *ṣafūḥ*, AsS: 996), "the one who accumulates [different] kinds of goodness (*ḫayr*), *šaraf* (i.e., high social status), and virtues (*faḍāʔil*) (LsA15: 602)"; "name of the one who accumulates all of what is praised (LsA12: 602)"; and "*šarīf* [a man of a high social status] (LsA12: 606)", which together with the meaning of *karīma* "*ḥasīb* (i.e., a man of many virtuous deeds) (LsA12: 605)" manifest the affinity of *karīm* with HONOR and as such relate to the meaning "honorable, noble; high-born" provided by Lane (1968h: 2999). Ibn Manẓūr also says that *karīm* is called *makramān* "if they ascribed him with generosity (*saḫāʔ*) and bravery (*saʕat aṣ-ṣadr*) (LsA12: 606)". This – quite genuinely – demonstrate the interplay between GENEROSITY and HONORABLENESS (from among which bravery also occupies an important place) in the cultural schema of *karam*. Ibn Manẓūr (LsA12: 606) also lists some GOODNESS- EXCELLENCE- related meanings of *karīm*, which all occur in the Holy Qurʔān: *qawl karīm* "easy, soft speech", *rizq karīm* "much, plenty profit/reward", *mudḫal karīm* "good (*ḥasan*) place (meaning the Paradise)", and *al-ʕarš al-karīm* "the great (*ʕaẓīm*) throne".

From among the analyzed lexemes, *karāma* seems to be the least elaborated in CAD. It is mentioned only in KtA and LsA. Beside defining *karāma* as a type of a plate (KtA4: 24; LsA12: 608), they explicate the lexeme as either an equivalent of *ʔikrām* – a verbal noun derived from the verb *ʔakrama* "to treat someone with honor or curtesy (cf. Lane 1968h: 2999)" (KtA4: 24), or as an equivalent of *karam*, the verbal noun of the verb *karuma* "being *karīm*" (LsA12: 602). Both meanings are mentioned also in *Encyclopedia of Islam*, which, so to say, approaches *karāma* as rather the synonym of *karam* being the verbal noun of the verb *karuma*. The verb itself is defined in there as "to be *karīm* "generous" in the widest sense (EoI: 744)". This "widest sense" seems to be particularly interesting considering the elaboration of the schema *karam* discussed further in this chapter. It suggests in fact that *karam* (i.e., being *karīm*) is a wide range of noble behavior, as it might be interpreted from the continuation of the definition of *karāma* in EoI (744) as "exhibition by Allāh of his generosity, favour, protection, help towards anyone", and also "the miraculous gifts and graces with which Allāh surrounds, protects and aids his Saints". The meaning posited by KtA4 – *karāma* as the verbal noun of *ʔakrama* – in EoI (744), is represented as "a noun of similar meaning to *ikrām* and *takrīm*, to show one's self *karīm* to any one". This would suggest that in fact, *karāma* as paying honor to someone, treating someone with honor and respect is equal to being *karīm* to someone. Additionally, Ibn Manẓūr defines *karāma* as a synonym of the verbal noun *ʕazāza* (LsA12: 604) derived from *ʕazaztu ʕalay-hi* "I exceeded him in generosity/nobleness (cf. Lane 1968e: 2030)". Such definition seems to be related to the explication of the concept as BEING *karīm* TO SOMEONE.

All in all, the meaning of lexemes *karam*, *karīm*, and *karāma* presented in CAD and in Western dictionaries of CA might be summarized as follows (Tab. 3.):

Tab. 3. The meanings of *karam*, *karīm*, and *karāma* in CAD and dictionaries of CA

Lexeme	Meaning	Sources
karam	[A] generosity, liberality	AlG: 798; AsS: 996; Wehr & Cowan 1976: 821
	[B] noble nature, noble-heartedness	Wehr & Cowan 1976: 821
	[C] magnanimity, kindness, friendliness, amicability	
	[D] a fertile stoneless land	KtA4: 24, LsA12: 606
	[E] excellence; high-value [in "horses, camels, trees and other valuable things"]	LsA12: 602
	[e] being *karīm*	KtA4: 24; AlG: 798; AsS: 996; LsA12: 602
karīm	[a] generous; liberal;	Lane 1968h: 2999; LsA12: 602, 606
	[b] honorable, noble; high-born; *šarīf*	Lane 1968h: 2999; LsA12: 606
	[c] a noble, a high-bred, a well-born, or an excellent, horse, etc.; a horse of generous, high, or good, breed or quality	Lane 1968h: 2999;
	[d] a thing highly esteemed or prized or valued; excellent, precious, valuable, or rare	Lane 1968h: 2999; LsA12: 606
	[e] in high estimation at his owner (said about a camel)	Lane 1968h: 2999;
	[f] law-obeying	AsS: 996; LsA12: 606
	[g] the one who accumulates all of what is praised	LsA12: 602
karāma	[α] =*ʔikrām* "treat someone with honor or curtesy" (by being *karīm* to them)	KtA4: 24; EoI: 744; Lane 1968h: 2999
	[β] =*karam*	LsA12: 602; EoI: 744
	[γ] a type of a plate	KtA4: 24; LsA:12: 608
	[δ] exceeding someone in generosity	LsA12: 604

As one can see, the affinity of *karam* and *karīm* with HONOR is not straightforward – at least in the light of the dictionaries' explications. I believe bringing the cultural schemata reconstructed based on data acquired from CEPA can indeed help in providing the specifics of that relation.

While defining *karam* and *karīm*, I could not, of course, ignore their counterparts *luʔm* and *laʔīm*. However, CAD provide rather vague explications of the concepts to which they refer. LsA12 (627) defines *luʔm* as the opposite of *karam* and *ʕitq*, which somehow brings into the picture the concept of

GOODNESS-EXCELLENCE. On the other hand, its definition of *laʔīm* as *danīʔ* and *šaḥiḥ an-nafs* portraits it duality of GOODNESS-EXCELLENCE and GENEROSITY. Lane (1968c: 918) defines *danīʔ* as "low, ignoble or mean in his actions; not caring for what he does, nor for what is said to him; bad, corrupt or foul; one in whom is little or no good; contemned, contemptible, mean, paltry" (ergo, more in the context of GOODNESS-EXCELLENCE), whereas *šaḥīḥ* as "niggardly, tenacious, stingy, greedily or excessively desirous" (here, more in the context of GENEROSITY). On its turn, AsS (1021) seemingly relates *laʔīm* only to the concept of GENEROSITY. The relation to GOODNESS-EXCELLENCE of these concepts might be seen also in the etymological hypothesis presented by Guth (2016: 73). Attempting to reconstruct the semantic development of the root √LʔM, he notices that in fact the derivatives of this root in other Semitic languages normally pertain to the concept of COLLECT (cf. Akkadian *līmu* "one thousand", or Hebrew *ləʔūm* "people, nation"). The same might be said about some of its derivatives in CA, such as e.g., the verbs *talāʔama* and *iltaʔama* (*wa-qad talāʔama al-qawm wa-ltaʔamū: iǧtamaʕū wa-ttafaqū* "people gathered and came to agreement", LsA12: 627). Guth suggest that perhaps originally the concept COLLECT was predominant in Arabic, and the notion of BASENESS-LOWNESS in reference to someone's character stems from the metonymic development from "common, as other people" to "mean, base, low". Similar development might be observed, for instance, in the evolution of the adjective *vulgar* from the Latin- lexeme *vulgaris* meaning "common" (Guth 2016: 74). Furthermore, Guth (2016: 76) suggests that imaginably, the lexeme *ʔumma* "nation, people" might be in fact a derivative of √LʔM, and its current form is a result of a change *alluʔuma>alʔumma*. In such a case, we could hypothesize that *laʔīm* formerly referred to a concept of a common man – someone "from the people" – and that would allow us to say, that *karīm* was someone special, extraordinary, noble. Of course, with time – the hypothesis might go – the relation of *laʔīm* to COMMONNESS would fade, and, as a result of a contrast to *karīm*-EXCELLENT, the lexeme would begin to refer more to a concept of BASENESS-LOWNESS of someone. Its affinity with GENEROSITY (i.e., *laʔīm* = "meager, stingy") could be then a result of a metonymic shift motivated by the great deal of this value hold by pre-Islamic Arabs. To be sure, this is just a hypothesis based on no material data. Nevertheless, considering the results of my CEAP inquiry, it has some potential of plausibility.

4.2. CEAP data on *karam-karīm* and *karāma*

In the study on CEAP, I analyzed the following lexical items (all of which are nouns): *karam*, *karāma*, *karīm(a)* and its plural forms – *kirām* and *kuramāʔ*.

Tab. 4. The number of occurrences of the members of *karam* cluster within CEAP

<table>
<tr><th colspan="2">Item</th><th colspan="2">Number of Occurrences (NO)</th><th>Normalized Word Count (per 10,000)</th></tr>
<tr><td colspan="2">karam</td><td colspan="2">23</td><td>0.81</td></tr>
<tr><td colspan="2">karāma</td><td colspan="2">13</td><td>0.46</td></tr>
<tr><td rowspan="4">karīm</td><td></td><td>125</td><td rowspan="4">=216</td><td rowspan="4">7.64</td></tr>
<tr><td>karīma</td><td>9</td></tr>
<tr><td>kirām</td><td>81</td></tr>
<tr><td>kuramāʔ</td><td>1</td></tr>
</table>

Within the CEAP, it was the most frequent analyzed HONOR- related lexical cluster with regard to occurrences. Together, the items occurred within the corpus 251 times – hence the normalized frequency (per then thousands) of all the members of the cluster is 8.81.[1] The detailed information about the frequency of the cluster within CEAP is presented in the table below (Tab. 4.).

Within the corpus, not all the meanings listed in CAD occurred. The meanings absent in the EAP were the one related to the land, i.e., [D], and two of the meanings of *karāma*, i.e., [γ] and [δ]. Remaining meanings were present in the corpus and were placed within the cultural model of *karam* I postulated on the basis of the analysis, or were identified as metonymies.

4.3. Role schema of *karīm*: the script of NOBILITY, the code of HONORABLE CONDUCT

The data from CEAP show that the lexeme *karīm* refers mostly to a single man. It can refer also to a woman (NO:4) – as in the examples (1) and (2) – or to a group of individuals. In the latter case, either the item *karīm*(*a*) is used to refer to a collective noun, or its plural forms are at play.

(1) شقّت على العُلْيا وَفاةُ **كريمةٍ** شقّت عليها **المكْرُماتُ** بُرُودَها

The death of **a noble woman** (*karīma*) deeply grieved the nobles – [the death of the woman] whose garments were torn by the **noble deeds** (*makrumāt*) (cf. t21B:51)

1 Such frequency corresponds, roughly speaking, to the frequency of such English words as *most* (8.9), *just* (8.87), *any* (8.76) or Polish *również* (8.93), *jako* (8.88) or *jeśli* (8.83). Based on the corpora *English Web 2015* and *Polish Web 2015* available on *SketchEngine* (https://www.sketchengine.eu [7-12-2020]).

(2) ألا رُبَّ يومٍ لو سقِمتُ لَعادَني نِساءٌ **كِرَامٌ** مِنْ حُيَيٍّ ومالِكِ
Isn't it true that if I got sickened, for many days, **good** women (*kirām*) of the tribes Ḥuyay and Mālik would [take] constant [care] of me (cf. t07A:95)?

(3) ولقدْ غدوْتُ على الجَزُورِ بفِتْيَةٍ **كُرَماءَ** حَضْرَةَ لَحمِها ، أزوالِ
Thus, early in the morning, I went forth – with **noble** (*kuramāʔ*), intelligent young men – towards the slaughtered she-camel, [to participate] in a feast made out of her meat (cf. t36A:191).

A *karīm* man or woman is furthermost someone, who performs a certain type of deeds. Such deeds are referred to by the lexeme *makārim* or *makrumāt* (sg. *makruma*), which we have already seen in the example (1). Based on the data extracted from CEAP, it seems that such deeds of *karīm*, *makārim*, might be classified under several categories, which are generosity and hospitality, magnanimity, bravery, loyalty, *ṣabr* (roughly speaking, "endurance"), custom obedience, *ḥilm* (roughly speaking, "reasonableness, moderation, forbearance"), and eloquence. As one can see, these categories almost perfectly correspond to what is known in the historical literature as honorable traits of *sayyid*, the tribal chief or lord. In other words, they might be seen as the code of the behavior expected from a *sayyid* (ʕAlī 1993b: 350). The term *sayyid* refers primarily to a tribal chief. Nevertheless, seemingly by means of metonymy, it also covered in a broader sense the concept of a tribal nobleman or an aristocrat, who had sometimes acquired much more renown than the chiefs of his tribe or clan themselves (ʕAlī 1993b: 587). Therefore, perhaps it is justified to say that this code of behavior constituted in fact a code of certain conduct that one could call *noble* in English. However, it should be read rather as an indication of certain EXCELLENCY attached to this behavior, or perhaps RIGHTEOUSNESS. Thus, the code of behavior of *sayyid*-tribal chief or lord became a model for respected or admired behavior that was perceived as certain ideal to be realized by a man (and possibly by a woman). In other words, this behavior fits neatly into the category of HONORABLE CONDUCT or even CODE OF HONOR, being a certain script of ideal(ized) behavior expected from members of a given (honor) group and serving as a nexus for their mutual recognition of RIGHT TO RESPECT. Consequently, the LEAP category of *karīm* should be than understood as a complex cultural role schema combining our understanding of EXCELLENCE and NOBILITY, and the notion of HONORABILITY. Being *karīm* meant then being someone EXCELLENT and NOBLE in their conduct, and by that deserving HONOR-RIGHT TO RESPECT. Therefore, I believe LEAP lexeme *karīm* might be rendered in English as either *noble* or *honorable*.

This cultural role schema subsumed then a certain script of behavior, which I will propose to interpret as the cultural script of the HONORABLE BEHAVIOR. This script seems to consist of several sub-scripts that could be understood as realization of traits of *sayyid*-tribal chief.

4.3.1. Generosity and hospitality – essence of *karam*

The first of these subscripts is certainly the script of GENEROSITY-HOSPITALITY. Having in mind that *karam*, i.e., "being *karīm*", might have referred to both, NOBILITY-HONORABILITY (cf. meaning B "noble nature, noble-heartedness"), and GENEROSITY (cf. meaning A), one must naturally ask the question about the relationship between these concepts and the motivation behind this obvious polysemy. In CEAP, the lexemes *karīm* and *karam* seem to refer 34 times – rather unmistakably – to the concept GENEROSITY or HOSPITALITY, which – to my taste – seem to a certain degree conflated in LEAP.

GENEROSITY and HOSPITALITY were clearly the most important values – the key values – of pre-Islamic Arabic society. Such importance of this obligation was an obvious result of the specifics of the environment of life of pre-Islamic Arabs – the harsh and unhospitable deserts and semi-deserts of the Middle East (ʕAlī 1993b: 576). If left alone, one would definitely die in such surroundings. Ergo, assisting someone in their need was a simple insurance policy – now, I help, so that I would be helped another time (ʕAlī 1993b: 576; Sławek 2011: 90). Thus, one can see them as the essential elements of the code of honorable conduct of pre-Islamic Arabs – *karīm*, a noble, honorable man must be always committed to them.

The pre-Islamic Arabic cultural script of GENEROSITY and HOSPITALITY seems to encompass a broad notion of READINESS TO SUPPORT SOMEONE – be they stranger or not – in any case by means of one's WEALTH. Thus, *karam* should be understood rather as one concept linked to a notion of FINANCIAL SUPPORT, and it could be seen as being further elaborated in different forms of GENEROSITY or BENEFICENCE as an answer to SEEKING charity or SUPPORT, or as the manner of HOSTING guests. GENEROSITY and HOSPITALITY should be seen more as profiles of this concepts rather as two separate conceptual entities (cf. e.g., t19:89). The fact that based on the data from CEAP, one could not have been depicted in LEAP as GENEROUS but not HOSPITABLE, and vice versa, confirms this statement. *Karīm* as a honorable man being GENEROUS-HOSPITABLE is depicted, for instance, in (4), the fragment of a poem by al-Aʕšà, and in (5), a verse from a poem attributed to al-Aswad an-Nahšalī, in which the HOSPITALITY profile is being foregrounded.

(4) وَلَكِنّ رَبّي كَفَى غُرْبَتي، بِحَمْدِ الإلَهِ، فَقَدْ بَلّغَنْ
(...)
كَرِيماً (...)
فَإنْ يَتْبَعُوا أمْرَهُ يَرْشُدُوا، وإنْ يسألوا مالَهُ لا يَضَنّ

However, my Lord satisfied my desire – praise be to Allāh – since truly I have met (…)
an **honorable man** (*karīm*) (…).
If someone followed him, they will be guided [the right way]; and if someone asked him [for support] from his wealth, he will not turn niggardly to them (cf. t28A:19).

(5) **كَريمٌ** ثَناه تُمْطِرُ الخَيْرَ كَفُّهُ كَثِيرُ رَمادِ القِدْرِ غَيْرُ مُلَعَّن
The palm of the **honorable man** (*karīm*) – [of the one] you have praised – rains with beneficence; [of the one who] feeds many guests with his cooking-pot, [and who] does not curse [others] (cf. t16A:64)

GENEROSITY-HOSPITALITY was considered an honorable deed especially in the time of scarcity or in a situation somehow difficult – like, for example, a journey (ʕAlī 1993b: 582). The most challenging time for pre-Islamic Arabs was winter, when the food shortage might have occurred (ʕAlī 1993b: 583). Hence, this was the time for *karīms* to prove their value (i.e., their *karam*). Such winter generosity is implied, e.g., in (6), a fragment of self-panegyric by ʕUrwa ibn al-Ward. Similarly, the generosity of a *karīm* in the time of famine is depicted by al-Ḫansāʔ in (7), a verse from her elegy on her brothers.

(6) (…) هل تَعلَمِينَني **كَريماً**، إذا اسوَدّ الأناملُ، أَزْهَرا
صبوراً على رُزْءِ الموالي وحافِظاً لِعِرْضِي حتّى يُؤْكَل النبتُ أَخْضَرا
(…) Do you know that I am an **honorable man** (*karīm*)? Whenever [others'] fingertips blacken, [i.e., when a sordid winter comes], I blossom,
enduring (*ṣabūran*) the calamities, [which falls upon my] protégés, protecting my honor– [and that's] until the flora gets green [again] (cf. t20A:35).

(7) ومُطْعِمُ القَوْمِ شَحْماً عندَ مَسْغَبِهم وفي الجُدوبِ **كريمُ** الجَدِّ ميسارُ
He fed people with fat during a famine or a drought. He was of **noble** ancestry (*karīm al-ǧadd*) and wealth (cf. t33A:47).

The exorbitant evaluation of GENEROSITY-HOSPITALITY made some people to go to extremes (ʕAlī 1993b: 576). That, perhaps, could explain why camel meat was considered such an important part of one's LIBERALITY (ʕAlī 1993a: 13). The excessive generosity was not though a problem – at least for the generous agent and the society that judged his deeds. Moreover, it seems it was considered a very noble deed, as we can see in (8), a fragment of the panegyric of Ḥasan Ibn Ḥadīfa by Zuhayr Ibn Abī Sulmà, where the excessiveness of Ibn Ḥadīfa is brought out by the depiction of his women's complaints. The figure of such a complaining woman – or women – is a frequent motive of eulogies in EAP (Kowalski 1997: 68).

(8) يُفَدّينَهُ طَوْراً وطَوْراً يَلُمْنَهُ وَأعْيا فَما يَدْرِينَ أينَ مَخاتِلُهْ
فأقْصَرْنَ مِنْهُ عَنْ **كَريمٍ** مُرَزَّإٍ عَزُومٍ على الأمْرِ الذي هوَ فاعِلُهْ
أخي ثقةٍ، لا تُتْلِفُ الخمرُ مالَهُ ولكنَّه قَدْ يُهْلِكُ المالَ نائلُهْ

> For a moment, [his wives] were giving up, [only to] reprehend him again [for his excessive generosity]. [Thus], he got fatigued, but still, they didn't know how to outwit him.
> So, they left him alone – [him], an **honorable** (*karīm*), very generous man, determined to persist in doing his deeds,
> trustworthy, whose wealth is not corrupted by wine, but by himself, who makes his wealth perish, by giving it away [to others] (cf. t22A:59).

In fact, GENEROSITY-HOSPITALITY was a kind of requirement in pre- Islamic Arabic society (ʕAlī 1993a: 17), hence no wonder it was clearly depicted as a stipulation on being, becoming, or staying *karīm* in eyes of other people. We can observe how GENEROSITY-HOSPITALITY preserves *karam* of someone in (9), a verse from al-Ḥuṭayʔa, who depicts respecting the custom of hospitality as the factor, which keeps someone *karīm* and brings onto him respect of others. The essentiality of hospitality for being *karīm* is well foregrounded in (10), a passage from Ḥassān Ibn Ṯābit, or in (11), a fragment from a poem attributed to ʕĀmir Ibn aṭ-Ṭufayl. In general, it seems that GENEROSITY-HOSPITALITY is an essential part of being *karīm*, and *karam* as a whole.

(9) فَباتُوا **كِراماً** قَد قَضَوْا حَقَّ ضَيفِهِم فَلَم يَغْرَموا غُرْماً وَقَد غَنِموا غُنْما

They stayed **honorable** (*kirām*), by respecting the guest rights. Thus, [not only] did they not lose anything, but they gained a reward of [respect] (cf. t39A:396).

(10) أولئكَ قومي فإن تسألي **كرامٌ** إذا الضيفُ يوماً ألمّ

Those are my people – if you ask [about them, I will tell you]: whenever one day, a guest arrives at [their] abode, they [act] **honorably** (*kirām*) (cf. t38A:270).

(11) وُجِدْنا **كِراماً** لا يُحَوَّلُ ضَيفُنا إذا جَفّ فَوْقَ المَنزِلاتِ جَليدُهَا

We are considered **honorable** (*kirāman*) [by people] – none of our guests have ever been turned away in the time, when their abodes dried out in freezing (cf. t29A:45–47).

4.3.1.1. The major cultural metonymic model of *karīm*

Therefore – what is clearly seen in (9), (10), and (11) – one can perceived GENEROSITY- HOSPITALITY as simply the bare minimum of NOBLE/ HONORABLE BEHAVIOR. It could derive from the cultural significance GENEROSITY-HOSPITALITY enjoyed in al-Ǧāhiliyya. This, however, might actually explain the motivation of the polysemy of *karam* and *karīm*, which depending on the context, can refer to either GENEROSITY- HOSPITALITY or HONORABLENESS. Consequently, this polysemy should be seen as arising from a metonymic model of highly culture-specific nature.

This cultural metonymy can be rendered as *karīm*-GENEROUS-HOSPITABLE FOR *karīm*- NOBLE- HONORABLE and it corresponds to the metonymy *karam*-GENEROSITY- HOSPITALITY FOR *karam*-NOBILITY- HONORABILITY. It can be classified as a *part-for-whole* metonymy, in which a part of the script from a role schema – here, a part of the CODE OF HONOR – was socially recognized as a default for the whole script (cf. Radden & Kövecses 1999: 31–2, 34). In other words, *karam*-GENEROSITY-HOSPITALITY was perceived by pre-Islamic Arabs as a prototype of HONORABLE BEHAVIOR – or even its archetype (cf. Sławek 2011: 90). Thus, stereotypically, in al-Ǧāhiliyya, a NOBLE, HONORABLE man was GENEROUS and HOSPITABLE. Perhaps, even the script of GENEROSITY- HOSPITALITY was an ideal or typical example of HONORABILITY, meaning that a *karīm*-HONORABLE man was always expected to be *karīm*-GENEROUS-HOSPITABLE in any circumstances (cf. Radden & Kövecses 1999: 48–9).

In other words, a notion of a *karīm*-GENEROUS- HOSPITABLE man started being used to call up the whole schema of a MAN OF HONOR – a person who deserved to be RESPECTED by their EQUALS. An important hint about such a relationship can be found in *Encyclopedia of Islam* (EoI: 744), which defines the verb *karuma* "to be *karīm*" as "to be *generous* in the widest sense". This "widest sense" seems to be exactly the notion foregrounded in the metonymy in question. It foregrounds the special high evaluation of GENEROSITY-HOSPITALITY in the concept of HONORABLENESS. In other words, *karīm* as a MAN OF HONOR was "generous in the widest sense", meaning he was the BEST in terms of the values hold important for pre-Islamic Arabic society. The BEST should be read here in the sense of AS GOOD AS GENEROUS-HOSPITABLE. Thus, RESPECT enjoyed by a NOBLE-HONORABLE man was equal to the RESPECT people paid to someone GENEROUS-HOSPITABLE.

Although such a reasoning seems perfectly plausible, one can point towards its major weakness – the uniqueness of such a conceptualization. Although a situation, in which a prototype stands for the entire category – here, the entire cultural script – is ubiquitous, a situation, in which this category does not have a proper designation, seems to be extremally rare. And such a situation takes place in the case of the metonymy *karam*-GENEROSITY-HOSPITALITY FOR *karam*-NOBILITY- HONORABILITY. Because what is the proper denotation of HONORABILITY in LEAP? Some probably would say that it could have been referred to as *murūʔa*, which is used by ʕAlī (1993b: 574) to refer to the honorable traits of *sayyid*, defined above as traits of *karīm*. Personally, however, I see this lexeme more as referring to a certain potentiality of HONORABLE BEHAVIOR – MANLINESS – which predisposed one to be HONORABLE, rather than to this behavior itself. As noticed by Radden and Kövecses (1999: 18), metonymy sometimes operates only as a mental phenomenon, which is especially noticeable in the case of stereotypes (Radden and Kövecses 1999: 27). Then the designation of the whole category (e.g., *mother* designating the category MOTHER) is used to imply the stereotypical sub-category (e.g., MOTHER-HOUSEWIFE) – socially recognized as a default one – which does not have any proper designation. I believe that we can also see the encodement of the typicality in the metonymy *karam*-GENEROSITY-HOSPITALITY FOR *karam*-HONORABLENESS as operating in a similar fashion. Nevertheless, the situation here is the opposite: the whole – the category of HONORABILITY – seems to be lacking a proper denotation, whereas the sub-category has its own name.

Perhaps, we can interpret this peculiar situation as in fact a culturally motivated phenomenon. Possibly, if we assume that the core of the pre-Islamic Arabic virtuous conduct consists of GENEROSITY-HOSPITALITY, the remaining elements of the code of honorable conduct were augmented with time as a kind of extension of the core value of *karam*-GENEROSITY-HOSPITALITY. This would imply a culturally specific conceptualization of HONORABLE CONDUCT as generosity – so to say – in "the widest sense", a kind of extended GENEROSITY-EXCELLENCY, which was embodied in the behavior of a MAN OF HONOR. To put in yet in other words, primarily, *karīm* was used to refer to a generous, liberal man, who was RESPECTED by others for his GENEROSITY-HOSPITALITY. With time, however, the lexeme began to be used to refer to other men, who were RESPECTED in the society. Thus, *karam*-GENEROSITY-HOSPITALITY served for a model – a prototype – of NOBILITY-HONORABILITY, which granted one the RIGHT TO RESPECT by their peers.

Of course, the alternative metonymical mapping – with reversed source-target vector – might be possibly proposed. Such a metonymy – *karam*-NOBILITY-HONORABILITY FOR *karam*-GENEROSITY-HOSPITALITY – would follow a different schema – *whole-for-part*. In this metonymy, the whole – the script of HONORABLE BEHAVIOR – would be used in the reference to its stereotypical or typical part, i.e., the script of GENEROSITY-HOSPITALITY. It would resemble then the aforementioned Lakoff's example of *mother*-MOTHER FOR MOTHER-HOUSEWIFE. In other words, a GENEROUS and HOSPITABLE man could be referred to as HONORABLE, since HONORABILITY was stereotypically seen as consisting first and foremost of the script of GENEROSITY-HOSPITALITY. The problem of the proper designation of the whole category would disappear, and the detonation of the part – as we saw – is not of that importance after all. Nevertheless, even if it was, within LEAP lexicon, GENEROSITY-HOSPITALITY had many of their proper denotations (e.g., *ǧūd*, *saḫāʔ*).

However, such a metonymic mapping – *whole-for-part* – seems to me less accurate than the metonymy *karam*-GENEROSITY- HOSPITALITY FOR *karam*-NOBILITY-HONORABILITY. The historical[2] and comparative data (cf. Guth 2015: 178) suggest temporary precedence of the concept *karam*-GENEROSITY-HOSPITALITY over the *karam*- NOBILITY- HONORABILITY. As noted by Guth (2015: 178), the fact that in Ethiosemitic languages, √KRM is elaborated in the lexis pertaining to the meaning of "rain season" might make one "think that 'plenty of rain' is the more original value [of it], making 'to be generous' the secondary, figurative use (*'to be like the sky/clouds that give plenty of rain' > 'to be generous')". Thus, I believe, it is rather unlikely that NOBLE-HONORABLE and NOBILITY-HONORABILITY were primary significations of the lexemes *karīm* and *karam*. In other words, the extension from GENEROSITY-HOSPITALITY to HONORABLENESS was probably motivated by cultural perception of the former as the core – the prototype – of the code of honorable behavior. A reverse statement – although still possible[3] – would actually imply that the shift *karam*-HONORABLENESS > *karam*-GENEROSITY-HOSPITALITY must have happened quite early in the history of the development of Semitic languages. The lack of √KRM derived lexis relating to the concept of HONORABLENESS in those languages – except from Arabic – might suggest that after all such a statement is not correct.

Moreover, it seems that at least in CA, another metonymy following the schema *pars pro toto* and targeting at *karam* existed. It was *ḫīr* FOR *karam*. The concept of *ḫīr* seems to encompass primarily the notion of GOODNESS, GOOD QUALITIES of a man (cf. AlG: 594), but – as indicated by LsA (LsA4: 310) and AsS (352) – it was also used as a metonymical signification of *karam*.[4] In the case of this metonymy, one can observe a similar motivation of the category extension. The concept of *ḫīr*, GOODNESS, GOOD QUALITIES, as bestowing someone

---

2 In OCIANA – *Online Corpus of the Inscriptions of Ancient North Arabia* – *krm* occurs only in four inscriptions, from among which three are instances of a proper name (cf. search of "krm" in http://krcfm.orient.ox.ac.uk/fmi/webd/ociana, [24-06-2021]). The only inscription, in which *krm* seems having different meaning suggest its reading as "generous" or "magnanimous" rather than "honorable" (http://krc.orient.ox.ac.uk/ociana/corpus/pages/OCIANA_0012438.html, [24-06-2021]). Nonetheless, the scarcity of data doesn't allow drawing any definitive conclusion.

3 For instance, English lexeme *generous* is historically, via French, derived from Latin *generosus* "of noble birth, well-born, noble, eminent" and it began to pertain to the concept of GENEROSITY in 17th c. (Hoad 1993: 191). Thus, GENEROSITY being referred to by this lexeme must have been associated with NOBILITY and as such with certain HONORABLENESS associated traditionally with aristocracy.

4 LsA (LsA4: 310) suggests that *ḫīr* is also metonymically used in reference to *šaraf*. Based on the samples from CEAP (cf. t28A:92–97; t33A:58; t38A:150; t20A:45), I presume that in fact its metonymical use is rather restricted to the concept of *karam* only.

with RIGHT TO RESPECT, was with time employed to call up the schema of the whole complex of behavior giving someone such a RIGHT, i.e., the cultural script of *karam*.

All in all, the metonymy *karam*-GENEROSITY- HOSPITALITY FOR *karam*-NOBILITY-HONORABILITY is highly culture-specific. It is motivated by the great significance of the cultural script of GENEROSITY-HOSPITALITY for the society of pre-Islamic Arabs. Its existence suggests that primarily, following this script was upon what one could base their RIGHT TO RESPECT. With time, this RIGHT began to be allocated according to more and more extended code, a cultural script, which was referred to by the same lexis – *karam* and *karīm*. As a result, a MAN OF HONOR, an HONORABLE man, was perceived by Arabs of al-Ǧāhiliyya as a kind of extended version of a GENEROUS-HOSPITABLE one. In other words, in the eyes of those people, the prototype of the quality, for which one deserve RESPECT, was the cultural schema of GENEROSITY- HOSPITALITY – not that of BRAVERY, NOBILITY, or POLITICAL POWER.

4.3.1.2. Wealth helps one being *karīm*

Such a great estimation of GENEROSITY-HOSPITALITY depicted above must have resulted in a very positive evaluation of WEALTH. In fact, possessing wealth is even sometimes depicted as a requirement for someone who want to be seen as *karīm*, as it is intent in (12), a verse from a poet known as Uḥayḥa. This may be also deduced from (13), a fragment of a poem by Ḥātim aṭ-Ṭāʔī.

(12) إنّي أُقيمُ عَلى الزَوْراءِ أعمُرُها إنّ الكَريمَ عَلى الإخوانِ ذو المالِ
Truly, I dwell in [my land], az-Zawrāʔ, [known as such because it is as rich as a deep well] – and I will stay in it for long – since, certainly, an **honorable man** (*karīm*) [must] possess wealth in front of his brothers (cf. t01A:79).

(13) (…) كريمٌ غِناها، مُسْتَعِفٌّ فَقيرُها
(…) the wealthy one among them is **honorable** (*karīm*), and the poor one is virtuous (cf. t19B:64).

Nevertheless, the same poet did not exclude the possibility that *karīm* – here in fact, the poet himself – can also be poor and in need, as it is the case in (14) (cf. also t19A:32). It is especially important in the context of so-called *ṣaʕālīk*, i.e., pre-Islamic Arabic vagabonds/road bandits, who considered themselves *karīm* despite the fact they did not have any possession.[5] Their pride as *karīm* folk was derived from the fact that they distributed any robbed property among others.

5 I would like to thank prof. Marek Dziekan, the reviewer of my Ph.D. thesis, for this important remark on *karam* of *ṣaʕālīk*.

Thus, they satisfied the core requirement of the NOBILITY-HONORABILITY, i.e., GENEROSITY. We could see this pride expressed in the verses (6) attributed to ʕUrwa Ibn al-Ward, one of the best known of *ṣaʕālīk*, pre-Islamic Arabic "Robin Hoods". Consequently, although important, wealth was not a requirement *sine qua no* for being described as *karīm*. Rather, it should be interpreted as a mere – yet still important – facilitation of the *karīm* behavior.

(14) **كريمٌ** لا أبِيتُ الليلَ جادٍ أعَدِّدُ بالأنامِلِ ما رُزِيتُ
إذا ما بِتُّ أشرَبُ فَوْقَ رِيٍّ لِسُكْرٍ في الشَّرابِ فلا رَوِيتُ
[I am] an **honorable** (*karīm*) man in need. I do not sleep over night, counting on my fingers how much [of my wealth] I have lost.
And when I cannot sleep, I drink – more than [I need to] quench [my thirst] – to get drunk drinking, and [never could] I satisfy my thirst (cf. t19A:31).

4.3.2. Magnanimity, noble-heartedness

Moving further from the center of the script of HONORABLE BEHAVIOR of *karīm*, i.e., from GENEROSITY-HOSPITALITY, one can find a subcategory yet somehow related to the core. It was the category I termed as MAGNANIMITY. The members of *karam* clusters occurred 26 times in the context of this notion. The name MAGNANIMOUS is probably the most suitable for the concept of someone who is of a noble heart, or who is simply a good man. One could argue that the extension of the category *karīm*, so that it encompasses MAGNANIMOUS men, is another instance of a cultural metonymy. Perhaps, *karīm*-GENEROUS-HOSPITABLE FOR *karīm*-MAGNANIMOUS is justifiable. Nevertheless, MAGNANIMITY seems to be simply a part of the conduct of honorable and noble men.

In these 26 contexts in CEAP, *karīm* is depicted as a gentle, easy-going, kind man – as, for instance, in (15), a verse attributed to Labīd Ibn Rabīʕa, or someone whom people can trust as in examples (16) by al-Aswad an-Nahšalī. *Karīm* is then also sincere as depicted in (17), a verse from by Ṭarafa Ibn al-ʕAbd. This means *karīm* is a simply good man – as in (18) – and therefore he is the one with whom others want to spent time.

(15) حُلْوٌ **كَريمٌ** وَفي حَلاوَتِهِ مُرٌّ لَطيفُ الأحْشاءِ والكَبِدِ
He was a sweet **honorable** man (*karīm*) – and in his sweetness there was [a drop] of bitterness. [He was] of good heart [lit. of gentle, courteous intestines and liver] (cf. t30B:51).

(16) كم فاتَني مِن **كريمٍ** كان ذا ثِقَةٍ يُذْكي الوقودَ بجَمْدٍ ليلةَ الحَلَل
So many of **honorable men** (*karīm*), who were trustworthy and [first] to light the fire-wood with a frozen [kindling] during a night stop; [so many of them] became beyond my reach (cf. t16A:57)?

(17) والصِّدْقُ يألَفُهُ **الكريمُ** [اللبيب] المُرْتجى والكِذْبُ يألَفُهُ الدَّنئُ الأخيَبُ

The honesty is what you can expect from an **honorable man** (*karīm/labīb*), when asked – whereas the lie is what you will get from a disappointing low man (*laʔīm*) (cf. t07A:115).

(18) تَعلَّمْ أبَيْتَ اللَّعْنَ أنَّكَ ماجِدٌ **كريمٌ**، فلا يَشقى لديكَ المُجانِبُ

Learn how to reject cursing [others, to show] that you are a glorious **honorable man** (*māğid karīm*), and none, who is beside you, will suffer misfortune (cf. t24A:20).

Such popularity of *karīm*, the fact that people enjoyed spending time with him, occurs in CEAP only in the context of wine consumption. By no means it is surprising that MAGNANIMITY of *karīm* should manifest first and foremost at such an event. Wine was a very important part of the life not only a young man of a noble descent, but in fact of all Arabs living before Islam (ʕAlī 1993b: 665). No wonder then that wine drinking was one of the recurring motifs of EAP (Bielawski 1968: 24). The great al-Aʕšà himself was attached to wine so much that he could not imagine converting to the new – alcohol free – religion (ʕAlī 1993b: 668). Thus, a *karīm* must have been a good drinking companion and as such this figure is depicted in (19), in which Labīd Ibn Rabiʕa recalls his diseased brother Arbad, and in (20), a fragment of a panegyric on his own tribe attributed to Ḥassān Ibn Ṯābit. Perhaps, such collocation of wine drinking and *karīm/karam* might be the rationale of the emergence of the folk etymology of *karm* "vine-grape" I mentioned earlier in this chapter.

(19) وإنْ تشرَبْ فنعِمَ أخُو النَّدامى **كريمٌ** ماجدٌ حُلْوُ النِّدامِ

Thus, when you were drinking [wine], the life of your companion cleared up, [since you were] a glorious **honorable man** (*karīm māğid*), with whom drinking was a pleasure (cf. t30B:202).

(20) مَع نَدَامَى بِيضِ الوُجوهِ، **كِرَامٌ**، نُبِّهُوا، بعْدَ خَفْقَةِ الأشْرَاطِ

Thus, they are **honorable** (*kirām*) to their respectable [lit. of white faces] dinking companions – they are still full of life at the time, when the stars [of the constellation of Aries] disappears from the night sky, [i.e., at the end of the night] (cf. t38A:166).

The good, noble-hearted *karīm* is also helpful – as in (21) – and as a result he does not let others down (cf. t04A:81). Of course, he cannot be misanthrope or hating as he is depicted in (22) by Zuhayr Ibn Abī Sulmà. As a result of that, *karīm* is not vilifying or cursing others, what is mentioned in (23) attributed to al-Ḥuṭayʔa – a poet that might be actually considered a quite spiteful one (Bielawski 1968: 67) – and he is not blaming someone for failing his responsibilities as it is depicted in (24).

(21) وإذا طَلَبْتَ إلى **كَرِيمٍ** حاجةً فَلِقَاؤُه يَكْفِيكَ وَالتَّسليمُ

Whenever being in need, ask a favor from an **honorable man** (*karīm*). Meeting him and [his] greeting will suffice [to satisfy your need] (cf. t37A:137)

(22) **كِرامٍ** فَلا ذو الضِغْنِ يُدرِكُ تَبلَهُ ولا الجارِمُ الجاني عَلَيهِمْ بِمُسْلَمِ
[They are that excellent because of] the **honorable men** (*kirām*), among whom you won't find any malevolent man knowing [only] spite, nor any wrongdoer committing an atrocity to them, leaving them without help (cf. t22A:75).

(23) **كرامٌ** أبى الذَّمَّ آباؤهم فلا يَجْعَلُونَ لِلَوْمِ سَبِيلا
[They are] **honorable men** (*kirām*), whose ancestors rejected dispraise, [and who themselves] do not make a path towards the blame (cf. t39A:69–70).

(24) أُقدِّمُ ما عِنْدَنا حاضِرٌ وإن لَمْ يَكُنْ غَيْرُ خُبْزٍ وَخَلّْ
فـأما **الكريمُ** فَراضٍ به وَأَمَّا اللَّئِيمُ فَمَا قَدْ أَبَلْ
I am offering you whatever we have – even if it was [only] bread and vinegar.
As far as an **honorable man** (*karīm*) is concerned, he will be content. As far as an ignoble one is concerned, he [simply] won't refuse [to accept my offer] (cf. t37A:122).

In other words, *karīm* treats others with respect – even those, who are rarely respected, such as slaves as, it is mentioned in (25).

(25) فَثِقْ بِمَوْلاكَ **الكريمِ** فإنه بالعَبْدِ أرْأَفُ على أبٍ بِبَنِيهِ
Thus, trust your **honorable** (*karīm*) protégé, since he is caring about his slave more than a father about his sons (cf. t37A:152).

Karīm is then someone who brings good to other people – thus he is someone people like, respect, and find pleasing. It seems that in pre-Islamic Arabic society, people saw being kind and amicable as entitlement for a good life – in other words, they believed good people should have good life. I believe that is what we could deduce it from the sample (26), in which the poet al-Aʕšà states that *karīm* – i.e., a good person – enjoys a blissful life.

(26) رَبّي كَرِيمٌ لا يُكَدِّرُ نِعْمَةً
My Lord, the wellbeing of an **honorable man** (*karīm*) is not [easy] to be distorted (cf. t28A:228–229).

4.3.3. Bravery

The first fully independent from GENEROSITY-HOSPITALITY subschema of the cultural script of HONORABLE BEHAVIOR of *karīm* is that of BRAVERY. A man considered *karīm* is seen as BRAVE and COURAGEOUS in the data from CEAP at least in 20 contexts, such as the verses (27) or (28). The fact that the BRAVERY was an element of the code of the noble conduct is not surprising – the environment of scarcity pre-Islamic Arabs used to live in must have naturally resulted in high estimation of one's ability to defend themselves as well as their tribe (ʕAlī 1993a: 271). ʕAlī (1993c: 345) claims that in fact battling, fighting was deeply entrenched in the character of pre-Islamic Arabs and were a part of their nature. Therefore, courage, bravery and manliness were the major theme of many Early Arabic poems, which praised tribal warrior as heroes and role models for all men (ˁAlī 1993c: 335). The stories of *ˀayyām al-ˁarab* "days [of glory] of Arabs" occupies a huge space within EAP, thus the concept of *karīm* could not be detached from the trait of fearlessness.

(27) رجالٌ **كِرامٌ** غيرُ مِيلٍ نَماهُمو إلى الغُرّ آباءٌ **كرامُ** المَخاصِلِ
[They are] **honorable men** (*kirām*) – not cowards. [Their] forefathers of **noble** (*kirām*) swords elevated them towards the nobility (cf. t24A:73).

(28) ومِنْ كُلِّ حَيٍّ قَدْ أَتَتْني فَوارِسُ ذَوُو نَجَداتٍ في اللِّقاءِ **كِرَامِ**
From each tribe, **honorable** (*kirām*) knights, [full] of courage in a battle, came to me (cf. t37A:129).

Karīm must be then not only brave, but also skillful in the warfare. As such *karīm* is depicted by a great warrior and possibly even greater poet ˁAntara Ibn Šaddād, for example in (29), or by al-Aˁšà in (30). In the latter, the poet accentuates the importance of STRENGTH OR FORCE (*ˁizz*) for BRAVERY of *karīm*. STRENGTH – *ˁizz* – was a crucial element of one's *murūˁa*-MANLINESS, since in the difficult environment of deficiency, any rights and any influence over others was acquired mainly by means of force (ˁAlī 1993b: 608). BRAVERY and STRENGTH were then what makes a man MANLY and what differs him from a woman (ˁAlī 1993b: 609). Therefore, *karīm* could not be weak. That is probably why in (31), Kaˁb Ibn Zuhayr states he cannot consider himself a *karīm* because of the fact that he is an old man.

(29) وضَرْبَةَ فَيْصَلٍ من كَفِّ لَيْثٍ **كَرِيمِ** الجَدِّ فاقَ على الرِّفاقِ
A strike of a sharp-cutting sword [wielded] in the hand of a lion of the **noble** (*karīm*) ancestry excels over his companions (cf. t21A:93).

(30) **بِمِثْلِهِمْ غَدَاةَ الرَّوْعِ يَجْلُو العِزَّ وَالكَرَمَا**
[When people fight] like them in the day of a battle, [their] **strength** (*ˁizz*) and **nobility** (*karam*) become apparent (cf. t28A:298–303).

(31) ما صَلاحُ الزَوْجَيْنِ عاشا جَمِيعاًبَعْدَ أن يَصْرِمَ الكَبِيرُ الكَبِيرا
فاصْبِرِي مِثْلَ ما صَبَرْتُ فإنّي لا إخالُ الكريمَ إلّا صَبُورَا
There is no good health for a married couple, who lives together after their senility separated them from each other.
Thus, become enduring (*iṣbirī*) in the same way, I learnt to endure (*ṣabartu*) – and truly, I do not consider myself as an **honorable man** (*karīm*) anymore – just as an enduring one (*ṣabūr*) (cf. t34A:22, t34B:26).

Moreover, it seems that killing a *karīm* in a battle was a great reason for pride. Contexts reflecting such a conceptualization occur frequently in CEAP, and as their good example we can consider (32).

(32) كَمْ قتَلْنا من **كريمٍ** سيّدٍ، ماجِدِ الجَدَّيْنِ مِقْدامٍ بَطَلْ
We have killed so many of **honorable men** (*karīm*), leaders (*sayyid*), [men] of glorious (*māǧid*) [parental and maternal] ancestors, brave and fearless (cf. t38A:216).

The culture, which hold bravery and courage in such a great estimation, must have naturally promote the idea of the death in the battle. In fact, such death was an ideal for a young warrior (Dziekan 2008: 85). Thus, there is no more suitable death for *karīm* than while fighting in the name of his tribe. In CEAP, such a conceptualization is manifested, for instance, in the verses (33) by al-Aʕšà and (34) by ʕAntara Ibn Šaddād. Such glorification of battle hazards must have resulted in the attempts of bravery which were brought to extreme – to recklessness. At least, in such light, the bravery of *karīm* was seen by a woman – like ʕAntara's mother, who – as it is depicted in the fragment (35) of his poem – was honestly worried about her son. Of course, it did not change the fact that her son considered his daring behavior as perfectly reasonable and the only one suitable for a *karīm*.

(33) فَمُوتُوا **كِرَاماً** بِأَسْيَافِكُمْ وَلِلمَوْتُ يَجْشَمُهُ مَنْ جَشِمْ

Die like **honorable men** (*kirām*), wielding swords [in your hands]. Truly, only a daring man can dare to seek death (cf. t28A:43).

(34) واختَرْ لِنَفْسِكَ منزِلاً تعْلو به أَوْ مُتْ **كريماً** تَحْتَ ظِلِّ القَسْطَلِ

Thus, either choose for yourself an abode, in which you will ascend [in rank], or die as an **honorable man** (*karīm*) in the shadows of dust [of a battlefield] (cf. t21A:110).

(35) تُعَنِّفني زَبيبةُ في المَلامِ على الإقدامِ في يومِ الزِّحامِ
تخافُ عليَّ أن ألقى حِمامي بطعنِ الرُّمحِ أو ضَربِ الحُسامِ
مقالٌ ليسَ يَقْبَلُهُ **كِرامٌ** ولا يَرضى به غيرُ اللِّئامِ

Zabība, [my mother], rebuked me sharply, reprehending [me] for my bravery on the day of the crowded [battle].
She is worried about me, [and she fears] that I will meet my death being pierced by a spear or slashed by a sword.
Such a speech is not acceptable for **honorable men** (*kirām*) and only base people (*laʔīm*) can accept it (cf. t21A:133).

4.3.4. Loyalty

Another element of the cultural script of behavior of *karīm* present in the CEAP is that of LOYALTY – a person rendered *karīm* must have been LOYAL. Yet again, such conclusion should not be found surprising. The environment of scarcity, in which pre-Islamic Arabs happened to live, forged their deep sense of loyalty towards the members of the group they belonged to (ʕAlī 1993a: 271). A man must have defended his tribe, his family, his associates, because in turn, he would not be able to survive without their support – his problems were then theirs, but in return, theirs became his (ʕAlī 1993b: 402). Such an environment-driven obligation of loyalty towards one's tribe and his kins manifested in a certain type of feeling called *ʕaṣabiyya* – a feeling of unbreakable blood bond with people one belongs to (1993b: 394). In fact, in the semi-anarchistic society of pre-Islamic Arabs, *ʕaṣabiyya* played the role of the foundation of the legal system and governed the tribe's activities (ʕAlī 1993b: 392). *ʕAṣabiyya* was the absolute LOYALTY of tribe members to any of their fellows in tribe membership – no matter a given person was the victim of injustice, which deemed to be avenged, or he/she was its perpetrator (LsA1: 707), bringing upon the whole tribe the vengeance of another kin-group. The LOYALTY of *ʕaṣabiyya* was gradual – first and foremost, it was the strongest in the matters of one's nuclear and more distant family – and becomes gradually weaker with the distance of blood relationship (ʕAlī 1993b: 393).

The LOYALTY was considered a part of the code of conduct of *karīm*. The NOBLE, HONORABLE man was LOYAL not only to his family or tribe, but – perhaps more importantly – to the people he pledged alliance and support. A promise of support or alliance in a form of an oath was a sanctity for pre-Islamic Arabs and its transgression was an unforgivable act (ʕAlī 1993b: 370). Anyone who broke an oath brought upon himself disgrace and dishonor, and the society took an active part in vilifying him. Among many ways of announcing someone's breaking an oath, pre-Islamic Arabs, for instance, were displaying a banner with the oath-breaker's name on it in the marketplace of ʕUkāẓ (ʕAlī 1993b: 403). Therefore, *karīm* is an epithet of a person, who fulfilled his allegiance or who answers the call for (military) assistance. We can find traces of this conceptualization in the verses (36) by Ibn Muqbil, (37) by Ḥassān Ibn Ṯābit, and (38) by Aš-Šammāẖ Ibn Ḍirār.

(36) وحَيٌّ نُمَيْرٍ إنْ دعَوْتُ أجابَني **كرامٌ** إذا شُلَّ السَّعَامُ المُصَبَّحُ

When I called the tribe of Numayr [for help], they answered my [call] – at the time in the morning, when camels are herded to the pastorage, they [showed how] **honorable** (*kirām*) [they are] (cf. t36A:25).

(37) لأنّا نَرَى حَقَّ الجِوَارِ أمَانَةً، ويحفَظُهُ مِنَّا **الكريمُ** المعاهِدُ

Since we consider safety as the right of [our] protégé, the **honorable man** (*karīm*) from among us, with whom [a man] allied, protects him (cf. t38A:86).

(38) دَعَوْتُ فلبّاني على ما يَنوبُني **كريمٌ** من الفِتْيانِ غيرُ مزلَّجِ

I had called [for help] and an **honorable** (*karīm*) young man, who does not hesitate to help, answered my [call] (cf. t32A:81).

Thus, the *karīm* was expected to be faithful in any kinds of contracts, as it is depicted by Zuhayr Ibn Abī Sulmà in the verse (39). As we could see in, e.g., the example (36) quoted above, within such contracts, military alliances occupied a prominent place. The loyalty of a *karīm* in a battlefield is depicted also in (40). A special instance of the contracts between strangers was a protégé or a client relationship between individuals as well as between tribes/kin-groups, which I will elaborate further later in this chapter. The stronger party – the protector – was accounted for the protection he provided to his protégé, and thus, evaluated as *karīm* when fulfilling this duty. *Karīm* understood as someone of such loyalty is meant, for instance, in (41).

(39) أبْلِغْ لدَيْكَ بَني الصَّيْداءِ **كُلَّهُمُ** أنّ يَساراً أتَانَا غيرَ مَغلولِ
ولا مُهانٍ، ولَكِنْ عِنْدَ **ذي كَرَمٍ** وفي حِبَالٍ وَفيِّ غَيْرَ مَجْهُولِ
Inform all of the people of aṣ-Ṣaydāʔ, who are with you, that Yasār, [my slave-boy] came [back] to us without a scratch,
and without a complaint. [You can tell them] that he has been with the man, who is **honorable** (*ḏī karam*), and who adheres to agreements, about which [he does not] forget (cf. t22A:49).

(40) نَصَحْتُمْ بالمَغيبِ ولَمْ تُعينُوا عَلَيْنا إنّكُمْ كُنْتُمْ **كِراما**
فلوْ كُنتُمْ معَ ابنِ الجَوْنِ كنتُمْ كَمَنْ أوْدى وأصْبحَ قد ألاما
Your absence [at the battlefield] was fair – you did not assist [our enemies] against us, since truly, you are **honorable** (*kirām*).
Had you however supported [the clan of] Ibn al-Ǧawn, [our enemies], you would have been destroyed [by us, and died] in disgrace (cf. t29 A:115).

(41) طَوِيلُ اليَدَيْنِ، رَهْطُهُ غَيْرُ ثِنْيَةٍ، أشَمُّ **كَريمٌ** جارُهُ لا يُرَهَّقُ
[Muḥliqa has] long arms, [i.e., he is generous]. His people are not those, who [are satisfied with] the second rank. [He is] a great **honorable man** (*karīm*). His neighbor-protégé is safe from any harm (cf. t28A:225).

To be sure, LOYALTY in the context of *karīm* should be translated rather in a broad way. *Karīm* was also a person who simply kept his promises, as Ṭarafa Ibn al-ʕAbd meant it in (17). The same conceptualization of *karīm* one can found also in (42).

(42) لا تُودِعِ السِّرَّ إلّا عِنْدَ **ذي كَرَمٍ** والسِّرُّ عِنْدَ **كِرَامِ** النَّاسِ مَكْتُومُ
Tell [your] secret only to a man who has **honor** (*karam*) – a secret [revealed] to **honorable** (*kirām*) people is well-kept (cf. t37A:136).

LOYALTY of *karīm* was something absolute. Someone rendered as *karīm* must have obey his obligations – be them *ʕaṣabiyya* driven or enacted by a contract or an oath. Therefore, even if the person he pledged support is fully responsible for his troubles, he cannot refuse his help – and in this manner, one should interpret the verse (43) attributed to al-Aʕšà.

(43) وَرُبّ بَقِيعٍ لَوْ هَتَفْتُ بجَوّهِ، أتَاني **كَرِيمٌ** يَنفُضُ الرّأسَ مُغضَبَا
So often, when I cry [for help] from a vast land, an **honorable man** (*karīm*) comes to [assist] me, shaking his head with anger (cf. t28A:114–5).

4.3.5. Endurance

The concept of *ṣabr*-ENDURANCE was another very important part of the cultural HONORABLE BEHAVIOR of *karīm*. As we could see in the example (31), if a man could not be fully *karīm* because of his weakness brought onto him by the old age, he should have at least tried to stay *ṣābir*, that is, a man of *ṣabr*. Nowadays, this lexeme is most commonly translated as "patience." In LEAP, however, its more appropriate English equivalent could be the concept of ENDURANCE. *Ṣabr* is then the quality of someone's character, which makes him able to endure, survive in the least manageable circumstance. Again, one could try to locate the environmental motivation of such a great esteem this value enjoyed in the Arabic society of al-Ǧāhiliyya. I believe that naturally, the harsh environment must have model character of pre-Islamic Arabs as enduring and patience in the face of scarcity, in which any calamity would turn to be a matter of the most basic survival.[6]

Therefore, *karīm* is also conceptualized as the one who is strong enough to ENDURE in any kind of turmoil. Being *ṣābir* – a man of *ṣabr* – could be considered as a general life approach of someone – especially facing death – as we can observe it in a verse (44), in which Taʔabbaṭa Šarran praises another famous poet, Šanfara. I believe, however, that the most important relation between *karīm* and *ṣabr* is a kind of natural disposition to be able to adapt. This is exactly the conceptualization manifested in (45).

(44) وَأَجْمَلُ مَوْتِ الْمَرْءِ إِذْ كَانَ مَيِّتاً وَلَا بُدَّ يَوْماً مَوْتُهُ وَهُوَ **صَابِرُ**
فَلَا يَبْعَدَنَّ الشَّنْفَرَى وَسِلَاحُهُ الْحَدِيدُ وَشَدٌّ خَطْوِهِ مُتَوَاتِرُ
إِذَا رَاعَ رَوْعَ الْمَوْتِ رَاعَ وَإِنْ حَمَى حمى معهُ حرٌّ **كريمٌ** مُصابِرُ

The most beautiful death is [the death] of a man, who [knowing that] one day, he'll certainly die, [stays] **enduring** (*ṣabūr*), [not fearing it].

Let aš- Šanfarà not depart (*lā yabʕadanna*), nor his weapon and his sword that followed him step after step;[7]

---

6 Although, it seems grounded in the specifics of environment and culture, the concept of *ṣabr* is rather conceptualized in a manner, which is to be found in many cultures and languages. ENDURANCE, as it is the case of *ṣabr* meaning primarily "holding something" (cf. AsS: 631; LsA4: 506), is frequently conceptualized as HOLDING (ONESELF) against difficulties (cf. English *to hold on* or Polish *wytrzymać* "lit. to hold through").

7 I would like to thank the reviewers of my Ph.D. thesis, prof. Janusz Danecki and prof. Marek Dziekan, for pointing towards the inaccuracy in my original translation. As noted by Tadeusz Kowalski (1997: 182–7), the phrase *la tabʕadanna* was used as a funeral formula that should not be translated literally. My translation of this verse is based on the translation by prof. Marek Dziekan published in Danecki (1997).

when he feared the death – [they] feared [with him]. When [they] were defending [someone, aš-Šanfarà], an **honorable** (*karīm*), **enduring** free-man, was defending [this someone] with them (cf. t03A:78–85; cf. also Danecki 1997: 16).

(45) وكم مِن **كرِيمٍ** قد أَضَرَّ بِهِ الهوى نفَعَوَّدَه ما لَمْ يَكُن يَتَعَوَّدُ

So many **honorable men** (*karīm*), after an affection caused harm to them, got used to what they [hadn't been] used to [before] (cf. t35A:27).

Karīm must prove his *ṣabr* first and forest while facing an enemy on a battlefield, as it is implied in (46) by Labīd Ibn Rabiʕa, who describes his readiness to fight with the people who harmed his protégé. But the CEAP showed that also in other contexts, such as while facing a reproach or offence, *ṣabr* is a quality expected from a *karīm*, as we can find it in (47) by Hudba Ibn al-Ḫašram.

(46) ويومَ ظَعَنْتُمْ فاصْمَعَدَّتْ وُفُودُكُمْ بأَجْمادِ فاثُورٍ **كريمٌ** مُصابِرُ

On the day, on which you departed and went forth, when you were reaching the hills of Faṯūr, I [was] **honorable** (*karīm*) and **enduring** (*ṣabūr*) man (cf. t30B:63)

(47) إذا سَبَّني أَغضَيتُ بَعدَ حَمِيَّةٍ وَقد يَصبِرُ المَرءُ **الكَريمُ** فَيَعرِفُ

When someone defiles me, I patiently hold annoyance after [a moment of] indignation, since when an **honorable** (*karīm*) man is **patient** (*yaṣbir*), he gets wiser (cf. t08A:123).

The importance of *ṣabr* might be even interpreted as a kind of essence of one's *karam*. This might be deduced, for instance, from (48), a verse attributed to Ibn Muqbil. *Karīm* is depicted there as a man formed as *karīm* by adversities and hardship. Perhaps, that's the reason why in (31) quoted above, the poet considers *ṣabr* a kind of substitute of *karam*. If you are unable to be *karīm*, try at least to show endurance while facing the misfortunes of your life.

(48) أبقى خُطوبٌ وحاجاتٌ تُضَيِّقُني وما جَنى الدَهْرُ مِن صَفوٍ ومِنْ كَدَرِ
مِثلَ الحُسامِ **كريماً** عندَ خِلَّتِه لِكُلِّ إِزْرَةٍ هذا الدَّهْرِ ذَا إِزَرِ

Any calamities, needs, which bother me, and anything – either clear [and easy] or turbid [and difficult], with which the fate has maltreated me – [all of it] has left [in me]
[marks] – like [marks] of sword [strikes] – [making me] **honorable** (*karīm*) and strong (*ḏū ʕizz*) in the face of poverty or other misfortunes (cf. t36A:74).

4.3.6. Customs obedience

The CEAP contains a few conceptualizations of *karīm*'s behavior, which I clustered under an umbrella term of CUSTOM OBEDIENCE. In fact, most of the manners of honorable behavior I have already mentioned fall in a certain way under the category of the obedience of pre-Islamic Arabic customs. This obedience might be seen as the element of the conservative nature of (nomadic) Arabs of al-Ǧāhiliyya (ʕAlī1: 279).

However, in this sub-section, I bear in mind mostly the actions which stems from one's feeling of *ḥayāʔ*, which will be more precisely elaborated in Chapter 8. Although it might be translated as "modesty" or "chastity" – in reference to both sexes – as I believe it might be rendered, for example, in (49) by Kaʕb Ibn Zuhayr, I think that we can expand this rough definition to the form of a concept of the intuition of how to behave and what behavior to avoid. Therefore, the obedience of the customs I meant is precisely such an application of a kind of MORAL SENSE to one's behavior. As one can observe in this verse, this MORAL SENSE is related to avoidance of vulgarity that mostly implied a foul speech.

(49) إنّي امْرُؤٌ أقْنِي الحَيَاءَ وشِيمَتِي **كَرَمُ** الطبيعةِ والتجنُّبُ للخَنا

Truly, I am a man – I apply my sense of shame, my natural temper is **nobility of character** (*karam aṭ-ṭabīʕa*) and avoidance of vulgarity (cf. t34B:11).

4.3.7. Reason, moderation, and forbearance – the concept of *ḥilm*

The next sub-category of the cultural script of HONORABLE BEHAVIOR of *karīm* was referred to in LEAP as *ḥilm*. The script it consisted of was yet another culturally specific behavior, which was in high estimation among pre-Islamic Arabs. Lane (1968a: 632) translates *ḥilm* as "forbearance, clemency, the quality of forgiving and concealing offences, or moderation, gentleness, deliberateness; a leisurely manner of proceeding, or of deportment, etc.; patience, as meaning contr. of hastiness; gravity, staidness, sedateness, calmness". I believe, however, that following ʕAlī (1993b: 351), we should understand it rather as a mixture of two qualities of one's conduct: their *ʔāna*, which is a concept of moderation, leisurely manner of proceeding (cf. Lane 1968a: 119), and their intelligence, wit, or the soundness of their judgement.

Nevertheless, *ḥalīm* – a man of *ḥilm* – is frequently depicted as the one who easily forgives. Forgiveness of *karīm* is portrayed, e.g., by Ḥātim aṭ-Ṭāʔī in (50). This habit was expected from a tribal chief (ʕAlī 1993b: 351) – the one who certainly must have been *karīm*. Forbearance and clemency, I think, should not though be seen as the direct translation of the trait of *ḥilm*. We should rather see them as resulting from *ḥilm* – the ability of considering and approaching matters without hastiness and unnecessary emotions (ʕAlī 1993b: 351). The *ḥilm* in a *karīm* man is what makes him successful – as al-Ḥuṭayʔa mentions it in (51) – that is his intelligence and strategical thinking, which originates from it. *Karīm* faces the adversities not only with *ṣabr* – which is the endurance resulting in surviving – but also with *ḥilm*, which provides him with tools of overcoming the problems.

(50) وَعَوْرَاءَ، قَدْ أعرضْتُ عنها، فلم يَضِرْ وذي أوَدٍ قَوّمْتُهُ، فَتَقَوّما
وأغْفِرُ عَوْراءَ **الكَرِيمِ** ادّخارَهُ وأصفَحُ مِن شَتْمِ اللئيم، تكرَّما
[As far as] shameful deeds [are concerned], I kept myself away from them. And there is no harm, [if] I straighten someone's tangled [paths], making [him] follow the right direction.
I do forgive shameful deeds of an **honorable man** (*karīm*), letting him [reflect] on them. I [also] turn away from a vile speech of a base man (*laʔīm*), [giving him a chance] to become honorable (*takarrama*) (cf. t19B:81).

(51) و لَولا أَصِيلُ اللُّبِّ غَضٌّ شَبَابُهُ **كريمٌ** لأيّام المَنُون عَرُوفُ
Thus, if he hadn't been an **honorable** (*karīm*), freshly young man of a steady judgement, he would have experienced days of ill-fate (cf. t39A:253–257).

Most often, the *ḥilm* of *karīm* is implied as either intelligence (as in 58) or clemency. Nevertheless – since *ḥalīm* forgives but only based on his sound judgement – *karīm* might get angry and punish someone, especially if such a person acted foolishly – as it is depicted by Ṭarafa Ibn al-ʕAbd in (53).

(52) وجَوْفاءَ يَجنَحُ فيها الضَّرِيكُ لِحِينِ الشِتَاءِ جُنوحَ العَرِنْ
مَلأْتُ، فأتْرَعْتُها تابِلي على عادةٍ مِن **كريمٍ** فَطِنْ
Thus, I [have filled] a deep well, into which a poor man keeps leaning during the winter, [the time of scarcity], as if he was [a camel] affected with a neck disorder;
I filled it up to the brim with my spice according to the ways of wise **honorable men** (*karīm*) (cf. t36A:214).

(53) أدُّوا الحُقوقَ تَفِرْ لكم أعْراضُكم إنّ **الكريمَ** إذا يُحَرَّبُ يَغضَبُ
[Thus] respect [my] rights, while your honor (*ʕirḍ*) is unoffended, [because] truly, when an **honorable man** (*karīm*) is provoked, he gets mad [and vilifies his offenders, damaging their honor] (cf. t07A:115).

4.3.8. Eloquence

Words and speech were quite important part of pre-Islamic Arabic culture. Arabs of *al-Ǧāhiliyya* feared words in form of magical formulas (Dziekan 2008: 115) or in reproaches – those day-to-day and those special in form of elaborate poetical satire (ʕAlī 1993b: 593). Words were then a weapon, but they were also tools of artistic creation, means of propaganda and simple entertainment. Thus, eloquence must have been an ingredient of *karīm*'s code of conduct. Nonetheless, it is only in few instances that such a conceptualization occurs in the CEAP. For instance, it might be deduced from (54) by Ḥātim aṭ-Ṭāʔī, or (55) by Ḥassān Ibn Ṯābit, where eloquence is presented by the poet as an essential element of behavior expected from a *karīm*.

(54) فأبشِرْ، وقرَّ العينَ منكَ، فإنني أجِيءُ **كريماً**، ولا ضعيفاً ولا حَصِرْ
Thus, rejoice and wipe your tears, since I am coming – truly – as an **honorable man** (*karīm*), not as a weakling, who does not know how to speak (cf. t19B:56).

(55) كَمْ مِنْ **كريمٍ** يعُضُّ الكلبُ مِئْزَرَهُ ثمّ يفِرُّ إذا أُلْقمتَهُ الحَجَرَا

So many **honorable men** (*karīm*) are [so honorable] that as soon as a dog bites a hem of their cloth, [they panicked and get scared]; and when you put a pebble into their mouth, [i.e., when you silenced them, while arguing], they flee away (cf. t38A:157)?

4.3.10. The deeds of *karīm* – *makārim* – and the expectations as for the conduct of *sayyid*

The scripts of behavior presented above clearly indicates that the essential part of the role schema of *karīm* is the code of behavior resembling what the tradition defined as a conduct expected from a *sayyid* – a tribal chief or lord. In the most famous formulation, these expectations were listed by Arabic scholar al-Ǧāḥiẓ († 868) as six traits of character: *saḫāʔ* "generosity and hospitality", *naǧda* "bravery and loyalty", *ṣabr* "patience", *ḥilm* "sound judgement, moderation, forbearance", *bayān* "eloquence", and *tawāḍuʕ* "humbleness" (Šukrī Al-Alūsī 2009: 187). As one can see, only the last one of them – *tawāḍuʕ*-HUMBLENESS – was not clearly associated with *karīm* in the texts of CEAP. This might be considered as another argument for considering the presence of this trait within al-Ǧāḥiẓ' listing as an anachronic attempt to adjust pre-Islamic Arabic morals to the later Muslim morality (cf. Pellat 1983: 10). I believe that this fact can further confirm that the record of EAP we possess is a faithful image of the authentic pre-Islamic poetry that after all has not been accustomed to the new cultural setting of Islam in the fullest.

As I have mentioned, a person who acted like *karīm* performed deeds referred to in LEAP as *makārim* or *makrumāt* (sg. *makruma*). One can see these lexemes used in CEAP in such examples as (56) and (57), or (1) quoted earlier. Otherwise, in LEAP, these deeds or acts are referred to as *masāʕī* (sg. *masʕāt*) (cf. t38A:229) or *faʕāl* as in (58) and (59), verses attributed to Ḥassān Ibn Ṯābit. The lexeme *faʕāl* seems to a manifestation of a quite interesting metonymy in form of *faʕāl*-DEEDS FOR NOBLE/HONORABLE DEEDS. Such a metonymy, in form of a *totum pro partem*, foregrounds the importance of *makārim* from the perspective of an individual. In other words, the noble deeds of honor as so important for evaluation of someone that in fact only they count – they are then the only deeds one should take into consideration.

(56) فَدَعِ **المكارِمَ**، إنّ قوْمَكَ أُسرةٌ مِنْ وُلْدِ شَجْعٍ غيرُ جِدِّ **كِرَامِ**
من صُلبِ خِندِفَ ماجِدٍ أعرَاقُهُ نجلتْ بِهِ بيضاءُ ذاتُ تمامِ

Give up on **honorable deeds** (*makārim*), since truly, your people are men that descend from brave juveniles, not from **honorable** (*kirām*) ancestors,
from the excellent [lineage] of glorious Ḫindif, from whose roots, white women give birth to [noblemen] (cf. t38A:263, t38B:216).

(57) وَقَد عَلِمَت سُلَيمى أَنَّ (...)
(...) **خَليقَتي كَرَمٌ** وأَنِّي إذا أَبْدَتْ نَواجِذَها الحروبُ
أُعينُ عَلى **مَكارِمِها** وأَغشى مَكارِهَها إذا كَعَّ الهَيوبُ
Sulaymà had known that (...)
(...) **honorability** (*karam*) is my natural disposition, and that – when wars show their teeth
– I support [my people in fighting for sake] of the **honorable deeds** (*makārim*) they, [the wars, could make us commit], and dealing with their horrors, when cowards [from among us] manifest their cowardice (cf. t08A:60–61).

(58) أبوكَ أبو **الفَعالِ**، أبو بَراءٍ، وخالُكَ ماجِدٌ حَكَمُ بْنُ سَعْدِ
Your father, Abū Barā?, was a man of **honorable deeds** (*fa*ʕ*āl*), and your uncle, Ḥakam Ibn Saʕd, was glorious (*māğid*) (cf. t38B:71).

(59) تَجِدْنا سبَقْنا **بالفَعالِ** وبالنَّدى، وأمرِ العَوالي في الخُطوبِ الأوائلِ
Thus, you will find us excelling in **honorable deeds** (*fa*ʕ*āl*), generosity (*nadà*), and wielding spears in the time of any adversities – [even] the worst ones (cf. t38B:187).

All in all, conduct of *karīm* in no more no less than the most genuine reason of one's pride. It is also what is praised in someone in panegyrics or elegies (ʕAlī 1993b: 588). This conceptualization is quite well manifested in (60), a verse from a *mu*ʕ*allaqa* by Labīd Ibn Rabiʕa or in (61) by an-Nābiġa aḏ-Ḏubyānī.

(60) أنكرتُ باطِلَها وَبُؤْتُ بحقِّها عندي، ولم يَفْخَرْ علَيَّ **كِرامُها**
I've disowned the wrong and boldly maintained the right as I saw it, and none of those **noble gentry** (*kirām*) could glory over me (Arberry 2017: 146)

(61) عَيَّرْتَني نَسَبَ **الكِرامِ**، وإنّما فَخْرُ المَفاخِرِ إنْ يُعَدَّ **كَريمَا**
You ascribed me with disgrace because of [my attachment] to the lineage of **honorable people** (*kirām*). Truly, [to be attached to them] is the greatest possible pride, when [this fact is] considered by an **honorable man** (*karīm*) (t26A:166)

4.4. Propositional subschemata of *karīm*

Besides the cultural script of HONORABLE BEHAVIOR of *karīm*, the role schema *karīm* encapsulate two important subschemata of propositional nature. They are {the CONDUCT of *karīm* is the IDEAL CONDUCT} and {*karīm* deserves RESPECT}. Their importance lies in the fact that they motivate perhaps the most significant metonymic extension of the category of *karīm*.

4.4.1. *Karīm* is EXCELLENT and DESERVES RESPECT

Since *karīm* is the man realizing the code of honorable – noble – conduct, naturally, a kind of NOBILITY of this figure must be a part of its cultural schema. This NOBILITY should not be interpreted in English terms as inherently implying noble descent. Rather, it ought to be seen as NOBILITY of one's CONDUCT – the notion I believe the most accurately expressed as HONORABILITY or perhaps INTEGRITY.

Karīm – as such a NOBLE man – was realizing certain ideal of a man persisting it pre-Islamic Arabic society. In other words, one could say that the role schema of *karīm* must have subsume a propositional subschema in form of {the CONDUCT of *karīm* is the IDEAL CONDUCT}. This subschema seems to have motivated a metonymic extension of the category *karīm*, making it encompass the notion of EXCELLENT or even THE BEST. The perception that *karīm* referred to the special – the best choice – of men could be seen, for instance, in the sample (62). More evidently, however, it is discernible in (63) attributed to Ibn Muqbil and (64) by Abū Ṭālib.

(62) أرى الموتَ يَعْتامُ **الكِرامَ** ويَصنطَفِي عقيلةَ مالِ الفاحِشِ المتشدِّد

The demise seems to choose [only] the **noble men** (*kirām*) and the best wealth, [the wealth so vast that is seems to be collected by] an exorbitant meager (cf. t07A:49).

(63) وحَيٍّ **كِرامٍ** قدْ تَلَغَّبْتُ سَيْرَهمْ بمَرْبوعةٍ صَهْباءَ مَجدولةٍ جَدْلا

In my ride, I exhausted [their] **best men** (*kirām*), riding on the swift, white-and-red, slenderest she-camel (cf. t36A:156).

(64) إذا اجْتَمَعتْ يوماً قُريشُ لِمَفْخَرٍ فعَبْدُ مَنافٍ سِرُّها وصَمِيمُها
فإنْ حُصِّلَتْ أشرافُ عبدِ مَنافِها فَفي هاشمٍ أَشْرافُها وقَديمُها
فإنْ فَخرتْ يوماً، فإنَّ محمَّداً هوَ المُصْطفى مَن سِرُّها **وكريمُها**

When [the people of] Qurayš gather to pride themselves, [the clan of] ʕAbd Manāf is the best and the purest among them.
And if the most noble men [descending from] ʕAbd Manāf are called upon, the most noble and the most ancient of them are among the [descendants of] Hāšim.
And if one day, they, [the sons of Hāšim], are priding themselves, Muḥammad is the purest one – he is their best part, **the best** (*karīm*) from among them (cf. t24A:82).

The notion of EXCELLENCY must naturally connect with the schema of RESPECT. Something worth our respect is something valued by us – something the best in our eyes. The existence of the propositional subschema encoding this relationship – {*karīm* deserves RESPECT} – might be deduced from several samples of CEAP. For instance, in (65) ʕAntara Ibn Šaddād complains about mistreatment of *karīm* which is attempted by a *laʔīm* (i.e., non-*karīm*) person. Nevertheless, the poet states that *karīm* sometimes might be a subject of disrespect, what in his eyes, seems to be wrong. In (66), al-Aʕšà talks about the way he entertained his *karīm* companion. Since they were *karīm*, they deserved to be treated with the best wine. The respect, which should be paid to *karīm*, is also depicted in (67). Here, the poet urges his listeners to not hesitate to be grateful to *karīm*. Therefore, I believe, in some contexts, one can render LEAP *karīm* even as English *venerable*.

(65) فكم يشكو **كريمٌ** منْ لئيمٍ وكم يَلْقى هِجانٌ من هَجينِ
Thus, so often does an **honorable man** (*karīm*) complain because of a base one (*laʔīm*) – so often, does an honorable man meet [on his way] an ignoble one (cf. t21A:150).

(66) وَأدْكَنَ عَاتِقٍ، جَحْلٍ، سِبَحْلٍ، صبَحتُ بِراحِهِ شَرْباً **كِراما**
In the morning, I treat my **venerable** (*kirām*) drinking [companions] with a matured wine from a big, black wine-skin (cf. t28A:197).

(67) وَإنْ أوْلاكَ **ذو كَرَمٍ** جَمِيْلًا فكُنْ بالشُكْرِ مُنْطَلِقَ اللِسانِ
Thus, if a **man of honor** (*d̲ū karam*) brings upon you something nice, in your thanksgiving, do not withhold your tongue (cf. t37A:145).

The RESPECT and VENERATION were manifested at the best within the poetry, which played an immense role in the society of al-Ǧāhiliyya. Being praised in a panegyric – *madḥ* – was the highest possible distinction and esteem one could attain. Veneration of *karīm* in form of panegyrics and elegies is depicted, for instance, in the sample (68). Consequently, one could expect that this conceptualization would translate to the prohibition of shaming *karīm* people. Clearly, such a notion is implied, for instance, in (69), a passage attributed to Ḥātim aṭ-Ṭāʔī. Naturally, it must have resulted in avoidance of satirizing *karīm* folk, as it is plainly said in (70).

(68) قلّدْتُكَ الشِعرَ يا سَلامةَ ذا التَّفْضالِ، والشّيءُ حَيْثُما جُعِلا
وَالشِّعْرُ يَسْتَنْزِلُ **الكَريمَ** كمَا اسْتنزلَ رَعْدُ السَّحابةِ السَّبَلا
With [my poetry], I followed you, Salāma, a man of many virtues. And [this was the case], whenever something happened.
[Since] an **honorable man** (*karīm*) makes poetry descend in the same way a lightning bolt makes rain poor down (cf. t28A:234–5).

(69) وإنّي لَمَذْمومٌ، إذا قيلَ حاتِمٌ نبا نَبْوَةً ، إنّ **الكريمَ** يُعَنَّفُ
سأبى ، وتَأبَى بي أُصُولٌ **كريمَةٌ** وآباءُ صِدْقٍ، بالمَوَدّةِ ، شُرِّفوا
Truly, I am dishonored, when one talks about Ḥātim with disdain – truly, they are viciously disgracing an **honorable man** (*karīm*).
I will rebuff [these vile words] in the way the **noble** roots (*ʔuṣūl karīma*) rebuffed me. My sincere ancestors gain high social status (*šurrifū*) by their kindness, [not by birth] (cf. t19B:71).

(70) لِمَ أَمرْتُمْ عَبْداً ليهجُوَ قَوْمًا ظَالمِيهِمْ مِنْ غَيْرِ جُرْمٍ، **كِرَامَا**
Why did you make a slave satirize **honorable men** (*kirām*), harming them, though they did not harm you (cf. t28A:246–7)?

Obviously, since *karīm* deserves RESPECT, he deserves to attain *karāma*, as it is implied in the sample (71). As I mentioned earlier, *karāma* might be seen as the concept of HONOR-PAID, i.e., a treatment with honor and respect. Such a treatment is naturally perceived as what is paid to someone who is considered to be of HONOR (of any type). *Karīm* as a man who follows the honorable conduct deserves *karāma*.

(71) **وَكَريمٍ** نالَ الكَرامِةَ مِنّا وَلَئيمٍ ذي نَخوَةٍ قَد أَهَنّا
Thus, an **honorable man** (*karīm*) has received from us **a good treatment** (*karāma*), [i.e., he was honored by us], and [because of us], a base (*laʔīm*) self-magnifying man has cried (cf. t01χ).

Naturally, this does not mean that *karīm* was untouchable. In fact, as I mentioned, killing a *karīm* in the battle was considered a great reason of pride, what we saw in the sample (32). Yet another example of such conceptualization is (72), a verse by ʕAntara Ibn Šaddād.

(72) فَشَكَكتُ بِالرُمحِ الأَصَمِّ ثِيابَهُ لَيسَ **الكَريمُ** عَلى القَنا بِمُحَرَّمِ
Thus, I pierced his hard armor with my spear – it is not forbidden to [impale] an **honorable man** (*karīm*) onto a spear (cf. t21A:117–124).

In other words, *karīm* as metonymically referring to EXCELLENT- THE BEST inherently implied the concept of DESERVING RESPECT of others. The source for this metonymic mapping, I believe, is ultimately the category *karīm*-NOBLE-HONORABLE, which is also based on a metonymic extension accentuating a kind of EXCELLENCE OR GOODNESS of a person judged based on their behavior. Thus, perhaps, to bring out the whole conceptual path directing the extension of the category *karīm*, one should formulate it rather as *karīm*-NOBLE-HONORABLE-AS GOOD AS GENEROUS-HOSPITABLE. All in all, this metonymy follows the model CATEGORY FOR DEFINING PROPERTY OF THE CATEGORY (Radden & Kövecses 1999: 35), and it highlights the aforementioned propositions – IDEALITY OF CONDUCT and DESERVING RESPECT. In other words, using the lexeme *karīm*, while referring to someone, one uses the whole schema to call up only these two of its parts and to ascribe them to the referent.

4.4.2. Further metonymic extension of *karīm*: EXCELLENT said about OBJECT

Consequently, the category *karīm*-EXCELLENT-THE BEST (and by that DESERVING RESPECT) as applicable to people underwent further development evident in many contexts in CEAP. The lexeme *karīm* is used in them in reference to all kind of OBJECTS, not only people, such as animals, things, or phenomena, which could be considered of the EXCELLENT quality and thus, RESPECTED. In fact, one can see this metonymy as a generalization process, which resulted in extension of the category from denoting PEOPLE only to being used in reference to other kinds of OBJECTS. It foregrounds then the distinctiveness of an animal or a thing, by directing the focus onto the distinctiveness of *karīm* person as EXCELLENT-THE BEST of people. It implies also that a given OBJECT deserves in a way one's RESPECT OR ADMIRATION. Thus, a *karīm* horse is simply the best from among horses and it possesses special qualities, which are admired at horses – in the same way, a *karīm* man possesses qualities admired at people. As an example of linguistic elaboration of this metonymy, one can consider passages (73) and (74) attributed to ʕUrwa Ibn al-Ward, who pictured the excellence of a she-camel and a horse.

(73) يناقلن بالشُمْط **الكرام** أُولي القُوَى نِقابَ الحِجَازِ في السَّرِيح المُسَيَّرِ

Those white-lipped, **excellent** (*kirām*), strong [she-camels] carried us swiftly through the hilly roads of Ḥiǧāz (cf. t20A:38).

(74) كأني حِصانٌ مالَ عَنْهُ جِلالُهُ أغَرُّ، **كريمٌ**، حَوْلَهُ العُوذُ، راتِعُ

(...) as if I were a horse, from which an overlay slipped, [a horse, which is] noble (ʔaġarr), **excellent** (*karīm*); [which is] surrounded by young mares; [which] eat what pleases it (cf. t20A:49).

Other instances of the metonymy *karīm* FOR EXCELLENT- THE BEST conceptualize the concepts somehow linked to the category *karīm*-GENEROUS-HOSPITABLE. In two samples – (75) and (76) – *karīm* is used to reference to hospitality or food offered in generosity. Here, the foregrounded information links to the GENEROSITY of a *karīm* man. Thus, the hospitality is THE BEST, EXCELLENT when it is conceptualized as hospitality enacted by a *karīm*. Such a conceptualization, I think, is expressed, for instance, in the verse (77) attributed to ʕAntara Ibn Šaddād. Perhaps, even more accurately, the HOSPITALITY of *karīm* is perceived simply as proper or decent – the only appropriate way of hosting someone. It could lead us to a conclusion that these two textual metonymies – from (75) and (76) – are more of elaborations of a special instance of *karīm* FOR EXCELLENT-THE BEST, i.e., they are surface manifestations of the metonymy *karīm* HOSPITALITY FOR HOSPITALITY OFFERED BY *karīm* TO *karīm*.

(75) فمَنْ يأتِنَا أوْ يَلْقَنا عنْ جنايَةٍ يجِدْ عندنا مَثوى **كريماً**، ومَوْئِلا
نُجِيرُ، فلا يخْشى البوادِرَ جارُنا، ولاقَى الغِنى في دُوْرِنا، فتمَوّلا

A man, who comes to us or meets us, [fleeing] from a wrongdoer, [always] finds at us a **decent, kind** (*karīm*) dwelling and a shelter.
We give protection [to people], and our protégé does not worry about [our] rebuke – he finds profusion in our abodes, so he prospers (cf. t38A:255).

(76) ولقد أبِيتُ على الطوَى وأظَلُّهُ حتى أنالَ بهِ **كريمَ** المَأكَلِ

I will stay sleeping on the mat, waiting until I was given from him the **decent** food (*karīm al-maʔakal*) (cf. t21A:97–98).

(77) أَثْوَى ثَواءَ **كَرِيمٍ**، ثُمّ مَتَّعَنِي يومَ العَرُوبَةِ إذْ وَدَّعْتُ أصْحابا

He hosted [me] in way [only] an **honorable man** (*karīm*) can host [others]. Later, on Friday, he entertained me, after I paid my companions a farewell (cf. t28A:365).

Moreover, possibly, we can consider the phrase *laḥm karīm* "the best sort of meat" from (78), attributed to Taʔabbaṭa Šarran, as an elaboration of a derivative from this special conceptual metonymy, realized in (75) and (76). The phrase could then be explicated as "the meat, which is as good as the meat offered by a generous *karīm*". Of course, in (78), the poet talks about his corpse after his death in a battle – therefore, I think yet another conceptualization – {*karīm* is a brave, skillful warrior} – might be here at play as well.

(78) وَإِنْ تَقَعِ النُّسُورُ عَلَيَّ يَوماً فَلَحْمُ الْمُعْتَفى **لَحْمٌ كَرِيمُ**

Thus, when the vultures descended one day upon my [death body], they will find meat worth [their descending], **the best sort of meat** (*laḥm karīm*) (cf. t03A:201–204).

I believe that the metonymy *karīm* FOR EXCELLENT-THE BEST is instantiated also in the concept of *karīma* "the best possession, what is the best in one's possession", which occurs in (79), a verse attributed to al-Ḫansāʔ. I propose to interpret it as resulting from an ellipsis of *ʔašyāʔ karīma* "the best things". Clearly, it derives then from this metonymy.

(79) آبي الهَضِيمةِ آتٍ بالعَظيمةِ مِتْلافُ **الكريمةِ** لا نِكْسٌ ولا وانِ

He was a man who objected any wickedness; who was bringing in greatness [to his people]; who possessed the **best property** (*karīma*). He was not a coward or a weakling (cf. t33A:111).

Similarly to the metonymy expressed in (78), in several instances in CEAP, the metonymy *karīm* FOR EXCELLENT-THE BEST is elaborated in the form of a link additionally calling up the conceptualization {*karīm* is a brave, skillful warrior}. All textual instantiations of such a subtype of this metonymy appear in three verses attributed to Labīd ibn Rabīʕa: (80), (81), and (82). The poet uses in them the lexeme *karīm* to refer to attribute a battle (cf. (80) and (81)) or a spear (cf. (82)). I believe that these three textual metonymies could be interpreted as an elaboration of the conceptualization, which connects to at least three elements of the role schema *karīm*. It links to the metonymy *karīm* FOR EXCELLENT-THE BEST (and thus DESERVING RESPECT), by pointing towards the great deal of IMPORTANCE of events (i.e., battles) and tools (i.e., weapons) for the people who can derive from them their claim of *karam*-NOBILITY-HONORABILITY and the consequent RIGHT TO RESPECT. Moreover, it also links the aforementioned proposition {*karīm* is a brave, skillful warrior}, since it highlights the association between those events and tools and the *karīm* people, who prove to be brave, skillful warriors during a battle and using a weapon. In other words, a battle was *karīm*, i.e., it was EXCELLENT, because it proved the *karam*-NOBILITY-EXCELLENCE and the RIGHT TO RESPECT of those, who bravely fought it. Thus, perhaps, one can even argue that what we observe here is rather a separate conceptual phenomenon, which might be found in many languages. For instance, in English, there is the phrase *a lucky day*, in which the attribute *lucky* conceptually links to the concept of a person who was lucky on that day. Ergo, a *karīm* battle was a battle, during which one manifested his *karam*, and a *karīm* sword, a sword one used to prove he is *karīm*. In English, I think, a similar attribution of at least a battle or a combat one can express by the adjective *glorious*. Again, *a glorious battle* conceptually links to the glory of people, who fought it. All in all, perhaps more accurately, one should consider these metonymical models in terms of conceptual integration (i.e., a blend).[8]

(80) تلاقَتْهُمُ من آلِ كعبٍ عِصابَةٌ لها مأْقِطٌ يَوْمَ الحفاظِ **كريمُ**
Thus, they were reached by a group of men from the clan Kaʕb, who on the day of the battle, won the **glorious** (*karīm*) **combat** (cf. t30A:196–197, t30B:181–183).

(81) منها حُوَيٌّ والذُّهابُ وَقَبْلَهُ **يَوْمٌ** بِبُرْقَةِ رَحْرَحَانَ **كريمُ**
(…) from among them [the battle] of Ḥuwayy wa-d̲-D̲uhāb, and before it, the **glorious** (*karīm*) **battels** of Burqa and Raḥraḥān (cf. t30B:157).

(82) وأعدَدْتُ مأثُوراً (…)
وأخْلَقَ محموداً نَجيحاً رَجيعُه وأسْمَرَ مَرْهُوباً **كريمَ المآزِقِ**
I made my ornate sword ready (…),
a smooth, admirable, swift-cutting [sword] and a spear – fear-spreading and **robust in fierce combats** (*karīm al-maʔāziq*) (cf. t30B:97).

Another example of the elaboration of *karīm* FOR EXCELLENT-THE BEST is its logical extension in form of *karam* FOR THE BEST QUALITY/GREATNESS/NOBILITY. Its linguistic manifestation one can find in (83) and perhaps in (49), both being verses attributed to Kaʕb Ibn Zuhayr. What is quite interesting, in (83), *karam* as a nominal head is supplemented with two (nominal) arguments – *nubuwwa* "prophecy" and *ǧudūd* "ancestors". Thus, it seems that the metonymy active in here has only one target – GREATNESS/NOBILITY – which might be difficult to render in English, since GREATNESS and NOBILITY are not the same concepts. I do not think rendering *karam* as simply "nobility" in this context is justified. It

8 For instance, to explain the utterance *That was Mark's lucky day*, one can postulate existence of a blend, in which there are two mental spaces – two events – (1) a day, in which some events were taking place, and (2) an attribution, in which Mark was described as *lucky*. The integrated space affording the blend would be the fact that (2) was performed based on the knowledge of (1). The blend *lucky day* would inherit from (2) the attribution (i.e., *lucky*), and from (1) the denotation of the whole event (i.e., *day*), which could be seen as a metonymy WHOLE-FOR-PART (since only certain subevents – situations on that day – were the basis for the attribution in (2). In a similar manner, one can explain the use of *lucky* applied to different kinds of objects – instruments employed in events – which could result in similar attribution as (2). In such instances, *lucky* used in reference to these objects would be an example of PART-FOR-WHOLE metonymy, in which the major instrument of an event (i.e., its active-zone, cf. Radden & Kövecses 1999: 31) stands for the whole event.

would translate *karam an-nubuwwa* as "nobility of [His] Prophecy", which I do not find the most accurate, since NOBILITY encompasses chiefly the quality of being distinguished by a rank/a title or moral excellency (cf. OD: 450).[9]

(83) مَسَحَ النَبْيُّ جَبِينَهُ فَلَه بَياضٌ بالخُدودْ
وبِوَجْهِهِ دِيبَاجةٌ كَرمُ النُّبوةِ والجُدُودْ
The Prophet rubbed his forehead. His cheeks are white,
and on His face, [you can see] the skin-beauty, the **greatness** (*karam*) of His Prophecy and [(nobility) of His] ancestors (cf. t34B:18).

4.4.3. *Karam* and nobility – a complicated relationship

The aforementioned metonymy is a good example of a close relationship of the concepts of EXCELLENCY and NOBILITY in the context of *karam*. As I mentioned, this relationship in the context of LEAP should be considered on its own terms. Someone termed as *karīm* was *noble* in the sense of NOBILITY-HONORABILITY, i.e., certain EXCELLENT-NOBLE conduct. Nevertheless, *karam*-BEING *karīm* is also closely related to the concept of NOBLE DESCENT, NOBILITY in terms of one's origin. I discuss this relationship in detail in the section 6.4. in the chapter on *šaraf*.

In CEAP, the lexeme *karīm* is frequently used as an attribute of an aristocrat – a noble by birth – a tribal lord, or chief. It can be seen in such samples as (60), (84), (85), and (86). In the last verse – (86), attributed to ʕAntara Ibn Šaddād, the ARISTOCRACY is implied by the metaphor *šumūs* "suns" that will be discussed further in Chapter 6.

(84) وأبْنَاؤهُ بِيضٌ كِرَامٌ نَمَى بهم إلى السُّورة العُلْيا أبٌ غيرُ تَوْءَمِ
His ancestors were white **noble** (*kirām*) [aristocrats], by whom [his] father, who had no equal, was elevated towards the highest ranks (*as-sūra al-ʕulyā*) [among people] (cf. t39A:89–90).

(85) فأصبحتُ ذا مالٍ كثيرٍ وعادني بَنُونَ كِرامٌ سادةٌ لِمُسَوَّدِ
Thus, I accrued significant wealth, and **noble** (*kirām*) lords, [sons] of lords, kept paying me visits (cf. t07A:53).

(86) من القَومِ الكِرام وهُم شمُوسٌ ولَكِنْ لا تُوارى بالدُجون
[He descends] from **noble people** (*kirām*), who are [like] Suns – but [the Suns], which are never blocked by thick clouds (cf. t21A:149–150).

9 On the other hand, the second argument – *ǧudūd* "ancestors" – could be govern by the noun *karam*-GREATNESS, since nobility of one's ancestry might be perceived as their greatness, i.e., excellency and distinctiveness. In my translation of (92), I chose the lexeme *greatness* to encompass both English concepts – NOBILITY and GREATNESS.

Moreover, this collocation seems to govern yet another mode of use of the lexeme *karīm*, which was a honorific title. In some places in CEAP, *karīm* does not seem to refer to a particular actual property, but it calls up the schema of RESPECT, by linking to the conceptualization {*karīm* deserves RESPECT}. This means, that in some context, *karīm* could be translated as "respected", "venerated", or simply "honorable" – all meaning the same: DESERVING RESPECT of others. In fact, such a use of *karīm* in CEAP is quite prevalent, and we can see it, for instance, in (87) attributed to al-Aˁšà and (88) by ˁAntara Ibn Šaddād. In general, *karīm* as an honorific title in CEAP is used in reference to a man (cf. t21A:75–76; t30B:26–28; t06A:71; t16A:60), a king/tribal chief (cf. t28A:315; t21A:92; t11A:35), envoys (cf. t30B:26–28), ancestors (cf. t30B:199), a whole tribe (*ḥayy*) (cf. t17A:151–152), or even drinking companions (cf. the example (66)).

(87) وَصَحِبْنَا مِنْ آلِ جَفْنَةَ أمْلاكاً **كراماً** بالشّامِ ذاتِ الرّفيفِ

The **esteemed** (*kirām*) lords of the clan Ǧafna have accompanied me into the fertile, green [lands] of aš-Šām (cf. t28A:315).

(88) وقادُوني إلى مَلِكٍ **كريمٍ** رفيعٌ قَدْرُهُ في العِزّ راقي

They brought me in front of his majesty, **noble** (*karīm*) king [Munḏir] – [oh, how] enormous his power is, and how elevated he is by his strength (cf. t21A:92).

Furthermore, the lexeme *karīm* occurs in the context of ARISTOCRACY yet in another form, by being applied to someone's ORIGIN. As we saw in the sample (69), in LEAP, one's origin – their roots – could have been described as *karīm* – *ˀuṣūl karīma*. Such an attribution should be seen as indicating the EXCELLENCY of one's ORIGIN, which seems to translate into NOBILITY-NOBLE ORIGIN by far. One's origin implied their *nasab* – a lineage, which was something pre-Islamic Arabs jealously protected and highly esteemed. In fact, it was as an important part of one's pride, as their honorable deeds (ˁAlī 1993b: 292), what I will discuss in the section 7.7. in the chapter on *ˁirḍ*. Thus, the aforementioned attribution seems to point not only towards the EXCELLENCE of the ORIGIN, but also to the fact that this ORIGIN was an essential part of the RIGHT TO RESPECT. In other words, *karīm* lineage is EXCELLENT lineage that is to be RESPECTED, granting by that the RIGHT TO RESPECT to its owners.

Similarly, frequently in CEAP, a person could be described as being of noble ancestors – e.g., *karīm al-ǧadd* "of a noble forefather(s)". Perhaps, such an expression served to bring out the assumption that one of such an origin can mimic the *karam* of their noble predecessors. This conceptualization might be seen as derived from a hypothetical propositional schema {*karīm* people bring up *karīm* descendants}. Thus, *karīm*, so to say, derives his *karam*-BEING *karīm* form his lineage, as it could be observed in the samples (89) and (90). *Karīm* was then born *karīm* by *karīm* parents, as it is meant in (91), attributed to Ḥassān Ibn Ṯābit.

(89) لوْ كنتَ ضَنْءَ **كريمةٍ** أبْلَيْتَها حُسْنى ، ولكنْ ضنءَ بنتِ عُقابِ

If you had been born by a **noble woman** (*karīma*), you would have been able to overcome it – but you are an offspring of ʕUqāb (cf. t38A:30–31).

(90) (...) وكان **كريماً** ماجداً لِهجانِ

(...) and he was an **honorable** (*karīm*), glorious (*māǧid*) man due to his noble origin (cf. t21A:146).

(91) وَإنّ سَنَامَ المَجْدِ مِن آلِ هاشِمٍ بَنُو بنتِ مَخْزُومٍ، وَوَالدُكَ العَبْدُ
وما وَلَدَتْ أفْناءُ زُهْرَةَ مِنْكُمُ **كَرِيماً**، ولَمْ يَقرَبْ عَجائزَكَ المَجْدُ

Truly, the highest glory [was brought into the tribe Qurayš] by the clan of Hāšim, sons of Maḫzūm's daughter. Whereas you father was a slave!
Thus, none of your mixed-blooded [women] of the clan Zuhra have given birth to an **honorable man** (*karīm*). Nor had the glory ever approached your old men (cf. t38A:110).

Similarly, in LEAP, one could describe *karam* – BEING *karīm* – as something inheritable, as one can observe it in the sample (92).

(92) أنا ابْنُ الذي لَمْ يُخْزني في حَياتِهِ ولَمْ أُخْزِهِ حتّى تغيّبَ في الرَّجمْ
فأُعْطِيَ حتّى مات مالًا وهِمّةً ووَرَّثَنِي إذ ودّع المجدَ **والكَرَمْ**

I am a son of the one who has not ashamed me in his entire life, nor have I made him ashamed, before he disappeared beneath a gravestone.
Until his death, he was growing in wealth and ambition. When he was paying me farewell, he made me inherit the glory (*mağd*) and the **honor** (*karam*) (cf. t34A:137).

This could mean that one might have been somehow predisposed to *karam* due to their noble origin. Such a conceptualization seems to be still persistent in some Bedouin communities, like the one examined by Abu-Lughod (1986: 45). As she notices, in this community, "nobility of origin is believed to confer moral qualities and character", what I think seems easily corresponding to traits making one follow the code of BEHAVIOR OF *karīm*. These qualities seem to be inheritable for people of both that Bedouin society as well as al-Ǧāhiliyya. Abu-Lughod (1986: 87) stated that in fact origin – *ʔaṣl* – was so strongly associated with one's ability to act HONORABLY, that it was "the primary metaphor for virtue or honor".

Perhaps, in this light, we could also interpret the pre-Islamic Arabic fixation on the purity of their lineage. Since, *nasab*-LINEAGE was the foundation of the tribal *ʕaṣabiyya*, a spirit of solidarity (ʕAlī 1993b: 352), keeping it pure was a good strategy to guarantee maximum success in a situation requiring assistance. Purity of the lineage must have translated into the possession of many *karīm* relatives, who inherited their predisposition to *karam* after their *karīm* ancestors, and who – as *karīms* – were perfectly equipped with the qualities sought at people one needs to be supported by.

Thus, it could suggest that *karam* – BEING *karīm* – was stipulated by *karam*-EXCELLENCY of one's LINEAGE. Such a conceptualization might be found, for instance, in the sample (56), attributed to Ḥassān Ibn Ṯābit. The poet clearly differentiates in it between "brave juveniles", in whom satirized Ibn Hišām prided himself, and *ǧidd kirām* "noble ancestors", whom he lacked and, as a consequence, he was unable to perform *makārim*. It seems then as if the courage itself did not grant a man the status of *karīm*. A similar conceptualization is entrenched in (93), in which *karam*-BEING *karīm* supported, so to say, by noble lineage is depicted as better than that of a man without NOBLE-ARISTOCRATIC ancestors, what finds it support also in the historical literature (cf. ˁAlī 1993b: 559). (93) is especially interesting, since, I believe, one can find in it both central and metonymic meaning of the lexeme *karam*. Obviously, the first instance indicates that lineages of a man are pure, the best, excellent – and thus, his *karam* – in the second instance meaning HONORABILITY– might be evaluated as better, of more worth.

(93) لِلّه دَرُّ فَتًى أنسابُهُ **كَرَمٌ** يا حَبَّذا **كَرَمٌ** أضْحى له نَسَبا
To God be attributed the lineages of a young man, [which are] **the best** (*karam*). My dear, the brighter **honorability** (*karam*) is [supported] by a lineage (*nasab*) (cf. t37A:48).

In CEAP, the relation between NOBLE ORIGIN or *šaraf*-HIGH SOCIAL STATUS and *karam* looks mutual. For instance in (94), the HIGH SOCIAL STATUS of the poet is described as achieved by belonging to *karīm*-HONORABLE people. In other words, *karam*-BEING *karīm* is predisposed by a NOBLE LINEAGE, and the NOBLE LINEAGE – that is such one of HIGH SOCIAL STANDING – is established based on BEING *karīm*. Therefore, in contrast to what is implied in the passage (56), it seems that also people of no noble-aristocratic blood could be referred to as *karīm*. Such a case is definitely described by Ḥātim aṭ-Ṭāʔī in (69), quoted earlier. The poet admits that he did not have noble roots – *ʔuṣūl karīma* – nonetheless, his ancestors became *šarīfs*, noblemen, based on their *karam*.

(94) إنّي لَأُنمى إذا اِنتَمَيتُ إلى غُرٍّ **كِرامٍ** وَقَومُنا شَرَفُ
بيضٌ جِعادٌ كَأَنَّ أَعيُنَهُم يُكحِلُها في المَلاحِمِ السَدَفُ
Truly, I am ascending [in eminence] by being ascribed to the best **honorable people** (*kirām*), since our people, are [my] **high social position** (*šaraf*)
–[they are] white, generous, and their eyes spring [like early flowers] in an advent of [every] battle (t01χ).

Nevertheless, based on the sample (93), I believe we should acknowledge that although BEING *karīm* was not stipulated by nobility of one's origin per se, more esteem was enjoyed by *karīm* who was of noble blood. The nobility of blood seems to be only auxiliary in one's RIGHT TO RESPECT. This conceptualization is perfectly expressed in both, (95) – a passage attributed to al-Mutalammis, and (96) by ʕAntara Ibn Šaddād. Al-Mutalammis clearly states that he does not consider someone being *karīm*, if he does not behave like a *karīm*, in a noble way. Further, he adds that the sole noble origin[10] does not protect someone from dishonor – being a low and dispraised man – if he does not take care of the *ḥasab*, i.e., roughly speaking, a count of *makārim*, honorable deeds. It seems he says that a nobleman – *šarīf* – is expected to prove his nobility in his deeds (cf. Pitt-Rivers 1965: 23), and only after having done that, he can claim respect. In (95), the poet defended himself against supposed reproaches he was facing because of his low-born mother. Similarly, on many occasions, ʕAntara repels attacks on his HONOR, in which the attackers use as a main argument the slavehood (and being Black) of his mother. The poet, being of impure blood himself, openly states in (96) that HONOR-RIGHT TO RESPECT is first and foremost acquired by one's *karam* (here, bravery) not merely by his noble ancestry.

(95) يُعيّرُني أمِّي رِجالٌ ولا أرى **أخا كَرَمٍ** إلّا بِأَن **يتَكَرَّما**
وَمَن كانَ ذا **عِرضٍكَريمٍ** فَلم يَصُن لَهُ حَسَباً كانَ اللَئيمَ المُذَمَّما

[There are] men, who disgrace me [because of] my mother [and her base origin]. I do not consider someone **being honorable** (*ʔaẖū karam*), if he does not **behave in an honorable way** (*yatakarram*).

The one, who is of **noble origin** (*ʕirḍ karīm*), and because of that he doesn't care about [his] merits (*ḥasab*), is a low (*laʔīm*) and dispraised man (cf. t10A:16).

(96) فأَما القائلونَ هِزَبْرُ قومٍ فَذَاكَ الفَخرُ لا **شَرَفُ** الجُدود

And when they say: [this one is] a lion of [his] people – it is [a matter] of pride, and not of **high social standing** of [his] ancestors (cf. t21A:44).

In the context of one's social status, the only stipulation absolutely imposed on being recognized as *karīm* is being free, i.e., non-slave. It seems – as we know from the history of ʕAntara – one could be a freed slave and enjoy respect, but – as it is implied in the example (44), quoted above – a slave rather could not be described as *karīm*. This, of course, derives from the broader cultural model of social strata functioning in the pre-Islamic Arabic society, in which the most important division is placed between free and enslaved people (cf. ʕAlīl: 262).

---

10 In (95), al-Mutalammis uses lexeme *ʕirḍ*, meaning here metonymically *nasab* "lineage". This matter will be elaborated further in Chapter 7 (cf. section 7.2.3.). Conceptualizations of *ḥasab* are presented in Chapter 5.

As we can observed in the sample (97) – a verse attributed to al-Aʕšà – the quality of *karīm* might be derived not only from the direct ancestors, but also in a broader sense from one's people – their tribe. This stems from the conviction that in fact a whole tribe is a family, and all its members trace back their lineage to a single ancestor (ʕAlī 1993b: 314). Sometimes, though, such derivation of the quality of *karam* is restricted to one's *bayt* "abode" meaning either tent – in the context of nomadic tribes – or house – in the context of sedentary people. The concept of HOUSE as a social unit is quite widespread metonymy found in many languages – also in Semitics. In Arabic society of al-Ǧāhiliyya, similarly to the modern Bedouin communities (cf. Abou-Zeid 1965: 253), *bayt*-HOUSE is a nuclear social unit, from which a man derived much of his HONOR-RIGHT TO RESPECT. Thus, it was also the source of a man's quality of being *karīm*, as it is meant by Abū Ṭālib in (98).

(97) **كَرِيماً** شَمَائِلُهُ مِنْ بَنِي مُعَاوِيَةَ **الأكْرَمِينَ** السُّنَنْ

[I met] an **honorable man** (*karīm*), [who derives] his tempers from [the clan of] Banū Muʕāwiya, [from the people] of the most **noble** (*ʔakramina*) traits (cf. t28A:19).

(98) أبْكى العُيُونَ وأذْرى دَمْعَها دِرَراً مُصابُ شَيْبَةَ **بيتِ** الدينِ **والكرَمِ**

كانَ الشجاعَ الجَوادَ الفَرْدَ سُؤْدَدُهُ لهُ فضائلُ تَعْلُو سادةَ الأمَمِ

The one, who was affected by the death of Šayba, cries out his eyes with heavy tears – [by the death of the man] from the **house** (*bayt*) of [custom] obedience (*dīn*) and **honorability** (*karam*).

He was brave, generous, and unique in [his] highest value. He had virtues ascending [to the level of virtues of] lords of nations (cf. t24A:89).

A bit different situation is described in (99), a verse attributed to Ḥassān Ibn Ṯābit. Here, the poet claims that attachment to *karīm* people also results in acquiring the quality of being *karīm*. By attachment, he means sticking to someone – perhaps, a more or less official relationship of protection. Therefore, it seems that becoming a protégé or client of someone was having the same effect as being biologically related to that person.

(99) والْزِمْ مُجالَسةَ **الكرامِ** وفِعْلِهِمْ، وإذا اتَّبَعْتَ فأبْصِرَنْ مَنْ تَتْبَعُ

Do adhere to the company of **honorable men** (*kirām*) and to their [way of] acting. If you [chose to] follow someone, [always] look at the one, whom you follow (cf. t38A:184).

I think we could hypothesize that such a conceptualization is an example of non-linguistic conceptual metonymy. Its source domain would be then the FAMILY or LINEAGE-BASED RELATIONSHIP, whereas its target would consist of the CLIENT-PATRON RELATIONSHIP. In other words, pre-Islamic Arabs considered such protection ties in the same terms as blood affinity. This client-patron relationship – in Arabic, *ǧiwār* – was in fact a very important part of social system of Arabs of al-Ǧāhiliyya, and its gravity is well described by historians (cf. ʕAlī 1993b: 360–371). The non-linguistic metonymy *ǧiwār*-RELATIONSHIP FOR LINEAGE-BASED RELATIONSHIP might be considered as a formal representation of this knowledge.[11] This conceptualization, however, is by no means purely pre-Islamic conception. As reported by Abu-Lughod (1986: 59–60) the client-patron relationship was perceived as mimicking the linage-based one also in the community of Bedouin studied by her in 80' of the last century. This perception was manifested in their speech, in which they referred to such a relationship as *garaba min l-galb*, i.e., "kinship from the heart". This suggests that *ǧiwār* was seen by those people as a voluntary kinship, kinship of choice. What is quite significant, many times, they tried to justify the existence of this relationship by reference to real or presupposed common ancestors, from whom both the client and the patron descend (Abu-Lughod 1986: 60). This further suggests that such a relationship was perceived in the simile to LINEAGE-based one.

Thus, I believe, it was possible to suggest – as Ḥassān Ibn Ṯābit did in (99) – that becoming a protégé or simply a companion[12] of *karīm* people could make someone *karīm*. Perhaps, a kind of further linguistic extension of the aforementioned conceptualization could be the metaphor BEING A MEMBER IS BEING A BROTHER, in which MEMBERSHIP is conceptualized by the concept of BEING A BROTHER of something (cf. Danecki 2012b: 59). Thus, *ʔaḫū tamīm* meaning "a brother of [the tribe] Tamīm" corresponds to the meaning "a member of [the tribe] Tamīm" (Danecki 2012b: 59). As noted by Danecki (2012b: 59), a further elaboration of this metaphor structures also the conceptualization of QUALITIES ascribed to someone. As we saw in (82), the expression *ʔaḫū karam*, "lit. a brother of *karam*" meant simply "[a man] of *karam*". Such an elaboration would require yet a metonymic model being at play: QUALITY FOR PEOPLE HAVING THIS QUALITY. In other words, the metaphoric use of *ʔaḫ* "brother" in the sense of "someone of a certain quality" derives from the original metaphor BEING A

11 Another elaboration of this non-linguistic metonymy might be also the custom of *istiḥlāq* (cf. ʕAlī 1993b: 357–359). I believe that a further argument in favor of existence of this metonymy is the fact that frequently, tribes, which were tied by the means of the *istiḥlāq* or even an alliance, eventually merged into one organism, which developed its new lineage bringing together lineages of the two formerly independent tribes. It was such a common phenomenon that scholars hypothesize that in fact the names of some of presumed ancestors of bigger tribes might have been originally names of alliances (ʕAlī 1993b: 385).

12 The companionship could be understood as a possible elaboration of the category *ǧiwār*-RELATIONSHIP.

MEMBER IS BEING A BROTHER, and conceptualizes the QUALITY as possessed by a collective of people. Another example of a linguistic elaboration of this metaphorical mapping is the phrase *ʔaḫū ṯiqa* "a trustworthy [man]" also found in the CEAP (cf. t28A:14–19; t22A:55–59).

Consequently, becoming a protégé of a *karīm* man could also be a mean of acquiring *šaraf*-HIGH SOCIAL STANDING, since *karam* was what leads to it at the first place. This proposition might be found, for instance, in (100), a verse by Ḥātim aṭ-Ṭāʔī. The poet encourages one to enter the client-patron relationship with *karīm*, since in this way one can use his resources to become *karīm* himself. At the end of the verse, the poet mentions that in such a way one can climb a ladder, which links to the conceptual metaphor SOCIAL STATUS IS A POSITION ON A LADDER together with *šaraf* IS ELEVATED PLACE I will discuss in Chapter 6.

(100) فجاوِرْ **كريماً**، واقتدِحْ مِن زِنادهِ وأسْنِدْ إليهِ، إنْ تَطاوَلَ، سُلّمَا

Do attach yourself as a client-neighbor (*ǧāwir*) to an **honorable man** (*karīm*). [Try] to light [the fire] using his wood-fire. Do relay on him, [while climbing the social ladder], if his ladder is tall enough (cf. t19B:81).

4.5. Other cultural conceptualizations of *karam*

The lexeme *karam*, as a verbal noun derived from the verb *karuma* "to be *karīm*", served as a general name denoting the role schema BEING *karīm*, i.e., NOBLE-HONORABLE, but also – by means of metonymy – EXCELLENT-and-DESERVING RESPECT. In other words, it referred to "compliance with the traditional patterns of behavior (Abou-Zeid 1965: 258)," being a certain CONDUCT: HONORABLE BEHAVIOR. Accordingly, we can propose to equate it with such English concepts as HONORABILITY or HONORABLENESS. This means, however, that it falls in the proximity of the concept of (HONOR)-VIRTUE. Therefore, *karīm* might be also seen as pertaining to the notion of VIRTUOUS MAN. In this sense, *karam* can be understood as realization of culturally defined ideals, and the figure of *karīm* will then be "the ideal type of man (Peristiany 1965: 10)".

The data from the CEAP suggest that the value of *karam* was gradable – men could be more or less *karīm*, as it is implied in the samples (101) or quoted above (60). The graduality of *karam*, I believe, should be interpreted more as the fact that it constituted a spectrum of certain qualities and actions. Thus, *karīm* performed more or less of *makārim* – noble deeds of honor – and as a result might have been perceived as more or less noble-honorable. Consequently, *karīm* could also violate the code of honorable conduct – as it is meant in (50), quoted before. In this passage, we can see that *karam* is something, which might be acquired also by someone who was not considered *karīm* – by *laʔīm*. This conceptualization brings out clearly the proximity of *karam* and VIRTUE. Moreover, Ḥātim aṭ-Ṭāʔī also states that clemency toward *karīm* who erred might bring him back to following the code of honor.

(101) وكَمْ مِنْ مَقَامٍ قَدْ شَهِدْنَا بِخُطَّةٍ نَشُجُّ ونَأْسُو، أَو **كَرِيمٍ** نُفَاضِلُهْ
We have seen so many of places in such a [bad] condition [that we had] to sew and heal [their wounds]. [How many of] **honorable men** (*karīm*) have we met, whom we excel in virtue (cf. t36A:180).

4.5.1. The image-schematic model of *karam*

In general, the most frequently reoccurring conceptualization of *karam* in CEAP is that in form of the image- schema OBJECT. Predominantly, such a *karam*-OBJECT was depicted as POSSESSED by someone – namely, by *karīm*. In other words, BEING *karīm* was conceptualized as POSSESSING *karam*. In most cases, the POSSESSION was expressed by the use of the lexeme *ḏū* "possessor, owner (cf. Wright 1896: 265)", as it is, e.g., in the sample (67), quoted earlier. As one can see, the POSSESSION of a certain script (here, *karam*-BEING *karīm*) was perceived as following it. A similar conceptualization might be found in CEAP at least in the case of OBEYING, FOLLOWING *dīn*-CUSTOMS (cf. t38B:199–200), which might be also expressed in the terms of POSSESSION (OBEYING, FOLLOWING *dīn*-CUSTOMS IS POSSESSING/BEING *ḏū*-POSSESSOR OF *dīn*). It could suggest that in fact in LEAP, one could find a more general metaphor ADHERING TO/FOLLOWING A SCRIPT IS POSSESSING/BEING *ḏū*-POSSESSOR OF THIS SCRIPT.[13]

Alternatively, *karam*, BEING *karīm*, was conceptualized as an OBJECT IS INSIDE SOMEONE, as in the example (102), a verse attributed to al-Ḫansāʔ.

(102) مَاذَا تضمَّنَ مِنْ جُودٍ وَمِنْ **كَرَمٍ** وَمِنْ خلائقَ مَا فيهِنَّ مُقْتَضَبُ
How much of generosity, **honorability** (*karam*), and [good] dispositions did [Ṣaḫr] contain in himself – [how much of those virtues], from which we are now separated (cf. t33A:17–18)!

This metaphor seems to be an elaboration of more general BEING OF A TRAIT/QUALITY IS HAVING THE TRAIT/QUALITY INSIDE, and on its turn, it can be considered an elaboration of even more general mapping in form of BEING ENDOWED WITH QUALITY/ TRAIT IS POSSESSING THIS QUALITY/ TRAIT.[14] In fact, more

13 Similar metaphor might be found in Polish, as in *On ma zasady* (roughly, "He sticks to principles", lit. "He has rules") or English *She has good manners* (meaning, "She adheres to the manners of proper conduct").

14 This LEAP metaphor corresponds with a fairly universal metaphor BEING OF A TRAIT/QUALITY IS HAVING THIS TRAIT/QUALITY, which seems to be functioning in many

frequently in LEAP, the lexeme *ḏū* served as the major mean of elaboration of exactly this general metaphor. As a consequence, it could suggest that perhaps, *karam* might have been perceived also as a QUALITY or a TRAIT of one's character, which enabled them to ADHERE to the script of the behavior of *karīm*. This, however, brings us very close to the notion of *murūʔa* and its relationship with *karam*.

4.5.2. *Karam* and *murūʔa*[15]

Even though CAD do not claim any relationship between the concepts of *karam* and *murūʔa* (cf. LsA1: 186; KtA1: 130; AsS: 1070), we could find some common elements they share. In fact, many historians depict *murūʔa* as the collection of the aforementioned noble traits of *sayyid* (cf. ʕAlī 1993b: 574), what would mean that *murūʔa* and *karam* were at least synonymous.

In general, in CAD, *murūʔa* is defined as "the perfection of manliness" (KtA1: 130) or "humanity" (*ʔinsāniyya*) – perhaps, a kind of virtue or morality, which makes us act appropriately, in accordance with a customary code of conduct (cf. LsA1: 186; AsS: 1070), or even acting in a way suitable for a human being (cf. LsA1: 186).

All these explications and additional evidence on the notion of *murūʔa* (or *muruwwa*) have been examined in several studies by modern Arabic philologists, such as Ignaz Goldziher (1888), Bichr Farès (1932), Charles Pellat (1983), and recently by Salah Natij (2017; 2018) and Jakub Sławek (2011). This shows how difficult it is to determine the actual content of this concept. As noted by Pellat, it might be so because of the long evolution of *murūʔa* being a certain virtue first of al-Ǧāhiliyya and then of the Islamic morality. Consequently, the meaning of it differed throughout the time (Pellat 1983: 2).

Goldziher (1888: 13) stated that "[b]y *muruwwa* the Arab understands all those virtues rooted in the traditions of his people that make up the glory of each individual and of the tribe, to which he belongs." Consequently, he saw these virtues as constituting the set of requirements as for the leader of a community. Following Farès, Pellat (1983: 4–5) criticized Goldziher for narrowing in such a

---

conceptual systems around the world. A linguistic elaboration of this metaphor is, for instance, the English phrase *He has a lot of intelligence*, or Polish *Ona nie ma cierpliwości* ("She has no patience"). In both cases, possession of a quality – intelligence or patience – implies being of that quality – being intelligent or patient.

15 I would like to thank prof. Janusz Danecki, the reviewer of my Ph.D. thesis, for providing me with important comments as for my understanding of the concept of *murūʔa*.

wat the notion of *murūʔa*, pointing towards the fact that its original, pre-Islamic meaning was modified and adjusted to Islamic morals (Pellat 1983: 11, 15).

It seems that *murūʔa* was an umbrella term for all attitudes, abilities, and skills, which "according to the Arabic tradition, one must possess so as to be considered a man of honor (Sławek 2011: 88)." More precisely, however, it occurs to have pertained to this aspect of one's concern for honor known as *masculinity honor* – "a concern for being able to live up to the standards set for males (e.g., being tough, able to take care of one's family, produce offspring (Osh et al. 2013: 335))." Therefore, Pellat (1983: 15) noted that it did not refer only to personal qualities of character traits, but it also encompassed a notion of ability to provide livelihood for oneself and their dependents, as well as lawful behavior (*ʕafāf*), loyalty to whom one pledged to protect, or vengeance (*ʔaḫḏ aṯ-ṯaʔr*). It means that the lexeme *murūʔa* referred to a complex cultural schema encoding the knowledge of who is a successful – perfect – male. This also seems to fit the definition provided in KtA: *murūʔa* was "the perfection of manliness (KtA1: 130)". Such perfection also entailed possession of praise-worthy qualities or character traits, enlisted by Pellat (1983: 15) as loyalty, bravery, generosity, sincerity, sense of shame (*ḥayāʔ*), confidence, endurance (*ṣabr*), intelligence, sharpness of mind, eloquence, and the aforementioned *ḥilm*. After the development of Islamic morality, the meaning of *murūʔa* was narrowed only to encompass the set of personal qualities (Pellat 1983: 16). By that it was transformed into a collection of virtues or even a script of spiritual attitude – morality or even asceticism (Sławek 2011: 89).

The aforementioned findings were based on the later Muslim tradition that passed the meaning of *murūʔa* from early Islam up to the modern time. Nowadays, similarly to the understanding of Islamic scholars, this term seems to refer to a collection of DISPOSITIONS/TRAITS/QUALITIES (conceptualized by the image-schema MASS) that make someone obey a code of decent behavior. One can observe it, for instance, in this fragment of *Mawt Ṣaġīra* (*A small death*) by Muḥammad Ḥasan ʕAlwān:

> يتكلمون بالخليع من القول ويمارسون الشنيع من الفعل وقد ذهب حياءهم وقلّت **مروءتهم**
> They were talking in foul speech and practicing abhorrent actions, [since] their sense of shame (*ḥayāʔ*) had gone and **their manliness** (*murūʔa*) had dwindled (ʕAlwān 2017: 458).

Although Pellat – following Farès – assumed that *murūʔa* was a broader schema for a perfect man, it is quite difficult to find its traces in CEAP – yet it is not entirely impossible. CEAP contains only 7 contexts, in which this lexeme occurs, what makes any results as for the original understanding of *murūʔa* highly inconclusive. Some of these contexts – such as the samples (103) and (104) – suggest that *murūʔa* is a collection of some admired QUALITIES, which is conceptualized in the simile to the modern conception in terms of the image-schema MASS. This collection – as in (103) – is related somehow to HONOR/HONORABILITY (here, by the concept of *mağd*-GLORY).

(103) أَبَنِي الحِماس أليسَ منكمْ ماجدٌ، إنّ **المُروءةَ** في الحِماس قلِيلُ

Banū al-Ḥimās, is there any glorious man (*māğid*) among you? Truly, there is so little **manliness** (*murūʔa*) among [the clan of Banū] al-Ḥimās (cf. t38B:210).

(104) أَيَّتُها النَفسُ اِجْمِلي جَزَعا إنّ الَّذي تَحذَرينَ قَد وَقَعا
إنَّ الَّذي جَمَّعَ **المُروءَةَ** وَالنَجدَةَ وَالبِرَّ وَالتُقى جُمَعا

My soul, persist and refuse to lose [your] endurance, since truly the man, for whom you had been caring, has died!
Truly, [he was] a man, who collected [in himself] all of **manliness** (*murūʔa*), bravery, kindness, and piety (cf. t14A:93–94).

In other instances, such as (105) and (106), *murūʔa* is depicted as a certain broader QUALITY, rather an inner one, i.e., a CHARACTER TRAIT, that makes someone behave in a particular way I interpret as simply being *karīm*-HONORABLE. This conceptualization seems similar to the one discernible in (103). Furthermore, as in (107), such a *murūʔa* is clearly depicted as a quality or a collection of qualities that makes one a good candidate for a tribal leader – despite of their poverty. This contradict clearly Pellat's critics of Goldziher's understanding of this notion.

(105) وكَم فينا إذا ما المَحْلُ أبْدى نُحاسَ القومِ من سَمْحٍ هَضُومِ
يُبَاري الريحَ لَيس بِجانَبِيٍّ وَلا دَفِنٍ **مُرُوءَتُهُ**، لئيمِ

Thus, when a drought, which manifest traits of people's characters, [comes], [you will find] among us so many liberal and generous [men],
[who] face the [freezing] wind, and do not turn away from their people; [who] neither are men of hidden **manliness** (*murūʔa*), nor of ignobility (*laʔīm*) (cf. t30B:186–187).

(106) وَذَلّ سُمَيْرٌ عَنْوَةً جَارَ مالِكٍ على رَغْمِهِ بَعْدَ التَخَمُّطِ والجَهْلِ
وَجاءَ ابْنُ عَجْلانٍ بِعِلْجٍ مُجَدَّعٍ، فأدْبَرَ مَنقوصَ **المُروءَةِ** والعَقْلِ

Sumayr humiliated by force the surprised protégé of Mālik that was so swaggering [in his] ignorance.
So, [Mālik] Ibn ʕAğlān arrived with a strong warrior of mutilated nose, leaving behind [that protégé, who] lacked **manliness** (*murūʔa*) and sound judgement (cf. t38B:190).

(107) نُسَوِّدُ ذا المالِ القليلِ، إذا بَدَتْ **مُرُوءَتُهُ** فينا، وإن كانَ مُعْدِما

For our chief, we [do sometimes] elect a man of little wealth, whose **manliness** (*murūʔa*) manifest among us – even if he was utterly impoverished (cf. t38B:219).

Nevertheless, in one context, *murūʔa* is listed among element of someone's value. This context – (108), attributed to Ḥassān Ibn Ṯābit – repeats words uttered by a woman, whose heart the poet tried to win. One can argue that this verse describes a perfect match as someone who is handsome, intelligent, well-born, and of *murūʔa*. Here, this notion might indicate – I believe – certain resourcefulness, "liv[ing] up to the standards set up for males (Osh et al. 2013: 335)," what can be seen as corresponding to Pellat's definition.

(108) أما الوَسامةُ و**المروءةُ**، أوْ رَأيُ الرّجالِ فقدْ بدا – حَسْبي
فودَدتُ أنّكَ لوْ تخبِرُنا منْ والداكَ، ومَنْصِبُ الشعبِ
When it comes to the handsomeness, **the manliness** (*murūʔa*), or the sound judgement of men – these are evident. They suffice me.
Thus, I would like you to tell us about your parents are and the roots of your people (cf. t38B:31–2).

All in all, the scarcity of CEAP data makes it difficult to confirm or disprove Pellat's understanding of *murūʔa*. It seems safe to assume that this notion was simply a cultural schema for a perfect man (or better: male) – an ideal – who was able to achieve certain thing in his life. From among those things – what is the most important for my study – was a certain mode of behavior. Pellat (1983: 15) termed this mode of behavior as *ʕafāf* that is the verbal noun denoting the action of abstaining from unlawful conduct (Lane 1968e: 2088). It is well discernible also today – as in the aforementioned quotation form ʕAlwān. In this passage, people behaved in an unlawful way, because their *murūʔa* dwindled, i.e., there was too little of it to hold them back from transgressions. In other words, the decent or proper behavior expected from a man was possible because the man was of *murūʔa*.

I would risk saying this mode of proper behavior can be actually quite close to the cultural schema of BEING *karīm*. It means then that *murūʔa* as certain ability was responsible for one's noble/honorable conduct. Thus, without it one did not act in the way allowing others to call him *karīm*. Consequently, however, as it was claimed throughout the history of Arabic scholarship, *murūʔa* was something that made a man a good candidate for a tribal leader, whose trait were summarized by al-Ǧāḥiẓ in the form of the six honorable qualities I discussed earlier. As noted by Sławek (2011: 88), *murūʔa* was then the condition *sine qua non* of being a man of honor, i.e., *karīm*-NOBLE-HONORABLE one. It was yet only a potentiality of HONORABILITY. This is quite well implied in the aforementioned sample (105) attributed to Labīd Ibn Rabīʕa, in the phrase *dafin al-murūʔa* "[a man] of hidden *murūʔa*". The PREDISPOSITION to *karam*-BEING *karīm* could have been only presupposed, claimed, yet not manifested in one's action. Thus, what is quite important, in (105), the poet placed "hidden *murūʔa*" side by side with being *laʔīm*, i.e., non-*karīm*.

Murūʔa is interesting also from a comparative point of view. It pertained obviously to the noun *marʔ* "a man", being then quite similar to Latin *virtus*, deriving from *vir*. Thus, in fact, one can render it as "manliness". This, however, brings it closer to MANLINESS referents in other languages, which all seem to be closely related to HONOR – especially in the Mediterranean Basin. For instance, Spanish *hombría* "manliness" was described by Pitt-Rivers (1965: 44–45) as a Spanish peasant's "concern for repute", i.e., for honor of him and his family. It was a kind of an ideal of man's character, related to courage, which enables him to take care of his honor. Nevertheless, the *hombría* itself did not make someone being of honor (*vergüenza*). Similarly, also Greek shepherds known as Sarakatsani consider *andrismos* "manliness" as a kind of ideal to realize by a man, in order to be considered as someone of HONOR (hohonCampbell 1965: 145), what quite neatly corresponds to the reflection mentioned earlier. In the light of these anthropological data, we could hypothesize existence of the relationship between these concepts – *murūʔa*, *virtus*, *hombría*, and *andrismos* – as being an inner quality, a trait of character, which makes a man able of acting in accordance with a code of honorable conduct. In the culture of al-Ǧāhiliyya, as I mentioned earlier, a similar enabling predisposition was also attributed to the concept *ʕizz*-STRENGTH/FORCE, which naturally also pertains in a way to the MANLINESS.

4.6. Cultural script of *karāma* (*ʔikrām*)

As we learned in the previous chapter, the English lexeme *honor* is ambiguous, as it is clearly noticeable in the difference between lexemes *honorable* and *honored*. The former pertains to the concept of HONOR-VIRTUE, upon which one claim their RIGHT TO RESPECT, whereas the latter is related to the HONOR-PAID, i.e., the RESPECT itself received for one's HONORABLE CONDUCT.

In LEAP, I believe, the concept of HONOR-PAID is referred to by the noun *karāma* or *ʔikrām*, which is a verbal noun of the verb *ʔakrama*. These lexemes served to express the meaning of honoring someone or of paying honor to someone, which could be further elaborated as recognizing someone as an equal. As we learned, EQUALITY was among the most central element of the schema HONOR in general, since HONOR-RIGHT TO RESPECT is usually in some relationship to EQUALITY/INEQUALITY of those, from whom someone expect this RESPECT. In other words, *karāma* is not only the scenario prescribing how one honors a noble and honorable one – a *karīm* – but first and foremost, the statement of recognizing this someone as EQUAL in HONOR, i.e., RIGHT TO RESPECT.

Lane (1968h: 2999) defines the aforementioned verb *ˀakrama* as "to treat with honor or courtesy", which makes the concept of *karāma* close to English COURTESY or simply GOOD TREATMENT. Similarly, EoI explains it as "to show one's self *karīm* to any one (EoI: 744)". Considering the data derived from CEAP, I believe that these definitions accurately define the concept in question. Namely, it seems that in fact the treatment lexicalized as *karāma* in LEAP involved some GOOD TREATMENT, implying to a certain degree reciprocity. Thus, *karīm* received respect in form of *karam*-BEING *karīm* of others. Consequently, the cultural script of *karāma* encapsulated for the most part the role schema of *karīm*, activating its more another-party oriented elements: generosity and hospitality, magnanimity and respectfulness, loyalty, sense of shame (especially towards women), and forbearance, clemency. In other words, to honor someone's equal was to treat them in the way they would be treated by *karīm*. Alternatively, we can state bluntly that *karīm* people were *karīm* for each other. This means then that by treating a person in a *karīm* way, one was recognizing their *karam*, i.e., their belonging to the community of the EQUAL *karīm* folk. Such a mutual recognition of *karam* of equals might be found, I believe, in (109) attributed to Kaˁb Ibn Zuhayr. In the second verse, the poet says that his noble father was honored (*ˀakrama*) by *karīm* men – in other words, in the act of their respect, he was recognized by them as an equal.

(109) أنا ابْنُ الذي قد عاشَ تِسْعِينَ حِجّةً فلَمْ يَخْزَ يَوْمَاً في مَعَدٍّ ولم يُلَمْ
وأكْرمَه الأكْفاءُ في كلِّ مَعْشَرٍ كِرامٍ فإن كذَّبتَنِي فاسألِ الأمَمْ

I am a son of the man, who lived 90 years, and [during that time] not even once has he gotten ashamed or reproached in [the clan of Banū] Maˁad.
He was **respected** (*ˀakrama- hu*) by men him alike from among **men of honor** [*kirām*] – and if you think I am lying, ask people [about it] (cf. t34A:137).

The fact that *karīm*, as DESERVING RESPECT, received it in form of *karāma* is well discernible in the samples (110) and (71). In (110), *karāma* – COURTESY, GOOD TREATMENT, RESPECT – was refused to be given to someone, who is depicted as very generous person, being by that stereotypically *karīm*-NOBLE-HONORABLE. A *karīm* man was supposed to receive or obtain (*nāla- yanāl*) *karāma*, as it appears, e.g., in (111) attributed to Ḥassān Ibn Ṯābit. The meaning of the phrase *nāla*[16] *karāma*, I believe, could be rendered in English as either "he got, earned respect" or even "he was respected", "he was treated well", depending on the context. As one can see, *karāma* is conceptualized by the

16 The meaning of the verb *nāla-yanāl* is "obtain, attain, reach" (Lane 1968h: 3039).

image-schema of POSSESSED OBJECT. It clearly derives from the more general schema of POSSESSION, in which an OBJECT could change its POSSESSOR only by means of a GIVE-TAKE transaction. Thus, *karāma* is something one had to OBTAIN or GAIN – in other words, earn – be ASKED FOR, as in (110), or could be LOST or even BOUGHT.

(110) فأظعنتَ من يرجو **الكرامةَ** منهُمُ وخَيَّبْتَ من يُعْطي العَطاءَ المُكَرَّما

Thus, you drove away the one who was [only] asking them for **a good treatment** (*karāma*), failing [by that] the one who was giving generous gifts (cf. t23A:139).

(111) كم من صَديقٍ لهمْ **نالوا كَرامتَهُ**، ومِنْ عَدُوٍّ عَليهِمُ جاهِدٍ جَدَعُوا

They have many friends, at whom they **earned respect** (*nālū karāma*) and many enemies, [who had sought their demise] and were humiliated.
(*or alternatively:* by whom they **are respected**) (cf. t38B:152)

On the other hand, as in (112) by al-Ḥuṭayʔa, *karāma* could signify only the RESPECT itself or a GOOD OPINION about someone. In this verse, the poet complains that by following the clan of Banū Sahm, he lost his *mawālī* (sg. *mawlà*), which in this context, we can render as allies or associates – i.e., people who are obligated to assist a man (cf. ʕAlī 1993b: 366–370). This loss meant in fact also a loss of his *karāma* (conceptualized here as a LIVING BEING, perhaps a *dābba* i.e., an animal upon which one can ride), which I believe might be interpreted as respect among people. In other words, the poet states that now he is unable to seek help from his associates since they do not consider him worth their assistance anymore. Moreover, the poet continues, now, he must try to survive on his own – he cannot count on anyone.

(112) تَبِعْتُهمُ وضيّعْتُ الموالي فألْقَوْا لِلضِّبَاعِ دَمِي وجِرْمِي
وضيّعْتُ **الكرامةَ** فا[رْ]مَأَدَّتْ وقَبَّضْتُ السِّقَاءَ في جَوْفِ سَلْمِ

I had been following them, [the clan of Banū Sahm], so I have lost [all] my allies, and [Banū Sahm] left my blood and my body for hyenas [to pray upon them].
I have lost the **respect** (*karāma*) [among others] – it has run away swiftly. Thus, I [was forced] to squeeze out [what was left] at the bottom of [my] water-bucket (cf. t39A:349–351).

However, this respect and good treatment must have been stipulated to a certain degree by one's ability of *karam*-BEING *karīm*. Thus, it seems losing one's wealth that helps in being *karīm*-GENEROUS, might have resulted in losing *karāma*, i.e., the respect and honor paid by others. The importance of wealth is portrayed by Ḥātim aṭ-Ṭāʔī in (113). The poet states that the inherited wealth will be the mean of purchasing *karāma* by descenders of the addressee of his verse. Once again, I believe we can interpret *karāma* as the respect paid to one for being *karīm* – here, generous. The conceptualization manifested in this verse – PURCHASING *karāma* – clearly derives from the aforementioned conceptualization of *karāma* in terms of the OBJECT of the GIVE-TAKE scenario.

(113) أهِنْ للذي تَهْوى التِلادَ فإنه إذا مُتَّ كان نَهْبًا مقسَّما
ولا تَشْتَقِيْنَ فِيه، فَيَسْعَدَ وارثٌ بِهِ، حينَ تَخْشَى أغْبَرَ اللّوْنِ، مُظلِما
يُقَسّمُهُ غُنْماً، ويَشْرِي **كَرامَةً**، وقد صِرْتَ في خطٍّ من الأرْض، أعْظُما
Do not bother yourself with those, who seek passionately your hereditary wealth, since after you die, it will truly become a bounty for share.
In the time you fear the grayest of all colors, [i.e., your death], truly, do not be upset [with the matters of your wealth] – its wicked heir will rejoice in it.
He will divide it with profit and thus, he will buy [himself] **respect** (*karāma*) – and you will become a great man thanks to this line [you are leaving behind you] on the soil, [i.e., your wealth inherited by your descendants] (cf. t19B:80).

The fact of being related to HONOR-PAID makes *karāma* – honoring someone, recognizing as an equal – be a kind of a REWARD, another elaboration of the GIVE-TAKE schema. It can be observed, for instance, in the sample (114) attributed to Ḥassān Ibn Ṯābit. Here, a clan of Banū Qurayš, Banū ʕAbd ad-Dād, is depicted as endowed or bestowed with *karāma* by a deity Manāt (a daughter or a wife of Hubal, the chief deity of Mecca). This *karāma* seems to be explicated in the second hemistich of the second verse as the control over the Meccan sanctuary – *bayt allāh* "the House of the God [Hubal[17]]". Thus, in this case, one can interpret *karāma* as an HONOR or a PRIVILEGE given to the clan by Manāt, the deity of fortune and fate (Dziekan 2008: 100). In other words, such a reading of this verse implies a strong affinity of *karāma* to the European conception of honor. I believe it might be an example of a metonymic extension in which the whole schema *karāma*-RESPECT-GOOD TREATMENT (that is given to those who are NOBLE-HONORABLE) is used to call-up its part encoding DESERVING THE RESPECT. Consequently, one can read (114) as stating that Manāt made Banū ʕAbd ad-Dār respected by others for their service as the acolytes of Hubal. The REASON for this RESPECT is accessed by means of a metonymy.

(114) كانتْ قريشٌ بَيْضةً فتفلّقتْ فالمُحُّ خالِصُه لِعَبْدِ الدارِ
ومَناةُ رَبّي خَصَّهمْ **بِكرامةٍ** حُجّابُ بيتِ إلهِ ذي الأستار
[The tribe of Banū] Qurayš were an egg that got broken, and the best of its yolk has [gone] to [the clan of Banū] ʕAbd ad-Dār.

17 In al-Ǧāhiliyya, the term *allāh* "the god" was used to refer to a chief deity of a given region – in the former Nabatean lands it was a denotation of the god Dū Šarà, whereas in the central Arabia of the god Hubal (Dziekan 2008: 100).

And Manāt of my lord [Hubal] bestowed them with **honor** (*karāma*), [an made them] the door-keepers of the vailed house of the God [Hubal] (cf. t38A:138; B:122).[18]

All in all, *karāma* as HONOR-PAID or simply RESPECT one was given as the indication of their recognition as an EQUAL might be in a way read as DIGNITY. Nowadays, the MSA lexeme *karāma* almost exclusively is translated precisely as English *dignity*. Nevertheless, LEAP *karāma*-DIGNITY must be understood in its native terms as DIGNIFICATION, i.e., being recognized as a DIGNIFIED person – a full member of the community of HONORABLE people. What is quite interesting, also the modern Arabic notion of *karāma* seems to encapsulate this very conception – RECOGNITION of one's EQUALITY in HUMANITY and the RESPECT, which must follow it (cf. Badry 2017: 59). The only difference between them lays only in the understanding of EQUALITY. The al-Ǧāhiliyya notion is restricted to the community of *karīm* free-folk, whereas the modern one is fully universal.

It is also in this manner, I believe, that one should read the Qurʔānic passage (A), which describes God granting a man dignity (Qurʔān 17:70) in the action referred to by the verb *karrama*. This verb seems denote the very script of *karāma*, thus it could be seen as synonymous to aforementioned ʔ*akrama* (cf. Wehr & Cowan 1976: 821).

(A) ۞ وَلَقَدْ كَرَّمْنَا بَنِىٓ ءَادَمَ وَحَمَلْنَٰهُمْ فِى ٱلْبَرِّ وَٱلْبَحْرِ وَرَزَقْنَٰهُم مِّنَ ٱلطَّيِّبَٰتِ وَفَضَّلْنَٰهُمْ عَلَىٰ كَثِيرٍ مِّمَّنْ خَلَقْنَا تَفْضِيلًا
Indeed, **We have dignified** (*karramnā*) the children of Adam, carried them on land and sea, granted them good and lawful provisions, and privileged them far above many of Our creatures.[19]

---

18 The interpretation of the second verse is particularly difficult, since the verb – *ḫaṣṣa* "bestowed", 3 sg. masc. – is not in agreement with its possible subject – *manātⁱ* "[goddess] Manāt", 3 sg. fem. The possible subjects of the verb can also be *rabbī* "my lord [Hubal]" or *ḥuǧǧāb* "the door-keepers". In both cases, the noun *manātⁱ* wouldn't have any complement, unless it would bear different case-ending (instead of nominative -*u*, genitive -*i*; cf. Górska 2015: 36), becoming by that a swearing "I swear to [goddess] Manāt". In such a case, only the phrase *rabbī* could logically served as a subject of the verb, and the alternative reading of this verse would be "I swear to [goddess] Manāt! My lord [Hubal] bestowed them with honor (*karāma*), [an made them] the door-keepers of the vailed house of the God [Hubal]". The phrase with *ḥuǧǧāb* as its head is unlikely to be the subject of the sentence since the verse obviously connects to the idea of distinguishing Banū ʕAbd ad-Dār as the best of Banū Qurayš. The control over the most important Qurayšite possession – the Meccan sanctuary – would be a reasonable token of such a distinction. The use of the phrase with *ḥuǧǧāb* would convey the meaning of respect paid by the acolytes of the sanctuary to this clan only.

19 https://quran.com/17, [31-08-2021].

This fragment is a statement that God honored the man, by making them God's representative on Earth. It seems then quite similar to the notion conveyed in (114). In fact, this Qurʔānic verse was used as an element of the discussion on the conception of Islamic DIGNITY in 20th c. and might be seen as the manifestation of modern Muslim conceptualization of this notion (Badry 2017: 51). Perhaps, however, one can interpret this passage also in line with my proposed description of the script of *karāma*. It would mean that by elevating humans from among the creation, God somehow recognized them as Their EQUALS – as the only creation, which resembles God in any way – which was created in the image of God.

4.7. Conclusions

Karam – BEING *karīm* – in LEAP is conceptualized as a script of certain behavior, which might be perceived as the code of honorable conduct persisting in the society of Arabs of al-Ǧāhiliyya. Therefore, one can see it as corresponding to such notions as HONORABILITY or HONOR-VIRTUE/INTEGRITY. It was then the script of behavior, which in pre-Islamic Arabic society, entitled someone to receive RESPECT in form of HONOR-PAID (cf. Stewart 1994: 23), referred to in LEAP as *karāma* – HONOR-GOOD TREATMENT-RESPECT. A man could not be *karīm* if he did not possess *murūʔa* – the virtue of the perfect man. MANLINESS made him able of providing for himself and his dependents, as well as it dictated him a certain mode of conduct. By behaving in the way imposed by *murūʔa*, a man behaved like *karīm*, a noble and honorable person.

Karam-BEING *karīm* might be perceived as one of the key concepts of the culture of Arabs of al-Ǧāhiliyya (Guth 2015: 179). This would imply that the role schema of *karīm* encoded the major estimate of the conduct evaluation in their society – evaluation of someone's "compliance with the traditional patterns of behavior (Abou-Zeid 1965: 258)". This compliance entailed manners of behavior, which was augmented to the core or prototypical value of *karam* – GENEROSITY-HOSPITALITY. These augmented modes of acting were manifestation or realization of the traits of character that society expected from a *sayyid*-tribal chief. They were magnanimity, bravery, loyalty, endurance, custom obedience, moderation-forbearance-clemency, and eloquence.

Consequently, it is safe to say that *karam* was actually a CODE OF HONOR or HONORABLE BEHAVIOR expected from an honor group of *karīm* people. Those people, as the members of an honor group (cf. Stewart 1994: 54), were considered equal to each other in their HONOR-RIGHT TO RESPECT. The only way to sustain this RIGHT – to hold the respect of the equals – was to stick to the code of *karam*. The group in question seems to have been encompassing only free people, what consequently means that the script of *karam* as an evaluation template was applicable only to free folk, non-slaves. This, of course, derives from the broader cultural model of social strata functioning in the pre-Islamic Arabic society, in which the most important division is placed between free and enslaved people (cf. ˁAlī 1993a: 262). Nevertheless, – as we know from the story of ˁAntara – one could be a freed slave and enjoy anyway respect of *karīms*. However, as this story proves, even being an ex-slave diminished one's WORTH, and this translated to higher expectations one was held to meet to earn respect.

Karīm meant first and foremost "honorable" or even "a man of honor". Nevertheless, what is quite interesting, the script of *karam* was also applicable to women, although CEAP does not provide too much data on the specifics of this application. The only 4 instances of reference of *karīm* to women indicate that it definitely entailed following the script of GENEROSITY-HOSPITALITY, and perhaps, MAGNANIMITY. Nevertheless, I think one can hypothesize that the whole code of *karam* could be applicable to women, perhaps except from more stereotypically manly behaviors, such as warfare. It could find its reflection in more modern data on some Bedouin communities, in which women – at least those of high social standing – were also expected to follow the code of honor (Abu-Lughod 1986: 109).

The role schema of *karīm*, which encoded the schematized knowledge about who might have been considered HONORABLE according to Arabs living in al-Ǧāhiliyya, is definitely grounded in a cultural metonymy. Thus, stereotypically, *karīm* was expected to be GENEROUS- HOSPITABLE. This suggests that NOBILITY-HONORABILITY and the RIGHT TO RESPECT derived from it was first and foremost founded on one's GENEROSITY- HOSPITALITY, to which – as a consequence – the RESPECT of equals was prototypically attached. Therefore, GENEROUS-HOSPITABLE should be accounted for as the prototype of the whole category of *karīm*. It is reflected in CAD, in which the concept GENEROSITY-HOSPITALITY is entangled with HONORABILITY (i.e., EXCELLENCE, GOODNESS) as two major meanings of *karam* and *karīm*.

As I mentioned, *karīm* due to his/her conduct was endowed with the RIGHT TO RESPECT by their equals. The HONOR-PAID – that is this very RESPECT – was subsumed in LEAP by the concept of *karāma*. Since *karāma* was the synonym of the verbal noun derived from *ˀakrama* "to show one's self *karīm* to any one (EoI: 744)", it must have implied a certain degree of reciprocity. Consequently, *karāma* as the script of RESPECT entailed by far many of the conceptualizations elaborating the role schema *karīm*. This is why in CAD, *karāma* is also defined as a synonym of *karam*. In other words, this interplay between *karam* and *karāma* means that *karīm* people were expected to be *karīm* for each other. Nonetheless, as we have seen, the concept of *karāma* was also a culturally specific schema encompassing approximates of such English concepts as GOOD TREATMENT, RESPECT, or HONOR(-PAID).

Karāma could be also understood as DIGNITY being DIGNIFICATION of someone, i.e., recognizing someone as an individual deserving respect. In al-Ǧāhiliyya, this conceptualization seemed restricted only to the honor group of *karīm* people. With time, however, it was extended to encompass the humanity as a whole. Thus, nowadays, *karāma* refers to more or less the same concept as the LEAP one, yet expanding the category of EQUALS deserving RESPECT onto all the people.

Karīm was NOBLE but, at the same time, he/she does not have to be of aristocratic blood. This conceptualization is enlisted within CAD (cf. LsA12: 602), as well as in CEAP (cf. the examples (95) and (96)). By realizing the code of the ideal conduct – in other words, by fulfilling the ideal, role model – *karīm* was naturally seen as being from among THE BEST people. Such NOBILITY (of conduct and/or character) was also seen as something hereditary – thus the notion {*karīm* was born noble}. What I would like to stress is the fact that such inherited nobility was related only to one's character (and as a result, to their behavior) and as we have seen in the examples (69), it was not the nobility proper – *šaraf* – the high social status. As stated in the sample (79), high, noble origin should be seen conceptualized as auxiliary to one's *karam*, not as replacing other grounds for their HONOR-RIGHT TO RESPECT.

Nevertheless, *karam* was stipulated as behavior expected from those of noble origin. This is why it frequently collocates expressions denoting aristocrats in CEAP. Consequently, it seems to have been used also as an honorific title. It could be considered a further metonymic extension of the category *karīm*. In such a case, this lexeme was employed to call up one of the subschemata of the role schema *karīm*, i.e., the conceptualization {*karīm* deserves RESPECT}.

This conceptualization together with the metonymy *karīm* FOR THE BEST, linked *karam* to the concept of GOODNESS-EXCELLENCE, which occurs in CAD. They are also an essential part of perhaps the most important of the extensions of the categories *karam* and *karīm*. These extensions might be summarized by the conceptual metonymy *karam* FOR THE BEST QUALITY/GREATNESS/NOBILITY. Its elaboration involves the metonymic use of the lexeme *karam* and *karīm* in reference to wide range of the concepts attributed by the notion of GOODNESS-EXCELLENCE. In other words, *karīm* meant sometimes "excellent", "the best", "the most valued", "the most esteemed," etc. I believe this is exactly why CAD list among the meanings of *karam* [E] "excellence; high-value (in horses, camels, trees and other valuable things)" and those of *karīm* [d] "a thing highly esteemed or prized or valued; excellent, precious, valuable, or rare" or [e] "in high estimation at his owner (said about a camel)".

Similarly, I think, one can approach the application of the lexeme *karīm* as an attribute of the Holy Qurʔān later in Islam. The great veneration to the Book of Books must have resulted in the use of *karīm* in reference to it. The Qurʔān is simply excellent – in any way – linguistically, theoretically, dogmatically, etc. Its excellence is accompanied by a great deal of veneration, which it enjoys. The attribution of *karīm* clearly calls up the two subschemata of *karam*, the {*karīm* is THE BEST} and {*karīm* deserves RESPECT}.

Alternatively, the early Islam took different approach in attributing God as *karīm*. In fact, I think, Allāh is meant to be *karīm* not in a metonymic or metaphoric way, but in a quite literal manner. *Karam* – as we learned – was gradable. Thus, as Ibn Manẓūr stated, "[God] is the absolute *karīm* (LsA12: 602)", that is, Allāh is simply the perfect, unsurpassed executor of the ideal conduct. Allāh is conceptualized as not only excellent and worth veneration – as the Holy Qurʔān – but as the most *karīm* being – unsurpassed in His *karam* – and as such possessing the quality of excellence and worth of veneration in an absolute sense. In such a way, the pre-Islamic ideal of a man of honor met the Islamic notion of the perfectness of One God.

5. Ḥasab – Ḥasīb

Perhaps, *ḥasab* is yet another example of an Arabic word, whose connection to HONOR might seem peculiar at the very first glance. Nowadays, its meaning does not really pertain to either HONOR or HONORABILITY for speakers of Arabic language. Usually, it is recalled only as a part of a common phrase – *lā ḥasab wa-lā nasab la-hu* – whose meaning might be rendered as "he is worthless; there is no good in him; there is nothing to praise in him". This phrase, however, might be traced back to al-Ǧāhiliyya, and in fact it had more or less the same meaning for pre-Islamic Arabs. As noted by Dziekan (2008: 36), *ḥasab* and *nasab* – "dignity and genealogy" were at very center of life of those people – or even more – they were "an issue (…) around which many problems of Arabic civilization revolved" in general. As we will learn further in this book, in the chapter on *ˁirḍ*, such importance of these two phenomena was founded by the fact that one's RIGHT TO RESPECT fully rested upon them. Thus, they were what one was proud of and what one used to pride themselves about (cf. ˁAlī 1993b: 292). And although, the Prophet Muḥammad officially outlawed priding in one's *ḥasab* and *nasab* (ˁAlī 1993b: 602), they persisted as one of the major "institutions" of Arabo-Islamic culture, whose original meaning has not been yet lost entirely (Dziekan 2008: 36).

In this chapter, I will try to take a closer look at the cultural conceptualizations of original, pre-Islamic *ḥasab*, which are discernible in LEAP. I postulate to see the concept of *ḥasab* as corresponding – roughly speaking – to the VALUE or WORTH of someone, based upon which in Europe, people used to assign HONOR-RIGHT TO RESPECT. As we saw in the chapter on HONOR, such a VALUE was a result of the EVALUATION performed by the community and might be seen as resting on one's realization of the ideal code of conduct. In Europe, such a VALUE had always two facets – internal and external one – and consequently, could be seen either as REPUTATION (i.e., e.g., one could defend their honor-GOOD NAME) or SELF-WORTH (i.e., e.g., one could have a sense of HONOR-WORTH). I believe, LEAP *ḥasab* covered these both elements. The CEAP data suggest that one was always expected to protect their *ḥasab* in front of other people, and at the same time this someone was aware of their *ḥasab* as a reason of pride. Being is such a close relationship with *ˁirḍ*-RIGHT TO RESPECT, it is no wonder that the concept of *ḥasab* could be metonymically referred to by the lexeme *ˁirḍ*. As we will learn further in this book, similar situation was taking place also in the case of the concept of *nasab* "lineage".

5.1. *Ḥasab* and *ḥasīb* in CAD

The root √ḤSB undeniably refers to the idea of COUNTING things. It is quite easy to infer from such its derivatives as *ḥasaba-yaḥsub* "to count" (cf. LsA1: 369), *ḥisāb* "a number of things; quantity" (cf. KtA1: 314) or *muḥāsaba* "estimation of the quantity" (cf. KtA1: 314). This general idea is being further extended by means of metonymies and/or metaphors into such concepts as *ˀaḥsabtu-hu* "I gave him what suffices him" (cf. AlG: 277) or THINKING/HAVING OPINION (i.e., *ẓanna-yaẓunnu*) (cf. AlG: 277). The development into HONOR-related notion of *ḥasab* is yet another example of such an extension.

Lane (1968b: 566) defines *ḥasab* as having at least four interrelated meanings, which are "numbered, counted, reckoned, calculated, or computed number", "amount, quantity, or value", "grounds of pretension to respect or honor, consisting in any qualities (either of oneself or of one's ancestors) which are enumerated, or recounted, as causes of glorying, and hence signifying nobility, rank or quality; honorableness, or estimableness, from whatever source derived", and "an honorable manner with respect to himself and the seller". Additionally, he defined the concept of *ḥasīb* as "a reckoner, or taker of accounts, or a sufficer, or giver of what is sufficient" and "characterized, or distinguished, by what is termed *ḥasab*".

As one can see, already the definitions provided by Lane accurately hint at the specifics of the cultural schema to which the lexeme *ḥasab* refers. As far as the Medieval CAD are concerned, in fact, only LsA provides extensive description of this notion. KtA, AlG, and AsS define it rather vaguely.

In KtA1 (314), *ḥasab* is described as *šaraf*, i.e., the high social standing of someone, which is based upon or derived from one's ancestors. AlG (AlG: 277) defines it in a similar way stating that it is ancestors' *maˀāṯir* (sg. *maˀṯura* "a generous [i.e., *karīm*] quality or action; so-called because related, or handed down, by generation from generation; cf. Lane 1968a: 20"). It means then that for both, al-Farāhīdī and Ibn Durayd, *ḥasab* was closely related to one's ancestors – perhaps their honorable deeds as it is in AlG. Moreover, it is also related to one's social standing, i.e., *šaraf*. AlG (AlG: 277) adds also that *ḥasab* equals one's *dīn*, which has a vast range of meaning and can be defined as "obedience (to God or customs)", "a religion (being obedience to God and religious laws)", "a particular law", "a system of usages, or rites and ceremonies, inherited from ancestors", and thus as "custom or habit" (cf. Lane 1968c: 944).

AsS (AsS: 247) is more elaborative and provides as first a literal meaning of *ḥasab* as synonym of *qadr* "the quantity, measure, magnitude, size, amount, sum or number attained of a thing" (cf. Lane 1968g: 2495). It also repeats the statement found in AlG that *ḥasab* is *maʔāṯir* of one's ancestors, however, after Ibn Sikkīt, al-Ǧawharī adds that one can have *ḥasab* even if their ancestors were not of *šaraf*, i.e., high social standing. Such a statement, as we saw in the previous chapter, was also what Ibn Sikkīt considered a property of *karam*. By this, actually, AsS differentiate between *ḥasab* and *šaraf*, which were equalized in KtA. Additionally, AsS (AsS: 247) sees *ḥasab* as synonymous to one's *dīn* and one's *māl*, i.e., wealth or possessions. In this instance, it seems, AsS somehow agrees with the anthropological data on HONOR in different cultures – frequently localized around the Mediterranean basin – which clearly depict one's VALUE/WORTH as strictly bound to one's wealth (cf. Stewart 1994: 131; Pitt-Rivers 1965: 65).

LsA (LsA1: 366) lists a few synonyms, which are supposed to help one understand what *ḥasab* is. Thus, it is seen as equal to *karam* or a collection, which consists of *karam*, *murūʔa*, *dīn*, and *ḫuluq* "temper, nature". It also defines it as *šaraf*, which might be either established upon one's ancestors as well as by this someone themselves. What is quite peculiar, later on, Ibn Manẓūr repeats after Ibn Sikkīt the statement mentioned also in the previous chapter: that *karam* and *ḥasab* do not have to be based upon one's ancestors, whereas *šaraf* and *maǧd* do. There is also the claim of *ḥasab* being one's *māl* "wealth", which I believe should be read in the light of what Ibn Manẓūr quoted after Ibn Sikkīt further in his definition. Namely, he says that *ḥasab* does not provide as strong claim of RESPECT as one's wealth does – simply stated, a poor man of *ḥasab* is not venerated by others in the same manner as a rich one with no *ḥasab* at all (LsA1: 366).

LsA gets, however, much closer than the remaining CAD to the actual meaning of *ḥasab*, which is to be found in CEAP. For instance, Ibn Manẓūr (LsA1: 366–7) defines *ḥasab* also as *faʕāl* – as we learned in the previous chapter, "the (honorable) deeds of someone". He added that those *faʕāl* are perfect, excellent, and might be "bravery (*šaǧāʕa*), generosity (*ǧūd*), virtuous traits (*ḥusn al-ḫuluq*), and loyalty (*wafāʔ*) (LsA1: 367)". Most importantly, he quoted the statement by al-Azharī, who stated that "truly, honorable deeds of a man (*masāʕī ar-raǧul*) and his ancestors' (*maʔāṯir ʔābāʔi-hi*) were called *ḥasab*, because when [Arabs] were competing with each other in pride, the one, who was priding himself counted [all] of what is to be praised in him (*manāqiba-hu*) and [all] of his ancestors' honorable deeds – [in other words] he *counted* them (*ḥasaba-hā*) (LsA1: 367)". The relationship of *ḥasab* to the concept of COUNTING was further supported by the statement (after al-Aʕrābī) that *ḥasab* is "what a man counts from his ancestors proudful deeds (*mā yaʕuddu-hu al-ʔinsān min mafāḫir ʔābāʔi-hi*) (LsA1: 366)". LsA (LsA1: 367) also explains this relationship stating that in fact, *ḥasab* is a count or a number – or simply, what was counted – the quantity, i.e., *qadr* (LsA1: 367). All in all, he saw such a count of honorable deeds of someone and their ancestors as a great reason of pride (cf. LsA1: 366).

LsA also as the only lexicon contains a definition of the lexeme *ḥasīb* pertaining to the concept of HONOR. Ibn Manẓūr (LsA1: 367) defines such a figure as "*karīm* by himself (*bi-nafsi-hi*)", which means that they do not have to be of noble ancestry to be *karīm*. Nevertheless, he also added that a *karīm* of an excellent origin is simply more *karīm* than the one who had no one to be proud of (LsA1: 367). Other than that, he stated that *ḥasīb* might also mean "the counting one, the estimating one (*muḥāsib*) (LsA1: 368)".

The table below (Tab. 5.) presents all the meanings of *ḥasab* and *ḥasīb* listed in CAD. In general, a quite comprehensive picture of them was provided by Wehr & Cowan (1976: 175), who defined *ḥasab* as "measure, extent, degree, quantity, amount; value; esteem, high regard enjoyed by s.o.; noble descent".

Tab. 5. The meanings of *ḥasab* and *ḥasīb* in CAD and dictionaries of CA

Lexeme	**Meaning**	**Sources**
ḥasab	[a] amount, quantity, what is counted	AsS: 247; LsA1: 367; Lane 1968b: 566; Wehr & Cowan 1976: 175
	[b] [a count of] honorable deeds of someone or their ancestors, which is one's grounds of pretension to respect	AlG: 277; AsS: 247; LsA1: 366–7; Lane 1968b: 566; Wehr & Cowan 1976: 175
	[c] *šaraf* "high social standing"; noble descent	KtA1: 314; AsS: 247; Wehr & Cowan 1796: 175
	[d] *dīn* "customs or obedience to customs"	AlG: 277
	[e] wealth, possessions (*māl*)	AsS: 247
	[f] *karam* "honorableness"	LsA1: 366
ḥasīb	[α] a counting, estimating [man]	LsA1: 368; Lane 1968b: 567
	[β] a man being *karīm* on his own	LsA1: 367

As one can see, in the table, I combine the last part of the definition by Wehr & Cowan – "noble descent" with the meaning *šaraf* "high social status". I did it, because the meaning "noble descent" certainly pertains to the statement from KtA that *ḥasab* is *šaraf* derived from one's ancestors. Although many researchers translate *ḥasab* as exactly "noble descent" (cf. Arberry 2017: 209; Witkowska & Danecki 1981: 124), I decided to present it as a part of *šaraf*, since other CAD seem to elaborate the statement from KtA explaining *šaraf* in terms of *maʔaṯīr*, inherited fame of honorable deeds of one's ancestors. Moreover, CAD as well as CEAP point towards the fact that *ḥasab* can be also something derived from one's ancestors (i.e., "noble descent"), ergo it would sound somehow cumbersome to see it as "noble descent" itself. Thus, *ḥasab* seems to be more a certain VALUE or simply DIGNITY of someone, which usually is based on one's honorable performance, but can be also derived from other factors, such as the "noble descent".

All in all, the meanings I presented in the table seem to be interrelated. *Ḥasab* being a COUNT of what one can be proud on clearly derives from the original meaning being COUNT/NUMBER/QUANTITY. Consequently, one can see *ḥasab* as a reason of pride. Thus, the remaining meanings might be explained as arising from a metonymic extension motivated by this fact.

5.2. CEAP data on *ḥasab*

Within the CEAP, the *ḥasab* cluster consisting of the lexeme *ḥasab* and its plural form *ʔaḥsāb*, as well as the lexeme *ḥasīb* with its plural forms (*ḥasībūna*, *ḥusabāʔ*), occurs 99 times. It means that its NWC is roughly 3.5. However, there is a vast disproportion between the NO of *ḥasab* subcluster and the one of *ḥasīb*. The former

Tab. 6. The number of occurrences of the members of *ḥasab* cluster within CEAP

Item		**Number of Occurrences (NO)**		**Normalized Word Count (per 10,000)**
ḥasab		64	=92	3.25
	ʔaḥsāb	28		
ḥasīb		7	=7	0.25
	ḥasībūna	0		
	ḥusabāʔ	0		

appears 92 times, whereas the latter only 7. NO: 92 translates to the NWC of 3.25.[1]

From among the meanings presented in the Tab. 5., in CEAP, I identified only few. Most significantly, CEAP seems not to contain any indication of the meaning

1 Such frequency corresponds, roughly speaking, to the frequency of such English words as *small* (3.26), *open* (3.25), and *food* (3.22) or Polish *został* (3.26), *dni* (3.25), *osoby* (3.20). Based on the corpora *English Web 2015* and *Polish Web 2015* available on *SketchEngine* (https://www.sketchengine.eu [08-07-2021]).

[a] "amount, quantity, what is counted" – other than that which is an inherent element of [b] "[a count of] honorable deeds of someone or their ancestors, which is one's grounds of pretension to respect". I believe one can interpret it as an argument for specification of the meaning of *ḥasab*, which lost its hypothetical original signification. I postulate to render the meaning [b] in English depending on the context, as either *merits*, which I believe, could roughly denote the sense of multiple honorable actions, or *dignity*[2] or *value* connecting to the latter part of the definition ("one's grounds of pretension to respect"). Remaining identified meanings were [f] and in a way [c]. Clearly, both are results of a metonymic extension of the meaning [b]. Whereas, both meanings of *ḥasīb* – [α] "a counting, estimating (man)" [β] "a man being *karīm* on his own" – were present in the corpus in the ratio [α] NO:5 vs. [β] NO:2.

5.3. *Ḥasab* is a count of honorable deeds

The most interesting from among conceptualizations I found in CEAP is that resulting in the specification of the meaning of *ḥasab* in from [a]>[b]. Only two of medieval CAD identified *ḥasab* as AMOUNT/QUANTITY, which might be seen as a hint that in fact, such an identification could be an etymological guess. Nevertheless, in CA, *ḥasab* is frequently in use in the meaning of *qadr*, i.e., that one of [a] (e.g., *ʕalà ḥasab* "in [accordance with] the estimation [of something]"). This could suggest that in fact, [a] was present in LEAP, yet it was not recorded in CEAP.

Therefore, I postulate that this conceptualization of *ḥasab* was structured by a metonymy *ḥasab*-AMOUNT/NUMBER/COUNTED (VALUE) FOR *ḥasab*-COUNT OF HONORABLE DEEDS. Although in CEAP, the concept of AMOUNT/QUANTITY was not actually referred to by the lexeme *ḥasab*, the collocation of this word strongly suggests that for LEAP speakers, the concept of *ḥasab* was related to COUNTABILITY. Consequently, it could be seen as structured by a metonymy, in which the most salient subevent of arriving at COUNT OF HONORABLE DEEDS – i.e., COUNTING those deeds – afforded access to this concept as a vehicle. Thus, it definitely was a kind of PART-FOR-WHOLE metonymic model, which represents SALIENT SUBEVENT FOR EVENT schema (cf. Radden & Kövecses 1999: 32). In other words, the cultural schema *ḥasab* is linguistically evoked by the reference to its part – a script of COUNTING.

---

2 I borrowed this translation strategy from Dziekan (2008: 36), who rendered *ḥasab* as *godność* "dignity" in Polish.

In CEAP, one can find many instances, in which *ḥasab* collocates with attributes describing NUMBER or QUANTITY. First of all, *ḥasab* is sometimes described as NUMEROUS by such words as *ʕidd* as in the example (115) by al-Ḥuṭayʔa or *ʔalaff* (cf. t01χ). In a similar fashion, *ḥasab* is described in TBD (cf. mHs12: 201). Alternatively, *ḥasab* is also portrayed as ABUNDANT or EXCEEDING, what is expressed by, e.g., lexeme *fāḍil* "exceeding (Lane 1968 f: 2413)", as it is the case in (116), a verse attributed to Abū Ṭālib. Interestingly, as possible attribute of a great *ḥasab*, TBD propose adjectives *namīr* and *ġamīr* (mHs12: 201), which regularly collocate WATER and mean, roughly speaking, "abundant". Perhaps, then, one can see them as manifestation of a cultural metaphor, in which *ḥasab* being a QUANTITY is elaborated as (QUANTITY OF) WATER. In other words, the source domain of WATER – being employed in conceptualizations of different HONOR-related phenomena – also served as a source for conceptualization of *ḥasab*. At last, the CEAP data clearly indicate that *ḥasab* was something one could MEASURE as it is implied in the samples (117) and (118).

(115) أتَتْ آلَ شَمَّاسِ بْنِ لأْيٍ وإنّما أتاهُمُ الأحْلامُ **والحَسَبُ العِدُّ**

[The tribe of Banū Saʕd] came to the clan of Šammās Ibn Laʔy – and truly, [those who] came to them [were people of] reason and **numerous merits** (*al-ḥasab al-ʕidd*) (cf. t39A:140–142).

(116) أشَمُّ منَ الشُّمِّ البهاليلِ يَنْتَمي إلى **حَسبٍ** في حَوْمةِ المَجْدِ **فاضلِ**

[He is] the most honorable among chiefs of honorable tribes. In [his] plenty of glory (*mağd*), he has asserted relationship to **ample** (*fāḍil*) **dignity** (*ḥasab*) (cf. t24A:63–72).

(117) **فَمَا حَسَبِي** إنْ قِسْتَهُ بِمُقَصِّرٍ (...)

Thus, when you are measuring [**merits** (*ḥasab*)] by [the amount of] meagerness, I don't have any (…) (cf. t28A:118–125).

(118) شِبْهُ الإماءِ فلا دِينٌ ولا **حَسَبٌ** لَوْ قامروا الزنْجَ عن **أحْسابِهِمْ قُمِروا**

They are similar to female slaves – they have neither respect to the customs (*dīn*), nor **dignity** (*ḥasab*). And when they gamble with black men, putting on the stake their **value** (*ʔaḥsāb*), they lose (cf. t38B:137)

As one can see, the conceptualization of *ḥasab* in terms of COUNTABILITY was seemingly present in the linguistic practices of EAP. Thus, I postulate to consider it as the concept of a COUNT OR ACCOUNT, NUMBER of one's deeds. The data from CEAP indicate that these deeds were simply *makārim* – the deeds of *karīm*-HONORABLE-NOBLE man. Thus, among such deeds COUNTED within one's *ḥasab*, there was GENEROSITY-HOSPITALITY (cf. example (119) and also t28A:118–125; t33A:29–30; t33A:110) – of course, especially during the time of distress (cf. t17A:159–160; t39A:247–249). Similarly, *ḥasab* could include CUSTOM OBEDIENCE, which could be seen as implied by the concept of POSSESSING *dīn*-CUSTOMS. As we learned in the previous chapter, it might be seen as a metaphor, by which

ADHERING TO CUSTOMS is conceptualized as POSSESSING them. I believe, such a conceptualization might be seen in the sample (120) (cf. also example (118) quoter earlier and t33A:110). Moreover, it could explain why TBD postulated *ʕafāf* "abstaining from what is unlawful" (cf. Lane 1968e: 2088) as a synonym of *ḥasab* (mHs12: 200). Such a synonymy seems correspond to its meaning [d] "customs or obedience to customs" proposed by CAD. Alternatively, CUSTOM OBEDIENCE is implied by such behaviors as BEING RIGHTEOUS (cf. t38B:106) or simply HAVING GOOD MANNERS (cf. t37A:37).

(119) لا ناقصي **حَسَبٍ**، ولا أيدٍ إذا مُدّتْ قِصارَهْ

[We are the people], who do not lack **merits** (*ḥasab*), and if [any one in need asks us for help our] hands are not short [in giving] (cf. t28A:152–157)

(120) ظَعَائِنَ مِنْ بَنِي جُشَمِ بِنْ بِكْرٍ خَلَطْنَ بِمَيْسَمٍ **حَسَباً** وَدِيْنَا

(...) in their carriages, the women from the tribe of Banū Ǧušam Ibn Bakr, who combine [the] beauty with **dignity** (*ḥasab*) and obedience (*dīn*) (cf. t12A:87–88).

Other deeds and modes of behavior, which could be COUNTED within one's *ḥasab*, and mentioned in CEAP were: *ḥilm*[3] (example (121), cf. also t33A:29–30; t39A:115–119), BRAVERY (example (122), cf. also t33A:110; t37A:34), *ṣabr*-ENDURANCE (example (123)), and ELOQUENCE (example (124)).

(121) يا حارِ إني لَمِن قَومٍ أولِي **حَسَبٍ** لا يَجهلون إذا طاشَ الضَغابِيسُ

Ḥāriṯ! Truly, I am from among people possessing [numerous] **merits** (*ḥasab*), who do not behave like fools, when weakened people lose their temper (*ṭāša*) (cf. t10A:95).

(122) يا هَوْذَ إنّكَ من قَوْمٍ ذَوِي **حَسَبٍ**، لا يَفْشَلُونَ إذا مَا آنَسُوا فَزَعَا

Hawḏa, you are from the people of **dignity** (*ḥasab*), who do not fail [to withstand fear], when they see the terrors [of an upcoming battle] (cf. t28A:102–108).

(123) إنّي أَقُولُ لِنَفْسِيُ وَهْيَ ضَيّقة" وقدْ أناخَ عليها الدَهْر بالعَجَبِ

صَبْراً على شِدّةِ الأيامِ إنَّ لها عُقْبَى وَمَا الصَّبْرُ إلّا عِنْدَ ذِي **الحَسَبِ**

Truly, I tell my soul in distress in the time when the evil fate had suddenly befallen her: you need some endurance (*ṣabr*), while facing the difficult days! Truly, she – [my soul] – has plenty of [endurance], since [no man is as full of] endurance as **the man having** [numerous] **merits** (*ḏī al-ḥasab*) (cf. t37A:31)

(124) كُنِ ابْنَ مَنْ شِئْتَ واكْتَسِبْ أَدَبًا يُغْنِيكَ مَحْمُودُهُ عَنِ النَّسَبِ

فَلَيْسَ يُغْنِي **الحَسيبَ** نَسَبَتُهُ بِلا لِسانٍ له ولا أَدَبِ

إنَّ الفَتى مَنْ يَقولُ ها أنا ذا ليسَ الفَتَى مَنْ يقولُ كان أبي

Be the son of whoever you want, but acquire good manners (*ʔadab*) – its praised [value] will enrich you [more] than [your] lineage (*nasab*).

---

3 I provided a rough explication of this behavior in the previous section (subsection 4.3.7). What indicates *ḥilm* in (121) is fact that the people of the poet do not behave like fools in the time, when others lose their temper.

[The fact that] I recognized a **man of [numerous] merits** (*ḥasīb*) as my son (*nasabtu-hu*), does not enrich [him, when] he doesn't have [cultural] language and good manners.
Truly, the young man is the one who says "This is who I am", not the one who says "[This is who] my father was" (cf. t37A:37).

As I mentioned, *ḥasab* is sometimes depicted as being MEASURED – cf. (117). This means that *ḥasab* of a man could be better or worse – in other words, could contain more or less *makārim*, HONORABLE/NOBLE DEEDS. Naturally, the most NUMEROUS *ḥasab* could have been referred to as *karīm* as it is in the sample (125) (cf. also t38B:237). Here, *karīm* served to denote the EXCELLENCY, BEING THE BEST of such a *ḥasab*. A person who possessed such an EXCELLENT *ḥasab* was referred to as *ḥasīb*.

(125) لننظُر كيف سمَّكَ بانِيَاهُ على حِبَّانَ ذي الحَسَبِ الكريم
Let us see what [grave] built the builders onto Ḥibbān, **the man of noble merits** (*ḏī al-ḥasab al-karīm*) (cf. t30B:162)

Ḥasīb as a POSSESSOR OF EXCELLENT *ḥasab* seems to be, however, a metonymic extension from the original meaning [α] "a counting, estimating (man)". I believe that although this meaning appeared only 2 times in CEAP – in both cases, in the dubious *dīwān* by caliph ʕAlī, and always in the reference to God, as in the sample (126) – it is much more sensible to propose such a vector of semantic development. Perhaps, *ḥasīb*-POSSESSOR OF EXCELLENT *ḥasab* is a result of a kind of ellipsis, which shortened the concept of someone who COUNTS their NUMEROUS HONORABLE DEEDS. Alternatively, one can see it as an independent derivation from two related etymons – that of *ḥasb*-COUNTING and of *ḥasab* – based on the matrix *faʕīl*, which is one of the most frequently employed adjective matrices in Arabic (cf. Danecki 2012a: 414).

(126) عَلِمتُكِ، واللهِ الحَسيبُ، عَفيفَةً منَ المؤمناتِ غيرَ ذاتِ غوائلِ
I knew you, [my deceased sister] – I swear to the God the **Reckoner** (*al-ḥasīb*) – as the most modest of the believers, not neglectful (cf. t38B:205).

Nevertheless, *ḥasīb* as a man of a NUMEROUS *ḥasab* played an important role within the pre-Islamic Arabic society. CEAP suggests that people benefited from a *ḥasbīb* (cf. t40A:52; t33A:110), and naturally – since he was an excelling *karīm* – they sought from help as it is depicted in (127) by al-Ḥuṭayʔa. We could infer that *ḥasab karīm* was expected necessarily from a tribal chief (cf. ʕAlī 1993b: 344). Perhaps, a man of such a *ḥasab* could serve as a chief also in the situation, when he had no noble origin (cf. ʕAlī 1993b: 350).

(127) إليك تناهى كلُّ أمْرٍ يَنُوبُنا وعند ظِلالِ المَوْتِ أنتَ حَسِيبُ

With all [evil] matters, which befell us, we used to come eventually to you. And when the shadows of death [came to claim you], you stayed **honorable** (*ḥasīb*) (cf. t39A:247–249).

Since *ḥasab* was perceived as being a subject of a MEASUREMENT, one can imagine that it was MEASURED for sake of COMPARISON (cf. (118)). In other words, people were competing with each other over the PRECEDENCE in a script of behavior, which was conceptualized by the domain MEASURING. One can find an argument suggesting it in (128) by Ḥassān Ibn Ṯābit. What is quite interesting in this passage is the verbal noun *taqāyus* derived from the verb *taqāyasa*. It follows the matrix of the form VI, which implies reciprocity of an action expressed by the form III (Danecki 2012a: 179–80) – in this particular case, *qāyasa*. The matrix of the form III, on its turn, indicates the quality termed by Ryding (2005: 503) as "associative", meaning that the verb usually involves another agent in the action it denotes. Thus, *qāyasa* being derived from the verb *qāsa-yaqīs* "to measure" could be interpreted as "to measure something possessed by another agent", whereas *taqāyasa* as the same concept but enriched by the element of reciprocity. Consequently, what the poet meant was that people could measure each other's *ḥasab*s, and by that establish a hierarchy of PRECEDENCE between them.

(128) فورِثْتَ والدَكَ الخيانةَ والخنا، واللّؤمَ عِنْدَ تَقَايُسِ الأحْسَابِ

Thus, after your father, you inherited the treacherousness and the vulgarity, and the baseness (*luʔm*), [which is what you can present], **when people compare their merits** (*taqāyus al-ʔaḥsāb*) (cf. t38A:44–45; t38B:41–42).

As we saw, *ḥasab* could be described as EXCELLENT, i.e., *karīm*, which also implies the fact of its MEASURABILITY – evaluation of its content. EXCELLENCY of one's *ḥasab* might have been also expressed by the use of other lexemes, such as *ṣamīm* or *libāb* (cf. t38B:118–119, and aHm: 44). These adjectives seem to derive from a conceptual metaphor WHAT IS THE BEST IS INSIDE.[4] TBD suggest also that *ḥasab* might be described as *nāṣiʕ* (mHs12: 201), which I think might be seen as manifesting the metaphor WHAT IS THE BEST IS WHITE,[5] perhaps deriving from

4 The lexeme *ṣamīm* has several meaning, which might be seen as interrelated, the most important being: "the bone that is the main stay or support of the limb or member or the like", "the thing that is the (main) stay, or support, of another thing", "the heart", and "the prime, principal, or most essential, part; the choice, best, or most excellent, part; of a thing of any kind" (Lane 1968d: 1723). *Libāb*, however, derives from the meaning *lubb*, being primarily a pip in a fruit, and metaphorically, the best part of something (cf. LsA1: 856).

5 Primarily, *nāṣiʕ* or *naṣīʕ* denotes the purest from among colors, usually white (LsA8: 422).

the conceptualization *karīm* IS WHITE/OF WHITE FACE, which I will discuss in Chapter 7.

Alternatively, as in the sample (129), *ḥasab* might be defined as *ṯāqib* (cf. also aHm: 44). Primarily, this adjective was an attribute of stars, lamps, fires, and other shining objects, and it meant "shining brightly or shining, glistening, or gleaming very brightly, as though piercing through[6] the darkness, and dispelling it". Perhaps, it derives somehow from the metaphor WHAT IS THE BEST IS WHITE. Nevertheless, it is apparently based on the conceptualization of EXCELLENCE as something SHINING BRIGHTLY, which I believe is to be found in many languages and cultures (cf. English concept of STAR as a FAMOUS PERSON). In other words, one's *ḥasab* might be SHINING BRIGHTLY and by that distinguishing this someone from among others. *Ḥasīb* was then someone special, extraordinary. I think that this conceptualization might be also found in (130) by Qays Ibn al-Ḫaṭīm, who seems to imply that the fact that even a man possessing *ḥasab karīm* must die might be surprising to someone.

(129) النبيّ الأغرّ **ذي الحَسبِ الثّاقبِ** والباعِ والكريمِ النَّجيبِ

(…) the most respected Prophet, **the owner of the shining value** (*ḏī al-ḥasab aṯ-ṯāqib*) and of a great power, an honorable nobleman (cf. t37χ).

(130) أبلغْ خِداشًا أنّني ميتٌ كلُّ امرئٍ ذي **حسبٍ** مائتُ

Tell Ḫidāš that I am dead. Every man of [numerous] **merits** (*ḥasab*) dies (cf. t25B:68; t25C:75/39).

As SHINING, *ḥasab* must have been also described in the simile to GOLD, as it is the case of the sample (131), a passage by Bišr Ibn Abī Ḫāzim al-Asadī. The poet depicts *ḥasab* as *nuḍār*, i.e., "pure", an adjective used usually in reference to GOLD. Therefore, one can conclude, *ḥasab* was perceived by pre-Islamic Arabs as GOLD itself.

(131) أبى لِبَني خُزَيمَةَ أنَّ فيهم قديمَ المَجدِ **وَالحَسَبُ** النُّضارُ

He rejected [the claim that there is dishonor among people of] Ḫuzayma, since their glory (*maǧd*) is ancient, and their **value** (*ḥasab*) is pure (*nuḍār*) (cf. t14A:64).

5.3.1. *Ḥasab* is a value

The conceptualization *ḥasab* IS GOLD might suggest that *ḥasab*-COUNT OF HONORABLE DEEDS could have been seen as a certain VALUE or WORTH of someone – their DIGNITY. Thus, it was something people could EVALUATE, and consequently,

6 The lexeme *ṯāqib* is an active participle of the verb *ṯaqaba-yaṯqub* "to pierce something, to make a hole in something" (cf. Lane 1968a: 341).

it was upon EVALUATION of what the community could assign the HONOR-RIGHT TO RESPECT. Thus, men tried themselves out by mutually measuring their *ḥasab* – to prove who is of more VALUE/WORTH, and who is more ENTITLED TO RESPECT of others. The evaluative nature of *ḥasab* might be inferred based on the expression *ḥasaban*, i.e., "in terms of *ḥasab*", "regarding *ḥasab*", "in regard to *ḥasab*", "when it comes to *ḥasab*", being an example of so called *tamyīz*, the accusative of specification (Górska 2000: 310). In other words, people were comparing themselves "in terms of *ḥasab*" – who is of more of it. An example of such a use of the lexeme *ḥasab* one can find in (132) by Ḥassān Ibn Ṯābit (cf. also t28A:129–33). Individuality of the *ḥasab* as a PERSONAL VALUE is accentuated by the use of plural form of the noun *ḥasab* – *ʔaḥsāb*.

(132) اللُّؤْمُ خيرٌ من ثَقِيفٍ كلِّها **حسباً**، وما يَفْعَلْ لئيمٌ تَفْعَلِ

The baseness (*luʔm*) is better in terms of **a value** (*ḥasaban*) than all of [the tribe Banū] Ṯaqīf – whatever a base man do, they do [that as well] (cf. t38A:248)

As a consequence, in order to estimate the VALUE/WORTH of an individual, one must have always asked them about their *ḥasab*. This conceptualization might be seen realized in questions about *ḥasab* asked by women to their suitors, as it is in the samples (133) and (134).

(133) هَلّا سألتِ بَنِي ذُبيانَ ما **حَسَبِي**، إذا الدُّخَانُ تَغَشّى الأشمَطَ البَرَما

Didn't you inquire the tribe of Ḏubyān about **my merits** (*ḥasabī*)? [Know, that] when a smoky [hunger] covers salt-and-pepper-haired [people, I am] the one who shares with them goods instead of living in prosperity (cf. t17A:160)

(134) هَلّا سألتِ، هَداكِ اللهُ، ما **حسَبِي**، أمَّ الوليدِ، وخيرُ القولِ للواعي

Weren't you, Umm al-Walīd – may God protect you – asking what **my merits** (*ḥasabī*) are? [What you will hear about me] is the best what one can hear (cf. t38B:156).

Ḥasab as the VALUE/WORTH of someone seems to be perceived as a kind of foundational element of one's self. For instance, TBD (mHs12: 200) suggests that it could be referred to also by the lexeme *ṣulb*. This word is used in reference to quite a few concepts, however, from the perspective of my study, the most important one is that one of "the back-bone, i.e., the bone extending from the base of the neck to the rump bone; the bone upon which the neck is set, extending to the root of the tail [in a beast], and in a man to the os coccygis [i.e., coccyx] (Lane 1968d: 1712)[7]". As one can see, such a metaphoric conceptualization defines

7 This meaning seems to be a metonymic extension from the most primitive physical one in form of "hard, firm, rigid, stiff, tough, strong, robust, sturdy, or hardy; syn. *šadīd* (Lane 1968d: 1712)".

a sort of essentiality of *ḥasab* for someone. Perhaps, it is so, since *ḥasab* – as I will elaborate on further – is a crucial element of one's *ˁirḍ*-HONOR-RIGHT TO RESPECT, which as we will learn in Chapter 7, conceptually pertain to the BODY (SIDE) of an individual. In other words, *ḥasab* was the backbone of one's HONOR.

Being that important, naturally, *ḥasab* must have been protected. It is mentioned, e.g., in (135), a passage by al-Mutalammis (cf. also t37A:34). It is already quoted verse, in which the poet, having been vilified for his mother's low descent, declared that a man of honor cannot claim RESPECT only based on the noble origin. As one can see, he states that a man, who – being of noble lineage – does not protect his *ḥasab*, is a man worth disrespect or dispraise (cf. also t21A:44).

(135) وَمَن كانَ ذا عِرضٍ كَريمٍ فَلم يَصُن لَهُ **حَسَباً** كانَ اللَئيمَ المُذَمَّما

The one, who is of noble origin, and because of that he doesn't care about [his] **merits** (*ḥasab*), is a low (*laʔīm*) and dispraised man (cf. t10A:16)

Such protection could be achieved mainly by following the code of *karam*, but also by avoiding non-*karīm* people (cf. t19B:90–91). The latter conceptualization links to the belief of acquiring the attributes of people one stick to, which I discussed in the previous chapter. Moreover, it can be seen as an example of the behavior described by Stewart (1994: 61–2) as avoidance of one's inferiors, aiming to protect one's HONOR-PRECEDENCE. In other words, one avoids people who are of worse VALUE/WORTH than him/her, in order not to compromise the RIGHT TO RESPECT he/she has because of the fact that he/she is better than them.

The need of protection might be why *ḥasab* seems to be also conceptualized as a LIVING BEING, hypothetically, as a CATTLE POSSESSED by someone. It might be seen, e.g., in (136) by Ḥassān Ibn Ṯābit, in which the poet mentions his *ḥasab* being fat (*samīm*), i.e., WELL FED or FATTENED with the HONORABLE DEEDS. Similarly, in (137) by the same poet, *ḥasab* is something, which need to be given shelter. These two examples clearly suggest the importance of *ḥasab* and its protection.

(136) وقد أكرَمتُكمْ وسكنتُ عنكم، سَرَاةَ الأوْس، لوْ نَفَعَ السُّكونُ
حياءً أنْ أشاتمكمْ وَصَوْنًا **لِعِرْضي**، إنهُ **حسبٌ** سمينُ

Chiefs of [Banū] al-Aws, I would have paid you honor and left you in peace, if [such] a peace had been of any advantage [to me],
[if my] sense of shame [had restrained me] against [getting involved in] mutual vilification with you, [and if I had thought of nothing but] to protect my honor (*ˁirḍ*) – but [my honor] truly, is [based on] plenty of **merits** (*ḥasab samīn*) (cf. t38A:313).

(137) فقَدْ يُصَادِفُ بَاغي الخيرِ حاجَتَهُ فِيها ويَأوي إليها الذِّكرُ **والحَسَبُ**

The one, who seeks goodness, will encounter it in [the house of ˁUṯmān] – in it, the good renown and **the dignity** (*al-ḥasab*) find shelter (cf. t38B:27).

5.3.2. Where does *ḥasab* come from?

Being a COUNT of one's *makārim*-HONORABLE-NOBLE DEEDS, *ḥasab* must have been perceived as first and foremost derived from the conduct of an individual. Nevertheless, as suggested in CAD, *ḥasab* is also seen as being rooted in one's lineage or – more precisely – one's ancestry. The fact of being rooted in something (*ṯābit fī*) is mentioned, e.g., in KtA (KtA1: 314), where *ḥasab* is defined as *šaraf* "high social status" rooted in one's ancestors, i.e., one's noble descent This would suggest a kind of image-schematic model conceptualizing *ḥasab* as an OBJECT GROWING/BEING SET UPRIGHT. In CEAP, however, the lexeme *ṯābit* or any other referring to BEING ROOTED is not present. Nevertheless, *ḥasab* is frequently completed by the prepositional phrase with *fī* "in" as its head. I propose to interpret this fact as suggesting an ellipsis, in which the reference to BEING ROOTED is achieved by use of the preposition only (i.e., instead of "*ḥasab* rooted in", there is "*ḥasab* in"). I translate this phrase, however, as "derived from".

Most frequently, in such a way, *ḥasab* is referred as ROOTED IN one's people, as it is, e.g., in (138) by Ḥassān Ibn Ṯābit (cf. also t08A:119; t10A:42–46; t40A:75). It could be also traced back more precisely to one's ancestors as in the sample (139). As such, in some places it is explicitly defined as something inherited (cf. t38B:118–119), which could be lost by one's foolishness (cf. t39A:121–138). All in all, I believe, the fact of being ROOTED IN one's tribe or lineage could be read as ability of an individual to ascribe oneself to a collective *ḥasab*, i.e., *ḥasab*s of people belonging to such a kin-group. Such a notion might be seen in (140), a verse attributed to Abū Ṭālib. It corresponds to the conception of heredity of predisposition to *karam*. In other words, *ḥasab* was perceived as something strongly related to one's *nasab* "lineage", since its content – honorable deeds – was perceived as something, to which people were not equally predisposed. It might be also seen in an expression of NOBLE ORIGIN, provided in TBD, in form of *manbat al-ḥasab* "a place of growing in *ḥasab*" (cf. aHm: 43).

(138) وكمْ قَدْ قَتَلْنَا مِنْ كريمٍ مُرَزّإٍ، لَهُ **حَسَبٌ في** قَوْمِهِ، نَابِهِ الذِكْرِ

We killed so many noble (*karīm*) and excellent men, who possess a **value** (*ḥasab*) [derived] **from** (*fī*) their people; [who are] worth mentioning (cf. t38B:114).

(139) لهُ في الذاهبينَ أرومُ صِدْقٍ وكانَ لكُلّ ذي **حَسَبٍ** أرُومُ

He is firmly rooted in his ancestors – and [firm] roots are what every man of **value** (*ḥasab*) possesses (cf. t22A:83).

(140) إنَّ علياً وجعفراً ثِقَتي عندَ اخْتدامِ الأمورِ والكُرَبِ
أراهُما عُرْضَةَ اللِّقاءِ إذا سامَيْتُ أو أنْتَمي إلى **حَسَبِ**

In truth, [I put my] trust in ʕAlī and Ǧaʕfar, when the matters will deteriorate, and disasters will come.
I see they are [always] ready for an encounter, [a combat], [which happens] when I compete [with someone] in pride or [when doing so], I ascribe myself to (*ʔantamī ʔilà*) [to a certain group] **value** (*ḥasab*) (cf. t24A:22)

Nonetheless, what we already saw in (135) by al-Mutalammis, sole noble origin was not enough for one to be RESPECTED. As it explicitly stated in the sample (124), *ḥasab* was first and foremost a personal matter – it is still up to an individual to keep up the *ḥasab karīm*. It is implied by Hudba Ibn al-Ḫašram in (141). This verse, although very picturesque, quite nicely defines the relationship between *ḥasab* of a man and the *ḥasab* of his ancestors. It is up to a man to keep the *ḥasab* full of honorable deeds, since the *ḥasab* of his ancestors is based on the opinion on them only (implied by the word *ṣāliḥ* "a man good, incorrupt, etc., in himself; cf. Lane 1968d: 1715"). This opinion is only an opinion – and a man can only catch up with it in his own honorable conduct.

(141) فإن يَكُ أنفي بانَ مِنهُ جَمالُهُ فَما **حَسَبي** في الصالِحين بأجدَعا

Thus, if by cutting my nose off, one [can] deprive it of its beauty, there is no **value of mine** (*ḥasabī*) [derived only] from (*fī*) good people, [my ancestors] (cf. t08A:119).

5.4. Image-schematic model of *ḥasab*: to POSSESS *ḥasab*

Since *ḥasab* was a certain VALUE/WORTH of an individual, upon which the community judged this individual's RIGHT TO RESPECT, the conceptualization of it in terms of the image-schema POSSESSED OBJECT should not be surprising. VALUE/WORTH is conceptualized in many languages in such a way, what can be seen is, e.g., in English (cf. *It had no value to him*; *worthless*, i.e., *without worth*, etc.). In LEAP, this conceptualization – *ḥasab* IS POSSESSED OBJECT – is indicated first and foremost by the particle *ḏū*, which implies POSSESSION (I discussed it in the previous chapter). In CEAP, it cooccurs with the noun *ḥasab* 15 times (cf. t24A:22; t28A:102–108; t37A:31; t37A:34; t37χ; t38B:83–84; t38A:230–231; t38B:237; t38B:118–119; t39A:201–203; t40A:52; t25B:68; t22A:82–83; t10A:95; t39A:115–119).

BEING POSSESSED is what somehow brings *ḥasab* closer to the concept of WEALTH. For instance, in (142) by al-Ḥuṭayʔa, *ḥasab* and wealth are depicted as being part of the same positive change, which the poet ascribed to the activity of his tribe. As we saw in LsA (LsA1: 366), wealth, being rich was as important as having *ḥasab*, and it was also what validated one's RIGHT TO RESPECT. It is similar to the anthropological descriptions, which postulate that POSSESSION OF WEALTH was an element of HONOR in many cultures, especially those in the proximity to the Mediterranean basin (cf. Pitt-Rivers 1965: 59, 65).[8] Thus, one can infer that for pre-Islamic Arabs the VALUE/WORTH of an individual could be founded onto *ḥasab* or WEALTH. Perhaps, this can explain the metonymic extension of *ḥasab* FOR WEALTH, which although unattested in CEAP, was postulated by CAD. Moreover, it can also explain the meaning [c] "*šaraf*-high social standing; noble descent" as yet another example of a metonymic extension following a similar development. Thus, *ḥasab* being a VALUE/WORTH and, as a consequence, a mean of VALIDATION for one's claim of RESPECT could serve as a tool of conceptualizing other such means VALIDATING one's RIGHT TO RESPECT, i.e., WEALTH, *šaraf*, or noble descent.

(142) أَخُو ذُبْيَانَ عَبْسٌ ثم مَالَتْ بنو عبسٍ إلى **حسبٍ** ومالِ

[The tribe of Banū] ʕAbs fraternized with [the tribe] of [Banū] Ḏubyān – after that the sons of ʕAbs turned towards **merits** (*ḥasab*) and wealth (cf. t39A:312).

Usually, *ḥasab* is POSSESSED by an individual (it is the COUNT of their and their ancestors *makārim*), but in several places it was described as owned by a group of people (cf. the examples (121) and (143)). Such a conception is also clearly discernible in the expression *bayt al-ḥasab* "the house of *ḥasab*" used by Abū Ṭālib in (144). It is based on a quite frequent social life metaphor, in which one's people are conceptualized in terms of one's HOUSING (depending on the lifestyle, LEAP *bayt* could mean either "a tent" or "a house"). Such a collectively possessed *ḥasab* seems to be no more no less a collection of *ḥasab*s of individual members of the group in question.

(143) كِرامٌ يَفْضُلُونَ قُرُومَ سَعْدٍ أُولِي **أَحْسَابِها** وأُولِي نُهاها

(…) the honorable men (*kirām*) – the best from among chiefs of [the tribe] Saʕd – owners of **their merits** (*ʔaḥsābi-hā*) and their reason (cf. t39A:115–119).

(144) زَعَمتُم بأَنَّكمو جيرةٌ وأَنَّكمو إخوَةٌ في النَّسَبْ
فكيفَ تُعادونَ أبناءَهُ وأهلَ الدِّيانةِ بيتَ **الحَسَبْ** ؟

You claimed that you are [their] neighbors, that you are [their] brothers in lineage (*nasab*),
so how [is it possible that you] are enemies of his sons and people of kinsmen [who belong with you to the same] house of **dignity** (*al-ḥasab*) (cf. t24A:17–18)?

What is quite interesting, the image-schematic model *ḥasab* IS POSSESSED OBJECT participate in some metonymies, which account for the semantic extension of the category *ḥasab*.

8 It is worth mentioning that Stewart (1994: 132) claimed that the Bedouins of Eastern Egypt in the 80'of the 20th c. didn't share this conceptualization.

5.4.1. Having *ḥasab* is to be *ḥasīb*

First of these metonymies is POSSESSING *ḥasab* FOR POSSESSING *ḥasab karīm*, which, in fact, could be seen as an ellipsis. In other words, as one can see in the example (145) by Ḥassān Ibn Ṯābit, by HAVING *ḥasab*, people usually used to mean possessing an excellent COUNT of HONORABLE DEEDS – either of one's self or of one's ancestors. The fact that *ḥasab* could not be *karīm*, i.e., numerous, excellent, and can be *laʔīm* (non-*karīm*) might be seen, e.g., in the sample (146). Thus, originally, one should see this concept as more or less neutral and encompassing the idea of unspecified COUNT of *makārim* only.

(145) والفقرُ يُزْري بأقوامٍ ذوي **حَسَبٍ** (...)

Thus, poverty lowers the value [even] of people of **many merits** (*ḥasab*) (…) (cf. t38A:230–231).

(146) أبَني لُبَيْنى لمْ أجِدْ أحَداً في النّاسِ ألأمَ مِنكُمْ **حَسَبَا**

Isn't [it true], Banū Lubaynà, that I have not found among people someone of lower (*ʔalʔam*) **value** (*ḥasab*) than yours (cf. t26A:4).

Nevertheless, more often, *ḥasab* more specifically referred to a NUMEROUS COUNT OF HONORABLE DEEDS. Such a *ḥasab* was a precious POSSESSION, which could have been lost or wasted, when its POSSESSOR did not take a proper care of it. Such a conceptualization might be seen, e.g., in the samples (147) or (148).

(147) جارٍ أبَيْتَ لِعَوفٍ أنْ يُسبَّ به ألْقاهُ قَوْمٌ جُفاةٌ ضَيَّعُوا **الحَسَبَا**

[For the sake of your] protégé, [myself], you didn't let ʕAwf to be dishonored by [words] thrown [onto him] by people without manners, who lost their **dignity** (*ḥasab*) (cf. t39A:121–138).

(148) وَرِثْنا المَجْدَ عنْ آباءِ صدق أسَأْنا في دِيارِهِمُ الصّنيعَا
إذا **الحَسَبُ** الرّفيعُ تَوَاكَلَتْهُ بُناةُ السّوءِ أوشكَ أنْ يضيعَا

We have inherited glory (*maǧd*) after our great ancestors – and we have spoiled [it] in their well-constructed houses.
When bad builders desert an elevated **honor** (*al-ḥasab ar-rafīʕ*), [it is as if] it almost perished (cf. t26A:56).

Such a *ḥasab* meaning NUMEROUS *ḥasab* is something one acquires by their deeds. It might be reached (*balaġa-yabluġ*) as Ḥassān Ibn Ṯābit describes it in (149) or it can come to someone as it is depicted in (150) by ʕUrwa Ibn al-Ward. In the latter, perhaps, one can see an example of the aforementioned image-schematic model *ḥasab* IS LIVING BEING.

(149) فكلُّ شيءٍ سِوَى أن تذكُرُوا شرَفاً أوْ تبلُغوا **حسَباً** منْ شأنكُمْ جلَلُ

And when it comes to everything, either [when you are trying to] say something about your high social position (*šaraf*), or to reach some **worth** (*ḥasab*) [for others], in your case it is [such an] enormous business (cf. t38B:201)

(150) دعِيني للغنى أسعى ، فإنّي رأيتُ الناسَ شَرُّهمُ الفقيرُ
وأبْعَدُهُمْ وأهْونُهُمْ عَلَيْهِمْ وإنْ أمسى له حسبٌ وخِيرُ

Let me pursuit the wealth. Truly, I've seen people whose [only] misfortune [was being] poor.
I keep myself away from them, being gentle with them, even if suddenly [one of them] became of some **dignity** (*ḥasab*) and virtue (*ḫīr*) (cf. t20A:45).

What is worth mentioning is the fact that WEALTH is sometimes presented as an important mean of acquiring *ḥasab*. It might be seen, I think, in (151) by al-Ḥuṭayʔa. Nevertheless, as one could see in the sample (150), it does not have to be a widespread conceptualization and for some *ḥasab* was in reach also for poor people. This, however, corresponds to the previously mentioned possibility that *māl* – wealth or possessions – plays only auxiliary role in BEING (cf. t19B:31, 32).

(151) وإني قَدْ عَلِقْتُ بِحَبْلِ قَوْمٍ أعانَهُمُ على الحَسَبِ الثراءُ

Truly, [whenever] I bind myself with a rope to some people, my wealth support them in [their pursuit after] **merits** (*ḥasab*) (cf. t39A:97–103–104).

5.4.2. *Ḥasab* as integrity

HAVING *ḥasab* is some places could also mean POSSESSING *karam*, the concept analyzed in the previous chapter as BEING *karīm* or BEING ABLE TO ACT LIKE *karīm*. The metonymy POSSESSING *ḥasab* FOR POSSESSING *karam* could be hypothesized as responsible for the semantic development resulting in the meaning [f]. It can be observed, e.g., in (152) by Abū Ṭālib and (120) by ʕAmr Ibn Kulṯūm, quoted earlier (cf. also t28A:102–108; t37A:31; t37A:34; t38B:83–84; t40A:52; t10A:95). I believe, this metonymy foregrounds the fact that *makārim* – honorable, noble deeds – being performed by a *karīm* are what constitutes his VALUE/WORTH in form of *ḥasab*.

(152) واللهِ لا أخذُلُ النبيَّ ولا يخذُلُه من بنيَّ ذو حَسَبِ

God is my witness, I will not desert the Prophet because of my sons, since one who possesses **integrity** (*ḥasab*) will not desert him (cf. t24A:22).

As we have learned in the previous chapter, *karam* could be seen as corresponding to European HONOR-VIRTUE or INTEGRITY. Thus, by means of this metonymy, *ḥasab* also could serve to evoke this schema. In other words, in saying that someone POSSESSES *ḥasab*, a LEAP user could mean simply that this someone is *karīm* or follows the CODE OF HONORABLE CONDUCT. This may allow us to see yet another metonymic use of the lexeme *ḥasab*, which could be seen in the expression *mawāṭin al-ḥasab* "the lands of *ḥasab*" from (153), a verse attributed to Zuhair Ibn Abī Sulmà, an obvious formula repeated also by al-Ḥuṭayʔa in t39A:103–4. By this, the poet meant more or less something like "matters of honor" – perhaps the code of honor itself. Consequently, *ḥasab* in this expression – although clearly metaphoric – can metonymically link to the concept of HONOR-VIRTUE.

(153) وَإِمّا أَنْ يَقولوا قَد أَبَينا فَشَرٌّ **مَواطِنِ الحَسَبِ** الإِباءُ

Truly, they will say: "We rejected [to return what we had taken from our guest]" – and [exactly] this rejection [of the obligations towards the guest was] a crime against **the matters of honorability** (*mawāṭin al-ḥasab*) (cf. t22A:11, 15; t22B:18).

POSSESSING *ḥasab* meant then BEING *karīm* or BEING ABLE TO ACT LIKE *karīm*. The latter is clearly discernible in the sample (154). Perhaps, this could be interpreted as a metonymy, in which *ḥasab*-COUNT OF HONORABLE DEEDS affords the access to the idea of the ability or disposition to PERFORM these DEEDS, which as I noted, was referred to in LEAP as *murūʔa*. Similarly, in another place (t38B:37), *ḥasab* is also depicted together with *ʕizz* "the strength" as enabling one to perform honorable deeds. Such *ḥasab* and *ʕizz* are also portrayed as something one can inherit (cf. t38B:118–119). This metonymy seems to be also realized in the expression of someone missing or lacking *ḥasab*, which one could find in (119) by al-Aʕšà, quoted earlier. This example quite clearly shows that POSSESSING *ḥasab* could have also linked to the concept of POSSESSING PREDISPOSITION TO *karam*. Such a relationship would be rather expected, since as I said, *karam*-BEING *karīm* could be understood as something inheritable. Thus, POSSESSING *ḥasab* – the COUNT of prideful deeds of someone and their ancestors – should naturally imply *karīm* origin, from which one can derive HONORABILITY.

(154) لا أَسْرِقُ الشُّعَرَاءَ ما نَطَقُوا، بَلْ لا يُوَافِقُ شِعْرَهُمْ شِعْرِي
إِنّي أَبَى لي ذَلِكُمْ **حَسَبي**، ومَقالَةٌ كمَقاطِعِ الصَخْرِ

I don't steal poems, which they compose, but [to be frank], their poetry does not equal mine.
Truly, **my honor** (*ḥasabī*) forbids me [doing] that – and my words are [sharp] like cuts of a rock (cf. t38B:106).

5.5. *Ḥasab* is a reason to be proud

All in all, it seems the more numerous one's *ḥasab* was, the better for their *ʕirḍ*-HONOR-RIGHT TO RESPECT. It is definitely visible in the metaphor, which might be assumed based on the expression of *ḥasab* by the noun *ʔizār*, literarily meaning "a wrapper which covers the lower part of the body; anything with which one is veiled, concealed, or covered (cf. Lane 1968a: 53)". This metaphoric model, proposed by TBD (mHs12: 200), suggests that *ḥasab* was understood in terms of a

CLOTH. This could imply that *ḥasab* could have been used as a protective measurement. What is important is that specifically, *ˀizār* referred to a garment used to cover the "lower part of the body", i.e., the most vulnerable parts of a man. Therefore, I believe, this metaphor might be seen as lending the structure to the schema of the relationship between *ḥasab* and *ˁirḍ*-HONOR-RIGHT TO RESPECT. It would suggest that *ḥasab* was actually protecting one's *ˁirḍ*, which on its turn, was perceived as vulnerable. I will discuss this relationship further in Chapter 7.

What is most important in here is that *ḥasab*, being one's VALUE/WORTH, was obviously conceptualized as something contributing to one's RIGHT TO RESPECT. In other words, *ḥasab* protected someone's HONOR against SHAMING, since it is difficult to shame someone of recognized VALUE/WORTH validated by their HONORABLE DEEDS. Thus, possessing excellent *ḥasab* must have been a great reason of pride – no one could challenge *ḥasīb*'s RIGHT to be RESPECTED in the community. Such a conceptualization might be perhaps seen in a metonymic use of the adjective *fāḫir* "proud" in reference to *ḥasab*, as it takes place in (155) by Ḥassān Ibn Ṯābit. Obviously, "proud *ḥasab*" stands in here for the *ḥasab*, of which someone can be proud.

(155) فَلَوْ يَصْدُقونَ لأنْبَوْكُمْ بِأنّا ذَوُو الحَسَبِ القَاهِرِ
(…)
ورثتُ الفعالَ وبَذْلَ التِّلادِ والمَجْدَ عنْ كابِرٍ كابِرِ
وَحَمْلَ الدِيَاتِ، وَفَكَّ العُنَاةِ، والعِزَّ في **الحَسَبِ** الفاخِرِ
And if they, [Banū Qurayš], had told [you] truth, they would have made you know that we are in possession of the subduing **value** (*al-ḥasab al-qāhir*).
(…)
I inherited honorability (*faˁāl*), ancestral wealth, and glory (*mağd*) from my great [ancestors].
[And I inherited the obligation to] pay the bloodwites, and release the hostages; [and I inherited] strength in the proud **merits** (*al-ḥasab al-fāḫir*) (cf. t38B:118–119)

Of course, the opposite is also true – one *ḥasab*, when not being numerous, could be also a reason for shame, i.e., could be someone's *ˁār*-DISHONOR, as it is implied by the use of the verb *ḫazà-yaḫzī* "to dishonor someone; to humiliate someone[9]" in the sample (156).

(156) فَإِنّني رَجُلٌ لمْ يَخْزِني **حَسَبِي** وَلا أصْلِي
Truly, I am a man, who is not ashamed by his **value** (*ḥasab*) and his roots (cf. t27A:339).

9 Based on the data from CEAP, one can explicate the verb *ḫazà-yaḫzī* as "being a proof/trial that someone is worth *ˁār*-DISHONOR/DISGRACE".

As we have learned earlier, people MEASURED their *ḥasab*s for sake of comparing who has their RIGHT TO RESPECT more ample. One could see in the very interesting derivation of the verb *qāsa-yaqīs* "to measure" in form of *taqāyasa* (v.s.). Such an activity should be than seen as an example of *tafāḫur* (*mufāḫara* or alternatively, *munāfara*), i.e., a kind of public competition, in which men were trying to overshadow others with their pride-triggering qualities: their *karam*-HONORABLENESS, lineage and deeds of their ancestors, and their wealth. The lexeme *mufāḫara* refers to a whole cultural event schema, which entails priding oneself in front of a neutral judge or judges. Sometimes, it could lead to a more or less physical confrontation (ʿAlī 1993b: 589–592). An example of the use of *ḥasab* as an element of *mufaḫāra* one can find in (140) quoted earlier.

Since *mufāḫara* was a very competitive event, its conceptualization in terms of WAR is more than appropriate. I think this is why, in aforementioned (155), Ḥassān Ibn Ṯābit calls *ḥasab* not only *fāḫir*, but also *qāhir* "subduing, overwhelming, overpowering, prevailing". Again, by means of a metonymy, the poet suggests that the *ḥasab* he is talking about is what will make a competitor in *mufāḫara* winning in a definite fashion.

5.6. Conclusions

To sum it up, the most important cultural conceptualization pertaining to *ḥasab* is the metonymy *ḥasab*-AMOUNT/NUMBER/COUNTED (VALUE) FOR *ḥasab*-COUNT OF *makārim* ("honorable deeds"). It defines the specifics of the whole schema *ḥasab*, being someone's VALUE/WORTH COUNTED or ESTIMATED based on their CONDUCT. Although CEAP does not present any examples of the use of the lexeme *ḥasab* in the sense of AMOUNT/NUMBER/COUNTED (VALUE), the data it provides strongly suggest COUNTABILITY of the concept it refers to. Therefore, one can interpret this conceptualization as a metonymic model, in which the most salient subevent – COUNTING – served as a vehicle affording the access to the concept of COUNTED VALUE BASED ON HONORABLE DEEDS. All in all, because of that, whenever a context suggest multiplicity of *ḥasab*, I rendered it in English as *merits*.

Being simply a COUNT of one's HONORABLE DEEDS, *ḥasab* could be more or less numerous or ample. The excellent *ḥasab* could be referred to as *karīm*, and someone, who was characterized by it was denoted by the lexeme *ḥasīb*. In general, *ḥasab* covered both the DEEDS of someone and of their ancestors. Nevertheless, even if someone's ancestors left one as an inheritance a great deal of such DEEDS, he or she was always expected to prove being worth them and to keep the COUNT of their own *makārim* properly filled up.

Ḥasab as a COUNT of all the HONORABLE DEEDS one could see as attached to someone was what constituted the VALUE or WORTH of this someone. It was their own, individual VALUE (thus, *ḥasab* was referred to in singular as well as plural), which could be, however, also perceived as a VALUE of the whole kin group, such as a *bayt*-HOUSE. It corresponded to both INTERNAL and EXTERNAL aspects of HONOR-related evaluation. The INTERNAL element of *ḥasab* could be inferred based on its role in PRIDE of an individual, whereas its EXTERNALITY could be seen in its vulnerability – one must have always had to protect their *ḥasab* against SHAME and DISHONOR. Thus, the translation of LEAP *ḥasab* as English *dignity* in many places of CEAP seems justifiable. Nevertheless, the sense of such *dignity* should be differentiated from the sense of *karāma*, i.e., DIGNITY-DIGNIFICATION. *Ḥasab*-DIGNITY accentuated the POSSESSION of a certain VALUE or WORTH rather than the recognition of someone as DESERVING RESPECT.

Being VALUE/WORTH of someone, *ḥasab* was in fact the essential element of one's HONOR-RIGHT TO RESPECT. It was what validated one's claim of HONOR in eyes of the community. Possibly, such an essentiality of *ḥasab* was expressed by the metaphor *ḥasab* IS *ṣulb*-BACK BONE, which is suggested by the data from TBD. This metaphor derives in fact from conceptualization of LEAP *ˁirḍ*-HONOR-RIGHT TO RESPECT in terms of BODY (SIDE). Thus, *ḥasab* was a BACKBONE of one's HONOR – it was the most important, essential, fundamental part of it. And as such it must have been protected by all means. Moreover, because of that, ample, numerous *ḥasab* – *ḥasab karīm* – must have been conceptualized also as what protects *ˁirḍ*.

Since the lexeme *ḥasab* referred to the concept of the VALUE/WORTH legitimizing one's RIGHT TO RESPECT, it seems with time it started to be used in reference to the concepts of other means of such legitimization. Thus, in CAD, *ḥasab* seems to mean also *šaraf* "the high social standing" or *māl* "wealth". Both were very important factors which were being taken into consideration while allocating the RIGHT TO RESPECT.

Furthermore, we should not forget that since *ḥasab* was conceptualized as something quantitative, it was also MEASURABLE. MEASURING *ḥasab* served to publicly establish a social hierarchy of PRECEDENCE in terms of the NUMBER of reasons for PRIDE. It was then the most important part of *mufāḫara*s, priding competitions, in which men were boasting and swaggering in an attempt to prove others their higher VALUE.

And since *ḥasab* was a VALUE, it could be obviously seen as a POSSESSED OBJECT. This image-schema participated in important metonymic extensions of the meaning of the lexeme *ḥasab*. First and foremost, although it might be seen a mere ellipsis, I think, *ḥasab* is sometimes used to refer to specifically numerous *ḥasab*. I believe, the CEAP data allow us to say that basically, *ḥasab* was a concept of a COUNT whether numerous or not, and only in some places it indicates more narrow notion of the ample *ḥasab*. Such a *ḥasab* was an important POSSESSION, which could have been LOST or WASTED.

At last, POSSESSION of *ḥasab* sometimes meant POSSESSING *karam*, i.e., BEING *karīm* or BEING ABLE TO ACT LIKE *karīm*. Simply stated, one who HAS *ḥasab*, IS *karīm*. Alternatively, a man of *ḥasab* was then not only the one who acted in accordance with the script of *karam*, but also the one who possessed important inner qualities, traits, which made him follow the code of honorable conduct.

6. Šaraf – Šarīf

Ḥasab was then the VALUE/WORTH of someone, which validated their RIGHT TO RESPECT. In other words, it was what placed them in a hierarchical system of RESPECT, in which some of people are more or less WORTHY being RESPECTED by the community. This system is what is the essential element of the cultural schema referred to by the lexeme *šaraf* – the word, which is probably the most obvious mean of referring to HONOR in Arabic language.

In MSA, the use of the lexeme *šaraf* sometimes indicates that its content is very similar to that of European lexemes referring nowadays to HONOR. For instance, in the first volume of his monumental work *Cities of salt (Mudun al-Milḥ)*, Abdel Rahman Munif (2019: 517) uses this lexeme in the way indicating that *šaraf* is INSIDE of someone, and it makes one act in a certain way. Of course, such a usage indicates that *šaraf* – similarly to modern English *honor* – refers to more or less HONOR-VIRTUE or simply INTEGRITY and does not have too much in common with the notion of RIGHT TO RESPECT. Consequently, the use of the lexeme *šaraf* in MSA seems similar to the phraseology of European words referring to HONOR. Thus, it might be used in such a phrase as *kalimat šaraf* "a word of honor" or in the expression of "swearing to one's honor", as it might be found in the book *Men in the Sun* (*Riǧāl fī aš-Šams*) by Ġassān Kanafānī (1980: 26). Nevertheless, the similarity might be illusory or only partial. In another book, *Returning to Haifa* (*ʕĀʔid ʔilà Ḥayfā*), Kanafānī also uses the lexeme *šaraf*, but clearly in a different way than that mimicking European wording. The interesting passage is as follows:

> إنّ دوف هو عارنا، ولكن خالد هو **شرفنا** الباقي
>
> That's true – Dov is our shame (*ʕāru-nā*), but Ḫālid – he is the **pride** (*šarafu-nā*) that remained us (Kanāfanī 2013: 77).

Translating this passage, I rendered the lexeme *šaraf* not as *honor*, but as *pride*, what I believe reflects in the accurate way the intention of the author. He seems to juxtapose *ʕār* "dishonor, disgrace, shame" and *šaraf* being ascribed to two sons the main protagonists of the book, in the sense of ENTITLEMENT TO PRIDE or perhaps better to the RESPECT. This juxtaposition seems to me confirming that in fact, *šaraf* in modern Arabic literature still pertain to the schema of RIGHT TO RESPECT. Consequently, it does not share the fate of European referents of this notion, which with time, devaluated and nowadays, they usually signify a concept of INTEGRITY or VIRTUE rather than that of HONOR. *Šaraf* is then the HONOR *per se*, i.e., the original notion, which is in process of decline in the Western cultures.

The pre-Islamic concept of *šaraf* pertained similarly to the RIGHT TO RESPECT, although it seems to be closely related to the social stratification and hierarchy. Describing the HONOR in the community of Bedouins in Egypt in the mid of the 20th c., Abou-Zeid (1965: 245) explained the original signification of *šaraf* as "highness" – both, in physical and social sense – what might be seen as a very accurate definition. The lexeme *šaraf*, as we will see in this chapter, has never lost its primary sense of HEIGHT/ELEVATED PLACE, thus its metaphoric use in the conceptualization of RIGHT TO RESPECT seems to correspond to the widespread metaphor of HONOR-PRECEDENCE IS HIGHNESS/ELEVATED POSITION. In many cultures and languages, people who deserve RESPECT due to a certain quality – innate or endowed – such as, noble birth, serving at a state office (e.g., being a judge), are frequently conceptualized as being ABOVE others, and thus, referred to as *high* (e.g., English *your highness* or Polish *wysoki sądzie* "the high court (judge)"). In this, LEAP did not differ at all.

Thus, the only difference between LEAP and MSA seems to be the elaboration of what the RIGHT TO RESPECT is based upon. It occurs that pre-Islamic *šaraf* referred rather to the subschema of PRECEDENCE or vertical/rank/competitive honor, as it was termed by Stewart (1994: 59). The MSA lexeme, in turn, seems to pertain to the whole – perhaps undifferentiated – schema of RIGHT TO RESPECT (cf. Stewart 1994: 132).

As I said, Stewart termed HONOR-PRECEDENCE vertical honor, since in general, such a RIGHT TO RESPECT was not derived directly from following a certain code of behavior, for which one's equals pay them respect. The RESPECT of EQUALS is what horizontal honor entitles one for, and it is in fact, an acknowledgement of one's membership in their community. The vertical honor accentuates the INEQUALITY of the RIGHT TO RESPECT. One can define it more or less as "the right to special respect enjoyed by those who are superior, whether by virtue of their abilities, their rank, their service to the society, their sex, their kin relationship, there office or anything else (Stewart 1994: 59)". As one can see, the most important notion encapsulated in this schema is that of SUPERIORITY, which is either bestowed (by means of rank,[1] office, etc.), innate (i.e., based on sex or origin) or gained (by the virtuous conduct or the service to the community). From among these elements, LEAP *šaraf* encompassed only the innate and

1 Latin *honor* could sometimes refer to the concept of "the right to the special respect that arises from superior rank" (Stewart 1994: 60).

gained SUPERIORITY, since the bestowed one obviously links to the firm statehood, which was not a part of pre-Islamic Arabic social organization. By this, it seems to be akin to the notion of Ancient Greek *tīmē*, which was also the RIGHT TO RESPECT derived from the fact that one either proved to be better than others in his or her action (Stewart 1994: 60) or belonged to the aristocracy (Korus 2017: 33). What is quite important to stress here is that the virtuous conduct mentioned in the definition of HONOR-PRECEDENCE must be read as a special, exemplary, or extraordinary conduct – a certain merit of an individual – which proves that someone is better, and thus, deserves to be respected by everyone – not only by their equals. Although, as we will see, the virtuous conduct – in LEAP, we would say, *karam*, i.e., being *karīm* – was expected from those of vertical honor, earning it was rather related to the extraordinariness of such behavior (in LEAP, one could call it, e.g., *mağd*) and not simply with observing it on the daily basis. These two modes of honorable, noble behavior – extraordinary and normal – correspond quite accurately to the two main profiles of HONOR: vertical and horizontal one – in LEAP, *šaraf* and *ʕirḍ*.

Nevertheless, these two types of HONOR might have been seen as in a way interrelated. One's horizontal honor, for instance, made one protect – not compromise – their HONOR-PRECEDENCE by avoiding fraternizing with their inferiors (Stewart 1994: 61). One can find examples of such behavior also in CEAP (cf. t19B:90–91). Thus, the code of HONORABLE CONDUCT entailed preserving the status of a RESPECTED man by assuring the distinction of someone from those, who were considered without honor by his equals. Moreover, one's ability of increasing the HONOR-PRECEDENCE, i.e., attaining "higher" social standing, was possible only within the frame of one's horizontal honor (Stewart 1994: 62). In other words, one could become of more significance and of higher status only among their equals – for the inferiors, their status was unchangeable and undisputable. Only equals could question one's pretension to SUPERIORITY. HONOR functioned similarly also in the community of Eastern Egyptian Bedouins as described by Abu-Lughod (1986: 85–98).

There is, however, quite a few important differences between horizontal and vertical profile of HONOR. One is definitely the approach to EQUALITY. As we learned, horizontal honor highlights the EQUALITY of people who enjoy the RIGHT TO RESPECT and who PAY this RESPECT. Of course, these two groups contain each other. HONOR-PRECEDENCE by definition accentuates the INEQUALITY between people. The fact that one could increase it only among their EQUALS is consistent with this statement – by increasing one's vertical honor, one changes the EQUALITY group, by which – and in the terms of the standards of which – their behavior will be now evaluated. This INEQUALITY had a very important implication to the HONOR- PRECEDENCE. Namely, it was not reflexive. As we will learned in the following chapter on *ˁirḍ*, the horizontal honor was by far a reflexive in nature, i.e., it was very sensitive, and it required a proper response to any offence. HONOR-PRECEDENCE was not like that – if a superior – a man of a higher social standing – was offended by his inferior, he was not expected to react at all. Any reaction from his side would indicate the relation of EQUALITY between him and his inferior, and by that, it would diminish his RIGHT TO RESPECT derived from PRECEDENCE in the social hierarchy (Stewart 1994: 66). An offence requires EQUALITY to be effective (Pitt-Rivers 1965: 31).

The historical data seem to indicate that this was not entirely the case of pre-Islamic *šaraf*. Arabs of al-Ǧāhiliyya were very punctilious about their social status – one could say to their *šaraf* – and to the way it was acknowledged by proper PAYMENT of RESPECT (cf. ˁAlī 1993b: 541, 573, 674). This punctiliousness could motivate the existence of plethora of lexical tools used in reference to differentiate between those of *šaraf* and those inferiors to them (ˁAlī 1993b: 544). This could seem odd at the very first glance to those, who think of Arabs as men who loved freedom and cherish equality by all means. It is, however, quite a simplistic way of understanding the society of pre-Islamic Arabs. Its stratification existed by all means and consisted first and foremost of the differentiation between free folk – *ˀaḥrār* (sg. *ḥurr*) – and slaves (ˁAlī 1993b: 541). But freemen folk itself was deeply stratified – although, in fact, nomad Arabs not that much (ˁAlī 1993b: 545). The stratification followed wealth and origin (ˁAlī 1993b: 544–5) and it placed on the top tribal chiefs, i.e., leaders of groups of different sizes and different position in hierarchies of tribal units. Just below them, the people of *šaraf* – *ˀašrāf* (sg., *šarīf*) – were located (ˁAlī 1993b: 558), and they were followed by the rest of *karīm* people. The latter were simply people who being free were expected to follow the code of *karam*. By following it, they were consider being the equals group, within which the HONOR – vertical and horizontal – functioned as a part of the social life. Outside of this group – outside of the free folk – no HONOR was possible.

In this chapter, I will explore the notion of LEAP *šaraf* as it was functioning in the society of Arabs of al-Ǧāhiliyya. The following description will contain several cultural schemata, from among which the most important one, *šaraf*-HONOR-PRECEDENCE IS ELEVATED PLACE, is clearly an example of a nearly universal metaphor. The cultural conceptualizations will be described based on the data I acquired from CAD, but most importantly from CEAP and TBD.

In the case of that last source – TBD – *šaraf* was in fact the only HONOR-related concept, which was quite extensively elaborated in it. Thus, the description of schemata I will reconstruct below derive by far from the metaphorical and metonymic expressions presented in TBD – more precisely in aHm – as synonymous to *šaraf* and *šarīf*. In fact, such TBD data on *šaraf* is so abundant that I decided to present most of its examples in separate tables, presenting by this the whole range of linguistic expressions grounded in given conceptual metaphors and metonymies. All the expressions presented below are derived from aHm (44–45, 199–201).

6.1. *Šaraf* and *šarīf* in CAD

CAD clearly depict the root √ŠRF, from which *šaraf* and *šarīf* are derived, as pertaining to the idea of ELEVATION. It might be inferred from such its derivatives as *mašraf* "elevation, elevated place" (KtA2: 325), *istašrafa* "he raised his head looking at something" (KtA2: 325), or *šurfa* "the tallest/ most elevated thing" (LsA9: 204). The concept of *šaraf* naturally realizes this idea as well.

In general, *šaraf* meant simply "a high, elevated place", "the tallest/most elevated place" (KtA2: 325; LsA9: 204), or "elevation" (AsS: 593). LsA specifies, moreover, that it is "any high, elevated piece of the earth which overlooks from above its surrounding, (…) either [heap] of sand, or a mountain, it may be 10 or 5 ells (i.e., elbows) tall (LsA9: 204)". In fact, it was the only explicit meaning provided in KtA (cf. KtA2: 325) and AsS (cf. AsS: 593). On the other hand, however, AlG (729) does not provide this meaning at all, whereas in LsA (cf. LsA9: 203–4), it is definitely less salient than the HONOR-related one. Such a situation might reflect a kind of change in the salience of the meanings of *šaraf* in time. Perhaps, original meaning pertaining to the physical ELEVATION, with time was less and less important and – as one can notice in LsA, it became significantly diminished by the HONOR-related one.

When it comes to this HONOR-related meaning, at least AlG and LsA provide an explicit definition of *šaraf* in its terms. AlG (729) defines *šaraf* as "the elevation (*ʕulūw*) of *ḥasab*" or "being the tallest from among people", clearly using the concept of ELEVATION in explicating the HONOR-related notion. Nonetheless, it does not provide any characteristics of it. In fact, even usually more elaborative Ibn Manẓūr provided in LsA very similar explication of *šaraf*. He saw it as "*ḥasab* in one's ancestors", stressing that together with *mağd* "glory" it could be attained only through one's ancestry (LsA9: 203).

As one can see, none of the definition of *šaraf* as pertaining to the schema of HONOR are satisfactory. We can read them as stating that *šaraf* was a VALUE/ WORTH of a man derived from his ancestors, upon which he could claimed RESPECT of his EQUALS. Of course, such an explication is not to be explicitly found in CAD.

Besides these two major meanings, KtA adds that *šaraf* meant also "a tree possessing red dye" and something like "the brink, verge or point of some event of great magnitude, or of any importance (Lane 1968d: 1537)" (cf. KtA2: 325).

When it comes to the definition of *šarīf*, only LsA (LsA9: 203) defines it as referring to the man of *šaraf*. Both AlG and AsS do not provide any definition of this noun. KtA, however, explicitly states only that *šarīf* is "the tallest mountain in the land of Arabs" (KtA2: 325).

All in all, it seems that the concepts of *šaraf* and *šarīf* must have been quite intuitive for the compilers of CAD and thus, their definition did not seem to be of that importance. Alternatively, one can hypothesize that neither *šaraf* nor *šarīf* were important as such to them at all. Such an explanation, however, does not seem plausible to me. The significance and salience of these concepts in the Modern Arabic communities definitely suggests that cannot be the case.

The table below (Tab. 7.) presents all the meaning of *šaraf* and *šarīf* presented in CAD. Although Lane (1968d: 1537–8) provides a much longer list of their significations, I decided not to include all of them due to the obvious semantic development, distant from LEAP, they present.

Tab. 7. The meanings of *šaraf* and *šarīf* in CAD and dictionaries of CA

Lexeme	Meaning	Sources
šaraf	[a] highness or eminence in rank, high birth, nobility	AlG: 729; LsA9: 203; Lane 1968d: 1537; Wehr & Cowan 1976: 467
	[b] elevation	AsS: 593
	[c] an elevated place, any piece of ground that overtops what is around it	KtA2: 325; AsS: 593; LsA9: 204; Lane 1968d: 1537; Wehr & Cowan 1976: 467
	[d] a kind of trees, having a red dye	KtA2: 325; Lane 1968d: 1537
	[e] the brink, verge or point of some event of great magnitude, or of any importance	
šarīf	[α] high or eminent in rank; high-born, noble	LsA9: 203; Lane 1968d: 1538
	[β] the tallest mountain in the land of Arabs	KtA2: 325

As one can see, in fact only the meaning [d] "a kind of trees having red dye" does not fit the group of significations of *šaraf* and *šaraf*, which all pertain in a way to ELEVATION – either physical or social in nature. We can consider it as possibly derived from another etymon.

6.2. CEAP data on *šaraf* and *šarīf*

The cluster *šaraf* consists of the lexemes *šaraf*, *šarīf*, and the plural forms of the latter – *ˀašrāf* and *šurafāˀ*. The lexeme *ˀašrāf* sometimes refers in CEAP to the plural of *šaraf* meaning "an elevated place", nevertheless I have not included it in the overall count of the lexeme *šaraf*. I kept it only in the count for the term *šarīf*. What is actually surprising in the low frequency of the vocabulary from this cluster in CEAP. In total, they occurred only 49 times, which equals NWC: 1.73, and is the lowest result from among all LEAP HONOR-related terms (sic!).

In general, the lexeme *šarīf* seems to be very rare in the corpus. It occurs only 7 times, and together with 4 occurrences of *ˀašrāf* being a plural form of *šarīf*, it appeared in total only 12 times (NWC: 0.42). The lexeme *šaraf* could be found in the corpus a bit more frequently – 33 times (NWC: 1.17[2]). Still, both results seem to be unexpectedly low, taking into consideration the signification of words *šaraf* and *šarīf* for the modern conceptualization of HONOR.[3]

It might mean then that as a theme pertaining to the schema of HONOR-RIGHT TO RESPECT, PRECEDENCE – i.e., *šaraf* – was not that salient or significant for pre-Islamic Arabs. Perhaps, one can interpret it through the social situational context of EAP, which was focused on praising and shaming. As such, it was more concerned with people's behavior and achievements, which are normally encompassed by the schema of *karam* and *maǧd* "fame, glory". It would explain the high frequency of the clusters of *karam* – NWC: 8.81 – and *maǧd* – NWC: 8.67. PRECEDENCE as an ENTITLEMENT to RESPECT possibly was not that important for poets of al-Ǧāhiliyya, since both *karam*-HONORABLE CONDUCT and *maǧd*-FAME OF HONORABLE CONDUCT definitely were much more foregrounded in the RIGHT TO RESPECT schema. Moreover, as we will learn in this chapter, both had fundamental value for the *šaraf*-PRECEDENCE, thus the latter could have been omitted by means of metonymy. In other words, while praising or shaming someone, the position this someone achieved was not important – more important was

---

2 NWC of 1.17 corresponds to the frequency of English words *interested, investment, difficult, primary,* and *guide,* and Polish *ilość, myśli, zresztą, minut, wciąż,* and *cena.* Based on the corpora *English Web 2015* and *Polish Web 2015* available at *SketchEngine* (https://www.sketchengine.eu [08-07-2021]).

3 It is worth noting that in the corpora of MSA texts, *šaraf* and *šarīf* are also of low frequency. In Arabic Web 12 corpus (8 322,097 229 words; available at https://www.sketchengine.eu [22-07-2021]), *šaraf* is of NWC: 0.74, whereas *šarīf* (including *ˀašrāf* and *šurafāˀ*) of NWC: 1.33. In arabiCorpus (173 600 000 words; available at https://arabicorpus.byu.edu/ [22-07-2021]), the numbers are as follow: *šaraf* – NWC: 1.10, *šarīf* (including *ˀašrāf* and *šurafāˀ*) – NWC: 1.17.

the repertoire of means of achieving this position, i.e., the high or low social status. Those means were encoded in the cultural script of *karam*, HONORABLE CONDUCT.

All in all, the statistical data on the *šaraf* cluster were presented in the table below (Tab. 8.).

Tab. 8. The number of occurrences of the members of *šaraf* cluster within CEAP

<table>
<tr><th colspan="2">Item</th><th colspan="2">Number of Occurrences (NO)</th><th>Normalized Word Count (per 10,000)</th></tr>
<tr><td>šaraf</td><td></td><td colspan="2">33</td><td>1.17</td></tr>
<tr><td rowspan="3">šarīf</td><td></td><td>7</td><td rowspan="3">=12</td><td rowspan="3">0.42</td></tr>
<tr><td>ʔašrāf
(pl. of šarīf)</td><td>5</td></tr>
<tr><td>šurafāʔ</td><td>0</td></tr>
</table>

From among the meanings presented in the Tab. 7., only [a] "highness or eminence in rank, high birth, nobility" and [c] "an elevated place, any piece of ground that overtops what is around it" of *šaraf*, and [α] "high or eminent in rank; high-born, noble" of *šarīf* were to be found. What is quite interesting in the results for *šaraf* is that the signification [a] and [c] were almost equally represented (NO: 18 for [a] vs. NO: 13 for [b]). Moreover, twice in CEAP, *šaraf* refers to a proper name.

6.3. *Šaraf* is the "high" social status

The aforementioned statistical data suggest that *šaraf*-ELEVATED PLACE and *šaraf*-PRECEDENCE were still well associated in LEAP. It could suggest that the whole schema of *šaraf*-PRECEDENCE was structured by the metaphoric model *šaraf*-PRECEDENCE IS ELEVATED PLACE. As I mentioned, such a conceptualization is a quite widespread phenomenon. In fact, one should see it as only a part of a broader schema of SOCIAL STRATIFICATION, which obviously is shaped by the source concept of LADDER. More precisely, SOCIAL STATUS is frequently conceptualized as a POSITION (Lakoff, Espenson & Schwartz 1991: 59), which is usually perceived in terms of UP-DOWN image-schema. This schema is a nearly universal mean of conceptualization of GOOD-BAD distinction (Lakoff, Espenson & Schwartz 1991: 187), and in the case of SOCIAL STRATIFICATION it serves to depict the evaluation of one's STATUS-POSITION on the social LADDER. Thus, one could be of HIGH (i.e., better) or LOW (i.e., worse) social status, i.e., POSITION on that LADDER.

LEAP conceptualization of HIGH SOCIAL STATUS was no different. The SOCIAL STRATIFICATION was conceptualized as a something like LADDER or STAIR, and one's STATUS as a STEP on it – *daraǧa* or *rutba* (cf. Lane 1968c: 869 and 1025). The HIGH SOCIAL STATUS, i.e., the PRECEDENCE over others, was conceptualized as ELEVATED POSITION, which could be elaborated in a few ways. The most obvious one was *šaraf*, which referred to an ELEVATED PLACE – a hill, a mound, etc. Nevertheless, a more abstract idea of ELEVATION could also serve in the conceptualization of PRECEDENCE, which is indicated mostly by such lexemes as *ʕulūw* or *sumūw*, being verbal nouns derived from verbs *ʕalā-yaʕlū* and *samā-yasmū* both meaning "to ascend, to be elevated, lifted". Other means of expressing the concept of ELEVATED POSITION were such nouns as *naǧwa* "an elevated piece of land (Lane 1968h: 3028)", which was used in CEAP also as clearly referring to PRECEDENCE-HIGH SOCIAL STATUS (cf. t30A:66). Moreover, *šaraf* might have been also referred to by the expressions pertain to the schema STEP on a LADDER/STAIRS, and thus it could have been terms *daraǧa rafīʕa* or *rutba rafīʕa*, meaning "elevated step (on a ladder)". The table below (Tab. 9.) presents other lexical expressions of PRECEDENCE-HIGH SOCIAL STATUS in terms of ELEVATED PLACE or ELEVATION provided in TBD.

6.3.1. REACHING *šaraf* IS CLIMBING UP

The metaphor PRECEDENCE-HIGH SOCIAL STATUS IS ELEVATED PLACE structured also the event schema of how one could become *šarīf*, i.e., a man of high social standing. As one can guess, such an activity was mostly referred to by lexemes referring to the script of ASCENDING or CLIMBING (UP), which must have resulted in REACHING the ELEVATED PLACE, i.e., *šaraf*. Thus, the concept of BECOMING *šarīf* was referred to by such lexemes as *ṣaʕida-yaṣʕad* or *raqà-yarqī* meaning simply "ascending, climbing up". The goal of these activities – *šaraf* – was conceptualized as something one can REACH, what was lexically expressed by the verb *balaġa-yabluġ* also in CEAP (cf. example (158) below). Additionally, *šaraf* could have also been referred to by pointing to the very process of ascending or being lifted. This might be seen as an example of metonymy in metaphor, where *šaraf* stands for ACQUIRING *šaraf*. Consequently, also *šarīf* – as a man who was ASCENDING towards the HIGH SOCIAL STATUS – was frequently conceptualized as an ASCENDING or BEING ELEVATED, such as it is the case of the active particle *sāmī*, derived from the verb *samā-yasmū* both meaning "to ascend, to be elevated, lifted". The example of its use might be found in the passage (157) by Ibn Muqbil.

Tab. 9.

Meaning	Expression	Literary Meaning
šaraf	*rutba baʕidat al-maṣʕad*	a step on a ladder of a distant place, towards which one ascends (= a step placed high above, distant while ascending towards it)
	rutba baʕidat al-murtaqà	
	rutba bāḏiḫat aḏ-ḏurà	a step on a ladder of the lofty highest points (= a step placed high above, distant while ascending towards it)
	ʕulūw	ascending, becoming high or elevated
	ʕalāʔ	
	sumūw	
	rifʕa	high position

(157) وعَاقِدِ التَّاجِ أوْ سَامٍ له **شَرَفٌ** مِن سُوقةِ الناسِ نالَتْهُ عَوالِينا
Any crowned king or any **elevated man** (*sāmī*) of **high social standing** (*šaraf*), and any leader of people – our spears [know how to] reach [all of them] (cf. t36A:235).

The table below (Tab. 10.) presents other lexical expressions, which elaborate the metaphor ACQUIRING HIGH SOCIAL STATUS IS ASCENDING/CLIMBING (UP).

Tab. 10.

Meaning	Expression	Literary Meaning
acquiring *šaraf*	*ʕalat manzilatu-hu*	his position became elevated
	tawaqqala ad-daraǧāt ar-rafiʕa	he climbed elevated ladder steps
	tawaqqala fi maʕāriǧ aš-šaraf	he was climbing on the ladder of *šaraf*
	tasawwara šurufāt al-ʕizz	he ascended the heights of strength
	tasannama ḏirwat aš-šaraf	he rode upon the uppermost of the camel-hump of *šaraf*
	ṣaʕida furūʕ al-ʕulà	he climbed the highest (branches) of heights
	balaġa ʔilà rutba lā yasmū ʔilay-hi ʔamal	he reached a ladder step, towards which any hope does not ascend (= there is no hope to ascend that high)
	balaġa ʔilà manzila lā yataʕallaqu bi-hā darak	he reached the position, to which no rope is attached
	tawaqqala ʔilà al-ʕulà	he climbed towards the heights
	tasawwara ʔilà aš-šaraf	he climbed towards *šaraf*
	balaġa qimmat aš-šaraf	he reached the pick of *šaraf*
	waṯaba ʔilà qimmat aš-šaraf	he sprang/leaped onto the pick of *šaraf*

Tab. 10. Continued

Meaning	Expression	Literary Meaning
šaraf	*irtifāʕ*	ascending
	irtiqāʔ	ascending, climbing (the ladder)
	busūq	from *basaqa* "(the palm-trees) were, or became, tall, and full-grown, or exceedingly tall"
	sanāʔ	from *sanā* "(about fire) it became high in its light" [ergo: becoming high in light]
šarīf	*sanī*	shining and ascending upwards (like fire)
	ṭallāʕ ṯanāyā	wont to ascent difficult mountain roads
	ṭalaba al-marātib as-saniyya	he sought, pursued the higher positions
	ṭalaba ad-darağāt ar-rafīʕa	he sought, pursued the elevated step on the ladder

Climbing towards *šaraf* could also be what structures the conceptualization of {*ḥasab karīm* leads one to *šaraf*}, which encodes the very important knowledge that an excellent count of honorable deeds could have been seen as participating in both arriving at and persisting in the high social status. It can be definitely seen in (158) attributed to Ḥassān Ibn Ṯābit. In this verse, *ḥasab* is conceptualized as something, one could cut off – perhaps a rope or a ladder – which one can climb on towards the *mağd* and "heights", which naturally by means of the aforementioned metaphor indicate *šaraf*. This particular passage might be read as a statement that a *ḥasab*-count, which does not contain enough *makārim*-honorable deeds, cannot lead one to the social recognition or the high social standing.

(158) قدْ عِلِمَتْ أسْلَمُ الأنْذَالُ أنّ لهَاجاراً سيقتلهُ في دارهِ الجوعُ
وَأنْ سيمْنَعَهُمْ ممّا نَوَوْا **حسَبٌ**، لَنْ يبلُغَ **المجدَ** والعَلْياءَ مقْطُوعُ

[The tribe of] base people of [Banū] Aslam had known that they have a client [people], who would be killed by famine,
and that when they wanted [to help those people], they were stopped by a cut-off (*maqṭūʕ*) **honorability** (*ḥasab*), which will [never] reach **glory** (*mağd*) and heights [of social status] (cf. t38B:162).

The conceptualization of *ḥasab* in terms of object extending upwards, perhaps a rope or a ladder, seems to have found its reflection also in the idiomatical expression pertaining in Arabic to *šaraf*. In the table below (Tab. 11.), I presented some expressions from TBD, which refer to *šaraf* by means of commenting on one's *ḥasab* in terms of elevation.

Tab. 11.

Meaning	Expression	Literary Meaning
šarīf	*sanī al-ḥasab*	of shining and ascending upwards (like fire) *ḥasab*
non-*šarīf*	*sāqiṭ al-ḥasab*	of fallen-down *ḥasab*
	waḍīʕ al-ḥasab	of put-down *ḥasab*

6.3.1.1. Possessing *šaraf*-elevated place

After having CLIMBED UP and REACHED the *šaraf*-PRECEDENCE-ELEVATED PLACE (ON A LADDER), one seems to take it into their POSSESSION. Thus, *šaraf* as a mark of a social position was additionally conceptualized as a POSSESSED OBJECT. *Šaraf* – still being a PLACE – was then also a POSSESSION of someone. It is quite interesting that the conceptualization of HIGH SOCIAL STANDING in terms of POSSESSION persists in MSA. Also nowadays, while referring to someone, who enjoys such a high position, one usually uses the noun *ṣāḥib* "the owner", as in the expression *ṣāḥib as-sumūw* "[his] highness (lit. the owner of elevation/elevating)". In CEAP, the POSSESSION of *šaraf* was either expressed by the prepositional phrase with *li-* (i.e., *la-hu* "he has"), as in the sample (159) (cf. also t36A:225–235; t38B:170; t38A:200), or by the noun *ḏū* "owner" (discussed in Chapter 4), as in (160), or (161). Moreover, *šaraf* is depicted as something that could have been possessed either by an individual – as in (160) and (161) – or an entire group, as in (159) (cf. also t38B:170; t38A:200; t28A:100–102).

(159) وَيَصْحَبُنِي من آلِ عَبْسٍ عِصابةٌ لها **شرفٌ** بين القبائل يَمْتَدُّ

I am accompanied by a group [of men] from the clan of ʕAbs. They have a **high social position** (*šaraf*), which is extended, [well-known], among tribes (cf. t21A:49).

(160) لوْ ينطِقُ التيْسُ ذو الخُصْنَيَيْنِ وَسْطَهُمُ لَكانَ **ذا شَرَفٍ** فيهِمْ وَذا شانِ

If a white-fur buck had spoken up among them, he would have become [instantly] **of the high position** (*ḏā šaraf*) [in their tribe] and the one, who [is responsible for their] affairs (cf. t38A:248).

(161) وَاسْتَشْفَعَت من سَراةِ الحَي **ذا شَرَفٍ** فَقَدْ عَصاها أبوها والذي شَفَعَا

Thus, [his daughter] asked the noblemen (*sarā*) of the tribe to support her in convincing [her father], **the owner of the high social rank** (*ḏā šaraf*), [to keep him from constant traveling] – but her father opposed her and those, who assisted her [in trying to persuade him] (cf. t28A:101, 104).

Consequently, alongside the more LOCATION-bound source in form of REACHING, becoming of a HIGH SOCIAL POSITION could be also structured by the script of OBTAINING/RECEIVING. It is an obvious derivation from the schema POSSESSION, to which *šaraf* as POSSESSED OBJECT pertained. The image-schema OBTAIN in this particular case is called up by the verb *nāla-yanāl*, which I have already discussed in Chapter 4, while describing the schema of *karāma*. Therefore, *šaraf* was an OBJECT, which must have been took in one's POSSESSION in the more general terms. An example of this conceptualization in CEAP can be (162) by ʿAntara Ibn Šaddād.

(162) لِلهِ دَرُّ عَبْسٍ لقدْ بلَغوا كلَّ الفَخارِ **ونالوا** غايةَ **الشَرفِ**

To the God be praise for the excellency of [Banū] ʿAbs – they have achieved all of the pride and **obtained** (*nalū*) the limits of the **eminence** (*aš-šaraf*) (cf. t21A:88).

CEAP provides the examples of only two ways of OBTAINING *šaraf* – one could do that either by themselves or by derivation from their ancestors.

As observed by Abou-Zeid (1965: 252–3), Bedouins of Eastern Egypt derived much of their *šaraf* – referring to both HONOR-RIGHT TO RESPECT and PRECEDENCE – from their kin group. In Arabic society of al-Ǧāhiliyya, the situation looked quite similar. First and foremost, one derived their *šaraf*-HIGH SOCIAL STANDING from their people: a kin-group of a various size. It is depicted in the sample (94).

(94) إنّي لأنمى إذا إنتَمَيتُ إلى غُرٍّ كِرامٍ وَقومُنا **شَرَفُ**
بيضٌ جِعادٌ كَأَنَّ أعيُنَهُم يُكحِلُها في المَلاحِمِ السَدَفُ

Truly, I am ascending by being ascribed to the best honorable people (*kirām*), since our people, are [my] **high social position** (*šaraf*)
– [they are] white, generous, and their eyes spring [like early flowers] in an advent of [every] battle (t01χ).

This passage is quite interesting, since the poet states that his people are *šaraf*. We can read it as the statement that their kin-group was the source of their HIGH SOCIAL STATUS. Alternatively, one might see in here a metonymy, in which *šarīf* people are referred to by *šaraf*, as it takes also place elsewhere in CEAP (cf. t26A:75). Indeed, such a metonymy could bring forward the conceptualization that *šarīf* men are the reason of *šaraf* of the whole kin-group. Perhaps, this is how one should interpret the expression *baḍʿat aš-šaraf* "a lump of *šaraf*", which TBD presents as a mean of reference to a *šarīf* man. In other words, a *šarīf* is conceptualized as a CHUNK of MASS, being *šaraf* of the whole group. This metonymy seems to encode in LEAP the conceptualization that the whole community can derive a HIGH SOCIAL STANDING (among other communities) based on their *šarīf*s, who – collectively – are seen as the MASS of *šaraf* possessed by the group, and individually, as LUMPS of this MASS.

Alternatively, one could OBTAIN *šaraf* also from being affiliated to a *šarīf* ally by means of an alliance or a client-patron relationship. This could be seen, for instance, in the passage (163) by ʿAntara Ibn Šaddād, in which the poet described being a client of Sasanian shah Khosrow I Anushirvan as something bringing in HIGHER SOCIAL STANDING. This conceptualization seems to derive from the hypothetical non-linguistic metonymy, I discussed in Chapter 4, namely *ǧiwār*-RELATIONSHIP FOR LINEAGE-BASED RELATIONSHIP.

(163) مَلِكٌ حَوَى رُتَبَ المعالي كلَّها بِسُمُوِّ مَجْدٍ حَلَّ في إيوانِه
مَوْلًى بِه **شَرُفَ** الزَّمانُ وأهلهُ والدَّهْرُ نالَ الفَخْرَ من تِيجَانِه
[He is the] king, who fills the steps of all heights [of precedence] with the highness of the glory (*maǧd*), which occupies his palace.
A client (*mawlà*) [of his becomes] due to him [a man] of **high social position** (*šarufa*), and his people, and [his] times, become full of pride because of his crown (cf. t21A:141).

Nevertheless, *šaraf* could be also OBTAINED by means of one's deeds – one's honorable behavior. The same can be said about HONOR in Easter Egypt Bedouin communities studied by Abou-Zeid (1965: 245) and Abu-Lughod (1986: 85–6). Although, it seems *šaraf* was primarily derived from one's origin or one's tribal and other affiliation, in CEAP, one can find examples of becoming *šarīf* based on one's conduct only. This is definitely the case of the ancestors of Ḥātim aṭ-Ṭāʔī, described by him in (69) as people, who became *šarīf*s – *šurrifū* – on the basis of their MAGNANIMITY, which might be here read as a metonymic reference to *karam*.

(69) وإنّي لَمَذْمومٌ، إذا قيلَ حاتِمٌ نبا نَبْوَةً ، إنّ الكريمَ يُعَنَّفُ
سآبى ، وتَأبَى بي أُصُولٌ كريمَةٌ وآباءُ صِدْقٍ، بالمَوَدّة ، **شُرِّفوا**
Truly, I am dishonored, when one talks about Ḥātim with disdain – truly, they are viciously disgracing an honorable man (*karīm*).
I will rebuff [these vile words] in the way the noble roots rebuffed me. My sincere ancestors gain **high social status** (*šurrifū*) by their kindness, [not by birth] (cf. t19B:71).

6.3.2. *Šarīf* is ABOVE, non-*šarīf* is BELOW

Consequently, the conceptual model *šaraf*-PRECEDENCE IS ELEVATED PLACE structures the conceptualization of *šarīf*, a man of HIGH SOCIAL STANDING. As I already mentioned, *šarīf* could be perceived as an ASCENDING or a CLIMBING man, but first and foremost, this figure was conceptualized in the terms of the already taken POSITION. Thus, *šarīf* was ELEVATED, or of ELEVATED POSITION (on the social LADDER) or occupying a PLACE SO ELEVATED that it was NOTICEABLE from distance (cf. *malḥūẓ al-manzila* "lit. of a noticeable position"). As such, *šarīf* must have been conceptualized as ABOVE others, which in LEAP, was elaborated, for instance, by means of the lexeme *ḏirwa* (pl. *ḏurà*) meaning "the uppermost part of a camel-hump". Clearly, it is an example of a cultural metaphor, in which an element of the specific socio-environmental milieu of pre-Islamic Arabs was employed. In other words, *šarīf* was perceived by them as someone positioned on the UPPERMOST PART OF A CAMEL-HUMP or one who was climbing such one, which could be also found in CEAP (cf. t07A:43; t24A:81–82; t28A:162–169; t38A:301; t38B:161–162; t38B:207–208). Consequently, a *šarīf* might be also imagined as something that occupies a HIGH/ELEVATED PLACE. For instance, in the sample (86), *šarīf*s are referred to as *šumūs* "Suns".

(86) من القَومِ الكِرام وهُم شمُوسٌ ولكِنْ لا تُوارى بالدُّجون

[He descends] from **noble people** (*kirām*), who are [like] Suns – but [the Suns], which are never blocked by thick clouds (cf. t21A:149–150).

The schema of BEING ABOVE OTHERS seems to be elaborated in more physical metaphors pertaining to the schema of BODY. Thus, *šarīf* was conceptualized also as a man whose NOSE was ABOVE others, like in the expression *ʔašamm al-ʔanf*, which is to be found in the CEAP in two places (in form of plural *šamm al-ʔunūf* in t38A:246 and *šamm al-ʕarānīn* in t36A:245). This expression literarily means that someone is of high nose or of elevated nose bone, which was considered a symbol of nobility (cf. Lane 1968d: 1593–4). Moreover, *šarīf* was also seen as *ʕālī al-kaʕb* "of elevated ancle-bone", which could indicate that he was simply TALLER than others. The table below (Tab. 12.) presents other lexical expressions of the metaphors *šarīf* IS ON ELEVATED POSITION and *šarīf* IS ABOVE OTHERS.

Tab. 12.

Meaning	Expression	Literary Meaning
šarīf	*ʕalī, ʕilya*	high, elevated, lofty
	rafīʕ al-mazila	of high, elevated position
	rafīʕ ad-daraǧa	of high, elevated step on the ladder
	sāmī ar-rutba	
	ʕalī ar-rutba	
	malḥūẓ al-manzila	of a noticeable position
	huwa fī ḏurà	he is in the uppermost part of camel-humps
	ḏirwa	the uppermost part of a camel-hump
	ʕālī aḏ-ḏirwa	of elevated uppermost part of a camel-hump
	ṭālat ḏirwatu-hu	his uppermost part of camel-hump became tall
	faraʕa ḏirwat al-maǧd	he ascended the uppermost part of a camel-hump of glory (*maǧd*)
	ʕalī al-kaʕb	of elevated ankle-bone

The conceptualizations of non-*šarīf*, i.e., *laʔīm*, also derived from the same metaphorical system. Thus, a person who was of low social standing was perceived simply as either LOW or FALLING (DOWN) or as of LOW (or FALLING DOWN) POSITION. Interestingly enough, such a person is mostly conceptualized as one who failed to acquire higher status in a kind of RACE for it. One can see it, e.g., in the expressions such as *mutaḫādil* "left behind" or *muʔaḫḫar al-manzila* "[a man] of a position behind [others]".

The most important conceptualizations of NON-*šarīf* in form of expressions deriving from the metaphor *šaraf*-PRECEDENCE IS ELEVATE PLACE are presented in the table below (Tab. 13.).

Tab. 13.

Meaning	Expression	Literary Meaning
non-*šarīf*	*sāfil*	low
	sāqiṭ	low; one which is falling down
	waḍīʕ	put down, placed down [= *maʕwḍūʕ* (LsA)]
	ḫafī al-manzila	of obscure, invisible position
becoming non-*šarīf*	*ittaḍaʕat rutbatu-hu*	his step on the ladder became put down, was low
	inḥaṭṭat darağatu-hu	his step on a ladder became low, put down (like a load from a camel's horse's saddle)
	saqaṭat manzilatu-hu	his position fell down (=became lowered)
non-*šaraf*; LOW SOCIAL STANDING	*ḍaʕa*	being put down, low
	suqūṭ	falling down
	safāl	[opposite of *ʕulūw* "ascending, becoming high, elevated" (LsA)]
	inḥiṭāṭ	being put down, low

Furthermore, a logical consequence of the aforementioned conceptualizations of *šarīf* and non-*šarīf* must have been the GRADUALITY of *šaraf*-HIGH SOCIAL STATUS. As one can see in the passage (164), one's *šaraf* might have been still ASCENDING. It might suggest that it was always a subject of DECREASE or INCREASE – being made LOWER or HIGHER, ASCENDING and DESCENDING, as the date from TBD suggest. Thus, the HIGHER one's *šaraf*-ELEVATED PLACE was, the more of PRECEDENCE they were, i.e., they were located HIGHER on the social LADDER.

(164) ألمْ ترَنا أوْلادَ عَمْرِو بنِ عامرٍ، لَنا شرَفٌ يَعْلو على كلّ مُرْتقي

Sons of ʕAmr Ibn ʕĀmir, don't you see that we have a **high social position** (*šaraf*), which ascends [higher] towards all the highest [of social hierarchies] (cf. t38A:200).

Moreover, the metaphor conceptualizing *šarīf*-OF HIGH SOCIAL STATUS in terms of being ABOVE others also encoded the conceptualization {*šarīf* was someone important}. Of course, it might sound as a truism since the HIGH SOCIAL STATUS implies IMPORTANCE in general. Nevertheless, as it is described in TBD, conceptualizations of *šaraf* and *šarīf* folk seem to accentuate this fact a lot. Thus, *šarīf* could be also referred to as *ẖaṭīr* "important[4]" or in a less abstract manner, as BIG – *kabīr*, *ʕaẓīm* "big, large" – or BULKY/LARGE – *ğalīl* "lit. bulky, thick (applied to substances, cf. Lane 1968b: 437)". The last example is especially interesting, since *ğalāla* – referring to state of BEING *ğalīl* – still nowadays persist as a mean of reference to PRECEDENCE, normally while addressing a king (i.e., cf. *ğalālat al-malik* "your highness"). Moreover, as a synonym of *šarīf*, TBD provide the lexeme *quṭb* (pl.*ʔaqṭāb*) meaning "the axis of iron of a mill (Lane 1968g: 254)". Here, the IMPORTANCE of this figure is metaphorically implied by an elaboration of the image-schema BEING AT THE CENTER. In details, the conceptualizations of *šarīf* (and *šaraf*) in terms of IMPORTANCE are presented in the table below (Tab. 14.).

4 The noun *ẖaṭīr* itself, as well as the noun referring to the abstract state of BEING *ẖaṭīr* – *ẖaṭar* – are a very interesting example of metonymic development from seemingly original concept of a JEOPARDY, RISK, or HAZARD. Meaning that, *ẖaṭar* developed by means of a metonymy, generalization, and specification of meaning, etc., into a cluster of concepts, from among which IMPORTANCE is one of the most salient (cf. Lane 1968'2': 764–5).

Tab. 14.

Meaning	Expression	Literary Meaning
šarīf	*ẖaṭīr*	[derivative of *ẖaṭar* (v.i.)]
	kabīr	big, large
	ʕaẓīm	
	ʕaẓuma qadru-hi	his size, measure, magnitude became large, big
	ḍaẖuma ʔamru-hu	his affairs became large, bulky, fleshy
	ǧalīl al-qadr	of large, bulky size, measure, magnitude
	faẖīm aš-šaʔn	of large, big, bulky affair
	quṭb, ʔaqṭāb	iron axis of the mill
šaraf	*ẖaṭar*	importance (<=*metn*= {an affair, or event, or a case, of moment or importance or magnitude <=*metn*= {a perilous, important, momentous affair}})
	ǧalāla	bulkiness, thickness

6.3.2.1. ***Šaraf*** **is the PRECEDENCE in LEADERSHIP**

This IMPORTANCE, however, came definitely from the PRECEDENCE of *šarīf* folk in leadership, which in pre-Islamic society was exclusively limited to the social strata of people of HIGH SOCIAL STATUS. It can be interpreted, for instance, from the passage (165) by al-Ḫansāʔ. *Šarīf* folk was then equal to crowned heads and were perceived as the leading class of the pre-Islamic Arabic society (cf. t36A:225–235). Thus, *šarīf* person, occupying the high social position, was responsible for the affairs of his people, as it is implied in (160), a verse of a satire by Ḥassān Ibn Ṯābit, quoted earlier.

(165) ما لِذا المَوْتِ لا يَزالُ مُخيفًا كُلَّ يَوْمٍ يَنالُ مِنّا **شَرِيفًا**
مُولَعاً بالسَّراةِ مِنّا، فَما يأخُذُ خُذُ الّا المهذَّبَ الغطريفا
فلَوَ أنّ المَنُونَ تَعْدِلُ فينَا فتنالُ **الشَّريفَ** والمشروفا

How comes that every day, the permanently terrible death gets from us a **nobleman** (*šarīf*)!
[How comes that it is so] eager to [claim] from among us [our] aristocrats (*sarā*) – and d it takes only the courteous leaders!
But, if the fate was to be just for us, [anyway] it would [be able to] get [from us only] a **nobleman** (*šarīf*) and a man elevated [above others – since this is all we have in our tribe] (cf. t33A:89).

The fact that *šarīf* man was in charge of the tribes' affairs could be also found encoded in a number of metaphors and metonymies, which conceptualizes this figure in terms of a LEADER of his people. The most obvious from among such concepts are those which employ the schema BODY in conceptualizing TRIBE. Thus, a *šarīf* could be referred to as a HEAD of his people (*hāma*). He was also perceived as their TONGUE or FACE, which I believe, can be interpreted as the encodement of the fact that *šarīf*-LEADER was the spokesmen of his tribe, its representative (cf. ʕAlī 1993b: 547). This conception might be seen as encompassed by several conceptualizations, which are all included in the table below (Tab. 15.). It depicts the metaphorical and metonymic models pertaining to the relationship between *šaraf* and LEADERSHIP.

Tab. 15.

Meaning	Expression	Literary Meaning
šarīf	*hāma*	head
	nāṣiya	the place where the hair grows in the fore part of the head; and hence, the hair of that part; the hair over the forehead (Lane 1968h: 3033)
	lisān qawmi-hi	a tongue of his people
	ʕayn qawmi-hi	an eye of his people
	waǧīh	[derivative of *waǧāha* (v.i.)]
	waǧh qawmi-hi	a face of his people
	sahm qawmi-hi an-nāfiḏ	a perforating, piercing though arrow of his people
	taṭmaḥu ʔilay-hi al-ʕuyūn	eyes (of others) are raised towards him
	tarnū ʔilay-hī al-ʔabṣār	eyes (of others) gaze towards him
	rumiya bi-l-ʔabṣār	he was thrown in front of the eyes (of others)
šaraf	*waǧāha*	rank, position, estimation <=*derived from*= {*waǧh qawmi-hi* "a face of his people" <=*metf*= {"(in) the front of (the people)" <=*metn*/*metf*= {"the face"}}}
	ǧāh[a]	

[a] "Rank, station, or dignity, with, or in the estimation of, the Sultán; probably Arabicized from the Persian جَاه; also but said to be formed by transposition from *waǧh*; this being first changed to *ǧawh*, then to *ǧawah*; and then, to *ǧāh* (Lane 1968b: 491)".

Šarīf folk was then the elite of the pre-Islamic Arabic society. They play the role similar to European aristocrats, who had the real political power and virtually unlimited access to holding offices and controlling the government. Similarly, a chief – being *šarīf* at the first place – must also have had to consider opinions of other *šarīfs* of his tribe (ʕAlī 1993b: 351), who usually formed a council known as *šurà* (cf. ʕAlī 1993b: 349). Moreover, similarly to what we could have seen in the past in Europe, pre-Islamic Arabic tribes used to marry their *šarīfs* with *šarīfs* of other tribes, cementing alliances in such a way (cf. ʕAlī 1993b: 633). Perhaps, this could explain the metonymic model, which might be seen in the TBD, which claim that *šarīf* people could be also referred to as simply *malaʔ* "an assembly". It could indicate that in fact, by means of *totum pro partem* schema, the elite could be referred to as the assembly of the tribe, highlighting thereafter the fact that *šarīfs* were, in fact, those who made any decisions, who "owned" the matters of their people.

6.3.2.2. ***Šarīf* is from the best of his people**

Naturally, the aforementioned conceptualizations could be summarized in a form of a statement that *šarīf* folk were simply the best from among their people. As we saw in the chapter on *karam*, being *karīm* also indicated similar quality – EXCELLENCE, BEING THE BEST. I believe such a similarity in perceiving *šaraf* and *karam* is very meaningful. Namely, *karam* – as we will learn in the following subsections – was required from *šarīf* people. Thus, as it was, for instance, in the sample (166) (cf. also t26A:75), whenever an important matter was to be handled in a tribe, the best people and *šarīfs* were expected to take care of it.

(166) تَجِدنيَ من **أشْرَافِهِم** وَخيَارِهِم حفيظاً على عوراتهمْ غيرَ مُجْرِمِ

(…) you will find me among **their noble** (*ʔašrāfi-him*) and best men, protecting their vulnerabilities and not wrongdoing [them] (cf. t26A:124).

The belief that *šarīf* people are simply the best of people seems to be encoded in a number of metaphorical models, which all derive in a way from the metaphor THE BEST IS PRECIOUS. Thus, the simplest way one could refer to a *šarīf* was to say that he is a decoration, a jewel of his people – *zāna qawma-hu* "he adorned, ornamented his people (Lane 1968c: 1204)". The PRECIOUSNESS sometimes might be metonymically evoked by the schema of SHINING, which I believe is why *šarīf* could also be conceptualized by the source concept of SHINING START, *naǧm ṯāqib* "a star shining brightly[5]". This metaphor also clearly activates the schema of ELEVATION.

5 Cf. footnote 6, page 179.

Tab. 16.

Meaning	Expression	Literary Meaning
šarīf	*zāna qawma-hu*	he decorated his people; he was a jewel of his people
	šihāb qawmi-hi as-sāṭiʕ	a shining, gleaming star of his people
	naǧm qawmi-hi aṯ-ṯāqib	a brightly shining star of his people
	badr qawmi-hi aṭ-ṭāliʕ	a rising full-moon of his people
	faḍala qawma-hu	he excels his people
	šāʔa qawma-hu	he precedes his people

As the BEST, *šarīf* people were perceived as in a way unique or special. This fact might be seen encoded in a way in a metaphor presented in TBD, where non-*šarīf* people were conceptualized as *ġawġāʔ* "(sound of) locusts". This metaphor is by no means the only evidence of such a conceptualization. The historical literature provides several examples of how pre-Islamic Arabs considered their *šarīfs* special. For instance, a belief that blood of a *šarīf* has curative properties against rabies was widespread in al-Ǧāhiliyya (ʕAlī 1993b: 543). This, of course, was derived from the more general rule of blood equivalence, which has to be paid as a compensation for killing a *šarīf* person. By the rules, a killed *šarīf* required to be avenged by killing a *šarīf* from a tribe of the perpetrator – no matter what the status of such a one was, and what was his relationship to *šarīfs* of the tribe (ʕAlī 1993b: 399). Similarly, the blood of *šarīf* "costed" more of the financial compensation for a killing (which could replace revenge-killing), known as *diya* (ʕAlī 1993b: 542).

This special status of *šarīf* folk – their uniqueness – was not limited to the men only. In fact, a *šarīf* woman – *šarīfa* – enjoyed freedom non-*šarīf* women did not. For instance, in the marriage, such a woman experiences a significant amount of liberty and – by that – a much better treatment from her husband (ʕAlī 1993b: 616). It was so, since the family of *šarīfa* was of a great importance in a given community, and because of that, no one wanted to be on bad terms with them. Simply, the woman was protected by the status of her kins – obviously, her male agnates. Moreover, *šarīfa* was of much more control over her getting married than the common, non-*šarīf* women. She could refuse the candidate as she pleased (ʕAlī 1993b: 636). She also had much more freedom in divorcing her husband and getting remarried (ʕAlī 1993b: 636–7).

6.3.2.3. Šaraf and nobility

The aforementioned conceptualizations might naturally suggest that *šaraf* could also correspond to English notion of NOBILITY. *Šarīf* people enjoyed PRECEDENCE in LEADERSHIP, and they derived their HIGH SOCIAL STANDING primarily from their lineage. It all seems to fall in proximity of what one can understand as NOBILITY OF ARISTOCRACY. As we saw, CAD usually similarly define *šaraf* as related to one's ancestors. One could see this conceptualization, for instance, in (64) by Abū Ṭālib, in which the hint about NOBILITY implied by *šaraf* might be observed in the juxtaposition of two attributes, *ʔašrāf* (i.e., *šarīfs*) and *qadīm* "ancient, old". It could be read as a statement that *šaraf* indicates long tradition, long line of ancestors, based on which one can be distinguished from others. In other words, one could say that *šarīf* folk were no more, no less than the aristocrats of Arabic society of al-Ǧāhiliyya.

(64) إذا اجْتَمَعتْ يوماً قُريشُ لِمَفْخَرٍ فعَبْدُ مَنافٍ سِرُّها وصَمِيمُها
فإنْ حُصِّلَتْ **أشرافُ** عبدِ مَنافِها فَفي هاشِمٍ **أَشْرافُها** وقَديمُها
فإنْ فَخرتْ يوماً، فإنَّ محمَّداً هوَ المُصْطفى مَن سِرُّها وكريمُها

When [the people of] Qurayš gather to boast on themselves, [the clan of] ʕAbd Manāf is the best and the purest among them.
And if the **noble men** (*ʔašrāf*) [descending from] ʕAbd Manāf are called upon, the most **noble** (*ʔašrāf*) and the most ancient of them are among the [descendants of] Hāšim.
And if one day, they, [the clan of Banū Hāšim], are priding themselves, Muḥammad is the purest one – he is their best part, the best (*karīm*) from among them (cf. t24A:82).

Consequently, *šaraf*-HIGH SOCIAL STANDING was something one could inherit, what is also confirmed by TBD (*la-hu šaraf mawrūṯ* "he has an inherited *šaraf*"). This is fully compatible with the European perception of HIGH SOCIAL STATUS, in which it is frequently conceptualized as an inherited property – normally in agnatic line (Pitt-Rivers 1965: 53). This must have been yet another reason, for which keeping the purity of *nasab*-lineage was of such importance for pre-Islamic Arabs (ʕAlī 1993b: 573). In other words, *šarīf* folk held themselves back from marrying people who were not in their league (ʕAlī 1993b: 639–40). I believe this conceptualization might be observed also in CEAP, in the passage (167) by ʕAntara Ibn Šaddād. The poet is famous of his tragic love to his cousin ʕAbla, who being from *šarīfs* of his tribe, was not a suitable match for a half-slave. As we know, ʕAntara managed to prove the world that despite the fact he is not *šarīf* by blood, he can be *karīm* in an exemplary way – what he is accentuating in many verses of his poems (cf. the example (96), quoted below). Thanks to that his dream of marrying ʕAbla came eventually true.

(167) أبصرتُ ثمَّ هويتُ ثمَّ كتمتُ ما أَلقى وَلمْ يَعْلَمْ بذَاكَ مُناجي
فوَصلْتُ ثمَّ قَدَرْتُ ثمَّ عَفَفْتُ من **شرَفٍ** تناهى بي إلى الإنضاج

I saw [her], then I fell in love [with her], then I kept in secret what happened to be, so that even my trustee didn't know that.
Finally, I came to her, then I was able [to marry her], then abstained [from doing so], because of [my] **social position** (*šaraf*), which kept me from attaining my goal (cf. t21A:32).

Moreover, in one of the TBD definitions, *šarīf* was defined as someone *min ʕilya d̲awī al-ʔansāb* "from among the highest of possessors of lineages". This expression also implies that one's PRECEDENCE-ELEVATION can be grounded on their origin. Thus, sometimes, one could be described as *šarīf* simply by stating that their *manṣib* "origin, source (lit. the place of erection, of setting something upwards)" was *šarīf*, i.e., their ancestors (being their source) were *šarīf*. What is quite interesting, as suggested by Lane (1968h: 2801), with time the very lexeme *manṣib* began to refer to *šaraf* itself. This development – possibly a result of a further metonymical extension – implies even stronger that one's SOCIAL STANDING is firmly tied to one's ORIGIN. Interestingly, this conceptualization persists in Bedouin communities, such as that studied by Abu-Lughod (1986: 87).

Additionally, as indicated in other place in TBD, *šaraf* was not only perceived as inherited after someone, but also as something to be inherited by one's descendants. Thus, in TBD, a *šarīf* man is also defined as one whose *ʔāt̲ār* "traces, footprints, marks left behind" are large (*ʕaẓumat ʔāt̲āru-hu*). This expression derives obviously from the aforementioned metaphorical model *šarīf* IS LARGE/ BIG, encoding the IMPORTANCE of *šaraf*.

6.3.2.4. Society venerates *šarīf* people: *šaraf* is the reason of PRIDE

Being an IMPORTANT part of the society, being its ARISTOCRACY, *šarīf* people deserved RESPECT. It is a quite obvious implication of PRECEDENCE, which was another mean of ENTITLEMENT to the RESPECT of others (not only their EQUALS). The implication of this ENTITLEMENT might be seen, e.g., in the passage (168), in which the poet seems to suggest that it is wrong when *šarīf* folk is not better suited than non-*šarīf*s. If fact, PAYING RESPECT, or VENERATING *šarīf* people was something well-defined in the pre-Islamic culture[6] and could have many symptoms.

---

6 Of course, PAYING RESPECT to one due to their PRECEDENCE is a widespread phenomenon, which is well-defined not only in pre-Islamic Arabic culture. An example of such well-defined PAYING RESPECT script is the protocol (not only the diplomatic one) (cf. Pitt-Rivers 1965: 55).

(168) أَرَى حُمُرًا تَرْعَى وَتَأكُلُ ما تَهْوَى وأسَداً جِياعاً تَظْمَا الدهرَ ما تَرْوى
وَأَشْرَافَ قَوْمٍ ما يَنالُ قُوَّتَهم وَقَومًا لِئامًا تَأكُلُ المَنَّ والسَّلْوَى

I see grazed donkeys, which eat whatever please them, and [I see] lions, which are hungry and thirsty for a long time, not able to satisfy their thirst.
[Similarly, I see] the **noblemen** (*ʔašrāf*) of people, who do not benefit from their power, and [I see] low (*liʔām*) men, who eat best sorts [of food] and quails (cf. t37A:152)

First of all, the *šaraf*-STATUS could be manifested while dining. *Šarīf* had always a special place at eating area, which was precisely ordered in accordance with banqueters' social standing (ʕAlī 1993b: 541, 573). It seems that the SOCIAL LADDER also stipulated somehow the obligation of serving the dining companions. For instance, a story of the poet ʕAmr Ibn Kulṯūm suggests the custom of serving those who are higher in the social hierarchy (Witkowska & Danecki 1957: 110). The story also shows how hypersensitive pre-Islamic Arabs were regarding the acknowledgment of their status (Witkowska & Danecki 1957: 110; cf. also ʕAlī 1993b: 573).

Another example of PAYING RESPECT to *šarīf*s was to rise while one of them entered the tent or another place (ʕAlī 1993c: 30). The tent itself was usually also a status symbol, which normally was indicated by the spaciousness of one's abode (ʕAlī 1993c: 6). Thus, VENERATION of a *šarīf* could also take form of preparing a proper abode for him. As such a proper tent, pre-Islamic Arabs considered either so-called *qubba* (*ḥamrāʔ*) being a dome-like shaped tent made from skin, or *miḍrab*, a large tent made from camel (or sheep/goat) hair (ʕAlī 1993c: 7). In fact, the latter – *miḍrab* – became with time a clear indication of one's *šaraf* (ʕAlī 1993c: 8).

As we learned in the previous chapter, CAD saw *ḥasab* as possibly referring to *šaraf*. Perhaps, we can read it as a metonymy, in which a salient property of HIGH SOCIAL STATUS served as a vehicle affording access to this concept as a whole. This salient property was exactly the aforementioned conceptualization that *šaraf* granted one certain RIGHT TO RESPECT. As we saw, *ḥasab*, being a COUNT OF HONORABLE DEEDS, constituted a VALUE/WORTH of an individual, which served as justification for such a RIGHT. Perhaps, then, the metonymy *ḥasab* FOR *šaraf* was encoding the knowledge that *šaraf* could be seen also as one's VALUE, which provided rationale for the RESPECT PAID by others. This metonymy was then parallel to the previously discussed one, which encoded *māl*-WEALTH/POSSESSION as a similar VALUE-rationale for RESPECT.

Similarly, the conceptualization {*šaraf* is a reason of PRIDE} is expressed in (169) by Ḥassān Ibn Ṯābit (cf. also ʕAlī 1993b: 589). This passage is quite interesting, since it seems also indicate to pertain to the schema of VENERATION, i.e.,

RESPECT-PAID by others. Furthermore, *šaraf* might have been perceived – perhaps metonymically – as a kind of a merit or something one achieved, which granted this someone RIGHT TO RESPECT, and consequently, reason of PRIDE. Such a conceptualization, perhaps a metonymy *šaraf*-PRECEDENCE FOR *šaraf*-REASON OF PRIDE, one can observe, e.g., in the fragment (170) by al-Aʕšà. As we saw at the beginning of this chapter, this conceptualization of *šaraf* persists in MSA.

(169) دعْ ذا وَعَدِّ القريضَ في نَفَرٍ يَرْبَحُونَ مَدْحِي وَمَدْحِيَ **الشَرَفُ**

Let it be – [that they left me – I'm stronger than that] – thus, spread [my] poetry among the people, who benefit from my eulogy – and my eulogy is an **honor** (*aš-šaraf*), [a reason of great pride] (cf. t38B:169).

(170) لَوْ أنّ كُلَّ مَعَدٍّ كانَ شارَكَنا في يومِ ذي قارَ ما أخطاهُمُ **الشّرفُ**

[Even] if each a single one [of the whole folk of] Maʕad had accompanied us in the battle of Ḏī Qār, none [of them] would miss the **honor** (*šaraf*), [a great reason o pride, derived from that great battle] (cf. t28A:310–11).

Nevertheless, the sole *šaraf* – especially that derived only from one's noble origin – seems (at least to some poets) a lesser reason for pride than the actual HONORABLE, i.e., *karīm*, BEHAVIOR. As one could see in (96), quoted earlier, *karam* – here, BRAVERY – seems to be a better pretension to be proud than *šaraf* itself. It definitely connects with the fact that *šarīf* must constantly validate his position by a proper – i.e., *karīm* – conduct, what we will discuss later in this chapter.

The belief that *šaraf* is a reason of pride was perhaps encoded by a metaphor manifested in the TBD expression *quṭb al-faḫr* "the axis of pride" referring to a *šarīf* man. It might be seen as a conceptualization of the fact that *šarīf* is AT THE CENTER of the PRIDE of his people, being – as we learned – a CHUNK of their collective *šaraf*.

Consequently, *šarīf* could also be seen as FAMOUS. In this place, the FAME of *šarīf* should be understand more as POPULARITY or INFLUENCE rather than FAME-GLORY, referred to by *mağd*. The fact that *šaraf*-PRECEDENCE encapsulated such elements like POPULARITY or INFLUENCE is again quite natural, since in many cultures, the HIGH SOCIAL STATUS implies such qualities. In Arabic, however, this fact might have been perhaps more silent, since as it is presented in TBD, reference to BEING WELL-KNOWN was commonly used also to evoke the schema of *šaraf*-PRECEDENCE. Thus, in CEAP, *šaraf* metonymically could be referred to also as *ṣīṭ* "fame, reputation" (cf. t38A:299). All the expressions of conceptualization of *šaraf* in terms of FAME are presented in the table below (Tab. 17.).

Tab. 17.

Meaning	**Expression**	**Literary Meaning**
šarīf	*nabīh*	eminent, celebrated or well known
	nabīh aḏ-ḏikr	of eminent, celebrated, or well-known reputation
	bayḍat baladi-hi	an egg of his country ["He is like the ostrich's egg in which is the young bird; because the male ostrich in that case protects it, or he is unequalled in nobility; like the egg that is left alone, or he is a celebrated, or well-known, person (Lane 1968a: 282)"]
non-*šarīf*	*ḫāmil*	obscure, of no reputation
non-*šaraf*; LOW SOCIAL STANDING	*ḫumūl*	being obscure, of no reputation
	ġumūḍ	being obscure

The FAME of *šarīf* could also be profiled as INFLUENCE, which might be encoded in the metaphor suggested by TBD in form of BEING INFLUENTIAL IS HAVING VOICE HEARD FAR AWAY. Thus, *šarīf* could be also referred to simply as *baʕīd aṣ-ṣawṭ*, the one of a distance voice.

Furthermore, the lexeme *šaraf* seems sometimes to be used in reference to a kind of FAME or perhaps a common opinion that someone is of *šaraf*, as it is, e.g., in (159), quoted earlier. In this verse, *šaraf* is conceptualized as a STRETCHABLE OBJECT, which could extend "among tribes". This conceptualization encodes the fact of widespread acknowledgement of this *šaraf*, i.e., the high social status. Such an acknowledgment should be understood as knowledge of what is the *šaraf*-STATUS based upon. Similarly, *šaraf* as an opinion or knowledge of the grounds for one's *šaraf*-PRECEDENCE is to be found in (149) by Ḥassān Ibn Ṯābit. The poet says that *ḥasab*-WORTH/ VALE, being here the AMPLE COUNT of the HONORABLE DEEDS of one and their ancestors, can be reached (*balaġa-yabluġ*), whereas *šaraf* must be recalled or mentioned (*ḏakara-yaḏkur*). In other words, according to the poet, the shamed tribe is unable to achieve impressive number of honorable actions, nor it is able to properly name the grounds for their *šaraf*-PRECEDENCE. I believe the juxtaposition of reaching *ḥasab* and mentioning *šaraf* suggests that one's grounds for *šaraf*-STATUS could be assured always only by one's HONORABILITY.

(149) فكلُّ شيءٍ سِوَى أن تذكُرُوا شرَفاً أوْ تبلُغوا حسَباً منْ شأنكُمْ جلَلُ

And when it comes to everything, either [when you are trying to] say something about your **high social position** (*šaraf*), or to reach some worth (*ḥasab*) [for others], in your case it is [such an] enormous business (cf. t38B:201)

6.4. *Karīm* and *šarīf*: *šaraf* must be constantly proved in *karam*

As we saw in the aforementioned example (149), reaching a decent COUNT of HONORABLE DEEDS and mentioning one's grounds of HIGH SOCIAL POSITION were perceived as two compatible activities. This suggest that HONORABILITY was something constitutional for one's *šaraf*. We have already seen this notion in the passage (69). In other words, *karam* led to obtaining *šaraf*. Similarly, as in (171) by al-H̱ansāʔ, BEING *karīm* is depicted as the mean of ELEVATION over others, what clearly elaborates the conceptual metaphor *šaraf* IS ELEVATED PLACE. The conceptualizations expressed in this verse seem to be also manifested by a metaphor provided in TBD as a possible reference to *šarīf*. This metaphor was *huwa farʕ min ʔaykat al-karam* "he is the tallest branch in the tamarisk thicket of *karam*". As one can see, it is a very jam-packed notion, in which *karam* is conceptualized as a THICKET OF TAMARISK, from among which the TALLEST BRANCHES are occupied by *šarīfs*. Clearly, one can see that the HIGH SOCIAL STATUS was achieved by EXCELLING in *karam*. Consequently, one can say that *šaraf*-HIGH SOCIAL STATUS was acquired by EXCELLENCY of one's HONORABILITY.

(69) وإنّي لَمَذْمومٌ، إذا قيلَ حاتِمٌ نبا نَبْوَةً ، إنّ **الكريمَ** يُعَنَّفُ
سآبى ، وتَأبَى بي أُصُولٌ كريمَةٌ وآباء صِدْقٍ، بالمَوَدّة ، **شُرِّفوا**
Truly, I am dishonored, when one talks about Ḥātim with disdain – truly, they are viciously disgracing an **honorable man** (*karīm*).
I will rebuff [these vile words] in the way the noble roots (*ʔuṣūl karīma*) rebuffed me. My sincere ancestors **gain high social status** (*šurrifū*) by their kindness, [not by birth] (cf. t19B:71).

(171) مُوَرَّثُ المَجْدِ مَيْمُونٌ نَقيبَتُهُ ضَخْمُ الدّسيعَةِ في العَزّاءِ مِغوَارُ
فَرْعٍ منَ القَوْمِ **كريمِ** الجَدا أنْماهُ منهُمْ كلُّ محضِ النِّجارْ
He was an heir of the glory (*mağd*), a man of fortunate mind, very generous in the time of scarcity, gallant.
He was a lord of his people, **honorable** (*karīm*) in his generosity, which elevated him above others of noble origin (cf. t33A:47).

This could mean that *šarīf* people were stereotypically perceived as "natural" *karīms*. It would concur with the conceptualization of *karam*-BEING *karīm* as a hereditary property. In other words, a *šarīf* as someone who was born NOBLE was expected to be NOBLE – *karīm*-HONORABLE – by default. Consequently, the NOBILITY of *šarīf* had double characteristics; it was the NOBILITY of one's ORIGIN as well as of one's CONDUCT. Such conception is not, however, specific to the pre-Islamic Arabic culture only. NOBILITY as HONORABILITY is expected in many cultures from those who are NOBLE in the sense of HIGH SOCIAL STATUS (cf. Pitt-Rivers 1965: 23). As Pitt-Rivers (1965: 23) put it, "the well-born are assumed to possess by inheritance the appropriate character and sentiments which will be seen in their conduct (…)". Thus, *šarīf* men were the elite of the pre-Islamic Arabic society, because they were stereotypically perceived as EXCELLING in HONORABILITY. Consequently, only they could be perceived as suitable to bear PRECEDENCE in LEADERSHIP. The belief in EXCELLENCY of aristocrats was so widespread among many cultures, because in short, the (actual or presumed) EXCELLENCY was what justified the INEQUALITY inherently implied by the notion of PRECEDENCE. Thus, those who enjoyed the high social status were not only believed to be of EXCELLENT quality, but in fact, they must have constantly proved that it is so. The PRECEDENCE must have been continually confirmed in the conduct of the elite members – especially those, who derived their pretension to it from their noble birth (Peristiany 1965: 11). In general, a person of high social standing could not act against the virtuous conduct, because it would imply that they admit they are not of EXCELLENCE, and their whole pretension to PRECEDENCE – or further, to LEADERSHIP – would be immediately dismissed as invalid (cf. Pitt-Rivers 1965: 23). In other words, the virtuous conduct – we could say, the honorability – was what provides a nexus "between the ideal order and the terrestrial order, validating the realities of power and making the sanctified order of precedence corresponding to them (Pitt-Rivers 1965: 38)". Therefore, in al-Ǧāhiliyya, a *šarīf* person must always be honorable, i.e., *karīm*. *Karam* was not only what granted a man HIGH SOCIAL STANDING, but also what was constantly validating further his grasp on it on the social LADDER of pre- Islamic Arabic society.

Thus, *šarīf*s must have validated their PRECEDENCE-born RIGHT TO RESPECT, and their exclusivity of exercising the power, their right to DOMINANCE. As we know, pre-Islamic Arabs hated being subjugated – they disdain power and consequently, they tried to avoid its grasp as far as it was possible (cf. ʿAlī 1993b: 285). They all competed for the PRECEDENCE, so a natural effect of that must have been the rigorousness of the expectations formulated to their leaders. Perhaps, this system of accepting leadership was similar to that one described by Abu-Lughod (1986: 78–117) as existing in the Eastern Egyptian Bedouin community known as Awlād ʿAlī. In this community, the acceptance of the subjugation was always preceded by acknowledgment of exemplary honorability of those who issued the claim to leadership. Such people could only maintain their power if they were sticking to the code of honorable behavior. In other words, as far as some external qualities – origin, age, gender – established the status of those who were entitled to press such a pretension, it was not validated unless in their honorable conduct. In such a way, those who let such people to subjugate them, those who became inferior to such honorable men, preserve their sense of inner VALUE, due to the fact that the subjugation was voluntary and preceded (and justified) by acknowledgment of HONORABILITY of the leaders.

In al-Ǧāhiliyya, the situation must have been similar. The tribal leaders were expected to be *karīm* at any time (ʕAlī 1993b: 344–5). It was that since a chief must have been accepted by the tribesmen (ʕAlī 1993b: 669). They must have seen him suitable for the role, that is, he must have proved in front of them his *karam*-HONORABILITY, i.e., the reason for which he should be accepted as a leader. Thus, as it also took place in pre-Islamic Arabic society, sometimes, a tribal chief was elected from among the most *karīm* folk (ʕAlī 1993b: 350). In such a case, the NOBLE CONDUCT outweighed the NOBLE ORIGIN – i.e., innate PRECEDENCE – in the evaluation of one's fitness to the role of *sayyid*, a tribal leader.

Perhaps, this expectation of *karam* from such a leader could be seen also in the passage (160) quoted earlier. As one can see, the satirized people are of that little *karam* that they choose for their leader a white-fur buck. *Karam* seems to be indicated in it by the concept of WHITENESS, which encoded the knowledge that *karīm* men are of FREE BLOOD and have their *ʕirḍ*-HONOR kept CLEAN with *karam*-HONORABLENESS.[7] It may well be the case that the concept of *ġurra*, which according to the TBD, also connects to *šaraf*, could be explain in a similar fashion by the means of this conceptualization. The lexeme *ġurra* refers primarily to "a white mark on the forehead of a horse; a whiteness on the forehead of a horse (Lane 1968 f: 2238)", and thus it could code the concept of *šarīf* as both WHITE-*karīm* & FREE and AT THE CENTER-BEING IMPORTANT (maybe, a LEADER).

In several instances, such as the sample (172), CEAP confirms that all *šarīf* people – not only those being leaders – were expected to be *karīm*. This verse suggests that a *šarīf* man must be able to execute generosity. *Šarīfs* were also defined as expected to be brave, loyal, and magnanimous (cf. e.g., t26A:124), reasonable (cf. t38A:238), as well as enduring hardship (cf. t08A:94–95).

(172) وحِفَاظُ جارِك لا تُضِعْه فإنَّه لَا يَبْلُغُ **الشَّرفَ** الجَسِيْمَ مُضَيِّعُ

Do not lose the protected possession of your protégé [for which you are responsible], since he won't reach a substantial **social standing** (*aš-šaraf*), having it lost (cf. t37A:100).

The fragment (172) is especially important, since it clearly states that lack of wealth made one's path to the *šaraf*-HIGH SOCIAL POSITION difficult. This conceptualization is another widespread assumption about the PRECEDENCE. Generosity was commonly a mean of acquiring the higher standing among others (Pitt-Rivers 1965: 60) – in fact meagerness was always considered unaristoctratic (Pitt-Rivers

---

7 I will elaborate these conceptualizations in detail in the next chapter.

1965: 65). In al-Ǧāhiliyya, the WEALTH was a crucial part of one's HONORABILITY, which was in a way seen as a mere extension of the GENEROSITY-HOSPITALITY. Consequently, as we saw in the previous chapter, the wealth could be actually used as a mean of VALIDATING one's RIGHT TO RESPECT, and perhaps this was the reason why e.g., the Prophet Muḥammad's tribe, Banū Qurayš, considered such a lucrative occupation as trade, the only suitable one for a *šarīf* man (ʕAlī 1993b: 547).

The stereotypical expectation of *karam* formulated towards *šarīf*s was encoded eventually in a number of metaphorical and metonymic models, some of which pertain to the schema of LEADERSHIP (they encoded the expectations from a *šarīf* in terms of his responsibility for PROTECTION and SUPPORTING his community). Quite interestingly, the most noticeable expression of this stereotype was the collection of the references to non-*šarīf*, i.e., *laʔīm*, presented in TBD. Clearly, in the notion of *laʔīm*, two concepts – non-*karīm* and non-*šarīf* – eventually conflated, and in fact, it might be even futile to postulate any delimitation between them. This could support further the argument for the existence of the stereotype of *šarīf* as *karīm*-HONORABLE. In other words, as long as *karīm* and *šarīf* might be still rendered as two independent – yet interrelated – role schemata, *laʔīm*-non-*šarīf* and *laʔīm*-non-*karīm* are simply one unitary culture-specific concept of a man who is not HONORABLE, and as a consequence, who by no means can be consider of HIGH SOCIAL STATUS. It seems, however, that *laʔīm* was more non-*šarīf* than non-*karīm*, since a non-*šarīf* man still could be considered HONORABLE. Nevertheless, the concept of *laʔīm* always imply lack of HONORABILITY. In the table below (Tab. 18.), I presented all the expressions of *šarīf* and *šaraf*, which exemplify the aforementioned stereotypical expectations of *karam* from *šarīf* folk.

Tab. 18.

Meaning	Expression	Literary Meaning
šarīf	*ʔaḥyà qawma-hu*	he keeps his people alive and in a good condition
	taqifu ʕalay-hi ʔāmāl	hopes, expectations (of others) are standing, resting on him
non-*šarīf*	*raḏl*	(about a thing) bad, corrupt, or disapproved
	huwa fī ḫummān an-nās	he is among what is bad of household goods, form among people
	huwa fī ḥuṯālat an-nās	he is among things removed from food, inedible (<=*meff*= {a midget sand}) of people
	huwa fī quṣālat an-nās	
	huwa fī ġuṯāʔ an-nās	he is among the rubbish (such as particles of things, rotten leaves borne upon the surface of a torrent) of the people
	ǧilf	rude, coarse, churlish
	ṭaġāma min ṭaġām	foolish, stupid
	ʕāǧiz ar-raʔy	of weak judgement
	waġd	light, stupid, weak in intellect (<=*metn*= {weak person, who serves for the food of his belly <=*metn*= {a slave}})
	huwa fī hamaǧ an-nās	he is among small flies, like gnats, of people

It seems that this constant need of prove that a *šarīf* man deserves the PRECEDENCE was also a part of a conception that he should seek goals appropriate to his standing – appropriate ambitions (LEAP *himma*, pl. *himam*) – he should aim "high" (sic!). This conceptualization might be seen also in CEAP, in the samples (53) and (92). Perhaps, this appropriation should be read as a kind of higher standards, which were held for the evaluation of the conduct of *šarīf*s. In other words, as it was also noticed in the community of Egyptian Bedouins studied by Abou-Zeid, the more of *šaraf*-HIGH SOCIAL STATUS one had, the more obligations and responsibilities he must have faced (cf. Abou-Zeid 1965: 252).

(53) وَصَانَ عَنِ الفَحْشَاءِ نَفْسًا كَرِيمَةً أَبَتْ **هِمَّةً** إلّا العُلى وَالمَعاليا
[The one who keeps himself safe should] protect [his] honorable (*karīm*) self against any vulgarity, by rejecting any **ambition** (*himma*), which is not high or noble (cf. t37A:155).

(92) أنا ابْنُ الذي لَمْ يُخْزِني في حَياتِهِ ولَمْ أُخْزِهِ حتّى تغيّبَ في الرَّجمْ
فأُعْطِيَ حتَّى مات مالًا و**هِمَّةً** ووَرَّثَنِي إذ ودَّع المجدَ والكَرَمْ
I am a son of the one who has not ashamed me in his entire life, nor have I made him ashamed, before he disappeared beneath a grave stone.

> Until his death, he was growing in wealth and **ambition** (*himma*). When he was paying me farewell, he made me inherit the glory (*mağd*) and the honor (*karam*) (cf. t34A:137).

The knowledge of such a presumption as for the appropriate goals one had to face being *šarīf* seems to be encoded also in a number of conceptualizations, one can infer from the expressions provided in TBD. They conceptualize extraordinariness of *šarīf*'s goals and amotions in terms of DISTANCE (e.g., *šarīf* equals *baʕīd al-himma* "[a man] of a distant, i.e., far-reaching, goal/ambition"). Similarly, this conceptualization can be also seen in the expression synonymous to *laʔīm*, non-*šarīf* – *istanāma ʔilà aḍ-ḍaʕa* "he relied upon the low position" or perhaps even "he felt comfortable with [his] low position". It could suggest that non-*šarīf* occupies the social position he has, because he feels comfortable in it. This means then that, in order to be considered *šarīf*, one supposed to be aiming high in their life. It seems consistent with the aforementioned observation of Abou-Zeid – the more *šaraf* you claim, the higher you have to aim. All the conceptualizations of the *šarīf* as a man who must seek appropriate goals and ambitions were presented in the table below (Tab. 19.).

Tab. 19.

Meaning	Expression	Literary Meaning
šarīf	*taḥuṯṯu-hu ʕalà ṭalab al-ʔumūr al-ʕāliya*	he is hastened, urged to seek elevated affairs
	balaġa ʔilà ġāya tatarāğaʕu ʕan-hā sawābiq al-himam	he reached the extremity, from which preceding him ambitious people retire
	baʕīd murtaqà al-himma	of a distant place, towards which his ambition ascends
	la-hu himma baʕīdat al-marmà	he has a ambition of distant place, towards which it aims
	tasmū ʔilay-hi al-himam	ambitions ascends towards him
non-*šarīf*	*qaʕada ʕam-mā taraqqà ʔilay-hi al-himam aš-šarīfa*	he abstained, held back from the things towards which the *šarīf* ambitions ascend
	qāʕid al-himma	of sitting, resting ambition
	ṣaġīr al-himma	of small ambition
	qaʕada ʕam-mā tasmū ʔila-hi an-nufūs al-ʕazīza	he abstained, held back from the things towards which the strong souls ascend

All in all, *šarīf* must have been then perceived as a person who surpass others in *karam*-HONORABILITY. This could concur with the Abou-Lughod's conclusions on why proud to be free Bedouins accepted anyone as their leader – or, in the broader sense, their superior. She noticed that the PRECEDENCE was not based on one's FORCE, but only on one's opinion as HONORABLE man – on one's *gīma*, obviously CA *qīma* "value" (Abu-Lughod 1984: 99). Thus, they did not feel forced – i.e., subjugated by means of violence – but they accept the superiority voluntarily (Abu-Lughod 1984: 104) – based on their opinion that someone was of HONOR (Abu-Lughod 1984: 85–6). TBD provides several expressions, which might be seen as derived from the conceptualization of this assumption of *šarīf*s EXCELLING in *karam*-HONORABILITY. I presented them in the table below (Tab. 20.).

Tab. 20.

Meaning	Expression	Literary Meaning
šarīf	*ʕirnīn al-karam*	the first portion (<=*metf*= {the upper part of the nose}) of *karam*
	huwa farʕ min ʔaykat al-karam	he is the tallest branch in the tamarisk thicket of *karam*
	taqammaṣa libās al-ʕizz	he clads himself with the cloth of strength

6.5. *Šaraf* and *mağd*

As I said, in CEAP, *šaraf* does not seem to be a very frequently occurring theme. It is especially noticeable, while comparing the NWC of it (1.73) with NWC of the clusters of *karam* (8.81) and *mağd* (8.67). I believe one can explain this by looking at the characteristics of EAP, which was all about praising and shaming, and thus, it was more important to depict one – while praising them – as *karīm* or *māğid* (or *mağīd*), since both, *karam* and *mağd*, were what assured and validated one's RIGHT TO RESPECT. The notion of this RIGHT – either *ʕirḍ* or *šaraf* – was not as important as the arguments supporting their guaranteed persistence at the subject of a praise.

Here, while considering the relationship to *šaraf*, the aforementioned fact means simply that *karam* and *mağd* were what guaranteed one's HIGH SOCIAL STANDING. *Mağd* seemed to play a similar role in ensuring and acquiring *šaraf* as *karam* did, since – to put it simply – one can describe the schema called up by this lexeme, by stating that *mağd* was simply an extraordinary *karam* – or a famous, glorious *karam* performed by an individual and their ancestors. Thus, *mağd* must have established one's HIGH SOCIAL STATUS, since as the metaphor *huwa farˁ min ˀaykat al-karam* "he is the tallest branch in the tamarisk thicket of *karam*" suggests, a mere following the code of *karam* was not enough – one must have EXCEL in it.

Before, however, diving into the details of the relationship between *šaraf* and *mağd*, I would like to present some of the most significant conceptualizations of *mağd* in LEAP. The description I will present is by far only a sketch, since the data from CEAP is abundant (the total NO of the *mağd* cluster members was 245) and thus requires a much better elaboration, for which I could not find place in this book.

6.5.1. A famous *karīm* builds *mağd* for his descendant – *mağd* is GLORY

The most significant and silent conceptualization of *mağd* is a conceptual metaphor *mağd* IS BUILDING, which might be found in a number of instances in CEAP,[8] such as in (173) by Samawˀal. This metaphoric model established a whole range of mappings, which obviously describes one's *mağd* in terms of a BUILDING, which can be BUILT (cf. e.g., t39A:165–169–174; t28A:237–239) or have its foundations laid down (cf. t30B:197) and can be DEMOLISHED (cf. t21A:50; t05A:79) or WELL-CONSTRUCTED (cf. t26A:56).

(173) وأوصى عاديا قِدْماً بأن لا تُهَدِّمُ يا سموألُ ما بَنَيْتُ
وبيتٍ قد بنيتُ بغيرِ طِينٍ ولا خشَبٍ ومجْدٍ قد أتَيْتُ

Long time ago, [my father] ˁĀdyā instructed me that I don't tear down what he had built.
Thus, I have built a house – without clay or wood – and I arrived at **glory** (*mağd*) (cf. t05A:79).

The metaphor itself seems to be an elaboration of a quite widespread more general metaphor PERSISTING IS BEING ERECT. The schema BUILDING elaborates more abstract image-schema of BEING ERECT, what translates in the conceptualization of *mağd* as something durable or persisting. Moreover, this elaboration – BUILDING – also encoded the fact that that *mağd* is something CONSTRUCTED by someone for their posterity to persist for generations to come. In other words, *mağd* is a mark of ELEVATION – the *mağd*-BUILDING is BUILT UPWARDS – which

8 cf. t05A:79; t39A:73a; t39A:73b; t39A:165–169–174; t39A:5–14–15; t39A:115–117–119; t39A:102–104; t17A:171–178; t21B:51; t34A:136–138; t28A:237–239; t28A:82–85; t30A:91; t30A:197.

is left as an inheritance for one's descendants, as it is implied by al-Aʕšà in (174). Thus, by building *maǧd*, the descendants receive a special distinction, in which they can pride themselves. This distinction is a FAMILY GLORY.

(174) كساكمْ عُلاثةُ أثوابهُ، وَوَرّثَكُمْ **مَجْدَهُ** الأحْوَصُ

ʕUlāṯa, [your father] covered you with his robes, and al-Aḥwaṣ, [your grandfather] left you **his glory** (*maǧda-hu*) as inheritance (cf. t28A:368–369).

Thus, *maǧd*-BUILDING-FAMILY GLORY is what one builds for the posterity by oneself, as it is implied in, e.g., (175) by Labīd Ibn Rabiʕa.

(175) يا مَيَّ قُومي في المَآتِمِ وَانْدُبي فتىً كانَ ممّن يَبتني **المَجدَ أرْوَعَا**

Oh Mayya, join the mourning women and weep for the young man, **the most marvelous** (*ʔarwaʕ*) from among those who build **glory** (*al-maǧd*) (cf. t30B:91).

As noticed by Dimitriev (2017: 109), the conceptualization of ACHIEVING GLORY in terms of BUILDING A BUILDING is a common metaphor functioning in many cultures in Mediterranean Antiquity. Perhaps, the most famous of its manifestation is the Horace's "Exegi monumentum aere perennius", in which the monument the poet built for the posterity was his odes and epodes. Quite similarly, Dimitriev (2017: 109) states that also *maǧd* was something closely tied to the poetry, which was the major pre-Islamic Arabic mean of communicating and preserving the information across the time and space. Consequently, this fact derives from a more general characteristics of GLORY/FAME as it was perceived in the Antiquity. The metaphor ACHIEVING GLORY IS BUILDING A BUILDING encodes that for Ancient Mediterranean people the major function of the GLORY was first and foremost the immortalization of an individual in the collective memory of their communities, of their descendants. Similarly, the function of BUILDING *maǧd* is seen by Dimitriev, who suggests that perhaps, the pursuit[9] for glory could be perceived as an equivalent of religious notion of immortality, which – according to him – has not developed in the society of Arabs of al-Ǧāhiliyya (Dimitriev 2017: 106).

In CEAP, however, *maǧd* is more frequently described as something one inherited from their glorious ancestors. It is then more a FAMILY GLORY, which grands one a pretension to RESPECT – or perhaps, it assures the RIGHT TO RESPECT and to PRECEDENCE. One can see this conceptualization, for instance, in the sample (176) by Ṭarafa Ibn al-ʕAbd. In other words, as it is described in

9 In fact, in CEAP, ACHIEVING GLORY/FAME is also frequently conceptualized as a RACE (cf. e.g., t22A:23–26; t24A:54; t25B:60; t28A:118–127).

(177) by Abū Ṭālib, *mağd*-(FAMILY) GLORY is always prepared – pre-BUILT – by one's ancestors.

(176) وأنمى إلى **مَجدٍ** تَليدٍ وسُورةٍ، تكونُ تُراثاً، عندَ حَيٍّ، لهالِكِ

I am ascending towards the hereditary **glory** (*mağd*) and social heights (*sūra*), which will be an inheritance in the tribe after [me, when I will be] gone (cf. t07A:96–7).

(177) سَيِّدٌ وابْنُ سادَةٍ أَحْرَزوا **المجْـدَ** قديمًا وشَيَّدوا **المكْرُماتِ**
جعلَ أللهِ **مجدَهُ** وعُلاهُ في بَنيهِ نَجابَةً والبنَاتِ

A leader, son of leading men, who long time ago, brewed [for him] **the glory** (*mağd*) and laid foundations for [his] **honorable conduct** (*al-makrumāt*).
The God made **his glory** (*mağda-hu*) and his high social rank (*ʕulā-hu*) [spread] among his sons and daughters, making them noble (cf. t24A:30).

The fact that *mağd* is something one inherits brings it closer to the already discussed conceptualization of heredity of one's predispositions to *karam*. In (103) by Ḥassān Ibn Ṯābit, lack of *murūʔa* "manliness" in tribe of Banū al-Ḥimās led to the fact than none *māğid* – a man building *mağd* – has raised among them. One can read this verse as implying that lack of *murūʔa* among Banū al-Ḥimās might be traced back to their ancestors – none of which left in the inheritance proper predispositions to HONORABILITY. Thus, the whole tribe is unable to BUILD *mağd* – to leave behind a mark of ELEVATION for their descendants.

(103) أَبَنِي الحِماس أليسَ منكمْ ماجدٌ، إنّ **المُروءةَ** في الحِماس قلِيلُ

Banū al-Ḥimās, is there any **glorious man** (*māğid*) among you? Truly, there is so little manliness (*murūʔa*) among [the clan of Banū] al-Ḥimās (cf. t38B:210).

Consequently, the metaphor *mağd* IS BUILDING established also a quite important mapping, by which it encoded how one could ACHIEVE-BUILD GLORY. It will not be by any surprise, that the BUILDING BLOCKS used in CONSTRUCTING *mağd*-BUILDING were simply *makārim* – the deeds of *karam*, discussed in Chapter 4. It is well implied in (173) by Samawʔal, quoted earlier, where the poet clearly points towards the fact that the house he built was not constructed from clay or wood. What he implied was that *mağd* is built with one's deeds. Thus, BEING *karīm* led to *mağd*-GLORY.

Nonetheless, it seems quite too simplistic. What is quite important, I believe, and what can be deduced from a number of instances in CEAP,[10] *mağd* is not achieved by "regular" *karam*, but by extraordinary or unusual performance following this code of HONORABLE BEHAVIOR. It might be indicated, for instance, by the frequent cooccurrence[11] of the lexeme *ʔarwaʕ* as an attribute of a *māğid* man,

10 cf. t24A:20; t08A:115–116; t30A:200–202; t38B:96b; t20A:40 t20A:35–38; t21A:145–146; t39A:300–305.

11 cf. t30A:91; t08A:115–6; t33A:43–4; t38B:234; t38B:49–50; t21B:57; t21B:207–209.

i.e., a man BUILDING his *mağd* (cf. (175)). The meaning of this lexeme implies a kind of a devout fear people feels, while looking at someone described by it, and that's because of the excellency of such a person (cf. LsA8: 162). In other words, *māğid* is someone extraordinarily perfect – or simply, extraordinarily *karīm*.

This extraordinariness is accentuated in many places in CEAP in the implication that *māğid* was simply a famous man – seemingly, famous because of his exceptional *makārim*, honorable deeds. Thus, as indicated in (178) by ʕĀmir Ibn aṭ-Ṭufayl, *mağd* might have been simply seen as a BATTLE GLORY, which definitely pertains to the remarkable execution of the code of *karam* by one's BRAVERY.

(178) ونَعُدّ أيّاماً لَنَا ومَآثِراً قِدْماً نَبُذّ البَدْوَ والأمْصارَا
مِنْهَا خُوَيٌّ والذّهَابُ وبالصّفَا يَوْمٌ تَمَهّدَ **مَجْدُ** ذاكَ فَسَارَا
By counting our victorious battles and ancient inherited glories, we surpass both nomadic and sedentary people
– [from among those battles] there are battles of Ḫuwayy, of aḏ-Ḏahāb, and of aṣ-Ṣafā, the **glory** (*mağd*) of which was easy [to achieve for us], and thus it went forth [and spread among Arabs] (cf. t29A:78).

At last, I'd like to mention yet another metaphorical model, which also participated in structuring this schema in LEAP. In some places in CEAP, *mağd* was depicted as a POSSESSED MASS, which one could COLLECT, in order to leave it as INHERITANCE to their descendants. I decided to comment of this metaphorical mapping, because it employs a quite culturally specific elaboration of the image-schema POSSESSED MASS, used in LEAP frequently in the context of HONOR. Namely, in several instances, one can find the conceptualization of ACHIEVING *mağd* as COLLECTING WATER. In this metaphor, *mağd* is perceived as WATER being amassed usually by some group of people as it is in (179) by Ḥassān Ibn Ṯābit. Such *mağd*-WATER is a precious POSSESSION, which has to be protected by all means – and can be wasted by foolish, irresponsible behavior.

(179) لاطتْ قريشٌ حِياضَ **المجدِ** فافترطتْ سهمٌ، فأصبحَ منهُ حَوْضُها صَفِرَا
وَأوْرَدوا، وحِياضُ **المَجْدِ** طامِيَةٌ، فَدَلَّ حَوْضَهُمُ الوُرّادُ فانْهَدَرَا
[Banū] Qurayš patched the tanks of [their] **glory** (*mağd*), but [Banū] Sahm, [a party of them], overlooked [that repair], and thus, their tank [of glory] is now empty.
They came to the watering place and the tanks of [their] **glory** (*mağd*) got filled up, [but then] the watering men redirected their tank, thus it got empty (cf. t38B:135).

Moreover, the cultural metaphor ACHIEVING *mağd* IS COLLECTING WATER, might explain an extension of the concept of *musāğala*, originally, a competition in drawing water bucket known as *sağl* (cf. Lane 1968d: 1311; ʕAlī 1993b: 591). With time, it also began to signify another type of a competition – the *mufāḫara*, the priding competition. In the lights of the aforementioned metaphorical model, one can quite easily notice the motivations and a course of this semantic development. One can observe its premises also in CEAP – for instance, in (180) by al-Ḥuṭayʔa, in which the ASSESSMENT of *mağd* is metaphorically depicted as EMPTYING huge BUCKETS OF WATER.

(180) إذا قايَسُوهُ **المجدَ** أرْبَى عليهِمُ بِمُسْتَفْرِغٍ ماءَ الذِّنابِ سَجِيلِ

When he is measured in terms of the **glory** (*al-mağd*), he surpass them, being the one who empties water, [of his glory], from enormous buckets (cf. t39A:8, 10)

6.5.2. *Mağd* assures *šaraf*

Ergo, *mağd* might be roughly explicated as extraordinary – or better, famous – *karam*-HONORABLE BEHAVIOR. It was then the GLORY of someone or their ancestors. Because of that, no wonder *mağd* was conceptualized as something assuring one's *šaraf*-HIGH SOCIAL STATUS. In fact, seeing GLORY as something assuring one's HIGH STANDING was by no means a pre-Islamic Arabic phenomenon only. The closest to this conception was Ancient Greek notions of *tīmē* and *kleos*. Similarly to al-Ǧāhiliyya Arabs, Ancient Greeks saw the social status – the vertical honor – as something one could derive not only from their noble origin, but also what one could earn by their admirable actions, by which they showed their superiority over others (Stewart 1994: 59–60). The admirable performance resulted in *kleos* "glory, fame", which implied one's *tīmē*-HONOR (Korus 2017: 32) – being both their VALUE/WORTH and the RIGHT TO RESPECT derived from it.

Pre-Islamic Arabic *mağd* played similar role to Ancient Greek *kleos*. It assured one's HIGH SOCIAL STANDING by grounding the opinion on *karam*-HONORABLENESS of a particular *šarīf*. GLORY simply implied the recognition of an individual as a *karīm*, thus, in case of *šarīf* people, it was nothing but a guarantee of their *šaraf*-ELEVATED PLACE in the social hierarchy. This conceptualization is manifested, e.g., in the passage (181) by ʕĀmir Ibn aṭ-Ṭufayl. The poet describes actually both *šaraf* and *mağd* in terms of places – settling in the heights of *mağd* was described as settling in the greatest *šaraf*. I believe one can interpret this verse, by reading the settling in the heights of *mağd* as the major event described by aṭ-Ṭufayl. His glorious bravery during the war made him dwell in the HEIGHTS of FAME/GLORY – the opinion on his superb conduct spread wide among free folk. The concept of HEIGHTS definitely links to the conceptualization of *šaraf* in terms of ELEVATED PLACE. Thus, the poet seems to be saying that he achieved the most ELEVATED PLACE, from among such PLACES, which could be granted to someone by means of GLORY. In other words, he settled down in these HEIGHTS-HIGH SOCIAL STATUS of GLORY, what could be described as settling down in the greatest of *šaraf*-ELEVATED PLACE-HIGH SOCIAL STATUS.

A similar conceptualization might be observed also in in (158) by Ḥassān Ibn Ṯābit, quoted earlier. In this passage, the poet comment on inability of the clan of Banū Aslam to CLIMB UP onto their *ḥasab*-COUNT OF HONORABLE DEEDS towards *maǧd* and *šaraf*, implied by it.

(181) قَدْ تَعْلَمُ الحَرْبُ أَنّى ابْنُها وأَنّى الهُمامُ بِها المُعْلِمُ
وأَنّي أَحُلُّ عَلى رَهْوَةٍ مِنَ المَجدِ في الشَرَفِ الأَعظَمِ

The war has learned that I am her son, and that during it, I am a leader and a skilled knight,

and that I have settled down on the heights of **glory** (*maǧd*) in the greatest **eminence** (*aš-šaraf*) (cf. t29A:119).

The example (158) might actually manifest a certain conceptualization, which resembles conceptual integration phenomenon, conceptual blend, which seems to have arisen due to this relationship between *maǧd*-FAME/GLORY and *šaraf*-HIGH SOCIAL STATUS. Similarly, for instance, in (176) quoted above, the poet perceived PURSUING GLORY as ASCENDING towards it, which links naturally to the conceptualization of HIGH SOCIAL STATUS in terms of ELEVATION. It could be read that PURSUING FAME/GLORY inherently implies ASCENDING-OBTAINING HIGH SOCIAL STATUS, what can be actually see in this verse, where the poet presents PURSUING *maǧd* as something parallel to ASCENDING towards HIGH SOCIAL STATUS, referred to by the lexeme *sūra*. The integrated space allowing for such a blend would contain the conceptualization of PURSUING GLORY/FAME as leading to or assuring HIGH SOCIAL STANDING. Thus, the blend would use the source of the metaphoric mapping of OBTAINING HIGH SOCIAL STATUS IS ASCENDING in conceptualizing PURSUING GLORY/FAME.

The word *sūra* itself is also quite interesting and perhaps, its use in reference to *šaraf* might be perceived as a result of a metaphorical conceptualization similar to *maǧd*-GLORY IS BUILDING. In fact, as in the sample (182), *šaraf* might be also described in terms of the BUILDING. It could suggest that it was perceived as something DURABLE/PERSISTING in the simile to *maǧd*, upon which it had been founded. Thus, the poet seems to be saying that he and his tribe/clan achieved hereditary HIGH SOCIAL STANDING that will last for generations.

(182) ونحنُ الحاكِمونَ بكلِّ أمرٍ قَديماً، نبتَني شَرَفَالمعالي

For ages, we have been the [best] judges in any matter, building the social position of the **highest ranks** (*šaraf al-maʕālī*) (cf. t38A:238).

The semantic development of the aforementioned lexeme *sūra* might have followed this metaphoric mapping. Its basic meanings seem to be "a row of stones or bricks of a wall", and by a metonymy, "what is goodly and tall, of structures" (Lane 1968d: 1465). It could also mean "eminence, or nobility, rank or station, or high, or exalted, rank or station; excellence (Lane 1968d: 1465)", which naturally pertains to the concept of *šaraf*-HIGH SOCIAL STATUS. I believe that the conceptualization of GOODLY TALL STRUCTURE could have been used to conceptualize *šaraf* only by means of the aforementioned notion of *šaraf* as a BUILDING. Thus, one's *sūra*-WELL CONSTRUCTED BUILDING implied one's long-lasting high social standing that will be handed down to the next generations. Other examples of conceptualization of *šaraf* in terms of a BUILDING are presented in the table below (Tab. 21.).

Tab. 21.

Meaning	Expression	Literary Meaning
šarīf	*madarat* ˁ*ašīrati-hi*	he is clay of his tribe
	ˁ*amīd bayti-hi*	he is a pillar of his house
	yabnī ḫiṭaṭ al-makārim	he is building marks (for building a house out) of his honorable deeds

All in all, *mağd* and *šaraf* persisted in a close relationship, what is encoded in several metaphoric mappings presented in TBD. I listed them in the table below (Tab. 22.).

Tab. 22.

Meaning	Expression	Literary Meaning
šarīf	*yataraqqà* ˀ*ilà ḏurà al-mağd*	he ascends on a ladder towards the uppermost parts of the camel-hump of *mağd*-GLORY/FAME
	taḏarrà sanām al-mağd	he climbed onto the uppermost part of the camel-hump of *mağd*-GLORY/FAME
	*fara*ˁ*a ḏirwat al-mağd*	he reached the top of the uppermost part of the camel-hump of *mağd*-GLORY/FAME
	*rafī*ˁ *al-mağd*	of high, elevated *mağd*-GLORY/FAME

6.6. Conclusions

In modern Arabic, *šaraf* is probably the most obvious choice while rendering European words pertaining to HONOR. Consequently, it seems that nowadays, the concept it refers to encompass more or less the whole range of RIGHT TO

RESPECT aspects, such as VIRTUOUS CONDUCT (cf. Abu-Lughod 1986: 87) or PRECEDENCE. In other words, it is what can serve to imply REASON OF PRIDE, obviously derived from the RIGHT TO RESPECT.

Nevertheless, *šaraf* in LEAP seems much more specialized, which means that pre-Islamic Arabic concept of *šaraf* was not as capacious as its modern descendant. In general, *šaraf* meant more or less what later anthropologist rendered as HONOR-PRECEDENCE or vertical honor, i.e., RIGHT TO RESPECT derived from one's SUPERIORITY over others – be it extraordinariness in their HONORABILITY, or more frequently reoccurring profile of it, NOBILITY. *Šarīf*s of Arabic communities of al-Ǧāhiliyya were therefore aristocrats in the sense resembling notion of NOBILITY, which have persisted throughout European history.

The major mean of encoding this fact was the metaphor *šaraf*-HIGH SOCIAL STATUS IS *šaraf*-ELEVATED PLACE, which could be seen as derived from a more general model conceptualizing SOCIAL HIERARCHY in form of a LADDER or STAIRS. It was then a PLACE, which could have been REACHED by those, who wanted to claim PRECEDENCE and LEADERSHIP over others. Yet, most frequently, it was a PLACE POSSESSED by someone, who OBTAINED it in different transactions, from among which INHERITANCE was one of the most often reoccurring one. All of this clearly codes the fact that *šarīf* people were aristocrats of pre-Islamic Arabic society, who gained their high social standing either by their exceptional conduct (cf. European tradition of ennoblement) or inheriting it after their noble ancestors of an ancient, famous race. Thus, *šaraf* – as explained by Lane (1968d: 1537) – could be seen as all of "highness or eminence in rank, high birth, nobility".

Therefore, *šaraf* was one's PRECEDENCE – one's HIGH SOCIAL STANDING – which confirmed one's IMPORTANCE within the social fabric of a community. The IMPORTANCE meant INFLUENCE over a group's affairs, which consequently, granted one privilege of PRECEDENCE in the claim of LEADERSHIP. Therefore, *šarīf* men enjoyed exclusivity in exercising the power.

Nonetheless, with great power comes great responsibility. In Arabic society – not only of the al-Ǧāhiliyya (cf. Abu-Lughod 1986: 85–98) – an individual did not subjugate easily. Thus, LEADERSHIP must have been always supported by VIRTUE of the one who claimed it. As we learned, assumption and then expectations of HONORABILITY formulated on NOBILITY were not a pre-Islamic Arabic phenomenon only. Therefore, similarly to other aristocrats, *šarīf*s were urged to prove constantly their *karam*-HONORABLENESS. This urge was especially visible in metaphors of special ambitions, which were suitable to a *šarīf*, who for his entire life was expected to aim high – since he was already occupying a HIGH POSITION. In other words, *šarīf* were accepted as the leading class due to their

EXCELLENCY, which was first presumed, and then expected to be constantly proven in their HONORABLE conduct.

At the same time, however, the *karam* expected from *šarīf*s was not a mere HONORABILITY. It seems that in fact, while discussing *šaraf*, one should always have in mind two profiles of HONORABLENESS – two modes of this script of behavior. So, first, *karam* performed by a regular *ḥurr*, a free-man, was the bare minimum of the HONORABILITY I described in Chapter 4. It was the minimum of behavior expected from one who wanted to be RESPECTED as a full member of his community – the community of equals. A *šarīf*, however, seems to be expected to do more than that. Since he occupied a higher social position within his community, he was naturally expected to prove being worth it by excelling in *karam*. This means that aristocrats of pre-Islamic Arabs must have been exemplary in their HONORABLENESS – or even extraordinary in executing it. Thus, *šaraf* was conceptualized as something to be gained and to be assured by means of *mağd* –GLORY of one's HONORABILITY.

Mağd persisted in a very complicated network of relations with *šaraf*. GLORY was something one was BUILDING by his own deeds to leave it as a beautiful INHERITANCE to their posteriority, for whom this BUILDING of GLORY will serve as a mark of their *šaraf*. Thus, first and foremost, by achieving – settling in – *mağd*-GLORY, one was PLACING oneself in an ELEVATED PLACE among others – one was OBTAINING *šaraf*-HIGH SOCIAL STANDING in his community. Moreover, by doing that one simply assured their already acquired HIGH SOCIAL STATUS, because *mağd* – extraordinary, glorious performance of HONORABILITY – was a great prove of one's undeniable *karam*. But *mağd*-GLORY/FAME was yet a BUILDING, which was supposed be "aere perennius" and to last for generations. Therefore, it was also what the descendants of *māğid*, a man of GLORY/FAME, will later use as their prove that they deserve *šaraf*-PRECEDENCE.

What is quite interesting, the fact that *šaraf* seems to be in a way dependent on *mağd* can be observed in the frequencies of analyzed word clusters in CEAP. The most frequent of them are *karam* (NWC: 8.81) and *mağd* (NWC: 8.67), while the rarest was *šaraf* (NWC: 1.73). It must look surprising, taking into consideration the fact that nowadays, any reference to HONOR other than *šaraf* is simply difficult to imagine in MSA. Nevertheless, the numbers do not lie. Perhaps, as an explanation, one can point towards the specifics of EAP. It would be difficult to understand, if pre-Islamic Arabic poets did not care for *šaraf* at all. Therefore, I believe, we should look at the data from the perspective of the importance of *šaraf* rather than its negligibility. In other words, *šaraf* is not mentioned to frequently in the poetry, because it always implied by *mağd* or *karam*. The poets were supposed to praise and shame people or tribes, so it seems much more plausible that they were talking a lot about someone's GLORY/FAME and HONOR-ABILITY. The lack of *šaraf* implies only the fact that the listeners of pre-Islamic poems were not in need of being informed that someone is *šarīf* – obviously, they must have known that. What they actually needed was the prove that someone should be considered as *šarīf* – and such a proof could be only provided by mentioning one's *mağd* or *karam*.

Thus, *šarīf*s – pre-Islamic Arabic aristocrats – were venerated in poetry. They were venerated and respected in their communities. Ergo, *šaraf* was a great reason of pride. In this, I believe, one can start looking for the motivation of further semantic development of this lexeme, which nowadays seems to indicate the whole spectrum of RIGHTS TO RESPECT – or REASONS FOR PRIDE – one can enjoy. Thus, with time, the PRECEDENCE, by means of metonymy, started serving as a model for the whole range of ENTITLEMENTS to RESPECT. Eventually, it encompassed such concepts as HONOR- VIRTUE (perhaps, influenced by European "decline" of HONOR) and RIGHT TO RESPECT enjoyed by equals in a community, the concept previously referred to by the lexeme *ʕirḍ*.

7. ʕIrḍ

Thus, *šaraf* could be seen as a RIGHT TO RESPECT, which was possessed by a SUPERIOR – it was their mark of a PRECEDENCE, their social ELEVATION above other, which granted its possessor the influence and consequently, priority in leadership. It was then a special entitlement, which could be gained by EXCELLING in HONORABILITY, or by means of *maǧd*-GLORY of an individual and their ancestors; and which must have been constantly reaffirmed in one's conduct. But all in all, *šaraf* was limited in its application – not all free men were *šarīf*. It was a special case of HONOR, gained and maintained with special means.

As we learned, however, HONOR was not an extraordinary phenomenon applicable to a small group of aristocrats – although, sometimes, one could see it that way. HONOR was – and perhaps, still is – a common, not special – RIGHT TO RESPECT, which one enjoys as being a member of a community. In other words, despite PRECEDENCE over other, HONOR was perceived as a kind of recognition of one's decency, which resulted in prolongation of their membership in their community. It was then a RIGHT TO RESPECT received from EQUALS, which did not imply a PRECEDENCE-triggered respect in form of special recognition, but a simple fact of RECOGNITION. Thus, to put it bluntly, man of HONOR was RESPECTED, i.e., RECOGNIZED as a member of the community of EQUALS. The HONOR he had was not any special RIGHT – a privilege or a RIGHT to special treatment or admiration. It was a mere statement that he was a decent man, who deserves to be a part of the community – being VALUABLE for it – and as such has the full MEMBERSHIP in all doings of it. It was then a recognition of someone as an EQUAL.

In LEAP, a schema of such a common, ordinary RIGHT TO RESPECT by one's EQUALS was referred to by the lexeme *ʕirḍ*. In pre-Islamic Arabic society, *ʕirḍ* was then a possession of all free folk, which indicated the decency of a free man – and by that, his or her continuous belonging to the RESPECTED free folk social stratum. As we learned, such a common RIGHT TO RESPECT functioned only within a honor group, which bond together people, who expect from each other following a certain code of behavior. In al-Ǧāhiliyya, this code of behavior could be described as the script of being *karīm*, which simply was what one could call nowadays a decent behavior – not a heroic one. Thus, *ʕirḍ* was the mark of one's civility – one's fitness to their community. *ʕIrḍ* did not entail one to any special respect other than that in form of not being scolded, disdained, shunned away, or simply – ignored.

Therefore, *ʕirḍ* by far seems compatible with the notion of personal horizontal honor proposed by Stewart (1994: 59). Although, in Europe, this type of honor persisted in a binary schema – either you have it or not – LEAP *ʕirḍ* referred rather to a its instance, which could not really be lost – yet it could be in better or worse shape. Perhaps, then, it could be seen as related to the concepts evoked by such lexemes as English (*good*) *name*, or Latin *exisimatio* (Stewart 1994: 56–7). It was a kind of REPUTATION of someone, which granted them the RIGHT to hold the MEMBERSHIP in their community. In pre-Islamic Arabic culture, this RIGHT was always in possession of someone – one could not lose it, but it could be more or less SOUND, i.e., UNQUESTIONABLE. This REPUTATION was founded on two factors – one's *ḥasab*, i.e., one's VALUE/WORTH estimated based on their adherence to the code of *karam*, and one's *nasab*, i.e., the lineage to which one was attaching themselves. The connection to these two factors was so strong, that sometimes, *ʕirḍ* could evoke one of them by means of a metonymic model.

However, what is perhaps the most visible in the data on *ʕirḍ* is its vulnerability – it seems that it was always on a verge of demise, and thus, it must have been constantly protected. I believe that this conceptualization might be seen as factored by the aforementioned definition of *ʕirḍ* in terms of what assured one's MEMBERSHIP in their community. Further in this chapter, I will hypothesize that this notion effect on the overall LEAP conceptualization of *ʕirḍ* was by far conditioned by the socio-environmental factors, which shaped the life – and mentality – of Arabs of al-Ǧāhiliyya. As a result, the understanding of the LEAP schema *ʕirḍ* was structured by embodied metaphor of *ʕirḍ*-HONOR IS BODY SIDE/PART. It clearly indicates that for those people, their HONOR was a principle of life and death.

In this chapter, I will represent the pre-Islamic knowledge on *ʕirḍ*-HONOR-RIGHT TO RESPECT (by EQUALS), which was encoded in LEAP. Consequently, I will discuss the CAD definitions of the analyzed lexeme –*ʕirḍ* – as well as all the conceptualizations of its concept derived from the data from CEAP and TBD.

7.1. The concept of Arabic *ʕirḍ* in anthropological and philological literature – a brief synopsis

However, before doing that, I feel compelled to present a brief synopsis of the existing findings on the concept *ʕirḍ*, which describe the specifics of the function of this phenomenon both in pre-Islamic and Modern Arabic context.

7.1.1. The phenomenon of *ʕirḍ* in pre-Islamic Arabic culture in the writings of Bichr Farès

When it comes to the pre-Islamic *ʕirḍ*, the most important analysis was that conducted by Bichr Farès (1932 & 1938). In a part, it seems to be compatible with my own findings. In my presentation of his conclusions, I will elaborate on his entry on *ʕirḍ* in the Encyclopedia of Islam (Farès 1938).

In this entry, Farès (1938: 96) described *ʕirḍ* in a quite poetic way as "a portion which separates its possessor from the rest of mankind", adding that "this portion is certainly fragile since it easily destroyed" (what can find its expression in such idioms as *hataka ʕirḍa-hu* "he torn his *ʕirḍ*"). Moreover, he added, it "is a kind of a barrier which shelters the individual or the group from attacks from outside; if lowered, this barrier opens the way to anything that might cause dishonor, i.e., insult (Farès 1938: 96)". In other words, Farès defines *ʕirḍ* in terms of a certain VALUE or WORTH, which distinguished an individual from among others and protected this individual from being insulted or shamed. As such, this VALUE – perhaps, REPUTATION – required also constant protection, since permanently it is threatened by insults, which are the most frequently cooccurring theme of *ʕirḍ* in EAP (Farès 1938: 96). It was also something closely related to strength – *ʕizz* – and what could be seen as encompassing such element as "rebellion, courage, liberty, vendetta, chastity of the wife, liberality, faithfulness to one's word, the non-captivity of the free woman, *ḥasab*, protection, hospitality, invulnerability of the abode (Farès 1938: 96)".

As such, Farès continued, *ʕirḍ* played an extraordinary role in the life of pre-Islamic Arabs. He described this role as resembling – or even replacing – the religious cult, in the following statement, quoted already in Chapter 3.:

> *ʕirḍ* took the place of religion at the gathering held for contests of honor called *mufāḫarāt* and *munāfarāt*, to keep alive among Arabs that state of intense social life in which their feelings underwent a transfiguration (Farès 1938: 96).

ʕIrḍ was then at the center of the life of Arabs of al-Ǧāhiliyya – it was "at the root of various aspects of the mental life, (…) even of social institutions (Farès 1938: 96)" of those people.

Based on my study, however, I must disagree with some of the conclusions formulated by the author of this entry on *ʕirḍ*. First and foremost, the claim that *ʕirḍ* was what separated an individual from others and what protected the individual against them, does not find its confirmation in the data, which I will present further in this chapter. Although *ʕirḍ* was a very personal item, it was by no mean a shield against insults or other attacks. It was rather something requiring a shield (cf. the example (212) below). Moreover, the use of the verb *hataka* "to tear" while describing SHAMING or INSULTING, should be rather linked with the whole range of expressions, in which *ʕirḍ* is being described as WOUNDED, ATTACKED, etc. The data from CEAP clearly indicates that *ʕirḍ* was not a vail, which covered a man (cf. Farès 1938: 96) – more than that – actually, it was *ʕirḍ*, which needed to be covered constantly by its possessor (cf. the example (201) below). Moreover, the notion of *ʕirḍ* as something what separates one from others seems contrary to what one can see in this concept in the light of anthropological findings on HONOR.

Farès is right that *ʕirḍ* was related to *ʕizz*-STRENGTH and, in a way, it encompassed all the elements listed above, since – as I will demonstrate – *ʕirḍ* was preserved only by means of *karam*, which naturally implied – in certain areas of the schema – the concept of STRENGTH. I think he was also right regarding the acknowledgment of the role of *ʕirḍ* in the social life of pre-Islamic Arabs. Although, personally, I do not share his belief in a semi-religious status of this phenomenon, I am strongly convinced that by far, the life of the society of al-Ǧāhiliyya was circulating around this concept in several overlapping contexts, such as *karam*, *šaraf*, *ḥasab*, and *nasab*.

7.1.2. Modern conceptualization of *ʕirḍ* – the data from 20th c.

In regard to the modern notion of *ʕirḍ*, I will mostly focus on the concise description by Dodd (1973), which covers the more widespread conceptualizations of this phenomenon as they were recorded in 80' of the later century. The description will be supplemented with conclusions from other authors, such as, e.g., Abiu-Zeid (1965). Additionally, I will briefly present the finding of Stewart (1994) on the function of *ʕirḍ* in a Bedouin community of Sinai living in a similar time frame.

As we have learned in the previous chapter, the most obvious choice of MSA lexeme in translation English *honor* would be rather *šaraf* than *ʕirḍ*. Additionally, the lexeme *ʕirḍ* does not appear in the Holy Qurʔān (Dodd 1973: 44). Nevertheless, the notion of *ʕirḍ* is persisting in the Arabic culture mostly in the contexts of tribal and rural communities (Dodd 1973: 40). It is also quite different in content from what one can describe as pre-Islamic *ʕirḍ*, which definitely covered much wider range of HONOR-related phenomena and could be seen more similar to the European notions of HONOR studied by anthropologists (Stewart 1994: 103).

In the modern times, *ʕirḍ* usually refers to HONOR of a family, which is strongly connected to the sexual purity and chastity of its female members (Dodd 1973: 40, 43). Although, it seems, a man also has an *ʕirḍ*, it is by large a mere reflection of the *ʕirḍ* of his family and his lineage (Dodd 1973: 44). In fact, a family *ʕirḍ* is owned by male members of a kin-group – nevertheless, its state is technically related to female members' conduct – especially their chastity. The ownership translates to responsibility of making sure that *ʕirḍ* is intact (Dodd 1973: 44). It seems then that one can actually see *ʕirḍ* as an opinion on sexual conduct of women belonging to a family, whose male members own this *ʕirḍ*.

In fact, the association of *ʕirḍ* with female chastity led to even further development of the concept of *ʕirḍ* in some Modern Arabic communities, such as those in rural Jordan (Dodd 1973: 42). Thus, sometimes, *ʕirḍ* means woman's dignity (Dziekan 2008: 36), or simply "female chastity, prudence and continence (Abou-Zeid 1965: 247)". In other words, *ʕirḍ* is sometimes a mere reputation of sexual conduct of a woman, which however, reflects on the *šaraf*-HONOR of a man related to her (Abou-Zeid 1965: 253). Nevertheless, it is up to the man to protect *ʕirḍ* of her female kin – and by extension, the *ʕirḍ* of his family. This protection is perceived mostly as the rigid control over women, reaching in some situations the point of violence or even a crime, the example of which is the honor killing (cf. Abou-Zeid 1965: 253–4). A woman's role in preserving (her own) *ʕirḍ*-HONOR seems to be purely passive – a woman is perceived as unable to adhere to the virtuous conduct without being controlled by her male agnates (Abou-Zeid 1965: 256–7). What is quite significant, since *ʕirḍ* pertains to the reputation of a family as a whole, it is not husband, but male members of a woman's kin-group (usually her *ibn ʕamm* "paternal cousin"), who are responsible for the control and any possible retaliation, if the control failed to assure the woman's proper conduct (Abou-Zeid 1965: 257). Therefore, *ʕirḍ* is tied with a lineage and its state affects *šaraf*-HONOR of any male agnates of a woman, whose sexual reputation is at its foundation, including her sons and their descendants (Abou-Zeid 1965: 257). Because of that, in some communities, people prefer to marry their children within their kin-group, what is seen as an assurance that any possible "stain" from a foreign mother's misconduct will not eventually contaminate their lineage *ʕirḍ* (cf. Abou-Zeid 1965: 257).

Thus, a man could get his family *ʕirḍ* affected only by means of his female relative sexual misconduct. His actions – in the context of chastity – also could have effect on the *ʕirḍ*, but only as an indication of the overall state of the chastity in his family, thus also his female relatives (Dodd 1973: 45). Nevertheless, it seems that regaining the *ʕirḍ* – once it was lost – is either impossible (Abou-Zeid 1965: 256) or it is very difficult (Dodd 1973:45). Moreover, it seems that *ʕirḍ* is a subject of DECREASE/INCREASE, i.e., a family chastity might be evaluated as more or less rigid (Dodd 1973: 45).

As I mentioned, *ʕirḍ*, although being so strongly connected to women's actions, was a possession of those women's male agnates (Dodd 1973: 44). The possession should be understood as responsibility, which on its turn connects to the *šaraf*-HONOR of those men. This is because being responsible for protecting the kin-group *ʕirḍ* (Dodd 1973: 44), at an event of failure of such protection, men are being perceived unmanly, and, as a consequence, their *šaraf*-HONOR is lowered. In the light of this, Gubser explains the exodus of Palestinians from the West Bank after the *Naksa* of 1967. The escape was first and foremost dictated by the need to assure protection of their women's *ʕirḍ*s, i.e., protecting them against the expected rapes by Israeli soldiers. The perception of *ʕirḍ* in terms of female chastity is so strong in the modern Arabic society that even in scientific papers on *ʕirḍ* in LEAP, some seems to interpret this pre-Islamic phenomenon in the terms, which does not entirely fit it (cf. al-Azzam & al-Kharabsheh 2013: 293–5).

It is worth noting that female chastity as an element of the complex schema of HONOR is not an Arabic phenomenon and might be found in many cultures (cf. Baroja 1965: 88; Campbell 1965: 146; Stewart 1994: 107–9). In Polish, for instance, the lexeme *honor* could refer in the past also to the female chastity, as an equivalent to the more common lexeme *cześć* (Grzeszczak 2017: 125).[1]

A different characteristic of *ʕirḍ* was presented by Stewart (1994) based on his onsite study on Bedouin community in Sinai, Egypt, performed in 70' of the last century. In fact, the notion of *ʕirḍ* described by him is slightly more resembling LEAP *ʕirḍ* (e.g., it does not have anything to do with vertical honor, cf. Stewart 1994: 132).

First and foremost, Stewart noticed that in fact the Sinai Bedouin schema of HONOR contains actually two subschemata, which are called up by lexemes *wağh* "face" and *ʕirḍ* (Stewart 1994: 99). The FACE being an element of conceptualization of HONOR is a well-known phenomenon (cf. Appiah 2010: 10). Here, it was a profile of HONOR, which was involved in insults or – to put it in Stewart's words – in "affronts to dignity" (Stewart 1994: 100). Such affronts do not really

---

1 It seems, however, that such an extension of the meaning of *honor* is nowadays quite rare. The data from *Narodowy Korpus Języka Polskiego* "National Corpus of Polish Language" (https://nkjp.uni.lodz.pl/?q=yds3ygx5, [03-08-2021]) on the collocation of the lexeme *honor*, suggests than in modern Polish, *honor* doesn't refer to sexual conduct of any kind. Nevertheless, in 14 places, *honor* occurs in the phrase *honor kobiety* "an honor of a woman", which clearly connotates female chastity (cf. https://nkjp.uni.lodz.pl/?q=yg28jjv3, [03-08-2021]).

affect a man's ʕirḍ, which seems to be reserved to a more grievous offences, such as sexual offences against a woman of whom that man was responsible (Stewart 1994: 99).

This could be interpreted as the fact that Sinai Bedouin ʕirḍ covered only a part of one's horizontal honor, and only more serious affronts could be seen as attacks on it (Stewart 1994: 101). This seems to be the major difference between such a notion of ʕirḍ and its ancestor in LEAP. Despite the sexual offence, ʕirḍ is also involved in one's credibility or reliability. In other words, one could lose his ʕirḍ, if he failed to fulfill duties or meet obligations towards others (Stewart 1994: 86–98; 134). In fact, even sexual offences should be read as a failure in fulfilling the duty of the guardian of a female relative.

Though, Sinai Bedouin ʕirḍ significantly differs from its LEAP predecessor, one can find several important similarities between these concepts. First of all, in both contexts, ʕirḍ was by no means a VIRTUE – it was something definitely POSSESSED, i.e., being a POSSESSION of someone. The fact is also supported by the countability of the lexeme ʕirḍ, which has frequently used plural form *ʔaʕrāḍ*, i.e., *ʕirḍ*s (Stewart 1994: 144). Perhaps, another similarity could be found in the fact of being a certain whole, which can be either lost or preserved (Stewart 1994: 123). Although, as we will see in this chapter, it is not entirely clear whether LEAP ʕirḍ could be lost. Perhaps, in this department, it resembled the Sinai Bedouin concept of FACE, of which one could not be actually stripped, but which could be offended, attacked, and as a result defected and diminished (Stewart 1994: 99).

Nevertheless, the association between ʕirḍ and female chastity or female sexuality in general seems to be dominating and it persists in nowadays Arabic societies. A good example of its prominence is the protest song *Manūʕa min al-ʕarḍ*,[2] publicized by Abʕād foundation[3] as a part of *#NotYourHonor* campaign in December 2019. A following verse, frequently repeated in it, well depicts the dynamic of HONOR in the modern Arabic communities:

عرضي منو جسدي
جسدي منو **شرفك**
My honor (*ʕarḍī*) is not my body,
my body is not **your honor** (*šaraf-ak*).

2 https://www.youtube.com/watch?v=c3arQigsHjk [11-08-2022].
3 https://www.abaadmena.org/ [11-08-2022].

7.2. *ʕIrḍ* in CAD

The root √ʕRḌ seems to be encompassing a quite abstract idea, which might be describe as roughly WIDENESS. It is noteworthy, though, that it clearly contains the indication of EXPOSURE and of a (FLAT) WIDE SURFACE.

All CAD agrees in defining the major meaning of the most basic derivative of the root as simply the opposite of height (*ḫilāf aṭ-ṭūl*, cf. KtA3: 131; AlG: 747; AsS: 753), which we can interpret as WIDTH. Nevertheless, other derivatives of √ʕRḌ suggest that it indicates a wide surface, which is exposed. The element of (FLAT) WIDE SURFACE might be observed in such derivatives as *ʕarḍ* "the slope of a mountain, its side" (AsS: 754), and *ʕurḍ* and *ʕarūḍ*, both meaning "side" (AlG: 747; AsS: 756). The EXPOSURE, however, is well-recorded in CAD in form of such derivatives as *ʕārаḍa* "offering or exchanging products" (KtA3: 131), *muʕāraḍa* "exchange" (AlG: 747), *ʕarḍ* "the goods, what is the subject of financial transactions" (AsS: 754), or some of meanings of the verb *ʕaraḍa* "showing something or appearing" (AsS: 753), and "browsing, inspecting (an army)" (KtA3: 131). Both elements – (FLAT) WIDE SURFACE and EXPOSURE – seems to be crucial also for understanding the motivation of emergence of *ʕirḍ* as the derivative of √ʕRḌ.

As for the lexeme *ʕirḍ*, in KtA, one can find only a brief definition of it as meaning simply *ḥasab* (KtA3: 133). This definition was then repeated also in AsS (758) and LsA (LsA7: 191–2). Nevertheless, AlG (747), AsS (758), and LsA (LsA7: 191–3) all describe *ʕirḍ* as either "body" or "body scent", or as a synonym of *nafs* "soul", which here seems rather denoting one's SELF.[4] Moreover, they also define it as either a proper name of a wadi in al-Yamāma (AlG: 747; AsS: 758), or simply a term denoting a wadi, its side (LsA7: 193), or a wadi with trees (AsS: 758; LsA7: 194).

Despite the brief definition of *ʕirḍ* as *ḥasab*, all of CAD somehow try to explain the HONOR-related concept it was referring to. It is quite obvious that for al-Farāhīdī this concept was quite self-evident, since having stated that it resembles *ḥasab*, he used it in a sentence *lā taʕriḍ ʕirḍ fulān* "do not do *ʕaraḍa* to *ʕirḍ* of someone", which he explains as "do not mention him evilly" (KtA3: 133). It suggests that *ʕirḍ* is something possessed by someone, which might have been exposed or inspected – that is, offended or insulted – by someone. Similarly, *ʕirḍ* is explained by Ibn Durayd, who explicates *ṭaʕana fulān fī ʕirḍ fulān* "someone

4 In Arabic, the noun *nafs* was grammaticalized as a mean of self-reference (cf. Wright 1898b: 272; LsA6: 281).

perforated ʕirḍ of someone [else]" also as "he mentioned him evilly" (AlG: 747). It is consistent with the definition provided by al-Ǧawharī, who defined *naqī al-ʕirḍ* "[a man] of a clean ʕirḍ" as "[someone] free from any insult or offense" (AsS: 758). As one can see, *ʕirḍ* is perceived as a part of someone, which might have been insulted (cf. LsA7: 191). Ibn Manẓūr, who provided the most extensive elaboration on what *ʕirḍ* was, extend this notion stating that is what is praised or shamed in someone (LsA7: 191).

The only remaining question, which Ibn Manẓūr tried to answer, by quoting statements of different Arabic philologist, was that about what was this something belonging to someone, which was the subject of the praise and the insult. He recalls the claim that what was really praised or shamed in a man is either himself (or his soul) or his body. Its major proponent was Ibn Qutayba, who used a fragment of hadith (C) as an argument supporting this claim. As we can see, this claim simply extends the meanings of *ʕirḍ*, discussed earlier, as encompassing the evaluative element too, clearly discernible in this lexeme.

(C) فَمَن اتّقى الشُبُهات استبرأ لِدِينِهِ **وعِرْضِه**

Who shuns the doubtful matters, seeks immunity for his religion and for **himself/his soul** (*ʕirḍi-hi*) (LsA7: 192).

However, Ibn Manẓūr himself points towards some inconsistence of this claim, by citing another fragment of hadith, the passage (D), in which as forbidden for a Muslim, the Prophet Muḥammad listed other Muslim's blood (*dam*), possession (*māl*), and *ʕirḍ*. He argues that in this fragment, the use of the lexeme *ʕirḍ* would be absolutely redundant, if it referred only to (one's) SELF. This is because, in this context, *dam* "blood" clearly suggests killing someone (LsA7: 193).

(D) كلُ المسلِم على المسلم حَرام دَمُه ومالُه **وعِرْضُه**

[For] each Muslim, it is forbidden to [act] against [other] Muslim's blood, [i.e., life], possessions, and ***ʕirḍ*** (LsA7: 193).

In other words, if *ʕirḍ* meant one's SELF or their SOUL, Muḥammad would outlaw killing someone twice. Thus, *ʕirḍ* was something else. As an explanation of its nature, he quoted two statements – by Ibn al-Aṯīr and Abū al-ʕAbbas – I rendered below:

العِرْض مَوْضِعُ المَدْح والذَمّ من الإنسان سَواء كان في نَفْسِهِ أو سَلَفِهِ أو مَن يَلْزَمُهُ أَمْرُه، وقِيل هو جانِبُه الذي يَصُونُه من نَفْسِهِ وحَسَبِه ويُحامِي عَنْهُ أن يُنْتَقَص ويُثْلَب

[Ibn al-Aṯīr said:] *ʕirḍ* is a locus of praising and dispraising a man – [it might be based] either on himself, or on his ancestors, or on the one, whose orders that man follows. It was [also] said [that *ʕirḍ* is] his, [this man], side (*ǧānib*) that he protects by himself and with his *ḥasab*, and he defends it against any reproach or insult (LsA7: 192).

إذا ذُكِرَ عِرْضُ فُلانٍ فمَعْناه أُمُورُه التي يَرْتَفِع او يَسْقُطُ بِذِكْرِها من جِهَتِها بِحَمْدٍ او بِذَمٍّ، فَيَجُوز أن يَكُون أُمورًا يُوصَفُ هو بِها دُونَ أسْلافِه وَيَجُوز انْ تُذْكَرَ أسْلافُه لِتَلْحَقَه النَقِيصةُ بِعَيْبِهم

> [Abū al-ʕAbbās said:] If someone's *ʕirḍ* is mentioned, the meaning of this is [that someone is mentioning] his matters, because of which he ascends – [if they are being] praised – or falls down – [if they are being] dispraised. It may be that these matters, by which one is described, might not [encompass information about] his ancestors. It could [also] be the case that his ancestors are mentioned [within those matters], so that a shame was attached to him due to their faults (*ʕayb*) (LsA7: 191).

LsA suggests also that perhaps *ʕirḍ* could also mean one's ancestors or their deeds (LsA7: 191–2), which I believe we can read as simply one's *nasab* "lineage". Perhaps, then, as suggested by Abū al-ʕAbbās, sometimes, *ʕirḍ* could also imply one's origin, which could be blamed for someone's disgracefulness.

Additionally, LsA provides yet three other meanings of the lexeme *ʕirḍ*: "a kind of trees, like tamarisks" (also *ʕarḍ*, LsA7: 193), "interior of a country/town" (LsA7: 193), and "a side, out- skirts of a land" (LsA7: 193), which I did not include in the table containing the CAD definition (Tab. 23.), since they seem to be separate derivatives form the root √ʕRḌ. This table does not also include most of the meanings of *ʕirḍ* listed by Lane (1968e: 2007–8) for the similar reasons. The HONOR-related meaning was rendered by me in form presented in Wehr & Cowan (1976: 604).

Tab. 23. The meanings of *ʕirḍ* in CAD and dictionaries of CA

Lexeme	Meaning	Sources
ʕirḍ	[a] *ḥasab*	KtA3: 133; AsS: 758; LsA7: 191–2; Lane 1968e: 2008
	[b] body	AlG: 747; AsS: 758; LsA7: 191–3; Lane 1968e: 2008
	[c] body scent	
	[d] *nafs* "self" or "soul"	
	[e] the wadi in al-Yamāma	AlG: 747; AsS: 758
	[f] a wadi with trees	AsS: 758; LsA7: 194; Lane 1968e: 2008
	[g] honor, good repute; dignity	KtA3: 133; AsS: 758; LsA7: 191–3; Lane 1968e: 2008; Wehr & Cowan 1976: 604
	[h] *nasab* "lineage"	LsA7: 191–2; Lane 1968e: 2008

Obviously, the meanings [e] and [f] must have been derived independently from the other significations, which seem clearly interrelated. Nonetheless, it seems to be quite difficult to specify the direction of the semantic development binding them together. Due to its most physical nature, the meaning [b] "body" or [c] "body scent" seem the most possible original significations. Thus, having in mind the hypothetical idea of the root √ˁRḌ, being WIDENESS with elements of EXPOSURE and WIDE SPACE, they would profile the concept of BODY as something EXPOSED – maybe something exposed to immediate evaluation (cf. "body scent"). Perhaps, however, it was not the case, and in fact we can observe here an example of a quite interesting – culture-specific to a certain extent – conceptual development of the notion of (EXPOSED, WIDE) SIDE of one's BODY, which could serve in conceptualization of one's HONOR or REPUTATION. In other words, it may well be the case that the primary signification of *ˁirḍ* was the meaning [g] "honor, good repute; dignity", and the rest – [a], [b], [c], [d], and [h] – its conceptual extensions, in which some of the specifics of the conceptualization of HONOR are forwarded.

As I said, it is difficult to reconstruct the semantic development of the noun *ˁirḍ* with precision. Such a reconstruction is, of course, by no means among any of the aims of this chapter, in which I will purely focus on reconstructing a defined stage of this development, i.e., the functioning of the lexeme *ˁirḍ* in LEAP. Nevertheless, I will use the hypothesis on the derivation of its HONOR-related meaning from the notion of (EXPOSED, WIDE) SIDE of one's BODY, since it clearly indicates the embodiment phenomenon, which I believe one can find in many places in CEAP and TBD. In other words, although I will hold myself from pressing any specific etymological claims, I will hypothesize that *ˁirḍ*-HONOR was by far conceptualized in bodily terms, and its conceptualizations seem indicating the derivation form the concept of (EXPOSED, WIDE) SIDE of one's BODY.

7.3. CEAP data on *ˁirḍ*

The cluster *ˁirḍ* consists of only two lexemes *ˁirḍ* itself and its plural form *ʔaˁrāḍ*. It means that *ˁirḍ* as HONOR was not a derivational base for terms denoting a MAN OF HONOR or concepts alike. In total, these lexemes occurred in CEAP 76 times (singular NO: 57, and plural NO: 19). The NWC for such a frequency equals approximately 2.69,[5] which is lower than *ḥasab* (NWC: 3.5), but definitely higher than *šaraf* (NWC: 1.73). The aforementioned data are represented also in the table below (Tab. 24.).

5 NWC of 2.69 corresponds to the frequency of English words *might, large,* and *department,* and Polish *coraz* (2.70), *swoją* (2.68), *przecież* (2.67), *życie* (2.67), and *dopiero* (2.67). Based on the corpora *English Web 2015* and *Polish Web 2015* available on *SketchEngine* (https://www.sketchengine.eu [08-07-2021]).

Tab. 24. The number of occurrences of the members of *ʕirḍ* cluster within CEAP

Item		Number of Occurrences (NO)		Normalized Word Count (per 10,000)
ʕirḍ		57	=76	2.69
	ʔaʕrāḍ	19		

From among the meanings presented in CAD, the most frequently occurring signification was that related to HONOR – NO: 71 – either [g] "honor, good repute; dignity" or [a] *ḥasab*. In fact, it was quite difficult to differentiate between them based on a particular context. The meaning [a], I believe, could be found 2 times in the corpus (t34A:130; t13A:70). Thus, the [g] seems to be implied in CEAP 69 times. Moreover, CEAP contains one occurrence of the meaning [e], i.e., the proper name of a wadi in al-Yamāma (t10A:123), as well as 2 instances of the use of *ʕirḍ* in reference to [b] "body" (t28A:79–80; t37χ). What is noteworthy, embodiment of the concept represented as [g] is well present in the corpus. Thus, in fact, the meaning [b] might well be seen as more represented in CEAP depending on a given interpretation. I believe in 3 passages (t30B:46–48; t30B:160–161; t22A:43–46) *ʕirḍ* was, moreover, used in reference to one's SELF, i.e., to the meaning [d]. Yet, again, the border between signification [d] and [b] "body" might be quite blurry (cf. t28A:79–80). Moreover, twice (t10A:16; t39A:9, 11), *ʕirḍ* was definitely used in reference to one's *nasab* "lineage", i.e., to [h].

As one can see, frequently in CEAP, it was difficult to delimit the meanings presented in CAD – especially in the case of [a] and [g]. It naturally should be seen as an example of blurriness of categories borders, which are fuzzy by nature. One can read it as an indication of quite prolific function of the lexeme *ʕirḍ*, which could call up different schemata at once by means of metonymy and metaphor, bringing out by that some important features of the concepts it recalled in a given context.

7.4. *ʕIrḍ*-HONOR-RIGHT TO RESPECT is one's EXPOSED SIDE

As we saw, Ibn Manẓūr (LsA7: 193) placed among many meanings of the lexeme *ʕirḍ* also that of "a side (of anything)". Perhaps, this particular claim, should be rather seen as registering a variant of another word – *ʕurḍ* – of exactly this signification (AlG: 747; AsS: 756). Nevertheless, I believe, the indication of referring to a SIDE is an important element of the understanding the motivation for the fact that lexicalization of the RIGHT TO RESPECT was derived from the root √ˁRḍ. As already mentioned by Ibn Aṯīr, *ˁirḍ* was one's *ǧānib*, i.e., "side", which must have been protected by someone – and this SIDE was the subject of the PRAISE-SHAME activities of others (cf. ˁAlī 1993b: 407). This PROTECTION was – as we will learn – frequently conceptualized as COVERING the *ˁirḍ*, which also could find its reflection in the expression quoted by al-Farāhīdī (KtA3: 133). As I mentioned it earlier, he presented a sentence *lā taˁriḍ ˁirḍ fulān* "do not do *ˁaraḍa* to *ˁirḍ* of someone" as meaning "do not mention someone evilly". In here, *ˁirḍ* is a subject of the action of *ˁaraḍa*, which means in this place rather "he made the thing apparent; he exposed it to view (Lane 1968e: 2003)". Thus, "to mention someone evilly" – that is, to INSULT someone, or to OFFEND them – was to EXPOSE their *ˁirḍ*.

In other words, *ˁirḍ* – as derived from √ˁRḌ – evoked an image-schema of a SIDE. This SIDE definitely links to one's BODY. It was the SIDE of one's BODY, which should have been kept protected – COVERED, and its EXPOSURE inevitably indicated a HARM or a DAMAGE done to it.

As one's BODY SIDE, it was conceptualized as a very fragile. I believe one can actually see this conceptualization as encoding what we refer to as the self-worth or self-esteem. Consequently, we might understand *ˁirḍ* as one's GOOD NAME or REPUTATION, which EXPOSED to EVALUATION might be DIMINISHED or REDUCED. This REPUTATION, however, was derived from a certain VALUE or WORTH, being also the basis for the SELF-ESTEEM of the individual. Altogether, the REPUTATION/ESTEEM and SELF-ESTEEM constituted the foundation of one's RIGHT TO RESPECT. In other words, one could claim RECOGNITION of their FITNESS in the community based on their GOOD NAME, derived form a certain WORTH of them – in their eyes and the eyes of their EQUALS in the community.

Therefore, it seems *ˁirḍ* referred to the complex schema of RIGHT TO RESPECT, which encapsulated several subschemata encoding the knowledge of the basis for this RIGHT. Thus, *ˁirḍ* was the very RIGHT to be RECOGNIZED as a full MEMBER of a community, as well as the HONOR-VALUE/ESTEEM/REPUTATION in its two major profiles, SELF-ESTEEM and ESTEEM enjoyed in the eyes of others. These two elements of the schema *ˁirḍ* – HONOR-RIGHT TO RESPECT and HONOR-ESTEEM/SELF-ESTEEM – were deeply conflated and I believe could not be easily separated or delimited.

The only situation, in which the delimitation was easily achieved, was the metonymic use of the lexeme *ˁirḍ*. As we learned, *ˁirḍ* might have simply meant one's *ḥasab* (KtA3: 133; AsS: 758; LsA7: 191–2) or their *nasab* "lineage" (LsA7: 191–2), what suggests that sometimes, *ˁirḍ* was calling up particular elements of its schema, following the metonymic model WHOLE FOR ITS PARTS (cf. Radden & Kövecses 1999: 32). In this way, the two elements of the schema clearly separated, and the HONOR- ESTEEM/ SELF- ESTEEM part was being foregrounded with the specification in form of its major profiles – *ḥasab* and *nasab*. In other words, *ʕirḍ*- ESTEEM/SELF-ESTEEM was constituted by one's *ḥasab*, i.e., VALUE/WORTH estimated based on their adherence to the code of *karam*, and one's *nasab*, i.e., the VALUE/ WORTH derived from the lineage to which one was attaching themselves.

Of course, one could see *ʕirḍ* as a mere synonym of *ḥasab* – as it was clearly promoted in CAD. I believe, however, that as noticed by Farès (1938: 96), *ḥasab* was only a part of the whole referred to by the lexeme *ʕirḍ* – and not its alternative name. As I said, it is true that sometimes differentiation between *ʕirḍ* and *ḥasab* in the contexts in CEAP was challenging, if not impossible. Yet, it does not mean the concepts these words referred to could not be delimited at all. As we could see, *ḥasab* was perceived as a COUNT of one's HONORABLE DEEDS, of one's *karam*-HONORABILITY – it was a quantifiable element of one's PRIDE. *ʕIrḍ* – as we will learn – was conceptualized in a different way: it involved the conceptualization in terms of embodiment and – what is more important – it was subject to constant attack, and it needed persistent protection. Thus, I think we can actually posit the thesis that *ʕirḍ* was more of a broader schema, whereas *ḥasab* constituted one of its parts, prominent enough to be called up by the means of metonymy WHOLE FOR ITS PARTS.

The fact that RIGHT TO RESPECT is something founded on one's VALUE might be observed in many cultures, including modern Arabic ones. For instance, Stewart was informed that whenever one's VALUE (*gimih*, CA *qīma*) was being diminished by an INSULT, the person faced some social repercussions in form of ostracism (Stewart 1994: 118).

The VALUE, on its turn, in the society of pre- Islamic Arabs, clearly derived from one's *ḥasab* – honorable conduct – *nasab* – lineage – and also one's *šaraf*- high social standing. It is seen, for instance, in the fact that while evaluating a candidate for marriage, a family always paid attention to these elements (ʕAlī 1993b: 544). It is also to be observed in the sample (108), in which a woman inquires the poet about his WORTH. This consists of his look, *karam* (here, *murūʔa*, i.e., ability to be *karīm*, and the sound judgement) and the specifics of his ORIGIN.

(108) أما الوَسامةُ و**المروءةُ**، أوْ رَأيُ الرّجالِ فقدْ بدا – حَسْبي
فودَدتُ أنّكَ لوْ تخبِرُنا منْ والداكَ، ومَنْصِبُ الشعبِ

When it comes to the handsomeness, **the manliness** (*murūʔa*), or the sound judgement of men – these are evident. They suffice me.

> Thus, I would like you to tell us about your parents are and the roots of your people (cf. t38B:31–2).

They must have then constituted one's VALUE – the way he or she was perceived by others, but also – I believe – by themselves. The SELF-ESTEEM element might be observed, for example, whenever one is priding themselves. As reported by ʕAlī (1993b: 292), Banū Qurayš, the tribe of Prophet Muḥammad, were always bragging about their origin and their *ʔaḥsāb*, i.e., COUNTS of HONORABILITY. This, of course, implies that these two elements were what they perceived as their VALUE. The SELF-ESTEEM encompassed in *ʕirḍ* sometimes is more discernible in CEAP. Therefore, Tadeusz Kowalski could render the lexeme *ʕirḍ* occurring in a poem attributed to Qays Ibn al-Ḫaṭīm even as German *Ehrgefühl* "the sense of honor" (cf. t25C:74; the sample (191)).

All in all, as noticed by Dodd (1973: 45), also nowadays *ʕirḍ* is a matter of REPUTATION. This part of the schema is so evident that some philologist, as William A. Clouston, rendered the lexeme *ʕirḍ* as simply *fame* (cf. al-Azzam & al-Kharabsheh 2013: 293). Nevertheless, I think such a treatment is an oversimplification. Obviously, the REPUTATION must have indicated something more important since it was so much in need of constant protection. This something, I believe, was RIGHT TO RESPECT by EQUALS, i.e., the RIGHT to be accepted within a group – and by that to stay within it and to not be exposed to the perils of the environment of pre-Islamic Arabia.

7.4.1. One's *ʕirḍ*-RIGHT TO RESPECT might be DIMINISHED

As noted by Stewart (1994: 123) RIGHT TO RESPECT can be only LOST or SAVE. However, *ʕirḍ* – being a POSSESSION of someone – does not really seem to follow this scenario. The only indication that *ʕirḍ* could have been lost might be found in (183), attributed to Ḥassān Ibn Ṯābit. The poet mentions two kinds of PRECIOUS POSSESSED MASS – his WEALTH or simply POSSESSIONS, and his *ʕirḍ*. Both are described as possible agents of the action referred to by *ʔawdà* that LsA (LsA15: 450) presents as a synonym of *halaka* "to perish, to cease to exist; to pass away, to die". Therefore, clearly, Ibn Ṯābit suggests that *ʕirḍ* can disappear in the same manner as one's POSSESSIONS. Still, he evidently sees the LOSS of *ʕirḍ* as something way more difficult to reverse than the LOSS of one's WEALTH.

(183) أحتالُ للمالِ، إن أَوْدى فأَجْمَعُهُ، ولسْتُ **لِلعِرْضِ** إن أوْدَى بمُحتالِ

> I am acting clever with [my] wealth – [so], if it perishes, I collect it [again with easy]. [But], in case of [my] **honor** (*ʕirḍ*), I cannot [retrieve it easily, simply by] being clever (cf. t38A:231).

Nevertheless, it was actually the only instance, in which *ˁirḍ* is described as perishable. Perhaps, it is so, because it was conceptualized as PRECIOUS POSSESSED MASS, which resembled one's *māl*-WEALTH-POSSESSIONS. Thus, *ˁirḍ* might also be given away (cf. t07A:169), put as a stake in a bargain (cf. t10A:42–45), or simply wasted, exhausted (cf. t21A:117–123). Consequently, in CEAP, *ˁirḍ* is frequently depicted in the simile to *māl*-WEALTH-POSSESSIONS, as it is, e.g., in the example (184) by ˁAntara Ibn Šaddād.

(184) فإذا شرِبْتُ فإنّني مستهلَك مالي **وعِرْضي** وافِرٌ لَمْ يُكْلَمِ

Thus, truly, whenever I was drinking [wine], I was squandering my wealth (*māl*), leaving **my honor** (*ˁirḍī*) abundant (*wāfir*) and unharmed (cf. t21A:122; cf. also Arberry 2017: 181).

Perhaps, such a conceptualization emerged as a blend deriving from the fact that WEALTH – another example of such PRECIOUS POSSESSED MASS – was so crucial for the preservation of one's RIGHT TO RESPECT. I will comment of this further in this chapter.

The conceptualization of *ˁirḍ* in terms of the image-schema PRECIOUS POSSESSED MASS might be also observed in the expressions of INSULTING/OFFENDING someone provided in TBD, such as *ˀaḫaḏa min ˁirḍi-hi* "he took [something] form his *ˁirḍ*", *ˀaḫaḏa min ǧānibi-hi* "he took [something] form his side", (cf. aHm: 32; cf. also t30A:265) and *nāla min ˁirḍi-hi* "he attained (something) form his *ˁirḍ*" (cf. aHm: 32; cf. example (197)). They seem to imply that one's *ˁirḍ* – being also referred as their SIDE (v.s.) – is a certain WHOLE – a MASS – from which one could chunk off a piece, DIMINISHING and DAMAGING it in the process. It is also compatible with a collocation of the lexeme *ˁirḍ* by derivatives of the verb *wafara* "it was full, complete, whole, entire (Lane 1968h: 2955)", as we could see it in (184), in the attribute *wāfir*, i.e., "ample" (cf., also t07A:115; t22A:63–76). In other words, HONOR – being a RIGHT – was more or less AMPLE, i.e., more or less supported and thus, guaranteed. One's RIGHT TO RESPECT could be founded on thinner grounds than the RIGHT of others, and therefore could be much easier to be challenged, and consequently, dismissed.

Since *ˁirḍ* was a PRECIOUS POSSESSED MASS, it could also be a subject of COMPARISON (cf. t38A:159; t28A:138– 143; t30A:265). Such a conceptualization must derive from the fact that *ḥasab* – by far its constitutive PART – was frequently a subject of MUTUAL MEASUREMENT, i.e., COMPARISON, during the time of *mufāḫarāt* (cf. section 5.5.). Of course, in both cases, the goal of the COMPARISON was to prove who is BETTER, thus, who deserves the PRECEDENCE (i.e., *šaraf*) among others. However, as one can see in (185) by al-Aˁšà, sometimes, participating in such a COMPARISON of men's *ˁirḍ*s might be a sign of *safah*, i.e., foolishness, irresoluteness. I believe it might be so, since ʕ*irḍ*-HONOR was perceived as something extremally vulnerable, and its purposeful EXPOSURE might have been a symptom of irresponsibility.

(185) عَلْقَمَ لا تَسْفَهْ وَلا تَجْعَلَنْ **عِرْضَكَ** للوارِدِ والصّادِرِ

ʕAlqama, do not act foolishly (*lā tafsah*), and do not make **your honor** (ʕ*irḍa-ka*) [a subject of comparison] for [everyone] – the one who aims the watering place and the one, who returns from there (cf. t28A:142–3).

All in all, it seems that ʕ*irḍ*-RIGHT TO RESPECT was not entirely losable, yet it could suffer being DIMINISHED. I think one can try to understand it also in the simile to the WEALTH, which is a POSSESSION no matter how large or small it is. In other words, by saying that someone lost his *māl*-WEALTH-POSSESSIONS, we actually employ metonymy stating that this POSSESSION became little, and as a consequence, its POSSESSOR is now poor. Nevertheless, even being poor, POSSESSOR still has some *māl*-POSSESSIONS, although it is now a mere shadow of the past affluence. The situation with ʕ*irḍ*, I believe, must have been similar. Thus, one never really lost their ʕ*irḍ*-RIGHT TO RESPECT, yet it could have gotten reduced significantly.

The REDUCTION of one's ʕ*irḍ*, the process of DIMINISHING it, implied that ʕ*irḍ* was becoming DEFECTED or DAMAGED, and as such it does not serve its original purpose with the same effect. In other words, ʕ*irḍ* was not that potent in gaining RESPECT of one's EQUALS, once it was DIMINISHED, i.e., made DEFECTIVE. This, I believe, derives from the embodiment model, I will discuss further in this chapter. It means that ʕ*irḍ* as being BODILY cannot be fully REMOVED, but can be made DEFECTIVE, i.e., of less effectiveness in claiming the RESPECT of others.

This DAMAGING was done by INSULT or OFFENCE, which implied an accusation of dishonorable behavior. Such an accusation was referred to in LEAP by the lexeme *ḏamm*, which might be seen as the opposite of *madḥ*-PRAISING (cf. LsA12: 256). It was than DISPRAISING someone, by ascribing them with dishonorable traits, actions, or facts. A more specific profile of this action was *šatama*, one can see, I believe, as referring to the concept of SHAMING. One can observe it, e.g., in (186), a verse by Ḥassān Ibn Ṯābit (cf. also t21A:117–127). In fact, *šatama* is a lexeme quite frequently cooccurring with ʕ*irḍ*. By looking at the derivatives of the root √ŠTM, based on which it is formed, one can find in it a discernible notion of FACE DISFIGURATION (cf., e.g., *šatīm* "(a donkey or a lion) of an ugly face", or *šatāma* "difficult character accompanied with an ugliness of the face"; cf. KtA2: 305, AlG: 399, and LsA12: 371).

(186) أمّا الحِماسُ فإنِي غيرُ شاتمِهِمْ، لا هُم كِرامٌ ولا **عِرْضِي** لهمْ خَطَرُ
قَوْمٌ لِئامٌ أَقَلَّ أُلله عِدَّتَهِمْ، كما تساقَطَ حَوْلَ الفَقْحَةِ البَعَرُ

As far as [the clan of] al-Ḥibās is concerned, I do not shame them – [simply stated,] they are not honorable men, and **my honor** (*ʕirḍī*) is [far from being] like theirs. They are base, low people – shall God belittle their number in the manner the dung drops down from a wide anus (cf. 1.8A:159).

This colocation, then, brings *ʕirḍ* closer to the aforementioned conception of FACE, persisting in the communities of Sinai Bedouin studied by Stewart (1994). What is quite interesting is that similarly to what we observe in LEAP *ʕirḍ*, Sinai Bedouin HONOR-FACE could not be entirely taken away, but only could be defected and diminished – by means of INSULT or OFFENCE, referred to as "blackening" (Stewart 1994: 137). The blackening simply means an accusation of dishonorable behavior, which for those Bedouins was not a matter of *ʕirḍ*, but FACE. What is noteworthy here is also the fact that FACE in general was a very important element of conceptualization of HONOR in many cultures around the world (cf. English *to lose face*, or Irish *enech* "honor"[6]).

The action of *šatama* was usually performed as an element of *hiǧāʔ*, i.e., satirizing or vilifying someone in a poetic composition. One can find this conceptualization implicitly expressed in (187), a passage by Ibn Muqbil. As one can expect the means of such SHAMING via poetry was normally belittling of one's *ʕirḍ*-VALUE (cf. t03A:101), as well as use of vulgarity (cf. t07A:51)

(187) هَلْ كُنْتُ إِلَّا مِجَنًّا تَتَّقُونُ به قَدْ لَاحَ في **عِرْضِ** مَنْ باذَأَكُمْ عَلْبِي

Was I anything else than a shield you use to protect yourself? [Didn't] marks of [my tongue's] smites show up on the **honor** (*ʕirḍ*) of those who abusively offended you (cf. t36A:245)?

In fact, in other cultures, such as in the culture of rural Andalusia, words – in form of a public oral performance known as *burla* – were also used in DIMINISHING one's HONOR (Pitt-Rivers 1965: 47–8). In the case of both pre-Islamic Arabic *hiǧāʔ* and Andalusian *burla* the main goal was to publicize the INSULT. As we know Early Arabic Poetry was the major mean of transporting information in space and time in the society of al-Ǧāhiliyya. Thus, satires were simply as important public institution as penitential pillars, pillories, conical hats, flogging, all being means of publicizing one's DISGRACE in deferent cultural and temporal contexts (Baroja 1965: 103). The reason why they were so substantial is the fact that disgrace – a social death – must have been made widespread, so that it was effective (cf. Stewart 1994: 113).

6 https://www.oxfordreference.com/view/10.1093/oi/authority.20110803095751621 [06-08-2021].

7.4.2. *ʕIrḍ* is reflexive HONOR

Of course, as we know, *ʕirḍ*, being fragile, was to be protected. Thus, any attack on it – any INSULT, OFFENCE – any SHAMING, must have been met with an appropriate reaction. The fact that OFFENCE to the *ʕirḍ* was perceived as something calling for immediate reaction indicates that *ʕirḍ*-RIGHT TO RESPECT was reflexive (cf. Stewart 1994: 56–5) – in the same way as European version of this notion. The sensitivity of the reflexiveness of HONOR varies from culture to another. It seems, in Europe, HONOR was a very sensitive matter and in fact – in many European cultures, such as in that of Medieval Islandic warriors – it covered much of one's personal self-worth, or self-esteem (cf. Stewart 1994: 101). It means that in fact any failure in showing one RESPECT was considered as an OFFENCE or INSULT, which demanded reaction.

The reaction was also more or less culture- specific. Nevertheless, when reaching the extreme, it was always violent. In Europe, as noticed by Pitt-Rivers (1965: 29), "the ultimate vindication of honour lies in physical violence (…)" – in other words, European HONOR "feeds on blood (Stewart 1994: 140)". In contrast, as noted by Stewart (1994: 139), the mid 20th c. Sinai Bedouins rarely resorted to the violence in avenging their *ʕirḍ*, choosing usually to satisfy the offence by means of customary laws and customary trials. Nevertheless, their notion of *ʕirḍ* was reflexive – what could not be said about the aforementioned HONOR-FACE.

Pre-Islamic *ʕirḍ*, however, resembled by far the European notion of HONOR. It was highly sensitive, what accounts for the fact that not only grievous offenses against one's HONOR, but also common insults required a proper response (ʕAlī 1993b: 407). Moreover, even those imaginary insults – those supposed mockeries, interpreted from one's eye blinking or smile – also were seen as calling for avenge (ʕAlī 1993b: 407). And the response was rarely contained within peaceful dealing and – as one can see in (188) by Ṭarafa Ibn al-ʕAbd – usually required blood (cf. ʕAlī 1993b: 547). This, however, should be read literarily rather than as a figure of speech. As ʕAlī (1993b: 547) describes it, pre-Islamic Arabs considered cutting one's throat or cutting off one's head as a proper mean of the revenge, which aimed to *wash away* the disgrace with the blood of the offender.

(188) وإن يَقذِفوا بالقَذع **عِرْضَك** أسقِهم بشَرْبِ حِياضِ الموت قَبْلَ التهدُّد

If they are throwing mud, [vulgarities] onto **your honor** (*ʕirḍa-ka*), I will not utter threats. I will make them drink from the pond of death (cf. t07A:51; Witkowska & Danecki 1981: 61).

Of course, not only INSULTS could DIMINISH one's *ʕirḍ*. As I said, it covered the whole range of personal honor, so naturally INSULTING was only the least harmful – yet requiring avenge – ATTACKS on one's HONOR. The *ʕirḍ* could have been also OFFENDED, e.g., by violation of the *ḥurma* "sanctity" of one's abode, by breaking the rules of good guest (ʕAlī 1993c: 25–6), including misbehaving in front of the host's women (ʕAlī 1993c: 57).

7.5. Embodiment of HONOR in pre-Islamic Arabic culture – *ʕirḍ* is BODILY

Thus, HONOR was perceived as something more than an added value or an advantage – in cultures of both pre-Islamic Arabs and Europeans. The fact that its offence was demanding violent response could suggest that, in fact, it was as precious as life itself (Stewart 1994: 139). This means that frequently people felt a strong connection between their physical person and their HONOR (Pitt-Rivers 1965: 29). Ergo, HONOR was always in a way deeply related to one's BODY.

The conceptualization in terms of embodiment is the most basic cognitive procedure, in which our concepts of the words are being shaped by means of our body-based physical experience of the world (cf. Kövecses 2005: 18). When we are getting ANGRY, we feel it as if TEMPERATURE within our BODY was RISING, thus we conceptualize ANGER as RISE OF TEMPERATURE or PRESSURE in a CONTAINER that serves us to imagine our BODY. In such a way, our conception of ANGER takes form of a metaphor, which can be found manifested in our linguistic practices in such expressions as *You make my blood boil* or *He's just blowing off steam* (Lakoff, Espenson & Schwartz 1991: 149).

The conceptualization of HONOR should be then seen also in similar fashion. As noted by Sławek (2011: 87), already Aristotle noticed the relationship between BODILY and HONOR, considering the latter in the terms of FEELING SHAME. Namely, it seems, European conceptualizations of HONOR focus on the EXPOSURE element of this notion, usually employing the concept of FACE in structuring it. Therefore, when we read that someone *lost face*, we understand that one's HONOR, being based on their REPUTATION, is implied. In other words, one LOST their FACE-APPEARANCE of an HONORABLE, thus HONOR-deserving individual – they lost their good name, good opinion, based on which their RIGHT TO RESPECT was founded. This embodied conceptualization must derive from our experience of FACE as the main mean of PRESENTING ourselves or simply, DISPLAYING our emotions. LOSING FACE implies a lost ability to keep showing the appearances of SHAMELESSNESS, being the indication of HONORABILITY. It derives then form the aforementioned observation by Aristotle. In other words, our FACE DISPLAYS our FEELING of SHAME, implying by that the loss of HONOR-VALUE.

Other than that, European conceptualizations of HONOR do not seem to employ bodily idioms. It finds its expression in the collocation of the American

English *honor* and British English *honour*. In general, none of bodily vocabulary collocate them, even though they are still accompanied by such lexemes as *defend* or *avenge*, suggesting the great appreciation of the concept they refer to.[7]

In LEAP, the situation is different. I believe *ʕirḍ*-HONOR-RIGHT TO RESPECT, as based on a REPUTATION/SELF-ESTEEM derived from a certain VALUE of someone, was by large conceptualized in the terms of embodied cognition. This conceptualization, however, forwards the perception of *ʕirḍ* as something vulnerable rather than as something indicating one's standing – as in European metaphors in terms of FACE. Thus, pre-Islamic Arabic seems to have been imagined it as the SIDE of the BODY (perhaps the most fragile of its parts) or BODY in its FRAGILITY/VULNERABILITY. Consequently, one can consider this conceptualization as an example of a cultural embodiment, in which "physiology, function, and neural basis of body parts are imaginatively exploited and hijacked by culture" (cf. Maalej 2008: 396–7). It means that the culture of al-Ǧāhiliyya, HONOR was a very sensitive and delicate matter.

What is quite interesting, CAD suggest that the bodily conceptualization of *ʕirḍ* pertain to the whole BODY rather than its specific part (cf., e.g., LsA7: 191–2). Perhaps, then, *ʕirḍ* could be better described as a profile of the schema BODY, which foregrounds its FRAGILITY/VULNERABILITY as being EXPOSED to a harm. Nevertheless, the interpretation of *ʕirḍ* as indicating BODY SIDE finds its support in related metaphoric mapping *ʕirḍ*-HONOR-RIGHT TO RESPECT IS *ǧānib*-BODY SIDE (cf. Lane 1968b: 468). It was lexicalized in the aforementioned expression *ʔaḫaḏa min ǧānibi-hi* "he took [something] form his side", (cf. aHm: 32; cf. also t30A:265) denoting the script of an INSULT. It may well be the case that *ʕirḍ* denoted in LEAP a profile of BODY in the consequence of a metonymic *pars-pro-toto* mapping, in which the BODY SIDE afforded access to this particular profile of the whole – the BODY – its FRAGILITY/VULNERABILITY.

Whatever was the case, the bodily conceptualization of *ʕirḍ* encoded cultural perception of it terms of this particular trait: FRAGILITY/VULNERABILITY. Despite the clues derived from CAD definitions, one can also find many instances in CEAP and in TBD, in which *ʕirḍ*-HONOR- RIGHT TO RESPECT is evidently depicted as BODILY. Most of those instances pertain to metaphorical expressions, in which INSULTING/OFFENDING one's *ʕirḍ* is depicted in the terms of different kinds of PHYSICAL ATTACKS. It strengthens the argument that *ʕirḍ* profiled the schema BODY in terms of its FRAGILITY/VULNERABILITY, since these expressions clearly foreground the part of the schema BODY that can be termed as BEING

7 cf. *English Web 2015* on *SketchEngine* (https://www.sketchengine.eu [08-07-2021]).

OBJECT OF PHYSICAL ATTACK. Consequently, other elements of this schema, such as GROWING, BEING AFFECTED BY DISEASE, DYING, etc., were not employed at all.

The embodiment of *ʕirḍ*-HONOR might also explain the problem with the LOSS of one's HONOR in LEAP. As we saw earlier, it is not quite clear whether one could actually LOSE their *ʕirḍ*. It seems that it might have been in a deplorable state, yet it was always somehow present. Thus, LEAP *ʕirḍ* resembles rather the conceptualization of 20th c. Sinai Bedouin HONOR-FACE, which also could not be LOST, but definitely could be defected and diminished (Stewart 1994: 99). As one can see, this conceptualization contradicts the European notion of HONOR-FACE, which was by all means losable. The similarity between Sinai Bedouin FACE and *ʕirḍ* might be explained by the fact that in LEAP *ʕirḍ* seems to encompass both HONOR schemata functioning in those Bedouin communities (v.s.). As I said, *ʕirḍ* must be seen as a RIGHT TO RESPECT yet firmly bound to one's VALUE-ESTEEM/SELF-ESTEEM. Consequently, this duality should have found expression also in the conceptualization of HONOR LOSS. In other words, HONOR-RIGHT could be exhausted, wasted, squandered, etc., as in (183), but HONOR-VALUE was always in place – no matter how HIGH or LOW it was. Consequently, the FRAGILE/VULNERABLE *ʕirḍ*-BODY (SIDE) could not be LOST – but could be DAMAGED, and also WASTED, SQUANDERED, etc.

The metaphor *ʕirḍ*-HONOR-RIGHT TO RESPECT IS BODY (SIDE) can also by supported by the fact that in CEAP at least in two places – one being the example (189) by al-Aʕšà – the lexeme *ʕirḍ* was used clearly in the meaning "body". Although, the commentary to this passage suggests reading *ʕirḍ* rather as "oneself" or "soul", I believe, "body" is much more accurate, since the poet implies physical rather than any other repercussions, which the addressee would face. Nevertheless, this reading is a very good example that it is virtually impossible – in many instances – to delimit the concept of one's BODY and ONESELF/SOUL.

(189) أَبَا ثَابِتٍ لا تَعْلَقَنْكَ رِمَاحُنَا، أبَا ثَابِتٍ أَقْصِرْ **وَعِرْضُكَ** سَالِمُ

Abū Ṯābit, [I promise] our spears won't reach you – oh Abū Ṯābit – [but only if] you gave up. Thus, **your body** (*ʕirḍu-ka*) will be intact (t28A:79–80).

Moreover, the embodiment of *ʕirḍ* could be also supported by the fact that everyone had their own *ʕirḍ* – a concept of a general HONOR did not exist. As one can see in the example (190) by al-Ḥuṭayʔa, *ʕirḍ*-HONOR can be depicted as an individual possession, what is implied by the use of the plural form *ʔaʕrāḍ*. Thus, *ʕirḍ* might be also seen as a GOOD NAME – a personal honor of someone. What is quite important, even when implying the HONOR of the whole group – e.g., of a tribe – still the plural form could be preferred (cf. t19A:79). It is noteworthy that the use of the plural form corresponds to the similar situation of the lexeme *ḥasab*. In other words, it could imply that in the same fashion as everyone had their own VALUE, everyone had their own HONOR derived from it.

(190) لَسْتُ بِمَحْنُوٍّ (بِمَحْبُوٍّ) وَلَا جَدِّ مُكْرَمٍ ثَوَائِي إذا لَمْ أَهْجُ آلَ مُخَرَّمِ
أَأَجْعَلُ **عِرْضِي** دُونَ أَعْرَاضِكُمْ لَكُمْ وأَكْلُمُ **عِرْضاً** كان غيرَ مكلَّمِ

I won't gain any benefit (or: No one will pity me), nor will I [earn] a respectful standing, if I won't satirize the clan of Muẖarram.
Am I placing my **good name** (*ʕirḍ*) near your **good names** (*ʔaʕrāḍ*), [lowering myself] for you? [If so], I am wounding **honor** (*ʕirḍ*), which hasn't been yet wounded (cf. t39A:88–89).

The fragment (190) is important also because it clearly depicts the employment of the notion BEING OBJECT OF PHYSICAL ATTACK, the only salient element of the schema BODY used in the structuring of the concept of *ʕirḍ*. More precisely, the most salient mapping of the metaphor *ʕirḍ*-HONOR IS BODY (SIDE) was that of OFFENDING ONE'S *ʕirḍ* IS PHYSICALLY ATTACKING ONE'S BODY (SIDE).

As we saw in the example (190), the most frequent of the elaboration of the PHYSICALLY ATTACKING ONE'S BODY schema is WOUNDING (cf. t21A:117–123; t36A:245; t39A:88– 89). In other words, most usually SHAMING, i.e., INSULTING one's *ʕirḍ*-HONOR, was perceived as WOUNDING one's *ʕirḍ*-BODY (SIDE). Sometimes, the WOUNDING is yet further elaborated, as for instance, in (191) by Qays Ibn al-Ḫaṭīm. In this verse, apart from the more general WOUNDING scenario indicated by the verb *kalama*, a more specific one is invoked by the use of the verb *ẖadaba* "to bite (about a serpent), or to cut (the flesh, without cutting the bone), or to smite (with a sword)". This reading is also to be found in other variants of the verse recorded in the tradition, in which the verb *ẖadaša* "to scratch with fingernails" occurs (cf. t25B:65). Perhaps, such an elaboration pertains to the aforementioned primary conceptualization of *ʕirḍ* as an EXPOSED (FLAT) WIDE SURFACE of one's BODY. In other words, the poet might imply the fact that *ʕirḍ* is a SURFACE, which might be BITE/ CUT/ SMITE/ SCRATCH in the same way one wounds the SKIN.

(191) ولستُ ناسيَهمْ إنْ جاهلٌ خَطِلٌ خَنا، وما خَدَبُوا **عِرْضي** وما كَلَمُوا

And I don't forget them, when a coarse boor speak vulgarity [about them]. They didn't bite (or cut, or smite) my **sense of honor** (*ʕirḍ*), nor did they wound [it] (cf. t25C:74/38).

Similar profile of BODY is implied also by a number of expressions provided in TBD as pertaining to the SHAMING script (cf. iSk: 179; aHm: 32). Some of them elaborate the WOUNDING in form of TEARING something. These expressions, such as *mazaqa ʕirḍa-hu* or *hataka ʕirḍa-hu*, both meaning "to tear someone else's *ʕirḍ*", and especially, *mazzaqa ʔadīma-hu* "he torn his skin" clearly indicates the profiling of BODY as SKIN, i.e., an EXPOSED (FLAT) WIDE SIDE of the BODY. As we learned, Farès (1938: 96) saw this kind of idioms more as an indication that *ʕirḍ* is a vail, which covers someone. However, I do not think he is entirely correct in this statement. As we will see further in this chapter, *ʕirḍ* is frequently described as something, which was to be COVERED, VEILED, or simply PROTECTED. Therefore, I find it more suitable to read these expressions more as indicating embodiment of *ʕirḍ* rather than its conceptualization in terms of CLOTH.

Alternatively, WOUNDING, as the source of conceptualization of INSULTING, was in LEAP also profiled as CUTTING something, which also indicates SKIN-like profile of the BODY schema, perhaps again, the BODY SIDE. The most important of the expressions manifesting this metaphor was the verb *sabba-yasubbu*, which literary meant "to cut" and with time started pertaining simply to the notion of OFFENDING someone (cf. t10A:191; the sample (245) below). In CEAP, *ʕirḍ* occurs as the patient of this verb only once in CEAP, in (192) attributed to al-Ḥuṭayʔa, where it appears in a nominal form *masabb*, referring to the action of CUTTING. Perhaps, it presents the original form of this metaphor, i.e., the conceptualization of INSULTING in terms of CUTTING one's *ʕirḍ*. With time however, *sabba-yasubbu*-INSULTING lost its complement in form of *ʕirḍ* – possibly because of an ellipsis. I believe the same might be said about other examples of such elaboration of the script WOUNDING presented in TBD (cf. aHm: 32; iSk: 180), which together with the TEARING-related idioms are all included in the table below (Tab. 25.).

(192) مَسَبُّ ابْنِ لُقْمانَ **عِرْضَ** امْرِىءٍ شَدِيدِ الأَنَاةِ بَعِيدِ الغَضَبْ

[I heard about] an offence (*masabb*) [done by] Ibn Luqmān to **honor** (*ʕirḍ*) of a man of exceptional clemency, [of a man] far from easily angered (cf. t39A:297).

Tab. 25.

Meaning	Expression	Literary Meaning
INSULTING (someone)	*ṭaʕana fī-hī*	he pierced, perforated (in) him
	bakkata	he struck (with a staff or stick)
	ġamaza	he pressed
	sabba	he cut
	ʔafrà	
	qaṣaba	
	mazzaqa ʕirḍa-hu	he torn his honor
	harata ʕirḍa-hu	
	mazzaqa ʔadīma-hu	he torn his skin

Another example of the elaboration of WOUNDING script was that of DEVOURING or EATING the FLESH. In other words, SHAMING or INSULTING one's ʕirḍ was also conceptualized as DEVOURING or EATING it, as one can observe it in (193) by Ḥassān Ibn Ṯābit (cf. also t38A:115–116). Obviously, this elaboration brings out even better the embodiment of ʕirḍ-HONOR – it seems to indicate that ʕirḍ was perceived as FLESH upon which one could graze. This metaphor is also well present in the expressions presented in TBD as referring to INSULTING or SHAMING others (cf. aHm: 32). I rendered them in the table below (Tab. 26.).

(193) وأجْعَلُ مالي دونَ **عرضي** وقايةً، وأحْجُبُهُ كي لا يَطِيبَ لآكِلِ

I place my wealth near **my honor** (ʕirḍī) for [its] protection, and I cover it, [my honor], so as not to be tasty for the one who eats [it] (cf. t38B:188).

Tab. 26.

Meaning	Expression	Literary Meaning
INSULTING (someone)	*ḍarrasa*	he clenched canines / molars
	sabaʕa	he caught a pray; (about lion) broke/crashed its neck'
	ʔalǧama ʕirḍa-hu	he bridled his honor
	rataʕa fī ʕirḍi-h	he pastured on his honor
	lasaʕa bi-lisāni-hi	he stung him with his tongue
	ladaġa-hu bi-lisāni-hi	he bit him (like a snake) with his tongue
INSULT	*qāriṣa*	(she) biting one

The script PHYSICAL ATTACK ON ONE'S BODY was also elaborated in form of an actual ATTACK, such as THROWING something towards the ʕirḍ-BODY (SIDE) of someone – or perhaps even SHOOTING at it. It could be interpreted from the sample (194) by Ḥassān Ibn Ṯābit, who complains that he was under attack from the poets of another tribe. Those were shooting at him with their *luʔm*, i.e., baseness, ignobility. I believe one can read this verse as implying that the adversaries of Ibn Ṯābit were SHOOTING at him with *hiǧāʔ*, i.e., the poetic satire. The ʕirḍ-HONOR is here implicitly implied, being largely the major target of a satire. It seems then that the poetry – and in general, words – were conceptualized in pre-Islamic Arabic society as WEAPON, which might have been used to DAMAGE – ATTACK – someone, i.e., their ʕirḍ (cf. ʕAlī1: 264). Ergo – as the legendary poet of al-Ǧāhiliyya, Imrūʔ al-Qays, once said – "the wound inflicted by a tongue is like a wound inflicted by a hand" (Dziekan 1993: 58).

(194) فَجَعَلْتَني غَرَضَ اللّئامِ، فكُلُّهُمْ يرمي بلؤمهِ بَالِغاً كمُقَصِّرِ

Thus, you made me an aim for ignoble men. They all shoot [at me] with their baseness like mediocre [archers] (cf. t38A:116).

This conceptualization must derive from the phenomenon called by Dziekan (1993: 80) "words magical power", which was a very important element of the mentality of pre-Islamic Arabs. In general, they were awed by words and wording, and consequently perceived them as more magical than human only powers. This awe also included a known behavior, while facing an insult. Namely, once someone offended another man, that man usually was ducking down, thereby avoiding "the hit" of the insulting word (Dziekan 2008: 115). The "words magical power" could also be observed in the belief that every poet had their own jinni, which was making them able to compose the poetry (Dziekan 2012: 18). As one can see, the poetry was that much venerated that it was seen not a humanly but almost a divine creation.

The last elaboration of the script PHYSICAL ATTACK ON ONE'S BODY is probably the least obvious, however, it seems to connect pre-Islamic Arabic conceptualization of HONOR the closest to its European counterpart. It was STAINING or SOILING one's *ʕirḍ*-BODY. In other words, INSULTING someone was perceived as making them or their *ʕirḍ* DIRTY or STAINED. One can observe this conceptualization directly in (195), a passage by as-Samawʔal.

(195) إذا المَرءُ لَم يُدْنَسْ مِنَ اللُّؤمِ عِرضُهُ فَكُلُّ رِداءٍ يَرتَديهِ جَميلُ

If **honor** (*ʕirḍ*) of a man is not grimed by wickedness, any cloth he is wearing is beautiful (cf. t05A:90).

As I said this conceptualization seems similar to some HONOR-related metaphors persisting in European cultures, such as Polish *zbrukać czyjś honor* "to grime one's honor" or English *throw mud at someone*. Both perhaps pertain to the schema of FACE, being more an indication of VALUE OR REPUTE of a person, who based on it, claims RESPECT. In LEAP, this conceptualization was much more elaborated. Thus, an OFFENCE was perceived as FILTH or something DIRTYING, and *ʕirḍ* itself – or a person themselves – could be described as DIRTY OR CLEAN, depending on the state of their HONOR. Therefore, people who do not protect their *ʕirḍ*s are simply GRIMED – as it is said in (196) – and the deeds of such men are seen as DIRTY too (cf. t24A:79).

(196) قومٌ مَدانِيسُ لا يمشي بعَقْوَتِهِمْ جارٌ، وليسَ لهمْ في مؤطِنٍ بَطَلُ

[You are] grimed people, whose yard is not visited by any neighbor or client; and who does not have any fighter in their land (cf. t38B:201).

All in all, the conceptualization of INSULTING one's *ʕirḍ*-HONOR in terms of STAINING/ SOILING it could be also found among the expressions presented in TBD (cf. aHm: 115). I rendered them in the table below (Tab. 27.).

Tab. 27.

Meaning	Expression	Literary Meaning
INSULTING (someone)	*ʕarra*	he dunged, manured
MARK OF SHAME	*ʕurra*	dung
	maqḏar	dirt, fith
WASHING DISGRACE AWAY	*raḥaḍa*	he washed (away)
	ġasala	

7.5.1. One's HONOR and one's SELF

As we could see in the example (190), sometimes delimitation between BODY and SELF could be difficult, if not impossible. In that passage, the poet clearly threatens with physical violence, thereby indicating that the harm will affect the opponent's BODY. However, naturally, it in a broader sense the harm is done to this man himself. It is naturally a widespread phenomenon and such a lack of clear boundary between SELF and BODY can be noticed in many languages. Let us consider two English phrases: (x) *I wounded him* and (z) *I wounded his body*. Of course, one can see (x) as expressing much wider sense than (z), but literarily, it actually conveys the same message, since the major activity is defined strictly as WOUNDING, which – in the literary sense – can be done only to one's BODY. The wider sense of (x) seems to derive from a metaphoric extension of the script WOUNDING, which can serve as a source of conceptualization of, for instance, events of HARMING one's FEELINGS or OFFENDING someone. Nevertheless, primary – i.e., in the literary sense – (x) and (z) express the same meaning. Thus, it seems (x) expresses a certain metonymy, in which the WHOLE is represented by its salient, active-zone PART, i.e., BODY. Being active-zone means that BODY is the PART of the WHOLE, which in a particular context is activated. In (x) and (z), the context – the event of WOUNDING – clearly implies the involvement of BODY as the major patient of the action (cf. Radden & Kövecses 1999: 31). Consequently, due to bidirectionality of metonymic mappings, SELF can be access by the reference to its PART in form of BODY, and BODY can be referred to by the notion of the WHOLE it belongs to, i.e., the SELF. Thus, it is no surprise that metonymies BODY FOR SELF and SELF FOR BODY are observed in use in many languages (cf. Wolk 2008: 272).

In LEAP, the most obvious model of SELF is that with *nafs*-SOUL as its vehicle. It seems to be rather grammaticalized and well entrenched in the linguistic system of Arabic (cf. Wright 1898b: 272; LsA6: 281), although further research in the extent of this entrenchment in LEAP is definitely needed.[8] As we could see, CAD postulate that the lexeme *ʕirḍ* could also refer to the concept expressed by the word *nafs*, primarily interpreted as *nafs*-SOUL. Although, one could read this as the suggestion that *ʕirḍ* linked somehow to one's spirituality and meant perhaps simply one's SOUL (cf. Sławek 2011: 87), personally, I think this particular notion of *nafs* mentioned in CAD should be rather seen as a conflated concept of SOUL-SELF. Consequently then, *ʕirḍ* as an HONOR-denoting term could also refer to one's SELF, or perhaps more precisely to one's global SELF (cf. Wilson & Lewandowska-Tomaszczyk 2021: 457). In CEAP, however, *ʕirḍ* seems to serve such a reference only in three passages, from which two are traditionally attributed to Labīd Ibn Rabīʕa (t30B:46–48; t30B:160–161).

In the first of them – (197) – the poet uses *ʕirḍ* as the patient of the verb *ʔakrama*. I treated it as an instance of the reference to one's SELF based on the definition provided by Lane (1968h: 2999). For him, the phrase *ʔakrama ʕirḍa-hu* (*ʕan-hu*) meant "to preserve oneself (from something)."[9] The verse (197) might be then interpreted as stating that Labīd kept himself from being defamed, thanks to his high social standing, referred to by the lexeme *naǧwa* "an elevated place" (i.e., *šaraf*, cf. section 6.3.). Nevertheless, I believe, reading the lexeme *ʕirḍ* as the HONOR of the poet could be fully justified. And this ambiguity might be of great importance.

(197) أكرَمتُ **عِرْضي** أن يُنالَ بنَجْوَةٍ. إنَّ البريءِ مِنَ الهناتِ سعيدُ

By means of the elevated [social] position, [at which I arrived], I kept **myself/ my honor** (*ʕirḍī*) from being reached [by an insult], [since] truly, [only] a man free form any abuse is happy (cf. t30A:66).

The meaning proposed by Lane might seem strange, especially considering what I have said about the verb *ʔakrama* in Chapter 4. (cf. section 4.6.). As we learned *ʔakrama* referred in fact to the cultural script of *karāma*, i.e. PAYING RESPECT to

---

8 A further investigation over the delimitation between *nafs*-SOUL and *nafs*-SELF in LEAP could be definitely of many benefits (not only for the proper understanding of the concept of HONOR). It is certainly worth examining whether it actually existed and what its extent was. The results of such an examination could bring in valuable implications for our understanding of pre-Islamic Arabic conception of SELF and their theory of spirituality.

9 Alternatively, one can read the verb *ʔakrama* literarily as derived from the form I verb *karuma* "to be *karīm*" based on the pattern *ʔafʕala*. Verbs following this pattern are form IV verbs and they usually are causative of form I verbs (Ryding 2005: 515). It would mean that by *ʔakramtu ʕirḍī*, Labīd meant "I made my *ʕirḍ*/myself *karīm*", what could be also an appropriate reading.

karīm people. Thus, the phrase used by Labīd – *ʔakramtu ʕirḍī* – should be rather interpreted as "I paid honor to/I respected/I treated with curtesy my *ʕirḍ*-HONOR/SELF". Perhaps, one can read this in the same way we interpret such an English utterance as *he doesn't respect himself*, which implies an INDECENT behavior. It would mean that the script of RESPECTING ONESELF is used in English in reference to a proper conduct (in LEAP, we would say *karam*), and for Kövecses (2007: 56) it is clearly a metaphor derived from a more general conception in form of AN EVALUATIVE SUBJECT–SELF RELATIONSHIP IS AN EVALUATIVE SOCIAL RELATIONSHIP. It encodes the understanding of our self- evaluation in terms of the external, social evaluation. In other words, we perceive ourselves – our VALUE OR WORTH – in parallel to what we imagine or expect that other would evaluate them. Thus, *ʕirḍ* in the quote (197) definitely follows this schema in a more elaborate form of conceptualization, in which perhaps, both HONOR-RIGHT TO RESPECT and SELF conflated.

The poet seems then to be saying that by holding *šaraf*-HIGH SOCIAL STATUS, i.e., proving being worth it, he was respecting himself – his SELF – which is no more no less than his HONOR. Thus, he is simply stating that he adhered to the script of *karam*, expected from *šarīf*, and by that he made it impossible that someone would insult or reproach him. In other words, he treated his SELF/HONOR as a *karīm* property, which deserved RESPECT, and thus, he was constantly reassuring his HIGH SOCIAL STANDING, making his *ʕirḍ* immune from any OFFENCES.

The reading of *ʕirḍ* in (197) as referring to SELF (though – as it is in a conceptual metonymy – still calling-up the schema *ʕirḍ*) could be supported by the fact that in CEAP the verb *ʔakrama* is to be found also with the patient expressed by the lexeme *nafs*, i.e., "soul/(one)self". In fact, *ʔakrama nafsa-hu* occurs in the corpus 5 times, whereas the complement in form of *ʕirḍ* was used only once – in (197).

The second instance of the metonymy ONE'S *ʕirḍ*-HONOR FOR ONESELF is the verse (198), also by Labīd Ibn Rabīʕa.

(198) وَلَقَدْ عَلِمْتِ لو أنَّ عِلْمَكِ نافِعٌ وسمِعْتِ مَا يتحدَّثُ الأقْوامُ
أنّي أُكاثِرُ في النَّدَى إخْوانَهُ وأعِفُّ **عِرْضِي** إنْ ألَمَّ لِمامُ
Thus, you had known, if only you would have been finding any benefit in knowing [that], and if you had been listening to what people say,
[you had known] that in generosity, I could contend for superiority with his brothers, [and that] I keep **myself** (*ʕirḍī*) behaving properly, whenever I pay a courteous visit (cf. t30B:160–161).

Here, the poet makes *ʕirḍ* a patient of another verb *ʔaʕaffa*, which similarly to *ʔakrama* is derived from a form I verb based the patter *ʔafʕala*. Verbs following this pattern – form IV verbs – usually are causatives of the form I verbs (Ryding 2005: 515). In case of *ʔaʕaffa*, such a form I verb is *ʕaffa* "to abstain from unlawful behavior; to behave properly", what would mean that by *ʔuʕiffu ʕirḍī*, Labīd intended "I make my *ʕirḍ* abstain from unlawful behavior" or "I make my *ʕirḍ* behaving properly". This, I believe, unquestionably suggests that the lexeme *ʕirḍ* refers rather to the concept of (ONE)SELF.

Nevertheless, because of (198), one can ask why I postulate the metonymy, in which the vehicle is one's *ʕirḍ*-HONOR and not their *ʕirḍ*-BODY. Perhaps, though, Labīd referred to himself by hinting at the fact that his BODY – as the active-zone PART – behaves properly, while he is paying a visit. Moreover, as I mentioned, the concept of BODY FOR SELF seems quite widespread phenomenon and perhaps it would be more reasonable to postulate the metonymy in this form. As we know the most important element of a conceptual metonymy is the encoded information, which is brough forward, while using this conceptual devise.

In the case of the use of *ʕirḍ* in reference to one's SELF, I believe, a very important such information was encoded. Namely, this cultural metonymy could serve as the conceptualization that one's SOCIAL SELF is as important as one's (INNER) SELF. In other words, it coded the fact that one saw themselves in the eyes of others. It seems compatible with the fact that in the schema *ʕirḍ* the VALUE-REPUTE, upon which RIGHT TO RESPECT is founded, definitely has two aspects conflated – the external ESTEEM and the internal SELF-ESTEEM. Consequently, it could mean that ONE'S *ʕirḍ*-HONOR FOR ONESELF encoded that there is no other VALUE than the VALUE ascribed by the society, i.e. the external ESTEEM. By using the lexeme *ʕirḍ*, which evoke the whole schema RIGHT TO RESPECT, the poet might have simply hinted at the substitution of one's SELF by one's HONOR – or to put it in other way – at the fact that one's HONOR and one's SELF might seem the same or indistinguishable, as we could observe it in (197). Ergo, we can think of it that by ATTACKING a man's HONOR – by OFFENDING it – a pre-Islamic Arab in fact ATTACKED that man himself – a WOUND to his HONOR was then a very real WOUND inflicted on his BODY and thus, his SELF. This reading could also allow us to reconcile between BODY and SELF element brought forward in this metonymy. Thus, this conceptualization would strengthen argument for the claim of the embodiment of the schema RIGHT TO RESPECT, which I believe is the most important structuring principle of it as a whole.

It is perhaps for this reason that, in many expressions I presented in the previous subsection, the script WOUNDING, which served as a source for conceptualizing INSULT, did not involve *ʕirḍ* at all. Thus, although an INSULT was a WOUND inflicted on one's HONOR, it was also a WOUND inflicted on someone and consequently, on one's SELF. Therefore, in those expressions, *ʕirḍ* did not have to be mentioned at all – simply stated my *ʕirḍ* is myself – by ATTACKING it, you ATTACK me. It seems to me that the same principle, which we could observe in the aforementioned English examples (x) and (z), is at play in a culture-specific way also in this conceptualization. Therefore, we could deal here in fact with a bidirectional metonymy, in which ONE'S *ʕirḍ*-HONOR stood for their SELF, and their SELF for their HONOR.

Thus, in (197) and (198), Labīd Ibn Rabīʕa could have hinted at this very fact. In (197), he says he hold his HIGH SOCIAL POSITION to pay respect to his SELF/HONOR, that is, to keep it from being insulted. His SELF and HONOR were though the same in the context of HONORABLE BEHAVIOR and HONOR as a general schema. In other words, his SELF in the schema of HONOR was evaluated in the same manner as his RIGHT TO RESPECT – these two concepts from the point of view of the community of EQUALS were undistinguishable.

In (198), Labīd says I am keeping myself abstaining from unlawful behavior or I behave in a proper way, while paying a visit. The use of *ʕirḍ* brings forward the fact that during such a visit – when he is being evaluated by EQUALS, when his *karam* is evaluated – his SELF, his behavior, conflates with his HONOR-RIGHT TO RESPECT. Again, from the perspective of evaluation there is no difference between someone themselves and their HONOR. Ergo, the action of my SELF – of mine – are only meaningful in the context of their effect on my RIGHT TO RESPECT.

In the light of this, I think, one can read (199) by Zuhayr Ibn Abī Sulmà – the last passage, in which I believe one could observe the aforementioned metonymy ONE'S *ʕirḍ*-HONOR FOR ONESELF. In this verse, the poet calls a man who kidnapped his herdsman not to act foolishly with (*bi-*) his *ʕirḍ*, what I believe should be read as acting foolishly in one's name, i.e., by ONESELF. In other words, Zuhayr seems to say: your behavior was foolish, since you put your *ʕirḍ*-HONOR at stake, and thus now it can be harmed – you acted in your name, i.e., on your account, openly, making others to evaluate your action accordingly. This fragment brings also out the aforementioned conception that one's behavior was always evaluated in terms of HONORABILITY, i.e., the effect it has on one's *ʕirḍ*-RIGHT TO RESPECT.

(199) أُرْدُدْ يَساراً ولا تَعنُفْ عَلَيهِ وَلا تَمْعَكْ **بِعِرْضِك**، إنّ الغادِرَ المَعِكُ

[Ḥāriṯ], return Yasār, and do not make him harm! Do not do stupid things whit your **honor** (*ʕirḍ*) [at stake]. Truly, [your] treachery would be stupid (cf. t22A:43–46)!

Nevertheless, it is important to note that not always *ʕirḍ* and one's (global) SELF conflated in LEAP. As one can see in (200) by Ḥātim aṭ-Ṭāyʔī, keeping one's *ʕirḍ*-HONOR unchallenged or uncompromised was a way to protect ONESELF. Yet, naturally, one can still perceive even this conceptualization as compatible with the metonymic mapping we discussed in this section.

(200) وأَجْعَلُ مالي دون **عِرْضي**، جُنّةً لنَفْسِي، فأَسْتَغْنِي بما كان من فَضْلِي
And I place my wealth near **my honor** (*ʕirḍī*), making a protective wall for my-self.
And [for that], my excessive possession suffices me [by far] (cf. t19B:75).

7.6. COVERING the *ʕirḍ*: RIGHT TO RESPECT must be PROTECTED

The metonymy ONE'S *ʕirḍ*-HONOR FOR ONESELF is compatible with the metaphor of *ʕirḍ*-HONOR with BODY as its source. It seems even to accentuate its central role in structuring the whole schema of RIGHT TO RESPECT in LEAP. Its next entailment might be presented as SECURING ONE'S *ʕirḍ*- HONOR IS COVERING ONE'S BODY (SIDE), which seems encoding the conceptualization that *ʕirḍ*-RIGHT TO RESPECT as something VULNERABLE/FRAGILE must be protected by different means parallel to those one undertakes in order to protect their VULNERABLE/FRAGILE BODY (SIDE). This seems to find its parallel in the observation by Abu-Lughod (1986: 114–5), who noticed that in the Bedouin community she studied EXPOSURE was the major vehicle of conceptualization of the VULNERABILITY. It could be observed, for instance, in the concept of EVIL EYE, a widespread phenomenon, which implies constant EXPOSURE of a human being, i.e., its VULNERABILITY. In other words, COVERING *ʕirḍ* meant that it was in need to be protected against EXPOSURE, what indicated its FRAGILITY.

The script COVERING is the main source of the conceptualization of such a PROTECTION (cf. t10A:16; t39A:75–76; t19B:75; t38B:186–188; t30B:67; t37A:90; t38A:311–313; t20A:33–35). One can see it used in (201) by Ḥassān Ibn Ṯābit, in which while describing HIGH SOCIAL STATUS of his people, the poet depicts their action of COVERING their *ʕirḍ* against *ḏamm*, i.e., OFFENCE or INSULT. The hint about the COVERING-CLADDING schema might be also found in a way in the verse (188).

(201) وتلقى لدى أبْياتِنا، حينَ نُجتدى ، مجالِسَ فِيها كُلُّ كهلٍ مُعمَّمِ
رَفِيعِ عِمادِ البيتِ، يسترُ **عِرضَه** مِن الذَمّ، ميمونِ النَقِيبةِ خِضْرِمِ
And whenever you ask us for a favor, you will find in our abodes seats taken by middle-aged men, attired with turbans,
who are elevated in their nobility, who cover their **honor** (*ʕirḍ*) against the insult, who are blessed by prosperity, who [will be thus] generous [to you] (cf. t38A:293).

The COVERING, i.e., PROTECTING or SECURING of one's RIGHT TO RESPECT seems to be done in a number of ways, including the violent response to an insult I mentioned while describing the reflexiveness of LEAP ʕ*irḍ*.

An important mean of this PROTECTION was also the poetry, what is clearly implied in (202) by al-Aʕšà. As we learned earlier in this chapter, pre-Islamic Arabs were awed by words to the extent of ascribing them magical properties, what consequently, resulted in conceptualization of WORDS (and by extension, POETRY) in terms of WEAPONS. This metaphor can be easily observed in both examples (187), quoted earlier, and (202).

(202) وَأَدْفَعُ عَنْ **أَعْرَاضِكُمْ** وَأُعِيرُكُمْ لساناً كمِقْراضِ الخَفاجيِّ مِلْحَبا

I will repel [any insult] from **your good names** (*ʔaʕrāḍi-kum*), by lending you [my] tongue, which cuts [as well as] shears [in the hand of a man from] Ḫafāǧa (cf. t28A:116–7).

Based on the aforementioned example (202), we can infer that someone could also protect ʕ*irḍ* other than their own. Frequently, in such a case, an individual was responsible for PROTECTING his or her (kin-)group HONOR – as it is depicted, e.g., in the sample (203).

(203) وإني اليومَ أحمي **عِرْضَ** قومي وأَنْصُرُ آلَ عَبْسَ على العُدَاةِ

Truly, I am defending today the **honor** (ʕ*irḍ*) of my people, supporting the clan [Banū] ʕAbs against their enemies (cf. t21A:24).

This must connect with a more universal rule of HONOR PROTECTION, which requires one's family (and thus, by extension, one's community, nation, etc.) to undertake a proper action once the HONOR of one of their kins was compromised – especially, when that someone does not or cannot react by themselves (Stewart 1994: 71). It is a consequence of a conceptualization – persisting also in pre-Islamic and modern Arabic communities – of the fact that an individual's HONOR by far conflate with the HONOR of their social group. Thus, the individual must constantly protect the HONOR of this group as much as they are responsible for their own RIGHT TO RESPECT (Peristiany 1965: 11). The pre-Islamic Arabic society seems no different. The offence to one's ʕ*irḍ* was a call for assistance of the entire kin-group they belonged to – and the assistance was in place until a proper avenge was achieved (ʕAlī 1993b: 574). In such a case, an INSULTED man was calling up others by means of the tribal solidarity spirit – the ʕ*aṣabiyya* (ʕAlī 1993b: 393) – the phenomenon known also in other cultures, such as among Basques (cf. Baroja 1965: 91).

By extension, it seems that in al-Ǧāhiliyya, one could not only PROTECT the HONOR of their kins or their tribesmen, but also of anyone else associated with them – as it was the case in the example (202) by al-Aʕšà (cf. also t37A:90). It definitely derives from the metaphoric extension I discussed in Chapter 4., which mediate between one's linkages based on blood and those initiated by attachment in form of client-patron relationship (cf. subsection 4.4.3.). Usually, such a PROTECTION is performed by means of one's own *ʕirḍ*-HONOR, what should be read as implying the fact that one's REPUTE derives by far from one's LOYALTY, being a component of the script of *karam* (cf. subsection 4.3.4.). In other words, a man was protecting another with his own *ʕirḍ*, because any failure of protection of that another man's HONOR, would cast a shadow on the HONORABILITY of the PROTECTOR. It might be seen as compatible with a more widespread phenomenon of swearing, taking an oath on one's honor (i.e., giving a word of honor). Such a conceptualization might be seen, for instance, in the sample (204) (cf. also t38A:9–12; t26A:124).

(204) لأنّي إذا **عِرضي** لكَ اليومَ دونهَمْ وحَتفُكَ فيما يَنْتِجُونَ به حَتْفِي

Since **my honor** (*ʕirḍī*) is today yours [to protect you] against them, your demise, which they [will attempt to] cause, will be my demise (cf. t40A:91).

As I mentioned, there were couple of ways to PROTECT and SECURE one's *ʕirḍ*-HONOR. Nevertheless, two of them bare the most significance: one's AMPLE *ḥasab* and one's *māl*-POSSESSION/WEALTH.

7.6.1. HONORABILITY is the VAIL for the *ʕirḍ*

The notion of AMPLE *ḥasab*-COUNT OF HONORABLE DEEDS connects with the logical implication of HONORABILITY, i.e., the fact that it was granting one's RIGHT TO RESPECT. In other words, one could protect their *ʕirḍ*-HONOR first and foremost by means of their *karam*-NOBLE/HONORABLE CONDUCT. It can be observed, for instance, in the passage (186) of a satire attributed to Ḥassān Ibn Ṯābit, in which the poet states that the lack of HONORABILITY among Banū Ḥimās make their *ʕirḍ*s far from his own. One can read it as the indication that the RIGHT TO RESPECT Ibn Ṯābit enjoyed was in better shape, i.e., it was much better grounded or supported, than the RIGHT of those people. And the only mean of securing the RIGHT mentioned in this passage is *karam*-HONORABILITY.

In other words, in the CEAP, *karam* is not only what grants one the RIGHT TO RESPECT, but also what assures and secures it. Consequently, HONORABLE CONDUCT protected one against DISHONOR and DISGRACE (cf. t34A:136–138). Similar notion was also observed by Abou-Zeid (1965: 245), who noticed that in the community of Eastern Egyptian Bedouins, in mid-20th c., SHAME always befell upon someone, who failed "to observe the rules of good manners", that is – in our case – when they do not behave like *karīm*. This notion is present in (205) by Abū Ṭālib, in which the poet seems to imply that actions of someone can be shameful in the light of *karam*, ergo – *karam* set some standards of what is and what is not disgraceful.

(205) إلى الرَحْمٰنِ **والكَرَمِ** استَذَمُّوا وكلُّ فَعالِهم دَنِسٌ ذَميمُ

They committed shameful [atrocities] against Raḥmān and **honorability** (*karam*) – all of their deeds are soiled and shameful (cf. t24A:79).

As we could see, in this verse, Abū Ṭālib depicts the shameful actions as dirty or soiled (*danis*), bringing about the conceptual metaphor INSULTING ʕirḍ-HONOR IS STAINING/SOILING IT, I discussed earlier in this chapter. This metaphor is at play also in (206), a fragment of a poem attributed to al-Aʕšà, depicting a very important moment in life of the legendary poet Samawʔal, in which he proved to be among the most loyal people known to pre-Islamic Arabs (cf. ʕAlī 1993b: 404). What is interesting, *karam* of Samawʔal's son seems to be what kept his ʕirḍ-HONOR CLEAN, i.e. UNCOMPROMISED. Similarly, "purifying" properties of HONORABILITY are portrayed by Kaʕb Ibn Zuhayr in (207).

(206) فشكَّ غيرَ قليلٍ، ثمّ قالَ لهُ: اذْبَحْ هَدِيَّكَ إنّي مانِعٌ جاري
إنّ لهُ خَلَفاً إنْ كنتَ قاتِلَهُ، وَإنْ قَتَلْتَ **كَريماً** غيرَ عُوّارِ
مالًا كثيراً **وعِرْضاً** غَيْرَ ذي دَنَسٍ، وإخوةً مثلَهُ لَيْسُوا بأشْرارِ
جَرَوْا عَلى أدَبٍ مِنّي، بِلا نَزَقٍ، ولا إذا شَمَّرَتْ حَرْبٌ بأغْمارِ

Thus, he hesitated a lot, and afterwards he said: slit [the throat] of your hostage, [my son], since I [choose] to protect [the belongings] of my ally- neighbor (*ǧārī*), [the poet Imruʔ al-Qays].
Truly, if you killed him, he has replacement [from among my sons in my abode]. By killing him, [you kill] an **honorable man** (*karīm*), not a weakling or a coward;
[you kill a man, who possesses] vast wealth, an unsoiled **honor** (ʕirḍ), and brothers, who are like him, not worse.
[They all] inherited after me good manners and no foolishness, no inexperience [in the matter of warfare], when a war calls [them] up to fight (cf. t28A:180–1).

(207) هم الأصل مني حيثُ كنتُ وإنني من المُزَنِيِّينَ المُصَفَّيْنَ **بالكَرَمْ**

They are my roots, wherever I go – truly, I am of parents, both from [the clan] Muzayna, who purified themselves in **honorability** (*karam*) (cf. t34A:138).

7.6.1.1. *Karīm* has WHITE CLEAN ʕirḍ – *karīm* IS WHITE/OF WHITE FACE

The conceptualization of *karam* as the mean of CLEANING, WASHING, or PURIFYING one's ʕirḍ, connects to the very important metaphor, which is to be observed in many places in CEAP, as well as noticed in CAD. As we saw, al-Ǧawharī expressed the meaning of "[someone] free from any insult or offense" by the phrase *naqī al-ʕirḍ* "[a man] of a clean ʕirḍ" (AsS: 758). It means that a man of SECURED – UNCHALLENGED OR UNQUESTIONED – ʕirḍ-RIGHT TO

RESPECT was perceived as someone's whose *ʕirḍ* was CLEAN, what seems to imply the CLEANNESS achieved by one's HONORABLE CONDUCT. This conception is further encoded by a metaphor, in which WHITENESS served as a source of conceptualization of the SECURED HONOR-RIGHT TO RESPECT.

More precisely, people, who by means of their HONORABLE BEHAVIOR, possessed UNDISPUTABLE RIGHT TO RESPECT, were frequently conceptualized in terms of WHITE FACE or WHITE SKIN. In the table below (Tab. 28.), I gathered all the linguistic expressions, which manifest this conceptualization, I found in CEAP, while performing my study.

Tab. 28. Examples of surface manifestations of the conceptualization *karīm* IS OF WHITE FACE/SKIN

Expression	Literary meaning	Location in CEAP
bīḍ al-wuǧūh	of white face	t38A:218–219; t38A:166; t24A:38–39
ṣalt al-ǧabīn	of bright, clear, white forehead	t36A:97
ʔabyaḍ *bayḍāʔ* *bīḍ*	white	t38A:130–131; t28A:179–181; t38B:216; t39A:88–90
ʔabyaḍ ka-l-hilāl	white like the crescent	t38A:238
la-hu bayāḍ bi-l-ḫudūd	he has whiteness in [his] cheeks	t34B:18
munīr al-waǧh	of shining face	t38A:238
wāḍiḥ as-sunna	of clear, bright face	t38B:28

At the very first glance, one could think of it as encoding the most important social division of pre-Islamic Arabic society, that divided people into free folk – *ʔaḥrār* (sg. *ḥurr*) – and slaves (ʕAlī 1993b: 541). The fact that BLACKNESS was associated with SLAVEHOOD might be seen in the poetry of the Black poet ʕAntara Ibn Šaddād, as for example in (208). Thus, consequently, WHITENESS could have been used in conceptualization of BEING FREE MAN, yet – as we can see it (208) – such a conceptualization indicated strongly also the association with HONORABILITY.

(208) وإنْ يعيبوا **سواداً** قد كُسِيتُ بهِ فالدُرُّ يسْتُرُهُ ثَوْبٌ مِن الصَّدَفِ
Thus, if they vilify [me because of the] **blackness**, in which I am covered, the pearl, a cloth of the mother-of-pearl, [i.e., the purest whiteness] will conceal it (cf. t21A:87).

In other words, if this conceptualization associates the WHITE color with the FREE MEN[10] and BLACK with SLAVEHOOD, it would simply code that only FREE people can be *karīm*, i.e., can belong to the honor group, which adhere to the code of HONORABLE BEHAVIOR. Consequently, it would imply that only free people could enjoy RIGHT TO RESPECT. It could be then seen as compatible with ʕAlī's claim that in fact the concept of WHITENESS was used in LEAP only as indication of CLEANNESS of one's *ʕirḍ*-HONOR. It explains then, why BLACKNESS OF FACE was used later in the Holy Qurʔān to indicate humiliation and shaming (Al-Jallad, N. 2010: 100).

Moreover, the aforementioned conceptualization encodes also the perception of SLAVEHOOD in terms of heredity. As we learned in Chapter 4., in al-Ǧāhiliyya, *karam*-HONORABLENESS was perceived as a hereditary property – *karīm* people were giving birth to *karīm* people. Thus, the BLACKNESS as a vehicle could actually encode the indication of the lack of innate predisposition to *karam*. In the light of this, one can interpret the verse (208) as a statement, that ʕAntara proved being worth RESPECT by his HONORABLE DEEDS, even though he was not predisposed to them by his ORIGIN. The HONORABILITY was then implied by WHITENESS, the CLEANNESS of his *ʕirḍ*. In other words, he seems to say: I was not born FREE, but nevertheless I managed to become a part of the honor group of *karīm* EQUALS.

Furthermore, the fact that CLEAN-UNQUESTIONED *ʕirḍ*-HONOR was perceived as WHITE links to a certain observation one can made while looking at the list provided in Tab. 28. As we see, it contains a number of instances of the reference to FACE, which as we learned, is a common source of metaphoric mappings targeting at HONOR. It seems then that pre-Islamic Arabic society profiled this conceptualization in an interesting, culture-specific way, by which the definition of the honor group as consisting of free folk seems to have been somehow forwarded.

7.6.1.2. One COVERS their *ʕirḍ* with a CLOTH of *ḥasab* – *ḥasab* makes up one's HONOR

Sometimes, however, in CEAP, the SECURING of one's RIGHT TO RESPECT, COVERING it for PROTECTION, is implied as possessing proper skills or predispositions to *karam*, which is well discernible in (209) attributed to Aws Ibn Ḥağar.

10 The perception of the skin color in pre-Islamic Arabic culture is a quite complicated issue. It was discussed in detail by ʕAlī (1993b: 308–12).

(209) فإنّا وجدنا **العِرضَ** أحوجَ ساعةً إلى الصَّوْنِ من رَيْطٍ يَمانٍ مُسَهَّم
أرَى حَرْبَ أقْوامٍ تَدِقُّ وحَرْبَنا تَجِلُّ فَنَعْرَوْرِي بِها كُلَّ مُعْظَمِ

[During the war], we were sometimes encountering **the honor** (*al-ʕirḍ*), which needed protection by means of a stripped Yemeni garment.
I see the war [skills] of [other] people flimsy – whereas our war [skills] are great. Thus, we stripped off the clothes from every great man [who fought against us] (cf. t26A:121).

The passage indicates that *ʕirḍ* could be COVERED-PROTECTED simply by BRAVERY, a subschema of the script of HONORABILITY. However, what is quite interesting in (209) is not the target of the expressed metaphor, but its source, i.e., a CLOTH, a GARMENT, or a VEIL. The same source seems to be also employed in the conceptualization of *ḥasab*-COUNT OF HONORABLE DEEDS.

TBD suggest that this schema could be also called up be the use of the lexeme *ʔizār* "a wrapper which covers the lower part of the body; anything with which one is veiled, concealed, or covered (cf. Lane 1968a: 53)" (mHs12: 200). It could be read then as a metaphoric model in which in understanding what *ḥasab* is, one uses the tangible concept of a CLOTH or a VEIL, that – what is quite significant – served specifically for covering the "lower part of the body", i.e., the most vulnerable parts of a man. This metaphor might be seen as lending the structure to the schema of the relationship between *ḥasab* and *ʕirḍ*-HONOR-RIGHT TO RESPECT.

Being one's VALUE/ WORTH derived from HONORABILITY, *ḥasab* must have been obviously conceptualized as something SECURING one's RIGHT TO RESPECT. Simply stated, the person, who possessed an ample, numerous COUNT OF HONORABLE DEEDS had this RIGHT guaranteed by far. We can see the example of such a thinking in (136), in which Ḥassān Ibn Ṯābit presented himself as being immune against SHAMING due to the fact that his *ʕirḍ*-HONOR was a "well-fattened" *ḥasab* (cf. also t38B:37).

(136) وقد أكرَمتُكمْ وسكنتُ عنكم، سَرَاةَ الأوْس، لوْ نَفَعَ السُّكونُ
حياءً أنْ أشاتمكمْ وَصَوْنًا لِعِرْضي، إنهُ **حسبٌ سمينُ**

Chiefs of [Banū] al-Aws, I would have paid you honor and left you in peace, if [such] a peace had been of any advantage [to me],
[if my] sense of shame [had restrained me] against [getting involved in] mutual vilification with you, [and if I had thought of nothing but] to protect my **honor** (*ʕirḍ*) – but [my honor] truly, is [based on] **plenty of merits** (*ḥasab samīn*) (cf. t38A:313).

Thus, the metaphor *ḥasab*-COUNT OF HONORABLE DEEDS IS A VEIL COVERING ONE'S *ʕirḍ* encoded the knowledge that HONOR-RIGHT TO RESPECT was something bodily and vulnerable, whereas *ḥasab* was the major mean of its PROTECTION.

Ḥasab must have been seen as the best way to COVER-PROTECT one's ʕ*irḍ*-HONOR, since as a COUNT of *makārim*-HONORABLE/NOBLE DEEDS it was a sheer manifestation of one's HONORABILITY. In other words, one's honorable actions secured their RIGHT TO RESPECT by their EQUALS.

The importance of *ḥasab* for ʕ*irḍ* could be observed also in the conceptualization of the *ḥasab* in terms of one's *ṣulb*-BACKBONE, which I discussed in Chapter 5. (cf. section 5.3.1.). As we learned, it implied that *ḥasab* was a BACKBONE of one's ʕ*irḍ*-HONOR-BODY. This indicates that *ḥasab*-COUNT-VALUE was not only a mere mean of PROTECTION of one's HONOR, but in fact, it was what was constituting the basis on which someone's ʕ*irḍ* was founded, i.e., their REPUTE-VALUE-ESTEEM/SELF-ESTEEM. In other words, the protective properties of *ḥasab* are rooted in the fact that it was what made up by far the VALUE of someone, upon which their RIGHT TO RESPECT was established. Thus, the metaphor of CLADDING one's ʕ*irḍ*-HONOR with *ḥasab*-ʔ*izār*-VEIL should be interpreted as encoding the knowledge that the more AMPLE one's *ḥasab*-COUNT OF *makārim* was, the SAFER, more SECURE, his or her RIGHT TO RESPECT was. We saw this conceptualization expressed by Ḥassān Ibn Ṯābit in the passage (136), quoted earlier. The poet clearly states that his ʕ*irḍ*-HONOR is not easy to be INSULTED, since – truly – it is constituted by an AMPLE *ḥasab*-COUNT OF HONORABILITY, by "plenty of merits".

Thus, ʕ*irḍ* could metonymically refer also to *ḥasab*, and – it seems so – *ḥasab* is sometimes used in reference to ʕ*irḍ*. This bidirectional metonymy might in fact be seen as an instance of a PART FOR WHOLE – WHOLE FOR PART schema (cf. Radden & Kövecses 1999: 31), since *ḥasab* was what ʕ*irḍ* actually consisted of. The metonymy is clearly seen in CAD and TBD (mHs12: 200). It could also be observed in at least two places in CEAP, but as I said, sometimes it was difficult to distinguish between these two meanings of the lexeme ʕ*irḍ*. For instance, an example, in which *ḥasab* is referred to as ʕ*irḍ*, is (210) by Kaʕb Ibn Zuhayr. I believe, *ḥasab*-DIGNITY, perhaps meaning here simply *karam*-INTEGRITY suits this passage very well, since clearly, the poet has in mind a decent or a nice way, in which a woman of ʕ*irḍ* cuts the relationship with a man. It could mean that one can observe in here another metonymy – ʕ*irḍ*-HONOR FOR INTEGRITY – which would encode the knowledge that a person, whose ʕ*irḍ*-RIGHT TO RESPECT is ample, was someone who always protects their HONOR, thus being someone of certain INTEGRITY.

(210) وذَاتُ **العِرْضِ** قَدْ تَأْتِي إذَا مَا أرادتْ صرمَ خُلَّتِها الجِمالا

A woman having **dignity** (ʕ*irḍ*) might come and cut a friendship, whenever she wants – [and she does it] in a decent way (cf. t34A:130).

Moreover, in one context in CEAP – (211) – the lexeme *ʕirḍ* seems to refer metonymically not only to *ḥasab*, but also to the sheer *makruma*, i.e., a HONORABLE, NOBLE DEED, subsumed by it. This context is the verse attributed to Aws Ibn Ḥağar, in which the plural form of *ʕirḍ* – *ʔaʕrāḍ* – is ascribed to one subject only, an unspecified member of the poet's clan. This man – although being still unexperienced – led life similar to that of *sayyid*, tribal chief/leader. This similarity is expressed in the statement that he managed to achieve abundance of his *ʕirḍ*s (*tabaḥbaḥa fī ʔaʕrāḍi-hi*; cf. Lane 1968a: 191). Based on what I have said about the expectations as for the candidate for a tribal leader, *sayyid*, I believe it is safe to say that by *ʕirḍ*s, the poet actually meant *makārim*, i.e., the HONORABLE/NOBLE DEEDS. Consequently, one can read this verse as saying that even the most unexperienced member of the poet's tribe was as HONORABLE as a stereotypical *sayyid*. In other words, *ʔaʕrāḍ* stands in this passage for *makārim*. Perhaps, one can interpret this usage as a further metonymic extension deriving from the aforementioned model *ʕirḍ* FOR *ḥasab*.

(211) تَرَى النَّاشِىءَ المجهولَ منّا كسيّدٍ تبحبحَ في **أعراضهِ** وتأثّلا

Among us, you will see [even] an unexperienced boy as a [good candidate for] a tribal leader, [since even] he achieved abundance and plenty of **his proudful deeds** (*ʔaʕrāḍi-hi*) (cf. t26A:91).

On the other hand, the alternative situation, in which *ʕirḍ* is referred to by the lexeme *ḥasab* is depicted in TBD (aHm: 45) in the expressions synonymous to *šarīf*. I rendered them in the table below (Tab. 29.). Perhaps, since TBD were composed much later than the EAP, one can see this conceptualization as a later development grounded in the schema of *ʕirḍ*. Nevertheless, our general knowledge of how metonymies function suggests that a WHOLE FOR PART schema might work – and frequently it does – in both directions (cf. Radden & Kövecses 1999: 31).

Tab. 29.

Meaning	Expression	Literary Meaning
non-*šarīf*	*fī ḥasabi-hi maġmaz*	there is a dent in his *ḥasab*
	fī ḥasabi-hi maṭʕan	there is a perforation in his *ḥasab*
	mawṣūm al-ḥasab	of cracked *ḥasab*
	fī ḥasabi-hi waṣm	there is a crack in his *ḥasab*

The importance of *ḥasab* – the *ṣulb*-BACKBONE of one's *ʕirḍ*-HONOR-BODY – translated into the conviction that it must have been protected in the same way one protects their ˁirḍ (cf. section 5.3.1.). It could even suggest that perhaps ˁirḍ and *ḥasab* were one and the same phenomenon, as it was also suggested by CAD. Nevertheless, I believe one should actually distinguish between *ˁirḍ*-RIGHT TO RESPECT based on a certain REPUTATION-VALUE and *ḥasab*-VALUE, which constituted by far this very REPUTATION. Such understanding of this delimitation might be supported by the reading of (145) by Ḥassān Ibn Ṯābit. Although, *ˁirḍ* is not mentioned in this verse, it is implied by the verb *ˀazrà bi-* meaning more or less "to hold something or someone in little estimation". Obviously, it links to the schema of *ˁirḍ*, which was the embodiment of one's REPUTE-ESTEEM.

(145) والفَقْرُ يُزْرِي بِأقْوامٍ ذَوِي حَسَبٍ

Thus, poverty lowers the value [even] of people of **many merits** (*ḥasab*) (cf. t38A:230–231).

Thus – as the poet says – even people having *ḥasab*, might be of DIMINISHED WORTH, and consequently *ˁirḍ*-RIGHT TO RESPECT, if they are being POOR. This, however, brings us to another major mean of PROTECTING one's HONOR – the *māl*-WEALTH-POSSESSION.

7.6.2. One KEEPS their WEALTH NEAR to or UNDER their *ˁirḍ*

As we learned in the previous chapters, one's WEALTH was an important component of their ability to be *karīm* and thus of their HONOR (cf. sections 4.3.1.2., 5.4., and 6.4.). In fact, it could also be perceived as an important estimate of one's VALUE. Thus, as we saw, CAD suggest even the existence of a metonymic mapping between *māl*-WEALTH and *ḥasab*. It seems then that to a certain extent, WEALTH was also perceived as what one's REPUTATION, granting them *ˁirḍ*-RIGHT TO RESPECT, could have rested upon. One can realize how far-reaching this concept is by recalling a usual squabble all of us had while arguing who should pay for drinks in a bar. The ability of paying a bill is deeply connected with the struggle for superiority among equals (Pitt-Rivers 1965: 59), and surprisingly, it is far more common than we think.

Of course, at least ideally, one's WEALTH was so highly priced because of its impact on GENEROSITY-HOSPITALITY, which – as we know – was in fact a template for the NOBILITY-HONORABILITY. Therefore, the conceptualization of *māl*-WEALTH-POSSESSIONS –acquired or inherited (cf. t30B: 67) – as a mean of PROTECTING one's *ˁirḍ* seems well justified.

The script of this PROTECTION derives from several image-schemata, by which WEALTH is conceptualized as an OBJECT or MASS which is PLACED in PROXIMITY to or UNDERNEATH one's *ˁirḍ*-HONOR. The PROXIMITY or UNDER schema is called up by the preposition *dūna*, which frequently cooccurs with *ʕirḍ* in CEAP. The expression *ǧaʕala māla-hu dūna ʕirḍi-hi* "he made his wealth be close/near or underneath his *ʕirḍ*" might be seen in several places in the corpus (cf. e.g., t19B:75; t22A:63–76; t38B:186–188; t19B:71). The image-schema evoked by *dūna* seems impossible to be reconstructed with precision, thus we should simply keep seeing the whole script as indicating SUPPORTING or PROPPING one's *ʕirḍ*, by PLACING one's WEALTH NEAR or BENEATH it. We can see it even as the action of MAKING FOUNDATIONS of one's *ʕirḍ* with the WEALTH one has.

This conceptualization of PROTECTING one's *ʕirḍ*-HONOR, PLACING WEALTH NEAR/BENEATH it might be found, e.g., (193) and (200) quoted above. They clearly indicate – especially (193) – that the script described by this image-schema encodes PRESERVATION of one's HONOR. As I said, one should read this PRESERVATION in terms of ability to be *karīm* in the stereotypical sense, i.e., GENEROUS-HOSPITABLE, what – as we learned – was a *conditio sine qua non* of HONORABILITY.

The GENEROSITY-HOSPITALITY schema is implied as a PROTECTIVE measurement, for instance, in the sample (6), in which the poet brags about his HONORABILITY accentuating that he was GENEROUS during the time of scarcity.

(6) (...) هل تَعلَمِينَني **كَريماً**، إذا اسوَدّ الأنامِلُ، أزْهَرا
صبوراً على رُزْءِ الموالي وحافِظاً لِعِرْضِي حتّى يُؤكَل النبتُ أخْضَرا
(...) Do you know that I am an **honorable man** (*karīm*)? Whenever [others'] fingertips blacken, [i.e., when a sordid winter comes], I blossom,
enduring (*ṣabūran*) the calamities, [which falls upon my] protégés, protecting my honor– [and that's] until the flora gets green [again] (cf. t20A:35).

More precisely, this conceptualization might well be observed in the passage (212), a fragment of the *muʕallaqa* by Zuhayr Ibn Abī Sulmà, in which the poet states quite explicitly that by placing GENEROSITY[11] close to one's *ʕirḍ*, one makes it *wāfir* "ample", i.e., unchallenged. In the translation by Arberry presented below, the script of PLACING something NEAR/ BENEATH one's *ʕirḍ* is expressed as "making shield" for it, what expresses the PROTECTION schema, which was meant by Zuhayr.

(211) وَمَن يَجعَلِ **المَعروفَ** مِن دونَ **عِرضِهِ** يَفْرِهِ وَمَن لا يَتَّقِ الشَتمَ يُشتَمِ
Whoever makes of **benevolence** a shield for his good name (*ʕirḍ*) enhances **his honour** (*ʕirḍi-hi*); whoever is not wary of abuse soon gets it (translated by Arberry 2017: 117; cf. t22A:63–76).

11 In (211), GENEROSITY-HOSPITALITY is referred to by the lexeme *maʕrūf*, meaning literarily "known" or "well-known", which can also be used in reference to *ǧūd* "generosity" (LsA9: 286).

In his translation, Arberry definitely derived the imagery from more elaborative schema of PROTECTING ʕirḍ by means of WEALTH, in which by doing so, one created a SHIELD for or a protective WALL around one's HONOR (cf. the sample (200)). The former was used by Ḥātim aṭ-Ṭayʔī in (213).

(212) ذَرِيني يكُنْ **مالي** لعِرْضِيَ جُنّةً يَقي المالُ **عِرْضِي**، قبل أن يَتَبَدّدا

Give me peace, [woman, do not complain about my generosity] – let **my wealth** (*mālī*) – before it got dispersed – be a shield for **my honor** (*ʕirḍī*). The wealth is protecting **my honor** (*ʕirḍī*) (cf. t19B:40).

Despite of PROTECTING the *ʕirḍ*, one's WEALTH – as it is said by Labīd Ibn Rabīʕa in (214) – might be used to buy *ḥamd*-FAME, which clearly indicates *šaraf*-HIGH SOCIAL STATUS. Naturally, *ʕirḍ* is deeply involved in one's *šaraf*, since it is always *ʕirḍ*, which implies one's *karam*, being yet a necessary condition of preserving the HIGH SOCIAL STANDING – and also in acquiring it at the very first place (cf. t19B:71).

(213) أقي **العِرْضَ** بالمَالِ التِّلادِ وأشْتَري بهِ الحَمدَ إنَّ الطّالبَ الحَمْدَ مُشترِي

I protect [my] **honor** (*al-ʕirḍ*) with my inherited wealth and I buy with it fame (*ḥamd*). Truly, a man seeking fame (*ḥamd*) [can only] buy [it] (cf. t30B:67).

7.7. One's LINEAGE is one's HONOR

As we saw, CAD seem to postulate yet another metonymy – *ʕirḍ*-HONOR FOR *nasab*-LINEAGE. It might most probably be observed in the passage (95), attributed to al-Mutalammis, already quoted also in the previous chapters (cf. also t39A:5–11). In this fragment, the poet says that if a man possessing *ʕirḍ*, does not protect his *ḥasab* (i.e., keep it in a decent shape), he will be disgraced and dishonored. Naturally, in the light of what I said about the relationship between *ʕirḍ* and *ḥasab* earlier in this chapter, reading of *ʕirḍ* in the literary sense would be quite contradictory. As we learned in Chapter 4. (cf. section 4.4.3.), the meaning of this verse – in the whole contexts – might be rendered as rather implying someone, who – being of NOBLE ORIGIN – does not care about being *karīm*-HONORABLE. In other words, al-Mutalammis seems to criticize a belief – which might have been yet widespread in al-Ǧāhiliyya – that RIGHT TO RESPECT could be claimed only on one's NOBILITY in terms of LINEAGE, i.e., *nasab*.

(95) يُعيّرُني أمّي رِجالٌ ولا أرى **أخا كَرَمٍ** إلّا بأن **يتَكَرَّما**
وَمَن كانَ ذا **عِرضٍ كَريمٍ** فَلم يَصُن لَهُ حَسَباً كانَ اللّئيمَ المُذَمَّما

[There are] men, who disgrace me [because of] my mother [and her base origin]. I do not consider someone **being honorable** (*ʔaḫū karam*), if he does not **behave in an honorable way** (*yatakarram*).

> The one, who is of **noble origin** (*ʕirḍ karīm*), and because of that he doesn't care about [his] merits (*ḥasab*), is a low (*laʔīm*) and dispraised man (cf. t10A:16).

This supposed critics actually offer us a hint of the reason why the lexeme *ʕirḍ* might have been used in calling-up the schema LINEAGE, rather than that of RIGHT TO RESPECT. As we saw, similar situation could be observed in the relationship between *ʕirḍ* and *ḥasab*. It was so, because both – *nasab* and *ḥasab* – were simply the two pillars, upon which one's RIGHT TO RESPECT rested. In other words, they were the two factors, which constituted someone's EQUALS' opinion about him/her that was his/her REPUTATION.

But why *nasab*-LINEAGE was one of the estimates of one's REPUTE-VALUE, on the basis on which this someone claimed RIGHT TO RESPECT? It is a known fact that pre-Islamic Arabs paid assiduous attention to one's ORIGIN, what could be more primarily explained as arising from the fact that *nasab* was what kept the whole tribe together (ʕAlī 1993b: 313). The LINEAGE of forefathers traced back to a common ancestor made tribe members feel they are related – as if their tribe formed a huge complex family (ʕAlī 1993b: 314). *Nasab* was therefore the foundation of *ʕaṣabiyya* (ʕAlī 1993b: 352) – the tribal spirit of solidarity, stemming from the sense of blood relationship holding between tribe members. Consequently, its preservation was so important. Such preservation of one's lineage was done mostly by keeping it free from people who could be considered ignoble. This on its turn was achieved by rigid obedience of *nasab* purity requirement while marring outside of the kin-group. Most importantly, the purity meant lack of slave blood (ʕAlī 1993b: 541) – or any kind of association with slavery (that is why pre-Islamic Arabs disdained craftsmanship, cf. ʕAlī 1993b: 563). Therefore, even if a candidate for a husband was rich, without being of pure linage, he had no chance of getting married with a noble woman (ʕAlī 1993a: 276). Nevertheless, sole purity of *nasab* did not suffice to get married – a *šarīf* candidate should also be *karīm*, i.e., should prove his NOBILITY in his deeds (ʕAlī 1993b: 544; cf. also Abu-Lughod 1986: 92).

I believe the motivation behind the metonymic model *ʕirḍ* FOR *nasab* seems to come down to the aforementioned phenomenon of *ʕaṣabiyya* – a tribal spirit. It short one can understand it further as the ability to call up the entire agnatic kin-group to protect the right of an individual – when he was either the subject of injustice or its perpetrator (ʕAlī 1993b: 392–6). Thus, *nasab* could be a great deal of an asset – ergo, it must have been a part of one's overall WORTH. A person of a many male relatives – who were also considered in the society as *šarīfs*, i.e., the men exceling in *karam* – naturally translated into the position one had among others. Thus, pre-Islamic Arabs were very meticulous in the respect to their lineages – they know them by heart (ʕAlī 1993b: 352), and by all means they tried to protect it from being "spoiled" by un-*karīm* and un-*šarīf* elements (cf. ʕAlī 1993b: 541).

To sum it up, similarly to what Abou-Zeid (1965: 251–2) noticed among mid 20th c. Eastern Egyptian Bedouins, pre-Islamic Arabs derived much of their RIGHT TO RESPECT from their kin-group. It could also be seen in (215), where Ḥassān Ibn Ṯābit clearly indicates that a *karīm* man is someone, in whom relatives prided themselves. In other words, the poet derives his observation form a prepositional schema encoding the fact that one's sense of pride – SELF-ESTEEM – was derived by far from one's kin-group.

(214) فلا وَأخِيكَ **الكريمِ** الذي فَخَرْتَ بهِ لا تُرَى تُعتَلُ

I can't see your **honorable** (*karīm*) brother, in whom you have prided yourself [so much], pulling you [out of your troubles] (cf. t38A:237).

Of course – as al-Mutalammis wanted to remind us in (95) – *nasab*-LINEAGE was not the sole source of this RIGHT. A man who can claim the RIGHT TO RESPECT only due to his noble origin should not have been fully recognized as one deserving it. The noble origin without *ḥasab* was not enough to secure one's HONOR.

The impact of one's *nasab* on their *ʕirḍ* was not always positive only. Sometimes, when one's kin-group – or one's associates – were in disgrace, it was better to distance oneself from them. This is, I think, what one can read in (216). Thus, the derivation of one's HONOR worked in both ways – it could be something INCREASING the VALUE of a man, but it could well DIMINISH it as well. Consequently, however, if an individual's *ʕirḍ* was in a deplorable condition, the whole community saw it necessary to cut any ties with this person, expelling them from the group (ʕAlī 1993b: 574).

(215) إني سأقصُرُ **عِرْضِي** عنْ شِرارِكمُ، إنّ النّجاشي لَشَيءٌ غيْرُ مَذْكُورِ

Truly, I will make **my name** (*ʕirḍī*) cut from your wrongdoings. There is truly nothing to be mentioned about an-Nağāšī (cf. t38A:149–150)

Consequently, as we saw it in (216), a strong relationship was definitely holding between *ʕirḍ* of an individual and *ʕirḍ*s of his or her kins. Thus, as Ibn Ṯābit implies it, one's *ʕirḍ* was TIED to their group. This conceptualization can also be found in (217) by al-Mutalammis. This verse indicates further that this relationship is mutual. One derived their VALUE form their kins, yet their kins also should have had to protect this someone, because their *ʕirḍ*s were similarly TIED to this someone's VALUE. In other words, the members of the tribe should collectively protect all their kins – co-members – because if one member's HONOR is DIMINISHED, the HONOR of the rest – and of the whole group – suffered DIMINISHING as well. This is, I believe, exactly what the feeling of *ʕaṣabiyya* imply: one for all, all for one.[12]

(216) أَلا إِنَّنِي مِنهُم وَعِرضِيَ عِرضَهُمْ كَذِي الأَنفِ يَحمِي أَنفَهُ أَن يُكَشَّما

Isn't it true that I am one of them, and **my honor** (*ʕirḍī*) is **their honor** (*ʕirḍa-hum*)? [My honor is like a nose in their body]. Doesn't the owner of a nose protect it against being cut off (cf. t10A:21)?

7.8. Conclusions: why is *ʕirḍ*-HONOR so vulnerable in LEAP?

To sum it up, LEAP *ʕirḍ* was used in the reference to the schema of HONOR-RIGHT TO RESPECT. This notion, however, was conflated with the concept of one's REPUTATION, which might be seen as a concept of VALUE/WORTH, elaborated by two subschemata: INNER VALUE, i.e., SELF-ESTEEM, and EXTERNAL VALUE, i.e., REPUTE, GOOD NAME. As we have learned, the merger of these two elements might have also reflected on the further semantic extension of *ʕirḍ* in form of a metonymy ONE'S *ʕirḍ*-HONOR FOR ONESELF, what encoded that one's perception of their global SELF was deeply entangled with the external SOCIAL EVALUATION.

The REPUTATION, upon which the RIGHT TO RESPECT rested, was derived mostly from two major estimates: *ḥasab* and *nasab* – "dignity and genealogy (Dziekan 2008: 36)". Hence, one's WORTH, upon which one founded their HONOR, consisted by far from one's *ḥasab*-VALUE in terms of a COUNT of HONORABLE/NOBLE DEEDS, i.e., *makārim*. Nonetheless, *ḥasab* itself was not the only ground for the pretension to this RIGHT. Although, it was seemingly the most substantial factor in securing one's *ʕirḍ*-HONOR, one could also claim RESPECT based on their *nasab*-LINEAGE. Perhaps, some could have even been claiming RESPECT entirely on such a basis, what seems to be a subject of a critique by al-Mutalammis in (95).

The VALUE indicated by *nasab* seems to translate into the ability of calling to arms men by the means of *ʕaṣabiyya*. Therefore, one's *ʕirḍ*-HONOR was seen as tightly bond with *ʕirḍ*s of their kins. If a group failed to answer to the call of *ʕaṣabiyya* of a man, his personal *ʕirḍ* would suffer DAMAGE. Yet at the same time, by that, the whole group HONOR, would become DIMINISHED too – because his HARM was an indication that the group did not have STRENGTH to protect

---

12 In fact, by the means of derivation from √ʕṢB, the very concept of *ʕaṣabiyya* also implies BOND, i.e., something causing BEING TIED (cf. LsA1: 703–4, 707–8).

him. This, however, meant that their overall VALUE – their ʕirḍ-HONOR – was DECREASED.

Consequently, these two schemata – *ḥasab* and *nasab* – could be evoked by means of metonymic use of the lexeme *ʕirḍ*. Still, such a use – at least in the light of my interpretation of the analyzed data – was not widespread in EAP. Nevertheless, it was recorded, what confirms the prominence of these two concepts for the whole schema *ʕirḍ*. The importance of these two phenomena did not fade away with the culture revolution, which took place after the spread of Islam, thus they can be still seen as major "institutions" of Arabo-Islamic culture, whose original meaning has not been yet lost entirely (Dziekan 2008: 36). The use of the metonymic models in form of *ʕirḍ* FOR *ḥasab* and *ʕirḍ* FOR *nasab* served to hint at the fact that –in the particular context – *ḥasab* and *nasab* are mentioned in the sense of entitlements to HONOR-RIGHT TO RESPECT.

In contrast to European notion this RIGHT, *ʕirḍ* seems to be gradable and in constant process of INCREASE/DECREASE. In other words, in al-Ǧāhiliyya, one's RIGHT TO RESPECT could be more or less questioned by others. Consequently, *ʕirḍ* was not entirely losable, and it could be only DIMINISHED or DAMAGED. Thus, in such a way, it was more or less effective in making others – one's EQUALS – pay this someone RESPECT.

Such a conceptualization might be also seen as encoded in the fact that *ʕirḍ* was perceived as POSSESSED MASS. Consequently, QUESTIONING one's RIGHT TO RESPECT, by an INSULT, being an ACCUSATION of DISHONORABLE CONDUCT, was conceptualized as CHUNKING OFF a piece of this MASS. In CEAP, such *ʕirḍ*-MASS was depicted as belonging to either a man or an entire group. Only once, however, it was ascribed to a woman, what might seem striking, considering the association between *ʕirḍ* and female sexual conduct persisting in the modern Arabic communities until today. Moreover, this only instance was the passage (210) by Kaʕb Ibn Zuhayr, quoted earlier, in which, as we saw, the lexeme *ʕirḍ* refers to the noble conduct of the woman, and not to the RIGHT TO RESPECT or REPUTE.

INSULTING, i.e., QUESTIONING one's RIGHT TO RESPECT was predominantly conceptualized by means of such scenarios as HARMING or DAMAGING. I think such conceptualizations encodes the knowledge of usefulness of one's *ʕirḍ*. As I said, DAMAGED *ʕirḍ* was less effective in making one's EQUALS pay proper RESPECT to its POSSESSOR. The RESPECT, as we know, did not entitle any privilege or special treatment, but was a mere mark of recognition of an individual's RIGHT to MEMBERSHIP in his or her community.

What is crucial here is the fact that the survival of this individual outside that community was nearly impossible due to the harsh environment of Ancient Arabia. Being expelled from a group, one must have immediately attached themselves to another – otherwise, they could face demise (cf. ʕAlī 1993b: 410). This, however, I believe, is the reason why in the data on *ʕirḍ*, its most visible trait is its vulnerability – it seems that it was always on a verge of demise, and thus, it must have been constantly protected. In other words, we can read the loss of the full effectiveness of *ʕirḍ* as the loss of one's survival ability. And this is what I believe one can see in the culture-driven embodying conceptualization of *ʕirḍ*-HONOR in terms of one's BODY, profiled as VULNERABLE/FRAGILE, or as BODY SIDE – the most vulnerable/fragile of its part. Therefore, one's *ʕirḍ* was always endangered in the simile to one's fragile body living in the harsh and unhospitable environment of Arabia. Similarly, a harm, a wound done to it could have meant death – in the same way, the death could follow a wound in one's BODY. Thus, WOUNDING one's *ʕirḍ*, was like WOUNDING one's vital organ: in either case, its POSSESSOR could die.

Moreover, this relatedness of *ʕirḍ*-HONOR to persistence within the community is also compatible with the metonymy ONE'S *ʕirḍ*-HONOR FOR ONESELF. It encoded one's perception of their global SELF as entangled with the SOCIAL EVALUATION. As noted by Wilson & Lewandowska-Tomaszczyk (2021: 457), "[t]he central elements pertaining to this global self include acceptance or rejection by others, self-regulation, and self-evaluation." In other words, the fact that *ʕirḍ* was at the core of SOCIAL EVALUATION accounted for the conflation of this notion with the concept of one's global self – the heart of one's self-esteem.

Therefore, perhaps, in the culture of pre-Islamic Arabs, HONOR became a kind of obsession – or at least its entailment being one's VALUE. Arabs of al-Ǧāhiliyya, as ʕAlī (1993a: 265) describes it, were filled with the sense of personal dignity. Thus, priding, swaggering, boasting were of so much importance – to the point of semi-institutionalizing the priding itself in form of a competition (ʕAlī 1993b: 589–92). Pre-Islamic Arabs were – as said by al-Ǧāḥiẓ – "the proudest of nations" (ʕAlī 1993b: 307), and, as a consequence, they must have been easily agitated or angered by offences and insults (ʕAlī 1993a: 267). Nonetheless, it is worth noting that ANGER functioned as an HONOR-driven emotion not only in pre-Islamic Arabic culture. It seems to be a more universal phenomenon to be found in different societies, especially those that can be termed *honor cultures*. As noted by Mosquera, Manstead & Fischer (2016: 834), "attacks on one's honor [in such communities], as in the case of insults, appear to be a common anger-eliciting event" that "usually leads to retaliation against the perpetrator as a way of restoring one's honor."

Thus, it seems ʕirḍ-HONOR must have conflated with the SELF of its possessor. This might be observed as encoded by the bidirectional metonymy ONE'S ʕirḍ-HONOR FOR ONESELF. In other words, someone in a way always saw oneself in the terms of HONOR and HONORABILITY. Thus, all his or her actions linked always to *karam* or its opposite, *luʔm*. Similarly, any INSULTS issued to offend his or her HONOR were perceived as the simple attack on him or her – there was no difference between an INSULT and a PHYSICAL ATTACK. Consequently, one's SELF-ESTEEM could not differ from one's ESTEEM. Thus, in al-Ǧāhiliyya one's SELF-WORTH seems to have been entangled with the WORTH ascribed to them in the external SOCIAL EVALUATION.

Ergo, *ʕirḍ* was a very special, very precious POSSESSION. And it needed to be protected by all means. The easiest way of doing so was the proper conduct – *karam* – which would reflect on one's *ḥasab*-VALUE. What it means is that one could have been simply behaving in a way no one could ever find anything to reproach them with. In such a way, one could COVER or VEIL his vulnerable *ʕirḍ*-BODY-SELF in clothing – even in an armor – so that no INSULT, could WOUND it, i.e., make it DEFECTIVE, not fully functional. Perhaps, then, POSSESSING *ʕirḍ* could also metonymically serve to call up the schema of INTEGRITY. In other words, as we saw in the example (210), someone who had *ʕirḍ* ample – well protected – was a person, from whom one shall expect only HONORABLE behavior, proved in the fact of this PROTECTION. This, however, brings *ʕirḍ* very close to our modern understanding of HONOR, which by far is associated with one's INTEGRITY only.

Consequently, since *karam*-HONORABILITY was a mere extension of the core *karam*-GENEROSITY-HOSPITALITY, one could PLACE their WEALTH NEAR or UNDER their *ʕirḍ*, meaning one could use their financial resources to prove their VALUE as a man of honor. As we learned in many places in this book, WEALTH was as important element of one's WORTH. We can choose to believe that the reason for that was the importance of GENEROSITY-HOSPITALITY. However, as the history teaches us, WEALTH has been usually used for purposes different than those aiming to share blessings of one's life with others.

All in all, *ʕirḍ*-HONOR was precious and thus always in danger. It was as precious as one's BODY and one's SELF. Without it one could not live good life among people – as it was said in (197), being a fragment from a poem by Labīd Ibn Rabīʕa, in which the elderly poet shares his reflections on life. If one's *ʕirḍ* got WOUNDED, thus DAMAGED, it could not work properly anymore, and consequently, one was unable to demand their RIGHT TO RESPECT, their simple MEMBERSHIP card, without which one could not last long. Since, losing RIGHT TO

RESPECT was losing the RIGHT to stay in the community, outside of which one must have faced the perils of unhostile environment. Therefore, killing seemed such a justified retaliation for an INSULT. Naturally, one had to DISGRACE by all means – they had to dismiss all questions about their RIGHT to persist within the group.

8. Shame & dishonor[1]

As I mentioned, this book was meant to describe HONOR – the phenomenon, which can be defined as a key element of pre-Islamic Arabic life. Nevertheless, when asking about HONOR, one always asks in a way about SHAME. The traditional anthropological approach binds these two social phenomena together under one subsuming schema (cf. Peristiany 1965: 21). As Peristiany (1965: 9–10) stated, “honour and shame are two poles of an evaluation” of a community member’s behavior “by comparing it to ideal standards of action”. This evaluation takes place in front of the “court of reputation” formed by the opinion of members of the community (Peristiany 1965:27). SHAME is then the alternative pole of the phenomena I have analyzed in the previous chapters. Its elaborations in LEAP might be seen as elements completing the picture of the social evaluation of one’s behavior among pre-Islamic Arabs in terms of the “ideal standards of action” being the code of *karam*-HONORABILITY.

In this chapter, I will present the findings on fundamental pre-Islamic Arabic SHAME- and DISHONOR-related concepts I discussed in Pietrzak (2022). It that paper, I attempted to describe cultural conceptualizations linked to a sample of the lexical coverage of the English concept of SHAME[2] in LEAP. Their presentation in this place aims to provide a limited insight into the opposite of HONOR, which was the main subject of my analyses. My goal is then not to provide an exhaustive description of the subschema of SHAME and DISHONOR together with related linguistic frame, but only to present its general features that might enhance our understanding of the pre-Islamic Arabic conception of HONOR. The aforementioned discussion concerned only the concepts of *ʕayb*, *ʕār*, and *ḥayāʔ*, which might be seen as nuclear for the whole schematized knowledge of SHAME-DISHONOR in pre-Islamic Arabic culture. They might be considered as encoding knowledge on SHAME either as an ascribed value (SHAME or DISHONOR) or FEELING (FEELING ASHAMED). Consequently, I will not present in this chapter detailed conclusions on such concepts as INSULT/OFFENCE and SHAMING. They were partially covered in the previous chapter on *ʕirḍ*, in the context of their

1 This chapter contains repetition – sometimes verbatim – of the conclusions I presented in Pietrzak (2022).

2 SHAME is insightfully described in detail in Wilson & Lewandowska-Tomaszczyk (2021: 457–60).

conceptualizations related to the understanding of HONOR, mostly in terms of embodiment.

The following presentation is also important due to the hypothetical classification of pre-Islamic Arabic culture not only as *honor culture*, but also as a *shame culture*.[3] The notion of *shame-culture* was introduced to anthropology by Ruth Benedict (1947)[4] and it might be understood as characteristic of a culture group, whose members' behavior is regulated by shame that "is concerned with a man's failure to approach some ideal pattern of conduct (Campbell 1964: 327)." In the context of what I have presented in the previous chapter, pre-Islamic Arabic society could be described as somehow shame-driven in the sense presented in this definition. More precisely, a conduct of a member of this society was scrutinized in the respect to their adherence to the script of *karam*, i.e., to the code of BEING *karīm*. The failure to observe this code resulted in SHAME-DISGRACE that – as we will learn in this chapter – had highly negative effect of the state of one's *ʕirḍ*-HONOR. In other words, shameful behavior as contradicting *karam* could result in social ostracism that was the major factor affecting someone's behavior.

8.1. LEAP concepts of SHAME and DISHONOR.

As I said, in the following sections, I will represent – sometimes verbatim – the conclusions on pre-Islamic Arabic cultural schemata of SHAME and DISHONOR I discussed in Pietrzak (2022). They are those concerning conceptualizations that are crucial for more comprehensive understanding of HONOR in form of a knowledge model functioning in al-Ǧāhiliyya.

---

3 I would like to thank the reviewers of my Ph.D. thesis, prof. Janusz Danecki and prof. Marek Dziekan, for directing my attention to the shame-culture character of pre-Islamic Arabic society.

4 The notion of shame-culture into the Arabic studies was possibly first introduced in a highly controversial monograph by Raphael Patai, *The Arab Mind* (Patai 1973). I fully concur with the criticism of this work. Although, I must admit that in the department of the SHAME-DISHONOR model, Patai made some valid observations that corresponds with my findings. Nevertheless, I don't find his book meeting the standard of scientific research. I agree with some of the critics that Patai's monograph is not only unscientific, simplifying, but for the most part it is racist and simply offensive. For some more information cf. Mozaffar (2004) and Limon (2007).

8.1.1. The concept of *ʕayb*

The lexeme *ʕayb* (pl. *ʕuyūb*) and its verbal derivative – *ʕāba-yaʕīb* – are surprisingly rare in the CEAP, where they occur only 52 times (NWC: 1.92[5]). Moreover, CAD do not provide any decent explication of their meaning (cf. KtA3: 259–60, AlG: 369, AsS: 829, and LsA1: 741–3), what could indicate their relative intuitiveness for medieval Arabic philologists.

Primarily, the lexeme *ʕayb* seems to refer to the concept of DEFECT found prototypically in things, as it is in the sample (218), attributed to al-Aʕšà (cf. also t17A:28–32). This prototypical category – DEFECT IN OBJECT – extends to all sorts of elaborations of the image-schema OBJECT such as animals, but also abstracta (based on the metaphor ABSTRACT OBJECTS ARE PHYSICAL OBJECTS), which can be observed in (219) attributed to aš-Šammāẖ Ibn Ḍirār and (220) by Zuhayr Ibn Abī Sulmà (cf. also t36A:130 and t29A:19–20).

(217) لَهُ أكَالِيلُ بِاليَاقُوتِ زَيّنَهَا صُوّاغُها لا ترى **عيباً**، ولا طَبَعَا

He has crowns with sapphire, decorated by jewelers – you will not find in [those crowns] either **defect** (*ʕayb*) or dirt or soot (cf. t28A: 107–8)

(218) جُمالِيَّةٌ لو يُجْعَلُ السَيْفُ غَرْضَهَا على حَدِّهِ - لاستكبرَتْ أنْ تَضَوَّرَا
ولا **عَيْبَ** في مَكْرُوهِها غيرَ أنّهُ تَبَدَّلَ جَوْناً بَعْدما كانَ أزْهرا

She – [my she-camel] – is so loyal that if one made the joints of her saddle out of a sword – and [made them] at its edges – she would be too proud to cry [out of complaint].
And there would be no **defect** (*ʕayb*) in her, [even as] she was in such a pitiful state, except from the fact that [the sword used in her saddle] would turn from pure white into red-and-white (cf. t32A:134).

(219) أَرُونا سُنَّةً **لا عَيبَ** فيها يُسَوَّى بَيْنَنا فيها السَواءُ

Show us a law, in which there is no **fault** (*ʕayb*), and which will be just for us equally (cf. t22A:17).

Subsequently, the verb *ʕāba-yaʕīb* referred prototypically to the action of DAMAGING, MAKING DEFECTIVE (cf. t21A:50–51; t37A:54; t26A:88) or BEING DEFECTIVE (what has been claimed in CAD, however, cannot be found in CEAP).

The prototypical schema *ʕayb*-DEFECT subsumes a very important propositional subschema in form of {*ʕayb*-DEFECT lowers the VALUE of the OBJECT}, which could be observed elaborated in form of the statement presented in (219).

5 Such normalized word count corresponds to the NWC of such English lexemes as *mission*, *minister*, and *movement*, and Polish *trzy* and *centrum* (based on the corpora *English Web 2015* and *Polish Web 2015* available on *SketchEngine*, https://www.sketchengine.eu [08-07-2021]).

The poet describes a quite cruel proof of loyalty of his she-camel, stating that even being tortured, she will not lose her WORTH – she will stay DEFECT-less – there will be nothing to complain about her. This proposition might be seen as the motivation of metaphoric model, which accounts for the category extension linking the concept of *ʕayb* with SHAME-DISHONOR. The model might be represented as *ʕayb*-SHAMEFULNESS- SHAME IS *ʕayb*- DEFECT and it lends the structure for the subschema *ʕayb*-SHAMEFULNESS- SHAME subsumed by the aforementioned schema UNWORTHINESS.

In other words, some qualities of a person could have been considered by pre-Islamic Arabs as their DEFECTS, which in a way, lower their value. Therefore, *ʕayb* might be seen as a defect, because of which one should be ashamed, or as "something unsound, which makes someone defective, and thus, something for which one is reprehended, blamed, reproached (Lane 1968e: 2206)". Ergo, *ʕayb*-SHAMEFULNESS-SHAME was simply something shameful, which – based on the metaphoric model – decreased the value of a person. Something was someone's *ʕayb* only if it was perceived by others as lowering his overall WORTH. I think this conceptualization might be seen, for instance, in the sample (221), a passage attributed to ʕAmr Ibn Maʕd Yakrib (cf. also t21A:149–150), in which the poet implies that harassing men vilify a woman to diminish her WORTH and claim her for themselves. Thus, obviously, *ʕayb* was perceived as something, which decreases the value of an individual in the eyes of their community. In other words, the community could find this individual UNWORTHY, i.e., of worth, which did not justify keeping them around.

(220) وَرُبَّ مُحَرِّشٍ في جَنْبِ سَلْمى يُعَلُّ **بِعَيْبِها** عندي شَفيعُ

How many men, while approaching Salmà, harass [her], repeating all over again the **accusation of her faults** (*ʕayb*) – for me [these men are simply] suitors, [who themselves want to possess her, and thus, they try to make her repugnant to others] (cf. t31A:141).

In (221), *ʕayb*-SHAMEFULNESS was ascribed to the woman – Salmà – in the action of *ʕāba-yaʕīb*, which was referred to in this passage also by the lexeme *ʕayb*. The meaning of *ʕayb* as a verbal noun derived from *ʕāba-yaʕīb* is confirmed by CAD (cf., e.g., AlG: 369). Based on the metaphor *ʕayb*-SHAMEFULNESS-SHAME IS *ʕayb*-DEFECT, one could interpret the meaning of the verb *ʕāba-yaʕīb* by the mapping *ʕāba- yaʕīb*-ASCRIBING WITH *ʕayb*- SHAMEFULNESS- SHAME IS *ʕāba-yaʕīb*-DAMAGING-MAKING DEFECTIVE linguistically expressed in (222) by Ḥātim aṭ-Ṭāʔī and confirmed by LsA1 (742). In other words, ascribing someone with *ʕayb* was conceptualized as damaging someone or making them defective by pointing towards their *ʕayb*s-DEFECTS of different nature, as it was depicted by

Ibn Muqbil in (223) (cf. also t21A:75 and t21A:10). This consequently meant lowering their value, as we can see, for instance, in (224) by al-Ḥuṭayʔa, who states that he is unable to vilify (ʕāba-yaʕīb) a man, who is glorious and proud (cf. also t37A:47 and t21A:75).

(221) وكلمةِ حاسدٍ مِنْ غَيْرِ جُرْمٍ سمعْتُ فَقُلْتُ مُرّي فَانْقُذِينِي

وعابُوها علَيَّ، فلَمْ **تَعِبْني** ولم يَعْرَقْ لها، يَوْماً، جَبِيني

I have heard the [vilifying] word of an envying man – [and I was] of no fault – so I said: pass me, [oh vilifying word], and do not make harm to me.

[So many people] have **vilified** (ʕābū) me in such [envying words] – but these [words] did not **damage** me (lam taʕib-nī), nor did my forehead temples sweat because of them – even for a day (cf. t19B:90).

(222) واسْتَهْزَأَتْ بَرْبُها مِنّي فَقُلْتُ لَهَا: ماذا **تَعِيبانِ** مِنّي يا بَنْتَنَيْ عَصَرٍ؟

لو لا **الحَياءُ** ولو لا الدِّينُ **عِبْتُكُما** بِبَعْضِ مَا فِيكُمَا إذْ **عِبْتُمَا** عَوَري

Thus, her sister laughed at me, so I said: Why are you **laughing** (taʕībāni) at me, daughters of ʕAṣar?

If not for [my] sense of shame (ḥayāʔ), or [my] obedience to customs, I would **shame** both of you (ʕibtu-kuma) for some of [the faults], which are in you, since you have **vilified** (ʕibtukūmā) my weakness (cf. t36A:71).

(223) إنِّي نهاني أنْ **أَعِيبَكَ** ماجِدُ الجَدَّيْنِ فاخِرْ

Truly, I cannot **vilify** you (ʔaʕība-ka) – you are a glorious man [of the glory of your] ancestors [from both sides], a proud man (cf. t39A:169, 174).

The verb ʕāba-yaʕīb definitely refers to an action performed in speech as in (225) by ʕAntara Ibn Šaddād (cf. also t19B:90). Sometimes, it can even entail mockery as in the aforementioned passage (223) by Ibn Muqbil. Perhaps, it might be seen as a metonymic extension of the prototypical category. Since ʕāba-yaʕīb-ASCRIBING WITH ʕayb- SHAMEFULNESS- SHAME was structured by the schema ʕāba-yaʕīb-DAMAGING- MAKING DEFECTIVE, its linguistic expression might be complemented by the propositional phrase with the proposition bi- as its head, which can introduce instrumental (Danecki 2012a: 460). Nevertheless, more frequently (NO: 2 vs. NO: 6), its complement is a direct object expressed by the accusative case. Moreover, in three instances, poets employed passive voice of the verb – as in the example (226) by ʕAmr Ibn Maʕd Yakrib (cf. also t30B:34 and t37A:54) – which could support the assessment of ʕayb as an evaluative term.

(224) ومَنْ قالَ إني أسْودٌ **لِيُعِيبَني** أُرِيهِ بِفعْلِي أنهُ أَكذَبُ النَّاسِ

Thus, in my deeds, I will show that the one, who is saying that I am Black in order to **vilify** me (li-yaʕība-nī), is the most lying from among people. (cf. t21A:75).

(225) وَليسَ **يُعابُ** المرْءُ من جُبنٍ يوْمِهِ إذا عُرِفَتْ منهُ الشَّجاعةُ بالأمْسِ

The man **is not vilified** (yuʕāb) for the cowardice of his [now-a-]day, if his bravery is known from [his] yesterday. (cf. t31A:129).

Since *ʕāba-yaʕīb*-ASCRIBING WITH *ʕayb*-SHAMEFULNESS-SHAME results in devaluation of an individual, one can see it as related to the schema of *ʕirḍ*. In other words, *ʕayb*- SHAMEFULNESS- SHAME ascribed to someone diminishes this someone's *ʕirḍ*-HONOR-RIGHT TO RESPECT, which is based on their REPUTATION-VALUE. Thus, by *ʕāba-yaʕīb*, one aims to decrease someone else's WORTH and consequently, their RIGHT TO RESPECT, which is seen, for instance, in the sample (227), a passage attributed to Hudba Ibn al-Ḫašram. In this example, the poet states that the goal of the vilification is to *nāla-yanāl* "attain" someone. This concept clearly derives from the previously discussed metonymic model ONE'S *ʕirḍ* FOR ONESELF, standing for the expression *nāla min ʕirḍi-hi* "lit. he attained his *ʕirḍ*" meaning simply *ʕāba-yaʕīb* (cf. aHm: 32). As we previously saw, this conceptualization is based on the image-schematic model *ʕirḍ* IS A WHOLE, which structures the metaphor *ʕāba- yaʕīb*-ASCRIBING SOMEONE WITH *ʕayb*- SHAMEFULNESS-SHAME IS OBTAINING SOMETHING FROM THIS SOMEONE'S *ʕirḍ*. As one can see, this conceptualization neatly fits the understanding of *ʕirḍ* in terms of RIGHT, since OBTAINING SOMETHING metonymically links to DIMINISHING or REDUCING it, MAKING it SMALLER – in this particular case, the RIGHT TO RESPECT. Therefore, the more AMPLE someone's *ʕirḍ* is, the less *ʕāba-yaʕīb*-ASCRIBING SOMEONE WITH *ʕayb*-SHAMEFULNESS-SHAME can damage it (cf. t19B:90).

(226) **وَذي نَيرَبٍ قَد عابَني لِينالَني** فأَعيى مَداهُ عَن مَدايَ فأَقصَرا
وَكَذَّبَ **عَيبَ العائِبينَ** سَماحَتي وَصَبري إِذا ما الأَمرُ عَضَّ فأَضجَرا

A wicked man has **vilified** (*ʕāba*) me to **strip me [of honor]** (*li-yanāla-nī*), but his reach is too weak for my reach; it is much shorter.
My munificence and my endurance – which are my shelter in time of distress and grieve – has proven that the **vilifications** (*ʕayb*) of [my] **vilifiers** are lies (cf. t08A:97).

To sum it up, *ʕayb* is something devaluating a person and thus, reducing their RIGHT TO RESPECT received from others. Having *ʕayb* is then a subject of SHAMING, INSULTING, or OFFENDING by people (cf. t22A:19; t21A:19–20a). This means that *ʕayb* was a subject of gossips (cf. t22A:19; t39A:396). Therefore, for pre- Islamic Arabs, *ʕayb* must have been kept in secret. Divulging such secret was to shame – *ʕāba-yaʕīb* – a person, that is, to MAKE THEM DEFECTIVE (cf. t36A:69–71–72). This could link to the previously discussed conceptualization, in which EXPOSING one's *ʕirḍ* meant SHAMING them (*lā taʕriḍ ʕirḍ fulān* "do not mention someone evilly; lit. do not expose *ʕirḍ* of someone"; cf. KtA3: 133). In other words, as long as one's *ʕuyūb*-DEFECTS were HIDDEN, their effect on one's *ʕirḍ* was also unknown. The EXPOSURE of one's *ʕirḍ* indicates the divulging of everything that can affect its value. Consequently, it meant exposing also what lowered this value.

The subschema *ʕayb* SHOULD BE KEPT IN SECRET is structured by a metaphoric model KEEPING IN SECRET IS COVERING, HIDING, which might be observed in, e.g., (228) and (229). COVERING or HIDING *ʕayb* is a perfect example of the elaboration of metaphoric mapping of *ʕayb*-SHAMEFULNESS-SHAME IS *ʕayb*-DEFECT, where SHAMEFULNESS of something (mostly a trait of character) is conceptualized as PHYSICAL DEFECT. In fact, the domain COVERING is also used to structure yet another part of the schema *ʕayb*. One can COVER their *ʕayb* with WEALTH as in (230). As one can see, here, *ʕayb* is not kept in secret, but is somehow diminish or forgiven, forgotten due to the wealth of a man, which contributes – as we learned in the previous chapters – to his HONORABLENESS, BEING *karīm*.

(227) إذا الحربُ حلَّتْ ساحةَ القوْم أخرَجتْ **عيوبَ** رجالٍ يُعجبونَكَ في الأمنِ

When a war falls upon people, it pulls out the **defects** (*ʕuyūb*) of men, whom you admired in the time of peace (cf. t26A:130).

(228) يُنادي بالتَّضَرُّعِ يا إلهي أَقِلْني عَثْرتي واسْتُرْ **عُيوبي**

He is calling in humility: My God! Diminish my faults and hide my **shameful defects** (*ʕuyūb*)! (cf. t37A:47).

(229) يُغطي **عيوبَ** المَرْءِ كُثْرَةُ مالِه يُصَدَّقُ فِي مَا قَالَ وَهْوَ كَذُوبُ

The plenty of a man's wealth hides his **shameful defects** (*ʕuyūb*) as well as it authenticates what he said, while lying (cf. t37A:36).

From among the image-schematic conceptualizations of *ʕayb*, the most interesting one is the notion of *ʕayb* as OBJECT ON (THE SURFACE OF) ANOTHER OBJECT, i.e., as a flat, visible, superficial, two-dimensional OBJECT. It could connect to the aforementioned conceptualization of EXPOSING one's *ʕirḍ* as a mean of SHAMING someone. In other words, this might imply that *ʕayb* was a kind of stigma – a stain, something noticeable – that was placed on the *ʕirḍ* of someone. While EXPOSING one's *ʕirḍ*, this stigma was divulged and, as a consequence, the value of this *ʕirḍ* was diminished. Perhaps, it might be seen as an example of conceptual blend between the schemata *ʕayb* and *ʕār* (v.i.). This conceptualization was also linguistically expressed by a rare completion of the verb *ʕāba-yaʕīb* in form of the preposition *ʕalà* "on" as it is in (231) by ʕAntara Ibn Šaddād (cf. also t19B:90). As one can see, the agent shames in there the black color of ʕAntara's skin *alà* "onto" him, which might suggest that the action resembles THROWING the *ʕayb* color onto the poet and thus shaming him. Alternatively, one can interpret this conceptualization as derived from the model SHAMING IS THROWING SHAMING WORDS, which instantiates the well-observed conceptualization of WORDS by the image-schema (THROWABLE) OBJECTS.

(230) وما عابَ الزَّمانُ عليَّ لَوْني ولا حَطَّ السَّوادُ رَفيعَ قَدري

Thus, the time didn't **defame** (*ʕāba*) me (*ʕalayya*) with the color of my [skin] – [it didn't prove it was my shameful defect] – and [my] Blackness didn't put down the heights of my abilities (cf. t21A:66).

The metaphor *ʕayb*-SHAMEFULNESS- SHAME IS *ʕayb*- DEFECT is well present in LEAP also in form linguistic expressions of the elaborations of the category *ʕayb*-DEFECT. TBD (iSk: 179–80) provides several examples of members of this category, which take place in the conceptualization of *ʕayb*-SHAMEFULNESS and seem to correspond to the metaphoric models *ʕirḍ* IS WHOLE and ONE'S *ʕirḍ* IS ONE'S BODY (SIDE) structuring the schema of *ʕirḍ*-HONOR. Thus, *ʕayb*-SHAMEFULNESS might be referred to as *waṣma* (iSk: 179), implying the scenario of making a crack or fracture, which does not break up (cf. LsA12: 762), which, on the one hand, holds the SUPERFICIAL trait of *ʕayb* (cf. *ʕayb* is on someone), and on the other hand, relates to the image- schema of WHOLE structuring conceptualization of *ʕirḍ*. Similarly, this image-schema is called-up by the concept of *wakaf* "leaking" also participating in the conceptualization of *ʕayb*-SHAMEFULNESS (LsA9: 433).

The schema *ʕayb*-SHAMEFULNESS-SHAME is elaborated by several subschemas encoding the knowledge about what pre- Islamic Arabs considered to be shameful. Prototypically, the category *ʕayb*-SHAMEFULNESS- SHAME covered visible, physical defects of an individual, which might be observed in (232) by ʕAntara Ibn Šaddād (cf. also t30B:55–56). The historical data confirms that pre-Islamic Arabs used to shame people for all sorts of such physical defects (cf. ʕAlī 1993b: 304, 596. 660–1). However, the data from CEAP suggests that such shamed *ʕayb*s always indicated some devaluating traits of a person. For instance, in aforementioned (223) by Ibn Muqbil, the disability of the poet[6] is described as *ʕayb*. Perhaps, it is so, because it clearly points towards weakness, and as we learned in the chapter on *karam*, in pre-Islamic Arabic society, strength – *ʕizz* – was an important part of one's worth being the guarantee of respect and survival in the harsh environment of the homeland of Arabs (ʕAlī 1993b: 608).

(231) حوَى كلَّ حُسنٍ في الكَواعِبِ شَخْصُها فَلَيْسَ بِها إلّا عيوبُ الحَواسِدِ

Her posture is full with the beauty of her firm breasts – and there are no **defects** (*ʕuyub*) in her, except of [the fault] of envying [her] (cf. t21A:59).

Similarly, a physical defect indicating some devaluating trait and thus being *ʕayb* was the black skin color. For ʕAntara Ibn Šaddād, his black skin was what his opponents (and sometimes even his folk men) considered his *ʕayb*, as it was

6 Ibn Muqbil was blind on one eye (cf. t36A:3).

depicted by him in a number of instances, such as (16) or (225). Of course, the sole color is not as much shameful as the quality it implied, namely, the IMPURE BLOOD and the lack of ability to act HONORABLY it indicated, which I have discussed in the previous chapter.

As one can see, shameful physical defects were considered being someone's *ʕayb* only because they implied some faults in one's character. Thus, still at the center of the category *ʕayb*-SHAMEFULNESS- SHAME, yet less prototypically, there is the subcategory, which covers defects of one's character. Perhaps, such extension parallels the one of *ʕayb*-DEFECT IN OBJECT, which could also cover DEFECTS in abstracta (such as a law or custom) based on the metaphor ABSTRACT OBJECTS ARE PHYSICAL OBJECTS. Here, we can see the extension of the category SHAMEFUL DEFECT from physical – yet indicating abstract properties – traits to abstract traits *per se*, i.e., those of one's character. In general, the data from CEAP suggests that someone's character was only evaluated from the perspective of *karam*. Thus, any *ʕayb* being a SHAMEFUL DEFECT OF CHARACTER seems to indicate one's inability to be *karīm* as it is meant in (233) by Ḥassān Ibn Ṯābit, who juxtapose the lack of *karam* of Banū Huḏayl – their *luʔm* "baseness, lowness" – with their *ʕuyūb* (sg. *ʕayb*). Consequently, one can perceive *ʕayb* as DEFECTIVENESS of one's *murūʔa*. Therefore, in CEAP, *ʕayb* is meant when someone proved to not be eloquent (cf. t38A:9–13) or a coward without warfare skills (cf. t17A:28–32; t31A:129; t26A:130). Thus, one's *ʕayb*s made one unable to react in a proper – i.e., expected from *karīm* – way, which might be seen in (234) by ʕAntara Ibn Šaddād, who states that *ʕuyūb* perplex cowards by their SHAMEFULNESS. This must have indicated that *karam* – i.e., BEING *karīm* – can dismiss any accusation of being of *ʕayb* (cf. t21A:10; t21A:87).

(232) ولكنّ الرجيعَ لهمْ مَحَلٌّ بهِ اللؤمُ المُبَيَّنُ **والعيوبُ**

But they have their seat in [the water tank] of Rağīʕ, where [you will find] proved ignobility (*luʔm*) and **shamefulness** (*ʕuyūb*) (cf. t38A:42).

(233) وَدَعُوني أَجُرُّ ذَيلَ فخَارٍ عِندَما تُخْجِلُ الجَبانَ **العُيُوبُ**

Thus, they called me so that I pull [forward] a tail of pride – in the time, when **shameful defects** (*ʕuyūb*) were confounding the cowards (cf. t21A:20).

In the light of this, one can understand why the black skin indicating non-*karīm* origin was considered an *ʕayb*. If the origin was perceived as predisposing to *karam*, the impure blood could be seen as one's *ʕayb*, i.e., one's SHAMEFUL DEFECT. Therefore, someone of great ancestry cannot be easily ascribed with *ʕayb* as it is said by al-Ḥuṭayʔa in (224). All in all, now we can see why *ʕayb* was a SHAMEFUL DEFECT. As we learned in the previous chapters, *karam*, being *karīm* was the most important element of one's HONOR-RIGHT TO RESPECT. Ergo, if there is any DEFECT, which diminishes one's ability of performing *karam*, it must be SHAMEFUL, i.e., reducing one's HONOR.

Moving from the center of the category *ˁayb*-SHAMEFULNESS-SHAME, one can distinguish the subcategory covering the faultiness of actions. In other words, sometimes, this is someone's ACTION what is considered being DEFECTED. This extension relies on an elaboration of the metaphor ABSTRACT OBJECTS ARE PHYSICAL OBJECTS, and it can be found in CEAP in two places, one of which is (235) (cf. also t08A: 92–98). No wonder then that actions themselves might have been also seen as being someone's *ˁayb*. Such category, originated probably based on metonymic model, occurs at least in five passages from CEAP, such as (236) by ˁAntara Ibn Šaddād. Thus, sometimes, one's speech could be called *ˁayb* – either vulgar (cf. t30B:34) or simply inappropriate (cf. t36A:69–71–72). Quite importantly, in contrary to what Wikan (1984: 637) said about some modern Arabic communities, in LEAP, *ˁayb* meant a shameful action only occasionally. Perhaps, then, with time, this conceptualization has spread taking the place at the center of the category.

(234) بِكُلِّ كَسيبَةٍ **لا عَيبَ** فيها أَرَدتُ ثَراءَ مالي أَو صَلاحي

There is no **fault** (*ˁayb*) in any of my honorable gaining – whether I wanted to enlarge my wealth or my virtue (cf. t14A:46).

(235) حَسَناتي عند الزَّمانِ ذُنوبُ وفعالي مَذَمَّةٌ **وعيوبُ**

My good deeds are with time [seen by others as] crimes, and my honorable deeds [are considered as] reasons for shaming and [as] **faults** (*ˁuyūb*) (cf. t21A:19).

As one can see, the category of *ˁayb*-SHAMEFULNESS-SHAME covers a wide range of shameful markers, which diminish one's *ˁirḍ*-HONOR. Maybe, this was the reason of the statement that no one is really free from *ˁayb*, which one can find in the passage (237) from Ḥassān Ibn Ṯābit. Similar conceptualization is still widespread in the cultural group of Cairo poor (cf. Wikan 1984: 636).

(236) وَخَبِّرْ بالذي لا **عَيْبَ** فيهِ، بصِدْقٍ، غيرِ إخبارِ الكَذوبِ

Thus, tell [me] about someone there is no **fault** (*ˁayb*) in him – [do so] sincerely, not lying (cf. t38A:16).

8.1.2. The concept of *ˁār*

The notion of *ˁār* is frequently described in the literature on modern Arabic SHAME as a more grievous and serious than *ˁayb*. For instance, Abou-Zeid (1965: 247) describes it as an action that threatens the social equilibrium, providing as an example the crime of rape. Nonetheless, as noticed by Wikan (1984: 637), it seems that nowadays the concept of *ˁār* lost its presence in evaluation system of at least some Arabic societies. It also did not appear in the text of the Holy Qurʔān (al-Jallad N. 2010a: 105).

Nonetheless, it was not the case in the pre-Islamic Arabic society. The concept of *ʕār* was an essential element of the evaluation system, in which an individual was scrutinized by their WORTH or VALUE for the community. It was as important for pre-Islamic Arabs as the concept of *ʕayb*, what we can deduce based on the number of occurrences of the lexeme *ʕār* in CEAP: NO: 30 for *ʕār* vs. NO:31 for *ʕayb*. It seems *ʕār* was a stigma indicating UNWORTHINESS of a person, which had serious consequences for them. It was then DISGRACE or DISHONOR ascribed to someone, whose HONOR-RIGHT TO RESPECT was openly questioned or even denied. What is quite important here is that *ʕār*-DISHONOR was not by any means an opposite of *ʕirḍ*-HONOR: *ʕār* was what diminishes one's RIGHT TO RESPECT, which itself was more like a BODY PART – it could not be fully lost nor destroyed, but it could be damaged, i.e., reduced (cf. Stewart 1994: 129).

ʕār was a stigma that was ascribed to someone for their action or quality. It might be then seen as NOTORIETY or perhaps better, as INDICATION of NOTORIETY. It seems to be mostly a marker assigned to an individual; in some places in CEAP, however, it is also presented as extending onto their kin group (cf. t20A:50) or as being acquired by the entire group (cf. t26A:7–6; t38A:300; t40A:66–67). The extension of DISHONOR upon the entire kin group is a phenomenon recorded in many societies (cf. Campbell 1965: 145).

ʕār was ascribed to someone in the action of *ʕayyara*, which is derived from the same consonantal root √ʕYR. One can assume that the verb is a part of the linguistic frame associated with the schema *ʕār*, for instance, based on (238), a passage attributed to aš-Šammāḫ Ibn Ḍirār. The verb *ʕayyara* meaning thus "defaming, vilifying, i.e., deeming something an *ʕār* of someone" occurred in CEAP 23 times (NWC: 0.85), similarly to the verb *ʕāba-yaʕīb* (NO: 21; NWC: 0.76). Metonymically, it could also signify the meaning "to make someone be of *ʕār*" or "to bring *ʕār* onto someone" (cf. t32A:122). The verb was also used in reference to COMPLAINING about a behavior of someone (cf. t07A:94–95), which could be seen as another metonymy foregrounding that one should be ashamed of this behavior. Such an extension bore then some load of exaggeration in one's complain.

(237) تقولُ وقد بلَّ الدموعُ خِمارَها: أبى عِفّتي ومَنْصِبي أنْ أُعَيَّرا

She was saying, after tears had wetted her veil: My nobility and my origin reject [deeds, for which] I could be **defamed** (*ʔuʕayyar*) (cf. t32A:136).

ʕār was clearly linked with both EVALUATION and DEVIATION from the accepted way of behavior. Such a linkage might be assumed based on other derivatives of the root √ʕYR. The verb *ʕayyara* could also signify "weighing something in order to compare value". As reported by KtA3 (238), *ʕayyara* meant that one weighed two pieces of gold, one after another, evaluating their worth by this. EVALUATION is also a key element of the meaning of other derivatives of the root, such as *ʕāyara* "he measured or compared the measures of capacity, and the instruments for weighing, one by or with another (cf. Lane 1968e: 2208)" or *ʕiyār/miʕyār* "a thing with which another thing is measured, or compared, and equalized (Lane 1968e: 2209)" etc. Other derivatives, such as *ʕāra-yaʕīr* "to go astray, to get loose (LsA4: 716)" and *ʕāʔir* "astray (AsS: 830)", clearly refer to concepts deriving in a way from the idea of DEVIATION – mostly in the form of going astray (vs. obeying the owner) (cf. KtA3: 253; AsS: 830, LsA4: 716).

Ergo, one can assume that *ʕār* was a negative evaluative marker, which was assigned to a person in the action of *ʕayyara*, implying EVALUATION. What was then the subject of such an evaluation? Data from CEAP suggests two shameful factors, for which one could be ascribed with *ʕār* – actions/behavior and personal qualities – both being present in the sample (239).

(238) يَقُولُ النَّاسُ لي في الكَسْبِ **عارٌ فَقُلْتُ العارُ** في ذُلِّ السُؤالِ

People say that collecting wealth is **disgraceful** (*ʕār*) – and I say: **what is disgraceful** (*ʕār*) is weakness of the one [who has to] beg [people for help] (cf. t37A:120).

First and foremost, *ʕār* was ascribed to someone due to their behavior. In CEAP, such shameful behavior was almost exclusively related to the violation of the code of *karam* – the honorable behavior of *karīm*. Therefore, *ʕār* was ascribed to people because of their lack of warfare skills or cowardice (cf. t38B:213–215; t33A:45; t17A:89– 97; t16A:69; t17A:108– 111; t29A:71), from among which fleeing from the battlefield was definitely the most grievous of crimes – as it is depicted by al-Aʕšà in (240). In a similar fashion, one should interpret assigning *ʕār* for dying in the deathbed instead of on a battlefield – as in (241) attributed to the same poet – which is clearly related to pre-Islamic Arabic opinions on the matters of how a man should properly live and die (cf. Dziekan 2008: 85).

(239) فَقَدْ صَبَرْنَا، وَلَمْ نُوَلِّ، وَلَيْسَ مِنْ شَأنِنَا الفِرَارُ
وقدْ فرَرتمْ، وما صبرتم، وَذاكَ **شَيْنٌ لَكُمْ وَعَارُ**

So, we have endured [in the battle] – we did not turn back – because escape is not our habit.
And you fled – you have not endured – and this is your **disgrace** (*šayn*) and [your] **dishonor** (*ʕār*) (cf. t28A:282–3).

(241) فما مِيتَةٌ إنْ مِتُّهَا غَيرَ عَاجِزٍ **بعارٍ**، إذا ما غالَتِ النَّفسَ غُولُها

My death won't be a death in **disgrace** (*ʕār*), [since] it won't be [a death] of a weakling, [who dies] when the demise of [his] soul arrives [naturally] (cf. t28A:176–177).

In fact, link between lack of warfare skills and *ʕār* was the most visible in the data from CEAP. Other behaviors violating the code of *karam* mentioned in the corpus were lack of endurance (cf. t28A:280–282–283), lack of hospitality (cf. t24A:81), breaking an oath (cf. t28A:180), lack of a sound judgement (cf. t37A:34), envy (cf. t37A:120), and boasting/swaggering (cf. t28A:82–84–85).

The corpus suggests that *ʕār* could be conceptualized as a matter of choice of an individual, who always had a chance to behave properly, i.e., like *karīm*. This might be deduced from a metaphor VIOLATING CODE OF *karam* IS BUYING *ʕār*, which can be found in two verses attributed to al-Aswad an-Nahšalī (t16A:69) and al-Aʕšà (t28A:180). As one can see in (242) by al-Aʕšà, *ʕār* can be BOUGHT – i.e., exchanged – for *makruma*, an honorable deed, a deed of *karam*. Both *ʕār* and *makruma* are conceptualized by the image-schema OBJECT. Such an OBJECT could possibly become possessed by someone. *Makruma* can be easily conceptualized as a piece of one's wealth, possession, based on the previously discussed schema *ḥasab* IS A COUNT OF ONE'S *makārim* (sg., *makruma*). In other words, one's *ḥasab* is their HONOR-related possession, consisting of *makārim* – deeds of *karam*. Thus, while facing a challenge, one can choose between being *karīm* – and buying *makruma* – or violating the code of honor – and exchanging that possible *makruma* for an *ʕār*.

(241) وَقالَ: لا أشْتَرِي **عاراً** بِمَكْرُمَةٍ. فاختارَ **مَكْرُمةَ** الدُّنْيا على **العارِ**

And [Samawʔal] said: "I do not purchase **disgrace** (*ʕār*) in exchange for a deed of honor (*makruma*)." Thus, he chose the honorable deed (*makruma*), which world [will remember], rather than **disgrace** (*ʕār*) (cf. t28A:180).

One could be ascribed with *ʕār* also due to their attachment or joining to a tribe of a bad reputation (cf. t39A:313), also by marring into it (cf. t21A:44–45). This conceptualization reflects the pre-Islamic Arabic conception of equalizing belonging to a tribe by birth and by choice (cf. section 4.4.3.). Clearly, it also connects to the evaluation of low birth or mixed, impure origin. Interestingly, *ʕār* could be also assigned to someone because of their sedentary, farming life – as it is in (243) attributed to Aws Ibn Ḥağar. This, of course, reflects the well-known disdain of pre-Islamic Arabs towards such a lifestyle.

(242) **وَعَيَّرْتَنا** تَمرَ العِراقِ وبُرَّهُ وَزادُكَ أيْرُ الكلبِ شَوَّطَهُ الجَمْرُ

You **defamed** (*ʕayyarta*) us for the dates of Iraq and its crops – and your provisions [consist] of a dog penis smoked in the burning coal (cf. t26A:38).

Although, according to Abou-Zeid (1965: 247), in some Arabic societies of 20th c., *ʕār* was a shameful deed or atrocity, in CEAP, it is mostly a stigma assigned to someone for committing such a transgression. Nevertheless, at least in three places, *ʕār* refers also to ACTIONS themselves, what suggest existence of a metonymic model *ʕār*-DISHONOR FOR *ʕār*-DISHONORING BEHAVIOR, being elaboration of a frequently attested metonymy EFFECT FOR CAUSE (cf. Radden & Kövecses 1999: 38–9). Its expression can be seen, for instance, in the samples (239) and (245).

(244) وَفَرَرتُ خَشيَةَ أَن يَكونَ حِباؤُهُ **عاراً يُسَبُّ** بِهِ قَبيلي أَحمَسُ

Thus, I escaped out of the fear that publicizing that [poem] will be the **disgrace** (*ʕār*), with which my tribe, [descendants of] Aḥmas, will **be vilified** (*yusabbu*) (cf. t10A:191).

Alternatively, *ʕār* could be ascribed to someone because of their shameful qualities, which I believe one can simply call *ʕayb*s. This means that in CEAP *ʕār* and *ʕayb* are not equal – *ʕār* is a stigma, something which is ascribed to diminish one's RIGHT TO RESPECT, whereas *ʕayb* is something shameful, that is to say, something because of which one could be ascribed with *ʕār*. Most frequently, an *ʕayb*-SHAMEFULNESS-SHAME, for which people deemed someone of *ʕār*, was impure, mixed origin or in other words, ignoble lineage (cf. t17A:166; t34A:136–138). As we learned in the previous chapters, one's *nasab* "lineage" was a major component of their RIGHT TO RESPECT (cf. also Abou-Zeid 1965: 250) and its SHAMEFULNESS could be associated with the conception of heredity of predisposition to *karam*. Such a conceptualization might be observed, for instance, in (238) by aš-Šammāḫ Ibn Ḍirār, quoted earlier, in which a woman evidently states that she cannot behave in a way worth *ʕār* because of her origin. Thus, *ʕār* was assigned to people because of any indication of their low birth, such as their black skin – as in (246) by ʕAntara Ibn Šaddād – or ignobility of their mother – as in (95) by al-Mutalammis – which stems from her low birth or her foreign origin (cf. t20A:40).

(245) **تُعيِّرُني** العِدا بِسَوادِ جِلْدي وبِيضُ خَصائِلِي تَمْحو السَّوادا

The enemies **disgrace** me (*tuʕayyiru-nī*) for the blackness of my skin – but the whiteness of my character remove this blackness (cf. t21A:46).

(95) يُعيِّرُني أُمّي رِجالٌ ولا أَرى **أَخا كَرَمٍ** إِلّا بِأَن **يَتَكَرَّما**
وَمَن كانَ ذا **عِرضٍ كَريمٍ** فَلم يَصُن لَهُ حَسَباً كانَ اللَّئيمَ المُذَمَّما

[There are] men, who disgrace me [because of] my mother [and her base origin]. I do not consider someone **being honorable** (*ʔaḫū karam*), if he does not **behave in an honorable way** (*yatakarram*).
The one, who is of **noble origin** (*ʕirḍ karīm*), and because of that he doesn't care about [his] merits (*ḥasab*), is a low (*laʔīm*) and dispraised man (cf. t10A:16).

Another *ʕayb* – shameful defect – for which one could be assigned with *ʕār* was their old age. As we saw in (31), the passage from Kaʕb Ibn Zuhayr quoted earlier (cf. t34A:22, t34B:26), being old significantly decrease one's ability of performing *karam*, shaming them by this.

Perhaps, the fact that *ʕār* could be ascribed to someone because of their *ʕayb*-SHAMEFULNESS-SHAME, or shameful DEFECT, motivating metonymic extension in form of *ʕār* FOR *ʕayb*, which I believe can be observed in (247), attributed to ʕUrwa Ibn al-Ward. This metonymic model seems to be distributed in a limited way across the cultural group of pre-Islamic Arabs (cf. Sharifian 2008: 113), since it does not appear in other places in CEAP.

(246) وما بيَ من **عارٍ** إخالُ علمتُه سِوى أنّ أخوالي إذا نُسِبوا نَهْدُ

I think there is nothing **shameful** (*ʕār*) in me – as far as I know – except from the fact that when assigned to lineages, my uncles are of [Banū] Nahd (cf. t20A:26).

All in all, as one can expect, *ʕār* ascribed to someone negatively affects their REPUTATION – the foundation of one's HONOR. It is seen as something, which blemishes them as it is in (248) by al-Muhalhil, where the poet uses the verb *šāna-yašīn*, saying by this that *ʕār* can make someone look ugly or bad – it defiles them (cf. Lane 1968d: 1635). Similar relationship between *ʕār* and *šayn* "what makes one look ugly, disfigured (cf. Lane 1968d: 1635)" – derived from *šāna-yašīn* we could observe in (240) quoted earlier. Therefore, based on a metonymic model, *šayn* might be used as a synonym of *ʕār* (aHm: 115).

(247) وَحَادَتْ نَاقَتِي عَنْ ظِلِّ قَبْرٍ ثَوَى فِيهِ المَكَارِمُ وَالْفَخَارُ
لدى أوطانِ أروعَ لمْ **يَشِنْهُ** وَلَمْ يَحْدُثْ لَهُ فِي النَّاسِ **عَارُ**

My she-camel turned away from the shadow of the grave [of my brother Kulayb], in which [so many] honorable deeds and pride have settled down.
[They settled] in the homeland of a brave man, whom **disgrace** (*ʕār*) has [never] **defiled** (*lam yašin-hu*), and who never was disgraced in [the eyes] of people (cf. t04A:33).

ʕār is then a stigma, a bad name, which can stick – *ʔalḥaqa* – to someone (cf. t21A:44–45), and thus conceptualized by that as a visible OBJECT ON SURFACE, being one's *ʕirḍ*-HONOR perceived as their BODY (PART) or SELF. It can also be long-lasting – literally, *ṯābit* "well-established" (cf. t38A:300) – and thus, remembered by others for a long time. The use of the lexeme *ṯābit* is prescribed by the metaphor PERSISTING IS BEING ERECT I discussed before in case of *šaraf* and *mağd* (section 6.5.1.). It accounts also for the conceptualization of *ʕār* in terms of BUILDING/STRUCTURE as in (249) attributed to Aws Ibn Ḥağar.

(248) وصبّحَنَا **عارٌ** طويلٌ بِناؤهُ نُسَبُّ بهِ ما لاحَ في الأُفْقِ كَوْكَبُ

That morning, a tall **disgrace** (*ʕār*) fell upon us – we will be vilified with [this disgraceful tall] construction as long, as it shines like a star on a horizon (cf. t26A:6).

If *ʕār* diminishes one's REPUTATION, it must necessarily affect their RIGHT TO RESPECT. It is then with what people can be defamed in the action of *sabba-yasubbu* meaning "he reviled him, vilified him, upbraided him, reproached him, defamed him, or gave a bad name to him (Lane 1968d: 1284)". As we saw in the chapter on *ʕirḍ* (section 7.5.), the verb primarily means "to cut" and thus "to wound" someone, and it is used in the sense of DEFAMING based on the metaphoric model, in which OFFENDING one's HONOR was conceptualized as WOUNDING it. Naturally, *ʕār* – being a stigma, a bad name – must have been employed as a tool of DEFAMING someone. We can observe such a use of *ʕār* as the term defining the tool of *sabba-yasubbu* in, for instance, (249) and (245) quoted above (cf. also t28A:180). Therefore, the verb *sabba-yasubbu* might be in fact considered a synonym of the verb *ʕayyara*.

The effect of *ʕār* on one's *ʕirḍ* can be seen precisely as diminishing one's WORTHINESS for the community. Thus, trying to be kept within the group, people were avoiding *ʕār* as it is indicated by Abū Ṭālib in (250). Nevertheless, *ʕār* – although can be long-lasting – is not forever and it can be removed. It can fade away, for instance, as it is described by Ḥassān Ibn Ṯābit in (251) or it can be forgiven (cf. t40A:66–67). Of course, the bearer of *ʕār* can erase it by themselves. Such removal of stigma is conceptualized as CLEANING/WASHING, what evidently derives from the metaphor OFFENDING ONE'S *ʕirḍ* IS SOILING IT. *ʕār* is then perceived as something SOILING, which must be WASHED away as it is indicated in (252) by al-Ḫansāʔ, who compared *ʕār* to menstrual blood. As we learned in the previous chapter, the retaliation for an INSULT in al-Ǧāhiliyya usually required blood (cf. ʕAlī 1993b: 547), what should be read rather literarily. Therefore, pre-Islamic Arabs perceived cutting one's throat or cutting off one's head as an appropriate mean of the avenging their OFFENDED HONOR (ʕAlī 1993b: 547). The blood of the victim served to WASH AWAY the *ʕār*-DSIGRACE of the OFFENCE.

(249) ورَهْبَةُ **عارٍ** على أسْرتي إذا ما أتَى أرْضَنا المَوْسِمُ
لَتابعْتُه غيرَ ذي مِرْيةٍ (...)
[If not my] fear of **disgrace** (*ʕār*), which [would fall] upon my family, when [pilgrimage] season arrives to our land,
I would follow him – with no doubts (cf. t24A:81).

(250) إذا الدَّهْرُ عَفَّى في تَقَادُمِ عَهدِهِ على **عارِ** قومٍ كانَ لؤمُكَ في غدِ
As far as the fate erases **disgrace** (*ʕār*) of people in the passage of time, your ignobility will last forever (cf. t38B:97).

(251) لا نَوْمَ حتى (...)
(...) ترحَضوا عَنكمُ **عاراً** تَجلَّلَكمْ رَحْضَ العَوارِكِ حَيضاً عندَ أطْهارِ
There was no sleep until (...)

> you had washed away the **disgrace** (*ʕār*) – which fell upon you – in the manner, in which menstruating women washed away their menstrual blood on a day of purification (cf. t33A:55).

The conceptualization of *ʕār* as something SOILING is an elaboration of the most important image-schema structuring this concept. As I mentioned earlier, *ʕār* was conceptualized in EAP as a visible OBJECT ON SURFACE. That SURFACE implied the EXPOSURE of one's *ʕirḍ*-HONOR seen as their BODY (SIDE). Such a visible – EXPOSED – OBJECT was something decreasing one's RIGHT TO RESPECT, and consequently, something DEVALUATING this someone, thus SOILING. This image-schematic model accounts for the collocation of *ʕār* of such verbs as *ʔalḥaqa* "to stick to" as well as for the use of the preposition *ʕalà* "on, onto" while denoting the location of *ʕār* as it is in (250) quoted above. The fact that *ʕār* was and OBJECT ON someone explains the metaphor *ʕār* IS CLOTH/CLOTHING, which can be seen as instantiated in idiomatic expressions noted in some of TBD (cf. aHm: 115), in which something bringing in *ʕār* is conceptualized as what CLADS this someone with it (e.g., *ʔalbasa-hu al-ʕāra* "he cladded him with *ʕār*" and *sarbala-ha aš-šanāra* "he cladded him with *šanār*, i.e, *ʕār*").

8.1.3. The concept of *ḥayāʔ*

The lexeme *ḥayāʔ* together the verb *istaḥyà* derived semantically from it occurred 28 times in the CEAP (NWC: 1.03). As I mentioned earlier, some scholars (cf. al-Jallad N. 2010a: 102) named the concept *ḥayāʔ* "positive shame", what in a way, is a neat explication of the native, Arabic understanding of this feeling. It is so, because *ḥayāʔ* seems to refer to the sense of SHAME, which prevents one from engaging in SHAME-bringing actions. As al-Jallad N. (2010a: 83) noticed, in the Holy Qurʔān, such SHAME-triggering situations were somehow related to HONOR and social norms, against transgression of which *ḥayāʔ* was advocating. It is then a sense that someone should not do something (al-Jallad N. 2010a: 83), and this is perhaps the most straightforward definition of the meaning of this lexeme.

Judging by the explications provided in CAD, *ḥayāʔ* must have been well intuitive for the early compilers of Arabic dictionaries in the Middle Ages, since neither KtA1 nor AsS provided any explication of it at all. LsA14 (270), however, defines it as "what prevent [its possessor] from disobedience [to God] and from vulgarities", what in a way corresponds with my own conclusions derived from CEAP. Moreover, it seems the definitions provided by Ibn Manẓūr (LsA14: 270–2) link the concept of *ḥayāʔ* and *istiḥyà* with both the code of proper – i.e., accepted – conduct and the concept of *ʕayb*-SHAMEFULNESS-SHAME and *ʕār*-DISHONOR:

إذا لم **تستح** فاصنع ما شئت؛ المراد أنه إذا لم **يستح** صنع ما شاء لأنه لا يكون له **حياء** يحجزه عن المعاصي والفواحش
If you do not **feel shame** (*lam tastaḥi*), do whatever you wish [to do]. What is meant by this is that if one does not **feel shame** (*lam tastaḥi*), he does whatever he wishes [to do], because he has no **shame** (*ḥayāʔ*), which restrains him from deeds of disobedience and vulgarities.
إذا لم **تستح** من **العيب** ولم تخش **العار** بما تفعله فافعل ما تحدثك به نفسك من أغراضها حسنا كان أو ضبيحا
[After Ibn al-Aṯīr:] If you do not **feel shame** (*lam tastaḥi*) of the **shamefulness** (*ʕayb*) [of yours] and do not hide the **disgrace** (*ʕār*), [which is] in what you are doing, so do whatever your soul tells you [to do] – whether it aims a good or vile goal.

To sum it up, one can say that *ḥayāʔ* is a sense, which suggests that this someone should not do something. Moreover, this someone feels that commitment of this something will be negatively evaluated by others and thus, will result in *ʕār*-DISGRACE, as in the sample (253) by al-Ḥuṭayʔa, affecting their *ʕirḍ*-HONOR-RIGHT TO RESPECT, as in (136) by Ḥassān Ibn Ṯābit. Ergo, this someone behaves in a certain way because of *ḥayāʔ*, which in CEAP is expressed mostly by the noun *ḥayāʔ*" in accusative (i.e., *lam yafʕal ḏalika ḥayāʔan* "he didn't do this [feeling] *ḥayāʔ*; cf. t28A:356–357; t39A:147–152–153; t19B:68b; t21A:57–58; t32:215) or rarely by a prepositional phrase with *min* as its head suggesting causality (i.e., *lam yafʕal ḏalika min al-ḥayāʔ* "he didn't do this because of *ḥayāʔ*"; cf. t39A:394).

(252) لا يرفعُ الطَّرْف إلّا عِنْدَ مَكْرُمةٍ مِنْ **الحَياءِ** ولا يُغْفي على عَارِ
[I am a man, who] because of **sense of shame** (*ḥayāʔ*), does raise his sight only, while [committing] an honorable deed, and who is not resting on **disgrace** (*ʕār*) (cf. t39A:394).

(136) وقد أكرَمتُكمْ وسكنتُ عنكم، سَرَاةَ الأوْس، لوْ نَفَعَ السُّكونُ
حياءً أنْ أشاتمكمْ وَصَوْنًا لِعِرْضي، إنهُ حسبٌ سمينُ
Chiefs of [Banū] al-Aws, I would have paid you honor and left you in peace, if [such] a peace had been of any advantage [to me],
[if my] **sense of shame** (*ḥayāʔ*) [had restrained me] against [getting involved in] mutual vilification with you, [and if I had thought of nothing but] to protect my **honor** (*ʕirḍ*) – but [my honor] truly, is [based on] **plenty of merits** (*ḥasab samīn*) (cf. t38A:313).

The action, against which one is restrained by *ḥayāʔ*, is something UNLAWFUL, or perhaps better, SHAMEFUL, and thus, by obeying this sense one keeps themselves *karīm* against dishonor. We can find this conceptualization in (254) by al-Ḥuṭayʔa. Although, similarly to *ʕār*, the schema of *ḥayāʔ* is not structured by noticeable metaphorical models, the fact that *istaḥyà* might be expressed by the verb *ittaʕaba* "he contracted himself, he drew himself together, he shrank (Lane 1968h: 2913)" suggest that the RESTRAINT is an important image-schema constituting its conceptualization (cf. LsA1: 934).

(253) وأكرمْتُ نفسي اليومَ مِن سُوءِ طِعْمةٍ ويَقْنَى **الحياءَ** المَرءُ والرُّمحُ شاجِرُهْ

On that day, I kept myself away from any foul gain – a man keeps [his] **sense of shame** (*al-ḥayāʔ*), [even if] a spear is stuck [in his body] (cf. t39A:183, 188).

The data from CEAP strongly suggest that *ḥayāʔ* were restraining someone against the behavior considered unsuitable for either a man or a woman. Naturally, different expectations were formulated toward men and toward women, which found its expression in the schema of *ḥayāʔ*. Women were expected first and foremost to avoid the contact with stranger men (cf. the sample (255) by al-Ḥuṭayʔa) or being alone in a place (cf. the sample (256) by al-Aʕšà). This could account for the possible later semantic shifts of *ḥayāʔ*, which in a way began to encapsulate the concept of FEMALE CHASTITY or SHYNESS/BASHFULNESS expected from humble women. One can observe this semantic extension in, e.g., (257) by Ibn Muqbil and (258) by ʕAntara Ibn Šaddād. The SHYNESS element of *ḥayāʔ* might be also seen in the expectations that a woman must be nice and pleasant to her men or even to strangers (cf. t38A:121).

(254) ولمَّا رأتْ مَن في الرِّحال تَعَرَّضَتْ **حياءً** وَصَدَّتْ تَتَّقِي القومَ باليَدِ

Thus, when she saw who accompanied me, she turned [her face] on a side out of the **sense of shame** (*ḥayāʔ*), and veiled [her face] with [her] hand against [the sight of] people (cf. t39.A:147, 151–2).

(255) لا أراها في خَلاءٍ مَرّةً، وهي في ذاكَ **حَياءً** لمْ تُزَنْ

Not once, have I seen her [alone] in a place without other people – she [behaves] like this because of her **sense of shame** (*ḥayāʔ*), [which she keeps, so that no one could] judge [her as shameless] (cf. t28A:356–357).

(256) تَشَكَّتْ بِبَعْضِ الطَّرْفِ حتَّى فَهِمْتُهُ **حَياءً** ، وما فاهَتْ بهِ الشَّفَتانِ

[My wife] was complaining by [making a sign] with one of [her] eyes – her lips didn't utter [a single word] – until I understood [the fact that she is making signs with her eyes instead of speaking] as her **shyness/sense of shame** (*ḥayāʔ*) (cf. t36A:238).

(257) فولَّتْ **حياءً** ثُمَّ أرْخَتْ لِثامَها وقد نَثَرَتْ من خِدِّها رَطْبَ الوَرْدِ

Thus, she turned back because of her **shyness/ sense of shame** (*ḥayāʔ*). Then, she loosened her veil, spreading from her cheek moisture [like] rose [dew] (t21A:58).

Similarly to what one can find in CEAP, *ḥayāʔ* as SHYNESS was an important element of women's concern for HONOR yet in 20th c. Jordanian villages (cf. Dodd: 1973: 42). SHYNESS, however, was restricted mostly to women (cf. Dodd: 1973: 42) and it was considered SHAMEFUL for men (Abou-Zeid 1965: 246). Such female only sense of SHAME could be in fact found in many cultures, in which it is referred to as Spanish *vergüenza* or Greek *dropē* (Peristiany 1965: 42, 146). For the most part, all of them – *ḥayāʔ*, *vergüenza, dropē* – imply sexual shame (cf. Baroja 1965: 88; Campbell 1965: 146).

The Spanish concept of VERGÜENZA is especially interesting, since similarly to *ḥayāʔ*, it covers both a "concern for repute" – which links to one's HONOR – and SHYNESS/BASHFULNESS (Peristiany 1965: 42). It is then a similar sense of the right behavior and someone who does not have it – who is *sin vergüenza* – is of SHAME, is DISHONORED. The "concern for repute" can be more closely associated with male conduct. Thus, in this sense, both *ḥayāʔ* and VERGÜENZA could be seen as preventing behavior unsuitable for a man. In pre-Islamic Arabic culture such a shameful behavior mostly overlapped with the violation of the code of *karam*.

Only losing one's *ṣabr*-ABILITY OF ENDURANCE was prevented by *ḥayāʔ* at both men (cf. (259) by al-Aʕšà) and women (cf. 53 by al-Ḥuṭayʔa). Of course, as we learned in the chapter on *karam*, the code of *karīm*-noble behavior was also to a limited extent expected from a woman – especially from a *šarīfa*, noble woman, who also was required to be generous and hospitable, magnanimous and enduring, etc. Nevertheless, the full code of HONOR applied rather to men – or at least it was so in its more military and strength related elements. Thus, *ḥayāʔ* was restraining someone from being meager (vs. GENEROSITY) as in (261) by Ḥātim aṭ-Ṭāʔī, and from other *karam*-contradicting actions, such as not trusting a brother/companion (cf. t37A:37), non-magnanimity (t2:215; t36A:69–71–72; t38A:311–313), lack of hospitality (cf. t36A:111), but also opposing one's chief/leader during a war (cf. t10A:215–218).

(258) ألا **تقنى حَيَاءَكَ**، أوْ تَناهى بُكاءَكَ مِثْلَ ما يَبْكي الوَليدُ
[The poet addresses himself:] Isn't it [high time] to **apply** your **sense of shame** (*ḥayāʔ*), and stop crying like a crying child? (cf. t28A:320–1)

(259) تلك الرَّزِيَّةُ لا رَزِيَّةَ مِثْلُها فاقْنَيْ **حياءَكِ** لا أبا لكِ واصْبِري
This tragedy has no equal, so – girl who doesn't know her father – **keep** your **sense of shame** (*ḥayāʔ*) and endure! (cf. t39A:268–9)

(260) وإنّي **لأسْتَحيي** صِحابيَ أنْ يَرَوْا مكانَ يدي، في جانب الزادِ، أقرعا
Truly, I would **feel ashamed** (*ʔastaḥyī*) in front of my companions, [if] while placing my hand next to the provisions, I didn't put something in there (cf. t19B:68).

Therefore, one can perceive *ḥayāʔ* as a sense or a conscience directing someone to perform *karam* or to stick to the code of honorable behavior, as it is indicated by Kʕab Ibn Zuhayr in (49). It dictates then to avoid shameful behavior and commit only *makārim* – the honorable deeds (cf. t39A:394). Thus, having such a sense (i.e., proving that one follows it) must have been a reason for pride (cf. t37A:37). In a way, what could be observed in CEAP, *ḥayāʔ* was similar to other "moral senses" directing the behavior of an individual, such as *ʕafāf* "abstaining from unlawful behavior" (cf. t37A:37; t38B:81), *ʔadab* "good manners" (cf. t37A:37), or *dīn* "custom obedience" (cf. t36A:69–71–72). Perhaps, one can perceive them as subcategories of a broader schema of MORAL SENSE encompassing the knowledge about the character traits, which encourage appropriate – i.e., socially accepted – behavior.

(49) إنّي امْرُؤٌ **أقْنِي الحَيَاءَ** وشِيمَتِي كَرَمُ الطبيعةِ والتجنُّبُ للخَنا

Truly, I am a man – I **apply** (ˀ*aqnī*) my **sense of shame** (*ḥayāˀ*), my natural temper is nobility of character and avoidance of vulgarity (cf. t34B:11).

The SENSING *ḥayāˀ*-SHAME was referred to by the verb *istaḥyà*. More precisely, one can say that *istaḥyà* meant "feeling something because of the sense of *ḥayāˀ*; being/feeling ashamed because of some deeds, which *ḥayāˀ* deems unlawful", as it can be observed in (262) by Ibn Muqbil. Thus, *istaḥyà* falls in a proximity to English concept of FEELING SHAME or BEING ASHAMED, and its nominal derivative – *istiḥyāˀ* – might be considered referring to a concept similar to the English SHAME, being an emotion. This means then that *ḥayāˀ* itself was not SHAME *per se*, but it was only the sense, which could trigger this feeling, expressed by *istiḥyāˀ*.

(261) وإنّي **لأستحْيِي** وفي الحَقِّ مُسْتَحًى إذا جاء باغِي العُرْفِ أنْ أتَعَذَّرا

Truly, I **feel shame** (ˀ*astaḥyī*), and indeed, it would be something shameful (*mustaḥàn*), if a man seeking good had come [to me] and I refused to aid [him] (cf. t36A:111).

The verb *istaḥyà* was complemented either by a direct object in accusative or by a prepositional phrase with *min* as its head (cf. t19B:46). The first case scenario precluded compliment in the semantic form of a PERSON, and it expressed felling SHAME in front of someone because of the sense of *ḥayāˀ*, which dictates certain behavior directed towards this someone. In the latter scenario, the prepositional phrase expressed the reason of feeling SHAME, i.e., something, which is perceived by the sense of *ḥayāˀ* as unlawful. This second scenario could also – I believe – expressed meaning similar to the English construction *I would hate X to be Y*, what I find of the best use in translating (263) by Ḥātim aṭ-Ṭāˀī. As one can see in the examples (262) and (263), frequently, the expression ˀ*astaḥyī* "I feel shame; I follow my sense of shame" is accompanied by the intensification marker *la-* (cf. Górska 2015: 48–50), what could suggest the importance of stressing one's FEELING SHAME for their overall evaluation. At last, the verb *istaḥyà* in imperative mood (i.e., *istaḥyi!* "feel SHAME!") was also employed as an exclamation, which seems to expressed the meaning of the English exclamation "Shame on you!", as it is in (264) by al-Mutalammis.

(262) وإنّي **لأستَحيي** منَ الأرْضِ أنْ أرَى بها النّابَ تَمشي، في عَشِيّاتها الغُبْرِ

Truly, I **would hate** (ˀ*astaḥī*) to see [my] land, in which old she-camels wander and are left behind after the sunset (cf. t19B:46).

(263) خيرٌ مِنَ القَومِ العُصاةِ أميرَ هُم، يا قومِ **فَاستَحيوا**، النِساءُ الجُلسُ

Shame on you (*fa-staḥyū*), people – women sitting at home are better than men mutinying against their leader! (cf. t10A:218).

The sense of *ḥayāʔ* is structured by the image schema OBJECT and in general, it is perceived as something one POSSESSES. Thus, the noun *ḥayāʔ* referring to a POSSESSED OBJECT frequently collocates with the verb *qaniya-yaqnà* as, for example, in (265) by al-Aʕšà, as well as in the passages (259), (260), and (49) quoted earlier (cf. also t39A:180–183–188; t20A:35–36; t30A:97–98; t38A:121). The verb is considered a synonym of *lazima-yalzam* meaning "he kept it close, clave, clave fast, clung, or held fast to it; he preserved a thing (Lane 1968h: 3009)". This collocation instantiates the metaphorical mapping in form of APPLYING THE SENSE OF *ḥayāʔ* IN ONE'S BEHAVIOR IS PRESERVING *ḥayāʔ*, HOLDING IT FAST, NOT LETTING IT GO. In other words, *ḥayāʔ* is conceptualized as a POSSESSED OBJECT, which one has to HOLD FAST, i.e., OBEY it. This means that *ḥayāʔ* is conceptualized in parallel to one's wealth (cf. LsA15: 233–234). Therefore, as much as one can lose their wealth, one can also lose their *ḥayāʔ*, meaning by that one's failure in sticking to the proper behavior, what we could also see in (265) by al-Aʕšà.

(264) فَاقْنَ **حَيَاءً** أنتَ ضَيّعْتَهُ، مَا لَكَ بَعْدَ الشّيبِ مِنْ عَاذِرِ

So, **keep** (*fa-qna*) the **sense of shame** (*ḥayāʔ*), which you have lost, [since] besides your grey hair, nothing can be your excuse (cf. t28A:142–3).

Perhaps, this conceptualization of *ḥayāʔ* is still persisting in MSA, as in the already quoted passage from the book *Mawt Ṣaġīra* (*A small death*) by Muḥammad Ḥasan ʕAlwān, in which some people *let go* their *ḥayāʔ*, thus it *went away*, and they could not behave otherwise than shamelessly.

يتكلمون بالخليع من القول ويمارسون الشنيع من الفعل وقد ذهب حياءهم وقلّت **مروءتهم**

They were talking in foul speech and practicing abhorrent actions, [since] their **sense of shame** (*ḥayāʔ*) had gone and their manliness (*murūʔa*) had dwindled (ʕAlwān 2017: 458).

8.2. Conclusions

To sum it all briefly up, pre-Islamic Arabic SHAME-DISHONOR model subsumed at its core three notions: *ʕayb*, *ʕār*, and *ḥayāʔ*, which all pertained in a way to HONORABILITY encoded as the script for BEING *karīm*. The concept of *ʕayb* defined SHAMEFULNESS of someone's BODY, CHARACTER, or even ACTION, as preventing this someone from performing like *karīm*. The *ʕār* was a STIGMA – a mark attached to someone that failed at being *karīm*-NOBLE/HONORABLE. Its attachment DIMINISHED one's *ʕirḍ*-HONOR-RIGHT TO RESPECT, by indicating that they are not *karīm* people. Finally, *ḥayāʔ* was a special sense – a moral compass – that helped people navigate within the socially acceptable modes of behavior, prompting to follow the rules of *karam* and preventing the conduct that might be of *ʕayb* and – as a consequence – could result in *ʕār*.

This model clearly links to the model of HONOR, although this linkage is not direct. First and foremost, SHAME-DISHONOR cannot be placed as the simple opposite of HONOR. This is because none of the HONOR-pertaining concepts – *ʕirḍ* and *šaraf* – did have an anti-value. As noticed by Stewart (1994: 129), modern *ʕirḍ* does not seem to have a counterpart in the same fashion as European HONOR pairs with DISHONOR. He realized that – at least in modern Arabic – there is not such a concept as ANTI-*ʕirḍ*. Similarly, *ḥasab* does not pair with an opposite – in LEAP, as we saw, one could only have "low and dispraised" *ḥasab* (cf. t10A:16), meaning "a count of honorable deeds suitable for a base person". On the other hand, *šaraf* being the HONOR-PRECEDENCE, which granted RIGHT TO RESPECT based on one's social standing, seems to be accompanied by *luʔm* "lowness, baseness" as its counterpart. Nevertheless, as we learned, this relationship strongly derived from the conceptualization of the HONORABILITY, being stereotypically implied by HIGH SOCIAL STANDING. In fact, as we saw, *luʔm* was rather implying a conflated notion of BASENESS in both senses – social as LOW SOCIAL POSITION and moral as LOW, IGNOBLE BEHAVIOR. Thus, even this concept was not a precise counterpart of either *šaraf* or *karam*.

Nevertheless, the link between SHAME-DISHONOR and HONOR existed, and it pertained mostly to the evaluation of someone's behavior and the consecutive positive or negative assessment of it. This evaluation, as noted by Wilson & Lewandowska-Tomaszczyk (2021: 457), was "how one perceives how one is viewed through the eyes of others rather than just [positive or] negative assessment per se." These two models – positive and negative evaluation – I believe, can be subsumed within a broader one that will not be exactly SOCIAL EVALUATION OF ONE'S BEHAVIOR, but something resembling a more abstract scenario of SOCIAL EVALUATION OF AN INDIVIDUAL. I will discuss this model in detail in the following, concluding chapter.

In other words, not only one's CONDUCT was assessed in terms of their HONORABILITY, but also – so to say – their WORTHINESS as an individual for the whole group. Thus, while EVALUATING someone, the community always declared them either WORTHY or UNWORTHY of the persistence within its limits. Primarily, UNWORTHINESS implied DEFECTIVENESS, and this is exactly the most general SHAME conceptualized in LEAP – *ʕayb*-SHAME-DEFECT – being DEFECT of more or less physical nature. Similarly, the UNWORTHINESS might have been indicated also by one's stigma or notoriety deriving from their SHAMEFUL/DISHONORABLE BEHAVIOR or QUALITIE. Such a concept – SHAME-DISHONOR-NOTORIETY was referred to in LEAP by the lexeme *ʕār*.

The *ʕayb* and *ʕār* were then devaluating marks ascribed to an individual who was told to be of less VALUE and thus who should have had less RIGHT TO RESPECT. In the scientific literature on SHAME in contemporary Arabic societies, these marks are mostly assigned to behavior (Wikan 1984: 637) – or more precisely to one who failed "to observe the rules of good manners (Abou-Zeid 1965: 245)", in other words, rules of *karam*. Nevertheless, in the light of my study, I assume that in LEAP both *ʕayb* and *ʕār* had also non-behavioral component. In fact, *ʕayb* is most often a SHAMEFUL DEFECT rather than SHAMEFUL ACTION. Similarly, *ʕār* might have also been ascribed to someone due to the factors different than their conduct only. What I believe is present in the conceptualizations of LEAP, as well as of contemporary Arabic culture, is the fact that *ʕayb* is related to an individual, whereas *ʕār* can have extensional effect – it falls upon the individual together with their social group (cf. Abou-Zeid 1965: 252).

Finally, the schema of *ḥayāʔ* seems to have corresponded to English conception of SHAME-CONCERN FOR REPUTE or SHAME-REMORSE. It covers first and foremost what Nader al-Jallad (2010a: 39) calls "good shame", that is, a feeling which holds an individual against committing shameful deeds. One should understand it more as a moral sense activated in SHAME-triggering situation or in any "honor-threatening incidents (al-Jallad N. 2010a: 83)", which might be of "the focus of positive or negative attention (al-Jallad 2010: 83)". As noticed by al-Jallad N. (2010a: 82), in Qurʔān, such a moral sense is associated with sexuality and sexual conduct. In LEAP, however, it was of much broader use and could be seen as a moral compass, which dictates one to be *karīm*, to follow the code of *karam*.

The concept of *ḥayāʔ* is a base of conceptualization of all kinds of SHAME feeling, which are triggered by it, such as *tawba* resembling SHAME-REMORSE (cf. LsA1: 276 and KtA1: 191; cf. Wilson & Lewandowska-Tomaszczyk 2021: 457), *ẖağal* being PARALYZING, PERPLEXING SHAME (cf. t21A:20), and *ḥišma* approximating SHAME-WITHDRAWAL, AVOIDANCE (cf. Abu-Lughod 1986: 103–17; cf. Wilson & Lewandowska-Tomaszczyk 2021: 457; cf. also t38B:222). Moreover, the model of SHAME-DISHONOR must be yet completed by other SHAME related concepts – such as *ẖizy* "something that proves that someone is of *ʕār*", or INSULT/SHAMING/DISHONORING concepts (e.g., *lāma-yalūm* "blame, censure, reprehend" or *šatama-yaštum* "to revile, to vilify, to reproach, to defame"). Nevertheless, they all seem to relate to *ʕayb*, *ʕār*, or *ḥayāʔ* in one way or another.

9. Conclusions: HONOR and SHAME in LEAP

In this book, I have presented the conclusions of a case study, in which I applied the methodology of Cultural Linguistics in the examination of cultural conceptualizations of HONOR in LEAP. In other words, I aimed to depict the pre-Islamic Arabic perception of HONOR and the way, in which this perception affected the linguistic choices of LEAP offered to al-Ǧāhiliyya Arabs in the discourse on this phenomenon. Thus, in the previous chapters, I described in detail the most essential LEAP imageries of HONOR, defining culture-driven categorization of different social phenomena subsumed by this notion in European languages, as well as schematized knowledge encoded by the cultural categories. This knowledge might be seen as the basis of the encyclopedic meaning of the lexical items used in reference to these categories. Moreover, my description provided the information about structuring principles holding between the HONOR-related categories-schemata and other elements of the conceptual system of pre-Islamic Arabic culture. These principles were depicted as conceptual metaphors and associated image-schematic models. Additionally, by analyzing the metonymies, I pointed towards the encoded knowledge of the contiguity between different types of conceptual entities – cultural schemata and their elements. By this, I presented the perception of salience of some concepts in the broader conceptual context, as well as of special relationships between them. All in all, I characterized the specifics of the semantic frames for discourse about honor in LEAP.

Finally, in this chapter, I would like to integrate the conclusions presented in the previous chapters a bit further, postulating a sketch of pre-Islamic Arabic cultural model of HONOR. As we learned, a notion of model might be a bit confusing in CL, yet here after Sharifian (2008: 251) I will regard it as something, which "characterize[s] higher nodes of our conceptual knowledge and that encompass[es] a network of schemas, categories and metaphors". In other words, in the subsections below, I will subsume the previously rendered schemata (and other cultural conceptualizations) in a more integrated manner.

Consequently, by adding in my conclusions on pre-Islamic Arabic conception of SHAME-DISHONOR, I will postulate a broader cultural model that I believe, can afford better understanding of pre-Islamic Arabic interplay between HONOR and SHAME in the context of the society of al-Ǧāhiliyya.

9.1. The cultural model of HONOR in LEAP

The detailed conclusions on HONOR-related phenomena in LEAP were presented in chapters 4–7. At this point, I would like to briefly summarize them by depicting the most important relationship holding between different concepts encoding the pre-Islamic Arabic knowledge on these culture specific social institutions.

9.1.1. HONORABILITY – the essence of HONOR

As we know, in modern European languages, HONOR encompass the encodement of a certain type of behavior rather than the RIGHT TO RESPECT. This behavior is frequently mentioned in such phrases as *man of honor*, in which *honor* serves to denote a certain VIRTUE. This means that nowadays, HONOR in Europe is by far associated with VIRTUOUS CONDUCT or a kind of inner quality of INTEGRITY or even a MORAL COMPASS.

As we have seen, this semantic shift was definitely motivated by the fact that the "original" notion of European HONOR – RIGHT TO RESPECT – could be bestowed based on the positive evaluation of such VIRTUOUS CONDUCT. In other words, HONOR was based on HONORABILITY, i.e., following certain rules – known as CODE OF HONOR – which granted one the RIGHT TO RESPECT in their community. What is worth recalling is the fact that this CODE did not consist of an ideal script of behavior but was rather a bare minimum expected from the members of a given community. The fact that sometimes it could resemble heroic behavior is grounded in the community's perception of itself and its aspiration to be seen on the outside as a heroic one. Simply stated, the community set standards of behaviors, in terms of which it intended to be perceived.

In the pre-Islamic Arabic society, such standards of behavior persisting in different types of communities was referred to by the noun *karam*, the verbal noun denoting the action of *karuma-yakrum*, i.e., "being *karīm*". In other words, a man who followed these standards was termed *karīm*. At first glance, such a statement might seem controversial since these lexemes naturally evoke in the speakers of Arabic language the schema of GENEROSITY rather than that of HONOR. Nevertheless, as I attempted to prove, this was not entirely the case in LEAP.

Frequently, while commenting on pre-Islamic HONOR, researchers tend to see the concept of *murūʔa* as the closest approximate of HONORABILITY. Nonetheless, I believe this notion should be rather seen as a collection of certain qualities – material and more spiritual (i.e., being traits of character) – that made someone able to act like *karīm*. In the historical literature, *murūʔa* is often described as a predisposition expected from a candidate for a *sayyid*, a tribal chief or leader (ʕAlī 1993b: 350). Traditionally, this predisposition was described in form of a set of character traits. In CEAP, the enactment of some of these traits – that is generosity and hospitality, magnanimity, bravery, loyalty, endurance, custom obedience, reasonableness-moderation-forbearance, and eloquence – seems to at the center of the collection of the standards, which served the assessment of al-Ǧāhiliyya community members' RIGHT TO RESPECT (cf. Stewart 1994: 23). Consequently, I believe it is safe to say that the scripts encoding the enactment of these traits can be considered as an approximation of what one can termed pre-Islamic Arabic code of honor.

From among these scripts of behavior, GENEROSITY-HOSPITALITY held a prominent position. This was encoded in a highly culture-specific metonymic mapping *karam*-GENEROSITY-HOSPITALITY FOR *karam*-HONORABILITY. It seems then that GENEROSITY-HOSPITALITY was a prototypical value of HONORABLE/NOBLE BEHAVIOR, to which with time, remaining elements were augmented, forming in the process a full code of honor. Thus, by far, the RESPECT, which a *karīm*-HONORABLE person expected from others was an extension of the RESPECT paid to GENEROUS-HOSPITABLE people. It corresponds to the fact that GENEROSITY-HOSPITALITY was and still is held in high esteem by Arab people. This estimation translates to the fact that one cannot be considered HONORABLE or NOBLE, if not being GENEROUS-HOSPITABLE at the very first place.

The concept of GENEROSITY-HOSPITALITY, upon which the aforementioned metonymic model is founded, is often metaphorically structured by the concept of WATER (Guth 2018: 117–128, 134). For instance, GENEROSITY can be referred in Arabic as *nadà* "dew", and a GENEROUS man as *baḥr* "sea; a large body of water". What is quite interesting, this metaphor might be quite ancient since it finds its support also in the etymological data. It was suggested that the notion of GENEROSITY-HOSPITALITY could be derived from a primary more physical notion of COPIOUSNESS OF RAIN. This intriguing metaphorical conceptualization might actually provide some clues as for an interesting conceptual phenomenon observed in LEAP. Namely, many HONOR-related concepts, such as *ḥasab*-VALUE or *maǧd*-GLORY, are conceptualized in it by means of the notion of (ABUNDANCE OF) WATER. This could indicate the existence of a strong relatedness between GENEROSITY-HOSPITALITY and HONOR. In other words, the salience of GENEROSITY-HOSPITALITY within the model of HONOR resulted in "borrowing" the conceptual devices used in imagining the former in speaking about the latter.

The HONORABILITY of a *karīm* can be also perceived as a kind of NOBILITY but only understood in the native pre-Islamic Arabic terms. Thus, *karīm* was HONORABLE, i.e., NOBLE or even EXCELLENT for their adherence to the standards of the behavior set by their community. The EXCELLENCY of *karam* and *karīm* seems to derive from the conceptualization of RIGHT TO RESPECT as granted because of one's HONORABILITY. Thus, *karīm* as EXCELLENT/GOOD evoked also the whole script of RESPECT/VENERATION, which was to be paid to a man of honor. Therefore, the lexeme *karīm* started being used in reference to different kinds of phenomena and objects, which were deemed by Arab people to be worth their veneration.

All in all, *karam*-HONORABILITY was the major estimate of one's VALUE in the eyes of the community, which assessed its members in accordance with standards set for proper behavior. Because of that, in LEAP, this value was also lexicalized by means of a metonymy, in which the name for the whole scenario/category – *ḥasab*-COUNT – was employed to access a more specific scenario/category of COUNTING one's HONORABLE DEEDS, i.e., *makārim*. The COUNTABILITY – a kind of quantification – of one's HONORABILITY definitely originated as a result of a semi-institutionalization of priding in form of *mufāḫāra* contests, in which men were boasting over each other, *counting* their merits, trying to prove by that who is of more RIGHT TO RESPECT. Consequently, one's VALUE, by means of which they could claim HONOR, was conceptualized in LEAP as an ACCOUNT, what found its expression in the collocation of its denotation, i.e., *ḥasab*. The person of such an ACCOUNT being ample or numerous was referred to as *ḥasīb*.

What is quite important, *ḥasab* contained the whole range of HONORABLE DEEDS of an individual, including the merits of their ancestors. Nevertheless, such "inherited" *makārim* must have been proven being allocated at the right person, thus their heir was expected to show his or her *karam* as well.

Lexicalizing the VALUE/ WORTH, upon which one's RIGHT TO RESPECT was established, *ḥasab* was also metonymically used in reference to other means of claiming RESPECT, such as one's *māl*-WEALTH. It is quite important to note that nearly all of the HONOR-related concepts were somehow related to the notion of WEALTH. It seems to be the effect of prototypicality of GENEROSITY-HOSPITALITY for the HONORABLE BEHAVIOR. Naturally, WEALTH must have been perceived as the means of excelling in the realization of this script. Thus, it was perceived as further granting and securing HONOR of its possessor.

To sum it up, HONORABILITY in pre-Islamic Arabic society was assessed based on the enactment of scripts based upon the traits of a tribal chief. Prototypically, however, it was simply GENEROSITY- HOSPITALITY. Moreover, as an assessed VALUE, it was perceived quantitatively as a COUNT – *ḥasab* – based upon which, one pressed their claim of RESPECT.

9.1.2. RIGHT TO RESPECT

As we learned, the simplest understanding of HONOR implies its treatment as a RIGHT. More precisely, such a RIGHT entitled someone to RESPECT (Stewart

1994: 54). In both pre-Islamic Arabic and European cultures, however, this RESPECT seems to have two facets: ACKNOWLEDGMENT of one's RIGHT to persist within their community of EQUALS and ACKNOWLEDGMENT of one's RIGHT to PRECEDENCE. In LEAP, these two facets are delimited also in terms of lexicalization.

9.1.2.1. **ACKNOWLEDGMENT of one's WORTHINESS: horizontal honor**

The RIGHT TO RESPECT understood as one's RIGHT to persist within their community of EQUALS was referred to in LEAP by the lexeme *ʕirḍ*. More precisely, however, the scheme *ʕirḍ* seems to encompass two conflated notions of HONOR: RIGHT TO RESPECT and REPUTATION-WORTH/VALUE. In other words, in pre-Islamic Arabic society, the RIGHT to full MEMBERSHIP in a community did not differ from the REPUTATION of someone, who was claiming this RIGHT.

What is quite noteworthy, the notion of REPUTATION-WORTH/VALUE seems to encompass two subschemata, which perhaps can be delimited only analytically, i.e., they were in fact one and only phenomenon. These subschemata were INNER VALUE, i.e., SELF-ESTEEM, and EXTERNAL VALUE, i.e., REPUTE or GOOD NAME. The conflation of these notions could suggest that in al-Ǧāhiliyya, one's behavior was evaluated only externally, thus SELF-WORTH was mirroring the assumption of the SOCIAL EVALUATION rather than the actual self-assessment. It could explain the existence of a metaphoric mapping in the form of ONE'S *ʕirḍ*-HONOR FOR ONESELF.

The whole REPUTATION-WORTH/VALUE was established on two related factors, being *ḥasab*-VALUE-COUNT OF HONORABILITY and *nasab*-LINEAGE. By far, the RIGHT TO RESPECT was allocated based on the assessment of an individual in terms of their adherence to the script of *karam*-HONORABILITY. Thus, *ḥasab*-COUNT-VALUE was also conceptualized as *ṣulb*-BACKBONE of one's *ʕirḍ*-HONOR, its fundamental part. On the other hand, one's *nasab*-LINEAGE indicated the extent of one's ability of calling up to arms men by means of *ʕaṣabiyya*, the tribal spirit. It also suggested the information about the quality of these men, thus naturally affecting the QUALITY-VALUE of its possessor. All in all, then, both *ḥasab* and *nasab* clearly indicated one's VALUE, which might be understood as WORTHINESS, i.e., being a certain asset for the entire group/community. The essentiality of *ḥasab* and *nasab* for *ʕirḍ*- RIGHT TO RESPECT-REPUTATION was encoded in WHOLE FOR PART metonymies, which led to the semantic extension of the meaning of the lexeme *ʕirḍ*, which could have been also used in reference to these two estimates of one's VALUE.

Being a conflated notion of RIGHT TO RESPECT and VALUE/WORTH, *ʕirḍ* was conceptualized as a fragile and vulnerable possession. It could be explained by the simile to the conception of self-worth or self-esteem, which might be perceived also as something requiring protection. The vulnerability of *ʕirḍ* was also related to the fact of its entitlements, i.e., the RIGHT to persist within one's community. The harsh environment of the Island of Arabs must have played a role in such a conceptualization, on which I will comment yet further in this chapter. Thus, *ʕirḍ* was conceptualized as (VULNERABLE/FRAGILE) BODY or BODY SIDE, the notions in which the VULNERABILITY/FRAGILITY was especially salient. Consequently, this conceptualization encoded the knowledge that damage done to one's HONOR might have been as dangerous as a damage done to one's BODY.

In contrast to the European notion of RIGHT TO RESPECT, *ʕirḍ*-HONOR does not seem to have been losable. As a VALUE/WORTH, upon which such a RIGHT rested, it could have been only DIMINISHED, yet not erased entirely. Such a DIMINISHED – DAMAGED – *ʕirḍ* was conceptualized simply as less effective in making others pay proper RESPECT to its possessor. It was then imagined in a simile to one's BODY PART, which could have been more or less efficient.

One could DIMINISH someone's *ʕirḍ*-RIGHT TO RESPECT- WORTH mostly by an INSULT, in which the offender accused this someone of DISHONORABLE BEHAVIOR. In other words, the INSULT was a means of QUESTIONING one's HONORABILITY, and, as a consequence, their HONOR. The conceptualizations of INSULTING/OFFENDING were compatible with the model of *ʕirḍ* either as a BODY (SIDE) or PRECIOUS POSSESSED MASS. Thus, one could WOUND the HONOR of someone else, or they could CHUNK OFF a piece out of it. Either way, as a result, this HONOR suffered DIMINISHING and became DAMAGED and less efficient.

Similarly, one's HONOR could also be DAMAGED by SOILING or STAINING it. CLEAN *ʕirḍ* was then the mark of HONORABILITY. This conceptualization in fact could have conflated with the conception defining the honor group – the group of EQUALS adhering to the same code of honor – as the FREE FOLK. In fact, in many places in CEAP, HONORABLE people were referred to as WHITE or of WHITE FACES, which clearly contrasted with the notion of BLACKNESS conceptualizing SLAVEHOOD. In other words, WHITENESS could encode both concepts – the fact that only free people could be considered *karīm*-HONORABLE, and – as a consequence of that – only they could have their *ʕirḍ* CLEAN, i.e., unchallenged.

As I have said, the conflated notions of ESTEEM and SELF-ESTEEM, constituting one's REPUTATION-WORTH, suggest that in fact one's self-assessment must have mirrored the social evaluation of the community. This consequently suggests that one's HONOR could have been perceived as one's global SELF, which found its encodement in a conceptual metonymy ONE'S ʕ*irḍ*-HONOR FOR ONESELF. In other words, an individual seems to have perceived themselves by far in terms of their ʕ*irḍ*-HONOR and HONORABILITY. Consequently, all behavior was always seen as affecting one's RIGHT TO RESPECT, and from the perspective of this effect, all behavior was evaluated – not only by the "court of reputation" of the community, but also by the individual themselves. This could be also seen encoded in yet another metonymy mentioned in Chapter 4., i.e., *faʕāl*-DEEDS FOR *faʕāl*-HONORABLE DEEDS. This conceptualization evidently brings forward the fact that one's actions could have counted only, if considered in the context of the code of honor.

Thus, one can go farther and hypothesize that for pre-Islamic Arabs one's SOCIAL SELF somehow conflated with their (INNER) SELF – they became the indivisible *global* self. Consequently, it meant that an ATTACK launched on one's HONOR-REPUTATION was by far perceived as an ATTACK on its possessor themselves – a WOUND inflicted on one's HONOR was as real as the WOUND inflicted on themselves, i.e., their BODY. Therefore, the need of constant protection of ʕ*irḍ* was a natural and logical consequence.

This protection, however, could have been achieved in two different ways. First, the most obvious was the reflexiveness of HONOR, i.e., painstaking commitment to avenging any – even the most insignificant – affront to oneself. In al-Ǧāhiliyya, this reflexiveness was for the most part violent and cruel – similarly to past European conceptions, pre-Islamic Arabic HONOR "fed on blood". On the other hand, one could protect their RIGHT TO RESPECT, preventing any possible INSULT or OFFENCE, by adherence to the code of *karam*-HONORABILITY. In other words, the more ample one's *ḥasab*-COUNT OF HONORABILITY was, the less damaging an affront could be, having less effect on the overall REPUTATION of someone. Thus, one could COVER-PROTECT their ʕ*irḍ*-HONOR-BODY in the VEIL of *ḥasab*. An important consequence of this conceptualization is the role of one's WEALTH in PROTECTING the HONOR. As we saw, one could also physically SUPPORT their ʕ*irḍ* with their WEALTH, so that it was firmly holding against any ATTACK. Naturally, such an importance of one's WEALTH stemmed from the aforementioned perception of the affluence as a mean of performing HONORABILITY, which definitely links to the fact of the prototypical role of GENEROSITY-HOSPITALITY played within this cultural script of behavior.

The fact that HONOR-REPUTATION/WORTH was protected first and foremost by means of HONORABLE BEHAVIOR, must have translated into the metonymic use of ʕ*irḍ* in reference to INTEGRITY, indicated usually in LEAP by *ḥasab* or *karam*. This means that someone who POSSESSED ʕ*irḍ* was a person, who behaved in a certain way, avoiding breaking the rules of accepted behavior, and knowing how to deal with people. In other words, unchallenged HONOR indicated good PROTECTION, which was nothing else but a proper conduct.

9.1.2.2. **HONOR-PAID and ACCEPTANCE**

What was this RESPECT one was entitled to by means of their *ʕirḍ*-HONOR-REPUTATION/WORTH? As I said, I believe it was a fact of ACKNOWLEDGMENT of one's RIGHT to persist within their community of EQUALS. In other words, RIGHT TO RESPECT was the RIGHT to stay within a group, and the only HONOR-PAID for *ʕirḍ* was a simple recognition of this RIGHT derived from the positive evaluation of one's proper conduct.

In pre-Islamic Arabic culture, this recognition was referred to as *karāma*. It is a very interesting concept, since by far it encapsulates the script of behavior encoded as *karam*. This means that pre-Islamic Arabs recognized other FREE PEOPLE AS EQUALS by applying in their dealing with them the code of *karam*, or its more other-party related elements, such as GENEROSITY-HOSPITALITY, MAGNANIMITY, LOYALTY, FORGIVENESS, etc. In other words, free folk constituted a community of people mutually respecting each other – treating each other well, with curtesy. The concept of *karāma* implied then not a special treatment – a RESPECT PAID to someone in a visible way – but was the simplest rule of respectful coexistence. Thus, ACKNOWLEDGING that someone can stay within the group, was simply treating them in a good manner – not disdaining, scorning them, but living with them in peace. In a way, then, RESPECT-PAID was also indicating the EQUALITY between the group members.

Nevertheless, *karāma* could also be perceived as a certain REWARD – HONOR – being given to someone as a mark of their RIGHT TO RESPECT. Consequently, *karāma* also meant DIGNITY, i.e., being DIGNIFIED, recognized as someone deserving RESPECT, i.e., a good treatment. What is quite interesting, this meaning is in fact the most dominant signification of *karāma* in the modern varieties of Arabic language. The only difference lays in the perception of the range of people, to whom *karāma*-RESPECT should be paid. In al-Ǧāhiliyya, it was definitely restricted to the *karīm* folk, who were RESPECTED by other *karīm*s as EQUALS. *Karīm*s, however, were the only people who belonged to the honor group of *karam*, which as we learned, was perceived as limited to free men and women. This restricted understanding of *karāma* widened with time to encompass eventually the whole humanity, all humans – who deserve RESPECT of others as their EQUALS. In a way then the whole humanity became the community of *karīm*-HONORABLE folk.

The respectful coexistence implied by the script of *karāma* – mutual good treatment of the members of the group – brings us to the notion of ACCEPTANCE of someone as the full member of the community. As we learned, RIGHT TO RESPECT simply meant the RIGHT to be treated as someone belonging to the collective. The recognition of this RIGHT – in form of *karāma* – indicated simply lack of ostracism in any form. Thus, in al-Ǧāhiliyya, HONOR could be understood as simply MEMBERSHIP ACKNOWLEDGMENT.

9.1.2.3. **HONOR-PRECEDENCE**

Thus, as we saw, *ʕirḍ* being a RIGHT was not a matter of a privilege, but of ACCEPTANCE. Whenever the RIGHT TO RESPECT appeared to be a privilege, it became the RIGHT to PRECEDENCE, i.e., to SUPERIORITY over others and to LEADERSHIP. In LEAP, the schema of such HONOR was referred to by the lexeme *šaraf*. Therefore, *šarīf* – a man of *šaraf* – was simply a pre-Islamic Arabic aristocrat.

The main means of conceptualization of *šaraf*, being HIGH SOCIAL STATUS, seems to derive from a quite universal notion of a SOCIAL LADDER. Thus, one's position within their community was perceived by pre-Islamic Arabs as the STEP/STAIR they occupy. Consequently, *šaraf* was simply an ELEVATED PLACE within such imagined hierarchy, and acquiring it was conceptualized as CLIMBING UP or ASCENDING.

Pre- Islamic Arabic HIGH SOCIAL STANDING could have been achieved by means of either exceptional conduct – EXCELLING in the code of HONORABILITY, or by birth within a family of established high position. The EXCELLENCE of the HONORABILITY could have been understood as *maǧd*-GLORY, which by far was granting one the higher social place in the social fabric, by proving exceptionality of its bearer. Such GLORY was conceptualized in many ancient societies as a BUILDING, which was erected for posterity, who could be claiming their ELEVATED POSITION within their community based on this past *maǧd* of their ancestors. This conceptualization of *maǧd* – either of oneself or inherited from their forefathers – as well as its relationship to *šaraf*-PRECEDENCE, was deeply entrenched in LEAP. Perhaps, one can explain it by pointing towards the relationship between a tall, erected BUILDING and an ELEVATED PLACE. In other words, by BUILDING tall GLORY-BUILDING, one prepared for themselves and their descendants a PRECEDENCE-ELEVATED PLACE in their community.

The PRECEDENCE meant first and foremost the priority for LEADERSHIP. *Šarīf* people were simply aristocrats of pre-Islamic Arabic society, in which exercising the power was restricted only to them. Being yet accepted as leaders, they must have always proven their fitness to this role – they must have shown they deserve the PRECEDENCE. In many cultures, NOBILITY is assumed as indicating special moral qualities, which are expected to be manifested in the conduct of NOBLES. In al-Ǧāhiliyya, such a noble conduct was simply the code of *karam*-HONORABILITY. In other words, *šarīf* people were believed to be HONORABLE by default, i.e., by birth. Thus, they were naturally presumed to manifest this default mode of behavior in their conduct. This assumption is most visibly encoded in the conflation of the notion of non-*šarīf* with non-*karīm*, both lexicalized as *laʔīm*. In other words, insofar as not all *karīm* people were considered to be *šarīf*, each *šarīf* person must have always been *karīm*. Thus, *laʔīm* was not only the concept of COMMONNESS or LOW SOCIAL STANDING, but it deeply implied the fact of IGNOBILITY in terms of one's conduct.

What is noteworthy, HONORABILITY expected from *šarīf* people seems to have been a different mode of HONORABILITY, which preserved one's *ʕirḍ*-HONOR-REPUTATION. I believe we can hypothesize that *šarīfs* were supposed to perform *karam* in an exceptional way – not being a "regular" mode of simple adherence to this script of behavior. In other words, only EXCELLING in *karam* was seen as suitable for NOBLES. It could explain why it was *mağd* that granted one HIGH SOCIAL STATUS in the very first place. Perhaps, then such *karam* was supposed to prove one's SUPERIORITY in terms of AUTONOMY and FREEDOM, i.e., being able to survive on their own, without the community, which required "only" the regular *karam*. Such a conceptualization would correspond with the observations of Abu-Lughod she made, while studying Eastern Egyptian Bedouins in the last century (Abu-Lughod 1986: 79).

The fact that *mağd* and exceptional *karam* were indispensable for gaining and maintaining *šaraf* might explain the low frequency of the latter in CEAP. It seems that in EAP, one's HIGH SOCIAL STANDING was not as important to be mentioned as the grounds for its persistence. In other words, pre-Islamic poets shamed and praised people in terms of *mağd* and *karam* – far more present in CEAP – in order to argue against or in favor of their *šaraf*-HIGH SOCIAL STATUS.

Thus, pre-Islamic Arabic nobles were shamed and venerated in poetry, which translates to the fact that they were simply people of much interest in their communities. *Šaraf* was then the RIGHT TO RESPECT being a privilege, i.e., a special treatment, which stood in opposition to the concepts of *ʕirḍ* and its entitlements. Nevertheless, *šaraf* and *ʕirḍ* needed one another – at least in the context of NOBLE people.

First of all, ample, well protected *ʕirḍ* was a mark of one's HONORABILITY. Having such an *ʕirḍ* was to be perceived as a person of INTEGRITY, i.e., a person of honor. This naturally translated to the fact that *ʕirḍ* was also an estimate of one's eligibility for *šaraf*-HONOR-PRECEDENCE.

On the other hand, however, *šaraf* implied one's importance in the community – thus it constituted someone's VALUE/WORTH, upon which one could claim RIGHT TO RESPECT. In other words, *šaraf* assured *ʕirḍ*, protected it, and provided it with additional strong validation. Perhaps, this conceptualization might be the drive of hypothetical later metonymic development of *ḥasab* into the designation of HIGH SOCIAL STATUS. Furthermore, a recognized *šaraf* could be seen even as a compact argument for one's RIGHT TO RESPECT, implying, on the one hand, the exceptionality of one's HONORABLE CONDUCT, and on the other hand, the nobility of their ORIGIN.

9.1.3. HONOR and the group: role of *nasab*-LINEAGE

In collectivist cultures, one's HONOR persists in a binary relationship with their group – be it a family, a tribe, a town/village, or a nation (cf. Wilson & Lewandowska-Tomaszczyk 2021: 457). One of the aspects of the sense of honor is the concern for the repute of the family or the community of an individual. This is because the family/community is one of the major facets of one's social self. Consequently, one can say that these cultures – let us call them *honor cultures* – "can be characterized as having an interdependent (rather than an independent) notion of self (Mosquera, Manstead & Fischer 2016: 834)."

Similarly, in al-Ǧāhiliyya, HONOR – either *ʕirḍ* or even *šaraf* – was not only a matter of an individual, but also of their family or community. In the most basic sense, this individual was expected to stick to the code of honor not only for the sake of the RESPECT he or she received, but also in order to assure RESPECT for the community as a whole. In return, any member of the community could have claimed the HONOR this community enjoyed based only on the mere fact of belonging to it.

In fact, such a binary relationship boils down to the code of honor as the set standards for behavior within a group. As we learned, these standards, being a bare minimum expected from the group members, could sometimes been perceived as heroic or idealistic. This is because the community set the standards, which were supposed to exemplify the intended image of this community outside. In other words, expectations of HONORABILITY translated into the requirement of keeping up a certain image of the members of the group, which formulates these expectations. Thus, consequently one must have defended their own HONOR, preserving by that their GOOD NAME, which granted them the RIGHT to persist within a community of people who prided themselves in possessing a GOOD NAME.

On the other hand, as we saw, an individual could derive much of their HONOR – either *ʕirḍ* or *šaraf* – on the basis of their community. Most frequently, such a community was simply one's family or one's *nasab*-LINEAGE.

First and foremost, *nasab*-LINEAGE was the second most important estimate of one's REPUTATION/WORTH, which indicated the number and quality of supporters one could call up to arms if needed. It means it translated simply into one's power or strength derived from their family group, which could be exercised by means of *ʕaṣabiyya*, the tribal spirit. This phenomenon itself was deeply connected to the notion of HONOR, since it was based on a certain assumption. Ergo, if my kin will be left without support, his or her HONOR will be DIMINISHED. Consequently, such a situation will suggest that his or her kin-group was not able to assist and protect this HONOR. It will translate then to perception of the whole kin-group as weak, powerless, thus the HONOR of all its members – derived from the REPUTATION of this group – will be DIMINISHED too. As one can see, HONOR-REPUTATION of an individual was derived from the HONOR-REPUTATION of their community, which must have protected them in order to maintain this very REPUTATION.

Perhaps, this was the reason of the assumption that HONORABILITY was something one is predisposed to by birth. As I mentioned in earlier, *karīm* people were believed to rise *karīm* children – *karam* was simply something mimicked. Claiming RESPECT of other could then be based on one's ORIGIN only, what seems to have been a frequent situation in al-Ǧāhiliyya. Nevertheless, *karam* of ancestors must have been also proven in one's conduct. Thus, although *nasab*-LINEAGE was perceived as a supporting agent in one's HONORABILITY, after all, it was the adherence to the code of honor of an individual that was the main point of the social evaluation.

In other words, to sum it up, *nasab*-LINEAGE was seen by pre-Islamic Arabs as the source of HONOR in two complementary ways: as the mark of their WORTHINESS and as the predisposing factor in HONORABILITY, translating – after all – to this very WORTHINESS as well.

9.2. The cultural model of SOCIAL EVALUATION OF COMMUNITY MEMBER in LEAP: WORTHINESS

As we learned, in anthropology, HONOR is perceived as one of the "two poles of an evaluation (Peristiany 1965: 27)" which is takes place within a community. The second of these poles is SHAME. Traditionally, then, one can understand both HONOR and SHAME as a reward and a punishment given by the group to its members for the way they conduct themselves. They both pertain to the global self of an individual, which is a subject of "acceptance or rejection by others, self- regulation, and self- evaluation (Wilson & Lewandowska- Tomaszczyk 2021: 457)"

Traditional anthropology perceives one's conduct as the subject of such a SOCIAL EVALUATION. However, based on the data I studied in this book, I would like to propose a different model, in which the community evaluates the individual as a whole. It means that in al-Ǧāhiliyya, one's behavior was only one of the elements evaluated by the group, which granted the RIGHT TO RESPECT – the RIGHT to stay within in – based on an assessed overall VALUE or WORTH of an individual.

In other words, pre-Islamic Arabic "court of reputation" was deeply interested in all the WORTHINESS of a member of the community – their *ḥasab* and *nasab* – which indicated certain qualities affording for the declaration that an individual should be kept within the group. What is quite interesting, the aforementioned bipolar relationship between HONOR and SHAME does not seem to apply to such a model. In short, HONOR – in this model, *ʕirḍ* – appears to be a certain "default" VALUE, which could DECREASE/ INCREASE, whereas SHAME seems to be only a means of DECREASING this VALUE. In other words, one can hypothesize that "by default", every member of the community was deemed VALUABLE/ WORTHY, and only "in vivo" he or she was constantly assessed as for their upkeeping this "default" WORTH. SHAME was only something affecting this WORTH, by being a manifestation of lack of HONORABILITY – actual or only presupposed.

The WORTHINESS/ UNWORTHINESS was not a mere abstract notion but a very tangible evaluation of one's fitness to their community. It was then the assessment of their VALUE for this community, which as simply as it is, considered any individual as WORTHY or UNWORTHY to be kept within. Thus, the pre- Islamic Arabic SOCIAL EVALUATION OF COMMUNITY MEMBER script would imply three major elements: *ʕirḍ*-WORTHINESS, estimates of this WORTHINESS, and RESPECT, being – as we learned – only the ACKNOWLEDGEMENT of the RIGHT to stay within one's group.

9.2.1. Default WORTHINESS: *ʕirḍ* is at the center of SOCIAL EVALUATION

Thus, as I said, *ʕirḍ*, being the RIGHT TO RESPECT founded on one's NAME/ REPUTATION (ESTEEM- SELF- ESTEEM), seems to have been a certain default VALUE of every single member of the community. This VALUE was then something, which could have been consequently INCREASED or DECREASED during one's life. Primarily, however, it derived from one's *nasab*-LINEAGE, i.e., in fact, from one's

SOCIAL STANDING, which could – but did not have to – be *šaraf*. Thus, the "zero" WORTH of an individual was always ascribed based on their ORIGIN.

Nevertheless, this default WORTHINESS was constantly (re)EVALUATED in terms of the conduct of an individual. Thus, the individual was required to adhere to the HONORABLE CONDUCT – *karam* – keeping or increasing their VALUE, derived from the *nasab*-LINEAGE. In the light of this one can understand why *ḥasab*-COUNT OF HONORABILITY contained in fact deeds of both the person themselves and their ancestors. It seems *ḥasab*, as the major estimate of one's WORTH, was seen as a continuous VALUE – the default, derived from the ancestry, and the added one, upheld by this person themselves.

Thus, the individual was responsible for PROTECTING-COVERING their WORTHINESS simply by sticking to the code of *karam*, especially to its prototypical value, i.e., GENEROSITY-HOSPITALITY. *Karam* was then the set-out standards, which defined the estimates of the WORTH for every single group member. I believe that these standards were – at least originally – some qualities, which made a person a good companion or a good community member. In other words, the script of pre-Islamic Arabic HONORABILITY prescribed mostly such behavior, which were positively evaluated as needed or simply useful for a given community as a whole. Thus, *karīm*-HONORABLE man was a man the group wanted to keep within, because of his qualities, which were advantageous for the group as a whole.

I think that the set of the standards of HONORABILITY was by far most influenced by environmental factors, shaping the life of pre-Islamic Arabs. Thus, GENEROSITY-HOSPITALITY was of so much importance, since it was so needed in the world, in which survival was always very difficult. As I said, it must have been somehow – perhaps even unconsciously – an insurance policy, in which one stuck to this script, hoping that when they will be in peril, someone else will stick to it as well. Moreover, GENEROSITY-HOSPITALITY justified one's *šaraf*-PRECEDENCE – the inequality was easier to bear when someone shared its blessing with the less fortunate.

Consequently, GENEROSITY-HOSPITALITY was a fundamental part of intra-group solidarity. The group members were simply expected to support each other no matter what. Similarly, the script of MAGNANIMITY was also of great importance, since it assured the maintenance of social equilibrium within the community. Thus, *karīm* must have been *karīm* to others – they must have lived together in peace. A member of the community was expected to be also resourceful, but also moderate, forgiving, and loyal. At last, they were also expected to obey the customs, meaning not to disturb the aforementioned social equilibrium, by violating the existing norms and modes of understanding of the world. This naturally translated into conservatism, which was to be observed in the pre-Islamic Arabic society (ʕAlī 1993a: 278–9).

Moreover, the code of *karam* consisted also of scripts, which were supposed to protect the community as a whole from outside. Thus, first and foremost, *karīm* men must have been brave and fearless. The strength of a group was important for the group's survival while facing other groups – not only on the battlefield. It could also establish the position of the group within the broader fabric of inter-tribal network of dependencies, in which the HONOR of the whole community – derived from the HONORS of its members – played a crucial role. Thus, eloquence was so valued in a man, since it was the mean of protecting the HONOR of the collective in speech – especially in the poetry that was the major means of communication in pre-Islamic Arabic society. Moreover, group survival depended also on its members' morale while facing harsh or more difficult circumstances. Thus, it was natural that *karīm*-HONORABLE man was required to be *ṣābir*, i.e., enduring.

All in all, as one can see, *karam*-HONORABILITY – the means of sustaining one's WORTH/VALUE for the community – was simply the script of actions, which were supposed to ensure the success of this community– its survival – in the particular environment of the harsh and unhospitable *Ǧazīrat al-ʕArab*, "the Island of Arabs".

9.2.2. SHAME: a statement of UNWORTHINESS

As we saw, *ʕirḍ* was not then a reward for proper conduct at all. It was a certain VALUE and a RIGHT founded on this VALUE, which were by default attached to a member of the community. In the course of life, this member could either get this VALUE INCREASED or DECREASED, and by that could have more or less secured the RIGHT to stay within their group.

Arabic SHAME should not then be seen as the opposite of HONOR, what was already postulated by Wikan (1984), yet on different grounds. In my understanding SHAME was simply a statement of a certain UNWORTHINESS, which was aiming to DECREASE the VALUE of a particular individual, and as a result, DIMINISHING their RIGHT to stay within a group. This statement was usually declared by an INSULT or OFFENCE, which always implied some sort of accusation of lack of HONORABILITY. The most explicit of such an INSULT is persists in the modern varieties of Arabic and it can be rendered as a statement *lā ḥasab wa-lā nasab la-hu* – he has no *ḥasab*, nor *nasab* – that is, he is worthless.

This declaration was simply a stigma, a mark of UNWORTHINESS, which in LEAP seems to be lexicalized as *ʕār*. It was attached to a person due to their DISHONORABLE, shameful behavior, or qualities, which could have indicated predisposition to such. The latter in LEAP was referred to as *ʕayb*-DEFECT, which further suggests that the subject of the SOCIAL EVALUATION in al-Ǧāhiliyya was one's WORTH in general – not only their behavior.

Shameful behavior was simply the violation of the code of *karam*-HONORABILITY. Whereas the SHAMEFUL DEFECTS – *ʕuyūb* – were what could be seen as making one unable to be *karīm*. Thus, they were some imperfections of one's body or one's character, which could indicate that someone is an ignoble person. At last, they were also DEFECTS of one's ORIGIN – i.e., DEFECTS within one's LINEAGE – simply meaning the possession of slave-related (or foreign) ancestors. This type of DEFECT, as we learned, implied lack of innate inclination towards the HONORABLE BEHAVIOR.

As we saw, individuals derived much of their HONOR – i.e., their WORTH – from their group, whose overall VALUE they must have protected as their own. This overall VALUE was simply a sum of individual VALUES of the members themselves. Thus, *ʕār*-DISHONOR must have had some extensional properties, and it could befall not only an individual but also their whole kin-group.

Of course, as a mark of SHAME, *ʕār* was primarily attached to the person. Still, the person was always deemed WORTHY staying within a particular group. By that, this group somehow declared that the WORTHINESS of this person meets the standards it set for its members. Consequently then, if DISHONOR befalls this person, it also befalls the entire group, which in a way – by accepting this someone within – manifested that the DISHONORED behavior/ quality/ trait is within its standard of HONORABILITY. In such a way, the HONOR of the group – its GOOD NAME – by far depends on the REPUTATION/WORTH of its members.

Thus, the only way, in which the group could avoid the DISHONOR of its member, is to remove this member from within – denying them the RIGHT to MEMBERSHIP. In most cases, the easiest way of doing so was *ṭard*, i.e., expulsion of the DISHONORED man (cf. Sławek 2011: 92). Nevertheless, if it was difficult or impossible to expel someone, the only way to WASH AWAY the group SHAME was to kill the one who brought it the DISGRACE.

Alternatively, when the accusation of DISHONOR was not justified or the DISHONOR was brought about as an ATTACK on the group member, the group was simply striking back, protecting the WOUNDED HONOR of this member and of itself. This was obviously one of the most important manifestations of the tribal spirit – *ʕaṣabiyya*. Thus, a BOND holding between the members of the tribe was inextricably linked to their HONOR and the HONOR of the tribe itself (cf. Sławek 2011: 91)

Moreover, as in many cultures, in al-Ǧāhiliyya, SHAME was not only the mark of DISHONOR and LOWERED WORTHINESS of someone, but – perhaps primarily – it was also the feeling arising from certain self-assessment in terms of socially accepted behavior. In other words, one also felt SHAME – in LEAP, *istiḥyāʔ* – for DISHONORING actions. The feeling of SHAME, however, was grounded in a special sense – a kind of conscience – which made one fully aware of the expectation of the group towards the individual. This sense – the sense of SHAME – in LEAP was referred to as *ḥayāʔ*. It was simply "what makes a person sensitive to the pressure exerted by public opinion" (Pitt-Rivers 1965: 42), or in other words, a certain – perhaps biological, yet culturally adjusted – mechanism navigating someone to fit the expectations and the standards posited by their community. It was then the sense of how to fit in, what consequently meant it must have been conceptualized as something one was supposed to hold fast, to not let go away.

9.2.3. The *shame-culture* of pre-Islamic Arabs

All in all, by integrating the conceptions of HONOR and SHAME-DISHONOR, I hope I depicted a certain subsuming model of SOCIAL EVALUATION. As I said, it was rather culture-specific due to the EVALUATION of OVERALL WORTHINESS of the assessed member of the community. I believe its culture-specificity can also be traced back to the specific of the environment of life of al-Ǧāhiliyya Arabs – of the inhospitable lands of Arabia. In their circumstances, not only the conduct was worth evaluations, but also the individual as a whole. The strong interconnectedness holding between members of a group – a family, a clan, a tribe – imposed such detailed assessment, since in such a group a failure of one could be a failure of all.

The model of SOCIAL EVALUATION persisting in the society of pre-Islamic Arabs suggest the treatment of the culture of those people not only as a kind of *honor culture* but also as a *shame culture* (cf. Benedict 1947). In such a culture, an individual's decision on an action was based on their assessment of its fitness within "some ideal pattern of conduct (Campbell 1964: 327)." This assessment, I believe, was referred to in LEAP as *ḥayāʔ*, whereas such an ideal pattern of conduct could be equated with the script for BEING *karīm*. In other words, pre-Islamic Arabic culture, similarly to pre-Christian Greek one, was a typical ancient Mediterranean culture that in the department on behavioral motivations was predominantly shame- rather than guilt-driven (cf. Lloyd-Jones 1973: 25–6).

At last, as a summary of my finding, in the figure below (Fig. 1.), I attempted to graphically represent the relationships defined in the previous sections holding between the main HONOR- and SHAME-related concepts. One can consider this sketch as a representation of the cultural model of SOCIAL EVALUATION OF COMMUNITY MEMBER in terms of HONOR and WORTHINESS as it was functioning in the shame-culture-like society of pre-Islamic Arabs.

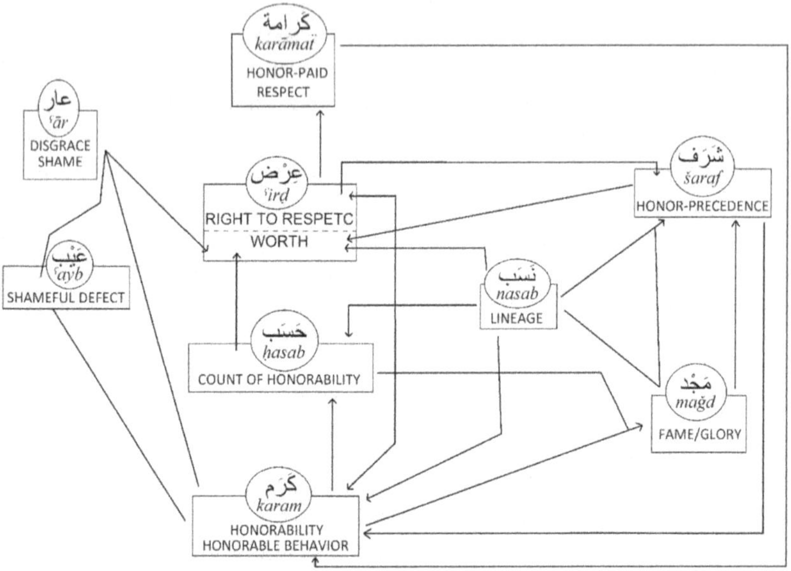

Fig. 1. A graphic representation of LEAP SOCIAL EVALUATION model

9.3. Further aspects of LEAP cultural conceptualizations of HONOR

In the previous sections, I have summarized my study in the form of two models containing the schemata, which I have discussed in the previous chapters of this book. However, at the very end of it, I would like to present some of my observations on the most interesting insight I made while studying HONOR in LEAP.

9.3.1. HONOR is like BODY

What was somehow the most striking for me was the plethora of physical attack scenarios associated by means of metaphors with the notion of ʕ*irḍ*-HONOR. Although the European concept of HONOR was also depicted as physical in nature, LEAP one was perceived as by far more fragile and vulnerable. This vulnerability, I think, indicates the existence of the metaphoric embodying conceptualization of ʕ*irḍ* in terms of BODY or BODY SIDE. In other words, as I mentioned it many times in this book, HONOR was experienced – and understood – by a pre-Islamic Arab in the simile to his or her BODY.

I hypothesized that this embodying conceptualization – like so many other conceptual phenomena discussed in this book – was motivated by the socio-environmental characteristics of life in al-Ǧāhiliyya. Namely, in the harsh environment of the terrain inhabited by pre-Islamic Arabs, the survival of an individual was bound to their persistence within a community. Being alone, secluded was a nightmare of those people, what must be a natural element of the life in such difficult circumstances (cf. Abu-Lughod 1986: 40). Therefore, HONOR must have been so bodily. If getting it DIMINISHED put one in danger of being removed from a group, it must have been seen as the BODY itself. As I said, similarly to one's BODY, DAMAGED, WOUNDED HONOR could have easily meant demise.

Consequently, HONOR conceptualized in bodily terms was FRAGILE, VULNERABLE. Perhaps, in this fragility one can look for the reason behind the exaggeration in pride, ascribed to pre-Islamic and medieval Arabs by al-Ǧāḥiẓ, who being an Arab himself, from a very proud tribe Banū Kināna, named them "the proudest of nation". Consequently, he described them as so easy to agitate by even the slightest of insults. This sensitivity must have been derived from the perception of HONOR as one's insurance policy – as something, which was protecting an individual against the threat of being an outcast. Thus, being so proud – so punctilious about one's REPUTATION – was a simple reaction to a danger posited by the scenario, in which someone could not find enough reasons to convince their companions to keep them within the group.

Moreover, I believe, one can add to this account another element: the notion of *relational mobility* used by Wilson & Lewandowska-Tomaszczyk (2021) in their explanation of the practice of honor killing in the modern Pakistani society. The relational mobility can be seen as the extent of one's ability to *flee* from their "court of reputation", especially however to terminate relationships inflicting the feeling of shame and replacing them with new ones (Wilson & Lewandowska-Tomaszczyk 2021: 459). In the pre-Islamic Arabic society – as it was the case of the communities of the past – such relational mobility was quite low, and one was rather restricted to one community as their "court of reputation" (cf. Wilson & Lewandowska-Tomaszczyk 2021: 459). As a consequence, a pre-Islamic Arab was more prone to SHAME, could not avoid it easily, and was more cautious as for their VALUE in the eyes of their companions. This, however, meant that protection of HONOR must have become an obsession of Arabs of al-Ǧāhiliyya: they had too few options as for the companionship – life-saving in the unhospitable environment of Arabia – to make light of their communal RIGHT TO RESPECT, their *ʕirḍ*. Thus, they were choosing different strategies of avoiding SHAME than *flight*: *fight* or *fright* (cf. Wilson & Lewandowska-Tomaszczyk 2021: 458) – they were quick to shed blood in defense of their *ʕirḍ*, and so worried about it that they perceived it as their own vulnerable BODIES.

9.3.2. Arabic-European contrast, which does (not) exist

As I mentioned in the introduction to this book, one of my intentions to examine LEAP expressions of HONOR was to find out about the way it contrasted with European notion I know as my own. In fact, I expected to discover highly culture-specific conceptualizations of this phenomenon persisting in the society of pre-Islamic Arabs. However, what I hope one could notice on many pages of this book, my expectations were not entirely satisfied. Interestingly, it seems HONOR of al-Ǧāhiliyya and HONOR of Europeans were surprisingly alike. Moreover, it turns out that while resembling the European notion, pre- Islamic Arabic conceptualizations of HONOR seem to differ in many ways from what HONOR is for nowadays Arabs.

The first similarity lays in violence being a part of the honor code. It is frequently assumed that Arabic HONOR is a violent, bloody affair, whereas the European one shall be seen as a matter of gentlemen's proceeding. Nevertheless, the violence – the blood-feeding HONOR (cf. Stewart 1994: 140) – was by far not only an Arabic phenomenon. European HONOR was as violent as its pre-Islamic Arabic counterpart, what might be seen reflected in its linguistic expressions – although, it is more noticeable in LEAP than in European languages.

Similarly, to what I found in LEAP, European HONOR was also conceptualized as a commodity as precious as the life itself (Stewart 1994: 139). Thus, this notion was similarly embodied, usually in the terms of FACE. Nevertheless, the embodiment of LEAP HONOR is far more discernible, which could be a result of one's much more life-or-death related dependency of the persistence within their community. Nevertheless, the difference here is that of degree only.

Moreover, in both pre-Islamic Arabic and European cultures, one can find the same conceptualization of PRECEDENCE/HIGH SOCIAL STATUS in terms of ELEVATION/ELEVATED PLACE, as well as such conceptions as the importance of one's ORIGIN/LINEAGE and WEALTH in acquiring and preserving their HONOR.

Nonetheless, I also found some differences, which do not seem, however, to be of great significance. What is interesting is the categorization of HONOR phenomena, which in LEAP, is much more precisely expressed than in European languages. All of the profiles of HONOR, such as RIGHT TO RESPECT, HONOR/RESPECT PAID, VALUE-REPUTE, PRECEDENCE, INTEGRITY- HONORABILITY, are well distinguished and referred to by different lexical tools. In most European languages, these profiles are usually referred to by lexemes derived from Latin *honor*, and almost always might be distinguished only on the basis of the context (cf. e.g., *He defended his honor*, vs. *He was given this honor by the king*, vs. *It was a great honor to us*).

Another difference – perhaps only in the sharpness of focus – is that of the role of GENEROSITY-HOSPITALITY in the code of honor, i.e., HONORABILITY. Evidently, in LEAP this role is much more salient, what is reflected in a culture-specific metonymic model. Of course, similarly GENEROSITY and HOSPITALITY are important elements of this code also in Europe, yet they have never achieved such a level of prominence as in al-Ǧāhiliyya (or in Arabic culture in general). Still, in some European cultures, one can perhaps also observe this phenomenon, such as in Serbo-Croatian lexeme *čast* "honor", historically derived from the meaning "a feast; food-sharing; a meal" (Sotirov 2017: 17–8).

Moreover, what seems to be quite important, in contrary to the way HONOR is conceptualized in Europe, LEAP HONOR – either *ʕirḍ* or *šaraf* – could not be fully lost. Of course, SHAME-DISGRACE diminished or reduce the value of one's *ʕirḍ*, nevertheless it did not remove it entirely. Whereas, as far as *šaraf* is concerned, the CEAP does not contain any instance of the conceptualization that can be lost or even diminished.

Of course, what one could definitely use against my claims of similarity between LEAP and European notions of HONOR is the fact that the conceptions of Western HONOR I used in my juxtaposition are only historical, not persisting nowadays. Perhaps, it is so, since – as noted by anthropologists – HONOR was always the preoccupation of small-scale communities, in which in Europe, we do not usually live anymore. Small-size groups are naturally much more sensitive in defining the standards of acceptable behavior. Consequently, it is much easier to keep evaluating the adherence to these standards, when a group consists of a number of people, who can all interact with each other on a daily basis. In modern societies, especially in the West, no one lives anymore in such secluded small communities, in which an individual is in constant contact with other members of the group. Therefore, naturally it is much more difficult to account any one for adherence to any particular standards of behavior, since in the individualized and atomized society, one is free from the constant examination of "the court of reputation".

9.3.3. The collapse of HONOR – is it really a thing?

As we learned, the situation I described above was termed by Stewart (1994: 51) as the collapse of the notion of honor, which from a real social institution deteriorated into the concept of merely INTEGRITY. It is true that such lexemes as *honor*, *dignity*, *sense of pride* are nowadays almost semantically void and serve in the high-register context only to express ideas, which seem to be too ideal or simply non-existent. Consequently, they are literary idioms used in books and speech of politicians, having no real significance for a regular speaker of, i.e., English language. Nevertheless, my study on the specificity of LEAP conceptualizations of these phenomena led me to some observations, which could perhaps change our perception of whether or not HONOR has actually disappeared from our life.

What is the most important to remember here is the notion of *ˤirḍ* as a certain REPUTATION, which being derived from one's adherence to HONORABLE CONDUCT, grants one the RIGHT TO RESPECT. As we learned, this RESPECT did not mean any special treatment or admiration but was a script of mutual recognition of membership within a community. This recognition – *karāma* – implied simply good treatment, aiming to uphold peaceful coexistence within this community. Moreover, we learned that the HONORABILITY, which made up one's REPUTATION calling for *karāma* towards this someone, was not an ideal code of conduct, but some standards of behavior established by this community as what it wants to manifest as the image of its ideals outside. As a whole, then, *ˤirḍ* and *karam* were not – by any means – schemata restricted to nobles, people of special abilities, etc., but they were the most basic rules of membership within a small-scale group.

Thus, I believe they can be easily translated into any notion of such a membership. In other words, any group – a community of professionals, researchers, a religious group of any type, even a friendship circle – is a subject of rules defined precisely in LEAP as *ˤirḍ* and *karam*. Any group seems to set some standards for membership, the adherence to which is constantly evaluated by all members of the collective. The community of researchers, academia, for instance, has very precisely defined such standards of scientific rigorousness as the code of "honor", following of which is the most important estimate of WORTHINESS of an individual as fitting (or not) this community. Similarly, these standards – the scientific rigorousness – is what the community of science wants to present outside as its group image. Consequently, as a reward for the realization of these standards, the individual – a researcher – receives *karāma*, i.e., a good treatment, a respect of his or her fellow researchers. Of course, for exceptional realization of the code of "honor", in any community, the reward is *šaraf*-PRECEDENCE, establishing the hierarchy of HONORS in terms of LEADERSHIP. Thus, the academia – similarly to pre-Islamic Arabic society – has its own *šarīf*s – professors – and its own *karīm* folk, their students.

As one can see, stating that, perhaps, we should reconsider our understanding of HONOR in terms of a literary world idiom and see in it as a more general principle of membership in a community, which is always assessed based on a certain code of behavior – be it scientific rigor, religious commands, or simply civil law. Maybe, the look at the LEAP conceptualizations of HONOR might sensitize our perception of this phenomena in a more general context of human unchangeable need to belong. Thus, it may well be the case that although we ceased to refer to certain phenomena as *honor*, they still could be understood by means of the very same schema I made the theme of this book.

***

I wanted to end this book with another observation – this time perhaps quite playful one. Maybe, the aforementioned conclusions on HONOR of the past and the present might be perceived as a manifestation of an old Arabic popular belief expressed by many medieval scholars, such as Ibn Fāris († 1005). This belief holds that Arabic is the most "eloquent", i.e., elaborative, language of the world. Because of this particular trait, God himself chose to reveal His Message to humanity in – as it is said in the Holy Qurʔān itself – *lisānin ʕarabiyyin mubīn* "an eloquent Arabic tongue (Q26: 195)". Ergo, perhaps, one can find a coincidental argument supporting this belief in the conclusions of this book. Who knows, perhaps even such a phenomenon as HONOR was actually much better elaborated – explicated – in this amazing ancient language. Therefore, perhaps, the analysis of the encodement of the knowledge of what HONOR is in Arabic language could be not only essential to our understanding of Arabic society, but also equally reveling for our perception of modern phenomena, which we ceased to refer to as *honor* a long time ago.

10. References

10.1. Corpus of Early Arabic Poetry (CEAP) – poetry compilations (*dawāwīn*) with commentary

t01A = Uḥayḥa (-), Mecca: Mecca Printing & Publishing CO.

t02A = Aš-Šanfara (1996), Bairūt: Dār al-kitāb al-ʕarabī.

t03A = Taʔabbaṭa Šarran (1984), Bairūt: Dār al-ġarb al-islāmī.

t04A = Al-Muhalhil (1993), al-Qāhira [Cairo]: Ad-dār al-ʕālamiyya.

t05A = ʕUrwa Ibn al-Ward & as-Samawʔal (1982), Bayrūt: Dār Bayrūt liṭ-ṭibāʕa wa-n-našr.

t06A = Imrūʔ al-Qays (1990), Bayrūt: Dār Iḥyāʔ al-ʕulūm.

t07A = Ṭarafa Ibn al-ʕAbd (2000), Bayrūt: Al-muʔassasa al-ʕarabiyya li-d-dirāsāt wa-n-našr.

t08A = Hudba Ibn al-Ḫašram (1986), Kuwayt: Dār al-qalam.

t09A = al-Ḫirniq Bint Badr (1990), Bairūt: Dār al-kutub al-ʕilmiyya.

t10A = Al- Mutalammis (1970), al- Qāhira [Cairo]: Ğāmiʕat al- duwal al-ʕarabiyya – Maʕhad al-maḫṭuṭāt al-ʕarabiyya

t11A = al-Ḥāriṯ Ibn Ḥilizza (1991), Bairūt: Dār al-kitāb al-ʕarabī.

t12A = ʕAmr Ibn Kulṯūm (1991), Bairūt: Dār al-kitāb al-ʕarabī.

t13A = ʕAdī Ibn Zayd (1965), Baġdād: Šarikat al-ğumhūriyya li-n-našr wa-ṭ-ṭabʕ.

t14A = Bišr Ibn Abī Ḫāzim al-Asadī (1994), Bairūt: Dār al-kitāb al-ʕarabī.

t15A = ʕAbīd Ibn al-Abraṣ (1994), Bairūt: Dār al-kitāb al-ʕarabī.

t16A = Al-Aswad an-Nahšalī (1970), Baġdād: Al-muʔassasa al-ʕāmma li-ṣ-ṣaḥāfa wa-ṭ-ṭibaʕa.

t17A = an-Nābiġa aḏ-Ḏubyānī (1991), Bairūt: Dār al-kitāb al-ʕarabī.

t19A = Ḥātim aṭ-Ṭāʔī (1994), Bairūt: Dār al-kitāb al-ʕarabī.

t19B = Ḥātim aṭ-Ṭāʔī (1981), Bairūt: Dār ṣādir.

t19C = Ḥātim aṭ-Ṭāʔī (-), al-Qāhira [Cairo]: Maṭbaʕat al-madanī – al-muʔassasa al-saʕūdiyya bi-Miṣr.

t20A = ʕUrwa Ibn al-Ward & as-Samawʔal (1982), Bayrūt: Dār Bayrūt liṭ-ṭibāʕa wa-n-našr.

t20B = ʕUrwa Ibn al-Ward (1998), Bairūt: Dār al-kutub al-ʕilmiyya.

t21A = ʕAntara Ibn Šaddād (2009), Bairūt: Dār al-kutub al-ʕilmiyya.

t21B = ʕAntara Ibn Šaddād (1996), Bairūt: Dār al-kitāb al-ʕarabī.

t22A = Zuhayr Ibn Abī Sulmà (-), Bairūt: Šarikat dār al-arqam Ibn Abi al-Arqam.

t22B = Zuhayr Ibn Abī Sulmà (1988), Bairūt: Dār al-kutub al-ʕilmiyya.

t23A = Ṭufayl (1997), Bairūt: Dār ṣādir.

t24A = Abū Ṭālib (1994), Bairūt: Dār al-kitāb al-ʕarabī.

t25A = Qays Ibn al-Ḫaṭīm (1967), Bairūt: Dār ṣādir.

t25B = Qays Ibn al-Ḫaṭīm (1962), Baġdād: Maṭbaʕat al-ʕānī.

t25C = Kowalski, Tadeusz (1914): *Der Dīwān Ḳais Ibn al Ḫaṭīm*, Leipzig: Otto Harrassowitz.

t26A = Aws Ibn Ḥağar (1980), Bayrūt: Dār Bayrūt liṭ-ṭibāʕa wa-n-našr.

t27A = al-Ḥādira (1969) [in:] *Mağallat maʕhad al-maḫṭūṭāt al-ʕarabiyya* 15 (2), pp. 269–388.

t28A = al-Aʕšà (-), al-Qāhira [Cairo]: Maktabat al-adab bi-l-Gamāmīz.

t29A = ʕĀmir Ibn aṭ-Ṭufayl (1979), Bairūt: Dār al-kitāb al-ʕarabī.

t30A = Labīd Ibn Rabīʕa (1993), Bairūt: Dār al-kitāb al-ʕarabī.

t30B = Labīd Ibn Rabīʕa (-), Bairūt: Dār al-kitāb al-ʕarabī.

t31A = ʕAmr Ibn Maʕd Yakrib (1985), Dimašq: Maṭbūʕāt mağmaʕ al-luġa al-ʕarabiyya bi-Dimašq.

t32A = aš-Šammāḫ Ibn Ḍirār (1968), al-Qāhira [Cairo]: Dār al-maʕārif bi-Miṣr.

t33A = al-Ḫansāʔ (2014), Bairūt: Dār al-maʕrifa.

t34A = Kaʕb Ibn Zuhayr (1989), Ar-Riyāḍ: Dār aš-Šawwāf li-ṭ-ṭibāʕa wa-n-našr.

t34B = Kaʕb Ibn Zuhayr (1997), Bairūt: Dār al-kutub al-ʕilmiyya.

t35A = ʕUrwa Ibn Ḥizām (1995), Bairūt: Dār al-ğīl.

t36A = Ibn Muqbil (1995), Bairūt: Dār al-šaraf al-ʕarabī.

t37A = Caliph Ali (-), al-Qāhira [Cairo]: Dār Ibn Zaydūn.

t38A = Ḥassān Ibn Ṯābit (2010), Bairūt: Al-maktaba al-ʕaṣriyya.

t38B = Ḥassān Ibn Ṯābit (1994), Bairūt: Dār al-kutub al-ʕilmiyya.

t39A = al-Ḥuṭayʔa (1958), Al-Qāhira [Cairo]: Šarikat maktabat wa-maṭbaʕat Muṣṭafà al-Bābī al-Ḥalabī wa-awaladi-hi bi-Miṣr.

t40A = Caliph Muʕāwiya Ibn Abī Sufyān (1996), Bayrūt: Dār ṣādir.

10.2. Classical Arabic Dictionaries (CAD) and Topic-based Dictionaries (TBD)

CAD

KtA = Al-Ḫalīl ibn Aḥmad (2003): *Kitāb al-ʕayn murattaban ʕalà ḥurūf al-maʕğam*, vol. I-IV, Bayrūt: Dār al-kutub al-ʕilmiyya.

AlG = Ibn Durayd (1987): *Kitāb ǧamharat al-luġa*, Bayrūt: Dār al-ʕilm li-l-malāyīn.

AsS = Al-Ǧawharī (2009): *Aṣ-ṣiḥāḥ. Tāǧ al-luġa wa-ṣiḥāḥ al-ʕarabiyya murattab tartīb^{an} alfabāʔīy^{an} wifq awāʔil al-ḥurūf*, Al-Qāhira [Cairo]: Dār al-ḥadīṯ.

LsA = Ibn Manẓūr (2009): *Lisān al-ʕArab*, vol. I- XV, Beirut: Dar Al-Kotob Al-Ilmiyah.

TBD

iSk = Ibn as-Sikkīt (1998): *Kitāb al-alfāẓ*, Bayrūt: Maktabat Lubnān Naširūn.

aHm = Al-Hamaḏānī (1991): *Kitāb al-alfāẓ al-kitābīyya*, al-Qāhira [Cairo]: Dār al-maʕārif.

mHs = Ibn Sīdah (1993): *Al-muḫaṣṣaṣ*, vol. 1–17, Bayrūt: Dār al-kutub al-ʕilmiyya.

10.3. Dictionaries & Encyclopedias

Lane, Edward (1968a): *An Arabic-English Lexicon*, vol. I, Beirut.

___________ (1968b): *An Arabic-English Lexicon*, vol. II, Beirut.

___________ (1968c): *An Arabic-English Lexicon*, vol. III, Beirut.

___________ (1968d): *An Arabic-English Lexicon*, vol. IV, Beirut.

___________ (1968e): *An Arabic-English Lexicon*, vol. V, Beirut.

___________ (1968f): *An Arabic-English Lexicon*, vol. VI, Beirut.

___________ (1968g): *An Arabic-English Lexicon*, vol. VII, Beirut.

___________ (1968h): *An Arabic-English Lexicon*, vol. VIII, Beirut.

Wehr, Hans; Cowan, J. Milton (1976): *A Dictionary of Modern Written Arabic*, Ithaca.

EAL&L = *Encyclopedia of Arabic Language and Linguistics,* (2008), Versteegh, Keek (ed.), vol. III, Leiden - Boston.

EoI = *The Encyclopedia of Islam*, (1927), Houtsma, M. Th.; Wensinck, A. J.; Arnold, T. W.; Heffening, W., Levi-Provencal, E. (eds.), vol. 2. London.

OD = *The Oxford English Dictionary*, (1989), Simpson, J.A.; Weiner, S.C. (eds.), vol. X, Oxford.

10.4. Corpora processing tools

SketchEngine, https://www.sketchengine.eu [15-09-2021].

10.5. Literature

Abou-Zeid, Ahmed (1965): "Honour and Shame among the Bedouins of Egypt", [in:] *Honour and Shame: The Values of Mediterranean Society*, Peristiany, J. G. (ed.), London: Weidenfeld & Nicolson, pp. 243–259.

Abu- Lughod, Lila (1986): *Veiled Sentiments: Honor and Poetry in a Bedouin Society*, Oakland: University of California Press.

Al-Azzam, B.; Al-Kharabsheh, A. (2014), "The theme of fakhr (self-exaltation) in the translation of Antara's Mu'allaqa", [in:] *Babel* 59 (3), pp. 288–309.

Alfaifi, Abdullah; Atwell, Eric (2016): "Comparative evaluation of tools for Arabic corpora search and analysis", [in:] *International Journal of Speech Technology* 19 (2), pp. 347–357.

Al-Ǧurǧānī (1984): *Kitāb Dalāʔil al-ʔIʕǧāz*, al-Qāhira: Maktabat al-Ḫāniǧī.

ʕAlī, Ǧawād (1993a): *Al-mufaṣṣal fī tāʔrīḫ al-ʕArab qabl al-ʔislām*, vol. I, Baġdād.

____________ (1993b): *Al-mufaṣṣal fī tāʔrīḫ al-ʕArab qabl al-ʔislām*, vol. IV, Baġdād.

____________ (1993c): *Al-mufaṣṣal fī tāʔrīḫ al-ʕArab qabl al-ʔislām*, vol. V, Baġdād.

Al- Jallad, Ahmad (2018): "The earliest stages of Arabic and its linguistic classification", [in:] *The Routledge Handbook of Arabic Linguistics*, Benmamoun, E.; Bassiouney, R. (eds.), New York: Routledge, pp. 315–331.

____________ (2020a): "*ʿArab*, *ʾAʿrāb*, and Arabic in Ancient North Arabia: The first attestation of *(ʾ)ʿrb* as a group name in Safaitic", [in:] *Arabian Archeology and Epigraphy* 31 (2), pp. 422–435.

____________ (2020b): "The Linguistic Landscape of pre-Islamic Arabia. Context for the Qur'an", [in:] *The Oxford Handbook of Qur'anic Studies*, Shah, M.; Abdel Haleem, M., Oxford: Oxford University Press, pp. 111–127.

Al-Jallad, Ahmad; Putten van, Marijn (2017): "The Case for Proto-Semitic and Proto-Arabic Case: A Reply to Jonathan Owens", [in:] *Romano-Arabica* 17, pp. 87–117.

Al-Jallad, Nader (2010a): "The semantic concept of '*shame*' in the Holy Qur'an", [in:] *Sacred Text. Explorations in Lexicography*, Monferrer-Sala, J. P.; Urban, A. (eds.), Frankfurt am Main: Peter Lang, pp. 81–106.

____________ (2010b): "The concept of shame in Arabic: bilingual dictionaries and the challenge of defining culture-based emotions", [in:] *Language Design* 12, pp. 31–57.

Alrabiah, Maha S. (2014): *King Saud University Classical Arabic Corpus*, Ar-Riyāḍ.

Al-Sharkawi, Muhammad (2017): *History and Development of the Arabic Language*, London – New York: Taylor & Francis.

Alsheddi, Abeer. 2016. *Edit Distance Adapted to Natural Language Words*. M.A. Thesis. Ar-Riyāḍ.

Appiah, Kwame Anthony (2011): *The Honor Code: How Moral Revolutions Happen*, New York: Norton & Company.

Arberry, A. J. (2017): *The Seven Odes. The first Chapter in Arabic Literature*, Edinburgh: Routledge.

Ar-Rāzī (1981): *Tafsīr al-faḫr ar-rāzī al-muštahir bi-t-tafsīr al-kabīr wa-mafātiḥ al-ġayb*, Bayrūt: Dār al-Fikr.

Athanasiadou, Angeliki (2017): "Cultural Conceptualisations of IRONY in Greek", [in:] *Advances in Cultural Linguistics*, Sharifian, Farzad (ed.), Singapore: Springer, pp. 111–124.

Badry, Roswitha (2017): "Arabic reflections on human dignity before and after 2011", [in:] *The world of Islam: politics and society*. vol. 2, Kończak, I.; Lewicka, M.; Skowron-Nalborczyk, A. (eds.), Toruń: Wydawnictwo Naukowe UMK, pp. 47–65.

Baranov, Kh.K. (1984): *Arabsko-Russkiy Slovar'*, Moskva [Moscow]: Russkiy Yazik.

Baroja, Julio C. (1965): "Honour and Shame: A historical Account of Several Conflicts", [in:] *Honour and Shame: The Values of Mediterranean Society*, Peristiany, J. G. (ed.), London: Weidenfeld & Nicolson, pp. 81–121.

Barska, Anna (2018): "Gościnność w kulturze/ kulturach Maghrebu", [in:] *Przegląd Orientalistyczny* 1–2, pp. 3–13.

Bartmiński, Jerzy (2006): *Językowe podstawy obrazu świata*, Lublin: Wydawnictwo UMCS.

_________ (2015–2017): *Leksykon aksjologiczny Słowian i ich sąsiadów*, vol. I–V, Lublin: Wydawnictwo UMCS.

Bauer, T. (2010): "The Relevance of Early Arabic Poetry for Qur'anic Studies Including Observations on Kull and on Q 22:27, 26:225, and 52:31", [in:] *The Qurʔān in Context – Historical and Literary Investigations*, Neuwirth, A.; Marx, M.; Sinai, N. (eds.), Leiden – Boston: Brill, pp. 699–732.

Benedict, Ruth (1947): *The Chrysanthemum and the sword: patterns of Japanese culture*, London: Secker & Warburg.

Berrada, Khalid; M'sik, Ben (2007): "Food Metaphors: A Contrastive Approach", [in:] *Metaphoric.de* 13, pp. 7–38.

Bielawski, Józef (1968): *Klasyczna Literatura Arabska: Zarys*, Wrocław – Warszawa – Kraków: Wydaw. Akademickie Dialog.

___________ (2012): *Klasyczna Literatura Arabska: Zarys*, Warszawa: Wydaw. Akademickie Dialog.

Blount, Ben G. (2009): "Anthropological linguistics", [in:] *Culture and Language Use*, Senft, G.; Östman J-O (eds); Verschueren J., Amsterdam – Philadelphia: John Benjamins Publishing Company, pp. 29–40.

Bobrowski, Ireneusz (1995): "Czy kognitywizm jest naukowy? O lingwistyce kognitywnej z punktu widzenia dwudziestowiecznych koncepcji nauki", [in:] *Biuletyn Polskiego Towarzystwa Językoznawczego* 51, pp. 19–24.

__________ (2010): "Lingwistyczny Obraz Świata", [in:] Górnikiewicz, J. (ed..), *W poszukiwaniu znaczeń…*, pp. 90–97.

Bourdieu, Pierre (1965): "The Sentiment of Honour in Kabyle Society", [in:] *Honour and Shame: The Values of Mediterranean Society*, Peristiany, J. G. (ed.), London: Weidenfeld & Nicolson, pp. 191–241.

Campbell, John Kennedy (1964): *Honour, Family and Patronage; A Study of Institutions and Moral Values in a Greek Mountain Community*, Oxford: Clarendon Press.

__________ (1965): "Honour and the Devil", [in:] *Honour and Shame: The Values of Mediterranean Society*, Peristiany, J. G. (ed.), London: Weidenfeld & Nicolson, pp. 139–170.

Casson, Ronald W. (1983): "Schemata in Cognitive Anthropology", [in:] *Annual Review of Anthropology* 12, pp. 429–462.

Cienki, Alan (2007): "Frames, Idealized Cognitive Models, and Domains", [in:] *The Oxford Handbook of Cognitive Linguistics*, Geeraerts, D. & Cuyckens, H. (eds.), Oxford: Oxford University Press, pp. 170–187.

Charmaz, Kathy (2006): *Constructing Grounded Theory*, London: SAGE.

Cohen, D.; Nisbett, R. E. (1994): "Self- protection and the culture of honor: Explaining southern violence", [in:] *Personality and Social Psychology Bulletin* 20, pp. 551–567.

Danaher, David S.; Głaz, Adam.; Łozowski, Przemysław (eds.) (2013): *The Linguistic Worldview: Ethnolinguistics, Cognition, and Culture*, London: De Gruyter.

Danecki, Janusz (ed.) (1997): *Poezja arabska. Wiek VI-XIII. Wybór* Wrocław-Kraków etc.: Zakład Narodowy im. Ossolińskich.

Danecki, Janusz (1998): *Klasyczny język arabski*, Warszawa: Wydaw. Akademickie Dialog.

__________ (2001): *Arabowie*, Warszawa: Państwowy Instytut Wydawniczy.

__________ (2012a): *Gramatyka języka arabskiego*, vol. I, Warszawa: Wydaw. Akademickie Dialog.

__________ (2012b): *Gramatyka języka arabskiego*, vol. II, Warszawa: Wydaw. Akademickie Dialog.

D'Andrade, Roy (1987): "A folk model of the mind", [in:] *Cultural Models in Language & Thought*, Quinn, N. (ed.), Cambridge: Cambridge University Press, pp. 112–148.

Da Silva, Augusto S.; Cuenca, Maria J.; Romano, Manuela (2017): "The Conceptualisation of AUSTERITY in the Portuguese, Spanish and Irish Press", [in:] *Advances in Cultural Linguistics*, Sharifian, Farzad (ed.), Singapore: Springer, pp. 345–368.

Deutscher, Guy. (2011): *Through the Language Glass: Why the World Looks Different in Other Languages*, New York: Henry Holt & Co.

Dimitriev, Kiril (2017): "Glory and immortality: the motif of *monumentum aere perennius* by Samawʔal b. ʕĀdiyāʔ", [in:] *Religious Culture in Late Antique Arabia*, Dimitriev, K.; Toral-Niehof, I. (eds.), Piscataway: Gorgias Press, pp. 105–122.

Dirven, Renè; Wolf, Hans- Georg; Polzenhagen, Frank (2007): "Cognitive Linguistics and Cultural Studies", [in:] *The Oxford Handbook of Cognitive Linguistics*, Geeraerts, D. & Cuyckens, H. (eds.), Oxford: Oxford University Press, pp. 1203–1221.

Dodd, Peter C. (1973): "Honor and the Forces of Change in Arab Society", [in:] *International Journal of Middle East Studies* 4 (1), pp. 40–54.

Durie, Mark (2019): "On the Origin of Qurʾānic Arabic", [*a draft paper, unpublished, available online*], https://www.academia.edu/37743814/On_the_Origin_of_Qur%CA%BE%C4%81nic_Arabic [15-09-2021].

Dziekan, Marek M. (1993): *Arabia Magica. Wiedza tajemna u Arabów przed islamem*, Warszawa: Wydaw. Akademickie Dialog.

__________ (1998): "Ǧāhiliyya między apologią a odrzuceniem", [in:] *Z Mekki do Poznania. Materiały 5. Ogólnopolskiej Konferencji Arabistycznej, Poznań, 9–10 czerwca 1997*, Jankowski, H. (ed.), Poznań, pp. 85–92.

__________ (2003): Gniewać się po arabsku, [in:] *Anatomia gniewu: emocje negatywne w językach i kulturach świata*, Duszak, A.; Pawlak, N., Warszawa: Wydawnictwo UW, pp. 139–147.

__________ (2008): *Dzieje kultury arabskiej*, Warszawa: PWN.

__________ (2012): *Pustynna muza: dwa studia o poezji staroarabskiej*, Warszawa: Polskie Towarzystwo Orientalistyczne.

Farès, Bichr (1932): *L'Honneur chez les Arabes avant l'Islam. Étude de sociologie*, Paris.

__________ (1938): "ʕIrḍ", [in:] *The Encyclopedia of Islam. Suplement*, pp. 96–97.

Fauconnier, Gilles (2007): "Mental Spaces", [in:] *The Oxford Handbook of Cognitive Linguistics*, Geeraerts, D. & Cuyckens, H. (eds.), Oxford: Oxford University Press, pp. 351–76.

Fillmore, Charles J. (1975): "An alternative to checklist theories of meaning", [in:] *Annual Meeting of the Berkeley Linguistics Society* 1, pp. 123–31.

__________ (1976): "Frame Semantics and the Nature of Language", [in:] *Annals of the New York Academy of Sciences* 280 (1), pp. 20–32.

Gilmore, David D. (ed.) (1987): *Honor and Shame and the Unity of the Mediterranean*, Arlington: American Anthropological Association.

Goddard, Cliff; Wierzbicka, Anna (2008): "Universal human concepts as a basis for contrastive linguistic semantics", [in:] *Current Trends in Contrastive Linguistics*, Gomez Gonzales, M.; Mackenzie, J. L.; Gonzalez Alvarez, E. M. (eds.), Amsterdam – Philadelphia: John Benjamins, pp. 205–226.

____________________ (2014): *Words and Meanings: Lexical Semantics Across Domains, Languages, and Cultures*, Oxford: Oxford University Press.

Goldziher, Ignaz (1888): *Mohammedanische Studien*, part I, Halle: Max Niemeyer.

Goossens, Louis (2003): "Metaphtonymy: The interaction of metaphor and metonymy in expressions for linguistic action", [in:] *Metaphor and Metonymy in Comparison and Contrast*, Dirven, R.; Pörings, R. (eds.), Berlin – New York: Mouton de Gruyter, pp. 349–371.

Górecka, Ewa (2009): *Znaczenie honoru kobiety w opinii współczesnego społeczeństwa jordańskiego*, Łódź: Wydawnictwo Ibidem.

Górska, Elżbieta (2000): *Studium kontrastywne składni arabskich i polskich współczesnych tekstów literackich*, Kraków: Wydawnictwo UJ.

__________ (2015): *Intensyfikacja treści we współczesnym arabskim języku literackim*, Kraków: Księgarnia Akademicka

Grady, Joseph E. (2007): "Metaphor", [in:] *The Oxford Handbook of Cognitive Linguistics*, Geeraerts, D. & Cuyckens, H. (eds.), Oxford: Oxford University Press, pp. 188–213.

Grzegorczykowa, Renata; Piotrowska, Agnieszka E. (2011): "*Świat jest teatrem niekończących się zmagań o ludzką godność.* Kształtowanie się pojęcia godności w dziejach polszczyzny", [in:] *Humanizm w języku polskim. Wartości humanistyczne w polskiej leksyce I refleksji o języku*, Janowska, A.; Pastuchowa, M.; Pawelec, R. (eds.), Warszawa: Neriton, pp. 79–148.

Grzeszczak, Monika (2017): "Honor w języku polskim", [in:] *Leksykon aksjologiczny Słowian i ich sąsiadów*, vol. V, Sotirov, P., Ajdačić, D., Lublin: Wydawnictwo UMCS, pp. 113–147.

Guillaume, Alfred (1934): "Review of *L'Honneur chez les Arabes avant l'Islam* by Bichr Farès", [in:] *The Journal of the Royal Asiatic Society of Great Britain and Ireland* 2, pp. 389–390.

Guth, Stephan (2015): "The Etymology of Generosity- Related Terms A Presentation of the EtymArab© Project – Part I", [in:] *Folia Orientalia* 52, pp. 171–201.

_________________ (2016): "The Etymology of Generosity- Related Terms A Presentation of the EtymArab© Project – Part II", [in:] *Folia Orientalia* 53, pp. 59–104.

_________________ (2018): "The Etymology of Generosity- Related Terms A Presentation of the EtymArab© Project – Part IV", [in:] *Folia Orientalia* 55, pp. 99–139.

Haiman, John (1993): "Life, the universe, and human language (a brief synopsis)", [in:] *Language Sciences* 15, pp. 293–322.

Haywood, John A. (1960): *Arabic Lexicography. Its History, and its place in the General History of Lexicography*, Leiden: Brill.

Hitti, Philip K. (1970): *History of the Arabs*, London: Macmillan.

Hoad, T. F. (ed.) (1993): *The concise Oxford dictionary of English etymology*, Oxford-New York: Oxford University Press.

Hoyland, Robert G. (2001): *Arabia and the Arabs: From the Bronze Age to the Coming of Islam*, London – New York: Routledge.

____________________ (2007): "Epigraphy and the Linguistic Background to the Qur'an", [in:] *The Qur'an in its Historical Context*, Reynolds, G. S. (ed.), London & New York: Routledge, pp. 51–69.

_____________________ (2017): "Reflections on the Identity of the Arabian Conquerors of the Seventh-Century Middle East", [in:] *Al-ʿUṣūr al-Wusṭā* 25 (1), pp. 113–140.

Jacob, Georg (1897), *Altarabishes Beduinenleben*, Berlin: Mayer & Müller.

Jackendoff, Ray (2002): *Foundations of Language. Brain, Meaning, Grammar, Evolution*, Oxford: Oxford University Press.

________________ (2009): "The Parallel Architecture and its Place in Cognitive Science", [in:] *The Oxford Handbook of Linguistic Analysis*, Heine, B.; Narrog, H. (eds), Oxford: Oxford University Press, pp. 645–668.

Joan, Eahr Amelia (2018): "600, Goddess Kaabou at Petra, Saudi Arabia", [in:] *Re-Genesis Encyclopedia: Synthesis of the Spiritual Dark- Motherline, Integral Research, Labyrinth Learning, and Eco- Thealogy*, Part I, available online at https://www.academia.edu/36599395/178_600_Goddess_Kaabou_at_Petra_Jordan_Plus_Mecca_Saudi_Arabia_pdf [23-08-2022], entry 178.

Kanafānī, Ġassān (1980): *Riğāl fī aš-šams*, ad-Dār al-Abyaḍ: al-Markaz aṯ-Ṯaqāfī al-ʕArabī.

_______________ (2013): *ʕĀʔid ʔilà Ḥayfā*, Bayrūt: Manšūrāt ar-Ramāl.

Knauf, Ernest A. (2010): "Arabo-Aramaic and ʕArabiyya: From Ancient Arabic to Early Standard Arabic, 200 CE – 600 CE", [in:] *The Qurʔān in Context – Historical and Literary Investigations, The Qurʔān in Context – Historical and

Literary Investigations, Neuwirth, A.; Marx, M.; Sinai, N. (eds.), Leiden – Boston: Brill, pp. 197–254.

Kollareth, Dolichan; Fernandez- Dols, Jose- Miguel; Russell, James A. (2018): "Shame as a Culture- Specific Emotion Concept", [in:] *Journal of Cognition and Culture* 18 (3–4), pp. 274–292.

Korus, Kazimierz (2017): "Timé (godność, honor) w starożytnej kulturze greckiej", [in:] *Leksykon aksjologiczny Słowian i ich sąsiadów*, vol. V, Sotirov, P., Ajdačić, D., Lublin: Wydawnictwo UMCS, pp. 27–50.

Kövecses, Zoltán (1995): "American Friendship and the Scope of Metaphor", [in] *Cognitive Linguistics* 6, pp. 315–46.

__________________ (2005): *Metaphor in Culture: Universality and Variation*, Cambridge: Cambridge University Press.

__________________ (2017): "Context in Cultural Linguistics: The Case of Metaphor", [in:] *Advances in Cultural Linguistics*, Sharifian, Farzad (ed.), Singapore: Springer, pp. 307–323.

__________________ (2021): "A Multilevel and Contextualist View of Conceptual Metaphor Theory", [in:] *Journal of Lauage and Communication* 8 (2), pp. 133–43.

Lewandowska-Tomaszczyk, Barbara (2007): "Polysemy, Prototypes, and Radial Categories", [in:] *The Oxford Handbook of Cognitive Linguistics*, Geeraerts, D. & Cuyckens, H. (eds.), Oxford: Oxford University Press, pp. 139–169.

Lakoff, George (1987): *Women, Fire, and Dangerous Things. What Categories Reveal about the Mind*, Chicago – London: University of Chicago Press.

Lakoff, George; Johnson, Mark (2013): *Metaphors We Live By*, Chicago: University of Chicago Pres.

Lancioni, Giuliano (2009): "Formulaic models and formulaicity in Classical and modern Standard Arabic", [in:] *Formulaic Language. Vol. 1. Distribution and historical change*, Corrigan, R.; Moravcsik, E. A.; Ouali, H.; Wheatley, K. M. (eds.); Amsterdam – Philadelphia: John Benjamins Publishing Company, pp. 219–38.

Langacker, Ronald W. (2006): "Introduction to Concept, Image, and Symbol", [in:] *Cognitive Linguistics: Basic Reading*, Geeraerts, D. (ed.), Berlin – New York: De Gruyter, pp. 29–67.

Larcher, Pierre (2010): "Pre-Islamic Arabic – Koranic Arabic – Classical Arabic. A Continuum?", [in:] n, *The Hidden Origins of Islam: New Research into its Early History*, Karl- Ohlig, H.; Puin, G-R. (eds), Amherst: Prometheus Books, pp. 263–282.

Leavitt, John (2015a): "Ethnosemantics", [in:] *The Routledge Handbook of Language and Culture*, Sharifian, F. (ed.), London – New York: Routledge, pp. 51–65.

_____________ (2015b): "Linguistic relativity: precursors and transformations", [in:] *The Routledge Handbook of Language and Culture*, Sharifian, F. (ed.), London – New York: Routledge, pp. 18–30.

Lloyd-Jones (1973): *The Justice of Zeus*, Berkley & Los Angeles: University of California Press.

Limon, John (2007): "The Shame of Abu Ghraib", [in:] *Critical Inquiry* 33 (3), pp. 543–72.

Maalej, Zouhair (2007): "The embodiment of fear expressions in Tunisian Arabic. Theoretical and practical implications (English – Arabic)", [in:] *Applied Cultural Linguistics: Implications for second language learning and intercultural communication*, Sharifian, F.; Palmer, G. B. (eds.), Amsterdam – Philadelphia: John Benjamins, pp. 87–104.

__________________ (2008): "The heart and cultural embodiment in Tunisian Arabic", [in:] *Culture, body and language. Conceptualizations of internal body organs across cultures and languages*, Sharifian, F.; Dirven, R.; Yu, N.; Niemeier, S. (eds.), Berlin – New York: De Gruyter, pp. 395–428.

__________________ (2009): "Metaphoric discourse in the age of cognitive linguistics, with special reference to Tunisian Arabic", [in:] *Journal of Literary Semantics* 28 (3), pp. 189–206.

____________ (2011): "Figurative dimensions of *3ayn* 'eye' in Tunisian Arabic", [in:] *Embodiment Via Body Parts: Studies From Various Languages and Cultures*, Ning, Yu; Maalej, Zouheir A. (eds.), John Benjamins Publishing Company, pp. 213–40.

Mahrān, Muḥammad Bayūmī (1990): *Dirasāt fī taʔrīḫ al-ʕarab al-qadīm*, al-Iskandiriyya [Alexandria].

Mejdell, Gunvor (2018): "Diglossia", [in:] *The Routledge Handbook of Arabic Linguistics*, Benmamoun, E.; Bassiouney, R. (eds.), London-New York: Routledge, pp. 332–44.

Monroe, James T. (1972): "Oral Composition in Pre-Islamic Poetry", [in:] *Journal of Arabic Literature* 3, pp. 1–53.

Mosquera, Patricia M. Rodriguez; Manstead, Antony S. R.; Fischer, Agneta H. (2016): "The Role of Honor-Related Values in the Elicitation, Experience, and Communication of Pride, Shame, and Anger: Spain and the Netherlands Compared", [in:] *Personality and Social Psychology Bulletin* 26 (7), pp 833–44

Mozaffar, Omer M. (2004): "Review of The Arab Mind by Raphael Patai" [in:] *The American Journal of Islamic Social Sciences* 21 (3), pp. 144–7.

Munif, Abdel Rahman (2019): *Mudun al-milḥ*, Maktabat "Telegram Network" (online).

Natij, Salah (2017): "Murūʾa – Soucis et interrogations éthiques dans la culture arabe classique (1ere partie)", [in:] *Studia Islamica* 112, pp. 206–263.

__________ (2018): "Murūʾa – Soucis et interrogations éthiques dans la culture arabe Classique (2e partie)", [in:] *Studia Islamica* 113, pp. 1–55.

Nisbett, R. E.; Cohen, D. (1996): *Culture of honor: The psychology of violence in the South*, Boulder: Westview.

Oakley, Todd (2007): "Image Schemas", [in:] *The Oxford Handbook of Cognitive Linguistics*, Geeraerts, D. & Cuyckens, H. (eds.), Oxford: Oxford University Press, pp. 214–235.

Osch van, Yvette; Breugelmans, Seger M.; Zeelenberg, Marcel; Bölük, Pinar (2013): "A different kind of honor culture: Family honor and aggression in Turks" [in:] *Group Processes & Intergroup Relations* 16 (3), pp. 334–344.

Owens, Jonathan (2006): *A Linguistic History of Arabic*, Oxford: Oxford University Press.

Palmer, Gary B. (1996): *Toward a Theory of Cultural Linguistics*, Austin: University of Texas Press.

_____________ (2007): "Cognitive Linguistics and Anthropological Linguistics", [in:] *The Oxford Handbook of Cognitive Linguistics*, Geeraerts, D. & Cuyckens, H. (eds.), Oxford: Oxford University Press, pp. 1045–1073.

Panther, Klaus- Uwe; Radden, Günter (1991): *Metonymy in Language and Thought*, Amsterdam – Philadelphia: John Benjamins.

Panther, Klaus-Uwe; Thornburg, Linda L. (2007): "Metonymy", [in:] *The Oxford Handbook of Cognitive Linguistics*, Geeraerts, D. & Cuyckens, H. (eds.), Oxford: Oxford University Press, pp. 236–263.

Paoli, Bruno (2001): "Meters and formulas: The case of ancient Arabic poetry", [in:] *Linguistic Approaches to Poetry* [*Belgian Journal of Linguistics* 15], C. Michaux & M. Dominicy (eds.), Amsterdam: John Benjamins, pp. 113–136.

Patai, Raphael (1973): *The Arab Mind*, New York: Scribner.

Pellat, Charles (1983), "Ḥawla mafhūm al-murūʾa ʿinda qudamāʾ al-ʿarab", [in:] *Al-Karmil*, 4, pp. 1–17.

Peristiany, J. G. (ed.) (1965): *Honour and Shame: The Values of Mediterranean Society*, London: Weidenfeld & Nicolson.

Petruck, Miriam R. L. (2013): "Advances in Frame Semantics", [in:] *Advances in Frame Semantics*, Fried, M.; Nikiforidou, K. (eds.), Amsterdam – Philadelphia: John Benjamins Publishing Company, pp. 1–12.

Pietrzak, Bartosz (2022): "Cultural Conceptualizations of SHAME & DISHONOR in Early Poetic Arabic (EPA)", [in:] *The Polish Journal of the Arts and Culture. New Series* 14 (2/2021), pp. 73–94.

Pitt-Rivers, Julian (1965): "Honour and Social Status", [in:] *Honour and Shame: The Values of Mediterranean Society*, Peristiany, J. G. (ed.), London: Weidenfeld & Nicolson, pp. 19–77.

__________________ (1977): *The fate of Shechem or the politics of sex: Essays in the anthropology of the Mediterranean*, Cambridge: Cambridge University Press.

Puzynina, Jadwiga (1992): *Język wartości*, Warszawa: PWN.

Rabin, Chaim (1951): *Ancient West-Arabian*, London: Taylor's Foreign Press.

___________ (1955): "The Beginning of Classical Arabic", [in:] *Studia Islamica*, 4, pp. 19–37.

Radden, Günter; Kövecses, Zoltan (1991): "Towards a Theory of Metonymy", [in:] *Metonymy in Language and Thought*, Panther, K-U.; Radden, G. (eds.), Amsterdam – Philadelphia: John Benjamins, pp. 17–60.

Raszewska-Żurek, Beata (2010): "Ewolucja niektórych elementów stereotypu psa w polszczyźnie", [in:] *Studia z Filologii Polskiej i Słowiańskiej* 45, pp. 65–80.

____________________ (2012): "O dwóch znaczeniach i jednym wartościowaniu leksemu czystość (na tle niektórych wyrazów pokrewnych i antonimów)", [in:] *Studia z Filologii Polskiej i Słowiańskiej* 47, pp. 99–124.

____________________ (2016): *ZGODA w rozumieniu Polaków czasów staro- i średniopolskich (analiza leksykalno- semantyczna)*, Warszawa: Instytut Slawistyki PAN.

____________________ (2019): "Metaforyzacja wartości w dawnej polszczyźnie na przykładzie metafory WARTOŚĆ TO BUDOWLA", [in:] *Pojęcie, kategoria, słowo w teorii i praktyce*, Dombrowski, A.; Żarski, W.; Rudnicka, M. (eds.), Kraków: Impuls, pp. 139–153.

Retsö, Jan (2003): *The Arabs in antiquity: their history from the Assyrians to the Umayyads*, London and New York: Routledge.

_____________ (2010): "Arabs and Arabic in the Age of Prophet", [in:] *The Qurʔān in Context – Historical and Literary Investigations, The Qurʔān in Context – Historical and Literary Investigations*, Neuwirth, A.; Marx, M.; Sinai, N. (eds.), Leiden – Boston: Brill, pp. 281–292.

___________ (2013): "What is Arabic?", [in:] *The Oxford Handbook of Arabic Linguistics*, Owens J. (ed.), Oxford: Oxford University Press, pp. 361–373.

Riemer, Nick (2003): "When is a metonymy no longer a metonymy?", [in:] *Metaphor and Metonymy in Comparison and Contrast*, Dirven, R.; Pörings, R. (eds.), Berlin – New York: Mouton de Gruyter, pp. 379–406.

Ryding, Karin C. (2005): *Modern Standard Arabic*, Cambridge: Cambridge University Press.

Sālim, ˁAbd al-ˁAzīz (1988): *Taʔrīḫ al-ˁArab qabl al-ʔislām*, al-Qāhira [Cairo].

Sapir, Edward (2003): "Język – przewodnik po kulturze", [in:] *Antropologia słowa. Zagadnienia i wybór tekstów*, Godlewski, G. (ed.), Warszawa: Wydawnictwo UW, pp. 77–82.

Sharifian, Farzad (2003): "On cultural conceptualisations", [in:] *Journal of Cognition and Culture*, 3 (3), pp. 187–207.

______________ (2008): "Distributed, emergent cultural cognition, conceptualization, and language", [in:] *Body, Language and Mind. Volume 2*: Sociocultural Situatedness, Frank, R. M.; Dirvern, R.; Ziemke, T.; Bernandez, E. (eds.), Berlin – New York: Mouton de Gruyter, pp. 109–136.

______________ (2011): *Cultural conceptualisations and language: Theoretical framework and applications*, Amsterdam – Philadelphia: John Benjamins.

______________ (2015): "Cultural Linguistics", [in:] *The Routledge handbook of language and culture, Routledge*, Sharifian, Farzad (ed.), London – New York: Routledge, pp. 473–492.

______________ (ed.) (2017): *Advances in Cultural Linguistics*, Singapore: Springer.

Sharifian, Farzad; Dirven, Rene; Yu Ning; Niemeier, Susanne (eds) (2008): *Culture, Body, and Language. Conceptualizations of Internal Body Organs across Cultures and Languages*, Berlin – New York: De Gruyter.

Sławek, Jakub (2011): *Jemen – świat wartości plemiennych*, Łódź: Ibidem.

Sotirov, Petar (2017): "Honor fundament słowiańskiego I europejskiego kanonu wartości", [in:] *Leksykon aksjologiczny Słowian i ich sąsiadów*, vol. V, Sotirov, P., Ajdačić, D., Lublin: Wydawnictwo UMCS, pp. 113–147.

Sotirov, Petar; Ajdačić, Dejan (eds.) (2017): *Leksykon aksjologiczny Słowian i ich sąsiadów*, vol. V, Lublin: Wydawnictwo UMCS.

Stewart, Frank H. (1994): *Honor*, Chicago: The University of Chicago Press.

Šukrī Al-Alūsī, Muḥammad (2009): *Bulūġ al-Arab fī Aḥwāl al-ˁArab*, al-Qāhira (Cairo): Dār al-Kitāb al-Miṣrī.

Sweetser, Eve E. (1987): "The definition of *lie*: an examination of the folk models underlying a semantic prototype", [in:] *Cultural Models in Language & Thought*, Quinn, N. (ed.), Cambridge: Cambridge University Press, pp. 43–66.

Szwedek, Aleksander (2018): "The object Image Schema", [in:] *Beyond Diversity: The Past and the Future of English Studies*, Żywiczyński, P.; Sibierska, M.; Skrzypczak, W. (eds.), Berlin: Peter Lang, pp. 57–89.

Tokarski, Ryszard (1995): "The Linguistic Picture of the World and some assumption of cognitivism", [in:] *Biuletyn Polskiego Towarzystwa Językoznawczego* 51, pp. 5–18.

Tuggy, David (2007): "Schematicity", [in:] *The Oxford Handbook of Cognitive Linguistics*, Geeraerts, D. & Cuyckens, H. (eds.), Oxford: Oxford University Press, pp. 82–116.

Turner, Mark (2007): "Conceptual Integration", [in:] *The Oxford Handbook of Cognitive Linguistics*, Geeraerts, D.; Cuyckens, H. (eds.), Oxford: Oxford University Press, pp. 377–399.

Ullmann, Manfred (1983): *Wörterbuch der klassischen arabischen Sprache*, Wiesbaden: Harrassowitz Verlag.

Wellhausen, Julius (1961), *Reste arabischen Heidentums*, Berlin: De Gruyter.

Wierzbicka, Anna (1992): *Semantics, Culture, and Cognition. Universal Human Concepts in Culture-Specific Configurations*, New York – Oxford: Oxford University Press.

____________________ (1996): *Semantics. Primes and Universals*, Oxford – New York: Oxford University Press.

Wilson, Paul A. (2017): "The Role of Shame in Conflict. A Cross-Cultural Perspective", [in:] Approaches to Conflict: Theoretical, Interpersonal, and Discursive Dynamics, Lewandowska-Tomaszczyk, B.; Wilson, P. A., Croucher, S. M. (eds.), Lanham: Lexington Books, pp. 55–78.

Wilson, Paul A.; Lewandowska-Tomaszczyk, Barbara (2017): "Pride in British English and Polish: A Cultural-Linguistic Perspective", [in:] *Advances in Cultural Linguistics*, Sharifian, Farzad (ed.), Singapore: Springer, pp. 247–288.

____ (2021): "Real-World Consequences of Devirtualization from Online to Offline Spaces: The Role of Shame as a Resource in the Honor Killing of Qandeel Baloch", [in:] *Shame 4.0: Investigating an Emotion in Digital Worlds and the Fourth Industrial Revolution*, Mayer, C.-H.; Vanderheiden, E.; Wong, P. T. P. (eds.), Springer, pp. 455–74.

Wikan, Unni (1982): *Behind the Veil in Arabia: Women in Oman*, Baltimore: Johns Hopkins University Press.

__________ (1984): "Shame and Honour: a contestable pair", [in:] *Man* 19, pp. 635–52.

Witkowska, Aleksandra; Danecki, Janusz (1981): *Siedem kasyd staroarabskich*, Warszawa: PIW.

Wolk, Daniel P. (2008): "Expressions concerning the 'heart' (*libbā*) in Northeastern Neo-Aramaic in relation to a Classical Syriac model of the temperaments", [in:] *Culture, body and language. Conceptualizations of internal body organs across cultures and languages*, Sharifian, F.; Dirven, R.; Yu, N.; Niemeier, S. (eds), Berlin – New York: De Gruyter, pp. 267–328.

Wright, William (1898a): *A Grammar of the Arabic Language*, vol.1., Cambridge: Cambridge University Press.

_______________ (1898b): *A Grammar of the Arabic Language*, vol.2., Cambridge: Cambridge University Press

Yaʕqūb, Imīl Badīʕ (1996): *Al-Muʕǧam al-Mufaṣṣal fī Šawāhid al-Luġa al-ʕArabiyya*, Bayrūt: Dār al-Kutub al-ʕIlmiyya.

11. Index of Authors

ŁÓDŹ STUDIES IN LANGUAGE

Edited by
Barbara Lewandowska-Tomaszczyk and Łukasz Bogucki

Vol. 1 Barbara Lewandowska-Tomaszczyk / Patrick James Melia (eds.): PALC'99: Practical Applications in Language Corpora. Papers from the International Conference at the University of Łódź, 15-18 April 1999. 2000.

Vol. 2 Lou Burnard / Tony McEnery (eds.): Rethinking Language Pedagogy from a Corpus Perspective. Papers from the Third International Conference on Teaching and Language Corpora. 2000.

Vol. 3 Barbara Lewandowska-Tomaszczyk / John Osborne / Frits Schulte: Foreign Language Teaching and Information and Communication Technology. 2001.

Vol. 4 Piotr Cap: Explorations in Political Discourse. Methodological and Critical Perspectives. 2002.

Vol. 5 Ewa Waniek-Klimczak / Patrick James Melia (eds.): Accents and Speech in Teaching English Phonetics and Phonology. EFL perspective. 2002.

Vol. 6 Barbara Lewandowska-Tomaszczyk / Kamila Turewicz (eds.): Cognitive Linguistics Today. 2002.

Vol. 7 Barbara Lewandowska-Tomaszczyk (ed.): PALC 2001: Practical Applications in Language Corpora. 2003.

Vol. 8 Corpus Linguistics by the Lune. A Festschrift for Geoffrey Leech. Edited by Andrew Wilson, Paul Rayson and Tony McEnery. 2003.

Vol. 9 Barbara Lewandowska-Tomaszczyk (ed.): Practical Applications in Language and Computers. PALC 2003. 2004.

Vol. 10 Imagery in Language. Festschrift in Honour of Professor Ronald W. Langacker. Edited by Barbara Lewandowska-Tomaszczyk and Alina Kwiatkowska. 2004.

Vol. 11 Seana Coulson / Barbara Lewandowska-Tomaszczyk (eds.): The Literal and Nonliteral in Language and Thought. 2005.

Vol. 12 Piotr Cap (ed.): Pragmatics Today. 2005.

Vol. 13 Jacek Waliński / Krzysztof Kredens / Stanisław Goźdź-Roszkowski (eds.): Corpora and ICT in Language Studies. PALC 2005. 2007.

Vol. 14 Krzysztof Kosecki (ed.): Perspectives on Metonymy. Proceedings of the International Conference "Perspectives on Metonymy", held in Łódź, Poland, May 6-7, 2005. 2007.

Vol. 15 Barbara Lewandowska-Tomaszczyk / Tomasz Płudowski / Dolores Valencia Tanno (eds.): The Media and International Communication. 2007.

Vol. 16 Krzysztof Kredens / Stanisław Goźdź-Roszkowski (eds.): Language and the Law: International Outlooks. 2007.

Vol. 17 Barbara Lewandowska-Tomaszczyk (ed.): Corpus Linguistics, Computer Tools, and Applications – State of the Art. PALC 2007. 2008.

Vol. 18 Barbara Lewandowska-Tomaszczyk / Katarzyna Dziwirek (eds.): Studies in Cognitive Corpus Linguistics. 2009.

Vol. 19 Barbara Lewandowska-Tomaszczyk / Marcel Thelen (eds.): Meaning in Translation. 2010.

Vol. 20 Łukasz Bogucki / Krzysztof Kredens (eds.): Perspectives on Audiovisual Translation. 2010.

Vol. 21 Piotr Stalmaszczyk (ed.): Turning Points in the Philosophy of Language and Linguistics. 2011.

Vol. 22 Stanisław Goźdź-Roszkowski: Patterns of Linguistic Variation in American Legal English. A Corpus-Based Study. 2011.

Vol. 23 Kamila Ciepiela (ed.): Identity through a Language Lens. 2011.

Vol. 24 Stanisław Goźdź-Roszkowski (ed.): Explorations across Languages and Corpora. PALC 2009. 2011.

Vol. 25 Krzysztof Kosecki / Janusz Badio (eds.): Cognitive Processes in Language. 2012.

Vol. 26 Alina Kwiatkowska (ed.): Texts and Minds. Papers in Cognitive Poetics and Rhetoric. 2012.

Vol. 27 Paul A. Wilson (ed.): Dynamicity in Emotion Concepts. 2012.

Vol. 28 Piotr Pęzik (ed.): Corpus Data across Languages and Disciplines. 2012.

Vol. 29 Mikołaj Deckert: Meaning in Subtitling. Toward a Contrastive Cognitive Semantic Model. 2013.

Vol. 30 Łukasz Bogucki: Areas and Methods of Audiovisual Translation Research. 3rd Revised Edition. 2019.

Vol. 31 Janusz Badio / Kamila Ciepiela (eds.): Language, Action, Interaction. 2013.

Vol. 32 Barbara Lewandowska-Tomaszczyk / Krzysztof Kosecki (eds.): Time and Temporality in Language and Human Experience. 2014.

Vol. 33 Iwona Witczak-Plisiecka (ed.): Cognitive and Pragmatic Aspects of Speech Actions. 2014.

Vol. 34 Małgorzata Anna Kamińska: A History of the *Concise Oxford Dictionary*. 2014.

Vol. 35 Łukasz Bogucki / Mikołaj Deckert (eds.): Accessing Audiovisual Translation. 2015.

Vol. 36 Joanna Jabłońska-Hood: A Conceptual Blending Theory of Humour. Selected British Comedy Productions in Focus. 2015.

Vol. 37 Krzysztof Kosecki / Janusz Badio (eds.): Empirical Methods in Language Studies. 2015.

Vol. 38 Katarzyna Stadnik: Chaucer's Choices. Through the looking-glass of medieval imagery. 2015.

Vol. 39 Paulina Pietrzak / Mikołaj Deckert (eds.): Constructing Translation Competence. 2015.

Vol. 40 Małgorzata Fabiszak / Karolina Krawczak / Katarzyna Rokoszewska (eds.): Categorization in Discourse and Grammar. 2016.

Vol. 41 Marcel Thelen / Gys-Walt van Egdom / Dirk Verbeeck / Łukasz Bogucki / Barbara Lewandowska-Tomaszczyk (eds.): Translation and Meaning. New Series, Vol. 1. 2016.

Vol. 42 Łukasz Bogucki / Barbara Lewandowska-Tomaszczyk / Marcel Thelen (eds.): Translation and Meaning. New Series, Vol. 2, Pt. 1. 2016.

Vol. 43 Łukasz Bogucki / Barbara Lewandowska-Tomaszczyk / Marcel Thelen (eds.): Translation and Meaning. New Series, Vol. 2, Pt. 2. 2016.

Vol. 44 Przemysław Łozowski / Katarzyna Stadnik (eds.): Visions and Revisions. Studies in Theoretical and Applied Linguistics. 2016.

Vol. 45 Marek Kuźniak / Bożena Rozwadowska / Michał Szawerna (eds.): From Motion to Emotion. Aspects of Physical and Cultural Embodiment in Language. 2016.

Vol. 46 Anna Rędzioch-Korkuz: Opera Surtitling as a Special Case of Audiovisual Translation. Towards a Semiotic and Translation Based Framework for Opera Surtitling. 2016.

Vol. 47 Mateusz Sajna: Video Game Translation and Cognitive Semantics. 2016.

Vol. 48 Kamila Ciepiela (ed.): Identity in Communicative Contexts. 2016.

Vol. 49 Mikołaj Nkollo: The Entrenchment of the 'unus alterum' Pattern. Four Essays on Latin and Old Romance Reciprocal Constructions. 2016.

Vol. 50 Paweł Rydzewski: Backness Distinction in Phonology. A Polish Perspective on the Phonemic Status of *y*. 2016.

Vol. 51 Piotr Pęzik / Jacek Tadeusz Waliński (eds.): Language, Corpora and Cognition. 2017.

Vol. 52 Janusz Badio (ed.): Events and Narratives in Language. 2016.

Vol. 53 Mikołaj Deckert (ed.): Audiovisual Translation – Research and Use. 2017. 2nd Expanded Edition 2019.

Vol. 54 Michał Szawerna: Metaphoricity of Conventionalized Diegetic Images in Comics. A Study in Multimodal Cognitive Linguistics. 2017.

Vol. 55 Artur Gałkowski / Monika Kopytowska (eds.): Current Perspectives in Semiotics. Signs, Signification, and Communication. 2018.

Vol. 56 Artur Gałkowski / Monika Kopytowska (eds.): Current Perspectives in Semiotics. Text, Genres, and Representations. 2018.

Vol. 57 Łukasz Bogucki / Piotr Cap (eds.): Exploration in Language and Linguistics. For Professor Piotr Stalmaszczyk on the Occasion of His 60th Birthday. 2018.

Vol. 58 Michał Kornacki: Computer-assisted Translation (CAT) Tools in the Translator Training Process. 2018.

Vol. 59 Marcin Walczyński / Piotr Czajka / Michał Szawerna (eds.): On the Verge between Language and Translation. 2018.

Vol. 60 Łukasz Bogucki / Paulina Pietrzak / Michał Kornacki (eds.): Understanding Translator Education. 2018.

Vol. 61 Marcin Walczyński: Psycho-Affective Factors in Consecutive Interpreting. 2019.

Vol. 62 Kamila Ciepiela (ed.): Language, Identity and Community. 2019.

Vol. 63 Olga Łabendowicz: Audiovisual Translation in Poland. Changing Audiences. 2019.

Vol. 64 Enrique Bernárdez / Joanna Jabłońska-Hood / Katarzyna Stadnik (eds.): Cognition in context. New insights into language, culture and the mind. 2019.

Vol. 65 Montse Corrius / Eva Espasa / Patrick Zabalbeascoa (eds.): Translating Audiovisuals in a Kaleidoscope of Languages. 2019.

Vol. 66 Barbara Lewandowska-Tomaszczyk / Valeria Monello / Marco Venuti (eds.): Language, Heart, and Mind. Studies at the intersection of emotion and cognition. 2020.

Vol. 67 Marta Chodkiewicz: Understanding the Development of Translation Competence. 2020.

Vol. 68 Urszula Paradowska: Developing Information Competence in Translator-Training. 2021.

Vol. 69 Luca Valleriani: Upper-class English in Natural and Audiovisual Dialogue. 2021.

Vol. 70 Michał Kornacki and Gary Massey (eds.): Contextuality in Translation and Interpreting. Selected Papers from the Łódź-ZHAW Duo Colloquium on Translation and Meaning 2020–2021. 2022.

Vol. 71 Monika Kopytowska / Artur Gałkowski / Massimo Leone (eds.): Thought-Sign-Symbol. Cross-Cultural Representations of Religion. 2022.

Vol. 72 Bartosz Pietrzak: The Concept of Honor in the Language of Early Arabic Poetry. A Cultural Linguistic Study. 2022.

www.peterlang.com

Lightning Source UK Ltd.
Milton Keynes UK
UKHW022004051222
413451UK00006B/133

9 783631 882900